HISTORY OF CEYLON

HISTORY OF CEYLON

FROM THE EARLIEST PERIOD

TO THE YEAR MDCCCXV;

WITH

CHARACTERISTIC DETAILS OF THE RELIGION, LAWS, & MANNERS OF THE PEOPLE AND A COLLECTION OF THEIR MORAL MAXIMS & ANCIENT PROVERBS.

BY

PHILALETHES, A.M. OXON.

TO WHICH IS SUBJOINED,

ROBERT KNOX'S

HISTORICAL RELATION OF THE ISLAND,
WITH AN ACCOUNT OF
HIS CAPTIVITY DURING A PERIOD OF NEAR TWENTY YEARS

ILLUSTRATED WITH A HEAD OF THE AUTHOR, WITH FIGURES, AND WITH A MAP OF THE ISLAND

GYAN

Published by

GYAN

Gyan Publishing House
5, Ansari Road
Daryaganj, New Delhi-110002
Phone: 011-47034999, 9811692060
E-mail: books@gyanbooks.com

Distribution Network
gyanbooks.com
India, USA, Canada, UK, Australia, France

ISBN : 978-81-212-3509-9 (PB)
First Published, Mangalore, 1817

2nd Impression 2020

Printed at: Gyan Press, Delhi.

History of Ceylon
Author: Philalethes

THE

HISTORY OF CEYLON,

FROM THE EARLIEST PERIOD

TO THE YEAR MDCCCXV;

WITH

CHARACTERISTIC DETAILS OF THE RELIGION, LAWS, & MANNERS OF THE PEOPLE AND A COLLECTION OF THEIR MORAL MAXIMS & ANCIENT PROVERBS.

By PHILALETHES, A. M. Oxon.

TO WHICH IS SUBJOINED,

ROBERT KNOX'S

HISTORICAL RELATION OF THE ISLAND,

WITH AN ACCOUNT OF

HIS CAPTIVITY DURING A PERIOD OF NEAR TWENTY YEARS.

ILLUSTRATED WITH A HEAD OF THE AUTHOR, WITH FIGURES, AND WITH A MAP OF THE ISLAND.

LONDON:

PRINTED FOR JOSEPH MAWMAN, LUDGATE STREET,

BY J. F. DOVE, ST. JOHN'S SQUARE.

1817.

Smith Sc. 63 High Holborn.

CAP^{T}. ROB^{T}. KNOX

Painted from the Life & Engraved by R. White. 1695.

Published by J. Mawman Novr 1816.

PREFACE.

The Island of Ceylon, though one of the most recent, is certainly amongst the most important, of the foreign possessions which are subject to the sovereignty of Great Britain. Whether we regard its internal resources, or its external relations, we shall find that it possesses singular advantages in a commercial, maritime, and political point of view. Its soil is rich beyond description, in almost every species of vegetable wealth; its forests abound with timber, fit for the construction of the most durable navy; its mountains, which have not yet been sufficiently explored, are believed to contain mineral treasures of the most valuable kind; and it is certain, that no country in the world can rival the fragrance of its cinnamon, and the beauty of its ivory.

But, whatever may be the wealth of Ceylon in vegetable, animal, or mineral products, in cinnamon, ivory, or precious stones, the circumstance, which renders the possession more particularly valuable to Great Britain, is the great facilities which it offers for the preservation of her naval superiority in that part of the world. The harbour of Trincomalée alone, is, in this point of view, an inestimable acquisition. Here, on the confines of a wide, perilous, and inhospitable ocean, the whole navy of Great Britain might ride in security, whilst the eastern monsoon was tempesting the neighbouring sea, spreading terror through the bay of Bengal, and covering with wreck the shores of the adjacent continent.

The Portuguese might covet the sovereignty of Ceylon, from the wide field which it offered for the propagation of the Roman Catholic faith; the Dutch might grasp at the possession with no less avidity, from its inexhaustible supply of cinnamon and precious stones; but, in a political point of view, it must be more particularly valuable to Great Britain, from its tendency to perpetuate her maritime superiority in the East. But, at the same time, I trust that, in the wise councils and magnanimous policy of Great Britain, moral considerations will not be overlooked in the midst of great political views, and that she will make her sovereignty of Ceylon contribute to the increase of civilization, to the encouragement of knowledge, the diffusion of Christian benevolence, and the consequent augmentation of the general happiness.

In detached instances, and for short periods, national prosperity may seem to be independent of all regard to moral obligations; but, look at human affairs in any connected series, and for any long interval, and you will invariably find that prosperity vanishes as virtue decays. Injustice may, for a season, spread its branches far and wide, and, according to a scriptural comparison, flourish like a green bay tree; but the time of storms and darkness will come, when the object, which once delighted the eye, will vanish from the sight. No truism can be more true, than that honesty is the best policy, both with respect to the conduct of individuals, and to the administration of states.

The territorial sovereignty of India may, hereafter, be wrested from this country, in the fluctuations of dominion, to which that part of the world has always been more particularly liable; but, whenever this catastrophe may occur, still the possession of Ceylon will, in a commercial and maritime point of view, be no inadequate compensation for the loss. For as commercial superiority must always be associated with that of maritime preponderance, and as the sovereignty of Ceylon must secure that preponderance in the great Indian Sea, the loss of our Indian commerce would not follow that of the territorial sovereignty. As long as we possess that great naval power in the west, which is likely to be coeval with our present free government, the harbour of Trincomalée will, more than any thing else, favour the permanence of the same power in the East. The dominion of the land may be more gratifying to the thirst of military distinction, but it is the dominion of the sea, which alone can afford security to commercial enterprise.

The wealth of nations may arise out of the soil; but of what little comparative importance is this wealth, without the facility of commercial exchange? or what can afford facilities to the prosecution of that commercial exchange by which nations are most enriched, equal to the dominion of the sea? The vital interests of Great Britain, in a national point of view, are principally concentrated in her maritime greatness; and they must, consequently, be more or less intimately combined with the sovereignty of this favoured isle.

The antient fables of the Singalese represent their country as having been first governed by a descendant of the sun; and I cannot but express a hope, that the wisdom, the justice, and the humanity of Great Britain, in the exercise of her sovereignty over Ceylon, may render that country, in modern times, what she might once have been in more ancient, the centre of a moral and intellectual light, which may scatter its beneficent rays over the whole East.

Ceylon offers the most auspicious theatre, and the most favourable opportunities for the gradual emancipation of the people from that state of degradation in which they are kept by the institution of casts. The institution of casts is the most formidable engine which was ever devised for perpetuating the subjugation of man; for sacrificing the many to the pride of a few; for keeping down the growth of the intellectual faculties, and for repressing the free expansion of all the social sympathies. It renders vain and abortive that germ of genius, which the great Father of all intelligence often imparts to particular individuals. It makes all mental culture impossible, except in a mode determined not by the ruling propensity of the person, but by the unalterable decrees of the state. It opposes an insuperable obstacle to the exercise of the active powers, which must be most successful where it arises out of preference, and concentrates most volition in the production of the desired effect. For the wisest purposes, and the most glorious ends, the Father of spirits has implanted in the bosom of every individual a desire to better his condition, and to add to his stock of enjoyment; but the elastic energy of this principle is relaxed and enervated by the institution of casts, which is equally at variance with the laws of God and with the welfare of man. But if, by the gradual operation of some discreet, rational, and benevolent system, this institution of casts could be abolished in Ceylon, the effect of the example must, sooner or later, diffuse itself over the continent of India. The great and solid chain can only be broken by degrees; but, if we can snap some of the links, the force of the whole will be diminished, till, in the course of ages, it will crumble into dust.

Whilst the Portuguese regarded Ceylon as a field that was highly propitious for the dissemination of the Roman Catholic faith, they disregarded the means in the prosecution of the end. Falsehood, injustice, and inhumanity, were practised, in order to plant the cross upon the ruins of the pagoda; but there are principles in human nature, which happily set limits to the operations of bigotry and ambition, and which cannot long be violated with impunity. The bigotry and oppression of the Portuguese missionaries, only added fresh fuel and increased constancy to the worshippers of Brahma and of Boodh.

The Dutch, actuated rather by the narrow parsimony and sordid selfishness of retail traders, than by the enlarged views and generous principles of great merchants, did not sufficiently consider, that the most efficacious means of securing their commercial aggrandizement would be by improving the condition of the natives, and by furthering their advances in knowledge, industry, and the refinements of civilized life. It would, perhaps, not be easy to determine, whether the people of Ceylon had more reason to execrate the insensate cupidity of the Dutch traders, or the ferocious bigotry of the Portuguese priests.

The example of what has happened to the Portuguese on the one hand, and to the Dutch on the other, ought to operate as a strong incentive to us, to pursue a more liberal and enlightened policy; which, whilst it is more conducive to the good of the Singalese, must at the same time be more advantageous to ourselves. In the intercourse between a sovereign country and her colonies, all benefits must be ultimately reciprocal. Their good must be the good of communion. In the conduct of states, as well as in that of individuals, there is no reaction so speedy, or so efficacious, as that of benefits.

As one who has often revolved, and humbly adored, the awfully-instructive administration of the moral world, I am deeply convinced that the cabinet of Great Britain will find it their safest policy, and their highest wisdom, to make the people of Ceylon experience the blessings of a government at once just, gentle, and beneficent. Under such a government, all the productive powers of the country will be augmented in an indefinite degree; and in those regions of Candy, which despotism rendered a wilderness, swarming with reptiles and wild beasts, or peopled only with a few half-famished and sickly individuals, the desert will be cleared, and the inhabitants be multiplied. Plenty will gratify the beholder at every turn, and health smile at every door.

Considered merely in a commercial point of view, the foreign possessions of Great Britain form beneficial ramifications of intercourse, through which her industry circulates, and by which her prosperity is increased; but, when we get upon higher ground, and, as philosophers or moralists, contemplate the subordination of one people, or kingdom, to another, we cannot but think it an imperious duty in the country, where the supreme power resides, to improve its various dependencies, not only in the arts, which add to the comfort, or contribute to the elegance of human life, but in that intellectual culture which, by elevating man in the scale of reason, exalts him in that of virtue and of happiness.

In delineating the History of Ceylon, I have endeavoured to render it as full and complete as the materials to which I could obtain access would permit; but I have never sacrificed truth to ornament, or blended it with any unauthorized addition of circumstances. I have not omitted the more early annals of the country, though they were barren of events, and little susceptible of interest; but I thought it right that the reader should be put in possession of all that is, or probably can be, known of those obscure periods, where tradition has supplied the place of regular records, and fiction has been busy in mutilating, in transforming, or in decorating truth.

Even national fables, though they are violations of truth, are often histories of manners and opinions. The records of credulity are far from being destitute of instruction. They occupy a large and prominent space in the history of the human mind; and though they may sometimes weary by insipidity, or disgust by exaggeration, they will often edify by moral inference, or amuse by ingenious combinations. The great Dutch work of Valentyn, the long concealed merits of which I have studiously laboured to bring to light in the course of the present history, has enabled me to exhibit a full and faithful picture of the mythological system and religious doctrines of the Singalese.

Ceylon appears to have been the early cradle of Boodhism, and was probably the point from which the doctrines of Boodh, which were anterior to those of the Brahmins, were diffused over a large part of the continent of India, from which, though they have been partially expelled, they have never been totally exterminated. They may not flourish as they once did on the banks of the Ganges, but they still occupy the kingdom of Siam, and the empire of the Birmans.

I have given only a very imperfect sketch of the natural history of the country, as my principal object was to make the reader acquainted with the civil and military transactions, the religion and manners of the people. The political, moral, and intellectual history of man, with all his deflections from virtue and all his aberrations from truth, is an object of higher interest and more general concernment, than any technical classification, or scientific description of quadrupeds and plants. Let me not therefore be condemned for not executing what I never designed to undertake, and never attempted to accomplish.

The moral maxims and antient proverbs of the Singalese, of which I have inserted a respectable collection in the present volume, will interest all descriptions of readers; for they contain truths, of that unvarying and permanent nature, which will touch some chord of sympathy in every breast. Among these proverbial sayings, there are many which penetrate the recesses of the human heart, and address themselves to those common sentiments, which constitute an indissoluble link of affinity amongst the scattered members of the human race. They prove that we are all parts of one moral scheme, which extends from pole to pole, and from earth to heaven.

PHILALETHES.

H. W. B.
November 13, 1816.

POSTSCRIPT.

In addition to the present history, the reader will find in this volume a republication of ROBERT KNOX's "HISTORICAL RELATION OF THE ISLAND OF CEYLON," with an account of his captivity during a period of nearly twenty years. This work had become so scarce, and has been so much in request since the possession of the Island by the English, that a new edition was requisite to gratify the demands of an increasing curiosity. Of Knox's work the merit is so well known, and has been so generally acknowledged, that it is superfluous to expatiate in its praise. His narrative exhibits a lively picture of the state of the country and the manners of the people; and the account, which he has given of what relates more immediately to himself, and particularly of his extraordinary escape from such a vigilant enemy, and in such difficult circumstances, combines the accurate details of a real transaction with the glowing interest of a romance.

PHILALETHES.

CONTENTS.

CONTENTS TO KNOX'S HISTORY.

PART I.

PART II.

PART III.

PART IV.

THE

HISTORY OF CEYLON,

FROM THE

EARLIEST PERIOD TO THE YEAR 1815;

WHEN

THE SOVEREIGNTY OF THE WHOLE ISLAND WAS CEDED TO THE

BRITISH CROWN:

WITH

CHARACTERISTIC DETAILS

OF THE

RELIGION, LAWS, AND MANNERS OF THE PEOPLE;

Topographical Notices;

AND A

COLLECTION OF MORAL MAXIMS AND ANCIENT PROVERBS.

By PHILALETHES, A.M. Oxon.

THE

HISTORY OF CEYLON.

CHAP. I.

Early Notices of Ceylon in Classical Writers—Arrian, Dionysius the Geographer, Ovid, Ptolemy, Pliny, Diodorus Siculus. Cinnamon not mentioned by these and other ancient Authors as the Production of Ceylon. The commercial Importance of Ceylon in the sixth Century, described by Cosma Indicopleustes. Ceylon visited by Marco Polo in the thirteenth, by Sir John Maundevile in the fourteenth Century.

THE first information respecting the Island of Ceylon, or Taprobane, as it is usually denominated in ancient writers, was brought into Europe by Nearchus and Onesicritus,* who were commanders of the fleet which Alexander dispatched from the Indus to the Persian Gulph. Gibbon remarks,† that the early geographers, and even Ptolemy, were so imperfectly acquainted with this remote region, that they "magnified above fifteen times the real size of this new world, which they extended as far as the equator and the neighbourhood of China." Dionysius, the geographer, mentions Taprobane as famed for its breed of elephants.

Μητερα Ταπροβανην Ασιηγενεων ελεφαντων.

v. 593.

* Arrian (de expedit. Alexand. lib. vi. p. 381, ed. Blancard. Amstel. 1668,) says that Onesicritus, in the account which he wrote of Alexander's expedition, falsely claimed the honour of having had the chief command of the fleet, as he only directed the helm of the ship in which Alexander himself sailed.

† Vol. iv. 8vo. p. 142.

Ovid has the following mention of Taprobane, as a part of the world removed almost beyond the limits of human intercourse; to which, he asks, of what advantage it could be for his fame to reach?

> Quid tibi, si calida, prosit, laudere Syene
> Aut ubi *Taprobanen* Indica cingit aqua.
>
> Pont. El. 5. l. 79.

In the time of Ptolemy the island was called Σαλικὴ, and the inhabitants Σάλαι. Hence we discern the origin of the modern name of Seylan, or Ceylon. The Arabians add to this name a termination, signifying island, Seylan-Dive, or Silendib.

Pliny* says that Taprobane was long supposed to be another continent, "alterum orbem terrarum;" and that it was not clearly known to be an island till the age of Alexander. He tells us, that Onesicritus had celebrated its elephants above those of India, on account of their greater bulk, and their more warlike properties; and that Eratosthenes had extolled the purity of its gold, and the size of its pearls.

Those who make this voyage, says Pliny,† cannot conduct their course by the observation of the stars, for the north pole is no longer visible to the eye. But the mariners, according to an ancient practice, carried birds in the vessel, which they set at liberty at intervals, in order to mark the direction they pursued to the land.

An accidental occurrence, in the reign of the Emperor Claudius,‡ contributed to make the Romans more acquainted with the Island of Ceylon, and to increase their intercourse with that part of the world.

* Hist. Nat. lib. vi. cap. 29. Pomponius Mela says, "Taprobane aut grandis admodum insula, aut prima pars orbis alterius Hipparcho dicitur;" that Hipparchus thought it either a very large island, or the commencement of a new continent.

† "Syderum in navigando nulla observatio."

‡ Claudius began his reign in 41, and died in 54.

One Annius Plocamus, a freedman, who farmed the customs in the Red Sea, having being blown in a violent tempest "off the coast of Arabia," was unexpectedly driven, after a passage of fifteen days, to the port of Hippuros, in the Island of Taprobane. Here he was kindly received by the king of the country, whose hospitality he experienced during a period of six months. In this interval, this European visitant had ample leisure to make the Ceylonese monarch fully acquainted with the majesty of Rome. He accordingly dispatched an embassy, consisting of four persons, to the imperial city.

These ambassadors from Ceylon gave, in some measure, an erroneous account of the island, or one that was rendered erroneous by the mistakes of Roman interpreters. They said that their country contained five hundred towns; that in Palæsimundo, which is represented as the capital, the palace alone could boast 200,000 inhabitants; that they had commercial dealings with the Seres (by some supposed Chinese), whom they described as men of gigantic size, with red hair, blue eyes, a shrill and piercing voice, and a language which they did not understand. They represented their traffic with the Seres to be conducted in much the same manner as the ancient commercial intercourse between the Phœnicians and the Britons, in which each party deposited in a certain place the goods which they designed to exchange, and which one relinquished to the other, when a satisfactory equivalent had been reciprocally obtained. But, says Pliny, though Taprobane is so far removed from the Roman world, still it is not free from the vices of Rome. Gold and silver are there objects of cupidity. They have variegated marble, jewels and pearls, which are of great beauty and in high esteem.

The ambassadors from Ceylon represented their wealth to be greater than that of the Romans, but said that the Romans turned theirs to more use. They mentioned that no one among them had any slaves. They did not take any repose after sun-rise, or during the day. Their houses were of moderate height. Provisions were never at an extravagant price; and they were free from the evils of judicial strife. For a king, they chose from amongst the people one, who was venerable for his years and his humanity; and who was without a family. But, if he should happen to have children, they compelled him to resign the sovereignty, lest the kingdom should become hereditary. The sovereign had a council of thirty persons assigned him by the people; and no one could be condemned to death except by a plurality of their suffrages. But the person, thus condemned, had a power of appeal from their sentence to the people; who, in that case, appointed seventy other judges to try the cause; and, if they acquitted the accused, the former thirty, by whom he had been condemned, were immediately disgraced, and never afterwards held in any estimation. If the king committed any outrage against his duty as a sovereign, he was condemned to suffer, not by the hand of violence, but by the universal detestation which he experienced. Every individual avoided his company; and he was left to perish in silence and in solitude. Their festivals were devoted to the chace; and they delighted most in that of the tiger and the elephant. Their fields were in a high state of cultivation. They had no grapes, but abundance of apples; and it was not uncommon for them to attain the age of one hundred years.*

If that part of the above account, which relates to the political state of Ceylon, be not entirely fabulous, it proves that the government of that island was formerly more free than it is at present, or has long been. But the statement of Pliny shews a greater degree of civil liberty, a greater regard for popular rights, and principles more adverse to the abuse of sovereign power, than perhaps ever existed in any of the regions of the East.

In the account of this island, which is found in Diodorus Siculus, lib. ii. there seems nearly an equal mixture of fable and of truth. He de-

* See Pliny ut sup.

scribes the inhabitants as characterized by an extraordinary longevity, and as little subject to disease.* He says that they have a severe law, according to which they put to death those who are mutilated, or labour under corporeal deformity. But, what is more remarkable, he adds, that they had a law to limit the duration of life; and that those, who had attained this period, took their leave of existence by a voluntary, but uncommon death. The country produced a plant, on which he who fell asleep expired without a struggle or a sigh.† The same historian relates, that the inhabitants of this island had a community of wives; that they regarded their children as a common stock, without any of the feeling of parental preference; and that the children were interchanged in their infancy, so that even mothers could not recognize their own.

The climate, though under the equinoctial line, is mentioned as so temperate, that the inhabitants are molested neither by the heat nor by the cold; and their fruits are said to ripen during the whole year. Thus, says the author, according to the poet—

Here clustring grapes and luscious figs appear,
With pears and apples, through the smiling year.‡

It is not a little remarkable that, in the ancient accounts of Ceylon, cinnamon, for which it is at present so celebrated, is never mentioned amongst its valuable products.§ Strabo ‖ speaks of Taprobane as sup-

* Πολυχρονιους δ' ειναι τους ανθρωπους καθ' υπερβολην, ως αν αχρι των πεντεχοντα και εκατον ετων ζωντας, και γινομενους ανοσους κατα το πλειστον. Diod. Sic. vol. ii. p. 163. Ed. Bipont.

† Εφ ἧς οταν τις κοιμηθη, και προσηνως προς υπνον κατενεχθεις αποθνησκει.

‡ Οχνη επ' οχνη γηρασκει, μηλον δ' επι μηλω
Αυταρ επι σταφυλῃ σταφυλη, συκον δ' επι συκω.

§ The account which Herodotus gives of this fragrant spice, lib. iii. c. iii. is well known. He mentions it as collected by the Arabs, who knew nothing of the country in which it was produced, except that it came from some of the regions of India. He gives an account of its having been used by birds in the construction of their nests, of which they were afterwards despoiled by strata-

‖ Lib. ii. p. 72. ed. 1620.

plying the Indian markets with large quantities of ivory, tortoise-shell, and other commodities; but cinnamon is not enumerated amongst the rest; though it could hardly have been omitted, if the country, which he mentions under the name of Taprobane, were the same as the modern Ceylon, and if that island were, in his time, as famed for the growth of that species of aromatic as it has since been. When the accurate geographer mentions Taprobane with a little more particularity in another place,* he speaks of its breed of elephants, but says nothing of its cinnamon. A very acute historian asks whether cinnamon, instead of being the aboriginal growth of Ceylon, were not subsequently naturalized in that island, as cloves were in Amboyna?†

In the sixth century Ceylon had become the chief seat‡ of the commerce of the Indian Ocean. Vessels entered its ports from the most remote parts of the East; and the merchants of Ceylon, in their turn, were not deficient in commercial enterprise. From China, called Tzinitza, they received "silk, aloes, cloves, the wood of cloves, sandal wood,

---

gem, which it is superfluous to relate. Herodotus speaks of the name, cinnamon, as derived from the Phœnicians.

The Persians, says a Dutch writer,* call this spice Dar-Cin, that is, Chinese wood; as the Chinese were the first who brought this and other eastern products to the Persian Gulph, from whence it was conveyed into Europe. Hence some supposed that Dar-Cin meant a Chinese tree; and that the bark of the cinnamon was one of the native products of China. As the Greeks procured cinnamon from the Arabian merchants who traded in the Red Sea, they, without farther inquiry, supposed it an Arabian product; and that it grew in the country of the people from whom they received it. In his Periplus of the Erythræan Sea, Arrian mentions pearls and precious stones, calico or muslin, and tortoise-shell, as commodities for which Taprobane was celebrated; but he says nothing of its cinnamon. Arrian. Blancardi, p. 176.

* P. 690.

† Macpherson, Annals of Commerce, Vol. I. p. 149.

‡ Ibid. p. 225. The work of Macpherson, to which I refer, is full of valuable information.

---

* Valentyn. Vol. V. p. 17. I have given some account of his great Dutch work on the East Indies in a note to the next chapter.

and other articles; from Male *(Malabar)* they imported pepper; from Calliena, now a place of great trade, copper, wood of sesame, like ebony, and a variety of stuffs; and from Sindu, musk, castoreum, and spikenard. All these articles, together with some spiceries,* and the hyacynths, for which the island was famous, were exported to every shore of the Indian Ocean. The Persian traders to Sielediv (Ceylon) appear to have been very numerous, since there was a church erected for them, the clergy of which received ordination in Persia. A principal part of their cargoes consisted of Persian horses for the use of the king."

These commercial particulars may be found in the account of Cosmas Indicopleustes, which, as Dr. Robertson remarks,† is the last which the

* But there is no mention of cinnamon as one of the products of Ceylon.

† Works, Vol. XII. ed. 1812, p. 131. Cosmas was an Egyptian merchant in the time of Justinian, who acquired the name of Indicopleustes from the voyages which he made to India. He turned monk in the latter period of his life. He calls Ceylon by the name of Sielediba. Though no information respecting Ceylon appears, according to Dr. Robertson, to have been received in Europe from the period abovementioned till the thirteenth century, still I cannot refrain from laying before the reader a short description of this island, which is found in "An Account of the Travels of Two Mohammedans through India and China in the ninth Century." This work did not make its appearance in any European language till the year 1718, when a French translation of it was published from the original Arabic by the learned Abbé Renaudot. The original appears to have been written about the middle of the ninth century. The following is what the two Mohammedan travellers say of the Island of Ceylon, as the reader may see in Harris's Collection of Voyages and Travels, Vol. I. p. 521, and in Pinkerton's more recent work of the same kind, Vol. VII. p. 179. "Beyond these islands (the Maldives), in the sea of Herkena (about the Maldives), is Serendib, or Ceylon, the chief of all those islands which are called Dobijat. It is all compassed by the sea, and on its coast they fish for pearl. In this country there is a mountain called Rahun, to the top of which it is thought Adam ascended and there left the print of his foot in a rock, which is seventy cubits in length; and they say that Adam at the same time stood with his other foot in the sea. About this mountain are mines of rubies, of opals, and amethysts. This island, which is of great extent, has two kings; and here are found lignum aloes, gold, precious stones, and pearls, which are fished for on the coast; as also a kind of large shells, which they use instead of trumpets, and are much valued. The inhabitants here have cocoa-nut trees which supply them with food, and therewith also they paint their bodies and oil themselves. The custom of the country is that no one

nations of the west received from any person who had visited that country till the thirteenth century, when the avidity of commerce began to awaken the spirit of curiosity, and the human mind, after the torpor of ages, was gradually roused into renovated activity.

In the latter part of the thirteenth century Ceylon was visited by Marco Polo, a Venetian, on his return to Europe from his long and celebrated travels. Marco Polo has justly been styled the Columbus of the East, as he was the first European who ever saw, or at least made

---

may marry till he has slain an enemy in battle and brought off his head. If he has killed two he claims two wives; and if he has slain fifty he may marry fifty wives. This custom proceeds from the number of enemies which surround them; so that he amongst them who kills the greatest number, is the most considered."——"When a king dies in this Island of Serendib, they lay his body on an open chariot, in such a manner that his head hangs backwards till it almost touches the ground, and his hair is upon the earth; and this chariot is followed by a woman with a broom in her hand, there-with to sweep dust on the face of the deceased, while she cries out with a loud voice, 'O man, behold your king, who was yesterday your master, but now the empire he exercised over you is vanished and gone; he is reduced to the state you behold, having left the world, and the arbiter of death hath withdrawn his soul; reckon therefore no more upon the uncertain hopes of life.' This proclamation, or some other like it, they continue for three days; after which the dead body of the king is embalmed with sandal wood, camphire, and saffron, and is then burned, and the ashes are scattered abroad to the wind."——"The king of this island makes laws, which are the fundamentals of the religion and government of the country; here are doctors and assemblies of learned men, like those of the Hadithis among the Arabs. The Indians repair to these assemblies and write down what they hear of the lives of their prophets, and the various expositions of their laws."——"In this same island there is a very great multitude of Jews, as well as of many other sects, even Tanouis, or Manichees, the king permitting the free exercise of every religion."——"Gaming is the usual diversion of the inhabitants here; they play at draughts, and their principal pastime of cocks, which are very large in this country, and better provided with spurs than cocks usually are." These travellers add, that the Singalese are so addicted to these pastimes, if so they may be called, that they will stake upon them all that they are worth; and that, when that is gone, they will "often play for the ends of their fingers." When they play, it is said that they have a hatchet placed ready for chopping off each other's fingers, which operation the winner resolutely performs and the loser patiently bears. Some of them gamble in this manner with so much frantic pertinacity, that before they part they have all their fingers mutilated.

known, the sea beyond China.* He left Venice in his way to Asia at the end of 1271, or the beginning of the following year; and he did not return till 1295. He passed the greater part of this long period at the court of Kublay, the great Khan of Tartary, on the frontiers of China. His father and uncle had previously spent many years in the dominions of the same sovereign; and on their return they took with them young Marco, who was then about nineteen years of age. Marco soon acquired the confidence of the khan, and was employed by him on several missions of great importance to the most distant provinces of his mighty empire. Marco diligently availed himself of these favourable opportunities to become acquainted with the productions and manners of the countries through which he passed; and, though he was formerly accused of exaggeration and fiction, yet subsequent research and the observation of later travellers have confirmed the general accuracy of his narrative. Tiraboschi,† with his usual candour, has vindicated his character, and paid a just tribute of praise to his veracity.

* See Harris's complete Collection of Voyages, 2 vols. folio, London, 1744, Vol. I. Modern Universal History, London, 1781, Vol. VIII. p. 16.

† Tiraboschi Storia della letteratura Italiana, Florence, 1806. Tomo IV. Parte I. p. 86—105. This admirable historian proves that many of the errors and inconsistencies, which have been censured in the works of Marco, may justly be imputed to those who transcribed his MSS.; as there are great diversities in the different copies. There was for some time a warm dispute whether the original was written in Latin or Italian; but Tiraboschi seems to have set this question at rest, and to have proved that it was composed in the dialect which was spoken at Venice in the thirteenth century. It was first printed at Venice in 1496; and afterwards inserted by Ramusio in his Collection of Voyages and Travels in 1559. Struvius, in his Bibliotheca Historica, Vol. I. p. 9. Lips. 1784, speaks thus of this celebrated traveller:—"Magnam Asiæ partem Mungalorum principi Kublai sive Hu-pi-lai serviens, peragravit, fideque singulari et candore quæ vidit audivitque, retulit. Partem in primis orientalem Asiæ accuratius, quam antea Europæi e Pauli itinerario cognoverunt. Insunt quidem et fabulæ; ideoque olim opus, quasi fictionibus rebusque anilibus scatens, contemnebatur: at salva est ejus præstantia atque integritas. Multa etiam oscitantiæ librariorum sunt tribuenda. Codices enim mirum in modum inter se discrepant."—Dr. Robertson has commended Marco Polo for the accuracy of his information and the fidelity of his descriptions, though he remarks, that some of his contemporaries gave him the name of *Messer Marco Millioni*, owing to the accounts which he gave of the numerous armies and immense revenues of the eastern princes. Vol. XII. p. 342—4.

Dr. Robertson,* speaking of Marco Polo, says, "He describes the great kingdom of Cathay, the name by which China is still known in many parts of the East, and travelled through it from Chimbalu or Peking, on its northern frontier, to some of its most southern provinces. He visited different parts of Indostan, and is the first who mentions Bengal and Guzzerat by their present names as great and opulent kingdoms. Besides what he discovered on his journies by land, he made more than one voyage in the Indian Ocean, and acquired some information concerning an island which he calls Zipangri or Cipango, probably Japan. He visited in person Java, Sumatra, and several islands contiguous to them, the Island of Ceylon, and the coast of Malabar as far as the Gulph of Cambay, to all which he gives the names that they now bear. This was the most extensive survey hitherto made of the East, and the most complete description of it ever given by any European; and in an age which had hardly any knowledge of those regions, but what was derived from the geography of Ptolemy, not only the Venetians, but all the people of Europe, were astonished at the discovery of immense countries open to their view, beyond what had hitherto been reputed the utmost boundary of the earth in that quarter."

Marco Polo says of Ceylon, that "it is the finest island in the world; the king is called Sendernaz; the men and women are idolaters, go naked, save that they cover their loins with a cloth; have no corn but rice, and oil of sesamino, milk, flesh, wine of trees, abundance of brasil, the best rubies in the world, sapphires and amethysts, and other gems. The king is said to have the very finest ruby that was ever seen, as long as one's hand and as big as a man's arm, without spot, shining like a fire, and not to be bought for money.† Cublai-Khan sent and

* Works, Vol. XII. p. 132.

† In his fifth volume, p. 352, Valentyn mentions the escape of two Englishmen, after a captivity of twenty-two years, from the capital of Candy to the Dutch fortress of Sitavaca, one of whom relates that he had seen a ruby that had been found by a peasant, which was of such immense size, that for some time he had in his simplicity used it for a whetstone without knowing what it was.

offered the value of a city for it, but the king answered, he would not give it for the treasure of the world, nor part with it, because it was his ancestors. The men are unfit for soldiers, and hire others when they have occasion."*

About half a century after Marco Polo, Ceylon was visited by Sir John Maundevile, who was a native of St. Alban's in this country. His work was first published in quarto in 1588, under the title of "The Voyage and Travaile of Sir John Maundevile, Knight, which treateth of the Way to Hierusalem and Marvayles of Inde," &c. A more complete edition appeared in 1727 in octavo. The author appears to have been better informed than preceding travellers respecting the dimensions of the island, the circumference of which he states at eight hundred miles, which is not far from the truth. He mentions that it contained a large portion of wilderness, and was infested by serpents, crocodiles, and wild beasts. He does not omit to notice its gigantic progeny of elephants; nor does he forget the celebrated mountain where Adam and Eve, after they were driven out of Paradise, wept for a hundred years, till they filled a lake with the effusions of their remorse. He adds, that the king was appointed by election, and that the island had two summers, two winters, and two harvests in a year.

* Harris's Collection of Voyages, Vol. I. p. 621. In another place Marco Polo mentions that a number of pilgrims from remote parts visited Adam's Peak, where some holy reliques were preserved of this great ancestor of mankind, consisting of his fore-teeth and one of his dishes. In the year 1281 the great Khan of Tartary sent an embassy to Ceylon, who were fortunate enough to succeed in obtaining from the king of the island two of the abovementioned teeth, the dish, and a lock of Adam's hair.

CHAP. II.

Singalese History from the earliest Period, as it is represented in their own Annals and Traditions. Vigea Raja, descended from the Sovereign of Tanassery, arrives in Ceylon, and founds the Dynasty of Singalese Emperors. His extraordinary Descent and high Pretensions. Vigea Raja, extraordinary Prediction respecting the Fate of his Daughter. Curious Precautions of the King to prevent the Accomplishment. The Princess escapes from her Place of Confinement. Her singular Adventures in a Forest. Is delivered of Twins, a Son and a Daughter. The Son learns the Story of his Birth. Some Feats of his early Life; marries his Sister; is raised to the Crown. Irregularities of his Two eldest Sons, whom he expels the Kingdom. They build a Town. The eldest Son marries a Daughter of the King of Madura, Tissanaon Ameti. Simit Comara. Pandu Vassaja marries a refugee Princess. Her Six Brothers hospitably received in Ceylon. Abeia Comara. Saguganatissa. Digagamonu. Pandu Cabaja puts his Nine Uncles to Death, builds Towns, and forms Rice-grounds. Muta Singa Raja. Deveni Petissa Maharaja erects numerous Pagodas, entertains eight princely Visitants. Suratissanam. Two Malabar Missionaries usurp the Government. Assalanam Raja puts them to Death, and is himself put to Death after a Reign of Fourteen Years by Etalanam Raja, who reigns for Forty-four Years. Gilinitissa Raja. Goluumbera. Ganatissa Raja. Some Nobles govern the Land in his Name for Thirty Years after his Death. Dutugeinunu Maha Raja performs great Feats upon his Elephant against the invading Malabars. Sedetissa Raja. Tullenam Raja. Lemenetissa Raja. Caluman Raja. Walagam Bahu Raja. The Island subjected to the Sway of Five Malabar Chiefs. Chonanga Raja. Bemminitissa. Maha Deliatissa. Chorawa humbles the Nobles, who put him to Death. Cuda Tissa Raja. Anularam Bisava Culavon. Tomo. Malutantissa; Excellence of his Government. Batia Raja. Madilimanna Raja, a royal Devotee. Adague Muwene Raja; permits no capital Punishment during his Reign. Cada Ambera Raja. Nalabissava. Elunna Raja. Sandamuhunu Raja. Asnapa Raja forms numerous

Rice-grounds and improves the Country. Vacnelisinam Raja. Bapa Raja; vast Strength of his Son Gaja Bahu Comara.

THE notices respecting Ceylon which have been preserved in the Greek and Roman writers are very vague and uncertain, and at the best furnish but little information. If the account which the Singalese themselves give of the early state and primary inhabitants of their island be sometimes fabulous and often inaccurate, it at least contains more varied details and more amusing combinations. The Singalese possess some written and some traditionary narratives of their primitive history, which have been preserved for many ages, and which are not undeserving the attention of the curious. Even in those instances in which these accounts appear to be only a tissue of fables, such fables will often be found to be only a veil thrown over real facts; and, at any rate, they will serve to throw some light on the genius and opinions of the people. In the three subsequent chapters I shall exclusively follow the authority of Valentyn in his famous work* on the East Indies, which is but

* The following is the title of Valentyn's work:—Keurlyke beschryving van Choromandel, Pegu, Arrakan, Bengale, Mocha, van 't Nederlandsch comptoir in Persien; en eenige fraaje zaaken van Persepolis overblyfzelen. Een nette beschryving van Malaka, 't Nederlands comptoir op 't Eiland Sumatra, mitsgaders een wydluftige landbeschryving van 't Eiland Ceylon, en een net verhaal van des zelfs keizeren, en zaaken, van ouds hier voergevollen; als ook van 't Nederlands comptoir op de kust van Malabar, en van onzen handel in Japan, en eindelyk een beschryving van Kaap der Goede Hoope, en't Eiland Mauritius, met de zaaken tot alle de voornoemde ryken en landen behoorende. Met veele Prentverbeeldingen en landkaarten opgebeldert. Door François Valentyn, Onlangs Bedienaar des Goddelyken woords in Amboina, Banda enz. Te Amsterdam by Gerard Onder de Linden, 1726.

This work is in five very large volumes in folio, and contains many hundred copper plates. The whole is written in the Dutch language, and it has never been translated, though there is no book extant which contains such a mass of valuable information respecting the parts of the world of which it treats. The knowledge of it, however, appears to be very circumscribed; and Pinkerton, who truly calls it an "inestimable work," speaks of it as "a treasure locked up in a chest, of which few have the key." See Pinkerton's Voyages and Travels, Vol. XI. p. 263. In the Bibliotheca Historica of Struvius, enlarged by Meuselius, Lipsiæ, 1785, Vol. II. p. 371, the following mention is made of this noble production of Valentyn: "Opus hocce carum æque ac rarum est dignissi-

very little known either in this country, or on the Continent, but which probably contains a mass of more valuable matter on the subjects of which it treats, than any other publication which has hitherto appeared.

The earliest traditionary accounts of the Singalese represent the people on both sides of the Ganges as living without laws or government, order or decency, in woods and caves, and, like inferior animals, feeding on grass and roots, without any trace of agriculture or civilization.

On a certain morning, in a length of ages past,* when the natives of Tanasserim, or Tanassery, were contemplating the rising sun, they beheld a figure of majestic form and beautiful appearance suddenly issue from the body of that splendid luminary. All who saw this attractive form ran towards it in an extacy of admiration. In a posture of homage and a tone of reverence they enquired who he was, whence he came, and what was the intention of his coming? The phantom replied, in the language of the country, that he was the progeny of the glorious sun, and that God had sent him to rule over the nations. The people of Tanassery, prostrating themselves upon the earth in humble adoration, said that they were ready to receive him as their chief, and to obey his laws.

---

mum, quod versionibus capitum præstantiorum plures in usus, quam hucusque factum, convertatur. Auctor enim munere ecclesiastes in insulis Amboina ac Banda functus, non solum, quæ ipse inde ab a. 1686 variis per plures Indiæ terras itineribus institutis observavit, diligentissime notavit, sed etiam scriptorum hodoeporicorum antecedentium, eorumque qui post illius reditum in Belgium Indiam viserunt, relationes cum suis contulit, optimaque ex iis selegit; varia insuper ex tabulario Societatis Belgo-Indicæ, in usum operis, illi tradita fuerunt, exceptis tamen ejusmodi scriptis, e quibus penitior societatis istius status cognosci posset. Quo factum ut partes Indiæ orientalis, a Belgis occupatas, curatius reliquis pinxerit." Valentyn died in 1727. In the "Bibliotheque Universelle des Voyages, par G. Boucher de la Richarderie," à Paris, 1808, it is mentioned that this work did not find its way into the National Library till the winter of 1796. M. Langlès expresses his surprise that it should have been so long unknown in France; but I am much more surprised that it should have been so little known in this country, where such a large mass of the community are more or less interested in every thing that relates to the East Indies.

* Valentyn vyfde deel, p. 60.

The first thing which this celestial visitant did, after he was received as the sovereign at Tanassery, was to induce the people to leave their savage and desultory life in the woods, and to build houses and villages, in order to live together in a state of civil subordination and social harmony. This king, having closed a long reign, left many sons, amongst whom he divided his dominions. His descendants, who are said to have continued in a long line of descent for 2000 years, were called Suriavas, or descendants of the race of the sun; amongst whom was Vigea Raja, who is celebrated as the first of the Singalese emperors.*

This Vigea Raja, one of the progeny of the sun,† is said to have made the first discovery of the Island of Ceylon, in the year of the world 1996. Accounts differ as to the part of the coast where he effected his first landing; but it is said that he disembarked with 700 men; and,

* In Valentyn the kings of Candy are always called keizers, or emperors. It is curious to observe how the name of the first usurper of the Roman diadem has impressed itself with so much force upon the languages north of the Danube and east of the Rhine, as to become the general term for sovereign, and even to obtain an ascendant over the more ancient and much more venerable name of kónig, koning, or king. The word keizer, or kaiser, which the Germans have generalized for emperor, when referred to its origin, can denote only an usurper. The word emperor, according to its primary signification, indicates a mere military chief, a man at the head of an army; but the word kónig, koning, or king, according to its etymological root, excites the ideas of wisdom and power. The German kónnen implies both wisdom and power; and these are the true attributes of sovereignty. The union of these ideas in the German kónnen, shews that this ancient people, long before they became metaphysicians, had the good sense to note, what the sagacity of Lord Bacon has been so much praised for remarking, that "knowledge is power." This observation has been so often quoted in the recent discussions about national education, that it has become quite familiar to the ear, and is no longer thought recondite, or profound.

† Valentyn remarks, that traces of a similar traditionary fable, with respect to their first Inca, were found amongst the natives of Peru. This is, with great probability, supposed to be of Chinese origin. The first Peruvian emperor, Inca Manco, with his wife, Coja Mama, appears to have been carried, either by design or accident, from China to America. Valentyn refers to Hornbeck de Convers. Indorum, and Hornius in Orig. Americ. lib. xv. cap. x. I agree with the learned writer in the Quarterly Review, Art. I. No. 27, in thinking, that there are numerous vestiges of the Chinese origin of the Singalese.

having proceeded to form a settlement at some distance from the shore, became the first sovereign of the island.

The most learned amongst the Singalese report that Vigea Raja was the son of a king of Tillingo, which borders upon Tanassery, and is a dependance upon the dominion of Siam. The priests, or astrologers, who read his history in the mirror of the stars, declared to his father, that, if he were suffered to remain in the kingdom he would, one day, prove the source of great public disturbance, or general distress; and his father accordingly, after mature deliberation with his wise men, ordered him to quit the kingdom, and, with a certain number of followers, to go in quest of some other place of abode.

As soon as Vigea Raja* arrived in Ceylon, he gave out that he was of royal extraction, but of the race of the sun, and the son of a lion. The oldest inhabitants of the island, at that time, along with the Malabars, worshipped the sun as their supreme god, under the denomination of Eswara; and they had so much respect for the professions of this foreign prince, that they immediately chose him for their king. Where the records of real history are wanting, national vanity, or busy credulity, is ever substituting some dazzling fiction, which passes current, till an age of scrutinizing inquiry succeeds to one of submissive ignorance.†

The emperors, or kings, of Ceylon, to the latest period called themselves, in their conquests, Suria Wangsa, or the race of the sun; and, in the list of their kings, we meet with some who took the name of Co-

* A subsequent account in Valentyn, and resting upon a different authority, ascribes the discovery of Ceylon to some of the descendants of this Vigea Raja, one of whom, named Vigea Comara, is represented as the first king of the country.

† Valentyn says, that it appears from some old books of the Singalese, which were then in existence, that the first king of the island was a Chinese, who was accidentally driven in a junk upon the shore, and that giving himself out for a son of the sun, which the natives at that time worshipped, they freely appointed him to the sovereignty.

mara Singa, which is said to signify a lion's tail. The name Singalese itself evidently alludes to some tradition respecting the lion,* as the word Singa-le denotes the blood or race of a lion, not only in their language, but in the Sanscrit, which appears to be the mother of all the eastern dialects.

Valentyn has exhibited a copious list of Singalese kings, which he procured from the ancient writings and traditions of the people themselves; and which, before his work appeared, had never been seen in any European publication. As the Dutch language, in which the work of Valentyn is composed, is very little known or studied in this country, and as his massy volumes, from their great cost and rarity, can be in the possession only of a few, I shall make no further apology for making a free use of his materials. If part of what I shall collect from his stores be thought dull and tedious, let me not be hastily accused of any undue attention to topics of little interest or importance. For in some of the following portions of Singalese history, it should be considered, that I am exhibiting much that has never appeared in any English work; and, if it be thought dull, it cannot be called stale. Nor ought it to be forgotten, that Ceylon is, at present, an integral part of the British dominions; and that under the humane, just, and wise government of this country, it may become in the south-east what Britain is in the north-west, the queen of isles. The fabled splendour of a descent from the sun, or of a kindred relation to the lion, may ultimately vanish in the true glory, the real prosperity, and the solid advantages, both commercial, moral, and intellectual, which she will derive from her union with the British crown.

From its soil, its climate, and its products, Ceylon is every way calculated to be the seat of plenty, and of happiness, to enrich its own in-

* The story of the lion-birth constitutes one of the national traditions of the Singalese, and will be detailed in the sequel. The royal race of Rome commences with twins who were nurtured by a wolf; but the imperial line of Ceylon has its fabled origin from the loins of a lion.

habitants, and to gratify others by its precious superfluities. Of such an island, particularly considered under its present political relations, even the most early history cannot well be destitute of interest; and if this interest be not so strongly experienced by those who reside at a distance from its deep forests and its lofty mountains, from its groves of cocoa-nuts and its gardens of cinnamon, still it must be vividly felt by numbers of our countrymen, who are settled in that region of beauty and delight, where Nature revels in all the gay luxuriance of vegetable life.*

In the 105th year of the Christian era, the southern coast was under the government of a king, named Vigea Raja, who married a daughter of Callinga Raja, by whom he had a daughter of the most exquisite personal charms. But the astrologers foretold that this paragon of beauty was condemned, by her evil destiny, to endure the caresses of a lion, and to be made the wife of that king of the forest.

Many of the courtiers ridiculed the prediction of this marvellous catastrophe, and could not be brought to believe that the daughter of a king would ever experience such a misfortune, as to have a lion for her spouse. The king, however, who yielded to the alarms of paternal solicitude, was not so incredulous about the truth of the prediction; and, in order to prevent the accomplishment, he ordered a royal mansion to be erected, which was to rest only upon one pillar, and to which no access should be allowed.

The king had provided this place of protection for the fascinating

* In a Spanish translation of Moreri's Dictionary, of which the second volume happens at present to be lying on my table, I find the following remark under the article Ceilan—"Llamanla los Indios Tenasirim ò Tenarisain, que en sue lengua significa tierra de delicias." I have no opportunity of ascertaining whether the word Tenasirim, or, as I have written above, Tanassery, means the "land of delight;" but if it does, it must be allowed that this island of exuberant fertility could not have a more appropriate appellation.

beauty of his daughter, with every thing requisite for her comfortable accommodation for a period of sixteen years. She was attended by some of her favourite women and domestics, who were to minister to her wants, and to relieve the languor of her solitude. The doors of the mansion were made fast; and, as an additional security, a guard of soldiers was stationed near the spot, on whose fidelity the utmost reliance could be placed.

When the abovementioned sixteen years of confinement had passed away, the king ordered the doors again to be opened; but, before he had ascertained whether his daughter were still alive, the fair captive, with some of her domestics, passed unobserved through the watch, and recovered her liberty. In the company of some other people, she made her way into the midst of the adjacent town, through which she proceeded till she overtook a caravan of merchants, who, after executing their business, were returning home. The track they followed led through a spacious forest, when the fair fugitive, oppressed by fatigue, sat down to rest herself for a short time by the way-side. In this situation, her lovely look and captivating form powerfully arrested the attention of one of the merchants, who determined to omit no persuasions, and to spare no efforts, to obtain her for his bride. Whilst he was meditating on the execution of this project, a lion, of tremendous magnitude, sprung forth from a neighbouring thicket. The whole company instantly fled with precipitation, with the exception of the princess, who, remaining motionless with fright, was immediately carried off by the king of the forest, and conveyed to his cave.

Whilst these events were taking place, Vigea Raja, not finding his daughter as he had expected, in her place of confinement, and not being able, after the most diligent inquiries, to learn any tidings respecting her from the watch, or from the people in the house, was oppressed with melancholy, and agitated with alarm. But, at last, he learned from a traveller, that a beautiful female, who was supposed to be the princess, had been carried off by a lion into a remote part of the forest, and had not since been seen.

The tradition proceeds to state, that after this act of violence, the princess was delivered of twins, a son and a daughter; to the first of whom she gave the name of Singa Bahu Comara, and to the other that of Singa Valli Comari, or children engendered by a lion, and having lion's tails.

The Prince Singa Bahu Comara, who had been nurtured by the lion, exhibited great strength, both of body and of mind, when he attained his fifteenth year. On one occasion, when he asked his mother how it happened that he and his sister were not like their four-footed father, she answered, that a long tale was attached to that circumstance, which, when he was older, she would unfold.—She subsequently informed him that she was the grand daughter of Calinga Raja; and that he and his sister were of that royal line.

As soon as the prince heard this, he felt a great repugnance to live any longer with the lion in the wilderness. He kindled with impatience to make himself known to his relations, and to repair to the court of his ancestors.

On one occasion, whilst the lion was from home, hunting for prey, the prince, in order to make a trial of his strength, took a large stone upon his shoulders, which he carried to a distance of seventy miles, and brought back again, before the lion had returned. On another occasion, when the lion was engaged in the chace, he rolled away the stone which covered the mouth of the cave, took out his mother and sister, who, like himself, were clothed in the skins of wild beasts, placed them on his shoulders, and bore them to the land of the king his grandfather.

When the lion returned, and found that his wife and children had abandoned the cave, he set up a dreadful roar; and, following the track which they had taken, he laid every thing waste in his way. Bodies of armed men in vain attempted to repress the ravages of this formidable enemy. The king, filled with alarm, and dreading some great catastrophe, directed his treasury to be opened, and some precious stones and pearls to be taken out, and exhibited about the town, by a man mounted upon an elephant, proclaiming them as the reward of any one by whom the furious animal should be destroyed.

The prince Singa Bahu, on hearing this, proposed to his mother and his sister to undertake this glorious achievement; but, considering that it was his father whom he designed to slay, they dissuaded him from perpetrating such a parricidal crime. Singa Bahu, nevertheless, determined to offer his services to the king; who, in addition to the proffered reward, engaged, in case of his success, to give him the half of the kingdom, and to associate him in the government.

The prince accordingly arming himself with his quiver and bow, marched out to meet the enemy. The lion, who recognized his son, imagined, at first, that the attack was rather jocular than serious; and it was not till after three arrows were stuck in his head that he discovered his mistake. But it was then too late to escape from death.

After the death of his lion-father, the prince began to reflect on the pious remonstrance of his mother and sister; when, penetrated with remorse, he bitterly reproached himself with what he had done. In the violence of his regret, he gave some of the attending courtiers a narrative of his whole life, from which they gathered that he was the son of the princess whom they had lost. Notwithstanding these emotions of remorse, the prince, after some internal conflict between conscience and ambition, proceeded to cut off his father's head. With this trophy of his prowess, which was destined to be rewarded with such a royal recompence, he made the best of his way to the palace, where he imparted to the sovereign the story of his birth, and the misfortunes of his family. His mother and sister were instantly ordered to be brought to the court, where they no sooner saw the lion's head, than the one began to bewail her husband and the other her father. The king, however, was overjoyed at the recovery of his lost child; and after having ordered her, with her son and daughter, to be apparelled in royal magnificence, he directed the body of her lion-spouse to be consumed, with all due pomp, on a funeral pile.

After this atchievement, the Prince Singa Bahu Comara, as he could find no other suitable match, married his sister, Singa Valli Comari, and he was afterwards crowned, according to the law of the country, which ordained that the marriage of the prince should precede his coronation. Hence also arose the custom, which afterwards prevailed in Ceylon, in conformity with which the emperors married their sisters.

This Singa Valli Comari proved very prolific; for she bore thirty-two sons. The first-born was named Vigea Comara, and his next brother Simit Comara. These two princes were educated along with two associates of the same age; but, as they grew up, they distressed the neighbourhood so much by their violent proceedings, that complaints were made to the king, who was requested to move either them, or the princes, to a different situation.

The king, who was a lover of justice, and who felt more concern for his obedient subjects than for his vicious sons, and their disorderly companions, commanded ships to be immediately equipped, on board of which he put them, and their 700 associates, who were thus compelled to seek their fortunes elsewhere. After a short voyage, they landed in a bay called Tammentatotte, or Tambuligamme, in the neighbourhood of Cotjaar. They found the country wild, and uninhabited; but they immediately set about building a town, which they called Tammena Nuwara.*

The Prince Vigea Comara, who was afterwards named Vigea Bahu Raja, having no wife, sent to solicit the hand of the daughter of the King of Madura, named Pandu Maharaja. With his daughter, who was designed for the royal bed, the King of Madura sent seven hundred female companions, besides eighteen couple of different casts, and five couple of artificers, consisting of goldsmiths, blacksmiths, carpenters, and masons.

The princess landed with her numerous attendants in the province of Cotjaar, where she was received with great pomp and rejoicings by Vigea Bahu Raja, who soon made her his wife; after which his coronation took place, according to the custom of the country.

This monarch next built a town called Utapissa, and, after a just and beneficent reign of thirty years, he died, leaving the kingdom to his brother. After the death of Vigea Bahu Raja, one of his nobles, named Tissanaon Ameti, rebelled against his brother Simit Comara, and obtained possession of the town of Utapissa, where he reigned for one year.

* I have represented Vigea Raja as the first sovereign of Ceylon, but that honour, as I have intimated, is also claimed for these princes, of whom Vigea Comara was the first. The primitive history of the Singalese, like that of other nations, which is made up of vague traditions, is largely blended with fable, and involved in uncertainty. It is vain to expect perfect consistency in the transmissions of oral history; and, in endeavouring to chuse between numerous contradictions and incongruities, it must often be impossible to decide in which there is the nearest approximation to truth. I have related no fact, in the whole course of this work, which does not rest upon authority; and though that authority was the best to which I could have access, yet I will not always answer for its credibility. All I can answer for is my own accuracy and fidelity, in making use of the documents in my possession. I lament, for the sake of the reader as well as for my own, that the materials out of which I have constructed the work, were not more copious, and the subject more susceptible of interest.

The Prince Simit Comara was crowned King of Ceylon,* after marrying his brother's widow, by whom he had three sons. He reigned in all twenty-two years.

His youngest son, Pandu Vassaja, having gone to the land of his grandfather, returned with thirty-two companions, with whom he surprised the town of Utapissa, and made himself master of the kingdom. Some time after this, a princess, named Baddacassaje, took refuge in Ceylon with some ships and a numerous retinue. She was well received and sumptuously entertained by Pandu Vassaja, who, having made her his wife, was invested with the royal crown.

Six princes, who were brothers of the new queen, afterwards landed in Ceylon, where the monarch gave them a hospitable reception, and permitted each of them to build a town in any situation he chose, over which they were to reign as feudatory sovereigns.

In the year 137 Pandu Vassaja had established his power over so many inferior kings and dependent chiefs, that he governed the island with absolute authority.† He had six sons, of whom the eldest was called Maja Comara, the second Saguganatissa Comara, and one daughter, who was the third in rank, and named Matsit Comari.

This princess was brought up in a house erected on one pillar, and married one of her cousins by the name of Digagamonu Comara, about the time that the Emperor Pandu Vassaja died, after a reign of thirteen years, leaving behind him a great and venerable name. His eldest son, who had taken the name of Abeia Comara, was his successor in the kingdom. His reign lasted for twenty years, and was no less glorious than that of his father.

* It was then called Lang-cauwn.

† It is asserted that he was the first who bore the title of emperor; but the native accounts are full of contradictions.

Saguganatissa succeeded his brother in the government, and reigned seventeen years. He was followed by his brother-in-law, Digagamonu, who governed well for thirty-seven years. The crown then descended to his son, Pandu Kabaja, who put nine of his uncles to death, and married the Princess Ranapalla (a golden jewel), who was a daughter of the King Mailkari Cudanan Raja. He was thirty-seven years old when he began to reign, and he reigned thirty-three years. In his time he rebuilt with great magnificence the town of Anurajapure. He also formed rice-lands, which he could overflow with water, and afterwards draw it off again, by artificial means. This part of the country was called Raja Veva. This monarch also directed the people where to erect strongholds and fortresses in the most eligible situations. After having ruled his people with wisdom and justice, he died with great piety* and devotion, and left a glorious name to after times.

His son, Muta Singa Raja, was his successor in the empire. He planted in the wilderness a great grove of cocoa-nut trees, to which he gave the name of Mahamuna. He governed his people as a father does his children; and died after a long reign of sixty years.

He was succeeded in the government by his son, Deveni Petisse Maharaja, who proved not only a prince of gentle disposition, but one who greatly feared God. He had been a scholar of Mihinda Mahatea, one of the priests, to whose memory he had ordered a pagoda to be erected in the middle of a wood. He afterwards caused many others to be built in different parts of the island. He also gave much alms to the poor.

It was during his reign that eight brothers and sisters, princes and princesses, came from the southern coast, out of a country called Ma-

* The old Ceylonese chronicler, whom Valentyn has followed, and whom I have followed through Valentyn, has quite left out of the account of this monarch's piety the massacre of no less than nine uncles, with which he began his reign. Some parts of this catalogue of the kings of Ceylon are as meagre and jejune as the Saxon chronicle.

danpadipe. In their retinue there were some who brought with them the tree of their Bodha, or god, Siermahabodi, which tree (says the writer) is still to be seen in the pagoda of the seven corles.

The Emperor Deveni Petisse Maharaja shewed great favour to the above princely visitants. He built several towns for them and their dependants; and, after a life of great piety, and a glorious reign of forty years, he died in a good old age.

He was succeeded by one of his brothers, named Suratissinam, whose reign lasted ten years. After this, two Malabar missionaries, who introduced horses into Ceylon, succeeded, contrary to all expectation, in usurping the government, which they preserved for twenty-two years by their good conduct and unanimity. But they were both ultimately put to death by Assalanam Raja, a younger brother of Deveni Petisse Maharaja. After recovering the throne of his ancestors, Assalanam Raja reigned for fourteen years, when he experienced a violent death, in a revolution which was effected in the government by Etalunam Raja, a chieftain who came from the coast of Malabar. This successful adventurer thus acquired the imperial crown of Ceylon, which he preserved for forty-four years.

The Singalese throne, which appears to have been regarded as the prize of ambitious chiefs, was next seized by Gilinitissa Raja, who kept it for twenty years, when he was succeeded by one of his cousins, named Golumbera Raja, who kept his court in the province of Roona, where he reigned fourteen years. His son, Ganatissa Raja, who had married a daughter of Gilinitissa Raja, was the next emperor who governed the empire of Roona, as it was then called by the Singalese, with much justice for four years. The great men of the land had the art to conceal the event of his death for a period of thirty years, during all which time they governed the country in his name. But his eldest son, Dutugcinunu Maha-Raja, having destroyed this usurping aristocracy, got possession of the throne of his father, just at the time that the country was overrun by the Malabars, and the religious worship of the island every where suppressed. But Dutugeinunu Maha-Raja soon found means to assemble an army of between eleven and twelve thousand men, when, mounting his elephant named Caddolhotu, he proceeded to the province of Roona, from which he had been compelled to fly. He attacked the Malabars in their thirty-two strong-holds in this province and in other parts of Ceylon, destroyed 129,000 of the enemy in the first battle, took the town of Anuraja Pure, slew Ellala the king of the Malabars, and cleared the island from the whole race of those invaders. After this event he received the imperial crown, and experienced a pacific reign of twenty-four years.

The last monarch was succeeded by his brother Sedetissa Raja, a sovereign of a gentle and devout disposition, who built the pagoda of Gunuditihera, and made ten beautiful rice-grounds, which could at pleasure be overflown or laid dry. His tranquil reign lasted eighteen years; during which there was not the smallest disturbance either from within or from without. His son and successor, Tullenam Raja, also built a pagoda in a village called Chamanda Landaru. He reigned one year, nine months, and ten days, when he was put to death by Lemenetissa Raja, who laid violent hands upon the crown.

This Lemenetissa Raja, having reigned thirty-nine years and eight months and a half, was succeeded by his brother Caluman Raja, who held the government for sixteen years, when his brother, Walagam Bahu Raja reigned in his stead. But this last sovereign had swayed the sceptre only eight months, when seven brothers, with seven different armies, came from the opposite coast of Malabar. They landed their troops in seven different bays of the island, fought against the emperor, and put him to flight; but no one knew the place of his retreat.

Five of these seven brother-chieftains now ruled over the island, but the two others returned again to their own country with the relics or bones of their idol Bodha. These five brothers had governed the country thirty-six years and seven months, when they were destroyed by Walagam Bahu Raja, who recovered the kingdom, which he afterwards governed for twelve years and five months. His son Chonanga Raja, who succeeded him, reigned for twenty-six years. One of the nobles, named Bemminitissa, then obtained violent possession of the government, which he conducted with great authority for twelve years.

Maha Deliatissa, a son of Caluna Raja, then ruled the kingdom for fourteen years; when Chorawa, the youngest son of Walagam Bahu Raja, succeeded to the throne. Though this prince manifested his impiety in destroying numerous pagodas, he nevertheless swayed the sceptre with great moderation and justice for twelve years. But he grievously harassed his nobles and courtiers; because he thought that they oppressed the people more than they ought. The nobles and courtiers accordingly rose up against him and put him to death, giving out that his soul was gone to hell, or, in their language, to Lovamahanara Caddia.

The son of Mahu Deliatissa, whose name was Cuda Tissa Raja, was next set upon the throne; which he had occupied for three years, when he was put to death by his wife Anularam Bisava, who reigned one year after his destruction. But Culavon, the secretary of her husband, made use of the same barbarous perfidy towards her, which she had practised towards her royal spouse. Culavon next seized the crown, which he kept during a short reign of eighteen months; when he was slain by another Malabar, named Tomo, who reigned only four months.

At this time Malulantissa, a son of the murdered Cuda Tissa Raja abovementioned, found means to establish himself upon the throne of his father, which he filled with much renown for twenty-six years. His gentle government caused him to be beloved by his subjects; and his active vigilance to be feared by his neighbours. Nothing escaped his observation; and he made such wise dispositions through all his dominions, and particularly in the vicinity of the coast, that not even a small vessel could come to anchor in his harbours or bays, without his knowledge or permission. No invader dared to approach the shore.

His son, Batia Raja, who next assumed the government, was a devout and pious person, who erected a magnificent pagoda, made many rich offerings to his gods, and, treading in the footsteps of his father, enjoyed a tranquil reign of twenty-eight years. He was succeeded by his brother, Madilimanna Raja, who built a beautiful pagoda in a village named Ambulu Vagala. Here he placed the images of his gods and the bones of his saints. He levied no taxes upon his subjects, but gave himself up entirely to religious observances, and ordered his people to pray diligently to the idols of his fathers. He embellished his favourite pagoda with a garden of flowers, and omitted nothing that could in any way contribute to increase the beauty or magnificence of his decorations.

His son, Adagu Muwene Raja, next mounted the throne. He formed two spacious rice grounds, paid great attention to the government of his people, and imposed upon them no other service, than that of serving their gods. During his reign, he did not suffer a single individual to be put to death. After a reign of nine years and eight months he was carried to the grave. His successor in the kingdom was his son, Cada Ambera Raja, who died at the end of six years.

His sister, Nalabissava, who succeeded him, reigned for the same period. She had married her mother's sister's son, Elunna Raja, who also held the sceptre for six years. After this, his younger brother, Sandamahana Raja was put to death by the Prince Asnapa Raja, in the sixth year of his reign. Asnapa Raja formed sixteen rice grounds, with very good water courses, built many pagodas, and reigned for forty-one years with great glory, as he had exceedingly improved the country and bettered the condition of the inhabitants. His son, Vacnelisinam Raja, who was his successor in the government, reigned only three years.

Bapa Raja, the son of the last monarch, next swayed the sceptre. He had a son named Gaja Bahu Comara, who was brought up along with Milo, a son of one of the cast of washermen, who was born on the same day as the prince. Both these children grew up to be strong as giants. The emperor, his father, had an iron walking stick or pole made for him, which it required sixty men to carry. It was as thick as twenty-two clinched fists, and was thirty-five span long. The handle was overlaid with gold, and the top of it blushed with a great and inestimable ruby. This walking pole was quite a plaything in his hand, and his giant foster-brother sometimes carried it after his lord. During the government of Bapa Raja, and whilst his son was only a youth, a great army landed from the coast of Malabar, which attacked the Singallese troops, and made 12,000 prisoners. With the exception of this disaster his reign was a peaceable period of twelve years.

CHAP. III.

Singalese History, as it is represented in their own Annals, continued till the Arrival of the Portuguese, in the Year 1505. Gaja Bahu, his Vengeance on the Malabars. Mana Raja. Hamatissa Raja. Cuda Raja. Venitissa Raja. Ambakeramun Raja. Sirina Raja. Vierdu Raja. Sangatissa Raja. Sirisanga Bodi Raja; a great Plague; fabulous Circumstances respecting an Invasion of his Dominions; submits to die for the good of his Subjects; his Head speaks after it was cut off. Lemini Golu Raja. Guwelaguwem Dettatissa. Malasen Raja. Guitsirimenaon Raja. Deva Tissa Raja. Upatissa Manam Raja; a great Sage visits Ceylon, his Doctrine widely diffused. Senam Raja. Leminitissa Raja. Visenan Curalsoo Raja. Seven Malabar Chiefs invade the Country and usurp the Government. Dacem Gulia Raja, builds many Pagodas, forms numerous Rice Fields. Comara Dahai Raja; he refuses to survive the death of a favourite Poet. Nine Emperors, of whom five suffered a violent Death. Dos Raja carried off by the Malabars. Ariacsi Chaccaravarti, King of Jaffnapatam, endeavours to subdue the whole Island with the Aid of the Malabars; the Country delivered by Alagues Vira Mandrim. Ruccale Praccaram Bahu Raja, builds a Palace at Cotta; shews great Favour to the Priests; vanquishes a large Army of the King of Canara; avenges an Affront of the Malabars; suppresses a domestic Rebellion; defeats an Attempt of the King of Jaffnapatam to make himself Emperor of Ceylon; obtains Possession of his Capital, and makes one of his Nephews King of the Country; closes a long Reign in Piety and Peace. First Arrival of the Portuguese in Ceylon in the Year 1505.

WHEN Gaja Bahu ascended the throne, and heard how the Malabars had carried off 12,000 of his father's subjects, he became agitated with rage, and vowed that he would revenge the affront. With no other attendant than his foster brother, Milo Jojada, and with no other weapon than his iron walking stick, he proceeded from the province of Roona, and from the town of Guliapura Nawara; and, without having recourse to boat or ship, he swam over to the coast of Malabar. Having dispersed the troops that opposed his landing, he marched towards the capital where the king held his court. That monarch, hearing of his approach, ordered all the gates to be shut; but the Emperor Gaja Bahu, having soon battered them to pieces with his club, went directly to the palace, set fire to all the doors and ransacked the apartments, till at last he discovered the king in a small room, where he was reclined on a bed. After sitting by the Malabar sovereign for some time, without saying a word, Gaja Bahu proceeded to lay his staff upon his stomach, which almost pressed his breath out of his body, and did not leave him power to utter a syllable. In the mean time his foster brother made great havoc in the town. He not only crushed all the men that came in his way, but slaughtered their horses in heaps, and laid their strongest elephants dead with a blow.

In this emergency the terrified King of Malabar, whom the lifting up of the iron staff enabled to breathe a little, asked the Emperor of Ceylon how large an army he had brought with him, when he replied, that he and his foster brother had come over by themselves, without any other attendants. He was then asked, what was the object of his expedition, and he replied, "I came here only to liberate 12,000 of my subjects, who have been carried into captivity." The King of Malabar, who was still half dead with affright, proposed to give up all the prisoners who were living, and to substitute others for those who were dead. But this offer did not satisfy the emperor. He required 24,000 captives, or threatened to lay the whole country waste. In order to escape these horrors, the king instantly complied with the emperor's demands, and furnished him with ships and provisions, that he might depart as soon as possible.

On his return to Ceylon, Gaja Bahu placed the 12,000 men in the land of Gale, and settled the rest in different parts of the island. Some of these took up their abode in Abu Curuwa, a part of the seven

Corles, and others in other parts of the same province. After this period Gaja Bahu conducted the government with great vigour; and, in the twenty-two years of his reign, was so formidable to his neighbours, that they trembled at his very name.

He was succeeded by Mana Raja, the eldest son of his mother's sister, who had an inactive reign of sixteen years. After him the sceptre devolved to Hamatissa Raja, who, during a reign of twenty-six years, left no other monument of his deeds than a pagoda, which he constructed for the relics of the saints. The names of the six following sovereigns were Cuda Raja, Venitissa Raja, Ambaheraman Raja, Sirina Raja, Vierdu Raja, and Sangatissa Raja, whose united reigns occupied a period of seventy-eight years.

Srisanga, or Sirisanga Bodi Raja, was the next emperor. In his time there was a great plague, which was occasioned partly by a devil, or evil spirit, called Ratenam Racsea, (which means a devil with red eyes) and partly by a great scarcity of rain. Sirisanga Bodi Raja asked the devil the meaning of this, and why he so tormented the country? The devil answered, that he wanted a certain number of the people for his servants, and that, when he had obtained them, the plague should cease. The king said, that he had no power to give his people over to him and to death, but that he would serve him in their stead, and that he was ready to do this for their sake. The devil answered, that not even a hundred devils would have the hardihood to kill a sovereign, who was so righteous and beneficent. Upon this the devil entered into a treaty with the emperor, in which the former agreed that the plague should cease; and that when any one fell sick, they should make some images of the devil, to whom they should be presented as offerings. The emperor undertook to maintain the observance of this compact, and to enforce these regulations.

In the life-time of this emperor, a king, named Lemeni Golu Amba Raja, invaded his dominions with a great force, with which he made himself master of the country. But not contented with this, he offered a reward for the emperor's head, besides putting to death great numbers of his people.

The emperor concealed himself in a pagoda, where he was discovered by a stranger, who told him that many of the nobles had lost their heads in order to preserve his from being delivered up to the enemy; and that if it were known that he had seen and spoken to his majesty, without taking away his life, according to the orders of the usurper, he should himself be put to death. The emperor, hearing this, and regarding his own preservation of less moment than the welfare of his subjects, told the stranger that he might freely take away his life; for that it was better that he should die for the good of his subjects, than that so many innocent people should be put to death on his account.

The stranger could not help admiring the magnanimity of the emperor, but, at the same time considering, on the other side, the danger which threatened himself, and the great reward which was offered for his majesty's head, he struck it off with his sword, and proceeding to the town of Roona, presented it to Amba Raja, who had recently usurped the title of emperor.

This prince, doubting whether it were the real head of the late sovereign, ordered the person who brought it to be put to death as an impostor; but he, lifting up the head, placed it before them, calling upon his gods to witness that it was the very head of Sirisanga Bodi Raja. When the head was lifted up, fire and smoke came from on high; and the head itself speaking, thus addressed the new emperor: "I am the head of Sirisanga Bodi Raja, who, through God's power, testify that I was cut off from my body by the man who has brought me here."

This unexpected declaration of the head quite disconcerted Lemini Golu Amba Rajà, as well as all the courtiers who were with him, and who were seized with a panic of apprehension. The emperor gave orders that the price, which had been set upon the head, should be immediately paid to the stranger who brought it, as otherwise he was afraid of being persecuted by the spirit of the murdered prince. The head itself he directed to be buried with great pomp, whilst he raised a magnificent pagoda over the grave in which it was laid. The usurper regarded these remains of the emperor, whom he had conspired to destroy, as his best and most precious relics, and one of his most potent idols.

After this event, Lemini Golu Raja lived very devoutly for twenty-two years. He built some more pagodas in Anuraja Pure, distributed much in charity, and governed his people with great justice and moderation. According to his desire, Guwelaguwem Dettatissa, the son of the former emperor, was placed upon the throne. This monarch ordered that eight of the most distinguished nobles and subjects of the preceding sovereign should be perpetually employed in servile labour, for having advised that chief to put his father to death. He restored every thing in the kingdom to the state in which it was in the time of his father, built many pagodas, and reigned ten years.

He was succeeded in the government by his brother, Malasen Raja, who gave himself up entirely to the service of demons. For this purpose he had himself instructed by the priests, who initiated him in the knowledge of all their subtle lore; by means of which he is said to have enriched his dominions with some hundreds of rice fields. This was the most remarkable atchievement in a reign of twenty-four years, which he devoted principally to the cultivation of the earth.

Up to this period, according to the Singalese records, which do not seem always very accurate or consistent in their chronological details,

846 years, nine months, and twenty days had elapsed since the time of Boodh.

The Emperor Guitsirimenaon Raja then ascended the throne, during whose reign a prince and princess, who were brother and sister, children of Mahasira Raja, came from the land of Calinga, and from the town of Dantapure. The name of the prince was Danta Comara, and of the princess Raon Valli. In the disguise of devotees and Brahmins they both escaped out of their native country with the relics of numerous saints, with which they fled to Ceylon, where they were very hospitably received by the emperor, and honoured with numerous presents.

Guitsirimenaon Raja built many pagodas, and governed very righteously for twenty-eight years. He was succeeded by his brother, Deva Tissa Raja, who with his own hands carved out of ivory and sandal wood the images of many idols and representations of Boodh, and with such exquisite skill and beauty, that they could not be excelled. He passed his time very happily and prosperously in the service of his gods, during the nine years of his reign.

His son and successor, Rajas Raja, invited into his dominions many priests, astrologers, physicians, and others whom he thought likely to be of any benefit to his subjects. Five hundred priests were fed by his bounty, and he had a righteous reign of thirty-one years.

In the reign of Utapissa Manam Raja, the next monarch, a renowned sage passed over into Ceylon from the coast of Choromandel. He distributed amongst the people many thousand copies of his doctrine in the Sanscrit tongue. They had been transcribed by 361,000 disciples, and contained a new religion, which they denominate Attua Catava. The present monarch was so much attached to this teacher and his opinions, that he exerted himself with great zeal during a reign of twenty-six years to diffuse them through his dominions. The Singalese throne was next occupied by Senam Raja, Leminitissa Raja, and Visenan Caralsoo Raja, each of whom had a reign of six years. But that of the last was forcibly terminated by the invasion of seven chiefs from the coast of Malabar, who conquered the country, over which they ruled for twenty-seven years. At the end of this period, their united domination was destroyed by the arms of Dacem Gulia Raja, who was wont to live in the wilderness as a jogi, or devotee, but who, on this occasion, found means to assemble a large army, and deliver his country from a foreign yoke.

Dacem Gulia Raja, having placed himself upon the throne, demonstrated his piety by the erection of eighteen pagodas, and the celebration of as many solemn festivals. He also formed numerous rice fields, with the requisite contrivances for irrigation. This devout prince was succeeded by his son, Comara Dahai Raja, who held the sceptre for twenty-nine years. This reign was distinguished by a catastrophe which evinced a more than ordinary sensibility of character. Comara Dahai Raja, who was himself a votary of the muse, had a great poet amongst his subjects, to whom he was much attached. This unfortunate bard was assassinated by a courtezan, when the grief of the emperor was so excessive, that he threw himself into the fire which was prepared to consume the corpse of the murdered Calidassa. But this feeling sovereign chose rather to have his ashes rest in the tomb with those of his friend, than to prolong his life in permanent agony of heart.*

I shall now pass over nine emperors, whose united reigns amounted to

* Valentyn's words are:—Zekere Hoer doodde in zyn tyd een Groot Dichter, van welken de Keizer zeer veel werk maakte, abzoo hy in die konst boven alle andren uytstak, en om de Vorst ook zelf een Liefhebber van de dichkonst was. Hy belastte niet alleen aanstonds die hoer om te brengen, maar sprong uyt liefde tot dien dichter wanneer hy zou verbrand werden, en uyt een onverzettelyke droefheid, mede in 't vuur, dat zyn lyk verteerde, verkiezende liever met zynen vriend Calidassa te verbranden, als zonder hem in geduurige hartzeer in 't leven te blyven.—Vyfde deel p. 70.

117 years, and five of whom appear to have suffered a violent death, when I come to the name of Dos Raja, who, in the sixth year of his reign, was made prisoner by a large army of Malabars, and carried off into that country. At this time, Jaffnapatam, in the northern extremity of Ceylon, was governed by a king, who was in possession of a larger army and a richer treasury than the Emperor of Candy. This prince, whose name was Ariacsi Chaccaravarti Raja, perceiving that there was no sovereign in the southern provinces, entertained the project of making himself master of the whole island. He marched accordingly into the territory of the Candians, giving out that he was only come to see the country, which he designed to subdue.

At this time there was a great chief, named Alagues Vira Mandrim, to whom the Singalese looked up with no ordinary respect. This chief, penetrating the object of the King of Jaffnapatam, retired with some followers to the town of Reygam, where he prepared for resistance. The King of Jaffnapatam, finding that a vigorous opposition was about to be made to his schemes of ambition in that and in other parts of the island, procured a large army of auxiliaries from the coast of Malabar. But these troops were attacked with such fury by the Singalese, who, it is said, fell upon them like lions, that most of the enemy were left dead upon the field. At this period, the above-mentioned chief, Alagues Vira Mandrim, mounted on his elephant, performed such feats of heroism, as greatly contributed to the deliverance of his country and the destruction of the foe.

The Singalese now chose for their king Ruccule Praccarum Bahu Raja, a prince who was descended from some of their most illustrious sovereigns, and had been educated in the pagoda of Vida Gamma. He was placed upon the throne on a Thursday, being the eighth day of the new moon, in the month of May, in the year 1958 after the death of Boodh, and 1453 since the birth of Christ. After remaining three years at

Reygam, he repaired to Cotta,* where he built a beautiful town, all of strong blue stone, with a magnificent palace of the same materials, and with shrines, for the demons and the idols whom he worshipped. He made this his residence, where his chief companion was a favourite priest. Here he preserved the relics of Boodh, and built a separate house or monastery for his priests. After shewing this favour to the priests, it need not excite our surprise that the daughter, of whom his royal consort was soon after delivered, should be distinguished by the name of Ulacudaganam Deva,† which Deva means goddess in the language of the Singalese.

Not long after this the emperor was suddenly attacked by a large army, which was sent against him by the King of Canara, but which he vanquished with a promptitude that diffused the splendour of his arms through the whole East, whilst it rendered him much beloved by his subjects at home.

On one occasion he sent a ship with cinnamon to the neighbouring coast of Malabar. This vessel anchored in the bay of Driampatam, where it was seized and plundered by a chief of the country, Raja Malavaragam, whilst the crew were made prisoners. The emperor, hearing of this affront, ordered the dominions of the raja to be wasted with fire and sword.

Whilst the affairs of the emperor in Ceylon were in a state of tranquillity, one of his tributary chiefs raised the standard of revolt. Supported by the people of the five provinces over which he presided, he resolved to shake off his dependance upon the emperor. In order to strengthen his influence, he distributed many villages and lands among his partizans, and lavished upon them many high sounding titles, to

* He is said, in Valentyn, to have been placed upon the throne of the emperors of Cotta.

† How nearly this approaches the Latin Diva, or Dea, and the Greek θεα.

which the Singalese are much attached. The emperor sent a great army against this rebellious foe, whose adherents he slew by thousands; and, having captured many of his nearest relations, and driven the chief himself out of Candy, he committed the conquered country to the government of one of his vassals, who was to pay him an annual tribute.

The King of Jaffnapatam, who had assumed the title of Emperor of Ceylon, alarmed by the increasing power of his rival, who was styled Emperor of Cotta, made preparations to avert the impending storm. But the Emperor of Cotta, who had resolved to make himself master of Jaffnapatam, marched an army into that country, previously informing the sovereign, that, as Ceylon could not contain two emperors, his general, Sappu Comara, was come to release him from the weight of that title; and, as he could not be at peace, nor remain contented with what he possessed, to take care that the general tranquillity should not in future be disturbed by his machinations. When the King of Jaffnapatam heard that the enemy was approaching, he sent three of his courtiers, one after another, to attempt to stop their progress; but these were all slain by Sappu Comara, who soon shewed himself before the walls of his capital, mounted, as the account says, on a blue horse, with a green mane.

The King of Jaffnapatam, terrified by the sight of this formidable foe, dispatched to the combat Varacara, one of his stoutest cavaliers, who had thought to have cut his adversary in pieces; but, before he could come up with him, he was himself run through the body by the enemy. In the mean time, Sappu Comara accomplished the conquest of the capital and of the surrounding country, over which the emperor made one of his nephews king.

After these events, this sovereign enjoyed a reign of profound peace for a long period of fifty-five years, passing the close of his days in the service of the gods. In the fifty-second year of this prince's reign,* Laurence D'Almeida, the son of the Viceroy of Goa, landed on the Island of Ceylon, and is the first Portuguese that ever visited the country.

* A. C. 1505. I need not revert to the gross incongruities which are very apparent in some of the Singalese historical and chronological details. They will, however, bring the reader acquainted with all that is known of their ancient history.

CHAP. IV.

Sterility of the Singalese Annals. Jaja Wira Praccaram Bahu. Mahapandita Praccaram Bahu Raja; his title disputed; dethroned and put to Death by Ambulvagala, who became Emperor. Darma Praccaram Bahu; his four Brothers. A Moorish Chief vanquished by these Brothers. Hostilities of the King of Candy against the Emperor of Cotta. A Portuguese Ship anchors in the Bay of Columbo. The Emperor makes a Treaty with the Commander. Death of the Emperor. Viga Bahu. Arrival of another Portuguese Ship; an Attack upon the Crew; Apology of the Emperor; Treaty of Amity. Sons of the Emperor and his Brother by a common Wife. They make War upon their Father, who is vanquished and put to Death. Bowaneca Bahu Maha Raja, Emperor, quells a Rebellion; marries his Daughter, whose eldest Son, Darma Palla, he recommends as his Successor to the Protection of the Portuguese. Hostilities of his Brother. The Emperor shot Dead. Darma Palla crowned by the Portuguese, who support him against his Enemies. The Viceroy of Goa brings Succours to the Emperor; returns to Goa. Feuds in the Court of Candy. The Emperor baptized by a Franciscan Priest; compelled to abandon Goa; takes Refuge with the Portuguese. Raja Singa Raja, Emperor.

THOUGH I am now arrived at the period when the state of affairs in Ceylon became changed by the arrival of the Europeans, I shall follow the example of Valentyn in continuing the scanty notices of the Singalese history, which have been furnished by their native writers, before I proceed to describe the commencement and progress of their intercourse with the Portuguese, the Dutch, and other nations; with the varied events which it occasioned, and the scenes of ravage and bloodshed which it too often produced. In the two preceding chapters, I am conscious that I have been traversing a desart, where there was hardly a blade of grass to relieve the eye, or a drop of water to moisten the lips.

In the present chapter, the prospect will not, I fear, exhibit more variety or interest: but, if the way is wearisome and oppressive, I shall endeavour to render it as short as possible; and the reader has this advantage over the author, that, if these three chapters have nothing to arrest attention, or to excite curiosity, he may get to the end of them easily by turning over the leaves. But the author must proceed step by step over the barren waste, and think it luxury if only one pleasurable sensation should occur to cheer his path or to alleviate his toils.

Ruccule Praccaram Bahu Raja, whose death I have mentioned in the last chapter, and who appears to have fixed the imperial residence at Cotta, was, in the year 1508, succeeded in the sovereignty by his grandson, Jaja Wira Praccaram Bahu. This monarch fell sick, and died, after a reign of seven years; when a young prince, whom he had brought up in the palace, became emperor of Cotta, under the name of Mahapandita Praccaram Bahu Raja. But his title was soon disputed by Ambulvagala, a first cousin of the former emperor, who raised an army against him, defeated his forces in the field, and besieged his capital of Cotta, which he took by treachery.*

The emperor, hearing of this disaster, ordered his queen and all her women to be deprived of life, that they might escape the profane violence of the enemy; but he himself, after a short reign of one year, was taken prisoner, and put to death by Ambulvagala, who reigned in his stead.

Ambulvagala enjoyed the sovereignty in peace for a period of twenty years, under the title of Wira Praccaram Bahu. At his death, Darma Praccaram Bahu, the eldest of his five sons, succeeded to the throne. His second son, Taniam Vallaba, became King of Candupiti Madampa; the third reigned over Manikravare, with the title of Siri Raja Singa; the

* Valentyn Byzondre zaaken van Ceylon, p. 74.

fourth became king of Reigam; and the fifth, who had the title of Saccalacala Valaba Raja, King of Udugampala.

At this period a Moorish chief, named Adiracarajan, anchored in the bay of Chilao with a large fleet and a considerable army. But his army was defeated and his fleet destroyed by the efforts of Saccalacala and his brother, King Taniam Vallaba. Saccalacala put the Moorish chieftain to death with his own hand.

The King of Candy, who was at this period a tributary to the Emperor of Cotta, began to throw off his allegiance, and to assume an independent authority. The emperor sent his brother, Siri Raja Singa against the rebellious chief, who reduced him to such straits, that he was happy to procure his pardon by a payment of money and elephants, and by abandoning his daughter to the pleasure of the emperor.

The emperor afterwards gave this princess in marriage to one of his chiefs, called Dequiravella, by whom she had six sons and a daughter, who was married to the Prince Jaja Vira Bandara.

Some years after this the King of Candy renewed hostilities against the Emperor of Cotta, who sent his brother Saccalacala against him with such a force, that he was soon compelled to throw himself prostrate at the feet of Saccalacala, and, stripped of all the insignia of royalty, to sue for peace in the most humiliating manner. He was again received into favour, but on much harder conditions than before.

In the life-time of this Emperor of Cotta, Darma Praccaram Bahu, and about the year 1530, the Singalese annals say, that a ship came from Portugal, which was the second that had anchored in the bay of Columbo. As soon as the emperor received intelligence of that event, he called together his four royal brothers, with whom he deliberated whether or not he should permit the strangers to land. Saccalacala, the King of Udugampola, said that he would first proceed in person to where the ship lay; when he was so much gratified by his reception, that he advised the emperor to make a treaty of amity with the Portuguese. Upon this the Portuguese sent a deputation to Cotta, with presents for the emperor, which were very favourably received; and a mutual league was the consequence. This is the account of the Singalese; but the embassy, which they have recorded, appears to have taken place in the preceding reign.

Darma Praccaram Bahu closed his life after a reign of twenty-five years, and appears to have been celebrated for liberality to his friends, and for charity to the poor. Saccalacala Valaba, who, though the youngest, was the wisest of the four brothers, would have been raised to the throne if he would have accepted the dignity; but his refusal caused the choice to fall upon the King of Reygam, who became emperor under the title of Viga Bahu. In his time another Portuguese ship anchored in the bay of Columbo; and, whilst the crew were engaged in unloading the cargo, they were attacked by a party of Singalese soldiers, who, however, were soon put to flight by a few shot. The emperor, who does not appear to have given any orders for this act of hostility, either felt, or affected to feel, great indignation at the conduct of his troops. He accordingly sent an embassy to the Portuguese to apologize for the outrage, and to represent it as originating in mistake. Two or three of the Portuguese soldiers were, at the same time, conducted with great ceremony to the residence of the emperor, where they were very courteously received; and a treaty was concluded, which professed to establish an eternal amity.

The Emperor Viga Bahu, and his brother Siri Raja Singa, are said, when young men, to have had only one wife between them, who was daughter of a chief called Quiravella Mahabisso Adassyn. By these two brothers this lady had four sons; of whom the first died when young. The name of the second was Bowanacu Bahu Maha Raja, of the third Para Raja Singa Raja, of the fourth Majadunna Raja. When the mother of these princes died, the emperor married another wife, of the family of Quiravella; who, upon her nuptials, had the title of Deva Raja Singa Comari.

This new empress, jealous of the regard which her husband evinced for his first family, conspired with two of the principal courtiers to remove them out of the way. But they had timely intimation of her sanguinary designs, and fled to a pagoda, where they were concealed by the priests. The two elder princes remained a considerable time in this sacred retreat; but the youngest repaired to Candy, where the reigning king, Jaja Vira Raja, had married his niece. He now invited his two brothers to join him, and, being furnished with a large force by the Candian monarch, they waged war upon the emperor their father, whom they reduced to great straits; and forced him to abandon to their vengeance the two courtiers who were implicated in the machinations of the empress against their lives.

But, not satisfied with this concession, they marched to Cotta, and having obtained possession of the palace, they carried off all the imperial treasure, and gave orders to have their father put to death, because he adhered to the party of his wife. Not one of his native subjects could be found who was willing to imbrue his hands in the blood of his sovereign; but, at last, they discovered a stranger, named Seelam, who perpetrated the atrocious deed. This emperor reigned eight years.

The morning after his death the eldest brother was crowned by the title of Bowaneca Bahu Maha Raja. A nephew of the last emperor, by one of his sisters, along with two chiefs and some other followers, opposed the claims of the new sovereign; but they were defeated, and their lands given to the Panneas, a caste, whose office it is to cut grass for the horses and elephants.

The emperor had a daughter named Samudra Deva, who had married a chief of Malabar extraction, named Vigea Bandara Raja, by whom she had two sons. Bowaneca Bahu had determined that the eldest of these grandsons, who was named Darma Palla, should succeed him on the throne; but his brothers had recourse to arms, in order to prevent the accomplishment of this design.

In the present exigency of his affairs, the emperor felt it politic to recommend his grandson and intended successor, Darma Palla, to the protection of the King of Portugal, in order to secure him against the arms of those by whom his title might be opposed. For this purpose he sent an embassy to Portugal, with a rich treasure and valuable presents.

The emperor's brother, who was King of Majaduna, having heard of this embassy, and at the same time being informed of the death of his brother, who was king of Reygam, called in the aid of the Moors from the opposite coast, who sent him some succours, in conjunction with which he laid siege to the town of Cotta; but the enterprise was rendered abortive by the vigorous opposition of the Portuguese. The King of Majaduna now sued for peace, which was offered upon condition that he would give up the two chiefs of his Moorish auxiliaries.. But, as he refused to comply with this demand, his army was furiously attacked by the emperor and the Poruguese, who put it to a total route; and the king was compelled to fly to Saffragam, with the loss of all his royal ornaments.

The King of Majaduna remained, for some time, concealed from the search of his pursuers; but afterwards returned, with the forces which he could muster, to his capital of Sitavaca, where he had resolved to renew the conflict. When this intelligence reached the emperor, he repaired with a large army to Calane, where the King of Majaduna had a sumptuous residence. After remaining some time at this place, the emperor, whilst reclining near the window, was shot through the head by a

Portuguese soldier; but without its being known whether the act were fortuitous or designed.

Darma Palla Maha Raja was now placed upon the throne, by the strong hand of the Portuguese. This was no sooner perceived by the King of Majaduna, than he marched to Cotta with a considerable army, and bravely attacked the force of the new made emperor and his European allies; but he was again vanquished, and forced to quit the field.

In the mean time Darma Palla sent an account of these events to the King of Portugal and to the Viceroy of Goa, who, at his request, dispatched more troops to his assistance. The viceroy himself, Don Louis de Taydo, with his nephew Don Juan, afterwards anchored in the Bay of Columbo, with a large fleet and a considerable supply of military stores. They proceeded to Cotta, where they experienced a very favourable reception.

After mature deliberation on the present situation of the emperor, the viceroy, De Taydo, marched to Sitavaca, from which the King of Majaduna was compelled to fly, leaving his palace a prey to the enemy. The Portuguese commander set fire to the town of Sitavaca, after which he returned to Cotta; and having left his nephew Don Juan with the emperor, he again took his departure for Goa.

Don Juan fell sick not long after he had been invested with this command; when he resigned his power to Diego de Melo, who became captain-general of the Portuguese. Some violent feuds about this period arose in the family of Jaga Vira, King of Candy, who finding one of his sons in rebellion against him, and supported by a powerful force, mounted his royal elephant named Aira Vatta, when, proceeding with his wife, his other children, and a large train of followers, to Sitavaca, he took the crown off his head, and threw it at the feet of the King of Majaduna. But this appeal to the sympathy of that monarch was not sufficient to induce him to support the King of Candy in the contest with his eldest son, whose claims to the crown he was endeavouring to set aside in favour of the children of a second wife.

In the reign of the Emperor Darma Palla, a Franciscan priest, John Villa da Conde resided for some time at Cotta, when he succeeded in persuading the emperor to be baptized, along with many of his nobles and people.

Peace was soon afterwards restored between the King of Majaduna, the emperor, and the Portuguese; but other contentions ensued, which finally proved fatal to the power of the Emperor Darma Palla, who was compelled to abandon Cotta, and take refuge with the Portuguese; whilst the youngest son of the King of Majaduna, who received the title of Raja Singa Raja, reduced all Ceylon under his power, with the exception of the Portuguese settlements at Columbo and Point de Galle. The astrologers are said to have early foretold that this prince would one day become master of the whole island; but the next chapter will exhibit more particulars of his conduct and character.

CHAPTER V.

Ceylon, how discovered by the Portuguese; State of the Island on their Arrival. Don Lorenzo d'Almeyda anchors in the Bay of Galle; enters into a Treaty with the King; stipulates for an annual Payment of Cinnamon. Lopez Suaar Alvarenga, in the Year 1518, *after some ineffectual Opposition from the Natives, erects a Fort at Columbo; forces the Emperor to pay an annual Tribute of Precious Stones, &c. to Emanuel, King of Portugal. The Singalese, exasperated by Injustice, lay Siege to the Fortress of Columbo; are finally dispersed, and the Emperor compelled to sue for Peace. The Fortress of Columbo demolished in* 1524. *A Moorish Chieftain endeavours by a Stratagem to get the Portuguese, who were left at the Factory, into his Power. The Emperor Darma Praccaram Bahu places his Grandson, Parea Bandara, under the Protection of the King of Portugal; sends an Embassy to that Court with an Image of the young Prince and a Crown of Gold. The Image ceremoniously crowned in* 1541. *Parea Bandara succeeds his Grandfather, but is forced by Raja Singa to fly from Candy and take Refuge at Columbo. Cruelties of Raja Singa; his Perfidy and Barbarity to Fimala Lamantia, one of his Chiefs. A Son of Fimala Lamantia sent to Goa, where he is baptized under the Name of Don John. The People of Candy, exasperated against Raja Singa, are disposed to unite with the Portuguese, who think by that Means to become Masters of the Island. The Portuguese first make themselves Masters of Jaffnapatam, and then march to Candy. The Candians terrified at their Proceedings; Don Philippo and Don John, Two Princes of the Blood-royal of Candy, dispatched to quiet their Fears. The Portuguese obtain Possession of Candy, where they raise Don Philippo to the Throne, but still in a State of Dependence upon the Portuguese. Rancour of Don John against the Portuguese excited by their Preference of Don Philippo; consults a Magician how best to get rid of his royal Adversary; Poison recommended. He executes his Purpose in the Absence of the Portuguese, who were watching the Motions of Raja Singa. His Adherents numerous, the Portuguese alarmed; Don John, elected Emperor, menaces the Portuguese, who surrender their Post at Ganoor. Details of the Conflict which ensued between Don John and Raja Singa; the last totally routed; Circumstances of his Death, his Inquietudes of Conscience, Expedients to ap-*

pease. Janiere Bandara, a new Competitor with Don John for the Sovereignty of the Island. The former obtains the Assistance of the Portuguese, to whom he surrenders his Independence. Their united Efforts. Don Pedro de Sousa sent to Ceylon. Don John, routed by the Portuguese, compelled to hide himself in a Wood. The Portuguese favour the Desire of the Singalese to have Donna Catharina, Daughter of Darma Palla Raja, for their Sovereign. She is sent for from Manaar. Inauspicious Commencement of her Journey. Her Entrance into Candy; her magnificent Coronation. A Price set upon the Head of Don John; daring Conduct of that Chief: the Insolence and Injustice of the Portuguese; they elude the Proposition of their Creature Janiere to marry Donna Catharina. Violence of his Resentment. An Interview with Don Pedro de Sousa. Janiere dissembles, but secretly corresponds with Don John; they agree to exterminate the Portuguese. The Portuguese discover the Plot; they resolve to assassinate Janiere; Mode in which they effected their Purpose.

IN the year 1505 Francisco d'Almeyda, viceroy of Goa, sent his son Laurence, or Lorenzo, with a fleet of nine sail, in order that he might fall in with some Moorish vessels which were passing by the Maldives. But this commander, instead of reaching the place of his destination, was driven by the wind to the coast of Ceylon, of which he thus, accidentally, effected the important discovery. The country appears at this time to have been divided into several kingdoms, the sovereigns of which were more or less dependent upon an emperor, but amongst whom there prevailed, at this period, the most violent dissensions and the most sanguinary feuds.*

* There are said to have been in ancient times no less than sixteen kings in Ceylon, who were wont to meet once a year to celebrate a great festival in the town of Sitavaca. The festival was continued for sixteen days, and thus allowed a day and a night of rejoicing to each of the kings with their wives and subjects. At the expiration of this period they brought out of the temple a gold bracelet, on which sixteen heads were engraved, representing the above-mentioned sovereignties. This was presented by the priest to the emperor, as a token of homage and service on the part of the other chiefs. The oldest of these kings was often chosen as the emperor; but his power did not much diminish the independence of the rest. By degrees, however, this choice of a superior fell into disuse; and the emperor found means to extend and to perpetuate his power, when the yearly meeting at

Don Lorenzo first cast anchor in the bay of Galle, which was then under the government of a particular chieftain or king, who sent an ambassador to him in the name of the emperor with a proffer of amity. This led to a treaty of alliance,* in which it was stipulated, that the Singalese monarch should pay to Emanuel, King of Portugal, an annual tribute of 250,000 lbs. weight of cinnamon. His Portuguese majesty was, on the other hand, to defend the emperor against all his enemies. In commemoration of this event, and no doubt with an intention to signify the subjection of the island to the Portuguese, Don Lorenzo erected upon the spot a marble pillar, on which were engraven the arms of Portugal.

In 1518 Lopez Suaar Alvarenga sailed to Ceylon with a fleet of nineteen ships, when he proceeded to erect a fort, according to orders which had been received from King Emanuel, and to a permission which had been obtained from the emperor. But the emperor had either never given such permission, or soon repented of the grant; for it was not long before some of the Singalese, who attempted to impede the progress of the work, were killed in a fray with the Portuguese.

Alvarenga was not to be appeased by a verbal apology for this outrage. Nor could he endure that his sovereign should be insulted by a black king. He accordingly attacked the Singalese with such energy, that they were compelled to accept of peace upon the following conditions:

1. That the Portuguese should be at liberty to erect a fort at Columbo.

2. That the emperor should pay to King Emanuel an annual tribute of a certain number of precious stones, with six elephants, and 120,000 lbs. of cinnamon.

Sitavaca was imposed as a mark of subjection to a paramount lord. See Extract uyt de consideratien van der Heer Van Rheed over Ceylon. c. xxii. Valentyn, p. 274.

* Valentyn, V. p. 90.

The first fort, which the Portuguese erected at Columbo, was a composition of clay and stone; but in 1520 they constructed fortifications of a more regular and solid kind. When these were finished, the Portuguese, presuming on their strength, committed various acts of violence upon the natives, which revived the late animosities, and caused acts of retaliation. The Singalese were so incensed, that they put to death every Portuguese that came in their way. The commander, whose name was Lopez Brit, for a time connived at these proceedings; but he afterwards fell upon the Singalese, and put them to flight. They returned, however, to the charge; and, after collecting a numerous host of 20,000 men, they invested the fortress at Columbo, and kept it besieged for the space of five months.

The Portuguese commander, Brit, who was a man of great courage, but whose inconsiderate facility had suffered his own people to involve him in these difficulties, sent a messenger to Cochin to inform the viceroy of his perilous situation. The viceroy accordingly sent to his aid Jacob Lopez Siqueira in a galley with fifty Portuguese. Upon receiving this little accession to his force, the brave Brit, who was on the point of perishing by famine, sallied forth at the head of 300 Portuguese, made himself master of the works of the enemy, and gave them such a signal overthrow, that the emperor was compelled once more to sue for peace. This Brit granted with the less reluctance, as he knew that his own people had been the aggressors in the late troubles; but he took care that they should treat the Singalese with more justice for the time to come.

In 1524, Emanuel, King of Portugal, gave orders to Ferdinand Gomes de Leme to destroy the fort at Columbo. Gomes afterwards left only a factor, a secretary, and fifteen Portuguese upon the island. A Moorish chieftain on the coast of Malabar, having learned that only these few Portuguese remained upon the island, and that he could easily get them into his power, accordingly set sail for Ceylon with 500 men in four ships. With this force he entered the bay of Columbo, when he informed the Emperor of Cotta that a general attack had been made upon the Portuguese throughout all their settlements in India, and that he had been sent on purpose to carry off all the people of that nation who had been left at this spot.

The Emperor of Cotta, who was embarrassed by this intelligence, was assured by the heads of the Portuguese factory that it was all false; and, if it were true, he had no power to comply with the demand. The emperor accordingly ordered the Moors to depart; but not satisfied with this determination, they made an attempt to carry off the Portuguese by force, but experienced such a vigorous repulse, that they abandoned the undertaking in disgrace.

A new fortress must about this period have been erected at Columbo, instead of that which King Emanuel had ordered to be demolished, though the Portuguese writers make no mention of the circumstance. It is certain that the Portuguese were now firmly established at Columbo, and that they constantly supported the interest of the Emperor Darma Praccaram Bahu, who is otherwise called Abu-Negabo Bandara, and who mounted the throne in 1536. This prince thought it expedient to place his grandson Parea Bandara, or Darmapalla, under the protection of the King of Portugal; and for this purpose he sent two messengers to that kingdom, along with a statue of the young prince, and a crown of gold. His Portuguese majesty was requested to place the crown upon the head of the statue; and this ceremony was accordingly performed with much pomp and magnificence in the great hall of Lisbon in the year 1541.

After the death of Darma Praccarum Bahu, the prince, whose statue had previously received the above-mentioned royal honours, succeeded to the power and dominions of his grandfather; but he experienced such a powerful enemy in Raja Singa, the King of Sitavaca, that he was compelled to fly from Candy, and take refuge at Columbo. Raja Singa accordingly made himself master not only of the kingdom of Cotta, but of that of Candy, where he afterwards practised the greatest oppression and the most revolting barbarities both upon the nobles and the people. These cruelties appear to have originated in the feeling of revenge. The Candians had taken part in the rebellion of one of Raja Singa's chiefs, named Fimala Lamantia, who had revolted against him, and, for some time, defied his power.* But what Raja Singa could not effect by force he accomplished by art. He made a treaty with his enemy on conditions that seemed very favourable to his ambitious views. Fimala Lamantia was hence induced to trust himself in the power of Raja Singa, who had him instantly arrested. He was afterwards ordered to be buried in the earth up to his head, which was left above ground and beaten with clubs till he expired.

A son of Fimala Lamantia had been previously sent by the Portuguese to Columbo, and thence to Goa, where he was instructed in the Roman Catholic religion, and baptized by the name of Don John, after Don John of Austria, brother of Philip the Second, King of Castille and Portugal. This Don John, as we shall afterwards find, makes some figure in the history of the Singalese.

The people of Candy, who were very much disaffected to Raja Singa, determined to form a union with the Portuguese, in order to destroy his tyranny. The Portuguese themselves were well disposed to comply with their wishes, as they hoped by this means to obtain possession of Candy, and to become masters of the whole island.

The Portuguese, however, after much deliberation, judged that, in order to obtain the object of their ambition, it was first requisite that

* This Fimala Lamantia, or, as it is otherwise written, Fimala Mantra, had been appointed Governor of Candy by Raja Singa; and the Candians had chosen him for their emperor, when he assumed the title of Fimala Darma Suria Adassyn, but his reign was short and his end miserable.

they should accomplish the conquest of Jaffnapatam. They accordingly sent a powerful fleet to that part of the island, under the command of Don Andrea Furtado de Mendoza, who made himself master of the kingdom by surprise, and forced the inhabitants to allow him to march as many troops as he pleased through their country to Candy; and the King of Jaffnapatam moreover stipulated to furnish them with all the aid in his power to further the execution of the project.

The people of Candy, who had not yet entered into any actual treaty with the Portuguese, when they heard that they had become masters of Jaffnapatam, were, at first, seized with considerable alarm. In order to allay this ferment, and to quiet their apprehensions, the Portuguese admiral resolved to dispatch to Candy, Don John; and Don Philippo,* a Singalese prince, who had also received Christian baptism from the hands of the Portuguese.

In addition to this measure, Don Andrea Furtado de Mendoza had resolved to set up Don Philippo as Emperor of Ceylon, to appoint Don John the general of his army; and also to enter into a treaty with the people of Candy to carry on hostilities against Raja Singa with their united forces.

Raja Singa, hearing of these movements, directed his march to another part of the island, without entertaining any apprehensions from the people of Candy, whom he had previously disarmed. But the Candians had secretly provided themselves with bows and arrows, which they had concealed in their houses. This intelligence induced Raja Singa to retrace his steps towards Candy; but, before his arrival, he found that the Portuguese had made themselves masters of the place, where they invested Don Philippo with the crown; and, at the

* Don Philippo was the son of Bandaar Raja, a prince of Cotta. He had been brought up by the Portuguese from a child.

same time, made Don John the commander-in-chief of the forces. But the Portuguese did not omit to stipulate, that these two princes, along with persons instructed by them in their faith, should enter into an engagement to marry none but Portuguese women; and that the people of Candy should take a solemn oath of obedience and fealty to the King of Portugal.

Don John, whose ambitious expectations had been disappointed by the elevation of Don Philippo to the crown, was greatly incensed against his rival; but still more violently against the Portuguese, by whom he thought that he had been treated with perfidy and ingratitude. But he concealed these sentiments of aversion in his breast, till a fit opportunity arrived for accomplishing the projects of vengeance which he entertained.

The town of Candy, which had suffered much from the ravages of Raja Singa, was repaired, strengthened, and embellished for the accommodation of the new emperor; whilst Don John, whose rancour was never dormant, consulted with a magician about the best mode of getting rid of his royal adversary. The prophetic sage recommended poison as the most advisable expedient.

When the Portuguese conducted the Emperor Don Philippo in state to his capital, he was welcomed into his palace by the acclamations of his subjects, and with every outward mark of respect and attachment. The Portuguese themselves, imagining that every thing was now settled on a footing of durable tranquillity, took their departure from the city, in order to watch the motions of Raja Singa, and free the Singalese from all apprehensions on that account.

Don John, judging the departure of the Portuguese a favourable moment for the perpetration of the horrid purpose which he meditated, lost no time in administering poison to his sovereign; and, not having patience to wait till it took effect, he repeated the dose with increased potency, when the unfortunate monarch immediately expired.*

The party of the successful usurper was soon joined by a considerable number of adherents, whom he allured by the most magnificent promises; and had the art to render himself much beloved by the Singalese. The Portuguese, who were encamped at Ganoor, beheld these proceedings with considerable anxiety, and began to regard the ambition of Don John as an object of serious alarm. They immediately dispatched an account of what had passed to Don John de Melo, the commander of the forces at Manaar, urging him, by repeated messengers, to send immediate succours, or their retreat would probably be cut off, and they would be placed in the most critical situation.

Don John, having prevailed upon the Singalese, or, at least, the people of Candy, to choose him for their emperor, he threw off the mask of friendship which he had hitherto professed for the Portuguese, and sent them peremptory orders to depart from their present situation within five or six days, or he would put them all to the sword. He upbraided them with their flagrant acts of perfidy and insincerity; and said that the only object of their policy was to make themselves masters of the lives and fortunes of the Singalese. He had, therefore, resolved, that not one of them should be suffered to remain in his dominions.

The Portuguese, who were posted at Ganoor, were not strong enough to make any effectual resistance to the above imperious mandate; and, despairing of assistance, they surrendered the fortress, and marched out with their side-arms, which was all that they were suffered to carry away.

On the following day, Don John de Melo arrived with reinforcements,

* "Waar van hy ten cersten quam te bersten." Valentyn.

but it was too late to recover what had been lost. Some of the Portuguese remained at Candy in the service of the usurper.

Raja Singa, in the mean time, having rapidly assembled his forces at Sitavaca, began his march upon Candy, where he determined at once to chastise both Don John and the inhabitants for their late rebellion against his authority. When Don John received this intelligence, and reflected that he was deprived of the aid of the Portuguese, he felt considerable alarm, particularly when he heard that the army of Raja Singa had arrived in the province of the four Corles. He hastened, however, to meet him with all the force that he could bring together. The two armies came in sight of each other at Walane, where Raja Singa told his adversary to expect the fate of his father, whom he had cut in pieces. Don John replied, that, if his father had been as conscious of his perfidy as he was, he would never have been the victim of his cruelty.

Don John moreover acquainted his adversary, that he entertained no doubt but that he should be able to inflict ample vengeance on the man who had put his father to such a cruel death. Raja Singa, enraged by this message, immediately gave orders for his army to advance. But he was much more disconcerted, when he learned that Don John, more brave than he, was already in motion for the encounter.

Don John himself soon appeared in sight with the Singalese ensigns of imperial power, two white umbrellas held over his head: when he made such a furious attack upon his adversary, that he fled with precipitation at the end of half an hour. Raja Singa took this unexpected and ignominious defeat so much to heart, that, in a moment of rage, he ran a sharp thorn into his foot, which brought on a mortification, of which he died. He had reached the great age of 120 years.*

* The Singalese are said to be long-lived, and often to preserve their strength and faculties in a sort of green old age. The above-mentioned monarch seems to have been an instance of this remark. There seems no reason to disbelieve the account which is given of his age; and the age of

As he became conscious of approaching death, he is said to have expressed deep regret for the different cruelties which he had committed upon the inhabitants of Candy, and particularly for those which he had afterwards perpetrated upon all the priests whom he could get into his power. But, before this period, he had caused almost all his nearest relations to be massacred. His father, his uncle, his mother-in-law, and his three brothers, who were born in wedlock,* were all put to death by his orders.

Oppressed by the recollection of these monstrous cruelties, he sent for the priests of Daldowanse to attend him before he left the world. He asked these ghostly counsellors, if such a man as he had been, might hope for pardon for his sins. The priests, with more uncourteous honesty than is usual on such occasions, particularly in the chamber of dying kings, replied, " that he could not hope to be forgiven."

The monarch, who had expected a softer answer, was so enraged by their presumption, or want of loyalty as he termed it, that he ordered them all, with the exception of the chief priest, to be shut up in a house and burnt alive.

After making this addition to his stock of impieties, the monarch sent for the priests of another pagoda, of whom he asked the same important question. But they, warned by the fate of their brethren, gave an answer of a more soothing kind. They said that such a sinner could hope for no forgiveness if he did not repent, but that, as his majesty had felt contrition for his enormities, they would bring

---

a king may in general be much more easily authenticated than that of any other man. The Portuguese were well acquainted with Raja Singa, with the circumstances of his life, and the vicissitudes of his history. We are now come to a period, when the events of the Singalese annals, by being incorporated more with those of Europeans, may be better ascertained. See Valentyn, 5. p. 94.

* Raja Singa was a king's son, but not by a legitimate bed. His mother was a dancing girl. The Portuguese say that he was a barber; but this is a calumny.

it to pass by the force of their prayers, that, after death, instead of being tormented by devils, he should be permitted to sojourn in some intermediate region between heaven and earth.

This answer served to compose the guilty inquietudes of the dying king; and he not only permitted those, who had given it, to live, but loaded them with presents, which they refused to receive. He requested them also not to think of the massacre of their brethren, which he had ordered in a paroxysm of rage. Upon receiving an assurance of their forgiveness, he soon after gave up the ghost.*

Don John, having heard of the death of Raja Singa, lost no time in concerting measures to render himself master of the whole island. But he found an enemy to his views in Xavier Wandaar, or, according to others Janiere Bandara, the secretary of his deceased rival. This Janiere, having obtained possession of all his master's treasure, entered into a treaty with the Portuguese, to whom he surrendered the whole kingdom; as he perceived that, without their assistance, he could not maintain himself against the opposition of Don John.

The Portuguese, elated with the prospect of becoming masters of the whole island, lost no time in sending to the viceroy of Goa intelligence of Raja Singa's death, and of the treaty into which they had entered with Janiere, requesting immediate and powerful reinforcements, in order that they might be able to repress the designs of Don John, and annex the dominion of the whole island to the crown of Portugal.

* The above Raja Singa, though a monster of iniquity, appears from the Singalese annals to have had some taste for literature, and to have patronized men of genius. For, we find that, during his reign, a great sage, named Vidumal, came from the coast of Malabar on purpose to pay his respects at the court of this sovereign. Raja Singa received his learned guest with great hospitality, showed him marked attention, and conferred upon him the honourable title of Manaperuma Mucavetic, or the Prince of the Poets. He made him also a Dessave or governor of a province; when he settled with his family in the dominions of his munificent benefactor. See Valentyn, p. 82.

In order to accomplish this purpose, Don Pedro de Sousa, in 1590, was sent to Ceylon with all the troops which the viceroy could spare, consisting of 1250 whites, besides mestizis and blacks. Before the reinforcement arrived, Janiere had already made himself master of all the low country, with the assistance of the Portuguese garrisons at Galle and Columbo. Don John, who was encamped at Walane, beheld the progress of the enemy in this quarter with great dissatisfaction, but he was so far from being able to prevent it, that he began to entertain serious apprehensions of danger to himself, from the union of the Portuguese troops, with those of the Singalese chiefs, who had armed against him.

Don Pedro, finding that the low lands had been already conquered, and thinking that little was left for him to do, was on the point of returning to Goa; but he was induced to desist from this precipitate resolution, upon the representation of the principal people, that he ought first to achieve the conquest of Candy, where the richest booty would reward his toils.

In the mean time Janiere had contrived to bring into the field an army of 151086* men, provided with seventy-five war elephants, and 1000 without teeth, a great body of coolies or porters, and a considerable number of baggage oxen. The army of Don Pedro consisted of 1474 whites, 1280 mestizis, 1224 natives or Singalese, forty-seven war elephants, and 20,000 oxen.

Don John, who could not muster more than 30, or 40,000 men, marched boldly to the conflict, with the superior force of the enemy; but the Portuguese attacked him with so much fury, and followed up their first success with such unremitting vigour, that Don John was compelled to hide himself in a wood along with his queen, where they subsisted on the wild roots and plants, which the place supplied.

* This is the force mentioned by Valentyn; but there is probably some mistake in the number.

The Portuguese, who had thus become masters of the country, began to require that the Singalese should take the oath of allegiance to the King of Portugal; but the Singalese themselves manifested such a strong inclination to have Donna Catharina, who was a daughter of their lawful Emperor Mahadassyn, or Darma Palla Raja, for their sovereign, that Don Pedro de Sousa, the commander of the Portuguese troops, was disposed to accede to the proposition. He consulted Janiere, who was commonly called king, upon the subject. Janiere, representing the services which he had rendered to the Portuguese, requested that he might be permitted to have the princess for his wife.

A considerable escort was accordingly dispatched, in order to bring the princess from her residence at Manaar. When every thing was ready for her departure, she got into a sumptuous palanquin, that had been prepared for her journey to Candy. But she had hardly been lifted up from the ground, when the bamboo poles, to which the vehicle was attached, broke in pieces. The princess, whose mind had not been divested of its superstitious tendencies by her Christian instructors, considered this as such an ill-omened commencement of her expedition, that she refused to proceed. Every argument was employed to persuade her that this was a mere fortuitous occurrence, which was totally beneath the consideration of one who had embraced the Christian faith. Her attendants moreover affirmed, that they would answer for her safe arrival at Candy. Upon these earnest solicitations and positive assurances, she at last consented to resume her seat in the palanquin, and arrived at Candy in eight days after her departure from Manaar.

Don Pedro, who had gone out to meet her with a large train of his principal officers and attendants, threw himself, with great reverence, at her feet, and warmly congratulated her on her safe journey and happy prospects. The native chiefs and nobles of Ceylon, according to their mode of shewing homage, prostrated themselves before her, with their faces flat upon the ground. She then returned to the palanquin, from which she had alighted, and was conveyed into the capital in splendid procession, whilst money was scattered amongst the people. After an interval of three days, she was crowned with great magnificence, and the ceremony is said to have cost no less than nineteen and a half tons of gold, which the treasures of Raja Singa were ransacked to supply.

When Donna Catharina had been thus elevated to her father's throne, with the universal consent of the Singalese, the country seemed likely to enjoy a period of profound peace; and all the subordinate kings and chiefs returned to their homes.

Don Pedro de Sousa, the Portuguese general, offered a reward of ten thousand pagodas for the head of Don John. But Don John was so little alarmed by this circumstance, that he occasionally came into Candy in the disguise of a beggar. At night he would set fire to the town in different places, without any body being able to discover the author; and, he was so expert in his machinations, that, whilst the people were employed in extinguishing it in one part, he contrived to kindle the flame in another.

The period of tranquillity, which late events seemed to promise, was not of long continuance. The Portuguese, elated with the idea of their prowess, and thinking their power irresistible, began to manifest their contempt of the Singalese, in numerous acts of injustice and oppression. Various complaints of their conduct were laid before the empress, who being very young and inexperienced, could afford them little protection or redress. They accordingly resolved to procure what satisfaction they could for themselves; and began to cut off the supplies of the Portuguese.

Don Pedro and Janiere perceived the storm that was gathering, but had not the virtue or the prudence to avert it, by changing that system of measures by which it had been produced. They endeavoured to intimidate by an ostentation of power, without, at the same time, labouring to conciliate by justice and humanity. They sent a force of 2000 Singalese and 1000 Portuguese troops into the principality of Uva; and 2005 native, and 200 European troops, into another part of the country called Laleluja,* in order to obtain a supply of rice. Though they were every where tolerably well received, they every where exhibited the most revolting scenes of outrage and oppression. The wives and daughters of the people were compelled to be the victims of their brutal passions; whilst those, who made any resistance to such acts of violence, were butchered by these merciless robbers, and had their villages burnt to the ground. The Singalese, exasperated by these enormities, secretly determined to make their persecutors feel the effects of their vengeance, upon the first favourable opportunity.

King Janiere Bandare at this time became very urgent in his solicitations to Don Pedro, to give him the hand of the Empress Donna Catharina in marriage, which the Portuguese commander refused, under the pretext, that it would be first necessary for him to write home, in order to procure the consent of the King of Portugal, without which he could not presume to give his own.

Janiere, who did not want sagacity to penetrate the reason of this insidious excuse, next requested of Don Pedro the hand of his sister's daughter, in which he also experienced a refusal. Incensed by this ungracious opposition to his aspiring hopes and fondest wishes, he scornfully asked the Portuguese general, if this was the reward of all his faithful services? At the same time declaring with an oath, that he should repent of the denial which he had given to his two requests. Don Pedro, observing the

* Valentyn, 5. p. 96.

mortified ambition of the Singalese chief, answered him in a way which inflamed his pride, and aggravated his resentment, saying, "It was not meet, that one, who was an empress born, should be given in marriage to an upstart king." Janiere deeply felt the bitter taunt, but repressing what he felt, he only replied, "That he could see through the designs of the Portuguese; and that, after having availed themselves of his assistance, to become masters of the island, they had determined to trample him under foot, but that the event would not correspond with their expectations." And, as if what he had just said, had been only the effect of momentary dissatisfaction, he terminated the interview with the most profound dissimulation. He reverted to other subjects, in order to induce a belief that what had passed had made but little impression on his mind, and would soon vanish from his thoughts.

But, the very same evening, he dispatched a messenger to Don John, who was still concealed in the woods, watching for a favourable opportunity of wreaking his vengeance upon the Portuguese, of which this communication of Janiere seemed to promise the speedy accomplishment. Janiere gave a circumstantial account of all that had passed between him and Don Pedro; invited Don John to aspire to the title of emperor; and promised to assist him in that enterprise, upon the condition that he should be king of the low lands, under his superior authority.

Don John, who little expected such a communication, agreed to all that Janiere had proposed. They accordingly entered into a treaty, in which they determined entirely to shake off the yoke of the Portuguese, and to put them all to death.

Don John now began to shew himself with less reserve, particularly to the people of Candy. He employed every means to augment their ill will, and exasperate their vengeance against the Portuguese, while he represented his elevation to the sceptre as the surest expedient to which they could have recourse, in order to deliver themselves from the insolent tyranny by which they were oppressed.

Janiere now gradually disclosed to his friends and partizans the engagements into which he had entered with Don John; but these intentions were not long kept secret from their enemies. The Portuguese had intercepted some letters of Janiere's, from which they discovered the plot that was hatching against them, and the critical situation in which they were placed. Don Pedro de Sousa saw clearly that he must either procure the hand of the Empress Donna Catharina in marriage for Janiere, or risk the loss of the island.

In a council of war, which the Portuguese held upon the subject, there was a great discordancy of opinion. Some were in favour of the marriage, others against it; a third party were for procuring Don John, or Janiere, to be assassinated; but the majority resolved, that the safest expedient was to get Janiere dispatched as soon as possible: and, in order to afford a plausible excuse for this violent measure, to give out that letters had been intercepted, in which he had expressed his resolution to take away the lives both of the empress and the commander of the Portuguese.

The opportunity selected for this purpose was an interview between Janiere and Don Pedro. In the course of conversation, the Portuguese commander requested permission to see the cross which Janiere wore, that he might give orders to have one made like it, and set with precious stones. Janiere, suspecting no evil, complied without any hesitation with Don Pedro's request, who professing to be particularly struck with the splendour and beauty of the cross, solicited the favour of retaining it for some time, till he could procure one to be made of a similar form.

Janiere had no sooner assented to this request, than, on a signal being given by Don Pedro, a poniard was plunged into his breast, and he was treacherously assassinated along with several of his suite. His guard, on hearing that their king had been murdered, raised a shriek of horror and indignation; but no attempt at retaliation was made, and all the Singalese, except the King of Cotta, fled with precipitation.

CHAP. VI.

The Empress Donna Catharina informed of Janiere's Assassination: her Prediction of its Consequences. Don John takes advantage of this favourable Juncture. Candy abandoned by the Portuguese; they take Post at Ganoor; fly to Walane. Don John attacks them in their Retreat; obtains a signal Victory. Death of Don Pedro. Don John follows up his Success; general Submission to his Power. He marries the Empress Donna Catharina; attends to the internal Improvement and Security of his Dominions. The Portuguese send Succours to Ceylon under the Command of Don Jeronimo d'Oviedo He commences his March to Candy, but is met by Don John on the Way, and suffers a severe Defeat. Dominicus Correa goes over to Don John, who sends him with an Army against Galle, where he is routed, made Prisoner, and perfidiously put to Death. Manner in which Don John avenged his Death. The Soldiers at Columbo Mutiny against Don d'Oviedo; his narrow escape from Assassination. Manuel Dias, a Candian Spy, in order to deceive the Portuguese, feigns a design to Assassinate Don John. The Portuguese caught in the Snare; the Consequences of their credulity. Manuel Dias greatly rewarded for his Services.

THE Portuguese conveyed immediate intelligence of Janiere's death to the empress; who, however, expressed no satisfaction at the crime, and foretold that it would prove the occasion of their fall, as the event shewed. The Singalese, who had previously sufficient cause of discontent, were now more than ever enraged; for, if kings were treated with so much barbarity, what lenity had the people to expect?

Don John, who knew how to turn events to his own advantage, found this conjuncture very favourable to his views. He every where summoned the people to avenge the cruelty and perfidy of the Portuguese. He himself rapidly assembled a large force, and marched towards Candy, from which the Portuguese, not daring to make a stand, fled to Ganoor. From this fortress they sent numerous messengers to hasten succours from Columbo. Many of these were intercepted on their route by the Singalese, who, in revenge for the cruelties perpetrated upon their wives and daughters, cut off their noses, ears, and other members, and sent them back in this state of suffering to their friends and companions, in order to shew them what treatment they might expect if they fell into the hands of the Singalese.

The Portuguese, in a state of the utmost consternation, left Ganoor, and fled to Walane, setting every thing on fire in their rear, in order as much as possible to impede pursuit. This event happened on a Sunday, in the year 1593, when Don John, informed of their flight, surrounded them in their retreat, and attacked them with so much fury, that the Portuguese, though they fought with the utmost desperation, experienced a total route.

Besides many who were slain, a great many persons of distinction were made prisoners; amongst whom were Don Pedro, with his son, and the Empress Donna Catharina, as well as numerous Portuguese officers and Singalese chiefs, who had espoused the party of the empress.

Don Pedro, who had been severely wounded in the battle, did not survive this catastrophe more than three days. A little before his death, he earnestly recommended his son to the compassion of Don John, who promised to send him to Columbo by the first opportunity; a promise which, to the general astonishment, he faithfully performed.

Don John, who had obtained a large and seasonable supply of arms and ammunition by this brilliant victory, followed up his success with unremitting activity. In a short time he obtained possession of all the Portuguese fortresses, except those of Columbo and of Galle. He made himself master of some by force of arms, in which case he put the whole garrison to the sword; and of others by capitulation, when he behaved with more humanity and moderation. His power seemed so irresistible, and so well established, that all the petty kings of the country submitted to his authority. With the most abject humility they went out to meet him at his approach with numerous presents, when they prostrated themselves before him upon the earth, holding their hands above their heads, in sign of the most unlimited submission to his will. They called Heaven to witness, that all which they had previously done against him was owing to the compulsion of the Portuguese; upon which assurance he received them into his favour, as he knew that they had never served those insolent masters either from affection or from choice.

When Don John had thus become paramount over the whole island, he still considered it a prudent policy, in order to remove all question about his title, to marry the Empress Donna Catharina. No magnificence was spared in the celebration of this event. The nuptial feast was continued for a hundred and ten days, in the celebration of which, the costly presents of individuals are reckoned to have amounted to 968,754 pagodas.

Don John had now some leisure to attend to works of internal security, and of regal state. He made three noble fortresses, and erected a new palace with strong bulwarks, besides many other fair buildings, in the construction of which he forced his Portuguese prisoners to labour as slaves, whilst, in token of his triumph, their conquered banners were seen waving on his flag-staffs and bulwarks.

Don John now enjoyed an interval of repose, without any hindrance from the Portuguese, who had been too much crippled by their late disasters for offensive operations. But when intelligence reached Goa that Don Pedro had experienced a dreadful overthrow, and was since dead of his wounds, the viceroy, after a long interval of deliberation, thought it advisable to send to Ceylon a large force of Portuguese and auxiliaries, under the command of Don Jeronimo d'Oviedo, or, according to others, d'Azevedo.

These reinforcements did not reach Ceylon till three or four years after the signal overthrow of the Portuguese. Upon his arrival in the island, Don Jeronimo exerted all his power to recover that footing in the island which the folly and temerity of his countrymen had lost. For this purpose he spared no pains to bring over the chiefs and princes of the low lands. He operated upon the minds of some by corruption, and upon those of others by fear; and he lost no time in restoring the strong places which Don John had demolished.

Don John himself did not remain inactive whilst this storm was gathering, that threatened the security of his power. The Portuguese general had taken post at Walane, whence he intended to proceed to Candy; after the conquest of which place he had determined to erect impregnable fortresses at Trikenam and in Palugam. But Don John did not leave his adversary time for the execution of these resolves; for, having come up with him at Walane, he immediately offered him battle, which Don Jeronimo did not think proper to refuse. The conflict between the two armies was begun with great fury, and maintained with persevering violence. For a long time victory hung in suspense between the combatants; but, at last, it declared in favour of the Singalese chief, who put his European foe to the route, and pursued him for five days, on his way to Columbo. Don Jeronimo, however, appears to have performed the part of a brave and skilful commander; for most of his troops arrived in good order at their place of destination. But he lost many of his principal officers in the battle, and was himself severely wounded; and, at one period, if he had not been concealed by the friendship of one of the native chiefs, he must have fallen into the hands of the enemy.

About this time Dominicus Correa, who had been treated with great barbarity by the Portuguese, went over to Don John, who gave him a very friendly reception, honoured him with the title of prince, and appointed him to the command of an army, which he sent against Galle. Here he was routed, and made prisoner by the Portuguese; who, contrary to a solemn assurance which they had given, perfidiously put him to death at Columbo. Upon this Don John ordered several of his Portuguese captives to be trodden to death by an elephant, and others, after having their noses and ears cut off, and being otherwise dreadfully mutilated, to be sent back to Columbo, with a message, demanding the release of the other Singalese prisoners who were there confined, or threatening, in case of a refusal, that the like vengeance should be inflicted upon all the Portuguese.

The soldiers at Columbo, who were informed of these threats, and observed the miserable looks and mutilated forms of their companions, threatened to put Don Oviedo to death, as the cause of all these calamities. A body of soldiers rushed upon him with their daggers, and, notwithstanding his loud and pitiful appeals to the mercy of his senhores soldados, or gentlemen soldiers, they would certainly have executed their ferocious purpose, if some priests, at the danger of their own lives, had not thrown themselves between him and his adversaries, and thus afforded the terrified general an opportunity to escape.

A Modelaar, named Manuel Dias, of great consideration in Candy, and who had formerly served in the army of the Portuguese chief, Don Pedro, was at this time in high favour at the court of Don John. This adventurer, in order the more effectually to deceive the Portuguese, feigned that he had formed a scheme for assassinating Don John, the means of effecting which he had come to propose to Don Jeronimo d'Oviedo. This proposition rendered him a very welcome visitor to the Portuguese, who were thus induced, instead of distrusting his sincerity, to place implicit confidence in every thing he said.

With five Portuguese, the principal of whom were Christian Jacobo, Alberto Primeiro, and Gaspar Pereyra, the artful traitor departed for Candy. They were to give themselves out as deserters, in order to find an opportunity of assassinating the emperor, whilst Manuel Dias, if the plot succeeded, was to have his head adorned with the Candian crown.

A great sum of money was given to Manuel Dias for the intelligence he had communicated, and the service he was going to perform. Before they set out, both the treacherous principal and his deluded accomplices took an oath of secrecy upon a silver cross. After this Manuel proceeded to Walane, and thence to Candy, where he made the emperor acquainted with the imposition which he had practised upon the Portuguese at Columbo. He informed his majesty, that some of their troops were hovering round Walane, in order to surprise that fortress, as soon as they received intelligence of his assassination.

In order to catch his adversaries in their own snare, Don John proceeded by night with some picked troops to Walane, where he lay concealed till the arrival of the five abovementioned Portuguese emissaries from Columbo. When these persons reached the town, they were received with great apparent cordiality by Manuel Dias, who had them immediately made prisoners, and hurried before the emperor. The concerted signal was then fired from the fortress for the other Portuguese, who were without the walls, to approach as soon as possible; but they had casually received some previous intimation of what had been transacting in the fort; and they accordingly made a precipitate retreat to Columbo, leaving behind them all their baggage and stores.

This piece of service brought Manuel Dias into such great favour with the emperor, that he made him his prime minister, and loaded him with honours; which this monster of perfidy seemed ambitious to deserve, by the torturing death which, after a long imprisonment, he inflicted upon the Portuguese prisoners, who were the victims of his artifice.

CHAP. VII.

The Dutch Admiral Spilbergen sails from Holland, arrives at Baticalo in 1602. The favourable Reception he experienced; Detail of his first interviews with the King; suspected of being a Portuguese. The King of Baticalo increases his Troops upon the Coast. The Dutch repeatedly disappointed in the Completion of their Lading. Spilbergen suspects Treachery. Means which he employs to elude the Machinations of the Singalese. He writes to the King, who sends back some Portuguese, whom he had detained, with professions of Amity. Spilbergen sends an Officer to the Emperor at Candy, who desires to see the Admiral in that Place. Spilbergen sets out for Candy; his Treatment on the Way. Vintana described. An Order of yellow Monks; various Particulars respecting. Gracious Reception of Spilbergen at Candy. Details of his several Audiences of the Emperor. Spilbergen permitted to inspect the Emperor's Pagodas; Dialogue after this Inspection between the Admiral and the Emperor. Spilbergen present at a magnificent Entertainment in the Palace; he sends the Emperor a Portrait of the Prince of Orange; the Emperor's desire to obtain information respecting the Dutch, and other European Nations. His singular condescension to Spilbergen. He offers Permission to the Dutch to build a Fort in any Part of his Dominions. The Admiral leaves Two of his Musicians with the Emperor; he departs from Candy with extraordinary Marks of the Emperor's Regard. Spilbergen returns on Board his Ship; visited by Manuel Dias. He captures three Vessels belonging to the Portuguese; sails from Baticalo. His wise Conduct.

I AM now arrived at the period when the Dutch or Hollanders first made their appearance in Ceylon, where they gradually supplanted and finally expelled the Portuguese. The brave Admiral Spilbergen sailed from Holland on the 5th of May, 1601, with three ships, called the Ram, the Sheep, and the Lamb. On the 26th of May, 1602, he doubled Cape Comorin, with only two of these ships, as he had parted company with the Ram, commanded by Guyon Le Fort, on the 24th of December, 1601, off the Cape of Good Hope.

On the 29th of May, 1602, Spilbergen entered the river of Baticalo. He anchored in a creek, and sent a boat to the land, where there was a village, and a pagoda, with a large grove of cocoa nut trees. Some of the natives left the shore in a prow, in order to speak to the people in the boat. The Dutch enquired after the town of Baticalo, and were informed that it lay more to the north. They made the natives a present of some knives, who promised on the following day to send some people to conduct them to Baticalo.

On the 31st, Spilbergen dispatched a messenger to Baticalo, in order to speak to the King Derma Jangadare. On the first of June some of the Singalese came on board with a Portuguese interpreter, who informed them that they might obtain a sufficient supply of pepper and cinnamon, and that the Modeliaar, who at that time conducted the king's affairs, had desired that the admiral would pay him a friendly visit on shore. About the same time, the messenger who had been sent to the king, returned with news that he had experienced a favourable reception.

The admiral presented the Singalese and their interpreter, who had come on board his ship, with some beautiful glass and other articles, before they returned to the shore. On the following day Spilbergen landed with three or four attendants. As he reached the shore, five elephants stood ready to receive him. By kneeling, and other signs, those noble animals had been taught to testify their respect for the Dutch admiral, whilst they raised some of the Singalese with their trunks from the ground, and placed them on their backs.

Spilbergen was received with great cordiality by the Modeliaar, and, at his departure promised, on the following day, to pay a visit to the King of Baticalo. He accordingly landed again on the 3d of June, when he took with him, not only a variety of presents for the king, but also a band of musicians with different instruments. At this time a prow made its appearance with a nobleman or chief on board, who had come from a more northern part of the island, where he expressed a great anxiety to see the Dutch, as the desire of profiting by their arrival had excited a general competition along the coast.

Upon the 5th, in the evening, Spilbergen repeated his visit to the king, whom he found attended by a guard of 1400 men. When the admiral returned on board his ship, he related with what state he had been received, and how the most distinguished nobles had conducted him into the royal presence.

His Majesty's body guards all stood in a line with drawn swords, as the admiral approached, and the king also welcomed his arrival with a naked sword in his hand. Spilbergen testified his respect for the monarch by many beautiful presents, and by the performance of some sweet music, at which he expressed great delight. He afterwards directed Spilbergen to be conducted to the house of the Modeliaar, where he and his suite were sumptuously entertained.

On the following day the king sent an order to the Dutch admiral and his attendants, to remain in the house where they had been placed; and towards evening he was carried before the king, when he was strongly accused of being a Portuguese. Spilbergen experienced a good deal of difficulty in convincing them that he belonged to another nation; upon which he was no longer detained as a prisoner, but received permission to go where he pleased. The day after the admiral returned to his ship, and remained on board that night. He now sent another deputation to the court, with more presents, in order to excite the chief to expedite the completion of his lading, which it was promised should be ready in fifteen days. Spilbergen after this went again ashore, in order to have an interview with the king, who now kept constantly near the coast; and was almost every hour collecting about his person a greater number of troops. Spilbergen again made enquiries about his lading, when the king informed him that he hoped the greater part would be ready in five days; and he requested, in the mean time, that the crew should unload the ship, and bring the goods to land.

The Singalese now pretended that they had sent a number of people and elephants to fetch the cinnamon, and other products; and the Modeliaar accordingly demanded that the Dutch should run the ship ashore: a request which was by no means reasonable in itself, and which caused Spilbergen to suspect that some treachery was meditating, which they were only attempting to gain time, in order the more effectually to execute. He was the more confirmed in his suspicions by the representations of some Moors, who told him that there was little or no pepper in the neighbourhood; and that they were not in the habit of trading in that article.

Spilbergen, finding that he and his companions were cut off from the ship, professed to accede to every demand which they made, even that of running the ship ashore; but for this purpose he required that some of the Singalese, and a pilot, should be sent on board, to assist in the execution. They gave him accordingly a pilot and some men, and permitted Spilbergen to go with them on board, but detained all his attendants on shore. They also demanded four other Portuguese, as hostages for their people. Spilbergen had to assure them again and again that they were not Portuguese, but Hollanders. He now departed for the ship, with eleven Singalese.

As soon as they had reached the ship, he requested their assistance in stowing some barrels and bales in the hold; when as soon as eight of them had gone down, the admiral had the hatches made fast over their heads. Spilbergen now sailed to another place, where, after having made a display of some of the sumptuous commodities which he had on board, he sent the interpreter on shore, with two Singalese, and told him to inform the King of Baticalo, that as soon as he had released the Dutch, he would send back his people, whom he had retained as hostages; and he directed them, moreover, to relate what costly articles they had seen, which were all designed for his majesty, if he would first supply them with a cargo of cinnamon and pepper.

Spilbergen also wrote a letter to the king, in which he warned him to beware of evil counsellors, and calumniators of their good intentions; and assuring his majesty that he should be amply remunerated for any pepper and cinnamon he might send. The Dutch admiral gave the prince to understand, that he had learned from the Singalese whom he had detained on board, that those, who had required him to run his ship and goods on shore, had no intention to give him any equivalent. He moreover represented, that their persisting in taking him and his crew for Portuguese, in spite of their most solemn assurances to the contrary, could proceed only from a design which they had formed of employing that fiction as a pretext for seizing on the cargo and the ship. The admiral finally declared, that if the king was inclined to act uprightly towards him, he, on his part, was disposed to shew all due honour and friendship to the king. As a proof of his sincerity, Spilbergen sent back the Singalese prisoners, with some presents, at the same time hoisting his colours, and firing a salute, with which mark of respect the king was highly gratified.

On the same day the king dispatched a prow to the admiral, with the interpreter, and a large supply of venison, fowls, butter, and fruit, adding, that he might make what use he pleased of his dominions. He also restored the Portuguese whom he had detained; strongly protested that he had never formed any design of seizing the ship and goods; and requested Spilbergen not to hasten his departure, as he was busy in collecting a supply of pepper; and said that he should have his lading ready in a short time.

After some further procrastination, in which the king found that he could neither perform his promise, nor execute his treachery, Spilbergen discovered that this King of Baticalo was a tributary of the Portuguese; that there was an emperor of the island, whose name was Don John, and who was now adorned with the splendid Singalese title of the Beloved Son of the Sun, or Fimala Darma Suria.

Spilbergen, on hearing that the island was subject to an emperor, had resolved to go himself in person to his court; but he was dissuaded from this measure by the King of Baticalo, who gave an alarming description of the length and difficulties of the way. The admiral therefore resolved, in the first instance, to send an officer to Candy, with presents for the emperor, and to wait till his return, before he determined what further measures to pursue.

In the mean time the admiral had every day numerous offers of precious stones, rubies, topazes, garnets, hyacinths, saphires, cats-eyes, and chrystals; but these were of small size and little value; and his greatest expense was occasioned by the presents which he was obliged to be continually sending to the King of Baticalo.

The admiral's messenger, who had left Baticalo on the fifteenth of June, returned again on the third of July, and gave a favourable account of the friendly reception and hospitable entertainment he had experienced. He also brought a letter to Spilbergen from the emperor, who had ordered two of his people to escort the officer on his return. The names of these two envoys were Gonsalo Rodrigos and Melchior Rebecca. They brought with them some presents of gold rings, with a few large arrows called segonsios, which are esteemed of great value, and considered as marks of distinguished favour to those upon whom they are bestowed. The emperor sent strong assurances of his friendship to the admiral, promised him as good a cargo as it was in his power to procure; and requested that he would not leave the island without paying him a visit at his capital.

The same evening the admiral was cheered by the arrival of the ship Ram, under the command of Guyon le Fort, from which he had been separated on the twenty-fourth of December, near the Cape of Good Hope, and had not since seen.

* It was now resolved that Spilbergen should proceed to Candy, and the rather as he had instructions to that effect from the Governors of the Dutch East India Company and from the Prince of Orange, who had ordered an offer to be made of a strict alliance, both offensive and defensive, between the chief sovereign of the island and the Dutch.

Spilbergen set out upon his journey on the sixth of July, taking with him various presents, and ten companions, amongst whom were some skilful musicians. After leaving the coast, the admiral and his suite were sumptuously entertained by the King of Baticalo, who made them presents of gold rings, and provided them with elephants, coolies, and palanquins. As they proceeded on their way, the whole company were liberally entertained free of all expense.†

When the escort entered the dominions of the emperor, they were met by a Modeliaar, with drums and pipes, who conducted them to a village, where they experienced the usual hospitality; and were placed in an apartment adorned with white hangings, an honour which is shewn only to persons of distinction.

As the admiral approached the town of Vintana, or Bintana, six Mo-

* As the Ram came to an anchor, she fired several salutes in honour of the emperor's envoys, when one of the guns, being overcharged, burst, and the gunner was killed.

† Several writers have remarked the close resemblance between the mode of entertaining ambassadors in Candy and in China. In both countries they are treated throughout as if they formed a part of the royal household, and were, like the domestics of the king, to be maintained at the public expense. The Candian institutions, in some other respects, bear a close resemblance to those of the Chinese. The former are probably a branch from the ancient Chinese.

deliaars came out to meet him, with a large concourse of people, who welcomed him with pipes, drums, horns, and other musical instruments. He was thus conducted to the lodgings which had been prepared for his reception, and hung with white calico.

The town of Vintana is situated on the Mahavala-ganga, where good ships are said to have been built. Besides several beautiful pagodas, which adorned the situation, and gratified the beholder, the admiral found a monastery inhabited by monks, dressed in yellow, who paraded the streets with spacious umbrellas over their heads, and attended by slaves. Their heads were without hair, with the exception of a bunch which was left unshaven on the crown. They had devotional formularies in the hand, which they kept muttering with a sort of busy continuity. The people held them in great veneration; and they were free from all secular toils, and all public impositions.

This monastery, like those which are found in the precincts of the Roman Catholic communion, was provided with various cloisters and galleries, with numerous chapels, gilded ornaments, and images of men and women, who, according to their report, had been patterns of blameless sanctity.

These images were tricked out in tissue of silver and gold; they held lamps in their hands, and wax candles were placed near them upon the altar, which were kept burning night and day. There were also chandeliers, supported by statues of naked children. The monks came every hour to recite their prayers and their breviaries. They also saw them celebrate their religious festivals, and make their processions along the street, in which the high priest appeared mounted upon an elephant, in cloth of silver and gold, and holding a gold staff with both hands over his head. Numerous monks paraded in order before him, to the sound of horns, trumpets, and cymbals, whilst there was a jingle of bells and basons to add to the harmony. Many lamps and torches were also borne in the line, with crowds of spectators, of both sexes.

The most beautiful among the young women were wont, at the commencement and termination of the procession, to display their surprising skill and activity in the dance. They were naked to the waist, with ornaments of gold and precious stones upon their hands and ears, and a richly embroidered petticoat on the lower limbs.

These people were seen every day in the chapels of the pagodas, throwing themselves down upon the earth, with their hands twisted over their heads.

From Vintana the admiral and his suite pursued their route till they came to a village which belonged to the emperor's son, at about a day's journey from Candy. To this place the emperor had sent his own palanquin, richly decorated, along with some elephants; when Spilbergen sent the other palanquins, bearers, &c. back to Vintana. The emperor himself was very liberal and frequent in his presents of provisions, fruits, and wine, made from a grape which he himself had planted in Candy, and which the Dutchmen thought as good as any that is produced in Portugal.

When the admiral arrived at the river, at a short distance from the town of Candy, he was obliged to wait an hour, till the arrival of the chief Modeliaar, Manuel Dias, whom I have mentioned above. This officer came escorted by numerous Portuguese, all of whom had suffered the amputation of their ears, but were now in the service of the court.

Spilbergen was received with great state, and conducted into Candy with a thousand soldiers and eight stand of colours, which had been taken from the Portuguese, whilst a loud concert was made with different musical instruments. He proceeded in this manner, till he reached his lodgings near the palace, where several salutes were fired to welcome his arrival.

When the admiral reached his lodgings he found every thing made ready for his reception in the Portuguese fashion. Manuel Dias, with his Portuguese suite, remained with him till the evening, when the emperor sent three horses very well caparisoned to bring him to the palace. The admiral accordingly set out, taking with him some beautiful presents. The emperor gave him a favourable reception, whilst the presents were laid on a carpet and exhibited to the view of the royal family.—The sovereign himself was dressed in white, and displayed, in his exterior appearance, the character of a high-minded prince. He walked with the admiral for a few turns up and down a great hall; and, after conversing with him on some subjects of importance, gave him permission to return to his lodgings, in order, as he said, to repose himself after his fatigue, when he was to return again to the palace the next morning.

Before Spilbergen took his leave, he ordered the musicians whom he had brought with him to play a lively tune, which gave great satisfaction to the emperor. On the following day this prince again sent his horses to bring Spilbergen back to the palace, where he accordingly proceeded, and was again very graciously received and sumptuously entertained.

The emperor discoursed on the trade in cinnamon and pepper; but he demanded so high a price for those products, that Spilbergen judged it best to draw off the conversation to some other subject.

When Spilbergen was preparing to take his leave, the emperor enquired what offer he would make for his cinnamon and pepper? The admiral replied, that he had not come to Ceylon for any purposes of traffic, so much as to execute the orders of the Prince of Orange, and to make an offer to his majesty of his highnesses friendship and assistance in his contentions with the Portuguese.

The emperor, on hearing this, repeated it to all his nobles and courtiers, amongst whom it diffused great satisfaction. In a transport of joy and gratitude the emperor took the admiral up in his arms, lifted him off the ground, and exclaimed—"All the pepper and cinnamon which I have by me is at your service;" but the whole stock did not amount to the value of more than 3000 crowns.

The emperor, however, readily accounted for his small supply of these commodities, by saying, that, before this, he had never paid any attention to the trade in cinnamon, but on the contrary had been wont to prohibit the collection of the bark, or to order the destruction, in order to prevent it from falling into the hands of his deadly enemies the Portuguese, and that the arrival of the Dutch had been too sudden and unexpected to allow him to procure a supply.

During his stay at Candy, Spilbergen had daily interviews with this monarch, in which he conversed with him upon a variety of subjects. He shewed the admiral the cuirasses, and other arms which he had taken from the Portuguese. He also admitted him to behold his magnificent pagodas, that were adorned with four or five thousand statues, some of which were of colossal size. They had beautiful towers constructed of the most costly materials, and arches resplendent with gold; and these sacred edifices are said to have been equal to the Roman Catholic churches, in the beauty of their decorations.

When Spilbergen returned to the emperor, after having seen these noble edifices, his majesty asked him what he thought of his pagodas, upon which Spilbergen replied, that he set a higher value on living men than on lifeless statues.

The emperor asked him if the Dutch churches, like those of the Portuguese, were adorned with images of the Virgin, of St. Peter, St. Paul, and the other saints? He moreover inquired if the Hollanders believed in Christ? Spilbergen replied, that the Hollanders were Christians, but not of the Roman Catholic communion like the Portuguese. He said that their temples consisted of bare walls, without any images; and that they worshipped God in their hearts.

The emperor proceeded to ask the admiral if the God of the Dutch ever died? The admiral remarked that no man, who was subject to death, could be like God. Spilbergen ventured to suggest to the emperor, that all the images in his pagodas, which represented nothing but dead men, were unworthy of his adoration; and that the only proper object of worship was the living God. The emperor touched upon other religious topics before the admiral took his leave.

The day after this conversation, Spilbergen was invited to a magnificent feast in a great hall of the palace, which was covered with carpets, provided with Spanish stools and a table; and in which every thing was conducted after the European fashion. The emperor also honoured his guest with some good music, in conformity with the custom of the Dutch.

Spilbergen now sent the emperor an equestrian portrait of the Prince of Orange, habited in complete armour, as he appeared in the field of battle, in Flanders, on the second of July, 1600. The emperor, who was much pleased with this mark of respect, asked the admiral to relate the particulars of this battle, and the other events of the war, which the Dutch had waged with the King of Spain.

The emperor, who appears to have been very anxious to obtain information about European affairs, gave strong proofs of this curiosity during the several days in which he conversed with Spilbergen. He was perpetually inviting him to talk about Holland and the Dutch. He ordered the portrait of the Prince of Orange to be hung up in the apartment where he usually lived. He, moreover, once introduced the admiral to the empress and her children, the prince and princess, who were dressed in the European fashion. This was an extraordinary honour; and, indeed, the annals of Candy will hardly furnish an instance of any ambassador to that court who was treated with any thing like the familiarity and condescension which Spilbergen experienced. The ceremonials of servile respect were no where more constantly exacted; and the reserve, the state, the contemptuous hauteur and crushing insolence of despotism were no where more rigidly maintained.

The emperor invited the states of Holland and the Stadtholder to erect a fort in any part of his dominions which they might choose to select. And he even condescended so far as to say if their high mightinesses and the Prince of Orange were desirous of forming such an edifice, that he the emperor with the empress, the prince and princess, would carry stones, mortar, and other materials on their shoulders, in order to assist in its accomplishment.

The emperor gave Spilbergen different letters for the states and the Stadtholder, and made the admiral his ambassador, in order to treat, in his name, with their high mightinesses and His Highness the Prince of Orange.

Before the departure of the admiral the emperor sent him some costly presents, and also invested him with various titles of honour, to which the Singalese are much attached. At the emperor's particular request, the admiral left with him two of his musicians, Hans Rempel and Erasmus Martsberger, from whom the sovereign himself learned to play on several instruments. The prince and the princess also made Martsberger their private secretary. Martsberger is mentioned as a person of respectable character and with a considerable knowledge of languages. The emperor, the prince, and the princess, seem at this time to have been so much gratified by their new visitant that they began to learn the Dutch language, and used to say that Candy had become another Holland.

When the admiral took his final leave of the Candian sovereign, he omitted no opportunity in his power of testifying his regard. He gave him many of his large arrows, called segonsios, as proofs of his undoubting confidence, and his lasting friendship, besides a large suite of attendants, elephants, and whatever could add to the convenience of his journey.—It is also mentioned, that he sent him a gilt umbrella with four or five slaves to wait upon his pleasure.

With these proofs of royal friendship and marks of royal munificence, Spilbergen regained the point of the coast from which he had set out, and returned on board his ship after an absence of twenty-two days, during which time, he had been entertained free of all expense.

On the 4th of August, Manuel Dias, the prime minister, was sent by his master with some other Modeliaars and 120 attendants in order to inspect the ship, and to assist Spilbergen in looking out for a better anchoring-place against his return. The prime minister was received on board with marked respect, and very sumptuously entertained.

Before Spilbergen left the coast he had an opportunity of furnishing a complete proof of his hostility to the Portuguese, by capturing three vessels belonging to that nation. The first of these was a galliot with forty-eight men on board, and laden with areca, pepper, and cinnamon. He made a present of this ship and the cargo to the emperor, which occasioned great joy in Candy.

The admiral sailed from Baticalo on the second of September, 1602. Before his departure he inquired of the people who were assembled in the market-place to the number of 200, whether they had any complaints to allege, or any demands to make against himself or any of his crew. Spilbergen certainly conducted himself with great good sense, firmness, and moderation, through the whole of this expedition; and if his successors had evinced the same probity, sagacity, and discretion, the power of the Dutch in Ceylon, of which he laid the original foundation, would have been more permanently established.

CHAP. VIII.

Sebald de Weerd arrives in Ceylon in 1602; his Reception at the Court of the Emperor Don John; he repairs to Achen, and returns in 1603; captures four Portuguese Ships on his Passage; the Release of which excites the Jealousy, and inflames the Rage of the Singalese Emperor. His Animosity aggravated, and his Fears alarmed, by the Representations of his Ambassador from Achen. The Emperor deliberates what Conduct to observe towards the Dutch; during the Debate Sebald de Weerd arrives at the Emperor's Quarters at Baticalo. Circumstances which led to the Assassination of De Weerd, with curious Details respecting that Event; his Attendants massacred. Laconic Message of the Emperor to the Dutch. Sickness of Don John; his Death; his Person and Character described.

SEBALD de Weerd was the next Dutchman who made his appearance at Ceylon. He landed in the neighbourhood of Baticalo, on the twenty-eighth of November, 1602. He immediately proceeded to the capital, where he received strong proofs of the favourable sentiments which Spilbergen had inspired in the royal breast. The emperor shewed him every mark of honour and regard.

Sebald de Weerd reaped great benefit on this occasion from the services of Martsberger, who had been appointed to the office of secretary to the emperor, and who gave the Dutch ambassador all the necessary instructions about his conduct at court.

From Ceylon Sebald de Weerd repaired to Achen, but returned again to Baticalo after a short absence. In his first visit he had entered into a treaty with the emperor, and had then proceeded to Achen, in order to procure a greater maritime force for the professed purpose of assisting his majesty against the Portuguese.

Upon his return De Weerd captured four Portuguese ships, intelligence of which having been communicated to Manuel Dias, he demanded that some of them should be given up to the emperor. De Weerd excused himself from complying with this demand, by stating that he had previously stipulated that they should be set at liberty.

The emperor, upon hearing of the capture of these ships, hastened in person to Baticalo; and when he heard that they had been released, he became greatly incensed, particularly as he had been informed by his ambassador, who had come from Achen with Sebald de Weerd, that the Dutch admiral had on all occasions shewn himself a friend of the Portuguese, and an enemy of the emperor.

The ambassador told his master that he himself had often experienced the contemptuous behaviour of De Weerd, who, at a magnificent entertainment, had placed the Portuguese at the head of the table, and himself at the bottom, though he was the emperor's representative. Hence he inferred that the Dutch had no other object than to deceive the court of Candy, and by stratagem to render themselves masters of the country; and he affirmed, that all their proceedings were in direct opposition to the treaty which they had lately made with the emperor.

The ambassador moreover warned the emperor to be on his guard against the design of the Dutch to inveigle him and his nobles on board their ships, and thus to become masters at once of his royal person and his dominions.

The emperor, who had heard the above report of his ambassador with a good deal of alarm, called a council of his courtiers and nobles; in which it was debated whether, after what he had heard, as well as the palpable violation of the treaty by the liberation of the Portuguese vessels, he ought to repose any further confidence in the sincerity of the Hollanders. It was finally resolved that an attempt should be made to induce the Vice-Admiral De Weerd to repair to Galle for the purpose of attacking the Portuguese in that quarter, and thus to ascertain whether they ought with De Weerd to regard him as a friend or a foe.

About the time of this discussion, De Weerd, attended by 300 armed men,* made his appearance at the emperor's quarters; and, after being hospitably entertained, requested his majesty to do him the honour of a visit on board, when he might gratify his curiosity by inspecting the interior of the ship. But the emperor, impressed by the late warnings of his ambassador, and fearing treachery, refused the invitation of the admiral, which he said that his nobles would not permit him to accept.

De Weerd, finding that the emperor could not be persuaded to venture on board, requested him to go down to the shore, in order to have a nearer view of the ship than he could in his present situation. The Dutchman added, that he had ordered a tent with white hangings to be fitted up at the sea-side for the reception of his majesty.

The emperor, whose suspicions were now more strongly awakened, and who became more assured that some attack was meditating upon his person, refused to comply with the wishes of the admiral. But De Weerd, who was a man of hot and hasty temperament, piqued by these two refusals of the sovereign, told him, without any reserve, that, as his majesty would not pay him the compliment which he had requested, he must not expect any assistance from him against the Portuguese.

Though the emperor was greatly enraged, yet smothering his resent-

* At the request of the emperor, De Weerd kept only a small part of this guard with him, and sent the rest towards the shore.

ment, he only replied, that he expected De Weerd would, according to his engagement, sail with his fleet to Galle, as he himself must return to Candy for the sake of the empress, who was left alone, by the departure of his half-brother, Cenuwieraat Adasseyn, for the frontiers.

Sebald de Weerd, who had been drinking to excess, replied with inconsiderate temerity and boorish coarseness, that the empress could not be in want of somebody to supply his place; and that, for himself, he should by no means set out for Galle till his majesty had paid him a visit on board his ship. The first part of this answer was a gross* insult upon the character of the empress, but the second part only confirmed the emperor in the suspicions which his ambassador had previously excited, that De Weerd had formed a design of making him prisoner.

The emperor, who was naturally choleric, and justly incensed by this unseemly and insolent answer of the Dutch admiral, instantly rose up from his seat, and exclaimed in an angry tone to his people, "Mara isto can," bind that dog.

Four of the nobles now attempted to seize the admiral, who made all the resistance he could in his present situation. He endeavoured to make his way to his men, who were stationed on the beach, and called out loudly for assistance; but, during the struggle, a Singalese courtier seizing him behind by the hair of his head, cleft it in two with a broadsword, and De Weerd instantly expired where he fell.

As the emperor had given orders only to bind De Weerd, and not to put him to death, none of the nobles durst at first acquaint him with the event; but, at last, the Prince of Uva had the courage to make it known.

* The Dutchman says, with more plainness than would suit the refinement of English ears, "Het eerste deel van zyn antwoord was een taal, die hy niet erger van een openbare snol en bordeel-hoer kon gevoerd hebben, en die hy nogtans van de Keizerin gebruikte."

As the emperor was asking earnestly, Why have ye not bound him as I commanded? the Prince of Uva said, that, as De Weerd had drawn his sword, he had put it out of their power to secure him in any other way than that which they had employed.

The emperor perceiving what had happened, said, "Well, if he is dead, don't let his people share a better fate than their master." These orders were immediately executed; and of those who came on shore with De Weerd, all were massacred with the exception of a few who swam to the ship, and of one young man of Flushing, named Isaac Plevier, whom the emperor took into his service.

After this barbarous transaction the emperor returned to Candy, and dispatched a short letter in Portuguese to the chief who was left in command of the Dutch. The following is given in Valentyn as a copy of the original;—" Que bebem venho naon he bon. Deos ha faze justicia. Si quisieres pas, pas; se quires guerra, guerra." He who drinks wine is good for nothing. God has executed justice. If you desire peace, let there be peace; if war, war.

The Emperor Don John did not long survive this unfortunate event. He was attacked with a malady, which occasioned such an intolerable and burning heat in his body, that he was obliged continually to lie in a vessel of water, which, according to the accounts, was so cold, that men could not hold it in their mouths, but of which he felt not any of the cooling powers.

In this miserable prelude to his latter end, he expressed deep regret for the massacre of the innocent Hollanders, who had given him no offence; but as, even in these last moments, he had not subdued the feeling of revenge, he said that Sebald de Weerd had only met with his reward, and had merited his fate.

During his sickness, he experienced such frequent paroxysms of pain, that he had no capacity to attend to public affairs, and he expired in the year 1604, leaving a son and two daughters, by his wife Donna Catharina.

In person, Don John was tall and slender. His complexion was black, his manner and conversation were very imposing. He was penetrating, crafty, and intelligent, and had become strongly impressed with the subtle policy of the Portuguese, whilst he was detained in their settlement at Goa. His military qualities were very conspicuous, and he displayed great energy, and performed great atchievements in his warfare with a vigilant and enterprising enemy.

In the distribution of his treasure, he was exempt both from parsimony and profusion, but employed it with much foresight and humanity, in works of public utility, in adding to the security and happiness of his dominions, in building forts against the incursions of the enemy, and choultries, or inns for the convenience of travellers. Great regularity and precision were remarked in all parts of his administration. The justice, which he exercised towards his subjects, was so strict and impartial, that few crimes were perpetrated during his reign; and his generosity was, at the same time, so great towards all who deserved it, that he was at once both beloved and feared. His great abilities made his friendship desired by all the Indian chiefs. He had a thorough insight into the character of the Portuguese, the only object of whose policy he knew to be the subjugation of his country. Nothing therefore could induce him to be made an instrument for the accomplishment of their ambitious views; and he regarded them with an antipathy, which nothing could soften or abate.

By birth Don John was a Singalese, but he had been early instructed in the principles of the Roman Catholic faith, which had not made any deep or lasting impression on his mind; and, what it might have made, was erased by the perfidy which he found to be practised by those who professed to believe in its sacred truths. The conduct of the Portuguese, and particularly their elevation of Don Philippo to the throne, in violation of their previous engagements with him, had instilled into his bosom a strong abhorrence of their religious ceremonial. When he himself ascended the throne, motives of policy induced him to comply with the religious prejudices of the Singalese, and to practise an exterior conformity to their worship, though he was convinced that it had no just claim to his belief. But, in process of time, he proceeded still farther in the career of skepticism, and regarding the diversities of religious opinion as a matter of indifference, he left them all at perfect liberty.

CHAP. IX.

Contention amongst the Nobles after the Death of Don John. Donna Catharina seizes the Government; her energetic Proceedings. The Portuguese attempt to negotiate with the Empress. Ambitious Intrigues of the Prince of Uva and Cenuwieraat; the former assassinated by his Rival. Transient Resentment of the Empress, who finally marries the Object of it in the Person of Cenuwieraat. He is crowned under the Title of Camapati Mahadassyn. He seeks the Friendship of the Dutch; a Treaty between them in 1612. Boschhouder, by whom the Treaty had been negotiated, detained; high Offices and great Honours heaped upon him by the Emperor. Ravages of a Party of Portuguese; revenged by the Troops of the Emperor. Great Preparations of Cenuwieraat for an Attack upon the Portuguese. Death of the Prince Mahestane, Son of Don John; his magnificent Funeral.

AFTER the body of the late sovereign had been placed under a magnificent canopy, and reduced to ashes according to the custom of the country, the nobles engaged in a violent contention for the crown. The Prince of Uva, by far the most powerful chief in the kingdom, immediately aspired to the vacant throne. His pretensions were opposed by Cenuwieraat Adassyn, the late king's half brother, who affected to be supporting the claim of his nephew, whilst he was secretly labouring to obtain the sceptre for himself.

Donna Catharina, in the mean time, observing the tumultuous ferment and bitter dissentions which distracted the kingdom, and judging herself to have the best claim to the administration of the government, as the mother and guardian of the young emperor, resolutely seized the helm, and instantly ordered some of those, who most loudly clamoured against her authority, or opposed her power, to be put to death. By these energetic proceedings, she repressed the public disorders and established a temporary tranquillity.

The Portuguese, who regarded Don John's death as an event very favourable to the further prosecution of their ambitious views, lost no time in making it known to the Viceroy of Goa, and immediately set their agents to work, in order to bring about a treaty with the empress, by means of which they might facilitate the final subjugation of the island. But the empress very wisely rejected all the overtures of the Portuguese.

As the Prince of Uva and Cenuwieraat were renewing their factious intrigues for the crown, the empress ordered the great body of the nobility to make their appearance at court, all of whom obeyed the royal summons, except these two aspiring chiefs. They were accordingly proclaimed traitors by a public act of the assembled nobles, and their estates were declared to be forfeited. But they had sufficient interest to get this sentence revoked, and they afterwards came to court as before; but each with a large body of retainers, and without any mutual confidence.

The Prince of Uva had formed a design of assassinating his rival, of marrying the empress, and of thus seating himself upon the throne, as soon as the assembly of the nobles was dispersed. But Cenuwieraat, who had obtained secret information of this plot against his life, omitted no precautions to prevent the execution; and in the mean time feigning a complete reconciliation with his adversary, he had resolved, along with some of the principal members of the government, to embrace the first opportunity of putting him out of the way.

These two competitors were both proceeding to court to take leave of the empress; but, whilst they were making some exterior demonstrations of ceremonious politeness to each other at the farther gate of the palace, and were reciprocally yielding, or professing to yield, the point of precedence, the Prince of Uva at last, as the eldest, consented to lead the way. But he had gone but a few steps, when Cenuwieraat stabbed him in the back, exclaiming, "Lie there, thou false traitor!" The followers of Cenuwieraat instantly carried off the dead body, while the retainers of the murdered chief set up a loud cry of "Treason! Treason!" and instantly fled. This cry caused it, at first, to be supposed that the empress herself had been assassinated. Many lives were lost in the tumult which ensued; but the uproar ceased as soon as the truth was known.

It was now loudly proclaimed that this daring outrage of Cenuwieraat in the sacred precincts of the palace, ought by no means to go unpunished; but the empress, who was fearful of producing greater distractions, thought it more politic to attempt the dispersion of the storm, by giving out that it was by her orders that the Prince of Uva had been put to death.

Tranquillity was thus restored. The empress, however, is said to have felt deep indignation at this act of violence, and only to have smothered her resentment till she could find a convenient opportunity for the gratification. But, in the mean time, Cenuwieraat had the art so effectually to insinuate himself into her favour, and to convince her that the murder he had committed, had only her good for its object, that she consented to choose him for her husband, and he was accordingly crowned in 1604, by the title of Camapati Mahadassyn.

After his exaltation to the throne Cenuwieraat, or Camapati Mahadassyn, anxiously sought to obtain the friendship of the Hollanders, that they might act with their united force against the Portuguese. But in the year 1609, the States General of the United Netherlands concluded a truce with the Archduke Albert, and the Infanta of Spain, which was to extend to their Indian settlements. During the continuance of this truce, the states general resolved to make every exertion in their power to fortify their eastern possessions, by cultivating the friendship and securing the alliance of the native princes. Directions were accordingly given to their supreme authorities in that quarter to enter into treaties, offensive and defensive, with the different kings and chiefs, in order to take every possible precaution against the future hostility of the Portuguese.

Letters were sent by the states general, and Prince Maurice of Nassau, to Cenuwieraat, Emperor of Ceylon, with strong professions of friendship, and to assure him that they had taken care to include his majesty in the truce which they had concluded with the Portuguese.* These letters were forwarded to the court of Candy in 1612, by Marcellus de Boschhouder, an officer of the second rank in the Dutch East India Company. Boschhouder was received by Cenuwieraat with much consideration; and a treaty was concluded between his majesty and the Hollanders, on the eleventh of May in the same year.

The treaty consisted of many articles, but the principal drift of it was, the union of the contracting parties in an offensive and defensive alliance against the Portuguese, in order, as far as possible to secure to the Dutch an exclusive trade with the Singalese; and to suffer no European whatever to enter the island without their consent. By this treaty the Dutch obtained permission to erect a fort at Cotjaar, the materials for building which were to be furnished by the emperor, who was also to provide magazines of stone for their goods and merchandize.

After the conclusion of the treaty, Boschhouder requested permission to depart to the coast with some elephants, which he had received for

* Portugal was at this time annexed to the crown of Spain. This annexation lasted from 1580 to 1640, when the Duke of Braganza recovered the independence of his country.

the factory of Tegenapatnam, and to make a report of what he had been doing at Candy; but the emperor refused to comply with this request. He represented it as one of the conditions of the treaty, that he should always have some of the Hollanders present in his councils; and he considered the meditated departure of Boschhouder as an infraction of that stipulation.

But in the mean time, in order to render the stay of the Dutchman as agreeable as possible, the emperor conferred on him various offices of honour, and some titular distinctions of great value in the opinions of the Singalese. Boschhouder was made Prince of Mingone, of Cockele Corle, Anaragipura, Miwitigaal, Chief of the Order of the Golden Sun, President of the Supreme Council of War, second in the Secret Council, and High Admiral; and was altogether in such favour with the emperor, and so high in his esteem, that he did nothing of the least moment without his advice or concurrence.

In the year 1612, Simon Correa, at the head of 1000 Portuguese troops and 3000 Indians, proceeded to Cotjaar by a secret path with which he had been made acquainted by the Singalese. Here he surprised and massacred the company of Hollanders whom Boschhouder had left in that quarter, and then retreated rapidly into the province of the Seven Corles, in order to anticipate the opposition which he was likely to experience from the emperor's troops.

As soon as the emperor received intimation of the above enterprise, he sent 5000 troops to Cotjaar, under some of his most distinguished officers, who came up with the flying enemy near the confines of the Seven Corles, cut many of them in pieces, set fire to numerous villages, and returned to Candy with considerable spoil.

After this the emperor was determined to make a powerful effort against the Portuguese, assembled the states of the kingdom, who agreed to raise an army of 50,000 men. One division of this force, under the command of the Prince of Uva, was destined to make an attack upon the town of Punto Gale; another, under the Prince of Mingone, to attempt to carry the fortress of Walane, and afterwards to march against Columbo; and thus to bring the whole force of the kingdom to bear upon the Portuguese.

The Portuguese also at the same time set a large army on foot, with which they marched to Jaffnapatam, where they were vigorously repulsed; but the exertions neither of the Singalese, nor of their European enemies, were at this time attended with any important results.

The Prince Mahestane, son of Don John and Donna Catharina, for whom the crown was professedly held, died on the twenty-second of August, in the year 1612, not without suspicions of having been poisoned by his step-father, Cenuwieraat, in order to secure the throne to a son of his own. But whatever might be the cause of his death, no magnificence was omitted in the celebration of his funeral obsequies. The body, preceded by the musicians of the deceased, was borne to the pyre amidst loud expressions of regret and lamentation. The corpse was placed on an elevation of seven stone steps, in the centre of which a hollow space had been made, which was filled with sandal wood, eagle-wood, (excaecaria agallochum) and many costly and fragrant aromatics. The bier was covered around to the height of several feet, with woods and spices of the same kind. Besides this there were three jars of cinnamon oil, which kept burning for half an hour. Over the hollow space a princely canopy was constructed, which was seven feet high, and decorated with sumptuous garments of embroidered gold.

Boschhouder, the Prince of Mingone, was deputed to set fire to the funeral pile, when the by-standers raised a loud shriek of woe. After the body of the deceased prince had been reduced to ashes, and all the funereal rites had been duly performed, the emperor and the nobles returned to the palace, in order to condole with the afflicted empress.

CHAP. X.

Boschhouder chastises a rebellious Chief; he defeats a Portuguese Fleet. Latter End of the Empress Donna Catharina; dying Scene. Sickness of Cenuwieraat; anticipates his Death; Two Chiefs appointed to rule during the Minority of his Son. Cenuwieraat recovers, proposes to marry his Step-daughter; the Match powerfully and successfully opposed by Boschhouder. Boschhouder's Embassy to Mazulipatam; he proceeds to Europe. His Hauteur disgusts the Directors of the Dutch East India Company; he repairs from Holland to Copenhagen; concludes a Treaty with the King of Denmark in 1618; he sets out on his Return to India; dies upon his Voyage. Some Danish Ships under Gule Gedde reach Ceylon; the Treatment they experience from the Emperor. Gule Gedde returns to Denmark. The Portuguese erect a Fort in Trincomalee; another at Baticalo. Constantine de Saa takes the Field; his miserable End.

AT the commencement of the year 1613 the favoured Dutchman, Boschhouder, was sent with an army of 35,000 men, to reduce to submission a rebellious chief, called the King of Panua, who had joined the Portuguese. He was brought a prisoner to Candy, where his head was cut off, whilst his followers were crushed to death by the elephant, which performed the office of public executioner.

In the same year Boschhouder had the good fortune to defeat the Portuguese fleet between Cape Comorin and Ceylon; and, after burning some of their ships, and taking others, to return with a prize of six tons of gold.

The Empress Donna Catharina, who was so much afflicted by the loss of her son that she had taken hardly any nourishment since his death, perceiving that her end was approaching, sent, in July 1613, for the princes of Mingone and Uva, and, after exacting from them an oath of fidelity, made them guardians over her children. Conscious of the rapid advances of death, she had her five children brought into her presence, and kissing them one after the other, she earnestly adjured the two chiefs above-mentioned to protect them with constancy and affection.

After this, casting her eyes upon her husband Cenuwieraat, who was present, she charged him with being the cause of her death, though it does not appear that there was any ground for the accusation; but he is said to have taken it so much to heart, that it impaired his health, and seemed to threaten his life. The empress breathed her last on the twentieth of July, in the year 1613. Before her death she expressed great contrition for her sins, and particularly that of having conformed to the rites of pagan worship. The day after her decease, her funeral obsequies were performed with great magnificence, in the same place where those of her son had recently received the same tribute of ceremonious regard.

After the death of the empress, the sickness of the emperor assumed such a dangerous aspect, that he assembled his principal nobles, and requested them to choose two of their order to govern the kingdom during the minority of his son. They selected the princes of Mingone and of Uva for this important trust; and they were accordingly appointed by a solemn act to exercise the supreme administration during the minority of the prince. The emperor himself at the same time earnestly admonished all his children to obey these guardians of the realm as long as they were subject to their control. This scene naturally leads us to expect that Cenuwieraat would soon breathe his last; but he appears to have survived for several years this delegation of the sovereignty to two of his chiefs. In the year 1614, we read that this same Cenuwieraat had formed a design of marrying his step-daughter, which the Prince of Mingone powerfully opposed. All the other nobles, who did not partake of his juster and more European sentiments of aversion, felt no repugnance to the match; but the Prince of Mingone is said to have made such a powerful appeal to the emperor's conscience upon the subject, that the tears rolled down his cheeks; and, what is more, the project vanished from his thoughts.*

Boschhouder, the Dutchman, who had thus acted a conspicuous part in the affairs of Ceylon, and become one of the greatest chiefs in the country, in the year 1615 obtained permission of the emperor to repair to Mazulipatam to procure some promised succours against the Portuguese. Boschouwer was invested with unlimited powers to conclude such treaties, and to form such engagements, with different powers, as he might judge good for the interest of his majesty, which he undertook accordingly to ratify.

Boschhouder, owing to the then state of the Dutch affairs in the East, having found it impossible to procure troops from Mazulipatam, or the other settlements, in order to act against the Portuguese, it was judged expedient to send him to the mother country, in order to make known his powers to the states general, the Prince of Orange, and the Directors of the Dutch East India Company.

When Boschhouder arrived in Holland, some little dissensions soon arose between him and the Directors of the East India Company. For the former, exalted above measure by the part he had acted in Candy, the influence he had acquired, the servility he had experienced, and the rank and the titles which he enjoyed, exacted more homage from the directors than they were disposed to yield to one whom they regarded as their servant and inferior. The Prince of Mingone, accordingly, listening more to the suggestions of vanity, than to the precepts of duty, repaired to Copenhagen, where, on the thirtieth of March, 1618, he con-

* Valentyn Vyfde deel, 114.

cluded a treaty with Christian IV. King of Denmark, which promised to secure to that monarch those advantages, of which the want of more condescension in the Dutch East India Company to their supercilious countryman had rendered them unworthy.

Boschhouder set sail with a ship and a yacht on his return to India in the same year. He was accompanied by his wife, who went by the title of the Princess of Mingone, some domestics, and a number of soldiers who were destined to be employed in Ceylon. But Boschhouder died upon his voyage, when most of his people ran away from the ship on the coast of Coromandel; and thus the whole expedition vanished in smoke.

Boschhouder had stipulated that the King of Denmark should be indemnified by the Emperor of Ceylon for the ship and the yacht which he had received. To these vessels the Danish East India Company at Copenhagen added five other ships, which were placed under the orders of a Danish nobleman, named Gule Gedde.

After a long and desultory voyage of twenty-two months, this fleet reached Ceylon in the year 1620, and anchored in the bay of Cotjaar. Gule Gedde immediately dispatched intelligence to the emperor of his arrival, of the death of the Prince of Mingone on the passage, and the number of ships he had brought, all of which he represented as having been built for the service of the emperor, and as then awaiting his orders.

But the emperor, who learned with grief the death of the Prince of Mingone, and who was irritated by the charge which was brought against him for these ships, declared that they had been sent without his orders; and that he would have nothing to do with them; nor could he by any means approve, nor would he ratify the treaty which Boschhouder had concluded with the Danes.

Gule Gedde, finding that he was not likely to obtain any compensation for his ships and other expenses, ascribed the whole loss to the account of the deceased Boschhouder, whose remains, as well as those of his son, who had also died on the voyage, were still on board. Gule Gedde accordingly declared all his property and effects forfeited to the King of Denmark.

After this the Danish admiral had the corpse of Boschhouder interred in a manner that marked the vindictive feelings which he harboured in his breast; but, though he evinced this contempt to the remains of the father, he exhibited a good deal of parade in the funeral obsequies of his son; as his majesty, Christian the Fourth, had stood sponsor at his baptism. Gule Gedde appropriated very little of her husband's property to the widow of the deceased Prince of Mingone, who was afterwards conducted to Candy with three maids of honour (staatdogters) and an old waiting maid. Here she remained about seven years, when, at the request of the Danish admiral, Rowland Carpe, and by the permission of the emperor, she, along with her companions, was conducted to Tranquebar.

Gule Gedde, after losing one of his ships, and entirely failing in the object of his expedition, returned to Denmark, to the great joy of the Portuguese, who after this commenced the erection of a fortress at the north-west point of the bay of Trincomalee, in order to prevent the access of other European settlers to that part of the island. The materials with which this fortress was built were taken from the ruins of a magnificent pagoda which once adorned the spot. The Portuguese began the erection of this fort in the year 1622; and prosecuted the work in silence during an interval of peace with the emperor.

The Portuguese afterwards erected another fortress at Baticalo, with which they had in all seven strong places in those parts of the island where a landing was most practicable; and thus they endeavoured to deprive the emperor of the means of holding any intercourse with foreigners.

In August, 1630, Constantine de Saa, the Portuguese chief, took the field with a large army against the Prince of Uva, Comara Singa Hastana, the eldest son of Cenuwieraat, who, in conjunction with his two brothers, was at the head of a powerful force. De Saa plundered the province of Uva; but, upon his return, he was deserted by all the Singalese whom he had in his army, whilst he was attacked by the three princes, who made great havoc in his rear. The rain, which fell in torrents, prevented the Portuguese from using their fire-arms; whilst the enemy put them to flight with their bows and arrows and pikes. In this scene of distress one of the revolted Singalese cut off the head of the brave De Saa, and carried it on a drum to the Prince Mahestane, or Raja Singa, as he was afterwards denominated.

CHAP. XI.

Death of Cenuwieraat; Division of his Dominions. Raja Singa becomes Master of the Whole; he calls in the Aid of the Dutch against the Portuguese. A Negociation begun; some Dutch Deputies sent to Candy; the Portuguese alarmed, resolve to March to that Capital. They reach Candy; their Retreat; their desperate Situation; Debate between the Chiefs De Melo and Bottado. The Portuguese attacked by Raja Singa, and cut to pieces; their Heads piled up in a Pyramid. De Melo and Bottado.

THE Emperor Cenuwieraat died not long after the abovementioned defeat of the Portuguese, and the destruction of their general. His dominions were divided amongst his three sons: Uva became the portion of the Prince Comara Singo Hastane; Mature of the Prince Viscapalla, and Candy of the youngest son, Mahestane, or Raja Singa Adassyn, who placed himself upon the throne of his father, and assumed the title of emperor. He afterwards obtained possession of the territories of his two brothers; the eldest of whom died in 1637; and the other, Visiapalla, who was wanting in intellectual capacity, went over to the Portuguese, amongst whom he lived neglected and despised.

Raja Singa,* finding that no durable peace could be maintained with the Portuguese, and that they were continually seizing every opportu-

* Valentyn says, that in February 1643, a vessel put into Punto de Galle, from the coast of Choromandel, having on board two princesses, daughters of a king of the Carnatic, who were intended to grace the nuptials of Raja Singa. There were some Moorish and Singalese ambassadors on board, who said that they had been nearly three years engaged in this expedition, and had expended four or five thousand pagodas. The Dutch, who were at this time masters of Galle, supplied the party with a yacht to convey them to Baticalo, which was the original place of their destination. Raja Singa expressed himself greatly obliged by this act of courtesy, which he promised to reward.

nity which offered of increasing their power, determined to call in the aid of the Dutch. He accordingly, in September 1636, dispatched a Brahmin with a letter to the commander of that nation, on the coast of Choromandel. The Brahmin, after having been detained six months at Jaffnapatam, where he was in continual danger of his life, at last found means of executing his commission.

Some Dutch deputies were accordingly dispatched to the Emperor of Candy, who remained at the place, where he then held his court, for eight days; and had an audience of his majesty twice every day; during which time they succeeded in convincing him of the gross misrepresentations of their power by the Portuguese.

The Portuguese having heard that the Dutch had had an audience of the emperor, and that they had determined to attack Baticalo with their united forces, resolved to lose no time in marching to Candy, and frustrating the project of their enemies. The Portuguese army, under the command of Diego de Melo and Damijao Bottado, set out on their expedition in March, 1638. They succeeded in reaching Candy, from which Raja Singa had previously retired. Having satiated their avarice and their cruelty, the Portuguese departed to Gameru, where they pitched their camp. Their army consisted of 2300 whites and Mestizos, with 6000 blacks. Raja Singa had had the precaution to block up the way to Walane, as well as to other places on their retreat, with large trees thrown across the paths. All the Singalese, who were in the Portuguese army, seeing the dreadful extremity to which they were reduced, deserted their standards; and the Portuguese themselves, discerning no chance of escape, sent a Franciscan and Augustinian monk to the emperor to endeavour to negociate a peace, on the condition that they might be permitted to return to Columbo without further molestation. But the answer they received was such as to convince them that they had not the smallest hope of safety except in the valour of their arms.

In this fatal extremity De Melo asked Bottado, who had first recommended this fatal expedition to Candy, what he would farther advise, in order to extricate them from their present difficulties? Bottado answered, that they had no other choice than to fight with desperation, and to sell their lives as dear as possible. But De Melo had no resolution to fight, and no inclination to die.

In the mean time Raja Singa, seizing the favourable opportunity, attacked them with such impetuosity, during a heavy rain, with his archers and spearmen, that not one of the Portuguese escaped, except the few whom the prince chose to spare. Whilst Raja Singa beheld the slaughter from a seat raised under a high tree, his troops brought him, as an offering, the heads of his enemies, which they piled up upon one another, in the shape of a pyramid.

No more than seventy Portuguese were left alive; these were made prisoners. Thus the brave Bottado, and the pusillanimous De Melo, both perished on the hill of Gameru; and the Portuguese long preserved the recollection of this memorable overthrow.

CHAP. XII.

The Dutch Admiral, Westerwold, wrests Baticalo from the Portuguese. In 1638 the Dutch conclude a Treaty with the Emperor. The Emperor lays Siege to Columbo. Trincomalee reduced. Negumbo taken and retaken. The Dutch, under Coster, carry Punto de Galle by Storm. Coster proceeds to Candy; his cold Reception; his impolitic Violence; his Assassination on his Return. The Emperor views the rising Power of the Dutch with Suspicion and Distrust; he accordingly relaxes his Exertions against the Portuguese.

IN May, 1638, Adam Westerwold, one of the council of the Indies,* attacked the Portuguese fortress of Baticalo with five hundred men and six pieces of cannon, and without much difficulty obtained possession of the place.

The Dutch, having succeeded in supplanting the power of the Portuguese in this part of the island, now entered into a treaty with the emperor consisting of twenty articles, in which they did not forget their own interest, or the means of establishing their future dominion. All the fortresses, which the contracting parties should take from the enemy, were to be garrisoned by Dutch troops, who were to be equipped at the expense of the emperor. The emperor was to supply gallies and smaller vessels for the protection of the coast and rivers. The arms and ammunition were to be provided by the Dutch, and paid for by the emperor with cinnamon, pepper, wax, cardamoms, and other products. The Dutch were to carry on their commerce in any part of the island which they chose, free of all tolls and imposts.

* Raja Singa sent this officer the sword of De Melo, in token of his recent victory.

No other Europeans were to be permitted to trade with any of his subjects, or to hold any intercourse with the coast. The emperor, in order to defray some definite expenses of the Dutch, was every year to send one or two ships to Batavia, laden with cinnamon, pepper, cardamoms, indigo, and wax ; and, when there was any overplus, it was to be paid for in money or goods. This treaty was concluded in 1638.

The emperor, with an army of 20,000 men, next proceeded to lay siege to Columbo, which was not, at the time, expected to hold out long, after the great disasters which the Portuguese arms had recently sustained. But the surrender of this place was delayed by subsequent events. The fortress of Trincomalee was reduced in 1639. Negumbo was taken in the following year by the Dutch troops, under the command of Philip Lucasson, but it was soon after recaptured by the Portuguese.

In March, 1640, William Jacobson Coster appeared with a body of Dutch troops before the town of Punto de Galle, which was a few days after bravely carried by storm. The native troops which were to have cooperated in the enterprise, seem purposely to have delayed their march. The Singalese had probably by this time begun to suspect that they had as much to dread from the ascendancy of the Dutch as from that of the Portuguese.

After having made himself master of Punto de Galle, Coster found it necessary to make a journey to Candy, in order to hasten some preparations which had been neglected, and to procure some supplies which had been withheld. Here he found so little attention paid to his reasonable demands, and experienced so much evasion and delay, that he suffered his anger and impatience to get the better of more prudential considerations. Instead of reflecting on the tragical end of Sebald de Weerd, which has been mentioned above, he began to make the officers of the palace the objects of his menaces and abuse. This outrage upon the decorum of a despotic court was immediately reported to the emperor, who sent Coster permission to depart from Candy, but without shewing him any of the customary tokens of friendship and respect. He was attended on his return to Baticalo by some Singalese, who murdered him on the road.

This atrocity, which was, no doubt, perpetrated by the command of the emperor, proves not only the resentment which was excited by the insolence or temerity of Coster, but the suspicious malevolence with which the rising power of the Dutch was beginning to be viewed by the Singalese. As a proof of this feeling of animosity and distrust towards the Dutch, the emperor, who had previously exerted himself to the utmost to drive the Portuguese from Columbo, at present gave them an opportunity of re-establishing their sway in that quarter, in order that they might be the better able to check the growth of the Dutch power and to diminish his fear of their exclusive domination.

CHAP. XIII.

The Armistice between the Dutch and the Portuguese in 1642 not extended to Ceylon. Negumbo again taken from the Portuguese. The Dutch carry off some of the Emperor's tame Elephants; how he avenges that Injury. Humble Overtures and hypocritical Professions of the Dutch, in order to effect Reconciliation with the Emperor. The Administration of Maatsuyker. The Portuguese driven out of Ceylon.

ON the separation of Portugal from the dominion of Spain by the Duke of Braganza, in the year 1642, an armistice for the space of ten years was agreed upon between the Dutch and the Portuguese, which was designed to include the respective territories in the East. But Ceylon did not enjoy the benefit of this truce, owing, as the Dutch say, to the bad faith* of the Viceroy of Goa, but probably not less to the impatient desire of the Dutch themselves to complete the work which they had begun, and to make themselves masters of the island.

In 1644, His Excellency Francis Caron, who commanded the Dutch forces in Ceylon, once more took the fortress of Negumbo from the Portuguese. After strengthening the works, he left in it a garrison of 500 men. In 1646, a temporary pacification ensued between the Dutch and the Portuguese.

Soon after this, the Dutch were involved in an open war with the Emperor of Candy. The Dutch commander at Negumbo had carried off some tame elephants belonging to his majesty, who was so enraged by this proceeding, that he resolved to avenge it with all his might.

* Valentyn, 5. p. 120.

He surrounded some troops of this nation in the Seven Corles; slew the commander, Adrian van der Stel, cut off his head, sent it in a silk bag for the inspection of his countrymen, and ordered 688 of the Hollanders into captivity at Candy.

The Dutch now exerted all their address to produce a reconciliation with the emperor. Their chief commander, Maatsuyker, strongly represented to his majesty that the elephants had been carried off without his orders, and were ready to be restored whenever his majesty should think fit. The Dutch pretended that their principal object was not to render themselves independent of his majesty, but to protect him against the Portuguese; and that, for this service, all they required was that their military expenses should be repaid; but that if the emperor could defend himself against the Portuguese, they (the Dutch) were willing to depart from his dominions. They called God to witness that they had no intention of establishing themselves in that country, but only to assist his majesty, and to receive the products of his territory at a reasonable price, according to a treaty which had been concluded with Westerwold. They prayed that his majesty would be pleased to appoint a place in which they might arrange their differences. They hoped that his majesty was wiser than to seek a war against those who had delivered him from the power of his enemies, and who still had in their possession four fortresses in order to render him farther service.

The above professions at least prove that, if the Dutch were wanting in sincerity, they discovered no deficiency of impudence. To tell the sovereign of a country that they had no intention of violating his independence, while they had garrisoned four fortresses in his dominions; and to assert that the possession of these very fortresses was designed only for his benefit; that is, to enable them to extend their own conquests, was to presume too much upon their own sagacity or upon the shortsightedness of the Singalese.

From the correspondence* which was carried on from 1646 to 1650 between the Dutch governor Maatsuyker and the court of Candy, it appears that the emperor often hesitated between the policy of uniting his interest with the Dutch or with the Portuguese. But in the end the Dutch shewed superior skill in the arts of deception; and triumphed over their opponents in the councils of the Candian sovereign.

Under the administration of Maatsuyker, the Dutch obtained quiet possession of Negumbo, Galle, and Matura, with the adjacent country; collected cinnamon, caught wild elephants, and, in other ways, promoted their commercial interests.

Maatsuyker was replaced in 1650 by Jacob van Kittensteyn, as governor of the Dutch possessions in Ceylon, under the title of President. In 1656 the Portuguese were driven out of Columbo, which they had possessed for 150 years. They were soon after deprived of their remaining settlements; and in 1658 they were finally expelled from the island.

* In some of Maatsuyker's letters, we find that presents of horses were amongst the means employed to sooth the jealous, or to conciliate the offended emperor. Thus, in a letter of March, 1649, Maatsuyker says, that a horse is arrived at Galle, well worthy of carrying a king upon his back. His majesty's orders are requested with respect to the sending it up to Candy. Some trinkets and fruits will also be forwarded to his majesty. The horse, abovementioned, which appears to have been an Arabian, is stated in another letter to have been sent to Candy with a Dutch saddle, on which no man had ever sat. If this steed, thus caparisoned, proved acceptable to his majesty, a still better was promised to excite further hope. See Valentyn, 5. p. 125—67.

CHAP. XIV.

The bad Policy of the Portuguese. The Commencement, Growth, and Destruction of their Power.

WHEN the Portuguese first arrived in India, they found the trade in the hands of the Saracens and Arabians, from whom they gradually wrested it by their naval superiority. But, not contented with acquiring the ascendancy at sea, they endeavoured afterwards to become masters of the land. For this purpose they had recourse both to stratagem and violence. After they had obtained permission to erect warehouses on the coast, they soon converted them into castles and fortresses, under the pretext of securing themselves against the incursions of robbers and pirates. They now sowed dissensions amongst the neighbouring chiefs; and, helping the weak against the strong, they at last obtained possession of the most important points upon the coast. These they enjoyed with little molestation till the year 1630.

In the trade with the East, the King of Portugal reserved to himself the cinnamon, pepper, musk, amber, gold, silver, and other precious commodities, and left the commerce in other articles in the hands of his subjects; but for which they had to pay various duties and imposts. Thus the sovereign amassed great treasures, by which he was enabled to support the expense of fortifications, garrisons, the equipment and the convoy of ships, &c.

The Portuguese flag was no sooner triumphant in the Indian Ocean, than they aimed at excluding almost all the Indians from any participation of the trade; or, if they gave permission of traffic to any of the native powers, they were obliged to purchase the license with large sums of money, and to pay high duties and exorbitant tolls in those places where the Portuguese had erected their castles and forts.

As their desire of domination increased with their means, they soon began to entertain less limited prospects of power and wealth. Hence they found it necessary to maintain a greater expenditure, more troops, and larger establishments. But the population of Portugal was not sufficient for these increased demands upon its stores. In order to supply the deficiency, the Portuguese had recourse to two expedients; these were marriages with the native women, and the conversion of the natives to the Roman Catholic faith. By these means they imagined that they should establish their power on the firmest basis, and render themselves invincible. But they forgot what both nations and individuals are not prone to remember, that no power can be stable which is founded on oppression; and that an agreement even of multitudes of the natives in the rites and ceremonies of their religion, would form but a weak bond of union, or a slender tie of submission, where the affections were alienated by inhumanity and injustice.

As the towns and castles of the Portuguese were confined to the coast, they were greatly inferior in numbers and power to the chiefs of the interior, who were able perpetually to frustrate their views and to humble their ambition. And as the settlements which they possessed were in remote situations, they were not able to send any efficacious support to each other, and consequently required more troops for their defence.

They had no inducement to cultivate the land in the vicinity of their factories, as the possession depended entirely upon the favour or the forbearance of the native chiefs.

In the towns which they occupied, the number of Portuguese was very small compared with that of the other inhabitants. The proportion was not more than that of 500 to 6000; and their establishments were filled with a refuse and disorderly population of slaves, of half-converted natives, and vagabond Moors.

The pride of the Portuguese, and the insolent habits which it produced, contributed also to accelerate their fall. All manual labour, which required either strength or skill, was reputed a degradation to a Portuguese. Thus the handicraft trades and useful employments were consigued to slaves. They taught the Indians to do every thing that they wanted to be done, and even to act as sailors on board their ships. A Portuguese was thought to be dishonoured by any but a military employment. These regulations of their policy might be productive of little inconvenience as long as they had no enemies to combat in the field; but, when a war broke out, they found their towns full of a tumultuary rabble, in whom no confidence could be reposed.

As soon as an enemy approached who was able to contend with them at sea, the King of Portugal lost all his duties, tolls, and revenues, and was compelled to support increased burdens with diminished means.

In the chiefs of the interior, whom they had by turns cheated and oppressed, the Portuguese could repose no more confidence than in their slaves. They were ready to practise, on every opportunity, the lessons of perfidy which they had learned from the example, if not from the precepts, of the Portuguese.

Thus the Portuguese lost, by successive alienations, their dominion in the Maldives, on the coast of Canara, in Ormus, Persia, Mascat in Arabia, with their trade in Abyssinia, Japan, and other places. But in Ceylon they maintained a long and desperate conflict, and, for a considerable interval, made head against their enemies, and delayed the overthrow of their power in that island of fertility and delight. Those treasures which the Portuguese had extorted by fraud, cruelty, and oppression, from impoverished millions, were lavished in support of their ambitious sway in this fair portion of the globe. But there is a term when fraud, cruelty, and oppression, cease to flourish; and, when the prosperity, which has been founded upon such crumbling materials, begins to decline, it soon vanishes like a dream of the morning, or a vision of the night.

CHAP. XV.

Animosity of Raja Singa against the Dutch. His Hostility rendered Abortive by their Sagacity and Perseverance. Raja Singa attacked by his own Subjects. Many of his Nobles slain; Design of the Insurgents; their Cowardice. The King escapes to the Mountains; pursued, but not taken. His Son proclaimed Emperor; Details of his Behaviour on the Occasion. The old Emperor's Sister joins her Brother with the young Prince; the Conspirators despair of Success. Origin of the Insurrection. One of the principal Insurgents sent to Columbo, to be tortured by the Dutch. Raja Singa orders his only Son to be poisoned; throws off the Weight of Gratitude, by putting his best Friends to Death. He shuts himself up at Dietlighy; his Detention of the Dutch Ambassadors; one of them departs without Leave; Details respecting. A French Fleet arrives on the Coast of Ceylon; opens a Correspondence with the Emperor, who gives the French Leave to build a Fort. Insolent Temerity of a French Ambassador at Candy; its Circumstances and Results. Raja Singa's Death; Description of his Person. Succeeded by his Son Mahestane; his Death. Wira Praccaram Narendra Singa. Decline of Ceylon in Military Power during the Reign of Mahestane.

AFTER the expulsion of the Portuguese, * Raja Singa perceived that he had contributed to raise up against himself a more subtle, active, and powerful enemy in the Dutch; with whom he continued on terms of open war, or secret hostility to the end of his reign. The Portuguese power was hardly exterminated from the island, before the Singalese sovereign found that his faithful servants and disinterested auxiliaries the Dutch, were determined, contrary to their recent professions and promises, to

* Knox, his father, &c. were made prisoners after this event. Raja Singa was sovereign of the country during the whole of Knox's captivity.

retain possession of all the towns and fortresses which they had reduced. This conduct so enraged the monarch, that he determined to embrace every opportunity of vengeance. Knowing the commercial cupidity of his present adversary, he gave orders to the inhabitants of the low lands, where the cinnamon grows, to carry it off to the hill country, to lay waste the groves and plantations, and reduce them to a state of desolate sterility, in order to force the Dutch to relinquish a territory, in which they had no prospect of gain. But the obstinate Hollanders were not to be so easily dislodged. More provident than the Portuguese, they made themselves masters, not only of the coast, but of the most valuable and productive portions of the adjacent country, which they secured against the incursions of their enemies.

In the year 1664, when Raja Singa had retired from Candy to the town of Nilobe, in order to prosecute his hostile designs against the Dutch, a rebellion broke out amongst his own subjects, which had nearly proved fatal to his authority and his life. On the 21st of December, a body of about two hundred men entered the town of Nilobe, at midnight, and proceeded towards the residence of the emperor.* They slew many of the nobles, who adhered to the king, and had resolved to treat him in the same manner, and to place his son upon the throne, who was a youth of from twelve to fifteen years of age.

The conspirators might readily have seized the person of the old king, if they had not been restrained by cowardice, as he was protected only by a mud wall, covered with straw, which served him for a breast-work. But as they delayed the attack till the morning, he had an opportunity of escaping, with about fifty followers, to the mountains during the night. The situation which he chose for his retreat, was so covered with bushes and underwood, that they were obliged to drive an elephant before, in order to trample down a path for the king to pass.

* Valentyn, 5. p. 198.

The conspirators pursued his majesty to this spot; but, as he was provided with some good musketeers, they took care to keep out of the reach of their fire. The king afterwards fled to the hill of Gauluda.* Here too his subjects might easily have made him prisoner; but the awe of the tyrant seems still to have operated upon their minds; their resolution was vanquished by their fears. They returned to Candy, and proclaimed the young prince emperor.

This unfortunate youth, who had never been out of the precincts of the palace, nor accustomed to any persons but his ordinary attendants, was seized with apprehension, when he beheld a number of persons prostrating themselves before him, saluting him as emperor, and telling him that his father had fled to the hills.

When the prince exhibited no signs of joy at this news, and shewed no disposition to co-operate in their designs, the conspirators were plunged deeper in irresolution and uncertainty. And as soon as they heard that the old emperor's sister had set out to join her brother, taking with her the young prince, they began to fly in different directions; and some of them turned their arms against each other.

This insurrection, which was conducted without vigour or intrepidity, originated in the cruelty and oppression of the sovereign; the object of whose reign seemed to be to devastate the country, and to destroy the inhabitants. He put his subjects to death in the most wanton manner, and by the most barbarous modes, as the caprice of the moment might suggest, or passion might impel.

After the above insurrection was suppressed, and most of the conspirators punished in various ways, it is not a little remarkable, that the inhuman tyrant sent a Singalese, named Ambom WellerauI, who

* Marked Garlenda in Valentyn's map, and close to Dietlighy.

had been one of the principal insurgents, to Columbo, where he thought that he would be treated with more cruelty by the Dutch, than his own imagination could devise. But the Dutch, instead of acting agreeably to the expectations of Raja Singa in this respect, set him at liberty, and treated him with kindness.

Raja Singa, perceiving that his then only son, though he had taken no part in the insurrection, had experienced the favour of the conspirators, and that they had designed to place him on the throne, determined to liberate himself from this apprehension for the future, and accordingly ordered him to be taken off by poison.

There are some persons, who have been so depraved, or so proud, as to be incapable of enduring the weight of gratitude; and this remark has, in various instances, been found applicable to sovereigns, whom a sense of obligation has humbled, by an uneasy sentiment of inferiority to those by whom it has been conferred. Raja Singa belonged to the class of ungrateful potentates; for he put to death, in the most barbarous manner, most of those nobles who had shared his flight, and assisted him in his adversity.

Late events had not contributed to teach Raja Singa either humanity or moderation. But though his government was not rendered more mild, those alarms, from which a tyrant is never free, were greatly augmented in his breast; and, after this insurrection, he kept himself in the town of Dietlighy, in which he expected to feel more security against similar attempts.

The Dutch made frequent attempts, by embassies and presents, to lull his suspicions, to soothe his animosity, and to conciliate his confidence. But these efforts were productive of little effect. He received their presents,* and detained their ambassadors. One of these ambas-

* In the year 1679, the Governor Van Goens sent the emperor a present of two black Persian

sadors, more intrepid than the rest, determined rather to die, than to linger in a protracted captivity. He accordingly formed a resolution, if he did not receive permission from the court, to depart by a certain day, not to wait any longer, but to set out upon his return. When the appointed day arrived, he girded his sword upon his side, proceeded to the palace, made a profound obeisance to the naked walls, and took a formal leave. As he was going away, he saw some English prisoners, who happened to be present at the scene, and to whom he gave money to drink his health. Two or three of his slaves accompanied him on his return. The emperor, instead of stopping his march, sent some of his courtiers to conduct him on the way; and he arrived safe at Columbo.*

---

horses, covered with green velvet trappings, hanging to the ground; and each horse led by two Malabar slaves. There were ten beautiful falcons, each borne by a Malabar, dressed in white; six musk or civet cats, each in a separate basket, borne by two slaves; six Tutocoryn hens, in elegant cages, all covered with green velvet; two Persian sheep, whose tails weighed from twenty to five and twenty pounds a piece; a case of Persian wine; a piece of sandal wood, weighing two hundred pounds, covered with fine white calico, and borne by slaves. There was also a letter for the emperor in a silver receptacle, which was carried by a sergeant bare-headed, and a canopy above, resting on four pillars, was borne by four Singalese noblemen, whilst, at each corner, four large wax tapers were displayed in much state by four noble Singalese. This magnificent present was escorted by a large party of Dutch and Singalese. At Ruanelli it was given up to the emperor's people, who came in great numbers with arms in their hands; and, when part of the Dutch, after having executed their mission, had crossed the river, the emperor's troops treacherously attacked those who remained behind. Some of the party succeeded in swimming to the other side, but a lieutenant and two soldiers were killed by the Singalese. This clearly shews the terms of amity, which at that time subsisted between the Dutch and the Singalese; and the contempt, in which the former were held by the latter, and which neither their presents nor their flattery could remove. In the year 1680, a succeeding governor endeavoured to propitiate his Candian majesty by a present of two lions, three tigers, twelve musk cats, all of which were enclosed in beautiful cages, covered with green velvet. There were also two black Persian horses, covered with the same, twenty falcons, borne by Malabars, with a letter carried by the ambassador himself in a silver dish under a gorgeous canopy, which was borne by four Singalese nobles bare-headed. In this procession there was an ambassador from the King of Persia, who travelled in a singular car, drawn by two white oxen, covered with white calico.

* See Valentyn 5. p. 201. The same incident is related in Knox. The event occurred in the year 1670.

In the year 1672, the French under Monsieur De La Haye, Viceroy of Madagascar, made an attempt to establish some commercial relations with the Emperor of Ceylon. De la Haye entered the Bay of Trincomalee with a fleet of thirteen or fourteen ships. He first dispatched three envoys to the capital, with valuable presents to the sovereign. The envoys were very graciously received, and each of them had a gold chain, a sword inlaid with gold, and a musket presented to him by the emperor.

One of the envoys was sent back to De la Haye with the emperor's answer, who, upon the receipt, sent an ambassador with six other Frenchmen to Candy. The French fleet in the mean time was amply supplied by the orders of the emperor with every thing of which it was in need.

The emperor at first seemed willing to comply with the wishes of the French. He gave them permission not only to build a fort in the bay, but he assisted them in executing the work, and let them have some of his subjects to assist in forming the garrison. The French admiral was now under the necessity of sailing for the coast of Choromandel, but he assured the emperor by the ambassador, that he would soon return; and in the mean time, he left in the fort, which he had built, a garrison of French troops and natives. Monsieur De la Haye, however, was not able to make good his promise of returning to Ceylon; for he was attacked by the Dutch, under Admiral Van Goens, who took four of the French ships,* and compelled the rest to take refuge in Surat. Van Goens after this made himself master of the fort which the French had erected in the bay of Trincomalee.†

The French ambassador, whom De la Haye had sent to Candy, conducted himself with such singular indiscretion, as to excite the indigna-

* When Knox wrote, he did not distinctly know the fate of De la Haye's fleet.

† Valentyn, Beschryving der Kust van Choromandel, p. 64.

tion of the emperor, and to bring great misfortunes upon himself and his suite. He persisted in making his entry into Candy on horseback, and in that manner even passing the palace in the way to his lodgings, in direct opposition to the earnest remonstrances of the courtiers, who represented that such a measure was not only unusual, but expressly forbidden by the emperor. These suggestions however could not prevent the Frenchman from sacrificing the success of his mission, to the gratification of his personal vanity. The emperor, though highly incensed at this violation of his orders, yet seemed willing to overlook it in this instance; and the ambassador and his suite were provided three times a day from the royal kitchen with every thing which they could need. After a short interval the ambassador was summoned to an audience of the emperor. A magnificent procession was formed to conduct him by torch-light to the palace; but as he was to be kept in waiting about two hours, according to the forms of the Singalese, the Frenchman regarded this as an intolerable affront, to which no consideration of policy or interest could induce him to submit. Some of the Singalese nobles, seeing him preparing to quit the palace, made a shew of stopping him by some elephants which were stationed about the gate; but, finding that he drew his sword and seemed determined to proceed, they let him pass, whilst his suite, surprised at his obstinacy, and alarmed for the consequences, left him and ran away.

This outrageous insult upon the grave decorum of his court, no sooner came to the ears of Raja Singa, than he ordered the ambassador and the other Frenchmen, except the two envoys who were first sent, to be well beat, and afterwards put in chains. The ambassador was kept in this situation for six months; but his companions were liberated upon an assurance that they had no participation in the indignity which had been thus wantonly offered to the sovereign.*

* The name of the ambassador, who made this signal display of egregious folly, was unknown to Knox. It was Monsieur Laisne de Nanclars de Lanerolle. He was a nobleman of considerable

Raja Singa did not die till the year 1687, when he had reigned about fifty-five years. He appears to have been at least eighty-seven years of age at the time of his decease. The person of Raja Singa was not above the middle size, but muscular and compact. His complexion a deep mahogany, his eyes large, rolling, and expressive of inquietude. Only a small portion of grey hair was scattered over his head, but he had a long shaggy beard. He wore a cap stuck full of feathers; and his dress was so fantastic, that he resembled a mountebank rather than an emperor. He was succeeded by his son Mahestane, under the title of Fimala Darma Suria Maharaja. Before his death Raja Singa is said strongly to have recommended it to his successor, to remain at peace with the Dutch, and he appears to have followed the advice. His character was inclined to superstition, and he was, in every respect, governed by his priests. He died on the fourth of June, 1707, and was succeeded by his son under the name of Wira Praccaram Narendra Singa. This prince was only seventeen years old when he began to reign, and he gave early signs of a turbulent disposition.

The military state of Ceylon had been very much neglected during the life of the former sovereign. The court was guarded only by some lascars, armed with pikes. The emperor had not 1000 soldiers who knew

---

consequence, and a Protestant. Valentyn mentions a letter which he had in his possession, written in Latin by this Monsieur de Lanerolle to a Dutch ecclesiastic, then in Ceylon, of the name of Cat. See Valentyn Byzondere Zaaken van Zeylon, p. 204. When Knox returned to England, he mentions in p. 375 of the 4to edition of his "Historical Relations," that he wrote to the French Ambassador, then in London, respecting his countrymen, who were thus detained in captivity at Candy. But it does not appear that any thing was done for their release; and the reformed faith which M. de Lanerolle had embraced, would operate against him at the court of Louis XIV. Bitter dissensions arose between this M. de Lanerolle and his captive fellow countrymen at Candy, who accused him as the author of their sufferings. Raja Singa, who shewed more humanity on this occasion, than on most others, made an attempt to reconcile the enraged parties, but without the desired effect. They ate his sweetmeats, but they retained their animosity. See Knox and Valentyn.

the use of fire-arms ;* and though they possessed some pieces of cannon, they were totally ignorant how to turn them to account.

The son of Raja Singa had about 300 elephants with teeth; but these were reserved merely for the parade of the court; and most of them were distributed in the neighbourhood of the pagodas, which his devotion caused him frequently to visit. When this religious sovereign went to pay his adoration on Adam's Mount, and to offer a salver (sombrero) of massy silver, with other presents, almost all these animals were exhibited in the monarch's pious train.

* At this period the Singalese manufactured their own gunpowder. They found at home the saltpetre, which was requisite for the purpose; but they were obliged to procure the sulphur from abroad. Valentyn, p. 344.

CHAP. XVI.

An Embassy of Condolence sent to Candy upon the Death of the Empress in 1721. Before his Audience at Court the Ambassador and his Suite required to throw off their Mourning and put on coloured Clothes. Introduction to the royal Presence, Details of the Ceremonial. The Ambassador opens his Mission of Condolence. Obsequious Compliance of the Dutch to the Emperor contrasted with their oppressive Conduct to his Subjects.

IN the year 1721, the death of the Empress of Ceylon caused the Dutch governor, Isaac Augustin Rumph, to dispatch an embassy to the court of Candy, in order to offer to the emperor the condolence of the East India Company, and of the governor and council of the island, upon that event. Cornelius Takel, who was the ambassador employed upon this occasion, wrote a circumstantial account of his embassy in a dispatch to the governor, which is preserved in Valentyn.* The ambassador and his suite were, of course, arrayed in mourning, as most appropriate to the object of their expedition. When they had arrived at their lodgings, at a short distance from the palace of the emperor, two nobles were sent to conduct them to the audience. These messengers were dressed in white, and informed the Dutch ambassador that old times were passed away, and a new year commenced; and that, at such a season, it would hardly be suitable for his excellency to appear before his majesty in the garb of woe. They said that his majesty had ordered all his courtiers to put off their mourning; and that it would therefore

* Byzondere zaaken van Zeylon, p. 352.

be proper for the ambassador to do the same. The ambassador represented that he had brought with him only one suit of coloured clothes, which he had been in the habit of wearing at Columbo; when it was settled that he should appear at court in that dress, and that his followers also should wear such coloured clothes as they might chance to have.

When the ambassador, attended by the first adigar, and different officers of the court, had come in front of the hall of audience, four curtains were thrown open, and the king was seen sitting upon his throne. The ambassador pulled off his cap, and kneeled down upon one knee; but all the other persons, with the interpreter, crossing their hands over their heads, fell down six times successively prostrate upon the earth. After getting up and proceeding five or six steps, they repeated these prostrations for a second and a third time.

The emperor now inquired concerning the health of the governor and council, and the treatment which the ambassador had experienced on his journey from Sitavaca to Maoye. After these questions had been put and answered, the ambassador had leave to sit down. The ambassador then, in the name of the governor and council, made formal inquiries after his majesty's health, and represented the ardent desire of the Dutch government to cultivate his friendship, and to promote his interest. The emperor signified his great satisfaction at these testimonies of respect on the part of the upright and faithful Hollanders, for whom he professed the most exaggerated regard, as long as the sun and moon endured.

The ambassador now proceeded to state the principal object of his mission, which was to present to his majesty the sincere condolence of the Dutch East India Company, and of the Governor and Council of Ceylon, on account of the decease of his majesty's late high-born, excellent, and all-accomplished queen. The ambassador, in the name of the governor and the council, implored the Almighty to comfort his majesty on this afflicting occasion; and, by other rich blessings, to compensate his calamitous loss. They prayed that his majesty might, for a long course of years, be preserved in perfect and permanent health upon his golden throne; and that his majesty's good subjects, the faithful and loyal Dutch, might long experience the favour and protection of his majesty.

Such were the external ceremonies of formal complaisance which the Dutch practised towards the Candian monarch, whom they were, all the while, confining as a sort of prisoner in the interior of his dominions; whilst those of his subjects, who were more immediately exposed to their sway, were suffering by their oppression, and impoverished by their rapacity.*

* Some of the Dutch governors practised more moderation than others; but the more moderate had not always the vigour to repress the exactions of their inferiors; and it is certain that, long before the arrival of the English, the native Singalese anxiously sighed for an opportunity of shaking off their yoke. One of the Dutch governors, of the name of Versluys, contrived to raise the price of rice to such a pitch as to cause a famine in order to gratify his avarice. The predecessor of Versluys, whose name was Vuist, made an attempt to render himself an independent sovereign; and, in the prosecution of that attempt, had recourse to the most atrocious cruelties. He had nineteen persons put to the torture, by which means he extorted a confession of crimes, the perpetration of which had never even entered their thoughts, Vuist was made prisoner, and sent to Batavia, where he was sentenced to be broken alive upon the wheel, his body to be quartered, and those quarters to be burnt upon a pile of wood, when his ashes were to be collected and thrown into the sea. Harris's Voyages and Travels, Vol. I. p. 288.—Modern Universal History, Vol. IX. p. 64. Vuist, the Dutch governor of Ceylon above-mentioned, succeeded Isaac Augustin Rumph, who governed the island with much humanity and talent from 1716 to 1723, when he died, as is said, of a fright, occasioned by the murder of the Fiscal Barent Van Simon and his wife at Columbo, in an insurrection of their slaves. In 1761, the oppressions of the Dutch caused a furious insurrection of the Singalese, who destroyed their plantations, and butchered the inhabitants. In 1763, the Dutch penetrated to Candy with an army of 8000 men. They retained possession of the capital for about nine months; but, at the end of this time, their force was so greatly reduced by the pestilential qualities of the climate, and by other causes, that they were compelled to abandon the town, and to retire with precipitation They suffered very much from the vigilant hostility of the Singalese during their retreat; and but a

small part of their original force survived to tell their tale at Columbo. In 1766, however, the Dutch compelled the King of Candy to treat with them on their own terms, and to cede to them those parts of the coast which they had not hitherto possessed. By one of the articles of this treaty, the humiliating prostrations to which the Dutch ambassadors had hitherto been compelled to submit at the court of Candy, were henceforth agreed to be relinquished. But in the embassy which the Dutch sent to condole with the Candian monarch on the death of his consort, the ambassador, instead of prostrating himself flat upon the ground, like the native Singalese, appears only to have kneeled upon one knee. The account which I have given of this embassy is taken from the Dutch dispatch of the ambassador himself, which may be found in Valentyn.

CHAP. XVII.

Temporary Possession of Trincomalee by the British in 1782. Mr. Boyd sent as an Embassy to the Court of Candy. The Country exhibits Signs of a scanty and poor Population. All the Supplies of the Embassy at the Expense of the Emperor. Two Individuals punished with Death for selling some Rice. Features of the Country during the Journey; Scenery near Lake Minary. Miserable Dwellings of the People. Mr. Boyd's House at Gunnoor. Conducted to the Court; his Description of the Interior of the Palace. The Hall of Audience, Person of the King, and Ceremonial of Introduction described. Humiliating Servility of the Prime Minister. Curiosity and Ignorance of the Singalese Courtiers. Termination of the Embassy,

IN 1782, a British fleet, under the command of Sir Edward Hughes, and some land forces, under that of Sir Hector Munro, made themselves masters of Trincomalee; of which, however, they were soon afterwards deprived by the French. During the temporary possession of this important place by the British, Lord Macartney, who was then Governor of Madras, sent Mr. Boyd on an embassy to the court of Candy; and, as Mr. Boyd himself has described his journey to that capital, and detailed the reception which he experienced, and the observations which he made during his route, I shall select a few of the particulars as far as they throw any light on the state of the country, and the manners of the people.

Mr. Boyd left Trincomalee on the fifth of February, 1782, and did not arrive at Gunnoor, which is stated to be five miles distant from Candy, till the fourth of March. The residence of Mr. Boyd was to be fixed at Gunnoor, whilst he was conducting his negociation with the court.

In his way to Gunnoor, Mr. Boyd remarked the visible signs of an impoverished and scanty population. The villages which he saw on his route were usually composed of only a few small huts; and the inhabitants generally fled at his approach. The excuse alleged was, that they were gone to the paddy fields; but the real motive was to escape the necessity of furnishing any supplies to the embassy. The ambassador and his suite, according to the custom of the country, were to be furnished with every thing at the expense of the emperor; but they nevertheless experienced great want of provisions at different stages of their journey; and they were never very abundantly supplied. All, however, which they did receive, they were to owe to the gratuitous hospitality of the sovereign; nor were the natives permitted to take any compensation for whatever they might furnish. At the village of Wishtegal, in his way to Candy, Mr. Boyd, who was in great distress for rice with which to supply the different persons in his suite, purchased about 500 measures of that grain, for which he paid twenty pagodas. But on his return from Candy, he found that the two inhabitants of Wishtegal, who had sold him this seasonable supply, had both been put to death for their temerity.

In part of his journey, Mr. Boyd describes the pathways as good, but overhung with wood, and interspersed with abrupt intervals of rock and precipice. In some places the wood formed such condensed bowers, as to cause a deep shade during the day, and to exclude the sight of the stars at night. Here and there the road was more open; and the varieties of the ground burst upon the view in all the charms of wild landscape. As he proceeded from Pulian-Caravvety to Wishtegal, along the margin of Lake Minary, he says that "the most noble scenes of nature rose on every side." The hills were of vast height and magnitude, exhibiting great diversities of form, and opening at different turns into vallies of great variety and extent.

Mr. Boyd was not impressed with any favourable ideas of the agriculture of the country, or the industry of the people. Despotism, indeed, so absolute and capricious as that of Candy at this period, could not but be very inauspicious to the efforts of individual diligence, and to general cultivation.

The huts of the people appeared to Mr. Boyd to be ill and clumsily constructed. Even at Nallendy-Caravvety, which is represented as a place of "particular estimation and consequence," the houses are described as consisting of huts of mud walls and straw, ranged in small squares, some within others, with one elevated in the centre, and larger than the rest.

When Mr. Boyd and his suite arrived at Gunnoor, where his lodging was to be fixed till the completion of his embassy, he found that the house, which had been prepared for his reception, was "a large building, consisting of a square within a square, and capable of containing five hundred persons." The walls were of clay, but "sufficiently strong and well finished." He describes the adjacent country as beautiful, varied, and highly cultivated.

Mr. Boyd was conducted to the precincts of the palace by one of the dessaves, or provincial governors, whom he describes as an old man of the most engaging manners; and, at the same time, he remarks, that he was surprised by a sort of courtly politeness, which he found to be universal amongst the people. He represents the palace as "a large stone building, with sixteen large stone steps leading up to the entrance, at each side of which was placed a bowman; two huge fellows fantastically dressed." The whole area below was filled with soldiers and elephants. Between forty and fifty of these animals were drawn up in a semi-circle, with two fine white ones in the centre.

After passing through an outer and an inner court, Mr. Boyd was directed to the front of a very wide and high arch, with a white curtain thrown across. The removal of this curtain exhibited to his view a long hall, divided by large arches in the centre, and two small ones on each side. These arches formed two aisles, within which the courtiers were sitting, not cross-legged, but with knees projecting straight forward. The hall was lighted by lamps, attached to the pillars of the arches, and large wax tapers burning at the upper end of each aisle. A secretary sat near one of these tapers, to record what passed.

The hall terminated in a large alcove, within which the king sat, upon a very high throne. He wore a large crown upon his head, and is depicted as a large black man, with an intelligent countenance, and about thirty-six or thirty-seven years of age.

The removal of the curtain, which concealed the interior of the hall, was the signal for those genuflections of the ambassador, and those prostrations of the courtiers who attended him, which I have before had occasion to describe; and which constituted a very essential ingredient in the ceremonial of the Candian court. Mr. Boyd gives a lively description of these prostrations. He says—"that those who performed them almost literally licked the dust; prostrating themselves with their faces close to the stone floor, and throwing out their legs and arms as in the attitude of swimming; then rising to their knees by a sudden spring from the breast, like what is called the salmon leap by tumblers, they repeated, in a very loud voice, a certain form of words, of the most extravagant meaning that can be conceived—'That the head of the king of kings might reach beyond the sun! that he might live a hundred thousand years,'" &c.

During the audience, Mr. Boyd observed an instance of humiliation in the prime minister of the sovereign, that was even more abject and debasing than any of the preceding, which appear to have been sufficiently servile. "Something happened which made it necessary for the minister to come to the lower end of the hall. I did not observe him set out," says Mr. Boyd, " but, turning my head by accident, I cannot express my surprise when I saw him, a venerable grey-headed old man, coming trotting down one of the aisles, like a dog, on all fours! He returned in the same manner to the foot of the throne."

Mr. Boyd remained nine or ten days at Gunnoor after this audience, during which interval he had several visits from persons about the court, and discussions with some of the ministers upon the subject of the embassy. In his conversations with the Singalese courtiers, Mr. Boyd found their curiosity very great, and their information very scanty and circumscribed. He mentions that they had never heard of America; and they were surprised that they now heard nothing of the Portuguese, whose power and bigotry were formerly such objects of their abhorrence and their fears.

The negotiation of Mr. Boyd terminated with hardly any other effect than bare professions of a pacific and friendly disposition.*

* The Government of Madras had sent Mr. Pybus on an embassy to Candy in 1763, in order to negociate an alliance, offensive and defensive, between the king, or emperor, and the East India Company. But, as the English were then at peace with the Dutch, the overtures of Mr. Pybus ended only in the disappointment of the Singalese in their subsequent hostilities with that people, and operated very much in disposing the court of Candy to accede to the propositions of Mr. Boyd. Mr. Boyd, who conducted the abovementioned embassy, was a man of genius and talents, and has been believed by some, though I think without any sufficient reason, to have been the author of the celebrated Letters under the signature of Junius. During six years and a half of a laborious literary life, from July, 1807 to December, 1813, my attention was, on several occasions, called to the examination of this subject; but I remember to have been much less impressed by the pretensions of Mr. Boyd, than by those of another gentleman, whose name has been seldom mentioned during the discussion of this interesting point of literary curiosity. The Letters which have been recently published, " proving a late prime minister to have been Junius," do not, I think, establish the authorship of the Duke of Portland; but they still render it highly credible that the Duke of Portland must have known who Junius was, and that Junius must have derived some of his information from the duke. The case of the Duke of Portland could never have been so repeatedly mentioned, and have formed such a prominent feature in the Letters of Junius, if the author had not written under the cognizance, and more or less at the instigation, of the duke. The direct mention of

the duke's case in so many Letters, and, above all, the reiterated allusion to it in so many more, prove it incontestably to have been a question of personal interest either in the author of the Letters or in the individual, with whose cognizance and under whose influence the Letters were composed. Now no proof has been adduced to shew that the duke himself had sufficient literary capacity for the authorship of the Letters; but there is certainly very strong presumptive evidence that at least some of them must have been written under his cognizance and inspection. Who then was the powerful agent, whose pen served to vindicate the claims of the duke, and to vilify both the sovereign and his ministers? Shall I invoke the manes of C****** L**** to reveal the disputed name? I had more than one conversation with the late Duke of Grafton concerning the Letters of Junius; but his grace certainly never entertained the smallest suspicion that the Duke of Portland was at all implicated in the composition.

CHAP. XVIII.

Dominion of the Portuguese and Dutch; Bigotry of the one, Avarice of the other; Degeneracy of both. Cowardice of the Dutch; their Singalese Settlements conquered by the British in 1796. Honourable Frederic North, Governor.

THE dominion of the Portuguese in Ceylon lasted for about 150 years; and that of the Dutch for nearly the same period, when it was added to the number of the British possessions in the East.

The conquest of Ceylon by the Dutch was in a great measure owing to the hatred which had been excited by the bigotry, intolerance, and cruelty, of the Portuguese. The Dutch soon shewed themselves as deficient as their predecessors in the great virtues of justice and humanity; but their tyranny was not, like that of the Portuguese, at all influenced by the desire to propagate an exclusive faith, but was the effect of unmitigated rapacity and avarice.

The Portuguese were under the influence of a sentiment of bigotry, which, when it becomes a predominant feeling in the human breast, equally disregards the suggestions of caution, the admonitions of prudence, and the higher considerations of humanity. It is a blind impulse, and it has all the effect of blindness both visual and mental, in the strange deviations which it causes from the straight path of virtue and of truth, and consequently of the best policy and the most stable interest.

The Dutch did not bend before the grim Moloch of religious bigotry, nor did they worship at the shrine of superstition; but cent per cent was their faith, gold was their object, and Mammon was their god. But this idol of the Dutch is as unfavourable to the growth of the softer virtues, and to all that tends to humanize the exercise of power, as that of the Portuguese. Avarice is a cold calculating feeling, and where it totally pervades the bosom, absorbing the affections, and concentrating the desires in a single object, it renders the heart as impenetrable as a stone to those moral considerations which are more particularly associated with a benevolent regard for the happiness of those who are placed in subjection to our will, or within the sphere of our influence. The insensate avarice of the Dutch proved as unfavourable to the happiness of the people of Ceylon, as the enthusiastic bigotry of the Portuguese.

Both the Portuguese and the Dutch, in the first instance, established their power by heroic effort and persevering enterprise; but neither of them long displayed the same energetic qualities in preserving what they had acquired. When the Portuguese were driven from the island, they had greatly degenerated from the vigorous, daring, and enterprising intrepidity of their ancestors; and, in the year 1796, the Dutch suffered this important settlement to be wrested from them by the British with a degree of contemptible imbecility and unresisting cowardice, of which the instances are not common in the annals of modern warfare. There is a high sentiment of honour operating in the bosoms of men in the present period, which is so active, as almost to counteract the effects of temperament in individual instances, and to render even cowards ashamed not to be brave. But, when the Dutch were called upon to defend their towns and forts on the coast of Ceylon against the attacks of the British, they seem to have lost both the thirst of distinction and the dread of shame; and to have felt none of those elevating sentiments which invigorate courage, and make men prefer even death itself to contumely and disgrace.

I shall not load my page with a detail of the operations by which, in 1796, the whole coast of this island became an easy conquest to the arms of Great Britain, under the conduct of Colonel Stuart. The sloth, lassitude, and pusillanimity of the Dutch,* formed a conspicuous contrast with the energy, intrepidity, and highmindedness of their adversaries.

The conquered provinces remained for a short time as an appendage to the presidency of Madras, when they were transferred to the crown of Great Britain, and rendered wholly independent of the East India Company. The Honourable Frederic North was sent to Ceylon in 1798, as governor of those parts of the island which the British had subdued.

* The Dutch surrendered Columbo to the British, without any resistance, though the number of the garrison was fully equal to that of the force sent against it; but, after the British troops had entered the fort, Mr. Percival says that he was assured, by an officer who was an eye-witness, that "the Dutch soldiers went so far as even to strike at our men with their muskets, calling them insulting and opprobrious names, and even spitting upon them as they passed. This behaviour," adds the same writer, "entirely corresponded with their former cowardice, and was equally despised by our countrymen." Percival's Account of Ceylon, p. 95.

CHAP. XIX.

Death of the King of Candy in 1798; his Successor raised to the Throne by the Arts of Pelemé Talavé. The Queen, her Brother, Mootto Sawmy, with the Relations of the deceased Monarch, protected by the British. Ambitious Projects of Pelemé Talavé. His Overtures to Mr. North. His Intentions developed to Mr. Boyd. General Macdonald's Embassy to Candy, Circumstances of, and Details respecting.

BEFORE the commencement of Mr. North's administration, a negociation had been set on foot between the government of Madras and the Court of Candy; but, though some important advantages were proposed to be conceded to the latter, the treaty, which had been actually signed by the Governor of Fort St. George, was subsequently refused to be ratified by the Candian sovereign. This monarch died in 1798, when the government was transferred by the treacherous intrigues of Pelemé Talavé, the chief adigar, or prime minister, to a young Malabar,* without any pretensions of birth or talents to the crown, but who appeared to be a mere puppet in the hands of the artful miscreant, to whom he owed his elevation.

The queen and all the relations of the deceased monarch were thrown into prison; but some of these, along with the queen's brother, Mootto Sawmy, afterwards made their escape, and solicited the protection of the

* Lord Valentia says, Travels, Vol. I. p. 279, that the abovementioned monarch was "a son of the late king by a Singalese mother, and consequently a bastard, since the King of Candy can only marry a Malabar, which is his own cast. The young man, therefore, had no rightful claim to the crown; and the adigar did not scruple to avow that he raised him to the throne, with the intention of removing him when convenient, and restoring the Singalese line, that is, of usurping the crown himself." This adigar is mentioned as the representative of one of the noblest Singalese families.

British government.* Mootto Sawmy, who was conceived to have the best title to the throne, was placed at Jaffnapatam under the charge of a British officer; and the other fugitives were kept at Columbo, in order to remove all reasonable ground of complaint from the established government at Candy.

In 1799, Pelemé Talavé, who has been just mentioned, began, in a mysterious manner, to try how far the British governor could be induced, by the most subtle misrepresentations and most complicated artifice, to co-operate with him in a scheme which he had formed for his own personal aggrandisement. His principal object was to depose the monarch whom he had raised to the throne, and to render himself the sovereign of the Candian territory, under the pretence that he would hold it subject to the supremacy of the English. Mr. North, however, indignantly refused to listen to these insidious overtures.

Pelemé Talavé, however, was not a man to be diverted from his purpose by slight obstacles. He afterwards found means of developing his projects more fully to Mr. Boyd, the secretary to the government at Columbo. He declared that, in raising the present puppet to the throne, his object had been to render the race of Malabar sovereigns contemptible, in order the more easily to effect its extermination, and to establish a native dynasty.

In order to ascertain as far as possible the real state of affairs in Candy, Mr. North deemed it expedient to send a special embassy to the court of the reigning sovereign. In March, 1800, General Macdowall was accordingly dispatched on this mission; of which, as it exhibits some curious details, I shall relate a few particulars, on the authority of Percival's Account of Ceylon, of the Asiatic Annual Register for 1804, and of an account of the embassy which is contained in the publication

* Cordiner, Vol. II. p. 160, &c. Asiatic Annual Register for 1804.

of Mr. Cordiner, and extracted from the manuscript diary of Mr. Macpherson, who was secretary to the embassy.

This embassy, which was attended by a numerous escort of Europeans and natives, besides pioneers and lascars, left Columbo on the 12th of March, with a letter from the governor to the king, and another to the first adigar. The letter to his Singalese majesty was treated during the whole route, with that sort of sacred reverence, which, in despotic governments, is often paid to all the circumstances of royalty. The letter, with all the requisite formalities, was placed upon the head of one of the appohamies; and, when the ambassador crossed the river near Sitavaca,* and entered the Candian dominions, a round of blank cartridges was fired over it by a corporal and six men.

Soon after the British had crossed the river, and the embassy had reached the choultry, which was appointed for its reception, the first adigar, who was encamped in the neighbourhood, advanced in great state by torch light, in order to pay a visit of ceremony to the ambassador. General Macdowall advanced to meet the adigar, who was attended by about a thousand men and seven elephants. "The ambassador went up to him with both hands open, the palms uppermost

* Sitavaca was the ancient residence of kings or rajas. The kings of Sitavaca were rulers of all the low lands, and were of such paramount importance, that the kings and chiefs of the hill and wood country were their tributaries. The kings of Sitavaca boasted that they were of nobler blood and purer descent than those of the high lands. They asserted themselves to be genuine descendants from the legitimate stock of a Prince of Tanassery, and a daughter of the royal race of Madura, whilst the Candian princes were only bastards, and of less honourable extraction. But it is certain that when the King of Sitavaca was conquered by the kings of Candy and Uva, they found it requisite to pay so much deference to the people in favour of the high claims of the extinguished dynasty, as to undergo the ceremony of inauguration in the ancient Palace of Sitavaca. This practice was still observed on the arrival of the Portuguese. Valentyn mentions, p. 229, that the palace at Sitavaca had been repaired by the Dutch, and that the gates, walls, and architectural embellishments attested its original magnificence; though he adds, that it was not to be compared with the ruins of the buildings left by Malabar sovereigns.

and joined; the adigar advanced and took hold of them." After this, the ambassador shewed the same mark of respect to the three mottiars, by whom the adigar was attended, and sprinkled rose water on a handkerchief, that each of them held in his hand. The ambassador then taking the adigar's left hand in his right, proceeded to the place in the residence where the king's letter was deposited; and, having testified their respect to this appurtenance of royalty, a conference ensued, which related rather to questions of ceremony, than to matters of importance.

Two days after this formal interview, the adigar waited on the ambassador in his customary pomp, and observing on his way some British officers and soldiers, who, in order to have a clearer view of the procession, had fixed themselves on an eminence, below which it was to pass, he expressed considerable displeasure, and desired that they might be ordered down; as no one in his presence ought to be placed higher than himself, in whom the majesty of the great King of Candy, the descendant of the golden sun, was represented.

Several flags and streamers were borne before the adigar, with a variety of musical instruments peculiar to the country, and a number of persons cracking immense whips, so as to produce a hideous discordancy.

The presents, which the embassy were conveying to his Candian majesty, were here delivered to the adigar at his desire. They consisted of an elegant state coach, drawn by six horses; a betel dish, with ornaments of solid gold, which had belonged to the late Tippoo Sultan, of rose water, and other articles.

The following day, the ambassador having ordered some alterations to be made in the road, which was too narrow, hollow, and precipitous, for the passage of artillery, the adigar, who appears to have regarded the embassy with considerable jealousy and inquietude, expressed his disapprobation of this proceeding, though he knew that the British escort could not advance, unless the road was improved. "The whole track," says Captain Percival, "which it was intended we should pursue, in our progress to Candy, was marked out by twigs and bushes, set up at proper distances." No intercourse was permitted between the natives and the English on the way; and the attendants on the camp were so reserved, either from terror or from choice, that no information could be obtained about the state of the kingdom.

Captain Percival says, that the adigar was acquainted with a more practicable road than that which was marked out for the British; but that he purposely selected this, in order to expose them to the greatest possible inconvenience. A large party of Candian troops, though kept out of sight, is said constantly to have watched their movements, and attended their march; whilst the inhabitants, in all directions, were assembled in arms. We cannot well be surprised at these suspicious precautions of the Candian court during the presence of an European embassy in its territory, with several pieces of artillery and a considerable number of troops. The Candians had experienced, for near three centuries, the perfidy, cruelty, and oppression of the Portuguese and the Dutch; and how could they tell that British bosoms cherished more pure and exalted sentiments of justice and humanity?

During part of their march, Captain Percival* complains of the inconvenience which the troops suffered from the multitudes of leeches by which they were infested on the way. "Most of the soldiers had their legs and different parts of their bodies streaming with blood. On taking off my gloves and boots, I found that I had not escaped; for what I had taken to be nothing more than excessive perspiration, now turned out to be the effects of these leeches." The officers and men,

* P. 387.

who were employed in clearing the jungles, seemed to be completely covered with blood. No precautions were sufficient to elude the attacks of these blood-suckers, which swarmed amongst the bushes and the grass. The Dutch used to represent them as one of the most pertinacious enemies against whom they had to contend.

The ambassador, having found it expedient from the difficulties of the road, to leave the greater part of his troops* behind, proceeded towards the capital on the thirty-first of March, with no other escort than two companies of sepoys, and two of Malays. The country, through which they passed, appears in general to have been highly cultivated, and much of the scenery was very varied and beautiful. But besides the badness of the roads, the troops were much incommoded in their march by the intensity of the heat, and by the almost constant rain, accompanied with violent storms of thunder and lightning.

* The troops which were thus left behind, were stationed in a tope of cocoa trees, called the King's Garden, on the banks of the Calany-ganga, within a mile of Ruanelli. Captain Percival says, that the detachment remained encamped in this situation for upwards of a month, during which, the rapid changes of temperature that the troops experienced, had the most pernicious effect upon their health. Heavy rain, with thunder and lightning, usually closed the evening, thick damp fogs loaded the atmosphere at night, and the early part of the day was marked by excessive heat. No circumstances could well have a stronger tendency to produce disease. "Dysenteries, fluxes, and liver complaints became frequent, and the jungle fever began to make its appearance." The encampment of the troops was surrounded by such deep and intricate woods, that no one could stir out without danger of irretrievably losing his way in the maze. "Having procured the adigar's leave," says Captain Percival, "to make shooting excursions, and also people acquainted with the country to conduct us, we had an opportunity of seeing several of their villages, most of which we found totally deserted by their inhabitants. On the approach of a red coat, the alarm was instantly given, and the natives, men, women, and children, fled directly into the woods. It was not till after some time, that we could persuade a few of them to remain in their habitations; but I never saw any thing in the figure of a woman, from the time I entered the Candian territory, to the moment of my quitting it. We found it very difficult to procure hogs, fowls, and fruits from the natives, although such articles were in great abundance in the country. This not a little surprised us, as the king's officers had expressly issued orders, directing us to be supplied with every sort of necessaries."

On the tenth of April the ambassador arrived at a place near the capital, where his residence was to be fixed during his stay. It now became necessary to settle the forms, to which the British ambassador might not think it beneath the dignity of his mission to submit, on his introduction to the Candian sovereign. The Dutch, who had never much regard for national honour, except as it was identified with the gains of their merchants, and the interest of their factories, had submitted to the most degrading ceremonies. They had sometimes endured to be led blindfolded into the capital; and had condescended to prostrate themselves on appearing in the royal presence. When the British ambassador was told that the King of Candy would not receive him standing, he answered with becoming spirit, that sooner than degrade the sovereign, whom he represented, by prostration, he would return to Columbo without proceeding farther in the object of his mission. The Candian monarch on this occasion gave way to the firm remonstrances of the ambassador.

After the requisite arrangements had been made for the grand ceremonial, the British ambassador, according to the intimation which he had received, left his house at nine oclock in the evening to proceed to the palace. Having crossed the Mahavillaganga in boats, General Macdowall and his suite were conveyed in palanquins, at a very slow rate, to a place where they halted, within the limits of the city, and half a mile from the palace.

The road to the palace was up a steep hill with narrow crooked paths. The crowd of natives, who early gathered round the procession, together with the glare of torches, made it impossible to take any accurate view of the city. The street, through which the embassy passed, was long and broad, and terminated by the palace, surrounded by an high wall and gardens.* The houses, though low huts of them-

* Percival, p. 401.

selves, were erected upon high banks on each side of the street, which forms an area below. Mr. Cordiner's account* says, "Upon the road we could only remark, that there were a good many houses upon each side of it, and that there were rice fields where there were not houses to obstruct the view. The road was pretty level, but bad from neglect in several parts. In four or five different places high palisades ran across the road, with gates in the centre of them; at each of these gates we found small guards of about twenty-five Malays each, and at three of them we observed two pieces of cannon mounted upon carriages, with their muzzles pointed at the moon."

The embassy were detained about an hour at the halting place, which has been just mentioned, when they proceeded through a drenching rain to the first gate of the palace, where they were compelled to wait half an hour longer before the first adigar came to announce his majesty's permission for the ambassador to enter the royal residence. When his excellency arrived at the second gate, he took the king's letter from "off the appahamy's head, and holding it in both hands level with his eyes, instead of putting it on his head, as was the practice of the Dutch ambassadors, he moved on to the hall of audience, the two adigars holding him by the arms."

As the embassy entered the hall † of audience, several curtains were removed, which exhibited a full view of the king upon his throne, in a recess at the farther end of the apartment. This was the signal for six of the nobles to prostrate themselves on the ground, and for the ambassador and his suite to kneel. The language of an Eastern court always

* P. 299.

† This state-room, says Percival, had alternate arches and pillars along its sides, and bore a considerable resemblance to the aisle of a church. The pillars and arches were adorned with muslin flowers, and ornaments made of the plantain leaf, which had a pretty effect. The king sat under one of the larger arches at the farther end of the hall, on a kind of platform covered with a carpet. That part of the hall where the king sat was not so well lighted as the rest, in order to impress more awe upon the beholder.

approaches more or less to that of religious adoration; and the exaggeration of the flattery is usually in proportion to the rigour of the despotism. In this instance, after the six nobles just mentioned had prostrated themselves several times before the throne, they exclaimed, in language which sounds like blasphemy in the ears of an European, "Oh, king, live for ever!"

These nobles having performed this ceremony of prostration, the ambassador, who was still held by the first and second adigars, advanced with the letter towards the throne. "Having reached the foot of the throne, the first adigar took off the muslin that covered the letter, and his majesty took the letter from the ambassador's hands, and laid it down on his left side. The ambassador was now led backwards to the spot, where we remained all the while kneeling. Having reached us, he kneeled also."

After his Candian majesty had kept the ambassador and his suite for some time upon their knees, the king at length condescended to let them sit down on the carpet.

The communication between the king and the ambassador was conducted through the medium of six, or, according to Captain Percival, five persons, and in three different languages. When the king had any thing to say, he addressed himself to the second adigar, who, after offering up a prayer that his majesty might live for ever, repeated the royal words to the dessave, or headman of Uva, who repeated them to the Singalese interpreter that attended the embassy, who repeated them in Portuguese to a person who explained them in English, as Mr. Cordiner says, or in French, as Captain Percival says, to the ambassador. When the ambassador made any reply to his majesty, the same tedious process of communication was obliged to be pursued.

After this audience, the ambassador was conducted by the adigar to a room which contained refreshments, consisting of balls of flour and honey, sweet cakes, and fruit. The ambassador was then attended as before to the halting place, about half a mile from the palace, where his excellency and his suite got into their palanquins, a little before five o'clock in the morning, and returned to the residence of the embassy at Gonaroova a little after six.

From the description which Mr. Cordiner has given of his Singalese majesty, he does not appear to have been far removed from an ideot; but other accounts are less in unison with such a supposition. "He seemed very vain of his dress, and very uneasy on his throne: he kept constantly shaking his head, to display the precious stones in his crown, and pulled down his vest or armour to shew off the jewels with which it was studded. He seemed particularly fond of a large round ornament, which was suspended from his neck." He had two attendants with fly-flaps, whilst he conversed and laughed at intervals with persons whose heads occasionally appeared. He was a young man, very black, with a light beard,* a large head, and a vacant countenance.†

* Percival, p. 406.

† Cordiner, Vol. II. p. 306. Percival says, "He was dressed in a robe of very fine muslin, embroidered with gold, fitted close at the breast, with several folds drawn round the waist, and flowing down from thence like a lady's gown. His arms were bare from the elbow downwards. On his fingers he wore a number of very broad rings, set with precious stones of different sorts, while a number of gold chains were suspended round his neck over a stiff frilled piece of muslin resembling a Queen Elizabeth's ruff." His Ceylonese majesty is sometimes termed, by way of distinction, the king who wears a crown, as the other Asiatic princes are prohibited from decorating their heads with that ensign of royal state.

CHAP. XX.

Return of the Embassy; failure of its Object. Machinations of Pelemé Talavé. Act of Aggression on the Part of the Candians; War unavoidable. Two Divisions of the British Army reach Candy; find it deserted by the Enemy. Description of the Palace, Town, and Vicinity. Mootto Sawmy placed upon the Throne; an impolitic Proceeding. Arts of Pelemé Talavé to entrap the British. Critical Circumstances of the British Garrison at Candy. Pelemé Talavé's Repetitions of Perfidy; General Macdowall deceived by his treacherous Overtures. Retires from Candy with Part of the Garrison. Pelemé Talavé amuses the Governor at Columbo by a Negociation; designs to seize the Person of Mr. North at a Conference; Progress of his Stratagems. Distress of the Garrison at Candy. Attempts to produce Desertion increase. Numbers of the Enemy.

THIS embassy, of which the former chapter has furnished some descriptive details, at last returned without effecting the purpose for which it had been sent. One of the propositions which the English ambassador made, appears to have awakened the jealousy of the Candian court. This was to make a sort of military road through the Candian territory, for the purpose of facilitating the communication between the British troops in the different garrisons on the coast. It appears evidently to have been the policy of the chief adigar, Pelemé Talavé, to amuse the British by the negociation, and to delude them with specious representations and perfidious offers, till he found what he thought a favourable opportunity of gratifying his ambition by making himself master of the interior, and expelling them from the coast. To assist in the execution of this scheme, he seems to have been long determined to bring on a war between the British and the Candians, calculating upon the unwholesome climate of the latter as a powerful auxiliary in the prosecution of hostilities and the extermination of the enemy.

In the spring of 1802, the Candians, who had for some time been secretly making preparations for war, began the first act of aggression, by detaining some British traders who had resorted to the capital, and by the violent spoliation of some native merchants, who were under the protection of the British government. Repeated promises of satisfaction for these acts of injustice were made by the Candian government, but which were as often violated, till the British had no alternative but that of base submission to a treacherous enemy, or of open war. In short, war, though adverse to the wishes and the policy of Mr. North, had become actually unavoidable.

The division of the British army from Columbo, under the command of Major-General Macdowall, which was destined to invade the Candian territory, was put in motion the thirty-first of January, 1803; and, on the fourth of February, another division, under Colonel Barbut, marched from Trincomalee for the same destination. Both these divisions of the army, which amounted to more than 3000 Europeans and Malays, arrived nearly at the same time at the capital of the Candian territory. They had experienced very little resistance on the way, though they had great obstacles to overcome in transporting their artillery, ammunition, and stores, through a country so destitute of roads, and so full of precipices and ravines.

When these divisions of the army, of which that from Columbo had performed a march of 103 miles, and that from Trincomalee of 145 miles, formed a junction at Candy; they found the city entirely deserted by the government and inhabitants, and occupied only by a few pariah dogs. The town had been set on fire* in several places; but the British

* Asiatic Annual Register for 1804, p. 12. Cordiner, Vol. II. p. 180.

arrived in sufficient time to extinguish the flames, though not before part of the palace had been consumed. The king had removed all his treasure, and the inhabitants had destroyed almost every thing valuable, which they could not carry away. A few days after this event, the enemy shewed themselves in considerable force near the city, but they were repulsed with little loss, and with great slaughter.

The palace is described as an immense pile of building, constructed of stone and wood, covered over with a white cement, called chunam. Some of the apartments,* which had been spared by the flames, contained elegant sets of glass and china ware, with some cups of gold, decorated with silver fillagree. One of the rooms was covered with pier glasses. The palace had been repaired and ornamented since the embassy in 1800. It comprehends within its walls two temples to Boodh, one Hindoo pagoda, a cemetery, and an immense variety of arsenals and storehouses. "Amongst some of the stores," says Mr. Cordiner, "was found a profusion of soft paper, made in the country, of the bark of trees: the sheets were rolled up, and some of them measured twenty feet in length."

The town of Candy consists of one broad street, which is two miles in length, with the palace at the end, and with numerous lanes branching from the principal thoroughfares. The houses are mostly of mud, thatched with straw and leaves, with small apertures instead of windows.

The surrounding scenery is rich and beautiful. The land is highly cultivated, interspersed with villages and rivulets. Some of the mountains are cleared to their summits, formed in ridges, and sown with grain. "The fields below are terraced in the most regular manner on different levels, so that not a drop of water can be lost." The vallies are enriched with areca, jack, cocoa-nuts, limes, oranges, plaintain, and

* Cordiner.

pumple nose trees, with fields of paddy and other grain, all fertilized by assiduous and skilful irrigation. The royal garden was enriched with abundance of vegetables, and the river near the city swarmed with fish.

As soon as the inhabitants in the northern and eastern provinces were said to be desirous of having Mootto Sawmy, the brother of the late queen, for their king, he was accordingly removed to Candy, and placed in the palace, where he enjoyed the transient parade of royalty; but none of the people of authority in the neighbouring country evinced any disposition to submit to his sway, or to support his power. This attempt of the British to place Mootto Sawmy upon the throne, appears to have been very inconsiderate and impolitic, even if we suppose it compatible with the previous negociations respecting the settlement of the government. Lord Valentia says, that Mootto Sawmy was ineligible to the crown on account of a fraud, for which the late king had subjected him to a public punishment.*

After abandoning Candy to the English troops, the adigar had posted himself, along with his royal puppet, at Hangaramketty, a strong post, about two days march from the capital. From this point the insidious minister began to exert his arts upon the honest simplicity of Colonel Barbut, who commanded the British garrison in that place. He accordingly made some specious overtures to that officer, to which he unwarily listened. The adigar promised, that if Colonel Barbut would send a sufficient force to Hangaramketty, he would deliver up the king to the British. A sufficient force was accordingly dispatched upon this disastrous expedition.

After experiencing repeated attacks and some loss, from parties of the enemy who were placed in ambush on the way, the British at last reached their appointed destination. But the monarch and his minister had

* Lord Valentia's Travels, Vol. I. 4to. p. 298.

previously taken flight before their arrival. Colonel Barbut began now to suspect the treachery of the adigar; but had he not before had sufficent experience of his perfidy? The colonel, however, returned with as much expedition as possible to Candy, before the adigar had time to complete the catastrophe which he meditated, by drawing the British still further into the country, till their retreat would have become impossible.

The British garrison at Candy soon found themselves in perilous and embarrassing circumstances. Numerous bodies of the enemy were posted in ambush round the city, and destroyed every straggler that came in their way. In order to stimulate the activity of their treacherous vengeance, the adigar promised ten rupees for the head of every European, and five for that of every native soldier in the British service.

About the end of March, when the rainy season had commenced, the adigar, who well knew that the sickliness of the climate would soon reduce the number of his enemies, determined to make farther overtures for negociation, in order, as much as possible, to relax the vigilance of the British, and to make still more sure of their destruction. As if he thought that nature had set no limits to English credulity, and that their confidence was never to be destroyed by his perfidy, he dispatched two letters, to propose pacific arrangements to the government at Columbo. He also, at the same time, sent the second adigar into the town of Candy, with a firelock and match wrapped up in white muslin, as an emblem of peace. General Macdowall, who was then at the head of the garrison, received this minister with marks of the most respectful attention; and, in their conferences, it was agreed that the king, who was to be deposed, should be placed under the protection of the British; that the supreme power should be vested in Pelemé Talavé; that a suitable provision should be made for Mootto Sawmy, who was to reside at Jaffnapatam, and that there should be a cessation of hostilities between the British and the Singalese.

Owing probably to the sense of security, which a trust in the fidelity of these engagements, on the part of the enemy, had unfortunately inspired, General Macdowall left Candy on the first of April, "taking with him his majesty's fifty-first regiment, the Ceylon native infantry, and part of the detachment of the Bengal artillery. At the same time, part of his majesty's nineteenth and Malay regiments set out on their march to Trincomalee." The garrison of Candy was thus reduced to about one thousand troops, of whom more than one half were Malays.

On the day after General Macdowall had retired from Candy, the chief adigar, eager to seize his prey, advanced with a large force within three miles of that place;* but he still had the art to masque his ultimate designs, and all the while kept amusing the government at Columbo with overtures for a definitive treaty of peace. In order to effect this purpose, Mr. North, at the particular desire of the adigar, on the third of May, actually admitted him to a personal conference at Dambadenia. During this conference, the insidious miscreant was remarked to exhibit much nervous agitation, which was ascribed to fear: but which, it afterwards appeared, arose from his hesitating diffidence about executing a plot that he had formed at this time, to seize the person of the governor. This attempt he was finally deterred from making, by the strength of Mr. North's escort, and by the unexpected arrival of Colonel Barbut from Candy, with a detachment of 300 Malays.

But, notwithstanding this intended plot, which was not discovered till afterwards, the adigar was so expert in dissimulation, that Mr. Cordiner says, "it was now thought that the adigar was sincere, and that he had at length determined to act with good faith." On this occasion, the adigar ratified with his signature and seal the terms of that conven-

* Mr. Cordiner says, Vol. II. p. 199, "But *the garrison remained in great tranquillity*, because it was confidently expected that the truce would bring about a peace agreeable to both parties."

tion, which had been previously arranged in Candy between General Macdowall and the second adigar.

Notwithstanding this treaty, which was intended only to deceive the British, the Candians drew their lines nearer to the city, and entrenched themselves in strong positions in the immediate vicinity. The garrison, which was under the command of Major Davie, began to suffer greatly from the pestiferous nature of the climate. Almost all the European troops were confined to the hospital. The swelling of the rivers, owing to the violence of the rains, had at the same time intercepted almost all communication between Candy and Columbo.

Great efforts were now made, by the emissaries of the adigar, to produce desertion amongst the Malays; and great praise is due, on this occasion, to the incorruptible integrity of Captain Nouradeen, a native officer, who commanded that corps, and who resisted the most flattering offers of the enemy.

Notwithstanding the repeated instances of perfidy in the conduct of the adigar, he still placed so much dependence on his own wiles, or had so much confidence in the credulity of his enemies, that, on the thirteenth of June, he sent a letter to the commandant of Candy, in which he represented that he had incurred the displeasure of the king, by his endeavours to serve the English, and urged the major to send another expedition to Hangaramketty, as the most efficacious means of putting an end to the war. Major Davie, however, was not, on this occasion, made the dupe of Candian artifice; but still his situation in the capital became every day more critical and precarious. Desertions became more frequent amongst the Malays, and death thinned the ranks of the Europeans; whilst the force of the enemy was augmented by new levies from all parts of the country.

CHAP. XXI.

The British Garrison at Candy attacked by the Enemy. Major Davie, the Commander, capitulates. The Garrison march out of Candy; Attempt in vain to cross the Mahavilla-ganga; surrounded by the Enemy; submit to dishonourable Propositions; Reflections upon their Conduct. The British Troops deliver up their Arms, and are all massacred, with the Exception of two Officers who escaped, and of two who were spared. Ensign Grant's Defence of Dambadenia; and Major Johnson's Expedition to Candy in 1804, *recorded in Note.*

THE palace at Candy, in which the British troops were quartered, was attacked by the enemy early in the morning of the twenty-fourth of June. The Candians were repulsed, and retired for an interval to the rising grounds near the city, from which they annoyed the garrison with their fire. The palace did not, at that time, contain more than twenty Europeans fit for duty; and there were 120 men of the 19th regiment in the hospital, who were too sick to be moved.

The Candians, gathering courage from their knowledge of the reduced and sickly state of the garrison, rushed forward to the assault with overwhelming numbers. Major Davie, despairing of the success of further resistance, offered to capitulate; and for this purpose he repaired, in conjunction with Captain Nouradeen, to the quarters of the adigar, who was stationed at a considerable distance from the town. It was agreed that the town, with the ammunition and stores, should be delivered up to the Candians; and that the British should march out with their arms, on the road leading to Trincomalee. The adigar was to supply the sick and wounded in the hospital wih medicines and provisions, till they were capable of being removed to one of the British settlements.

On the return of Major Davie, after the adigar had signed the capitulation, the garrison left the capital in the evening of the same day. The troops consisted of fourteen European officers, twenty British soldiers, 250 Malays, 140 gun lascars, with Prince Mootto Sawmy and his attendants. They proceeded to the distance of one mile and a half on the road to Trincomalee, where they halted for the night, on the banks of the Mahavilla-ganga. The next morning they in vain endeavoured to throw a raft over the stream. In the mean time the Candians began to gather round them on both sides of the river. Four head-men brought intelligence to Major Davie, that the king was incensed with the adigar for having permitted the English to retire from his capital; but that, if they would deliver up Mootto Sawmy they should be furnished with boats to pass the river, and with the requisite supplies for their march to Trincomalee.

Major Davie at first refused to listen to these dishonourable proposals, which were in direct violation of the late treaty. Another party of Candian chiefs then came, and declared that the king intended no violence to Mootto Sawmy, but would treat him as a relation; but the major still persisted in his refusal to deliver up the prince; and more honourable would it have been for his memory, if he had not suffered that resolution to be shaken by the subsequent menaces of the perfidious enemy. Another message was sent, to declare, that if the British commander still refused to deliver up the prince, the king would attack him with his whole force, and prevent their crossing the river. After deliberation with his brother officers, the major informed the unfortunate prince that he could protect him no longer. "My God!" exclaimed the unhappy man, who knew too well the fate that awaited him, "is it possible that the arms of England can be so humbled as to fear the menaces of such cowards as the Candians." He was taken before the king, who, after reviling him for his pretended treason, ordered him to be immediately executed.

On the following day, (26th of June,) a great mass of the natives bore down upon the British troops, when a dessave, or head-man, informed Major Davie, that the king commanded all the troops to lay down their arms and return to the capital. Death was threatened in case of a refusal. After the repeated proofs which the British had had that both the king and his minister were equally destitute of humanity and good faith, how could the major and the other officers expect that even a compliance with such ignominious proposals would be the means of preserving their lives? And, when the compliance itself manifested a high degree of pusillanimity, ought they, for a moment, to have hesitated between death and dishonour? Even, if the enemy had been less cruel than they knew him to be, still no British officer ought to think life worth having, at the expense of infamy.

If we were to allow any apology for the conduct of Major Davie and his brother officers, we must seek it in the previous influence of a malignant climate, which had debilitated their bodies, and deprived their minds of their wonted energy. It must be confessed, that the circumstances in which they were placed, and the horrors by which they were surrounded, were sufficient to shake the strong, and to cloud the brow even of the brave; but still whatever allowance we may make for human infirmity, no soldier ought, in any situation, to abandon the maxim, that death is preferable to shame.

If Major Davie and his brother officers had resolutely determined not to accede to the first perfidious proposition of the Candians to deliver up Prince Mootto Sawmy in violation of a treaty, the wax of which was hardly cold, such a generous vigour of resolution, if it did not make any impression upon the enemy, would at least have excited a glowing enthusiasm of resistance amongst the small band of troops under their command. They might indeed have been ultimately overpowered by numbers, but they would have sold their lives dear; and, whilst their death was not more painful, it would have been much more glorious than that which they finally experienced from a faithless foe.

To die in the field with his arms in his hand, is what a soldier ought always to contemplate as his probable destiny, that he may regard the event with cheerful acquiescence when the chance arrives. But, in the case of which I am speaking, Major Davie and his officers, in a moment of infatuated weakness, forgetting that it was their duty rather to face death, than to incur disgrace, submitted to the insolent and atrocious demands of the Candians, and consented to purchase a delusive security, by the sacrifice of all high and honourable sentiment.

The British troops, having given up their arms, and the Malays, according to orders, having grounded theirs, "They proceeded," according to Mr. Cordiner's account,* "all together towards Candy, accompanied by the Candian Malays, Caffrees, and a mob of armed natives. They had advanced only half way, when the Candian force was drawn up on each side of the road, and the British troops allowed to move to the centre of the lane; they were then ordered to halt, and the men of the Malay regiment were desired to march on; accordingly, they all proceeded, except four native Malay officers, and a few Malay servants, attending their masters, who refused to go on before the British officers. A Candian chief asked the Malays if they were willing to enter into the service of the King of Candy." Those who refused, were ordered to be bound and delivered to the Caffrees; those who consented, were conducted towards the town. The English officers were then separated from the private soldiers; and the whole, in divisions of two and two, were successively led out to be butchered, as the chief adigar had commanded. Whilst this horrid massacre was perpetrating, Captain Humphreys, laying hold of the arm of an assistant surgeon of the Malay regiment, rolled with him down the height upon which they

* Cordiner, Vol. II. p. 213.

were standing into the hollow beneath, into which the dead bodies of their slaughtered companions were precipitated. Here they remained till the fourth night, when the surgeon, going in quest of food, was recognized by the corporal of a Malay guard, whom he had formerly known when in the service of the Dutch. The corporal assured him of protection, and offered him refreshment, of which the surgeon said, that there was an English officer, who would be glad to participate. They were afterwards brought before the king, who ordered them to be separately confined.* Captain Humphreys, according to Mr. Cordiner, afterwards died in prison at Candy, but the surgeon fortunately effected his escape to Columbo. The only Englishmen, who were purposely selected to be saved from the general massacre, were Major Davie and Captain Rumley of the Malay regiment.†

* Asiatic Annual Register for 1805, p. 14.

† The major appears to have died of a dysentery at Hangaramketty, in the beginning of 1805; but Captain Humphreys and Captain Rumley, are mentioned at that time to have been in strict confinement. See the Asiatic Annual Register. When Mr. Cordiner wrote his Account of the Candian Campaign in 1803, he mentioned Major Davie, as still alive, in good health, and well treated, but closely confined.—Vol. II. p. 216. At the time that Candy was taken, the fort of Dambadenia, which was constructed only of fascines and earth, was assailed by a confused mass of several thousand Singalese; and, though it was defended only by fourteen convalescent English, and twenty-two invalid Malays, under Ensign John Grant, it held out for ten days against the open violence and perfidious machinations of the enemy, till it was finally relieved by succours from Columbo. This incident favours the conclusion, that if Major Davie had acted with the same vigour and heroism, he might probably have prevented the catastrophe which followed.

In September, 1804, Major Johnson, of the third Ceylon regiment, set out on his march from Baticalo to Candy, with a detachment of 300 troops, with 550 pioneers and coolies. Major Johnson reached the place of his destination on the 6th of October, and took possession of the capital, which had been previously deserted by the inhabitants. The major could obtain no intelligence of the other detachments, with which he expected to have formed a junction at this place; and he heard that the enemy were in great force in the neighbourhood, waiting till the effect of the climate had so reduced their numbers, or weakened their strength, as to render them an easy prey, as the troops under Major Davie had been the year before. Major Johnson found himself in a most critical situation. His troops were in some measure awed by the recollection of the recent massacre of their comrades in the previous year; and of this catastrophe, several of the apartments in the palace, in which they were quartered, contained mournful memorials in the hats, shoes, canteens, and accoutrements of the murdered soldiers, which were displayed on the walls; and many of them still marked with the ill-fated owners names. In these circumstances, Major Johnson, without wasting much time in deliberation, very wisely determined to cross the river that runs near the capital, and to take post on the left bank, where he might ensure his retreat. As he was proceeding to execute this resolution, the major passed on the outside of the town, a number of skeletons of massacred officers of Major Davie's corps hanging on the trees; and, when he reached the banks of the river, where that unfortunate officer had agreed to surrender to the enemy, he found the ground still covered with the bones of his butchered troops. The Candians, who had assembled on the opposite bank to oppose Major Johnson's movements, pointed to those bones, as a warning of the fate which they might expect. But Major Johnson, more determined, and more fortunate than his predecessor, after encountering and overcoming many difficulties, at last succeeded in getting his troops across the river. He now lost no time in prosecuting his retreat to Trincomalee, a distance of 142 miles. The Candians, in many parts of the rout, endeavoured to obstruct their march, by blocking up the way with large trees, which they felled for that purpose, or by raising breastworks to oppose their progress. They were, in other respects, greatly harassed by the enemy on their march, and suffered considerable loss. For some days, they were engaged in one continued skirmish, whilst they were, at the same time, exposed alternately to a scorching sun or a pelting rain. At length, however, the Candians slackened their pursuit, till the major and the residue of his detachment reached Trincomalee in a state of great lassitude and exhaustion, from the various privations which they had experienced, and the great fatigue which they had undergone, without mentioning the insalubrity of the climate, and the different extremes of heat, cold, and wet, to which they had been exposed. Major Johnson published a perspicuous and respectable narrative of his expedition.†

† London, Baldwin, 1810, 8vo.

CHAP. XXII.

Massacre of the Sick in the Hospital at Candy. Escape of George Barnsley. Noble Instances of Fidelity to the British Interest in two Native Officers of Malays. The King of Candy marches against Columbo; his Discomfiture. Desultory Hostilities and Ravage which ensued. Further Intrigues of Pelemé Talavé. The King of Candy seized with the Small Pox.

BEFORE the massacre, which I have just mentioned, was perpetrated, all the sick, to the number of 120 men, who had been left in the hospital at Candy on the faith of the capitulation, were murdered in cold blood. George Barnsley, a corporal of the 19th regiment, who had been left for dead amongst the slain, recovered sufficiently to make his escape. He crept into a thicket, and swam across the river during the night, when he arrived at Fort Macdowall, where he was the first to tell the dreadful tale.

Captain Nouradeen and his brother, who were native officers of the Malay regiment, were repeatedly solicited by the king to forsake the English, and to enter into the Candian service; but they refused to accept of life on such terms, and nobly preferred death to the violation of their oaths. Upon their last refusal, the king "turned his face from them in a rage," and gave orders for their immediate execution. The rites of sepulture were denied to their bodies, which were dragged into the woods, and left to be devoured by wild beasts.

On the evening of the wanton massacre of Major Davie's corps, the adigar, by whose nefarious artifices and atrocious treachery the whole had been contrived, ordered guns to be fired, and rejoicings to be made to celebrate the victory which he had obtained.

The enemy were greatly elated with the recent discomfiture of the English; and, in the pride of his heart, the King of Candy thinking that nothing could arrest the victorious progress of his arms, began to calculate upon their total expulsion from the island. He accordingly made preparations to attack them at all points, and conducted in person an expedition against Columbo, of which he appears to have entertained no doubts of the success. He had advanced within about twenty miles of the seat of the English government; but his progress was arrested by the determined resistance which he experienced* in an attack on a small fort called Hangwell, from which he was driven with great loss. His Candian majesty, however, had reckoned so little on this disappointment, that in front of a bungaloe, or temporary residence, which had been constructed for his reception in the neighbourhood, he had ordered the requisite instruments to be prepared for impaling the English prisoners. The enemy were pursued in their retreat; and his Candian majesty was so incensed at the ill success of his troops, though it was, in some measure, caused by his own cowardice, as he was the first who took to flight, that he ordered the heads of some of the principal officers in his army to be struck off, in order to expiate his rage.

It would be tedious and unprofitable to detail any further the desultory warfare of ravage and spoliation which followed the massacre at Candy. It was conducted on both sides with much barbarity and oppression. Numerous villages were burnt, and large tracts of country reduced to desolation; and, though the British were in some degree

* Cordiner, II. p. 233. This fort of Hangwell had been taken by the Candians in a prior expedition, and afterwards retaken by the troops under Lieutenant Mercer.

justified by the barbarities which they had experienced, yet who can justify retaliation when it is practised upon the innocent?

When we read that a detachment of the British troops "was employed in destroying all the houses, stores, and gardens in the rich province of Saffragam,"* and that many other parts of the country were exposed to similar horrors, we turn from the recital with disgust, and our hearts will not suffer us to admit, that the plea of vengeance could sanction such enormities.

In March, 1804, preparations were made by the Candians for a general invasion of the British possessions on the coast; but the meditated attack was anticipated by the vigilance of their adversaries. Pacific overtures were afterwards made, but without any beneficial result. Military operations were again commenced in the following September, when the chief adigar, who was stationed at this time with a considerable force in the province of Saffragam, made an attempt to renew the tissue of his treachery. But his present propositions were rejected with the scorn which his former ought to have experienced.†

In February, 1805, the British territory was again invaded by the

* Cordiner, II. p. 256. In the province of Saffragam above-mentioned there is a Hindoo pagoda, which is probably of greater extent and magnificence than any other which is left standing in Ceylon. The apartments of this pagoda, says Mr. Cordiner, "afforded excellent shelter for the troops, who found in several chests a greater quantity of silver and copper coins than they were capable of carrying away. The Malays, probably from motives of superstition, refused to receive any share of them; and almost all the indigent coolies (a sort of porters) disdained the sacrilege of either entering the pagoda or touching the coin." Every contemplative mind must, in the above instance, behold with pleasure the devotional feeling, however imbued with superstition, elevating a despised and ignorant class of our fellow creatures above the baser passions of rapacity and avarice.

† The adigar is stated, at this time, to have been on terms of very doubtful amity with the king.

Candians, who were repulsed, on all sides, with great loss. Soon afterwards the King of Candy was seized with the small-pox, which furnished the first adigar with a favourable opportunity for repairing to the capital and recovering his former influence in the government. After this, hostilities were suspended for an interval by a sort of tacit consent, which originated in the weakness of the enemy, but which was in unison with the wishes of the British government.

CHAP. XXIII.

In March, 1814, the chief Adigar, Eheilapola, takes up Arms against the Authority of the King; his Overtures to the English; the King generally abhorred; his unparalleled Barbarity against the Wife and Children of the insurgent Adigar, who takes Refuge at Columbo; his interesting Interview with General Brownrigg; his Sensations on a first View of the Ocean.

IN the month of March, 1814, the King of Candy summoned the first adigar, whose name was Eheilapola,* to appear before him, in order to answer for some real or imaginary offence. Eheilapola, who well knew how little he had to expect from the justice or the mercy of his sovereign, determined not to comply with the mandate he had received. He accordingly prepared for resistance; and was generally supported by the people of the province of Saffragam, of which he was governor, or dessave. This province he offered to surrender to the British government, whose succour he earnestly implored in the contest in which he was about to be engaged. But the Governor of Ceylon did not think it prudent to interpose in favour of the attempt of Eheilapola, till he had seen whether the insurrection, of which it was the commencement, was likely to become universal. The ruling sovereign of Candy had become generally odious by the cruelties and oppression which he had long exercised upon his subjects; and the abhorrence of his tyranny was diffused through his dominions.

* The writer of this is not at present aware that any thing certain is known respecting the fall of that perfidious miscreant, Pelemé Talavé, whom Eheilapola succeeded; but he has probably paid the forfeit of his crimes, and been sentenced to death by the despot whom he raised to the throne, and afterwards treacherously conspired to depose.

The tyrant no sooner received intelligence of the revolt of Eheilapola, than he determined upon an act of the most inhuman revenge. The wife and children of the chief had been left at Candy, according to the practice of the court, as hostages for his fidelity and allegiance. The children were five in number. The eldest was eighteen years of age, the youngest an infant at the breast. These innocent victims to the brutal rage of the royal monster were conducted to the market-place, where the head of the infant being first cut off, the distracted mother was actually compelled to pound it in a mortar. The other children were afterwards butchered in succession; and the mother herself was finally slaughtered, to consummate the tragedy.

These accumulated horrors seem, for a time, to have paralyzed both the body and the mind of the unhappy father. He could not exert his wonted energy. His partizans, who needed the animating force of his example, made but a feeble resistance, and were speedily overpowered by the troops of the sovereign. The adigar fled for refuge to Columbo; but it was some time before General Brownrigg appeared to espouse his cause, by admitting him to an interview. He was, however, finally favoured with a personal audience of his excellency at his country house.

The unparalleled misfortunes of Eheilapola rendered him in a peculiar manner an object of sympathy to every feeling heart. The reception which he experienced on the part of the governor, was such as was equally honourable to both parties. It was the respect and sensibility of a generous mind to a singular instance of the mutability of fortune, and of the extent of human suffering. As soon as Eheilapola was introduced to the British governor, the venerable chieftain, who had never been taught to subject his feelings to forms of ceremonial etiquette, burst into tears. The governor endeavoured to tranquillize his agonized bosom, by solemn assurances of favour and support. The rude and unrefined chief, who had passed his life upon the Candian mountains, expressed without reserve the gratitude which he felt. As the cruelty of his sovereign had stripped him of every kindred tie, he requested permission to call the governor father, and to consider him as the dearest relative that misfortune had not swept away.

This was the first time that Eheilapola had ever beheld the sea, except in a faint glance from a distant mountain; and the grand view of the expanded ocean which he enjoyed from the governor's house, that was situated on a rock overhanging the shore, affected him with feelings of wonder and delight. At the same time the furniture of the house, which differed so much from any thing he had seen before, excited his attention, and interested his curiosity.

CHAP. XXIV.

War, in which Candy was transferred to the Sovereignty of Great Britain. Preparations for attacking the English Settlements. Proclamation of the English Governor. British Troops on their March towards Candy. Insensibility of the King to his perilous Situation; deserted by his Subjects; his Cruelty to two Messengers of bad News. The Prime Minister, Molligodde, joins the British; his Example followed by other Chiefs. Interview between Molligodde and Eheilapola. Flight of the King from Candy. Candy occupied by the British. An English Captive recognized; his extraordinary History.

WE come now to the last* war, in which the British were engaged with the King of Candy, which terminated in his expulsion from the throne, and in the voluntary submission of the people to the British government. That government is, at present, happily extended over the whole island; and, considering it as better calculated to promote the real interests of the people, and to accelerate their moral and intellectual improvement than any native domination, I cannot refrain from expressing a wish, which is the wish of my heart, that the sovereignty of Great Britain, over this fair region of the globe, may last for ever; as far as this "for ever" can be applied to the instability of all human power, and the mutability of all human establishments.

The court of Candy, elated by its temporary triumph over the fugitive Eheilapola, began to make strenuous preparations for attacking the English settlements. At the same time it exhibited a shocking instance of the spirit by which it was actuated, by a most barbarous outrage

* In the account of this war, I have principally followed "A Narrative of Events," written by a gentleman on the spot. Egerton. 1815.

upon ten unoffending inhabitants of the British possessions, who were in the habit of trading within the Candian limits. These unfortunate individuals, without the smallest imputation of crime, or the shadow of any legal form, were captured and mutilated. Seven of them were destroyed by the severity of their sufferings; and the three, who did survive, arrived at Columbo, with their arms, noses, and ears, cut off—a spectacle too horrid to describe.

This barbarous outrage necessarily led to actual hostilities. Before the commencement of the war, the governor in council issued a proclamation, in which it was declared that the British arms were not directed against the Candian nation, but "only against that tyrannical power which had provoked, by aggravated outrages and indignities, the just resentment of the British nation, which had cut off the most ancient and noble families in the kingdom, deluged the land with the blood of his subjects, and, by the violation of every religious and moral law, become an object of abhorrence to mankind."

Whilst the British troops were marching from all points upon his capital, the Candian monarch, infatuated with an idea of his invincibility, remained for some time in a state of torpid inactivity, as if unconscious of the general disaffection of his subjects, and of the rapid and almost unresisted approach of the enemy. But, at length, he began to be conscious that those, on whose support he most relied, were deserting him; and that, in his falling fortunes, he was left, according to the common lot of tyrants, without a friend. But, as his situation became more desperate, his disposition became more cruel. In the last moments of his power he could not suppress the emotions of vindictive fury, which he had never previously endeavoured to control. Of two messengers, who brought disastrous intelligence, he ordered one to have his head cut off, and the other to be impaled alive.

On the morning of the eighth of February, Molligodde, the prime minister of the Candian monarch, revolted from his master, and came into the British camp. He brought with him several elephants, the insignia of the Four Corles, a banner, with the device of the sun and moon, to denote perpetual duration; and the rolls, or records, of his dessaveny. All the chiefs of the province, who had not previouly joined the British standard, followed his example.

After Molligodde had been received, he proposed to pay a visit to Eheilapola. When the two chiefs met, Molligodde exclaimed, that he was a ruined man. "What then am I?" said Eheilapola. These words suggested the most painful recollections; and both the chiefs burst into tears.

The British forces arrived on the fourteenth at the Candian capital, from which the king, awakened too late from his delusive dream of fancied security, had fled.

The British had hardly obtained possession of the city, when a man presented himself at head-quarters, in a Candian dress, but having the features of an European. His pale and haggard looks, and his long and matted beard, exhibited a melancholy appearance. This man, whose name was Thomas Thoen, said that he had marched with the British army to Candy in 1803, and that he was among the 150 sick who had been left in the hospital when the capital was surrendered to the enemy. When his fellow-sufferers were butchered, the barbarians, having torn off the blisters, which had been previously applied to his stomach in the hospital, felled him to the ground with the butt end of a musket, and left him for dead in the general heap. He recovered, however, enough to crawl to a neighbouring drain, when, on being discovered the next morning, he was hung up to a tree and left to perish. The rope, happily, broke; when he was again discovered, and again hung up in the same way. But, again the rope broke, when he contrived to crawl to a hut at a little distance, where he supported himself for ten days with nothing but the grass that grew near the door, and the drops of rain that fell from the roof. At the expiration of this interval, he was accidentally discovered by an old Candian, who, after looking at him, suddenly disappeared, but soon after came again with a plate of rice, which he put down and went away.

The king, who had never felt for human woe, was struck with the story which he received of Thoen's numerous and extraordinary escapes. Superstition, in the place of sympathy, made its way into the monarch's mind. He thought that Thoen would not have been so often preserved, if he had not been a peculiar favourite of Heaven; and he accordingly ordered him to be taken care of by one of the chiefs, and to receive every accommodation which he required.

The king allowed him a house in the town of Candy, in which he remained till the arrival of the British. He experienced no further ill treatment from the jealous tyrant; but the horrid barbarities which he beheld, and which the slightest offence was sufficient to excite, kept him in a state of constant inquietude and alarm. A woman, who had been detected in merely conveying a message from him to Major Davie, was instantly put to death.

The only source of solace, in which this unfortunate man had access in the dreary hours of his long captivity, was in the perusal of a detached portion of an English Bible, which contained some chapters of Jeremiah. The devotional sentiment in these chapters tended to sooth his melancholy, and to inspire a pleasurable confidence in the providential government of Jehovah.*

* A very able critic has truly remarked, that—"There is no incident in Robinson Crusoe told in language more natural and affecting, than Knox's discovery of a Bible in the Candian dominions. His previous despondency from the death of his father, his only friend and companion, whose grave he had just dug with his own hands, being now, as he says, 'left desolate, sick, and in captivity,' his agitation, joy, and terror, on meeting with a book he had for such a length of time not seen, nor hoped to see—his anxiety lest he should fail to procure it, and the comfort it afforded him in his affliction—are told in such a strain of true piety, and genuine simplicity, as cannot fail to interest and affect every reader of sensibility."

CHAP. XXV.

Some of the King's Women taken; his Retreat discovered; his abject Pusillanimity in his fallen Fortunes; his Life spared; Indignities heaped upon him by his Subjects. He is sent to Columbo; the Apartments prepared for his Reception; Circumstances of his Behaviour; his Person and Character; his Indifference to the Cruelties of his Reign. Effect of Despotism on the Heart. Shrewd Remark of the King's on a striking Difference between Despotism and limited Power. Frantic Barbarity of the King exemplified in a domestic Trait; his predominant Feeling in Confinement; Rancour against his Subjects.

ON the same day on which the Candian capital was taken, Major Kelly captured many of the females of the king's family, with a considerable treasure. The king himself was known to be in the neighbourhood, and it was hoped that he could not long elude the pursuit of his enemies. His retreat was soon discovered by some of Eheilapola's adherents, who surrounded the house, in which he had hid himself with two of his wives. The door was strongly barricaded, but they battered down the wall of the apartment, in which the tyrant was concealed, when he was exposed by the glare of torch light to the derision of his enemies.

The tyrant now shewed himself as obsequious and abject in misfortune, as he had been arbitrary and insolent in the period of his power. He implored that his life might be spared, though he himself had long sported with the lives of his subjects; and, as if Providence intended forcibly to admonish him, that cruelty is folly, he was constrained to solicit the boon of humanity for himself and his wives, from the followers of Eheilapola, whose wife and children he had destroyed, with circumstances of aggravated horror and ferocity. Though the life of the tyrant was spared by the magnanimous forbearance of his enemies, it was impossible to save him from the indignities of some of his infuriated people. They bound him hand and foot, reviled him, spit on him, and dragged him to the next village, with every species of insult and indignity.

After this, the deposed monarch was sent under an escort to Columbo, where a house had been prepared for his reception. In the largest of the rooms which were designed for his use, was an Ottoman or musnud, covered with scarlet cloth. As soon as the monarch entered the apartment, he is said immediately to have sprung forward, and placed himself upon this Ottoman, cross legged like a tailor, in which position he surveyed with great apparent satisfaction, the place allotted for his abode. " As I am no longer permitted to be a king," said he, " I am thankful for the kindness and attention which has been shewn me."

The description, which the author of " A Narrative of Events" gives of the king's person, physiognomy, and apparent intellectual character, is not quite in unison with that, which is furnished in the work of Mr. Cordiner. " Wikreme Rajah Sinha," says the author first mentioned, " is in his person considerably above the middle size, of a corpulent, yet muscular appearance, and with a physiognomy which is at all times handsome, and frequently not unpleasing. His claim to talent has been disputed by many, who have had an opportunity of conversing with him, but he is certainly not deficient in shrewdness or comprehension." He is said to unite good humour with the most insensate cruelty. He answered the questions that were put to him with a sort of unconstrained affability, whilst he related the barbarities of his reign with the most singular unconcern. " He passes with great rapidity from one story of court intrigue to another; but, it is to be observed, that the invariable issue of the whole of these anecdotes is the cutting off the offender's head, flogging him to death, impaling him alive, or pounding him in a mortar, as the caprice of the moment might have dictated; and all his surprise seems to be that the English should feel any great indignation at what he had always considered a mere matter of course and pastime."— Here we clearly see how uncontrolled despotism tends to convert the heart of flesh into a heart of stone; and how the human bosom, in which there is a natural repugnance to cruelty and oppression, soon becomes so altered by the exercise, or so hardened by the spectacle, as to regard, not only with indifference but with delight, the most torturing pangs and the most revolting sufferings.

The dethroned King of Candy made one remark on the difference between his own arbitrary sway, and a more restrained exercise of power, which does credit to his sagacity, and deserves attentive consideration. In a conversation with Major Hook, he said, "The English governors have one advantage over us kings of Candy;—they have counsellors about them, who never allow them to do any thing in a passion, and that is the reason you have so few punishments; but, unfortunately for us, the offender is dead before our resentment has subsided."

In the above remark, the late Candian monarch suggested a most unanswerable argument against unlimited power in any individual, unless he were exempted, by a sort of miracle, from the common imperfections of humanity. One of the most admirable contrivances of human wisdom is that part of the British constitution, which, whilst it secures the inviolability of the monarch, makes every one of his servants, whether high or low, responsible for his acts.

The following instance is well fitted to illustrate the nature of a character, where the will of the individual has never known restraint, nor experienced opposition. The captive king had requested that four of the usual female attendants might be permitted to wait upon his queens.

This was willingly conceded; and the same night one of these women was brought to bed in the house. The king no sooner heard of this, than he demanded that the woman should be instantly removed. Colonel Kerr very humanely refused to comply, and remonstrated on the cruelty of the proceeding, with a poor creature in her unfortunate situation. His majesty, however, who had not been used to have any of his desires contravened, however extravagant or barbarous they might be, flew about his apartment in the most frantic rage, vowing that "he would neither eat, drink, nor sleep, till he was satisfied." Colonel Kerr, becoming apprehensive lest the poor woman should be murdered by the tyrant, gave orders for her removal, though at the hazard of her life.

The author of "A Narrative of Events, &c." says that "the predominating feeling of the king's mind was indignation at the treatment he had received from his own subjects." Thus we find, that when Major Willerman had an audience of his majesty soon after his capture, "he pointed in proud indignation to the marks of a rope on his arm, and asked if that was treatment fit for a king." The unmitigated despotism he had so long exercised, the passive obedience he had so long experienced, made the idea of the recent resistance insupportable to his mind; and this sensation was still further aggravated by the consciousness that his vindictive feelings could no longer be appeased by their usual gratification.

The bitter rancour of the king against the conduct of his subjects, is said to have been favourable to the interests of the British, as it induced him to disclose the places of his hidden treasure, which was of great amount. He chose that it should become the property of his conquerors, rather than of those who had rebelled against his tyranny.

CHAP. XXVI.

A Convention of the British Authorities and Candian Chiefs. The reigning Sovereign formally deposed for Misgovernment; Substance of the Treaty. The Transfer of the Sovereignty beneficial to the Singalese. Radical Defects in the Policy of the Portuguese and Dutch; more enlightened Policy of Great Brituin. Dutch Administration of Justice, its Vices and Defects. Dutch Restrictions upon the Catholics removed by a more liberal Policy; Excellence of Mr. North's Administration.

AFTER the capture of the king, a grand convention was held of the British authorities and the Candian chiefs in the great hall of the palace in the capital. At this meeting a treaty was proposed and ratified by the assembly, by which the Malabar dynasty was solemnly deposed,* and

* In the treaty between " His Excellency Lieutenant-General Robert Brownrigg, governor and commander-in-chief in and over the British settlements and territories in the Island of Ceylon, acting in the name and on the behalf of his Majesty George the Third, King, and his Royal Highness George, Prince of Wales, Regent, of the United Kingdom of Great Britain and Ireland, on the one part; and the adigars, dessaves, and other principal chiefs of the Candian provinces, on behalf of the inhabitants, and in presence of the mohottales, coraals, vidaans, and other subordinate headmen from the several provinces, and of the people then and there assembled," the second article declared, " That the Rajah Sri Wikreme Rajah, by the habitual violation of the chief and most sacred duties of a sovereign, has forfeited all claims to that title, or the powers annexed to the same, and is declared fallen and deposed from the office of king; his family and relations, whether in the ascending, descending, or collateral line, and whether by affinity or blood, are also for ever excluded from the throne; and all claim and title to the dominion of the Candian provinces is abolished and extinguished." This furnishes a singular instance of a regular treaty between one sovereign and the people of another to deprive a king of his throne, and for ever to exterminate his dynasty, on account of the atrocities of his government. This treaty is a virtual acknowledgment, on the part of the British government, that an " habitual violation of the chief and most sacred duties of a sovereign," constitutes a forfeiture of the sovereignty.

the dominions of the whole Island of Ceylon vested in the sovereign of Great Britain. Every species of torture was abolished. No sentence of death was to be carried into execution without the written warrant of the British governor. The ancient religion of the people was declared inviolable, and its rites, ministers, and places of worship, are to be maintained and protected; whilst the administration of justice was to be exercised according to the usual forms and by the ordinary authorities.

There can be no doubt but that this transfer of the sovereignty of Ceylon to the British crown will be much more favourable to the general interest of the native inhabitants than the ancient government. There will be less fluctuation and violence in the interior administration; and the industry of the people will experience a degree of excitement from the secure possession of its products, which it never could have felt under that arbitrary sway, where the life and property of every individual in the kingdom was the sport of the most capricious tyranny, which was not only never checked by any legal restraint, but which was insensible to every sentiment of justice and humanity.

The Singalese were certainly oppressed rather than benefited by the conquests of the Portuguese and of the Dutch. The intolerant bigotry of the one, and the equally inhuman avarice of the other, were utterly at variance with any system of improvement which was to be founded on liberal ideas, and to exhibit enlarged views. The Portuguese regarded the extended domination of the Catholic faith of more importance than the morals, health, or subsistence, of the inhabitants. When the policy of a nation is under the direction of bigotry, no considerations of justice or humanity will be suffered to obstruct the execution of its designs. All the calculations of prudence will be despised, and the suggestions of wisdom will pass for the impulses of folly or impiety. One of the kings of Portugal * proposed to lead an army to

* Sebastian.

India, which was to be accompanied with a host of priests, who, by the terrors of the sword, were to force all the inhabitants to embrace the Catholic faith. Though this fanatical scheme was finally abandoned, yet the propagation of the Christian, or rather the Popish, faith, became the primary principle of the Portuguese policy in the East. Their settlements were filled with ecclesiastics; and, whilst commerce languished, virtue decayed.

The Dutch shewed less contempt than the Portuguese for the religious prejudices of the natives; but, what they wanted in the intolerance of fanaticism, they made up in the excess of mercantile cupidity; and both the one and the other tended to alienate the affections, and to impair the prosperity, of the people who were subject to their sway. The prosperity of Ceylon was never regarded by the Dutch any farther than as it was connected with a large supply of cinnamon.

Since the island has been in the possession of the British, a more liberal and enlightened policy has been adopted than was pursued by either of their European predecessors in their settlements on the coast, or within the circle of their influence. The Dutch * left the Singalese no other choice than to be poor and idle, or to work for nothing; but it must be allowed that, wherever the English form a settlement, they encourage industry by the security which they afford to its acquisitions.

The administration of justice, during the domination of the Dutch, was necessarily vitiated and corrupt, as it was usually entrusted to persons who were little qualified for the office by their education, their circumstances, or their character. Neither intellectual nor moral qualities were regarded in the selection of men for an office which was to determine the important questions of property, liberty, and life. The following is adduced as an instance, at least, of the carelessness of the Dutch criminal

* Lord Valentia's Travels, Vol. II. p. 305.

administration. A man, who was condemned to the works, presented a petition to the Honourable Mr. North, when governor, in which he stated that he had been three years and a half in that situation for a very slight offence. When the register of the judicial proceedings was examined, it was discovered, that the unfortunate culprit had been condemned to this punishment only for one year; but that the clerk, either by accident or design, had enlarged the period to ten.*

Under the government of the Dutch, the Catholic part of the population, whether of European extraction, or composed of converted natives, was subject to various restraints and disabilities. They were not permitted to have a separate burial-ground, and were compelled to pay extravagant fees for permission to inter their dead in the Protestant cemetery.† A tax was imposed on the marriages of Catholics, which almost amounted to a prohibition. Though persons professing the Catholic faith were very numerous in the European settlements in the island, they were excluded from all civil offices. These restrictions upon the Catholics, which had been imposed by the Dutch, had never been enforced since the island came into the possession of the English, and they were formally repealed in 1806. A regulation was then made, which was to take effect from the commencement of his majesty's birthday, the 4th of June, by which the Catholics were placed on a level in every respect with their Protestant fellow-subjects. They were allowed the unmolested profession and exercise of their religion in every part of the British settlements on the Island of Ceylon. They were admitted to all civil privileges and capacities. All marriages which had taken place within the above-mentioned settlements since the 26th of August, 1795, according to the rites of the Roman Catholic church, were to be deemed valid in law, although the forms appointed by the late Dutch government had not been observed.‡

* Lord Valentia's Travels, Vol. I. p. 305. † Lord Valentia, Vol. I. p. 309.
‡ Asiatic Annual Register for 1807.

The administration of Mr. North was, in the highest degree, mild, disinterested, and beneficent, and forms an admirable contrast with the unfeeling rigour and sordid avarice of most of the governors whilst the island was under the dominion of the Dutch. The native inhabitants, as well as the European settlers, seem to have been duly impressed with a conviction of his unsullied truth, justice, and humanity. The government of Mr. North was, indeed, truly paternal, and very characteristic of those amiable qualities which seem inherent in his family.

CHAP. XXVII.

Practice of Vaccination introduced into Ceylon.

AMONGST the benefits which have accrued to the Singalese from the establishment of the British dominion in the island, the introduction of the vaccine antidote to the small-pox is not one of the least conspicuous. Before the practice of vaccination, the constantly-recurring ravages of the small-pox were truly tremendous, and occasionally depopulated the country like a plague. From a letter of Mr. Christie,* the medical superintendant-general, in the Ceylon Government Gazette for February, 1809, it appears that the number of persons vaccinated throughout the different districts of Ceylon, during the year 1808, amounted to 26,207; which, added to 76,823, the number previously vaccinated, made a total of 103,030 persons, who had passed through the vaccine disease since its introduction into the island in 1802. The small-pox did not shew itself in any part of the British dominions in Ceylon during 1808, except in the district of Galle, when it was accidentally communicated by the crew of a Maldivian boat to two or three of the inhabitants in the neighbourhood; but this repression of its usual ravages must be ascribed to the influence of vaccination. This salutary practice has been, at present, so generally diffused throughout the island, that the recurrence of the small-pox need no longer be an object of alarm.

* Mr. Christie published "An Account of Ravages committed in Ceylon by the Small-Pox, previously to the Introduction of Vaccination," &c. in 1811.

CHAP. XXVIII.

Attention of the Dutch to the establishment of Schools; their judicious Regulations respecting. These Institutions restored and improved by Mr. North. His Plans obstructed by the injudicious Parsimony of Government.

HOWEVER sordid and contemptible may have been the policy of the Dutch in some respects, it must be recorded to their honour, that they established schools for the instruction of the natives in the rudiments of useful knowledge, and in the salutary principles of Christianity. These schools appear to have been placed under very judicious regulations. One school was erected in every parish throughout the provinces where the Dutch sovereignty was established. Each school had from two to four teachers, in proportion to the number to be taught. Every ten scholars were, at the same time, under the care of a superintendant, who examined the proficiency of the scholars, and the conduct of the teachers. There was likewise an annual visitation by nine of the Dutch clergymen,* each of whom had the schools in a particular diocese com-

* Mr. Cordiner has given a detailed account of the above annual visitation of the Singalese parochial schools. The following is part of his description:—"A large congregation attended in their best apparel. The children were ranged in the front lines. The minister began the business of the day by worshipping God, and preaching to the people. Then took place the examination of the school. The higher classes answered questions relative to the catechism of D'Outreir, and the twelve articles of the Creed. The lower classes repeated the catechism and prayers. The elder boys read a portion of the printed Singalese Bible, and wrote with a stylus on slips of the Palmyra leaf. The younger wrote with their fingers in sand spread on a bench, and, as they formed the different characters, they sung their names and particular marks by which they are distinguished."

mitted to his charge. The school-houses were at the same time employed for other useful purposes. They formed a place in which registers were kept of baptisms and marriages, and where divine service was performed. These schools were very numerous and flourishing under the Dutch; but, when the English obtained possession of the island, in 1796, the salaries of the masters were left unpaid for about three years, and the schools consequently fell into decay. At the termination of this period the Hon. Mr. North, who became governor of the island towards the end of the year 1798, spared no pains to re-establish these beneficent institutions. Under his auspices the parochial schools were enlarged in number, improved in management, and augmented in usefulness. He, at the same time, restored and new modelled an academy at Columbo, which Mr. Cordiner represents as in a very flourishing condition. The students, who are "Singalese, Malabar, and European, are all taught English, as well as other languages, by experienced masters. The Singalese scholars are sons of the Modelaars, and first class of the people in the country. They are possessed of industry and docility, and discover a strong ambition to acquire learning. Many of them converse fluently in English, and write, in a good style, very accurate translations from the Singalese."*

After contemplating the salutary arrangements which the enlightened mind of Mr. North had combined and executed for the intellectual culture and moral improvement of the Singalese, it is afflicting to behold the extent of their operations circumscribed, and the sum of their usefulness diminished by the inconsiderate parsimony of the governors at home. Parsimony is a great virtue in any government; but I am no advocate for that kind of parsimony which tends to stunt the intellectual growth, or to obstruct the moral improvement of mankind. In the year 1803, the annual expense of all the schools in the island was

* Cordiner, Vol. I. p. 161.

ordered to be limited to the sum of £1500. Now, as the whole expense of the beneficent establishments which Mr. North had restored, or new modelled, did not exceed £4,600 a year, and as the schoolmasters acted, at the same time, as notaries in their several districts, the saving was beneath the notice of a great people, when it could not be made without a sacrifice of the most general usefulness, and the most important interests.

CHAP. XXIX.

Missionaries sent to Ceylon. Number of Christians of the Protestant and Romish Communions. Circumstances tending to facilitate the Propagation of Christianity in Ceylon.

IN 1805, some missionaries were sent from England, for the purpose of instructing the Singalese in the principles of Christianity. Mr. Cordiner seems to think that the propagation of this beneficent doctrine in Ceylon would experience much fewer obstacles than in Hindoostan. In Ceylon the rites of the ancient religion are said to be almost totally forgotten; and the inhabitants, more ignorant than bigoted, and more simple than prejudiced, would readily admit any religious impressions which a devout teacher might make upon their minds.

In the year 1801, the number of native inhabitants, who professed the Protestant profession of the Christian faith, was calculated to exceed 342,000, whilst those of the Romish communion were reckoned to be still more numerous. Christianity is professed by natives of Columbo of the highest rank; and indeed it is not more devoutly to be wished, than reasonably to be expected, that, in a few years, the religion of Brahma and of Boodh will vanish entirely before the luminous and illuminating truths of the Christian system, if the education of the native Singalese shall be prosecuted with zeal, and the principles of Christianity taught by the reason, and enforced by the example of devout, honest, and well-informed missionaries.

Lord Valentia * remarks, that the attachment of the Singalese to their casts " is much more an affair of vanity than religion." But, perhaps this is not less the case in Hindoostan than in Ceylon. An attachment to the institution of casts, of which the exterior symbols consist in particular personal embellishments, must in all cases have a more intimate connexion with the gratifications of vanity, than with devotional sentiment, or pious veneration.† If the propagation of Christianity in the East should, though only in a limited degree, abolish the institution of casts, it would be of incalculable benefit. For no institution was ever devised, which is so adverse to political liberty, to social happiness, to the moral and intellectual improvement of mankind.

* Vol. I. p. 308.

† Lord Valentia, however, who intimates that the attachment to cast amongst the natives of Ceylon, opposes no insuperable impediment to the propagation of the Christian faith, mentions some instances, in which that attachment seems to have been traced upon the habits and affections in characters which would not be readily effaced. " The higher casts," says Lord Valentia, " are extremely jealous of their privileges, and severely punish those of the lower casts, who presume to usurp them. A man, who ventured to cover his house with tiles, without being entitled to that distinction, had it pulled down to the ground, by order of his superior ; and a poor tailor, whose love of finery led him to be married in a scarlet jacket, was nearly killed at the church door." The same noble author records a very ridiculous, but very angry feud between the casts of washermen and barbers, which became so inveterate, that the first were compelled to go unshaved, and the last to wear their foul linen, till Mr. North interposed to appease their deadly animosity.

CHAP. XXX.

Worship of Boodh; fabulous Account of his Nativity. His early Achievements; his Marriage. He retires into a Wood; a magnificent Seat dropped from Heaven. Hostility of the Devils to his Worship; their desperate Attack upon Boodh; their total Discomfiture. Boodh sheltered in a violent Storm by the flat Head of a huge Serpent. The Devils tempt Boodh in the Form of Women. He enters a Tower of Rubies; sees a Host of Angels; teaches his Doctrine at Sewetnure; retires to another Town, where he dies in a Fruit Garden. His Disciples comforted for his Loss. Inconsistency in the Accounts of Boodh. Saints or Deities subordinate to Boodh; Modes of Worship.

THE present worship * of the Singalese owes its origin to Boodh, who appeared in the island 623 years before the birth of Christ. The priests of the country assert that Boodh, whose footstep is still to be seen on the top of Adam's Peak, came to this island from the east, and left his laws for their instruction on tables of stone. His height was twelve feet, and each foot equal to two of ordinary mortals. They say that

* Valentyn has remarked, that the Singalese, in one part of the island, agree in the names of their deities and in their religious rites, with those of the people on the coast of Malabar; and, in another, with those of the Siamese. The places, in which they were formerly wont to celebrate their religious worship, were denominated pagodas. The antient kings of Ceylon had erected in the neighbourhood of Trincomalée a pagoda, which was celebrated through India for its great extent and magnificence, but which was demolished by the Portuguese in 1622, when the stones were used in the construction of a fort.

Valentyn mentions, that there was a very antient prophecy respecting this pagoda, current among the Singalese. This prophecy, which was originally discovered on an old stone, had deen decyphered by some of the sages of Ceylon, and was found to signify that Manica Raja had erected this pagoda to the honour of the god Videmal, in the year 1300 before the Nativity, but that a certain people, denominated Franks, should come and destroy the same, and that another king should afterwards restore the sacred edifice to its original magnificence.

this Boodh, before he came into the world, had his abode in the third heaven, where he ruled over millions of angels. He found that men were living in a sort of moral anarchy, without laws or institutions; and were plunged in an abyss of ignorance and misery. He accordingly ordered it so, that he should come into the world from the maternal bosom * of the Queen or Empress Mahamajedewi, and he first opened his eyes upon the light of this sublunary sphere, in a pleasure garden of the King or Emperor Zuddodene Raja. On his first appearance he seemed to be seven years of age. He made seven steps to the east, seven to the west, seven to the south, and seven to the north, where, lifting up his right hand, in a posture of supplication, and invoking God, he sunk into a cradle, and assumed the form of a new-born child. The king indulged in a transport of joy at the birth of this marvellous child, had him brought to his court, and called him by the name of Ziddatare Cumanca, or the prince who hopes to do whatever he desires.

He performed many wonderful feats before his sixteenth year, when the Emperor of Candy resolved to marry him to the Princess Jasodera, who had been born on the same day with Boodh. This princess was the daughter of the King Andusaek Raja, and the Queen Ammitanam Bisso, whose family was as ancient as that of the emperor and empress. After the celebration of his marriage, Boodh and his wife lived together for thirteen years, and had one son, to whom they gave the name of Rahule Cumane. Boodh, finding that, if he took proper care of this child, he should not have sufficient time to devote to the instruction of mankind, determined to abandon his family and to retire into a wood, where he spent six years in a state of great indigence and distress. Whilst he was in this lonely situation, a magnificent stool, covered with a blaze of diamonds, fell from heaven under a white tree, named Ze-

* "Hy quam," says the Dutchman, "uit het midden van haare borsten." His conception is said to have taken place on the full moon in the month of July, 622 years before the birth of Christ, and he was born on the full moon in the May of the following year.

remabod. The prophet sat down upon this sumptuous seat, and then went again out of the wood. On this occasion he assumed the name of Boodh.

Boodh had with him for a guard Thiakre Aramma Vishnu and Maheeschweere. They had each a dagger in their hand. The devils remarked that, after this none of their attempts upon mankind were successful; and that their power declined under the ascendant of Boodh. They accordingly resolved with their chief Wasse Mantimanda, to make a violent attack upon the author of this new sect, which threatened to cause a general apostacy from the worship of demons, and to become the universal faith.

The devils accordingly made their appearance like an embattled host, when they attacked Boodh with impetuous violence. But Boodh met them with a much more powerful army, whilst every blade of grass, tree, branch and leaf, converted into a shower of arms, assisted in the conflict. The devils could not long resist this accumulation of hostility. They vanished into smoke. After this victory, Boodh, in the joy of his triumph, assumed for a week the name of Gauteme Boodh, in order to denote that he had vanquished his enemies.

In the following week it began to rain violently, when the devils were very busy, although they did not dare to approach Boodh, whose prowess they had so lately experienced. But they saw, to their utter astonishment, that a snake of immense size had laid the flat part of its head on the head of Boodh, in order to protect him from the rain.

In the third week, the devils again showed themselves in the form of women, and practised all their wiles, in order to ensnare the affections of Boodh; but they were soon vanquished as before, and obliged hastily to retire.

In the fourth week, Boodh paid peculiar honours to the tree under which he sat.

In the fifth week, a tower of rubies descended from heaven, into which he entered, in order to receive the homage of his votaries.

In the sixth week, he left this tower, and retired under a tree, named Kiripallu-nunge, where he beheld a multitude of angels in the air, in whose presence he glorified God in the language of love and praise.

In the seventh week he withdrew to a town called Sewetnure, where the Emperor Cosele Maha Raja had a place prepared for his reception. Here he taught his doctrines to kings, princes, and subjects. He now added five apostles to his mission, two of whom he placed on his right hand, and two on his left, whilst the fifth was appointed to minister to his necessities. Besides these he had 500 disciples, whom he employed to announce his mission, to diffuse his doctrines over the whole world, and to eradicate the heresies of other sects. He also composed different books, which were designed to preserve his doctrine, and to furnish precepts for the regulation of conduct. Here he remained occupied for forty-five years, till he went into the town of Cussirana Nure, in the province of Mallewe, when he retired into a fruit-garden belonging to the king, where reclining on a couch, which had been prepared to receive him, he expired in the same place, the same month, and the same hour, in which he was born.

His disciples were disconsolate for his loss ; but they heard the admonitions of his spirit, saying, Do not lament because my time is come to depart out of the world. Burn my body, and lay my bones in the grave ; but, above all, be diligent in maintaining the doctrine I have taught. He ordered that Ceylon, Siam, and Arracan, should particularly engage their attention, as the sovereignty of those countries was vested in the descendants of the emperor, Zuddodene Raja.

Truth is uniform and consistent, but fiction is variable and incongruous; and therefore it is no wonder that the accounts* of Boodh, which are a tissue of fables, should be very dissimilar and inconsistent.

* "Hy is elf maanden in de buik van zyn moeder geweest." Valentyn, p. 369. Undecim menses in utero matris fuit; and all this time his brightness rendered him as visible as a silken thread, which is run through a chrystal. In their accounts of Boodh, or Buddha, learned men differ about the age in which he lived, and the country in which his religious doctrines were first promulgated. It seems, however, to be highly probable, that the system which he inculcated was anterior to that of the Brahmins, by which it had begun to be superseded about the commencement of the Christian æra, though it maintained its ground in some parts of the peninsula of India till a later period. It is at this day diffused over the empire of the Birmans, and the kingdom of Siam and Cambodia. But in those countries, in which the votaries of Boodh were extirpated by those of Brahma, the latter adopted many of the notions of their predecessors, and the two religions have thus been in some degree amalgamated. They both prevail in Ceylon, rather in a state of amicable union than hostile separation. If the Island of Ceylon did not form the first cradle in which the religion of Boodh was fondled into life, nurtured in its growth, and matured in its strength, it seems certain, that it was introduced into this country from the continent of India soon after its commencement. Sir William Jones supposes Boodh, or Buddha, to have been the same with Sesostris, who, about ten centuries before the Christian æra, rendered his conquests subservient to the extension of a new religion from the Nile to the Ganges. But if Boodh and Sesostris were two names for the same individual, the mighty conqueror must have wreathed his sword in the olive branch when he promulgated his doctrine in the East; for the religion of Boodh is essentially a religion of peace; and conquerors are not very likely to inculcate truths that represent their greatest achievements as vile and contemptible, exciting the displeasure of God, and meriting the abhorrence of mankind. According to the Hindoos, Boodh was the ninth avatar, or descent of the Deity in the character of preserver, or the ninth incarnation of Vishnu: and Sir William Jones asserts that the Boodh, or Buddha of the Hindoos, is the Fo, or Foe of the Chinese. This Fo is said to have been born in the kingdom of Cashmire in the year 1027, before Christ. Gaduma, Gautuma, or Gauda, is one of the appellations by which Boodh is often designated in the East. Kæmpfer, in his History of Japan, says, that a great saint, called Durma, and a twenty-third successor in the holy see of Seaka, Boodh, or Buddha, came over into China from Seilenseku, or from that part of the world which was westward with respect to Japan, and laid the first firm foundation of Boodhism in that populous empire. Though the worship of Brahma is a competitor for the palm of antiquity with that of Boodh, yet the priority of the latter appears to be the most credible, as the oldest books of the Brahmins make mention of Boodh, and so far establish the remote antiquity of his worship. A strong line of distinction is drawn between the Brahmins and the priests of Boodh by these peculiarities, that in the latter the priesthood is not indelible, that it does not constitute a caste, and that those who belong to it may eat flesh, though they may not put the animal to death.

The Singalese say that Boodh always wore a yellow dress, as a similar colour is still worn by his priests. They have also a tradition that he passed most of his time on Adam's Peak, where he resided at his death. They add, that he ascended to heaven from this spot; and they seem to have borrowed this circumstance of his history from some account which they had heard of the ascension of Christ.

In addition to Boodh, the religious calendar of the Singalese is distinguished by seven other saints or subordinate deities, to each of whom they ascribe peculiar powers and authorities. Of these they exhibit different external representations. One is seen in the shape of an elephant, another in that of the priapus of the ancients; one is figured as an ape, another as a beautiful horse; and all of them have the care of the water tanks.

They worship the images of all these saints; but this worship consists only in the form of placing their clasped hands upon the top of their heads, prostrating themselves three times upon the earth, and uttering this brief invocation: "Budhum Sarnaa Gochal;" O Boodh, think on me! This they never omit in their pagodas, but they practise no other forms of supplication; though, once in their lives, they pronounce three or four thousand prayers. But this solemnity they defer till they are very old; and it more especially belongs to a particular class of persons amongst them, who begin to accommodate themselves to the practice from early youth.

CHAP. XXXI.

Another Account of the Birth of Boodh, with a Variety of Mythological Details.

TWENTY-SIX Boodhs, according to the traditions of the Singalese, preceded the birth of Gautama Boodh, whose doctrine was in a very remote period diffused over a large part of the East. Gautama Boodh was born in heaven, under the name of Santusitte, but not till his birth had received the permission of the preceding Boodhs.

The sovereign of heaven, on this occasion, said to Santusitte—You have now received permission to become a Boodh: now therefore is the time appointed for you to appear in the world under that character. He was accordingly conceived in the womb of Mahamajadevi, the queen of King Suddenam Raddure. His mother was surprised by the pains of labour, as she was proceeding on an excursion of pleasure to a garden in the neighbourhood; and the birth of her infant took place under a tree named Halgas. As soon as he was born, Brahma brought some cloth of gold from heaven, in which he wrapped the child, who was to grow up a holy man, and without sin. Brahma, then taking up the infant, saluted the queen, as the glorious mother of a Boodh. But the mother survived her delivery only seven days, when she passed into heaven, which

* The names of these twenty-six Boodhs, or sages, were Tanhankere, Metankere, Saranankere, Dipankare, Condanje, Mangela, Sumana, Reewette, Soobiette, Anomadasja, Paduma, Naradde, Sommede, Sujaetje, Piadasse, Attodasse, Dammadasse, Siddatta, Tissa, Pussa, Wipassa, Seeki, Wessaboo, Kakalauda, Konagamme, Kaeikgramma.

is the destiny of all the mothers of the Boodhs, on account of their immaculate purity.

After this four heavenly beings appeared, named Pattenasto, Wirudde, Wirubaiksa, Waiissere Wema. They brought with them the skin of a tiger, which had been prepared in heaven, on which they laid the child, and fondled it in their arms; as did all the nobles of his father. After this the child raised himself up from the earth, and on whatever spot he set his right foot, there sprung up a red rose-tree, full of leaves and flowers.

The young prince fixing his feet on the ground, looked towards the east, when all the people and nobles shouted—There is no one so great and glorious as the being whom ye see: and the same exclamation was heard when he turned himself to the other three quarters of the world. Upon this the young prince, who appears to have had very little modesty for one so recently born, said to all the people, There is none so great as I am. He then declared, that he was the master, or teacher of all men; and that no instruction in wisdom was to be had except from him. Again he said—That no man was greater than he; and that all were his inferiors. A fourth time he exclaimed—There is none so great as I; when, advancing his foot seven steps, seven rose-trees instantly appeared, and the same thing happened throughout his whole life; so that wherever he set his foot roses grew. When Boodh had proceeded these seven steps, his father came and took him away, and he appeared as a new-born child.

The young prince was brought into the palace in great state, and much merriment ensued. There was, at that time, a celebrated priest, who frequently ascended into heaven, and was a constant visitor in the palace of the king. This priest, in one of his recent celestial excursions, having observed more than usual rejoicing in heaven, enquired the reason, when he was told that the Queen Mahamajadevi had been delivered of a son, who was destined to become a Boodh.

The priest proceeded with the intelligence he had obtained to the palace of Suddenam Raddure, when he asked the king about the birth of the young prince, whom he desired to behold. All men who were sinners used to testify profound reverence to this priest; but this holy child shewed no signs of homage, but put his feet upon the priest's head. The priest was greatly rejoiced, and, taking the prince in his arms, discovered in his hands and feet 216 tokens by which the Boodhs were always distinguished, along with thirty-two larger and eighty smaller marks in his body. The priest was greatly rejoiced at having thus verified the Boodhism of the child.

On another occasion, the king, having noticed some wonderful works which his son performed, called together forty-six of the most learned people in his dominions, out of whom he selected eight more learned than the rest; and of these he inquired whether this child would be a Boodh or a Brahmin. Seven of them, examining two of his fingers, said that he would become either a Boodh or a king; but the eighth, on looking at the forehead of the prince, saw a twisted hair, which, whenever it was touched, became as long as a man's arm, and then again curled up into its former state. By this sign it was determined that he would certainly become a Boodh.

When the prince was sixteen years old, his father resolved to procure him a wife; and he was to have a choice of wives such as no prince ever had before; for the king assembled no less than 40,000 princesses for the purpose. But multiplicity often makes preference difficult; and this appears to have been the case in the present instance; for the princess whom the prince took for his bride was not one of these 40,000, but a lady named Jasundere Devi, of extraordinary beauty and exalted family. She was the daughter of King Sopperabaedi.

Three palaces were erected for the prince and his consort; one for his residence during the hot season, another during the cold, and another during that of the rains. The king also had a delicious garden made for the recreation of the royal pair; and a large train of domestics was appointed to minister to their luxury and magnificence.

The king now consulted the wise men about the time when his son would become a Boodh; and they informed him, that it would take place when his son met an old man; secondly, a sick man; thirdly, a dead man; and fourthly, a sangatar, or priest, with a bald head.

The king, who had been apprised that if his son became a Boodh, a potent devil, named Wassawarti Marua, with many other confederate demons, would attempt his destruction, was anxious to delay or to avert the period of his inauguration; and he accordingly ordered the place where he resided to be surrounded by a wall with four gates, where a strict watch was to be kept, and no ingress to be given to any persons like those who have been described.

The prince, who had attained the age of thirty years, was one day proceeding to the garden which the king had provided for his recreation, when one of the heavenly devetas, who were anxious that he should become a Boodh, and who knew that the appointed period was at hand, descended from the celestial regions, and appeared before the prince in the form of an old man. The prince, who was in his carriage, observing this old man, asked one of his attendants if the person he beheld was born in that state, or had become so by gradual decay.

The attendant, who did not at the time think of the prohibition, which he had received, not to reveal such a circumstance to the prince, or to let him fix his eyes on such a form, said that it was an old man; and, when the prince proceeded to inquire whether he also should grow old, the attendant said, that all who were born, and lived, must one day become old. The prince said, if I am one day to exhibit such a picture of decrepitude and deformity as I have just beheld, what pleasure can I any longer derive from all the grandeur with which I am surrounded, and from all the means of gratification I possess? He accordingly ordered the driver not to proceed to the garden, but to return back to the palace.

The father remarking that his son had come suddenly back, without taking his usual recreation, asked the reason of his attendants, when he was told that the prince had met an old man, which had caused him to return. The king accordingly directed, that a watch of a thousand men should be posted at each gate, who were strictly enjoined not to suffer any persons of a particular description to have admission into the royal residence. At the same time, in order to dispel the melancholy, which had seized the mind of the prince, he directed that music and dancing should be provided as a remedy.

After an interval had elapsed, the prince, thinking no more of the above-mentioned occurrence, prepared for another excursion to the garden of delight. The devetas then dispatched one of their number in the form of a sick man, the sight of which caused the prince to make inquiries similar to those he had done before, when he again desisted from his purpose, and returned to the palace. His father now ordered 2000 watchmen to be placed at each gate, and the music and dancing to be renewed.

After some days, the prince met a dead body in a state of putrefaction, which the devetas exhibited to his view. On making inquiry respecting the loathsome spectacle, the prince was told, that his body would one day assume the same appearance, when he again returned, with grief and melancholy as before. His father again commanded that the watch should be increased, and that the expedient of music and dancing should again be tried upon the prince's mind.

The next time that the prince attempted to visit the garden of pleasure, he met one of the devetas in the form of a Sangatar on the way. He was told that this was an auspicious appearance, and a portent of good. The prince, delighted with this intelligence, continued his journey to the garden, full of hope and joy, to which he had long been a stranger. Whilst the prince was in this situation, his wife Jasundera Devi was delivered of a prince. His grandfather, having searched the planets and prefigured his future fortunes, made his son, who was still in the garden, acquainted with the result.

The prince, having seen the child, gave him the name of Rakulo, and said to his attendants—"What, though I have a son born, a magnificent court, and a large establishment, they cannot be supported without great exactions on the industry of my subjects, which must often be attended with injustice and oppression. The birth of a prince, therefore, is no just ground for the congratulations of the people."

When the prince returned from the garden, his attendants described to the king, the form which his son had seen on the way, and the joy it had produced. The king again ordered the dancing to be renewed in the palace, but the prince refused to be present at the festive scene; and, occupied with the thought of becoming a Boodh, retired to his chamber for meditation and repose. But his father said to the dancers, That as his son was sorrowful, they must exhilarate his spirits, and not depart till the effect had been produced.

The prince, however, persisted in refusing to admit the dancers to his presence, and they accordingly retired to a place of rest. The prince rose at midnight; and, whilst the whole palace was resplendent with torches, he beheld the musicians and dancers merged in profound sleep. Some of them were slavering at the mouth, others were lying in a state of perfect nudity; others were talking in their sleep. The prince, contemplating this scene, said within himself, "I must exhibit a spectacle, not less humiliating than this, when I fall asleep; and therefore, it is better for me to be released from this tenement of flesh."

The prince now prepared to leave the palace unobserved; but, as he was proceeding to open the door, he was accosted by one of the nobles, or officers of the court, to whom the prince said, that the period for his becoming a Boodh was at hand, and that he must fetch his horse Cantecanam. The prince mounted the horse, and ordered the officer to get up behind him.

Before they left the court, the horse neighed so loud, that the devetas, in order to prevent it from awakening the people in the palace, came and led it out of the gate. The gate was 100 feet high, and the door made of stone, to open which required the united efforts of 1000 men. But the devetas opened it so softly, that the prince departed unperceived by the watch.

The above-mentioned devil having noticed these proceedings, thought that it would be a great diminution of his dignity if the prince should become a Boodh. In order to prevent this from taking place, the devil appeared to the prince in a blaze of light, and said, That in seven days he should be exalted to the monarchy of the whole world, if he would abandon the attempt to become a Boodh. This assurance was repeated three times.

The prince asked the spectre who it was? When it replied, "I am Wassawarti Marua, the chief of all the devils." The prince said, "I have devoted my kingdom, my wife, my child, my eyes, and my flesh to the relief and solace of the poor; nor will I receive at your hands all the kingdoms in the world; and, though you and a thousand more should tempt me with this prospect of grandeur, you should not induce me to desist from the design of becoming a Boodh." Before the devil departed, he warned him not to make the attempt, and menaced the most dreadful vengeance if an opportunity offered.

The prince now travelled 120 miles till he came to the river Anomanam, which was a quarter of a mile broad. His horse sprung with him over the stream, and alighted on a bed of fine sand on the opposite side. The prince now thought, that if he were to become a Boodh, he must cut off his hair, which he proceeded to do without further delay. Taking the hair in his hand, he said, The hair of a Boodh, instead of falling to the earth, will mount to the sky. He accordingly threw it out of his hand, when it rose aloft, and a deveta or angel appeared, who conveyed it to heaven in a case of gold.

The prince then thought that his royal dress was not such as became a Boodh. This suggestion no sooner occurred, than Brahma brought him from heaven a yellow, or saffron robe, like what the Boodhs are wont to wear. The prince then threw off his royal apparel and put on the saffron dress, which had been so miraculously communicated. The suit which the prince had ceased to wear Mahobramma inclosed in a box of gold, and conveyed to heaven.

The prince now committed his horse to the care of his attendant, to conduct back to the palace; but the generous steed, unwilling to quit his master, sprung into the river and died.

The prince then wandered for six years through numerous regions, and traversed various wilds, without eating any thing, and experiencing every species of distress. The above-mentioned devil kept continually pursuing his footsteps, in order to watch an opportunity of vengeance, but none appears to have occurred. At the end of the sixth year, and at the period of the full moon in the fifteenth day of the month, the prince said, "Now shall I become a Boodh, and obtain a delicious repast, as all the Boodhs have done."

There was a town named Barnasnuru, in which a princess resided, who was wont, on this occasion, to provide a repast for the Boodh. This princess had 1000 cows, which were kept where the sweetest herbage grew. She took the milk of these 1000 cows, and gave it to 500 to drink. She afterwards gave the milk of these 500 cows to 250; of these 250 to 125; of these 125 to sixty-four; of these sixty-four to thirty-two; of these thirty-two to sixteen; and of these sixteen to eight. In the milk of these eight cows she boiled some rice; and she sent one of her maidens, named Fourre, to make preparations for the reception of the Boodh, under a tree called Nugagas. Whilst the maiden was thus employed, the Boodh appeared, when she went to inform the princess, who sent her back with the rice which she had cooked in a magnificent golden bowl. The Boodh took the bowl and proceeded to the river Neranjanam Ganga, where it is requisite on this solemnity for all those who become Boodhs to keep their feast. Of the rice which was in the bowl the prince made forty-nine cakes, which he put one after another in his mouth. After emptying the bowl he threw it into the river, when it rose to the top of the water, and floated to the point where the bowls of the other Boodhs lay. It then sunk to the bottom; and such a noise was made by the collision of the different bowls, that it was heard not only by the other Boodhs, but by Mahahella Naja Radjura, who was a king in Nagalove, or the world under the earth.

This subterraneous king, on hearing the clang of the bowls said, "Kakasomda has been a Boodh for some days; Kamagamma has been a Boodh for some days; this is the day in which Gautama is become a Boodh—we must go and celebrate the festival." He accordingly departed with 40,000 dancers, whilst the Boodh, leaving the place where he had thrown the bowl, had retired under the Bogas, or sacred tree. The Boodh was placed on a raised seat reclining against the tree, when the above-mentioned monarch made his appearance with his 40,000 attendants, who began to weave the dance. The devetas also came with dancers and musicians; and a Sakkrea, who was four miles high, brought a train of 10,000 dependants playing upon pipes which were fourteen cubits long. Brahma came also with 10,000 men, bearing white umbrellas. He himself held an umbrella over the Boodh, and the others stood round about him; after which other celestial forms appeared with flutes and a diversity of musical instruments. Whilst they were celebrating the festival, the rejoicing, with which it was accompanied, was heard by the devil Wassawarti Marua, who had so long in vain persecuted the prince, and who thought, that if he could not succeed in effecting his vengeance on this solemn occasion, the opportunity would be lost for ever. He accordingly ordered his drum, called Wassawarti Goza, to be beat, which uttered such a stunning sound, that it made the ears bleed of all his subordinate fiends. They all assembled, and asked why he had called them together, and if he wanted their services in any impending war. He replied, that they must exert themselves to do all possible injury to the new-made Boodh. They accordingly transformed themselves into snakes, crows, and other shapes, and departed to act against the Boodh. Wassawarti himself had 1000 hands and 500 heads; and in each of his hands he held arms of different kinds, whilst he sat upon an elephant, named Girinucalla, on which he led his host of devils.

This assemblage of fiends surrounded those who were celebrating the feast, who, being greatly alarmed, threw away their musical instruments and umbrellas, and fled with precipitation, leaving Boodh alone. The devils now hemmed him in on all sides: but, though deserted by all his friends, he felt assured, that the alms which he had given would stand him in good stead, and keep him from all harm.

Wassawarti now called forth a raging tempest, in order to tear up the tree by the roots on which Boodh reclined, and to carry both him and it into other realms: but, though all the neighbouring trees were beat down and dispersed by the wind, not a leaf of the Bogas was shaken. The devil had now recourse to an impetuous torrent of water, in order to effect his vindictive purpose, and next to a raging fire; but all these elements of destruction were employed in vain, as well as other expedients which his rage led him to try. He now made furious attacks upon Boodh with one of his arms, which was more powerful than the rest, and of a round form; but, instead of wounding the holy man, it remained suspended like an umbrella over his head.

Wassawarti, finding that all his attempts proved abortive, now claimed the seat on which the Boodh sat under the Bogas as his own, and called his devils to attest his right, which they proclaimed with a terrible cry. But the Boodh said that the earth should be his witness; and immediately a female form rose half above the surface, and declared the right of Boodh to the seat with such an appalling voice, that Wassawarti, with all his assembled fiends, instantly fled. The Boodh now remained here seven days without rising from his seat; but on the seventh day he arose, when he stood for seven days, looking up to the Bogas. Near this tree was a house of diamonds and rubies, in which he remained for seven days, meditating his law. He next went for seven days to a water-tank, which was frequented by a snake, named Musselindenam Nagea. Boodh now stood for seven days under the flat head of the serpent, which he employed as a protection from the rain. Hence he went under another tree, called Keripallugas, where he continued seven days; and next he proceeded to a tree named Halgas, under which he passed fourteen days.

The devil Wassawarti had three sisters, who, having heard that their brother had failed in all his attempts upon the Boodh, visited him with a company of 600 captivating females, who employed every feminine artifice to fascinate his affections and make him their slave. But he remained invincible even to all this variety of blandishments. Having passed through this terrible ordeal, he became established as a Boodh, and assembled his company of priests.

CHAP. XXXII.

Adam's Peak; Traditions respecting a Pagoda on the Top. Mode of ascending the Peak; Stone upon the Top with the Footstep of Adam, or Boodh. Adam's Footstep an Object of Devotion amongst the Siamese; a Representation of it in Gold. Valentyn's minute Description of the Figures on Adam's Peak. Ancient Denomination by the Singalese. Purification of the Pilgrims before they ascend the Peak; curious Mode of ascertaining whether they are sufficiently purified to pay their Homage to the Footstep. The Numbers who resort to this Place. The Tank of Fecundity. The Footstep attracts Moorish Devotees. Tradition of the Moors respecting Prince Sogomom Barcaon.

ONE of the most sacred places in the opinion of the Singalese is the mountain called Adam's Peak, which is situated in the centre of the broadest part of the island, and, according to Valentyn, at the distance of about fourteen German miles from Columbo. He says that it may be seen from sea at the distance of ten or twelve German miles; but at a greater, according to other calculations.

A beautiful pagoda formerly stood on the top of this hill, respecting which many traditions are circulated and many stories told. They say that it was the abode of Boodh, who was a disciple of the apostle Thomas. They add, that he stood with one foot upon this hill, and another upon a hill upon the coast of Madura, when such a flood of water burst forth as to separate the Island of Ceylon from the main land.

Pilgrims and travellers climb to the sacred summit of Adam's Peak by means of an iron chain which is fastened to the rock; and the links of which serve as the footsteps of a ladder to facilitate the ascent. On the top, according to Valentyn, there is an area of 150 paces in length, and 110 in breadth. In the centre of this plain there is a large stone, rising about three feet above the ground, and seven or eight feet in length, where the glowing imagination of the devotees discovers the sacred footstep of Adam or of Boodh. But some, who have seen this consecrated relic, affirm that they discovered nothing more than an excavation, smeared with the oil of the lamps which the pilgrims burn in that spot. When the pilgrims descend from the mount, they always carry with them a little of the earth, which they regard as very holy.

Baldeus says, that this impression of Adam's foot is not an object of adoration peculiar to the Singalese, for that the people of Siam possess a similar object of devotional regard. The Siamese, says the author just mentioned, exhibit a footstep impressed upon a stone on a mountain, which is an ell and a half long and three-fourths broad. The sides of it are covered with silver; and a magnificent temple is erected in the neighbourhood, round which many of the priests of the country and other persons dwell.

In March, 1654, according to Baldeus, these priests shewed to some Dutchmen, who had gone purposely to examine this sacred footstep, a representation of it in gold, and of similar dimensions, on which different images were engraven, which had before been exhibited upon the impression of the foot in the rock. But when these images had been pourtrayed in gold, they vanished from the stone.

M. Valentyn has given a very circumstantial account of the figures and images which are found on Adam's Peak, with the exact dimensions of their heads, eyes, ears, noses, mouths, shoulderblades, arms, palms of the hands, middle fingers, with the nails of the same, the great toes, and their nails, and the form of the chambers in which these colossal specimens of idolatry are placed. But, without entering into further details,

I shall content myself with referring the reader to the place where he may obtain as much of this valuable information as the heart of the most eager curiosity can desire.*

Diego de Couto, an accurate Portuguese writer, who collected the ancient opinions respecting this sacred locality, from the oldest inhabitants and from their vernacular books, says that the Singalese give to this hill the name of Hammanelle Siripade, or the Hill of the Footstep. It rises rapidly from the base; and in its ascent separates into two tops, on one of which is the sacred footstep; and from the summit of both some streams descend, which form a river in the plain below.

The pilgrims, who come to pay their homage to the footstep, bathe themselves in this purifying stream, which is called Sitegangele. This washing they regard as a sort of baptism.

On one of the tops of the Peak there is a small plain, in the midst of which is a cistern for water, called Wellemallacandure. It is raised upon two large stones; and in the middle of it there is a footstep, which they call Siripade. It is much larger than that of a common man, and seems an impression upon the stone like that of a seal upon wax.

Innumerable pilgrims flock to this spot from the most distant regions; and even the natives of Persia and China come to experience the virtues of these purifying waters. After their purification they climb up the precipitous hill; and at a little distance from the top they find some steps, or rather two upright columns, of stone, on which another stone is laid from one to the other. Here a bell is fixed, which, according to the fashion of the Chinese, is of the finest metal, with a large clapper in the middle. To this is attached a rope of leather, which each of the ascending devotees must pull, and make the bell strike, in order to

* See Valentyn Keurlyke Beschryving van Choromandel, &c. &c. Vyfde deel, p. 376, &c.

ascertain whether he is clean: for, if he is unclean, they believe that the bell will return no sound; and, in that case, the person must descend again to the foot of the hill, and practise with still greater solemnity the ceremonials of his purification. Thus it is that they keep off the assaults of the devils, with which the land abounds; but he is never pure, for whom the bell refuses to ring.

This hill is sometimes the resort of four or five hundred pilgrims at a time; who, when they reach the top, can do nothing more than kiss the stone with profound reverence and return again. For they are not permitted to climb up the cistern, or water-tank, which the Singalese term the tank of fecundity. When any women are unfruitful, they drink of this water, which is brought them by the jogis; for if they were to draw it themselves it would be an unpardonable sin.

This stone is frequented also by Moorish devotees, who say that it exhibits the footstep of Adam; and that this is the spot where he fixed his foot for the last time before he rose up into heaven. There is an old tradition in the East, that Adam, being driven out of paradise, was removed to a hill in India, called Serandive, which means the Island of Ceylon.

Marco Paulo says, that the Moors believe Adam to have been buried here. He farther adds, upon their authority, that the son of a king, named Sogomom Barcaon, despising the pomp of royalty, retired to this hill for the purpose of leading a holy life; that hence he ascended into heaven, and that his father ordered pagodas to be erected, and images to be made, in honour of his memory. But when the Singalese were interrogated upon these topics, they excited their derision, as a different account is exhibited in their old writings, and particularly in their national songs, in which they preserve most of their ancient transactions, and of which they perpetuate the remembrance by constant repetition.

CHAP. XXXIII.

Another Singalese Tradition respecting Adam's Peak. History of a Prince fated from his Birth to prefer the Life of a Devotee to that of a King.

THE Singalese retain a tradition about a king, who was sovereign of the whole East, who, after being married many years without having any children, at last obtained a son from God in a very advanced age. This son was unrivalled in majesty of stature and beauty of countenance. The father, who had recourse to the astrologers to cast the nativity of his son, was informed, that he would prefer a holy life to the possession of royal power, and would become a pilgrim (or a jogi) rather than a king. The father, who fondly hoped to avert this destiny, ordered his son, whom he designed for the sceptre, to be brought up in a garden, or park, surrounded by a high wall. Here he had no companions, but some noble youths of his own age; and guards were posted so as to prevent any communication from without, and to remove every cause of inquietude and alarm. Hence all the means of information which the prince possessed, were confined to the objects which he saw, and the conversation which he had, in the shady bowers within which he was immured.

Within this prescribed boundary the royal youth continued till he was eighteen years of age, without having acquired any ideas of sickness, misery, or death. But, with the expansion of his intellectual faculty, he desired to enlarge his sphere of information, and to pass the limits to which his existence had hitherto been confined. He accordingly requested permission of his father to indulge his curiosity in travelling over the kingdom. The father complied with his wishes, but ordered his attendants to watch him with scrupulous tenderness.

As he was proceeding on his journey, he met a cripple, and asked his companions what that object was? They answered that this was no uncommon occurrence in the world, as there were many who were lame, blind, &c. On another occasion, he saw an old man bent almost double with age, leaning on a staff, and shaking under the weight of years. The prince recoiled with horror at the sight; and, asking the reason of what he beheld, he was told that it was the common effect of time upon the human frame.

On one occasion he was met by a corpse passing to the grave with a procession of mourners dissolved in tears. He asked the reason of the heart-rending scene, and was told that it was what he himself must come to at last! The prince grew thoughtful and melancholy. Whilst his mind was absorbed in a state of pensive anxiety, a pilgrim appeared before him, whose suggestions inspired him with a contempt of the world, and incited him to lead a life of solitary and devotional meditation.

After this he found means to escape from his guard, and pursued his way into the interior of the country in the habit of a pilgrim. The Singalese have a tissue of fables respecting his flight; but, in the course of his wanderings, he came to Ceylon with a multitude of attending devotees, when he retired to the Hill of the Footstep, upon which he passed many years with so much sanctity, that the inhabitants adored him as a god. When he had resolved to depart from this island to other regions, his disciples entreated him to leave behind him some memorial which might serve to excite their reverence for his name. He accordingly fixed the print of his foot in the hollow of the cistern, which has been previously mentioned, and left it as a sacred relic for future devotees.

The Singalese histories ascribe several names to this prince, but his proper name, says De Couto, as quoted by Valentyn,* was Drama Raja; and after he became a saint he bore that of Boodh,† which means the wise.

* P. 381.

† I have before remarked, that there were many Boodhs, or Budhas. Valentyn mentions no less than the names of twenty-six before Gautuma Boodh. If we consider the term as a general appellative for sage, we need not wonder at the multiplication of the name.

CHAP. XXXIV.

Idolatry and Superstition. Conviction of a First Cause. Subordinate Deities of the Singalese; their Pagodas; their different Orders of Priests. High Rank and Privileges of the Tirinanxes. Celibacy of the Priests; on what Terms permitted to marry. Visit of a Priest to a scrupulous Devotee. The Priests called Coppuhs, the Jaddeses. Worship of Devils. Anxiety of the Sick to propitiate the tormenting Fiend. Supposed Inspiration of the Priests. Days of Worship. Festivals.

IDOLATRY converts spiritual agents into objects of sense, and consequently multiplies subordinate deities. Superstition peoples the earth, the ocean, and the air, with imaginary beings, but without the definite form which idolatry bestows. But neither idolatry nor superstition exclude gradations of power, or dependencies of causation: but graduated power supposes a higher and a higher, till we come to a highest; and secondary causes necessarily imply a first.

The idea of infinite power will present itself to the mind, however grossly it may contemplate the earth and the heavens: but infinite power must be essentially one and indivisible; for two omnipotents would involve a contradiction. Hence, as the mind labours to ascend to the beginning of all things, one supreme and only cause becomes an irresistible conviction, and is found generally prevalent both among the savage and the sage, the barbarous and the civilized. This conviction has not been withheld from the Singalese; and, though their theogony is composed of a numerous progeny of gods, yet, while they ascribe the direction of human affairs to inferior deities, they represent those deities rather as exercising a delegated trust, than an absolute and independent power. The inferior deities of the Singalese are supposed to be the spirits of good men, of transcendent piety and virtue. In the same manner, they suppose the spirits of wicked men, to be converted into devils; from whose malicious attacks they are protected by the subordinate deities, who have been just mentioned, of whom Boodh is the appointed chief.

Of their numerous pagodas,* some are magnificent structures, and seem to demonstrate that the Singalese, in some former period, had attained to a degree of excellence in the arts, and probably to a state of advancement in the scale of civilization, from which they afterwards declined.

Some of their temples exhibit painted staves, shields, and arms of various kinds, but no military instruments are suspended in the sanctuaries of Boodh, who was the advocate of peace.

Some of the pagodas are endowed with great revenues, and possess high privileges. Indeed, they were so enriched by the superstition or the bounty of different sovereigns, as in process of time to be possessed of more villages and estates than the crown itself could boast.

Of the great revenues which have been appropriated to particular temples, a great part is by the priests expended in offerings to their gods, before whose insensate images, they are continually placing an exuberant variety of viands, which afterwards serve to regale the appetites of those who are employed in the sanctuary. Some state elephants are also kept for the service of the temples, which give an imposing grandeur to their religious processions, and occasion a great expense. The priests of these holy places are exempted from

* See Valentyn, Vol. V. p. 402, &c. Knox's Relation, p. 144, &c.

all civil contributions to the wants of the state, or the exactions of the sovereign.

The Singalese temples, like the churches in some Catholic countries, served as places of refuge for criminals of every description; and the emperor himself had so much respect for the priesthood, as not to cause any persons to be taken by force from the consecrated walls, to which they had fled for protection.

Besides the larger and more sumptuous temples, the Singalese have numerous smaller, and some very diminutive sanctuaries, which they erect in their grounds or yards, upon a pillar or post, in which they place an image of Boodh; and where they burn lamps and make oblations.

The priests of the Singalese are distributed into three ranks or orders. Those who are above all the rest are called tirinanxes, and set apart for the ministration of Boodh, whose temples are denominated vehars. These high priests have a large mansion in the town of Dietlighy, where they meet together, and hold their consultations about the interests of the hierarchy and the affairs of the church. None but persons of noble birth, and of the best education and manners, are admitted into this class of priests; and, those who are admitted, though they nominally belong to the class, do not immediately obtain a place in the vehar or college at Dietlighy, which consists of only three or four persons. The tirinanxes were appointed immediately by the Emperor or King of Candy. They exercise an high authority over the other priests.

The large estates, which have been bequeathed or appropriated to their temples or vehars, are subject to their control. The rest of this first class of priests are called gonnis. These, as well as the tirinanxes, all wear long yellow robes, which are fastened by a fine linen girdle round the loins, and drawn over the left shoulder. The hair is shaven off the head, and they carry a round fan or umbrella in the hand, to protect them from the sun. They are permitted to wear the tallipot leaf with the broad end outwards, which was a mark of distinction, reserved exclusively for them and for the emperor.

These priests are objects of general respect amongst the Singalese, who shew them the same ceremonious homage which they pay to the images of their gods. When they enter a house, a mat is spread for their feet, and a white cloth thrown over a stool for them to sit upon, which are exterior demonstrations of respect, that the king or ambassadors only used to share.

This sacerdotal office is not compatible with any species of manual labour. The priests, as long as they continue to exercise their functions, are doomed to the most rigorous celibacy; though they are at liberty to renounce their sacred calling, if they resolve to enjoy the sweets of connubial life. But, in this case, they must strip off their robes, throw them into the river, and wash their heads and bodies, when they resume their place amongst the laity.

When any person is particularly anxious about the state of his soul, he has recourse to one of these high priests, for the solution of his doubts, or the dissipation of his inquietudes. Great parade is exhibited on the occasion. The priest walks to the house of the disconsolate devotee, under a sort of canopy, carried by four men, and preceded by drums and pipes, in such state as used to be permitted to no other person in the country except the emperor. When he reaches the place of his destination, he is sumptuously entertained for one or two days, and is then escorted back to his own house, with the same pomp as before, and accompanied by the presents by which his ghostly labours have been recompensed. Whilst the priest continues in the house, where he has gone to exercise his spiritual ministration, he keeps singing during the whole night certain hymns out of a book made of tallipot leaves. These he explains to the auditors as they relate to the mysteries of their religion; and the diction is so figurative and inflated, as to be quite unintelligible to the common people.

The order of priests next to the tirinanxes are commonly called coppahs; and their temples dewals. They minister in the worship of the other gods. These priests are not distinguished by their dress from the rest of the people, except in taking care when they perform their religious rites, that what they wear shall be neat and clean. They are chosen from amongst persons of noble rank, and derive no other emolument from their sacred functions than that of a certain piece of land, which has been bequeathed, or presented, to the dewal in which they minister.

The coppuhs engage in agricultural pursuits like the rest of the Singalese, except in the intervals when their attendance is required in the discharge of their sacred functions, which is usually morning and evening, as the revenues of each temple will permit. What they have to do, is to present to the idols the offerings which the devout lay down before the door of the temple. After the offering has continued some time before the idol, the priest carries it again out of the temple, when it is consumed by the drummers, pipers, and other officers. No flesh is ever offered to these idols; but every species of vegetable product.

The priests of the third order are called jaddeses, or priests of the spirits, which pass under the name of dajuntas, and their temples under that of covels, which form the smallest species of pagoda, and have no revenue set apart for their support.

When any individual affects extraordinary devotion, he builds a little chapel in his yard, of which himself becomes the priest. Various devices are painted on the walls, as well as figures with furious looks and menacing attitudes. These temples are much more commonly called houses of jacco, or the devil, than of God. On some extraordinary festivals, these priests cut off their beards in honour of the devil.

When any one is sick, it is usual to consecrate a young red cock to the devil, which, as the priest holds in his hand, he implores the fiend that the sick man may be restored to health. In case of his recovery, the cock is brought up in the yard where the covel stands, in order to be afterwards sacrificed, unless the priest think proper, under some other pretext, to convert it into money, as is frequently the case.

As the Singalese imagine that no other devil can cure any sickness but the one by whom it has been occasioned, their first object is to find out what particular devil, or evil spirit, is the author of the mischief. For this purpose they have recourse to certain magic observances, which never fail of success, under the sagacious management of the priest.

When the people are desirous of learning the will of Heaven in any particular conjuncture, the priests either become frantic, or counterfeit the appearance of frenzy, when they pretend that they are actuated by the Spirit of God: and their submissive votaries imagine that every thing which they utter, during this interval of real or personated delirium, is the undoubted word of God. At this time the priests receive as much homage as the gods.

Wednesdays and Saturdays are the days which they select for their pious ceremonials and different religious ministrations. Besides these ordinary days of worship, they have annual festivals, of which the most magnificent is that which is celebrated at Candy on the new moon, in the month of June or July, when there is a general meeting, which is called Perahar. But no compulsion is employed, and every one goes to the pagoda to which he gives the preference. A similar perahar is, at the same time, observed in other parts of the country; but in that at the capital the greatest magnificence is displayed. The particulars of the spectacle are detailed at length in Knox and Valentyn. The great festival, in honour of Boodh, is celebrated in the month of March, at the commencement of the Singalese year, both on Adam's Peak and under the Bogahah tree, which is found in the country of Anarodgburro, in the northern part of Ceylon. These solemnities are kept up for three or four nights, when they are terminated by the full moon.

CHAP. XXXV.

Introduction of Christianity into Ceylon. Mission of Xavier; Commencement of his Labours; his Discussion with the Brahmins. Wonderful Effects of Baptism on a Woman at Tutocoryn, with other Wonders. What kind of Conversions he effected. Xavier's numerous Baptisms at Travancore; he sends some Priests to Manaar; their Labours obstructed by the King of Jaffnapatam. This King's eldest Brother escapes to Goa, and is baptized. Xavier repairs to Manaar with a Fleet. The King of Jaffnapatam subjugated; revolts; persecutes the Christians; attacks Manaar; is entirely vanquished by the Portuguese, who multiplied their Converts as they extended their Dominion, till the Dutch attempted to substitute the Reformed Faith for that of the Church of Rome.

THE Christian formularies and doctrines which are maintained by the Church of Rome were first introduced into Ceylon in the year 1452, bythe celebrated Francis Xavier, who has been styled the Apostle of the Indians, and who commenced his devout labours in the neighbourhood of the pearl fishery.

As soon as he landed, he caused some portions of the Creed to be printed, with short explanations and prayers, which he formed into a sort of confession of faith. But what he more particularly taught the natives to repeat was the Paternoster, the Ave Maria, and the Credo; and, above all, made a forcible impression upon their minds by the austerity of his character and the temperate habits of his life.

Xavier entered into a variety of doctrinal discussion with the Brahmins in the neighbourhood of Madura, of whom he was never able to make a single convert. But he is said to have converted 40,000 persons of the common sort. Before his arrival, there are related to have been 20,000 persons who had the name of Christians, though they were heathens in superstition. These probably owed their origin to the Christians of St. Thomas; but the Portuguese say, that they were not to be compared with the Christians whose conversion was effected by the labours of Xavier.

After Xavier had sufficiently displayed his zeal, and exercised his mission on the coast of Madura, he retired to Tutocoryn, where he baptized a woman with child, but who had always hitherto had her wishes of progeny frustrated when on the point of being realized. But she had no sooner experienced the waters of baptism, than she was happily delivered. After this he baptized not only her new-born child, but all her family; and, finally, the whole town, which this marvellous occurrence had thrown into a state of pious consternation.

He also performed some other wonderful achievements in their neighbourhood. He released those who were possessed by the devil; and, in several instances, raised the dead. Hence he obtained the name of the Great Father; but he is said not to have been at all elated by the authority he exercised, or the celebrity he acquired.

Valentyn remarks, that the numerous converts which Xavier made from amongst the Indians, in so short a time, may well excite the surprise of those who have since found that several years were necessary in order to convert only three or four individuals. But much of the astonishment vanishes, when we consider, that these converts consisted principally of persons who had been taught only to repeat an Ave Maria or a Paternoster, but who had no further knowledge of Christianity. But what they had learned by rote,* and that with more repugnance

* Valentyn affirms, that the Indians are as slow in learning as they are rapid in forgetting

than inclination, they of course forgot as soon as Xavier had retired. Such were the Christians, of whose evangelical faith this zealous missionary had to boast.

In February, 1544, Xavier, who had gone back to Goa, returned again with Mansilla, and some other priests, of whom he left four at Travancore, where, in a single month, he baptized more than 10,000 of the heathen; on which account a persecution was raised against him by their priests, and by many Christians who had forsaken the faith.

The news of the great success of Xavier's preaching at Travancore caused him to receive solicitations from the inhabitants of Manaar, to whom he sent some priests, intending to appear amongst them in person as soon as his present converts were more established in the faith.

In the mean time, the priests whom he had dispatched to Manaar were very well received; but the King of Jaffnapatam beheld their progress with a jealous eye; and shortly after ordered a massacre of 600 persons of the island of both sexes, and of all ages. He sought, at the same time, an opportunity of destroying his elder brother, to whom the crown properly belonged; but he made his escape to Goa, where he was well received by the Portuguese, and admitted into the pale of the Christian faith.

Xavier now proceeded to Cochin and Cambaja, in order to obtain auxiliaries to co-operate with him in destroying the tyrant of Jaffnapatam. After having obtained the aid that he sought, he repaired, in April 1545, with a fleet to Manaar; but this enterprise was,

---

what they have learned, as soon as the effort ceases by which the impression was made. According to a common expression, they require to be kept constantly to it. But this incapacity of intellectual retention seems to prove rather that the teacher cannot interest, than that the scholar cannot remember, what he has been taught.

for the present, rendered abortive by an accident. The Portuguese, however, afterwards subjugated the whole kingdom of Jaffnapatam: but the king soon shook off the yoke, and commenced a persecution against the Christians. In 1590, he appeared with a considerable fleet in the bay of Manaar, when there were only sixty men in the fortress; but he was so vigorously repulsed by this small garrison, that he took to flight with considerable loss. In 1591 he renewed the attempt, when he was again vanquished, along with his auxiliary host of Malabar pirates; and all Jaffnapatam was reduced to submission by the brave Don Andrea Furtado de Mendoza, who had been sent there by Matthias Albuquerque, the Viceroy of Goa. From this period the Portuguese, gradually extending their dominion in Ceylon, had an opportunity of multiplying the number of their converts to the Roman Catholic faith.

As long as the Portuguese exercised their sway over the maritime parts of the island, the work of conversion was at different intervals prosecuted with more or less success by the zeal of their priests, till the arrival of the Dutch, who, becoming in their turn masters of the coast, laboured to substitute the Reformed faith for that of the Church of Rome.

CHAP. XXXVI.

A Regulation of the Dutch for the Diffusion of their Language in Ceylon. Reflections upon.

THE Dutch had not long obtained possession of the island before they made some wholesome regulations, for the purpose of diffusing their own language and eradicating that of the Portuguese. With this view, it was ordered that every planter or proprietor in the island should cause the hair of all his male slaves, who could not speak the Dutch language, to be cut off close to their heads; and that all those slaves who could speak the language should be suffered, by way of distinction, to wear long hair. It was at the same time ordained, that all those persons, who did not carry these regulations into effect within six weeks after the date of the same, should be amerced in a fine of three* reals, with the exception of those owners, whose slaves already understood the language, which it was the object of the government to diffuse.†

Valentyn thinks, that it would have been politic for the Dutch East India Company to have adopted resolutions, similar to those above-

* Valentyn. Vyfde deel, p. 414.

† I must here remark that, though I commend the attempt of the Dutch to naturalize their language in their foreign settlements, I do not think that they had recourse to the best possible expedient which wisdom or humanity might have suggested for that purpose. Let England adopt the principle, but improve the mode of effecting the end. Let her sedulously labour to diffuse her vernacular idiom through all her foreign settlements; and let her regard this as the best means of facilitating the greatest of all human works—the intellectual improvement of man.

mentioned, in all their settlements. And he adds, that if this measure had been universally adopted, the benefit which would have accrued, with respect to the intellectual improvement of the native inhabitants, would in the course of twenty years have been ten times as great as from the united efforts of all their preachers. Of their preachers, many either had not sufficient capacity or sufficient leisure to make themselves masters of the different languages; and those who with much difficulty did acquire the knowledge of one or two idioms, were often removed to situations where it was of little use.

Wherever a nation forms a settlement, nothing can contribute more to its security on the one hand, or its prosperity on the other, than the propagation of the language of the settlers through all parts of the settlement. No other expedient can so effectually facilitate the purpose of instruction, or the introduction of modes and sentiments, of which the natives have no knowledge, or to which they feel a repugnance; where their ignorance is to be enlightened, or their prejudices to be subdued.

The Romans established their power as much by the influence of their language as by the force of their arms. They did not learn the barbarous dialect of the conquered provinces, but they made it the interest of those provinces to learn the language of Rome. No nation ever possessed such singular facilities for transplanting its language, or a field of such wide extent for its growth and propagation, as the English; but they have not made the most of the auspicious opportunity. In their numerous settlements, and vast foreign domains, they have not adopted those means which policy might have suggested, for inciting the natives to become acquainted with the language which is spoken on the banks of the Thames. Instead of Englishmen learning the numerous dialects of Hindoostan, would it not tend more to the perpetuation of the British dominions in the East Indies, to hold out the highest encouragement to the natives to study the idiom in which the works of Shakspeare and Milton, of Bacon and Locke, were composed?

The institution of casts is what more than any thing else enfeebles the understanding, impairs the energy, and eternizes the degradation of the human species in the East. But what could so powerfully tend to break the spell of ages, by which the submissive myriads of the East have bowed their necks to this most oppressive and most pernicious institution, as to encourage the natives of all casts to think and speak in the idiom* of Britain, and to read those authors, whose writings breathe sentiments of the purest virtue, and the most diffusive benevolence; which impress the most exalted notions of the goodness of God and the dignity of human nature; which establish the independence of the mind, and destroy the chains both of superstition and of tyranny?

* When Valentyn wrote, he recommended that no other language than that of the Dutch should be employed in the whole extent of their Indian possessions. This would certainly have tended greatly to promote the propagation of Christianity; and it would at the same time have made a great addition to the strength and the security of their dominions in those regions. As the English possess at present what no other European nation ever did, the sovereignty of the whole Island of Ceylon, schools for teaching the English language should be established in all parts of the country. All places of power and distinction, which are bestowed upon the natives, should, after the expiration of two or three years, be conferred exclusively on those who had made themselves masters of the English language. A disposition to learn the language should thus as much as possible be excited throughout the island, till its use gradually superseded the ancient idiom of the country.

CHAP. XXXVII.

Physical and intellectual Characteristics of the Singalese; their Moral Qualities; Superstition; Resemblance to the Portuguese. Laxity of Sentiment with respect to Female Chastity. Different Characteristics of the People in the Hill-Country and on the Waste. Strong Prohibitions upon Marriages with Persons of inferior Cast. Marriage, Divorce, Polygamy; their Household Furniture. Principal Articles of Subsistence; their Meats. Drudgery of the Women. Belief in Sorcery. Healthy and long lived.

I SHALL now proceed to exhibit a brief, but characteristic representation of the native Singalese.* Their complexion is not entirely black, but of a deep chesnut, suffused with a yellow tint. Their ears are long and open; their form not robust, their bodies slender and agile, and their minds not deficient in sagacity. They display considerable ingenuity in many of their handicraft operations. They are naturally very hardy, capable of enduring fatigue, supporting life with simple food and little sleep. Their natural disposition is represented as friendly and humane; but this is very much circumscribed by the pride of cast. Where the institution of casts is established, it raises a wall of partition between the different members of the society, which is necessarily unfavourable to the mutual exercise of the kinder sympathies, and to the general operations of benevolence.

Though they are said to respect some of the moral qualities, to venerate probity, and to abominate thieving, yet truth, which lays the first basis of moral character, is not a particular object of their regard. To

* I shall here make liberal use of Valentyn, Keurlyke Beschryving, &c. vyfde deel. p. 43.

tell lies is with them thought no sin; and even a detection causes no shame.*

Superstition, which is a common characteristic of the Indians, prevails to an excessive degree amongst the Singalese. The most trivial occurrence is sufficient to make them relinquish any journey on which they have set out, or any undertaking which they have begun.

They bear a close resemblance to the Portuguese in the sombre gravity of their physiognomy, manner, and gait. They are clear in their ideas, and shrewd in their observations, but full of subtilty and stratagem; nor is any dependence to be placed upon their promises and engagements.

The want of jealousy in the men is not owing to the fidelity of the women. On occasional visits of their friends, they make no scruple of indulging them with the temporary caresses of their daughters, or even of their wives. But if a daughter should unite herself with a person of inferior rank, she must take care to keep out of the sight of her friends, as they would certainly take away her life; not from any respect for chastity, but from that feeling of pride, which eternizes the disparity of casts. With the exception of this prohibitory check, there is no sin more common amongst them, or which is less restrained, than that of fornication; and they even incite their children to the commission. In their mutual paroxysms of anger, the word w—— is never one of their terms of abuse; and adultery is so common amongst them, that a woman has little to fear from her husband, when she is not detected in the act; in which case he has a right to put both the offenders to death.

The Singalese who dwell upon the coast are described as of a more gentle and amiable disposition than the inhabitants of the mountains, who are more violent, insensate, and ferocious. The language and de-

* Liegen is by hen geen zonde, nog schande, &c.—Valentyn.

portment of the mountaineers are more polished and complaisant than those of the people who inhabit low lands near the shore; but they are nevertheless more distinguished by malevolence and perfidy.

Their marriages are never permitted to be contracted with persons of an inferior cast, whatever might be the advantages of such an union. But if a man has any casual intercourse with a woman of lower rank than his own, it is reckoned no disgrace to him, provided he does not eat or drink with her, or make her his wife; but, if he should marry into an inferior cast, the legal authorities would either punish him by fine or imprisonment, or by both; and he would remain for ever degraded to the level of the cast into which he had married. His own family would avoid him as a plague.

They marry their daughters at the early age of ten or eleven years, in order to increase the assurance that the bride has not been previously dishonoured; though little stress is sometimes laid upon that circumstance. The matrimonial contract is formed entirely by the parents, who give their daughters a portion according to their means. They occasionally think very light of a divorce; but, in that case, the bridal portion must be restored. They are not often contented with one wife, but take several, according to their means of maintaining them. The bridegroom is obliged to furnish the bride with her wedding-clothes; which, if he does not possess, he is compelled to borrow.

As they cannot eat nor drink with persons of an inferior cast, they have less sociableness in their meals than where this restriction does not prevail. When they drink, they do not apply the vessel close to their lips, but hold it above, and let the fluid drop into their mouths. Their household furniture consists of a few mats, two or three copper basins, some vessels of earthenware or porcelain, two or three wooden-stools without backs, a wooden pestle and mortar, with a hatchet or two, and some baskets. Instead of tables or table-cloths, the ground, or a mat, serves them for a table, and a plantain-leaf, which they can always have fresh and clean, is a convenient substitute for a cloth or a napkin.

Rice constitutes their bread; and they deem it luxury, when they can add to it a few stewed vegetables, with some pepper and salt, and a little lime-juice. To eat the flesh of the cow would be an abomination. They have not a large supply of meat or fish; and what they have, they are more inclined to part with for money, than to consume themselves. Parsimony and covetousness are qualities which they deem entitled to respect. They venerate him who knows how to live on a little, and to contract his wants within the narrowest compass. Rice, plantains, and some other fruits, with which the country abounds, form the principal articles of their subsistence. They have, or perhaps I ought rather to say had, but few hogs or poultry; for the officers of the government usually took them, without any compensation, whenever they came in their way; and the common people of course felt no inclination to multiply what they were not likely to enjoy. If they should breed more domestic animals or fowls, they would suffer much from the depredations of the civet-cats and tigers; and, whilst they had a native king, he was more desirous that his subjects should be poor than rich.*

The flesh of the goat is appropriated solely to the consumption of the chief, or the gratification of the stranger. Hence, the people in general subsist on the most simple products; and their bill of fare is composed of articles of vegetable growth.

The women are compelled to wait on the men at their meals, and to provide them with what is necessary; and when the men have satisfied their appetites, the women eat the residue. Their food is served on China plates, or merely on a leaf. Water is their usual drink. Their meals are marked by a taciturnity which experiences few interruptions.

* Valentyn, V. p. 45.

They wash the hands and mouth both before and after their meals. This they always do themselves; as to have it done by another would be reckoned a disgrace. They are scrupulously nice in preserving the body and the head from all impurities, and they subject both to frequent ablutions.

The women are treated more like the vassals than the equals of the other sex. They beat the rice, go to market, and fetch the fire-wood, which they bring home upon their heads. No woman is permitted to sit down upon a stool in the presence of a man; nor can she, at the hazard of forfeiting her tongue, command any one in the king's name, which can be done only by the men. But, on the other hand, it was the privilege of the women, with respect to inheritances, to be released from several impositions which the men had to pay.

They are very much in dread of sorcery; and there are people among them, who profess to know how to impose spells which they can again remove. To these jugglers they have recourse when any thing has been stolen from them which they are anxious to recover. The Indians are much addicted to this practice; and indeed it is common in all countries, where philosophy has not diminished the darkness of ignorance or broken the wand of superstition.

Different accounts agree in representing them as healthy, and preserving their vigour and activity to a great age. They have no regular medical practitioners; and, indeed, such a profession is not likely to be much wanted amongst a people whose diet is so simple, and whose lives are so regular. They are subject to few maladies, which they cannot cure themselves by very simple means.

CHAP. XXXVIII.

Different Potentates in Ceylon; Supreme Authority of the Emperor since the Time of Don John. The Emperor's Guard; his Revenues, when paid, and in what they consisted. Great Officers of State; inferior Servants. The Perils of Pre-eminence at the Court of Candy; Reflections on.

IN the more antient periods of the Singalese history, the island was under the domination of different kings or chiefs, who at times asserted an independent authority; and at others acknowledged the superior jurisdiction of an emperor. When the Portuguese first arrived in the island, they found the country divided by the influence, or disturbed by the dissensions of several minor or feudatory potentates; whilst the sovereign, who was styled emperor, as elevated above the rest, had transferred his residence to Cotta, where he exercised a nominal, rather than a real superiority. But, since the reign of Don John, who died in 1604, the sole authority of the emperor, or king of Candy, was acknowledged in all parts of Ceylon, where the European settlements had not established a separate and independent jurisdiction.

In the place of his residence the emperor had a strong guard for the protection of his person, composed of his principal servants, and a great number of soldiers under their respective chiefs. But he commonly placed more reliance on a body of Moors, who always kept watch at his chamber door. Besides these, he had many other younger guards, selected from among the bravest youths of the best families. They had long hair, went bareheaded, and usually attended him in his journeys and processions.

His revenues were considerable. Three times in a year he received the contributions of his subjects. The first was paid in March, at the commencement of the new year according to the reckoning of the Singalese; the second was collected from the first fruits of the earth; and the third took place at one of their festivals which was celebrated in November.

But, besides the more regular contributions, every one was obliged to supply gratuitously, whatever was wanting in the palace of the monarch. The nobles seized what was requisite for this purpose, wherever it was to be found; and, under this pretext, many acts of injustice were practised, and many atrocious extortions perpetrated with the awful sanction of the emperor's name.

All presents were conveyed to the emperor wrapped in white linen; and were first offered to the prince on the new year after he had washed his head, and undergone the ablution of the bath. On this occasion he was wont to exhibit himself in public to his army and his subjects, who were assembled for the purpose; when the guns were fired and great rejoicings made.

After this the nobles and people of all descriptions went to the palace with their presents, consisting of gold, silver, precious stones, arms, silks, and calicoes. They at the same time made the first payment of their taxes in money, palm-wine, oil, rice, honey, wax, iron, elephants' teeth, tobacco, and other commodities, but were often obliged to wait at court a long time till their respective imposts and offerings were received, either by the king or his ministers. This was wont to produce much tumult and inconvenience.

Besides his fixed revenues, the emperor had others which were fluctuating and contingent. Where a man died who possessed cattle, he was entitled by the law of the land to an ox, a cow, and a pair of buffaloes, which were deducted from the stock of the deceased by persons appointed for the purpose.

When the people got in their harvest, every individual reserved a certain measure of corn, or rice, as a present for the sovereign. This was indeed sometimes commuted for a sum of money; but such commutation was no longer permitted when Valentyn wrote. Besides this measure of corn, the farmers were obliged to pay a certain sum of money, from which those lands were exempt that belonged to the priests, or which had been devoted to eleemosynary purposes.

For all the imposts and oblations, which the monarch received in such various ways, he had several places of deposit in different parts of his dominions, where these various sorts of treasure were secured; but there have been exigencies in the Singalese history, when many of the jewels and valuables have been plunged into the bed of the Mahavillaganga, or thrown into the labyrinths of the forest, in order to secure them from the spoliation of an invading enemy.

Next in dignity to the emperor were two adigars, or chief judges, to whom the people might appeal when they thought themselves aggrieved by the inferior authorities. Numerous subordinate officers waited upon the adigars, who were easily distinguished by the pastoral staves, which they bore, and which were exclusively confined to their use. As much respect was shewn to these attendants of the adigar as to that officer himself.

In the scale of official dignity, the persons who came next the adigars were the dessaves, or provincial governors, who had not only to attend to the administration of justice in their several districts, but to take care that the revenue of the emperor suffered no defalcation. The dessaves were commonly selected from amongst the nobility, as the principal object of consideration in the choice was the birth of the individual. But none of the great officers of the government had power to inflict any capital punishment without the permission of the emperor, or to pass any sentence of death without his previous approbation.

Every village was wont to have a smith, a potter, a washerman, and an artificer of every other description. Each of these persons, as well as every occupier of land, besides the regular contributions to the emperor, had certain presents to make to the dessave, who reaped considerable emolument from the gratuities of those who had any need of his favour, or any occasion for his services. The dessaves indeed were usually incited to practise a good deal of extortion towards their inferiors, in order to satisfy the annual claims of the monarch upon the liberality of their contributions, without which his royal protection and regard could not readily be preserved.

As the dessaves were compelled to pass most of their time in servile attendance upon the court, they were under the necessity of appointing sub-dessaves, to whom they entrusted the administration of their provinces, and the care of their affairs. These sub-dessaves were denominated Coorli Vidanis, besides whom there were some other subordinate officers, called Congconnas, whose duty it was to attend to the coorli vidanis, and to give an account of the same to the dessave.

The coorli achila executed the orders of the coorli vidani, and undertook to provide all kinds of fruit for the emperor's table, besides superintending the different messengers to the court.

There was also in each province a liannah, or chief writer, who read, preserved, and executed all the correspondence relative to the government, and kept a register of every thing that was sent to the court.

There was an officer named Undia, who collected the emperor's money, and brought it together in a mass; and another called Monanhah, who measured all the corn that grew on his domain.

The villages which were appropriated to the pagodas and the clergy, were not subject to the authority of the dessave: nor were those villages which the emperor had bestowed upon his courtiers and favourites. Such lands were placed under the exclusive jurisdiction of the proprietors.

These persons, who were placed in situations of the greatest power and highest trust under the emperor, were usually in a less enviable situation than any other individuals in his dominions, as their lives were perpetually dependent on the capriciousness of a tyrant, whose suspicions or dislike they were more liable to excite, in proportion to their proximity to his person, or to the degree of their fancied elevation. Short was the interval between a sensation of displeasure in the royal bosom, and the destruction of his creatures or his favourites. But, though the posts of pre-eminence and distinction at the court of Candy were precipices of such perilous hazard and insecurity, yet we learn from Knox and other authorities, that they were not, on that account, less the object of eager desire and ambitious competition. The volatile cruelty of the tyrant had no sooner plunged one victim into the gulph below, than numbers were found ready to supply his place, and to take their station on the same giddy height, though they had no better chance of escaping the same abyss. In the lottery of ambition, as well as in other lotteries, whatever may be the preponderance of blanks, every individual flatters himself that he is more exclusively favoured by Fortune; and that chances, upon which he would think it folly in another to build one pleasurable hope, are a solid ground-work of confidence to himself. Such is the care which is exhibited in the moral administration of the world to prevent individuals from looking too much on the dark side of human affairs; or to have the spirit of enterprize rendered torpid, and their active powers paralyzed by gloomy calculations on the evils of life, and the contingencies of misfortune.

CHAP. XXXIX.

Laws of the Singalese. Form of Ordeal in doubtful Cases. Oaths. Modes of detecting Thefts; of forcing the Payment of Fines and Debts.

THE Singalese have certain established *national laws, or old customs, according to which most things are determined, where the will of the king does not interpose to make any alteration. The children inherit the landed property, which does not descend exclusively to the eldest son; but where the right of primogeniture is allowed, the individual is obliged to support the mother and children. All debts are doubled in the course of two years; and he, who has no means of paying them, passes into slavery with his wife and children. No man may marry a woman, who has run away from her husband, before the husband has married another woman. The children of a free man, by a mother who is a slave, are born slaves; but, on the other hand, the children of a slave by a free woman are free; so that the civil condition of the mother commonly determines that of the progeny. A thief, who cannot make a seven-fold restitution, becomes a slave. Old people, who run in debt, barter their children for the amount, or pawn them as a security for the payment.

In ambiguous questions both parties must take an oath in the temple before the images of their gods. This oath is accompanied with the most imposing solemnities; and the form of ministration in boiling oil, and burning cow-dung, is such as may appal even those who are supported by the consciousness of innocence.—Before the oath is taken,

* Valentyn, 48.

a permission* from the magistrate must be obtained. Both parties, after washing their heads and bodies, are shut up together for the night, and rigidly watched. Each of them has a cloth bound round his right hand, which is sealed, in order that no sorcery or other means may be employed to deaden the sensibility of the parts to the action of the fire. On the morning of the solemnity, after arraying themselves in their best attire, the parties, having the written permission of the magistrate fastened on their wrists, repair to a place under the Boghahah or god-tree, where the boiling oil and burning cow-dung are placed for the occasion. Here both the plaintiff and the defendant, in the presence of thousands of spectators, invoke the God of Heaven to witness their innocence. The cloths with which their hands were enveloped are now unloosed; when two of the fingers of each are dipped three times successively into the boiling oil and the burning cow-dung. After this part of the ceremony has been performed, the hands are bound with the same cloths as before, and the parties watched till the following day. The bandages are then removed, and the ends of the fingers examined, in order to see if the skin has been taken off. If that has been the case, the guilt of the person is thought to be established; and he is accordingly condemned to pay a heavy fine to the emperor. It is not said what expedient is employed to determine the question in dispute, when the fingers of both the parties have been alike flayed and blistered by the boiling oil. This of course would usually happen; but the priests probably have some secret means of protecting the individual whom they wish to favour; and thus, at the same time, of preserving the high authority of the ordeal in the estimation of the multitude.

On more common occasions, when they wish to confirm any assertion by an oath, they swear by the eyes of their mother, of their children, or by their own eyes; but little dependance is to be placed on these modes of adjuration; and, as I have intimated in another place, truth is

* Valentyn, V. p. 408.

not one of the virtues which occupies a distinguished rank in the moral code of the Singalese.

When any theft has been committed, the Singalese are wont to detect the thief by the following mode of sorcery:—They mutter some magical words over a cocoa-nut, which is held in the hand by the stalk, and placed at the gate, or opening where the robber made his escape. After the cocoa-nut has been thus enchanted, it is said to follow the track of the thief till it reaches his person, or arrives at his house. By this means numerous impositions are practised upon the simple, and various false accusations urged, where any ill-will is felt, or any pique is to be gratified.

Those who violate the laws are liable to be punished by fine or imprisonment. If the fine be not immediately paid, the individual is deprived of his sword, knife, cap, and doublet, and kept in confinement. If the payment is still deferred, he is condemned to carry a heavy stone upon his back, till it is discharged. Besides these, other expedients are employed to force the payment of a debt; of which that is not one of the least efficacious, in which the creditor threatens to destroy himself, and to load the soul of the debtor with the guilt of his death.

CHAP. XL.

The Malabars and Bedas.

WHEN Valentyn wrote his Description of Ceylon, the Malabars* were

* The Malabars speak a language which is totally different from that of the Singalese. The language of the Singalese is represented as very copious, particularly in the vocabulary of compliment. Thus it is said, that they can address the same individual by ten or twelve different titles, according to his rank or circumstances. They have seven or eight different ways of saying you or thou, each of which has a certain appropriation to the rank or condition of the person addressed. To the king or emperor, they used to give the title of Dionanxi, which is more exalted than that of God. Raja Singa permitted himself to be addressed by this title before the insurrection of his subjects, which is related above; but he forbad the use of it after that event. When they have occasion to speak of themselves before a chief or great man, they do not say I in the first person, but commonly give themselves the appellation of dog, and do not reserve for their family or relatives a more respectful name. "The Moors," says Thunberg, (Vol. IV. p. 188,) "who come hither from the coasts of the continent, are tolerably numerous in Columbo, and carry on an extensive trade. They are, for the most part, tall of stature, darker than the islanders, and well clad. Their dress resembles nearly a lady's gown, is most frequently made of white callico, very wide, and gathered up at the waist, and is bound round the body with a girdle of white cotton, tied on the right side. On the head they wear a turban. Their ears are commonly decorated with long ear-rings of gold, of various patterns, some being plain, others twisted, others set with precious stones of a red, blue, or green colour. Some are very large, being a full finger in length, others again are smaller. Sometimes one of these only is worn in the ear, sometimes more, even five or six together; so that with their weight, the foramen and tip of the ear are lengthened amazingly, insomuch that the ear reaches down to the shoulders. As soon as the children are three years old, one of these ear-rings is given them by way of ornament. It is properly the rich, who wear a number of rings in their ears; so that from the condition, size, and number of the ear-rings, one may form an estimate of the wealth and opulence of the wearers. Persons of rank among the Singalese, such as ambassadors and officers belonging to the court in Candy, wear long gold chains about their necks, which hang down upon the breast and stomach: such had the ambassadors who came to Columbo, and similar ones are given to the Dutch ambassador and his secretary, by the king, on their arrival at Candy. The chains do not consist of links, but of globules, which are hollow within, and pierced through in every part of their surfaces, and woven round with gold wire, like fillagree work. These balls are afterwards strung, either upon a silken cord or golden wire, to any length that is desired."

under the government of an independent prince, who was neither subject to the Dutch nor to the King of Candy, though he made the former an annual present of a few elephants. His subjects were held in as low a state of vassalage as those of the King of Candy, and were even oppressed by heavier imposts; but the sovereign of the Malabars paid his soldiers, whilst the King of Candy forced his troops to serve at their own cost. The Malabars, besides their dispersion over different parts of the island, possessed a small district in the vicinity of Jaffnapatam in the north. The products of their country are elephants, cattle, deer, wax, honey, milk and butter, a little rice, but no cotton: but they annually bartered large droves of cattle for bales of linen, which they carried to Nevecalava, where they procured a supply of cotton and rice, with which they returned home. Valentyn praises their manufacture of cotton, as superior to that of the Singalese. In this traffic with the Dutch they furnished themselves with salt, salt fish, copper vessels, and other commodities, of which they again disposed for other goods amongst the Singalese, who had no dealings with the Dutch.

Some of the Singalese, who are said to be the oldest inhabitants of the island, are named Bedas or Wedas. They dwell principally in the woods, in the northern and north-eastern parts of the island. Valentyn describes them of a black hue, with fiery eyes, of moderate stature, but well made and full of activity. They speak the same language as the rest of the Singalese, and subsist on venison, without rice, or any food but that which they procure by the chace. They have houses* and villages; but their ordinary abode is under the shade of a tree, or a bower made of some of the branches, by the margin of a river or a lake. They do not shave their heads, but tie up their hair in a large bunch, and let it hang in this manner from their shoulders. Some of them are much less civilized than others. Each individual has a peculiar allotment of ground, and his prescribed limits, within which they are very careful

* Valentyn, p. 50.

not to offer any violence to one another, as the offender would be put to death.

They preserve the venison, which they do not want for immediate consumption, in places of deposit, which they make in the trunks of trees, and then cover the opening with honey. When they marry their daughter, the portion which they give consists of some dogs fitted for the chase, in which the women also engage as well as the men. They appear to have been established here long before the time of the first King of Ceylon, and to have been subject to a queen, who, like another Medea, was skilled in magic arts.

CHAP. XLI.

Natural Products. Rice; the Tallipot Tree; the Cocoa Nut; the Kettule; the Cinnamon; the Areca, Bread Fruit, Banyan, Ficus Religiosa, Tulip, Tamarind, Teak Trees; Calaminder and Cadumberi; Oranges, Shadocks, Guava, Papai, Pomegranates, Plantains, Limes, Pine Apples, Custard Apples, Bullock's Heart.

I SHALL say a few words of some of the natural products of the country. Rice here constitutes the principal object of culture, for the purposes of human subsistence, as it is all over the East. No wheat is yet produced in the island, though it is probable that attempts will ere long be made to introduce that species of grain. The rice is of several kinds, one of which comes to maturity in six or seven, and the others ripen in three, four, or five months. But all the sorts are mentioned by Valentyn, as bearing the same price. The best tasted is that which is first ripe, and of this they have the least. They commonly sow the seed in July or August, after they have ploughed their lands with oxen. These oxen they employ afterwards to thresh or tread out the corn. Previously to the commencement of this operation, the women carry a bundle of rice upon their heads three times round the threshing floor, and afterwards perform some other mysterious rites, for which they are allowed to take away as much of the grain as they can lay on the magical stone which they carry to the spot.

Amongst their most remarkable trees is that called the tallipot, which is particularly straight, and shoots up to the height and the dimension of the mast of a large ship. It bears fruit only once during its existence, but its leaves are of great use in various respects.*

The circumference of this leaf is such, that it is large enough to preserve from six to a dozen persons † together from being wet in a pouring rain. When it is dried, it is very tough; but at the same time so supple and flexible, that notwithstanding its spacious dimensions, it may be folded up like a fan; and though it is as thick as a man's arm, it is so light, that a person may carry it a great way without fatigue. In its full expanse it displays a circular appearance; but, when cut in pieces, it has a triangular form. When a man lays it on his head in a journey, with the points projecting outwards, it serves to protect him through the bushes and thorns; whilst, in other situations, it assists in shading him from the scorching rays of the sun, and serves as a cover from the violence of a drenching storm.

The tallipot tree bears no blossoms till the last year of its growth, when some beautiful yellow flowers, of a strong but oppressive smell, appear on the wide-spreading branches of the top. These flowers are succeeded by a fruit as big as a large cherry, but which is used for no other purpose than as seed for the propagation of the trees.

Of that wonderful luxuriance with which Nature provides for the per-

* Thunberg says, in his Travels, Vol. IV. p. 253. "One of these leaves cut off about five feet in length, and of almost the same in breadth, decorated with various elegant embellishments, bears like the tree itself the name of tallipot, and is carried over the heads of people of distinction, both Indians and Europeans, by a slave, instead of the common parasols and parapluyes. One single leaf is generally large enough to shelter six persons from the rain. This beautiful palm tree grows in the heart of the forests, but is scarce. It may be classed among the loftiest trees, and becomes still higher when on the point of bursting forth into blossom from its leafy summit. The sheath, which then invelops the flower, is very large, and when it bursts, makes an explosion like the report of a cannon; after which, it shoots forth branches on every side, to the surprising height of thirty-six or forty feet."

† Valentyn says fourteen or fifteen; Thunberg six.

petuation of all her products, the tallipot tree furnishes a singular example; for, though it bears fruit only in the year in which it dies, it then bears enough to cover a whole province with its progeny.

When this tree is cut down for the sake of the seed, the pith yields a sort of meal, of which the natives make a cake, which tastes something like the finest bread. It serves as an occasional substitute for rice. They also write with an iron style upon the leaves, which they make up into books.*

The cocoa-nut tree is found in almost every part of the island in the vicinity of the coast, where it flourishes more than in the interior pro-

* "Both on the coast of the continent of Asia, and the Island of Ceylon," says Thunberg, Vol. IV. p. 250, "the leaves of the borassus palm tree (borassus flabelliformis) and sometimes of the tallipot tree (licuala spinosa), are used instead of paper, which the Indians do not prepare from the bark of a tree, as their neighbours more to the eastward do. The leaves of both these palm trees lie in folds like a fan, and the slips stand in need of no other preparation than merely to be separated and cut smooth and even with a knife. Their mode of writing upon them consists in carving the letters with a fine pointed style (stylus): and, in order that the characters may be the better seen and read, they rub them over with charcoal, or some other black substance, so that the letters have altogether the appearance of being engraved. The iron point, made use of on these occasions, is either set in a brass handle, which the Moors and others carry about them in a wooden case, and which is sometimes six inches in length; or else it is formed entirely of iron, and, together with the blade of a knife, designed for the purpose of cutting the leaves, and making them even, set in a knife-handle common to them both, into which handle it shuts up, so that it may be carried by the owner about with him, and be always ready at hand. On such slips are all letters, all edicts of governors, &c. written, and sent round open and unsealed. When a single slip is not sufficient, several are bound together, by means of a hole made at one end, and a thread on which they are strung. If a book is to be made, either for the use of the churches, or any other purpose, they look out principally for broad and handsome slips of tallipot leaves, upon which they engrave the characters very elegantly and accurately, with the addition of various figures delineated upon them by way of ornament. All the slips have then two holes made in them, and are strung upon an elegantly-twisted silken cord, and covered with two thin lacquered wooden boards. By means of the cords the leaves are held even together, and by being drawn out, when they are wanted to be used, they may be separated from each other at pleasure." Thus far Thunberg.—Valentyn says, that the few books which the Singalese possess are written on leaves, in the manner abovementioned, and treat principally of religion and the healing art; but in a language elevated above the common idiom. See Valentyn, Vol. V. p. 48.

vinces. With a trunk not more than a foot in diameter, it shoots up to the height of from seventy to eighty feet. There are no boughs or leaves, except at the top, where they expand like rays from a centre, and cover the head of the trunk with a circle of shade. The leaves, which are about twelve in number, are pinnated, twelve feet long, and from three to four broad. Of these leaves some are manufactured into mats, and others are used as brooms. The nuts are produced in clusters at the top of the tree, to the number of two or three dozen. They are covered with a thick tissue of fibres, which are manufactured into ropes and cables, and are, in some respects, preferable to those made of hemp. "The juice which is pressed from the kernel of the nut, after it is grated, is a principal ingredient in malakatanni, and all the Singalese curries; and the refuse, or dry substance, which remains, affords excellent food for poultry and hogs."* An oil is also expressed from the kernel, which is generally employed in the lamps of the East. The same oil is also used as an unguent, and a substitute for butter. At the top of the tree there is a shoot of about two feet in length and eight inches in diameter, which passes under the name of cocoa-nut cabbage, and furnishes a luxuriant vegetable. But as the tree dies when this shoot is destroyed, it is suffered to remain till it is deemed expedient to cut down the stem on which it grows. A fluid called palm wine exudes after incision from the buds at the top of the tree. This forms a cooling and a wholesome beverage, if drunk before fermentation, which exposure to the heat of the sun produces. When fermented, it acquires an intoxicating quality. The filaments at the bottom of the stem may be manufactured into a coarse cloth called gunny, which is used for bags and similar purposes. The leaves also supply a most grateful food to the elephant when they are fresh, and when they are dry they may be burned instead of a torch.

The kettule tree grows very straight, but not so tall as the cocoa-nut. It contains a pith like the tallipot tree, which yields an uncommonly

* Cordiner, Vol. I. p. 351.

sweet sap,* of very pleasant taste, and very wholesome qualities. A tree of the ordinary size will give out several quarts in a day. From this juice, after boiling, they prepare a brown sugar, and sometimes, when they employ particular care in the process, one that is not inferior to white. The leaves of this species of palm resemble those of the areca, and are attached to a strong skin, which is as hard as a board, but full of fibres. These they employ as thread, and make into cordage. The leaves keep falling off as long as the tree continues to grow, but when it has attained its full growth, they adhere for many years to the stem, and no fresh ones are produced. When the buds on the top become ripe and wither away, they are annually succeeded by others, which keep continually growing lower and lower down the branches till they reach the stem. The tree is then worn out; but, nevertheless, it will still remain for eight or ten years before it dies.

But the glory of Ceylon, the richest of its products, and staple of its commerce is, the cinnamon tree. The Singalese give it the name of Curundo-gas, and they denominate the cinnamon itself Curundo Potto.

The cinnamon tree sometimes grows to a considerable size. In an uncultivated state it is found from twenty to thirty feet in height. The trunk throws out numerous horizontal branches, which are covered with a thick foliage. The leaf resembles that of the laurel in thickness of tissue and in the colour of the surface: but, whilst the laurel-leaf has only one long vein in the middle, that of the cinnamon is distinguished by three principal fibres, which interrupt the green smoothness of the leaf. When the young leaves first make their appearance, they are as red as scarlet; and Valentyn says, that when rubbed to pieces in the hand, they smell much more like cloves than like cinnamon. The flowers, which are white, hang in clusters, and resemble those of the

* Valentyn, V. p. 50.

lilac. The fruit, which becomes ripe in April, has the form of an acorn, without any taste or smell, like the bark, and when removed from its socket its shape is like that of an olive, but it is not larger than a black currant. When this fruit is boiled it yields a fine oil, which congeals when cold into a substance like wax or spermaceti. Valentyn says, that it forms a very wholesome salve for pains and infirmities of the limbs. It may be either burned in a lamp or made into candles; but it was not employed for these purposes except by the King of Candy.

The cinnamon tree is indigenous to the island, where it grows wild like other native plants. According to Valentyn, it is chiefly found to the west of the river Mahavilla-ganga; but the growth seems principally confined to the south-west angle, formed by the sea-coast from Negumbo* to Matura. None is found in the province of Jaffnapatam, nor in the Island of Manaar; but the interior of the dominions belonging to the late King of Candy has not yet been sufficiently explored to establish the precise boundary which is auspicious to the growth. The bark of the tree is formed of two coats, or layers, of which the interior constitutes the true cinnamon. The outer and the inner bark used to be separated from each other by a nice operation of the knife whilst on the tree; but, at present, it seems that the two coats are not separated till they are removed from the trunk. The bark, after it is peeled off, is laid in the sun to dry, when it curls up into rolls as we commonly see it. The tree dies after it has been thus stripped of its bark. The wood, which is white and soft, almost like that of the fir, burns without yielding any perfume; but the islanders use it in the structure of their houses, and in some articles of cabinet work. The root, when macerated in water, imparts a smell of camphor; and camphor of a very strong kind may be extracted from the root.

* Valentyn says, V. p. 231, 232, that the best and finest cinnamon grows in the district of Negumbo or the Seven Corles.

The finest cinnamon is that which is peeled from the young and smaller trees. A more coarse sort is derived from the trees which are of larger dimensions and greater age: and there is a third kind, which goes by the name of the wood, or wild cinnamon, which is found on the coast of Malabar and in other places; but Ceylon alone seems the region which Providence has allotted for the production of this delicious aromatic in its highest purity and perfection. The soil and the climate are there happily adapted to its growth; and the artificial cultivation of any natural product will seldom be of much avail where these two great requisites, of appropriate soil and genial climate, are not to be found. The soil, indeed, may be meliorated or changed by industry and skill; but the influence of climate is less under the control of man.*

Amongst the trees which abound in Ceylon, and which are remarkable for their beautiful appearance, their stately growth, or their useful qualities, may be reckoned, in addition to those abovementioned, the

* The Europeans long believed, and the Singalese maintained, that no cinnamon could be good but what grew wild; and that the properties of the plant were impaired by artificial cultivation. The Dutch governor, Jman William Falck, made the first attempt to rear a plantation of cinnamon. This first attempt was rendered abortive by the hostility of the chalias, or cinnamon peelers, who feared that it might hurt their trade, and who accordingly poured hot water at night upon the plants. But this stratagem was detected; and Governor Falck was afterwards more successful in the horticulture of cinnamon. In its wild state, the propagation of the plant is effected by means of birds, who eat the soft berries, the kernels of which will not dissolve in their gizzards, and are consequently dispersed in the woods. See Thunberg, IV. p. 182, &c. Thunberg says, that the superfine cinnamon ought to be about the substance of royal paper, or a little thicker, of a light colour, making nearer approaches to yellow than to brown, with a sweetish taste, but not very pungent or hot upon the tongue. The chalias, or cinnamon peelers, who are mentioned above, constitute a distinct cast. Valentyn says, that they were despised by the natives; and they appear to have been oppressed by the Dutch. During the harvest, each of the chalias was obliged to procure two bars of peeled cinnamon, each bar consisting of 480 pounds. He received no compensation for one of the bars, and only 1½ rix dollar for the other. When the bundles or sacks of cinnamon are stowed on board the ships, black pepper is strewed over each layer of bundles, so as to fill up all the interstices. The pepper is said to improve the quality of the cinnamon by attracting the humidity, whilst it is itself improved by the contiguity of its associated aromatic.

areca; the jack, or bread-fruit tree;* the banyan, or Indian fig; the ficus religiosa bogaha, or god tree; the portia, or tulip tree; the tamarind; and the teak. The beauty of these and other trees, as far as it depends upon the foliage, is not occasional or evanescent, for it preserves its green as long as the plant retains its life.

Knox has described the bogaha, or god tree, and Valentyn has done little more than give a Dutch version of his account. This tree, which has sometimes been confounded with the banyan, or Indian fig, appears from very ancient times to have been an object of religious veneration amongst the Singalese. Its long, broad, and beautiful leaves, which are in the shape of a heart, are reported often to have furnished a cooling shade and soft repose to the divine Boodh when he was at liberty to relax from the devout labours of his mission. Hence tradition has consecrated it to his memory; and so holy is it esteemed, that the form of its leaves was not permitted to be painted on any article of furniture but what was designed for the palace of the king.

* There are two sorts of trees which produce the bread fruit; one of which yields a smaller fruit without seed, whilst the fruit of the other is larger, of more general growth, and in higher repute. The fruit of the smaller sort is about the size of a child's head; but that of the larger " weighs from thirty to forty pounds, and contains from two to three hundred kernels, each of them four times the size of an almond. The fruits are all over prickles, with a thick and soft rind: the internal part of the fruit only is used for food by the human race, and the rind is left for the hogs." The larger sort of bread fruit, which is almost universally used in Ceylon, is called by three different names according to the periods of its growth. " It is called pollos, when it has attained to the size of an ostrich's egg, and is a month or six weeks old; herreli, when it is half ripe, and of the size of a cocoa-nut; the pulpy esculent part is then still of a white and milky cast. At both these ages the fruit cannot be eaten without previous preparation. When it is perfectly ripe, it is called warreka; the pulpy part is then fit for use, and that which environs the seed has a sweetish taste, is yellow, and, without any preparation, both eatable and relishing."—" The seeds may be eaten either alone, like chesnuts, or together, with the pulpy part of the fruit itself, prepared in different ways: they are used for food, both boiled and roasted; the poorer sort generally boil and eat them with the scrapings of cocoa-nut and salt;" and the rich employ them in fattening pigs, geese, and other fowls. Thunberg describes the mode of preparing fifteen different dishes from the fruit of this beneficent tree." See his Travels, Vol. IV. p. 256—261.

The trees in the island, of which the wood is fit for a variety of mechanical and domestic uses, are very numerous. Mr. Cordiner mentions that specimens of these had been collected and sent to England. "The most valuable and beautiful," says Mr. Cordiner,* "is calaminder, which is extremely hard, of a dark chocolate colour, clouded like marble, streaked with veins of black and pale yellow, and receives a very high polish. Codumberi considerably resembles it, but is of lighter colour, and inferior beauty. Other species of ebony, satin, and nindoo wood, are very common."

Fruits and vegetables for culinary purposes are found in great exuberance and variety. There are two crops of oranges in the year, which are said to be extremely delicious for two months in each season. They do not acquire a yellow colour, except in a state of decay, but are green when perfectly ripe; and those of the best quality exhibit a russet tint. The pumple-nose, or shadock, which grows to the size of a man's head, abounds with juice of the most refreshing and agreeable kind. To these we may add the guava, papai, pomegranate, plantain, mango, limes, pine-apples,† custard-apples, the pulp of which has the taste and consistence of boiled custard; the bullock's heart, a fruit resembling the custard-apple, but of a different shape and colour; the billimbing, which has a strong acid taste, and is employed in tarts and preserves; with others of different kinds, and a diversity of vegetable products for domestic use.

* Vol. I. p. 381.

† "Pine-apples grow in greater plenty, and of a larger size, but not of so high a flavour as those of Hindoostan, where the degree of heat is greater, and the quantity of rain less. They are raised without any culture, farther than sticking the plants in the ground, and are sold in many places, at as low a rate as a penny a-piece. Their highest price does not exceed sixpence." Cordiner.

CHAP. XLII.

Elephants, Hunt of; Mode of ensnaring and taming.

AMONGST the different species of animals which this highly-favoured island exhibits, the elephant is that for which it has been celebrated from the most ancient times, and for which it is still renowned. The earliest writers, who seem not to have known Ceylon as the native region of cinnamon, mention it as famous for its breed of elephants and its export of ivory.

These elephants, which may be reckoned the gigantic aborigines of the island, are the largest, as well as the most sagacious and docile, which are found in all India. Some of those, which are spotted over the whole body, are said by Valentyn to have been particularly reserved for the use of the King of Candy, and to have been more prized by him than the elephants which had not such discriminating marks.

These noble animals, which are found in all the forests in Ceylon, usually go in droves; and many a traveller is said to have been trodden to death, who could not escape from their line of march. When they break into the cultivated country, they often occasion great loss to the inhabitants, by the injury which they do to their rice-fields, their plantations, and gardens.

Various accounts of the mode of entrapping elephants in Ceylon may be read in Baldeus, Thunberg, and other writers. One of the best descriptions of this interesting scene in any recent authority, is to be found in the first volume of Mr. Cordiner's publication. The great object of this mighty chase is to drive as many elephants as possible into a large triangular enclosure, formed of huge upright and transverse beams of the strongest timber, and purposely contrived to ensnare these noble animals. This enclosure, which is very * wide at the commencement, is gradually contracted till it terminates in a sort of funnel, or narrow passage, about five feet broad and one hundred feet long. The elephants are gradually impelled into this snare from the distance of thirty or forty miles, by thousands of hunters, alarming them with drums, shouts, fire-arms, flambeaus, and a variety of combustibles, sometimes uniting in an immense continuity of flame. Intimidated by these means, these enormous animals are, by slow degrees, and after the labour of many days, forced into the toil in which they are made prisoners, till they are at last subjected to the use of man.

The discharging passage, or the funnel of the snare, is not wide enough to admit more than one elephant abreast. As the mighty captive arrives at this point of his destination, " cross bars are shoved in behind him through the interstices of the stakes, and lashed down with ropes to the transverse beams, so that he can neither move forwards, nor backwards, nor sideways. His confinement is thus limited in order to contract the powers of his prodigious strength, and to allow the men to approach near enough to bind his legs, without being exposed to danger. The elephants which follow are separated from one another in the passage, and made close prisoners in the same manner."— " When the wild elephant is completely harnessed, two tame elephants trained to the business are brought to the gate and placed one on each side of it. These immediately survey the prisoner whom they have to conduct, feel his mouth to know whether or not he has tusks, and lay hold of his proboscis to know what degree of resistance he is likely to make. Ropes are passed through the collar of the wild elephant, and made fast

* Valentyn says four miles, and his miles are German measure.

to similar collars of each of the tame ones. The bars of the gate are then unclosed and drawn out; and the wild captive darts forward directly between the two tame elephants: he can, however, only advance a little way, as the ropes securing his hind legs still continue fastened to the strongest stakes of the toil. In this situation he remains until the riders mounted on the tame elephants have drawn tight the cords which bind him to the necks of his half-reasoning conductors. During this operation he endeavours to undo with his trunk some of the knots which have been made, and often attempts to give a destructive blow to the diminutive creatures so actively engaged in confirming his captivity. But the two tame animals, who are vigilantly observant of all his motions, never fail to prevent him from doing any mischief by gently lowering his proboscis with their own: and, if he continue long refractory, they batter him with their heads, and at last produce the most obsequious submission. The nooses of the ropes are then opened, leaving his hind legs at freedom, and himself entirely disengaged from the snare. The two tame elephants press close on each side of him, and proceed in pompous procession to the garden of stalls, where they deliver up their charge, to experience another species of hardship. The marching off of this venerable trio is a sight truly magnificent, and exhibits a noble specimen of the skill of man united with the sagacity of the elephant. At the commencement of the march, the keepers strike up a rustic song, something like whistling to oxen in the plough, which adds considerable effect to the striking scene. They are seated on the necks of the tame elephants, holding short inverted spear-hooks, struck perpendicularly into their collars. When they wish to turn them, they catch one of their ears with this instrument, and, by pressing it into their skin, make them move in any direction that is required. It is likewise highly gratifying to accompany them to the grove, and to observe with what expertness and ease they are securely bound in the most superb of all stables. Making him fast there is an operation as tedious as putting on his harness before he quits the toil. While that is doing, the tame elephants continue close on each side of him, and act their part with so much judgment, that their savage brother exhibits all the gentleness of a lamb."

When the tame elephants are removed from the custody of their wild companion, who is left alone secured in the stall that had been prepared for his reception, he usually makes the most desperate efforts to escape from the yoke of slavery. Whilst he was soothed by the presence of his tame associates, he preserved a tolerable degree of tranquillity and composure; but, on their departure, the horrors of solitude and the regrets of liberty seem to overwhelm his feelings; and he rages to break his bonds in all the violence of despair. The effort is so great that it often terminates his life. But, when the first orgasm of grief and rage has subsided, the surviving captive gradually becomes more calm, till the feeling of hunger induces him to eat some of his favourite leaves of the cocoa-nut tree, which are offered for his gratification.

The treatment, which is adopted in subjugating the wild elephant, varies a little in the means of security and precaution which are used, according to the size, strength, and ferocity of the animal. But there seems no necessity in a work of this nature to try the attention of the reader by more circumstantial particulars or more minute details.

CHAP. XLIII.

Wild and Tame Animals; Tigers, Wild Boars, Porcupines, Oxen, Sheep, Horses, Birds.

AMONG some of the other wild animals of Ceylon, we find tigers, bears, buffaloes, elks, deer, hares, civet cats, jackals, and monkies of various kinds.

The tiger is not of that large species, which is denominated royal, nor is this animal so tremendous or destructive here, as in other parts of the East. The Ceylonese tiger seldom ventures to attack a man. The woods are infested by wild boars, of considerable strength and ferocity, who boldly rush upon the traveller that comes in their way. Porcupines are also common in the forests, and are hunted by dogs, who are sometimes killed by their sharp quills, when they are too impetuous in the chace.

Deer are found in great numbers, and of different kinds and sizes, and there is one species which is not larger than a common hare. Mr. Cordiner says, "That it is very beautifully made, and as perfect in form as any deer in the world; nor is it less common in Ceylon, than hares in Great Britain. The natives bring these deer alive in cages to Columbo, where one may be purchased for two shillings." It is reckoned wholesome food.

The native Singalese kill no cows nor oxen for their own consumption, and when the wants of the British troops happen to be more than the island can supply, they are imported from the coast of Coromandel. The ox of the island is of a small size, and has a hump upon the shoulders.* They are employed in the plough, for drawing loads, and for the various kinds of military transport. The country, from some unknown cause, does not seem auspicious to the general health, either of the ox or the buffalo; for we are informed that an epidemic distemper occasionally destroys half the stock of these useful animals in the space of a few months.

There appears to be a plentiful supply of pork, which is a favourite article of food with the settlers of Dutch and Portuguese origin, but the English inhabitants are said to be more fastidious with respect to this species of animal food, and not to admit it to their tables without some previous assurance of the manner in which it has been fed.

Ceylon does not possess any native breed either of sheep or horses, but sheep † are said to thrive in the province of Jaffnapatam. No horses are used for agricultural purposes, or drawing burthens. The expense which attends their maintenance in the island limits them to the use of a few of the more wealthy Europeans.‡

* Mr. Percival says, that " The oxen of Ceylon are remarkably small, and in size scarcely exceed our calves of a year old. They are as inferior in quality as in size to the cattle of Bengal and the Coromandel coast, and are to be had for about one pound five shillings sterling. The beef is sometimes however fat, and tolerably good, and forms the chief food of the European soldiers stationed on the island." Percival's Account of Ceylon, p. 285.—Mr. Cordiner says, " Beef is sold at the rate of fourpence per pound." Vol. I. p. 425.

† " The common price of a sheep at Columbo (in 1804) was one pound twelve shillings. At the same time, one could have been purchased at Jaffnapatam for one shilling." Cordiner, Vol. I. p. 426.

‡ " A small horse, of good qualities, cannot be bought under sixty pounds sterling, and a fine Arab costs at least one hundred and twenty." Cordiner.—" Two attendants are constantly attached to each horse; one of them is employed in cutting and fetching him as much grass as he requires to eat, while the other takes care of him, cleans him, feeds him, and makes him ready for his master to mount. The last attendant never quits his horse, but follows him wherever he goes, and is ready on all occasions to take charge of him. Ihave seen some of those horse keepers, as they are called,

The feathered natives of Ceylon are more numerous than the quadrupeds. Amongst these I shall simply name the peacock, the pea-fowl, common fowl, the kite, the owl, the goose, the heron, wild and tame ducks, partridges, pidgeons, various kinds of parrots, plovers, bats, vultures, wood-peckers, sparrows, snipes, swallows, fly-catchers, with thousands of crows.‡ The island is at the same time not deficient in birds that warble their native wood notes wild.

---

keep up to my horse for twenty or thirty miles together, whilst I was proceeding at the rate of five or six miles an hour." Percival, p. 284.

* The inhabitants of Ceylon appear to understand the utility of this bird better than many of our English farmers, who persecute them with unrelenting vengeance, as a thievish race and incorrigible ravagers of the grain in a new-sown field. But in Ceylon, these same feathered marauders are found extremely useful to the settlements, in removing bones, dead insects, and all sorts of putrid substances. They are accordingly never molested, either by natives or by foreigners.

CHAP. XLIV.

Snakes; instinctive Hostility of the Ichneumon. Anecdote. Alligators. Scorpions. Leeches. Ants.

SNAKES are found in great numbers. Mr. Cordiner mentions only two species which are poisonous, but other travellers make them more numerous. The former gentleman says, that during the five years in which he resided in the country, he never heard of any individual who had suffered from the bite of these venomous reptiles. Against the multitude of snakes to which the Singalese are exposed, they have a powerful auxiliary in the ichneumon, which is said to wage a perpetual war upon the whole serpent race. Though a small animal it will venture to attack even the cobra di capello, the poison of whose bite is hardly equalled in danger by that of any other snake. It is confidently asserted, but does not appear to have been correctly ascertained, that the ichneumon is acquainted with some vegetable antidote to the poison of the cobra di capello, and other snakes; and that after being bitten it has immediate recourse to this salutary herb. Mr. Percival mentions an experiment, made at Columbo, in which an ichneumon was placed in a close room, where a snake had been previously introduced. The ichneumon, instead of darting upon the snake, ran peeping about the apartment, in order to discover some means of escape. "On finding none he returned hastily to his master, and placing himself in his bosom, could not by any means be induced to quit it or face the snake." But, when both were removed out of the house to a more open space, the ichneumon instantly flew at his antagonist, whom he soon destroyed. Mr. Percival adds, that, after this achievement, the ichneumon "suddenly disappeared for a few minutes, and again returned as soon as he had found the herb and eat of it." But as Mr. Percival did not witness the latter fact, what he says is only gratuitous supposition.

All the Ceylonese rivers are infested by alligators. One of these, of the largest size, was killed and conveyed to Columbo, when the stomach, on being opened, exhibited, according to Mr. Percival, "the head and arm of a black man not completely digested."

Thunberg says, that scorpions are found in great numbers, though they are seldom productive of injury. When it rains, these animals, as well as the scolopendra morsitans, issue from their places of concealment,, "and creep in shoals into those houses, the doors of which are left open on account of the heat."

Leeches swarm in particular situations, where they are found very vexatious to the traveller on his way, or to troops on their march. They are of a reddish brown colour, about the thickness of a knitting-needle, and an inch in length. They fasten on the feet, "and can suck out the blood through two pair of cotton stockings."

In this, as in other hot countries, the inhabitants suffer more real and habitual inconvenience from the smaller insects than from the larger reptiles or quadrupeds. The ants, which swarm in the earth, and from their countless myriads seem to breed in the air, are a particular source of vexation and distress. Mr. Cordiner says, that "many millions of the common red ant inhabit every house in Ceylon. They lodge within the walls, and are seen in every corner where any species of food is to be procured. If a bit of sugar, or any other eatable article, is dropped on the floor, it is almost instantly covered with them." Every species of food must be secured with the nicest precaution from the attacks of this domestic foe. If a loaf of bread be carelessly laid only for a few minutes, the heart of it will be found full of them. To protect the bread from their incursions, it must be placed on a stand, in some dish filled with water. The pillars of bedsteads are, for the same reason, placed on an elevation, in vessels of a particular construction, which are filled with water, in order to keep off the approach of the insidious enemy. The meat is sometimes suspended in a sieve, by a rope rubbed over with tar, which these vermin will not venture to touch.

It seems a fortunate circumstance, that one species of the ant is in a state of constant hostility with another. Two species therefore cannot exist together, or co-operate in any system of offensive warfare, upon the domestic comfort of mankind. Besides the ants, which I have mentioned, there are numerous hosts of insects of other kinds, which it would be superfluous to enumerate in a sketch of this kind, which does not profess to give more than a few detached features of the natural history of the country.

CHAP. XLV.

Precious Stones. Articles of ancient Import and Export.

THOUGH the island is supplied with various kinds of salt and of fresh water fish, there are none which merit a particular description, except perhaps the pearl-oyster, with the mode in which it is obtained. Of this I reserve the account till I come to some topographical details respecting a few of the towns and forts upon the coast.

The mountains of Ceylon probably contain a variety of mineral treasures, which it is reserved for the future researches of philosophy, or of avarice, to disclose. Among the precious stones of the island, the emerald, with the cat's-eye, are held in the highest estimation. "Cat's-eye is the name given to a very hard stone, which approaches more or less to a white or green, and is semediaphanous, with a streak of the breadth of a line in the middle, which streak is much whiter than the stone itself, and throws its light to whatever side soever this is turned. In this respect therefore it resembles a cat's-eye, whence it derives its name." Thunberg, to whom I am indebted for this description, says, that the largest specimen which he saw of this species of stone was of the size of a hazel nut. Mr. Cordiner tells us, that a perfect cat's-eye of this size is worth 1500 rix-dollars of Ceylon currency, or £150 sterling. Rubies, for which Ceylon was renowned at a very early period, are seldom found at present of any considerable size; and are not often larger than particles of gravel, or grains of barley. The Indians speak of them as more or less ripe, which means more or less high-coloured. In proportion as the ruby is of a deeper red it is more transparent, and consequently of greater value. The Moors, according to Thunberg, say, that they approach in hardness nearest to the diamond.

The Moors are here the chief dealers in precious stones, both in their rough and in their polished state; but they are said to be very dexterous in imposing counterfeit for genuine gems. The precious stones of Ceylon are found more especially in the region of Matura. Sometimes they are discovered on the surface of the earth, and in other places at the depth of from one, two, or three, to twenty or more feet.

The following articles of commerce were in ancient times imported into Ceylon, either to be purchased by foreign merchants, who resorted thither as to one of the great marts or emporiums of the East; or to be exchanged on the spot, for the different products of the island. Different coloured cloths, velvets, silks, of several sorts; red caps, porcelain, drugs of various kinds, amfioen or opium, camphor, spicery, steel, radix, China, tobacco, cotton, musk, eagle wood, called by the Portuguese pao d'aquila; saltpetre, sulphur, looking-glasses, glass bottles, &c.

The commodities of Ceylon, which constituted her principal means of exchange, were cinnamon, pepper, cardamoms, elephants, and elephant's teeth, ebony wood, red sandal wood, antimony, salt, rice, areca nuts, shells, pearls, precious stones of various kinds, as rubies, sapphires, emeralds, topazes, garnets, cat's-eyes, and crystals of many different species.

CHAP. XLVI.

Topographical Notices. Point de Galle. Road to Matura. Temple of Boodh. Province of Matura; Town and Fort. Dondra Head. Magnificent Ruins of a Hindoo Temple. Tengalle. Province of Mahagampattoe. Batticalo. A Singalese School.

I SHALL now exhibit a few characteristic notices of some of the principal places upon the coast, commencing with Point de Galle, at the southern extremity of the island.

Point de Galle is situated on a low rocky promontory, and backed by several ranges of hills, rising above one another, and covered with wood. Forests of cocoa trees abound every where in the vicinity. The fort, in which most of the Europeans reside, is more than a mile in circumference, and contains a variety of large and commodious habitations. Though it is situated within less than six degrees of the equator, the temperature is frequently as low as 72° of Fahrenheit's thermometer, and never above 86°. Hence Europeans are much less incommoded by the heat than in other parts of India. There is a manufacture of tortoise-shell at this place, and ropes are formed from the exterior fibrous covering of the cocoa-nut. Vast quantities of white coral are found along the coast. The disease termed elephantiasis is said to prevail a good deal amongst the poor residents of Point de Galle, and is ascribed to bad water and insufficient nourishment. The leg is the part affected by the disease, and this is sometimes swelled to four times its natural size from the knee to the ancle; but the patient often lives many years under its operation. Mr. Percival reckons Point de Galle about sixty miles from Columbo, and Mr. Cordiner states it to be seventy-eight. The road runs, for the most part, close to the shore; and the larger portion of the way is shaded by cocoa-nut and other trees, which reach the margin of the sea, and hang over the waves.

The road from Point de Galle to Matura, which is a distance of thirty miles, runs, for a large part of the way, through a forest of cocoa trees, and compensates for the want of extensive prospect by continuity of verdure and depth of shade. At intervals, where the road opens, hills are seen in the vicinity on the left, covered with lofty trees, rising from a mass of impenetrable brushwood. About half way between Point de Galle and Matura, and close to Belligam, on the summit of a hill, is a temple of Boodh, called Agrabuddhaganni. Here is a colossal statue of this venerable personage, in a recumbent posture. The walls of the temple are covered with paintings representing portions of the real or fabulous history of the country.

The picturesque beauties of the province of Matura may be readily conjectured from the following descriptive passage, which is extracted from the elegant work of Mr. Cordiner. "Sometimes venerable and majestic trees formed a shade over our heads; sometimes we travelled amidst flowering shrubs; sometimes through cultivated meadows and fields of smiling corn. Nature breathes around an eternal spring; flower blossoms and fruits adorn the woods at all seasons. A vast wilderness of noble plants rises in ten thousand beautiful landscapes, displaying a majesty and richness of scenery, and raising emotions of delight and admiration which cannot easily be described."*

Matura stands at a short distance from the sea, on the banks of the Neel-ganga, or Blue River. There is a square of good houses in the centre of the fort; and a street, which is inhabited by families of Dutch

* Cordiner, Vol. I. p. 187.

origin, extends along the banks of the river towards the sea. Landscapes of great beauty and luxuriance approach the vicinity of Matura. Game, according to Mr. Percival,* is plentiful in this place; and the surrounding country abounds with elephants, of which animals no less than 170 were caught in an elephant hunt in 1797.

Dondra Head, which forms the extreme point of the island towards the south, is a low strip of land, three miles from Matura, and covered with cocoa-nut trees. Here are seen the ruins of a Hindoo temple of great extent and magnificence. Two hundred of the columns are said by Mr. Cordiner to be still standing; some of which have curved bases and capitals, whilst others are kept in their original rough state. Near these ruins is a temple of Boodh, of more recent construction and smaller size, but which is said to possess such peculiar sanctity in the opinions of the Singalese, that an oath taken in this sanctuary is seldom violated.

The village of Tengalle, which is twenty-four miles distant from Matura, is principally inhabited by fishermen. It is embosomed in wood, and surrounded by hills on the land side. The road from Matura to Dickwell runs through a beautiful and well-peopled country; and thence to Tengalle the land is hilly, and covered with jungle, but not without many intervening spots of cultivated ground.

The province of Mahagampattoe, between Tengalle and Batticalo, is one of the wildest and least-cultivated districts; but those, by whom it has been traversed, describe it as one of the richest and most beautiful portions of the island. Part of the tract still exhibits vestiges of a higher degree of cultivation in a former period. It is at present very much infested by elephants, bears, leopards, and other wild animals, which add to the difficulties and insecurity of the way. Mr.

* P. 131.

Reeder, who travelled in 1801 from Batticalo to Tengalle, and from whose journal extracts are given in Mr. Cordiner's Tour, represents the country between Wammiemoodo and Karengekottotivo, as " charming beyond description. It reminded me," says he, " of the Capino at Florence, only that in place of pheasants, which are very numerous there, we have here peacocks and other beautiful birds crossing us in all directions. I walked with my gun for a quarter of an hour, and shot two, the tail of one of which measures one yard and a half in length. Had I been anxious to destroy them, I might with ease have killed fifty; but they are too valuable, being great enemies to the snakes, which abound in this part of the country. The other parts of the island which I have seen are not to be compared to the country between Batticalo and this place. The villages are neat and clean, and the people seem comfortable and happy: they mentioned never having seen a white man pass this road before." When Mr. Reeder arrived at Karengekottotivo, he says that the head man of the place came out to meet him with tom toms, &c. and that white calico was spread for him to walk upon, for about fifty yards, to the next " house, which was completely lined with cloth of a similar nature. Good fowls, milk, fruit, &c. were furnished me," says Mr. Reeder, " and I enjoyed a pleasant repast. I was treated in the same hospitable manner through the whole of the Batticalo district, and I shall ever hold these innocent people in the most friendly remembrance."

There is a small fort in the Island of Batticalo, with a little village near the walls. The island itself is about three miles and a half in circumference; Hindoos and Mahometans constitute the mass of the inhabitants; and the Malabar is the language in general use. The people here, as in other parts, wear gold rings of an enormous size. They are said often to be four inches in diameter. In order to accomodate their ears to these large appendages, they are bored at a very early period; and the orifice in the flap of the ear is enlarged by artificial means till it is dilated to the requisite dimensions. The necessaries of life may be procured at a cheaper rate at Batticalo and in the vicinity than in any other part of the island. Game is to be had in abundance; and Mr. Cordiner mentions fish to be so cheap, that a halfpenny would purchase enough to dine two hard-working men. The eye is, at the same time, highly gratified by the rich rural scenery with which this spot is adorned; where we find delicious shades well fitted to excite devotional musing, and to kindle those affections of the heart, which are inspired by the beauties of creation, when associated with the benevolence of the Creator.

Mr. Cordiner has given a pleasing account of a Singalese school, which is established on the main land, about two English miles from the Island of Batticalo. "The appearance of the children," says Mr. Cordiner, "was extremely gratifying, and the deportment of a teacher, only fifteen years of age, particularly interesting. His complexion was fair, and his manners denoted mild and amiable dispositions. The scholars are smart and tractable, displaying sweet serenity in their countenances. Their hair is nicely combed, plaited, and fixed in a knot, resembling a cockade with a silver pin in it; sometimes on the right, and sometimes on the left side of the head. A little thin hair is combed down upon the face, and at the back of the neck the hair is cropped quite close. The costume is handsome and becoming; but when the youth arrives at the age of puberty, the knot is tied behind, and all its elegance disappears. The children of the first class of inhabitants wear gold rings about their necks, legs, and arms, but no other articles of dress, excepting a piece of printed muslin about the waist. They sit upon the ground on mats, with their legs under them, seemingly very attentive to their tasks, which they read and repeat with as much vociferation as possible. The music of their voices resembles, in some degree, the quick notes of a harpsichord. They learn the letters in the same manner as the Singalese, and all the other nations of India, by writing them in sand upon the floor, or a stone bench, at the same time singing their names and the characteristics of their formation: as if in writing the letter A they were to say A is one line up, another down, and one across. Boys of five years of age write after this method with great facility and neatness. Those more advanced write, or engrave with a stylus, or piece of pointed steel fixed in a brass handle, on slips of tallipot, or Palmyra leaves, which are thicker than parchment, and of a nature no less durable. When the writing is finished, they sometimes rub over the leaf with a black juice, which fills up the characters, making them look bright and beautiful."*

The inlet of the sea, in which the Island of Batticalo is situated, runs thirty miles into the country, and contains several other islands of a similar size. The adjacent main land is level to some distance from the shore, where it gradually rises into a mountainous ridge of diversified forms and loftiest view.

* Cordiner, Vol. I. p. 258—9.

CHAP. XLVII.

Trincomalee; inestimable Advantages of its Harbour; Fort and surrounding Scenery. Village of Moletive. Jaffnapatam; the Fort, Town, and Country. Inhabitants. Vestiges of the Religious Zeal of the Portuguese. Curious Form of Swearing in a Criminal Process. Reflections.

THE harbour of Trincomalee is what gives a singular value to the possession of this island. The possession of this harbour is indeed of such importance, that it facilitates, if it does not ensure the command of the ocean in that part of the world. During the violence of the monsoons, no vessel can ride in safety on any part of the coast of Choromandel, or of Malabar. But this incomparable harbour offers a station of security at all times of the year, for any number of ships and of any size. It is so deep and spacious, that five hundred ships may lie at anchor in it, without any inconvenience. Though the water is deep, it is as transparent as glass, and seldom exhibits an agitated surface.

Its general tranquillity gives it the appearance of a lake, and this similitude is increased by the surrounding scenery, which consists of mountains of various forms, and shaded with foliage of perpetual green.

The proximity of Trincomalee to all the English settlements in the bay of Bengal, renders it of inestimable value to this country; and indeed if, in the revolutions of human affairs, the power of Great Britain should be annihilated on the peninsula of Hindoostan, the possession of Ceylon would of itself be sufficient to perpetuate her naval ascendant, and her commercial superiority in the East. Without the territorial dominion of India, Great Britain may safely defy every maritime or commercial rival in that part of the world, as long as this island continues one of the appendages of her crown.

Trincomalee is situated in 8° 28′ north latitude, and in 81° 28′ east longitude. The walls embrace a circumference of about three miles,* and enclose a hill immediately over the sea, which, according to Mr. Percival, is covered with thick jungle, and affords a shelter to wild deer and other game. Most of the houses are built on the lower ground, close to the landing place. Fort Ostenburgh, which protects the mouth of the harbour, is three miles to the west of Trincomalee, and was originally constructed by the Portuguese out of the ruins of a pagoda of great celebrity. It is at present strongly fortified, and indeed there is no military post in Ceylon, which is capable of being rendered so impregnable as Trincomalee.

The soil in the neighbourhood of Trincomalee is more sterile than in other parts of the island, but its productive powers have not been brought to the test of diligent cultivation. And, whatever may be its actual fertility, it seems agreed, that in beauty of scenery it is unrivalled by any of the other settlements. Since this important place has been in the possession of the English, it has been rendered more healthy by clearing the wood and draining the marshes in the immediate vicinity.

The small village of Moletive is situated about half way between Trincomalee and Jaffnapatam. The road from Trincomalee runs nearly in a line with the shore, and is in general wild, varied, and beautiful. The village of Moletive lies about a quarter of a mile from the sea. It contains some good houses, which are built of stone. The adjacent country exhibits a variegated picture of corn

* Percival, p. 41.

fields, cottages, trees, and meadows, along with features of a bolder and more rugged kind. Cattle and poultry are cheap; and the country furnishes an abundance of venison, as there are deer of three or four different species.

Jaffnapatam is situated on a neck of land towards the northern extremity of the island. Its latitude is 9° 47′ north, and the longitude 80° 9′ east. The fortress is an excellent structure. There is a square in the centre, the sides of which are occupied by the residence of the governor, by comfortable houses, which are tenanted by the officers, by barracks for the soldiers, and by one of the best churches in Ceylon. A street, which is inhabited by artificers and persons of inferior condition, runs at the back of one of the sides of the square. The pettah or town without the walls is large and populous. The principal street passes through the centre and is shaded by lofty trees. The houses, which are only one story high, with verandahs, are neat buildings, perfectly white on the outside, and covered with red pantiles on the top. The country in the vicinity is very fertile and highly cultivated, and the markets are well supplied with fruit, vegetables, game, and poultry. Though the soil is flat, the sensation of weariness or monotony is prevented by the varied luxuriance of vegetable life which it displays. The air is pure, and the temperature moderated by the vicinity of the sea. A constant intercourse is maintained with the coast of India, a passage to which from Point Pedro, at the northern extremity of the island, occupies only a few hours.

All the native inhabitants pass under the denomination of Malabars, one half of whom are nominally Christians, with a small portion of Mahometans. The most expert artificers are said to be found amongst those of the natives, who were originally of Portuguese extraction. The province of Jaffnapatam bears ample testimony to the religious ardour, which once animated the Portuguese when they were masters of the coast; for it exhibits the vestiges of no less than thirty-two churches, where the Romish religion was once celebrated. During the sway of the Portuguese in this island more attention was paid to religion than to trade; and, during that of the Dutch, more attention was paid to trade than to religion. Let us hope that the English will manifest a reasonable zeal for both.

The Portuguese were more tolerant in religion than the Dutch, but the Dutch were less tolerant than they ought. Under the mild dominion of the English, all religions at present enjoy the most perfect toleration.

Whilst Mr. Cordiner was at Jaffnapatam, he witnessed the administration of an oath, in a criminal process, to some natives of the place.* The ceremony was performed in the porch of a Hindoo temple. Some near relative was with each of the witnesses. Both the relation and the witness received from the officiating priest a small portion of consecrated ashes, which they rubbed upon the forehead, chest, and arms. " The relation then stretched himself upon the floor, with his face touching the ground. The person sworn repeated the words of the obligation, and stepped over him. If, after this ceremony, they should be guilty of perjury, they believe that some calamity will befal, either themselves or their relation. They are generally called upon by the adverse party to produce the person who is most dear to them, which they sometimes do with visible reluctance; but the ceremony is so affecting and impressive, that they seldom go through it, without a determination to speak the truth." It is a depressing consideration for the lover of his species, that, in order to induce people to speak truth, it should be necessary to have recourse to ceremonies, which are entirely independent of the moral obligation. But what motive ought to operate on the

* Vol. I. p. 329.

mind with more force than the obligation itself, or why should some exterior ceremony have more efficacy than the sanctity of truth? The serious and impressive ceremonial, with which all nations, whether more or less civilized, have associated the administration of an oath, whilst it shews the inestimable importance of truth, exhibits, at the same time, a melancholy proof of the proneness which there is in men to tell lies in questions, in which the heart is exposed to the sway of private interest.

CHAP. XLVIII.

Bay of Condatchy. Great Assemblage of Persons for the Pearl Fishery. Banks where the Oysters are found. Season of the Fishery. Simultaneous Departure of the Boats. Mode of Diving. Time which the Divers remain under Water. Produce of the Pearl Oyster. Classification of Pearls. Payment of the Divers; their Fondness for the Occupation. Forms of Conjuration to dissipate the Apprehension of the Shark. Dexterity of the Conjurors in maintaining the Reputation of their Art. Variegated Spectacle during the Fishery.

DURING the season of the pearl fishery, the bay of Condatchy is crowded with small vessels; and astonishing multitudes are seen assembled on the beach from all parts of India. During their stay they reside in temporary huts formed of sticks, mats, pieces of cloth, rice-straw, and Palmyra leaves. The huts are ranged in regular streets, and contain thousands of busy and animated inhabitants.

The banks, where the pearl oysters are found, are situated about fifteen miles from the shore, and occupy a considerable extent. These banks are divided into several portions, only one of which is fished in one season, in order to afford time for the oysters to attain a proper growth. The oysters are supposed to attain their maturity in seven years, when they sicken and die.

The season for the fishery commences in February, and ends in April; but various interruptions are occasioned by bad weather, and by the holidays of the different sects and nations, by whom it is frequented.

On Sunday all the divers, and others who are Christians, attend the Romish chapel at Aripo.

All the boats depart and return at a given signal. About midnight the whole fleet sails with the breeze which blows from the shore; and, after reaching their destined station, they cast anchor and await the dawn. The diving commences between six and seven o'clock in the morning. Each boat contains twenty men, besides the pilot, and two other persons. Of the twenty men, ten are employed in diving, whilst the rest assist them to re-ascend. Of the ten divers, five alternately relieve each other in the laborious operation. Each diver puts one of his feet into a loop, from which a heavy stone is suspended, in order to accelerate his descent; and he places his other foot in a basket of net-work suspended from the boat by a rope. When he reaches the bottom he disengages his foot from the stone, which is immediately drawn up. The diver now keeping himself as much as possible upon his face, puts every thing he can collect into his basket; and, when he is ready to re-ascend, he gives a signal, by jerking the rope, which is hauled up without delay. The blood sometimes gushes from the nose and ears of the diver after his emersion from the deep. The divers, according to the account of Mr. Cordiner, remain under water from one to one and a half, or two minutes. But Mr. Percival says,* that instances are known of persons who would remain under water for four or five minutes; and that, in 1797, a diver from Anjango actually remained "full six minutes" under water.

The diving continues for five or six hours; and on those days, on which three hundred boats are employed, the ear of the spectator is forcibly struck by the perpetual plunging in the deep. When the sea-breeze commences, a signal is given for the diving to cease; and the boats make for the shore, which they generally reach between four and five in the afternoon.

* P. 65.

The pearls are commonly found in the most fleshy part of the oyster near the hinge. One oyster generally contains several pearls; but pearls of a large size are of rare occurrence. Mr. Cordiner once saw the produce of 17,000 oysters, which weighed only three-quarters of a pound, and were contained in a vessel smaller than a common soup-plate. Out of that quantity not two perfect pearls were found of the first or second classes of size. The pearls are sorted according to their sizes by being put into perforated saucers or cullenders, which are denominated according to the number of holes they contain, as 20, 30, 50, 80, 100, 200, 400, 600, 800, and 1000; and, of course, only the largest pearls remain in the cullenders with the small numbers. The cullenders from number 100 to 1000 are denominated of the second order. The estimation of the pearl, however, depends not only upon the size, but upon the shape, colour, and other qualities.* The pearls which pass through the cullender which has 1000 perforations, are called seed-pearls, from their diminutive size.

The divers are usually paid by a certain proportion of the oysters which they procure; and, though this proportion is liable to several deductions, it does not appear to be an unprofitable employment, as every labourer in this branch of industry is said, at the end of the season, to have forty or fifty pagodas to carry home to his family. The diving itself does not excite the repugnance of those who are engaged in it, but

* Mr. Cordiner says, "A handsome necklace of pearls, smaller than a large pea, costs from one hundred and seventy to three hundred pounds sterling. But a very pretty necklace of pearls, about the size of a pepper-corn, may be procured for fifteen pounds. The former pearls sell at one guinea each, and the latter at eighteen pence. When the pearls dwindle to the size of small shot, they are sold at a very trifling price." Vol. II. p. 66.—"At the fishery the pearls of different sizes are sold together in a mass at two hundred pagodas (or eighty pounds sterling) per pound." In the year 1804 the fishery was let by the governor, for the season, to a native of Jaffnapatam. He was to fish for thirty days with 150 boats for the sum of 300,000 Porto Novo pagodas, or £120,000 sterling. But as the season proved a bad one, the government remitted about one third part of this sum; and, notwithstanding this deduction, the contractor is said to have been a loser by the bargain. The number of oysters brought on shore during this season did not average more than 3000 each boat.

is regarded rather as an agreeable pastime than an unpleasant toil. It seems, indeed, to operate upon the mind by the perpetual excitement of hope; and, though it is a sort of lottery, yet few lotteries are associated with so many probabilities of ultimate advantage. The only cause of painful apprehension to the divers seems to arise from the dread of the shark; but an efficacious remedy for this sensation has been found in the superstition of the people. Two conjurers are constantly employed for the purpose, whose charms are supposed to be capable of taming the voracious monsters of the deep. One of these dealers in sorcery always accompanies the fleet, whilst another remains on shore to mutter his incantations and perform his magic ceremonies. For this purpose, according to the account of Mr. Cordiner, which is somewhat different from that of Mr. Percival, "he is stripped naked, and shut up in a room, where no person sees him from the period of the sailing of the boats until their return. He has before him a brass basin full of water, containing one male and one female fish made of silver. If any accident should happen from a shark at sea, it is believed that one of these fishes is seen to bite the other."*

Mr. Percival says that, during the time of the fishery, the conjurers "stand on the shore from the morning till the boats return in the afternoon, all the while muttering and mumbling prayers, distorting their bodies into various strange attitudes, and performing ceremonies, to which no one can attach any meaning. All this while it is necessary for them to abstain from food or drink, otherwise their prayers would be of no avail. These acts of abstinence, however, they sometimes dispense with, and regale themselves with toddy till they are no longer able to stand at their devotions."†

As these conjurers are in high repute, and great faith is placed in the potency of their incantations, they are liberally rewarded by the credu-

* Cordiner, Vol. II. p. 52. † Percival, p. 66—7.

lity of their votaries; and, as accidents appear very seldom to happen, they readily manage to maintain their credit unimpaired. But on one occasion, since the island has been occupied by the British, one of the divers had his leg bitten off by a shark. The head-conjurer was of course called to account for this great deficiency in his art; but he saved the honour of his profession by replying, that an old witch, who owed him a grudge, had secretly come over from the coast of Malabar, and counteracted the force of his spells; but that, now he was aware of the hostile intrusion, he would shew the superiority of his art, by so binding up the mouths of the sharks, that they should do no more mischief during that season. And, as no more mischief happened to ensue, the reputation of the conjurer, instead of being impaired, was augmented in renown.*

During the season of the fishery, the bay of Condatchy exhibits a most interesting spectacle. At that period this barren spot displays a variegated assemblage of persons of different nations, religions, and manners, and from the most remote regions. It exhibits the commercial bustle of a great mart, and all the combined amusements of a fair on the largest scale. Here are artificers and traders of every description, mingled with jugglers, tumblers, female dancers, mendicants, sharpers, and pilferers of every class, form, and hue.

* Asiatic Annual Register for 1800, p. 122. Percival, p. 68.

CHAP. XLIX.

Country between Aripo and Putlam; between Putlam and Chilauw; Chilauw and Negumbo. Town of Negumbo; Situation; Cinnamon Gardens. Road to Columbo; Beauty of the Scenery. Rest-House at Jaellé.

THE country between Aripo and Putlam offers some beautiful views, but few traces of cultivation. The greater part of the road is bounded on both sides by dense and impenetrable woods, which form the undisturbed domain of wild beasts and reptiles, exempted from the intrusion of man. At Putlam, which is a village of considerable traffic, the Singalese barter areka nuts, cardamoms, black pepper, and coffee, for calicoes, muslins, salt, and dried fish. The country from Putlam to Chilauw is more open than that between Aripo and Putlam, but displaying little more cultivation. Between Chilauw and Negumbo the landscape assumes a more smiling and cultivated aspect, and is particularly grateful to the traveller who has lately passed through nothing but wilds and woods.

Negumbo is a large and populous town on the coast, twenty-four miles from Columbo, in a beautiful and healthy situation. About two miles north of Negumbo the soil becomes a rich mould, and the surface of the country displays the highest degree of vegetable luxuriance. An avenue, cut through groves of cocoas, conducts to the centre of a neat, large, populous town, diversified by the shade of intervening trees.

Areka nuts, betel, coffee, and black pepper, flourish in the neighbourhood; and a considerable trade is carried on with the interior of the

Candian territory. Fish, which are caught here in abundance, are a principal article of traffic. There is an inland navigation to Columbo, by lakes, rivers, and canals. The soil of Negumbo appears to be as favourable to the growth of cinnamon as any part of the island, nor is the quality at all inferior to that of Columbo. During Mr. North's beneficent administration, he formed some new cinnamon gardens* at Negumbo, which it was supposed would in time yield a sufficient quantity for the British market; so that the gardens at Columbo might be appropriated to other purposes.

The way from Negumbo to Columbo leads through scenes of the most delicious vegetation. It may indeed be truly called a garden of beauty and delight, where Nature seems to have lavished her captivating hues, and to have combined all her stores of gratification. Here she is seen to revel in all her prodigality of ornament, and to wanton in a boundless variety of trees and shrubs, fruits and flowers. I cannot here refrain from quoting Mr. Cordiner's description of this enchanting way:— "The jack, the bread-fruit, the jamboo, and the cashew-tree, weave their spreading branches into an agreeable shade, amidst the stems of the areka and the cocoa-nut. The black pepper and betel plants creep up the sides of the lofty trunks: coffee, cinnamon, and an immense variety of flowering shrubs, fill the intermediate spaces; and the mass of charming foliage is blended together with a degree of richness that beggars the powers of description. All the beautiful productions of the island are concentrated in one exuberant spot."†

At Jaellé, which is half way between Negumbo and Columbo, there is a neat and well-built rest-house, where travellers may regale themselves at a very cheap rate, with some of the most delicious fruits which India can boast. "Pine apples," says Mr. Cordiner, "are purchased at the rate of two for three halfpence, pumplenoses (the shaddock of the West

* Lord Valentia's Travels, Vol. I. p. 312.

† Cordiner, Vol. I. 345.

Indies) from threepence to fourpence a piece, oranges fourpence per dozen, jacks (the largest species of artocarpus, or bread-fruit) fourpence, and all other productions of the soil at corresponding prices." These prices, low as they may seem, were much lower before the arrival of the British in the island.

The traveller crosses the Calany-ganga river at the distance of three miles from Columbo, and in the intermediate way the country presents all the cheering features of industry and opulence.

CHAP. L.

Columbo. The Fort; Houses; Harbour. Healthiness of the Climate. The Pettah and Suburbs. The Lake. Slave Island. Adjacent Country.

COLUMBO, the capital of the British settlements in Ceylon, lies in 7° north latitude, and 79° 48′ longitude east of Greenwich. The fort is situated on a small projection of land, which is washed by the sea for about two thirds of its extent. The rest is bordered by a lake of fresh water, except in two places, where narrow slips of land form a connexion between the country and the fort. The fort itself is a mile and a quarter in circumference. The interior, which forms the principal residence of the Europeans, contains broad, straight and regular streets, intersecting each other at right angles, and planted on each side by double rows of the portia or tulip tree, which afford an agreeable shade and bear a yellow flower.

Before each house is a large open space or verandahs, covered with a sloping roof at top, and supported on pillars.* The houses are, in general, constructed with a hall or occasional sitting room in the front, and a chamber on each side. Another room at the back extends the whole length of the front, and varies from forty to one hundred feet. From the centre of the long room a back verandah projects, from which the two ranges of offices, or buildings for other purposes, run at right angles. When the English first obtained possession of Columbo in 1796,

* "Here," says Mr. Percival, p. 103, "it is customary to see the people walking about or lolling in a chair, with their feet supported against the railing, which is placed along the pillars, to the height of three or four feet."

all the houses had glass windows, but venetian blinds have since been generally substituted in their stead, which are more agreeable and better adapted to the climate. The houses have seldom more than one floor, but there are a few with two stories, which are highly prized for the fine prospects they command. Every house has a well of brackish water; but all the water which is fit to drink is brought from springs about a mile from the town, and conveyed by bullocks in leathern bags.*

The harbour of Columbo is an open road, which affords a safe anchorage for ships only for about six months in the year, or from the beginning

* When Mr. Percival was at Columbo, he complains that the roofs were so badly tiled, as to admit water to such a degree, as to render it difficult for an individual in the rainy season to find a dry place on which to lay his head. He mentions, that the mischief was partly occasioned by crows picking up bones, &c. in the streets, carrying them to the tops of the houses, and there fighting for the plunder till the tiles were broken or displaced in the fray. Monkies also are said by the above author to assist in the work of demolition. "While I was at Columbo," says Mr. Percival, "I recollect a very mischievous monkey, who used to run wild about the fort, and was so very cunning, that it was impossible to catch him. One day he suddenly made his entrance into my apartment, carried off a loaf of bread from my table, and made his escape. I immediately gave the alarm to an officer I observed standing at the next door; upon which, he ran in to secure his own breakfast; but, to his great mortification, found that the monkey had been before-hand with him, and was already scrambling up to the roof of the houses, with a loaf in each paw. Next day the same monkey snatched off a very fine parrot before the gentleman's face to whom it belonged, tore it to pieces, and then held it out to the gentleman, with many expressions of satisfaction and triumph at the exploit." Thunberg mentions an ape, that is a native of the island and called Rollewai, which he says that many Singalese kept tame in their houses. "When this ape," says the traveller just mentioned, "sees any of his acquaintance, he directly comes jumping to him, fawns upon him, grins, and with a peculiar kind of cry testifies his joy. He is of a very friendly and gentle nature, and is very loth to bite any one, unless he is immoderately irritated. If any one kisses and caresses a child, he seeks to do the same; if you beat a child, he rears himself up upon his hind legs, grins and howls in a wretched manner, and, if let loose, will attack the party that beats the child. He leaps faster than he runs, because his hind legs are longer. He eats fruit of every kind; as for instance, cocoanuts, apples, pears, greens, potatoes, bread, &c. He is very delicate and tender with respect to his tail, which is longer than his body. In size, he is nearly upon a par with the Lemur Catta, or somewhat larger." This ape appears to be very sensitive of cold, and to die upon coming into a more rigorous climate.

of October to the end of March. The west wind blows from the ocean during the other six months with such violence, as to render all intercourse with Columbo by sea impracticable during half the year. During this period, this part of the island is exposed to torrents of rain, to dreadful storms of thunder and lightning, and to all the fury of the winds. In the rainy season, which is of longer duration in Ceylon, than on the coast of Malabar or Choromandel, the Singalese are more particularly subject to a disorder, to which they give the name of berry-berry, a species of dropsy of the most fatal kind.* It appears to proceed from a low, meagre diet, bad water, and a climate perpetually damp. Mr. Cordiner, however, bears strong testimony to the healthiness of Columbo. He says, "That no climate in the world is more salubrious, and that a person, who remains within doors while the sun is powerful, never wishes to experience one more temperate. During five years residence," he continues, "I rarely heard of any person being sick, unless those, whose illness was caught in the interior of the country. Before the commencement of hostilities with the King of Candy in 1803, a fnneral was not a common occurrence at Columbo, and out of a thousand British soldiers, it often happened, that one man was not lost in the space of two months. The air is, at all times, pure and healthy, and its temperature uncommonly uniform. Farenheit's thermometer usually fluctuates in the shade about the point of 80°. It seldom ranges more than five degrees in a day, and only thirteen during the whole

* This disorder, according to Mr. Cordiner, "First became known to the English surgeons in Ceylon, by breaking out in a regiment of Madras native infantry, which had served several years in the island. It raged amongst them with great fury, carrying off one half of their number, and continued its ravages until the remainder were transported to the coast of Choromandel, where change of air and a more generous diet contributed to their recovery. Rice was almost their only food in Ceylon, mutton being sold there at so extravagant a price, that they could not afford to purchase it; beef forbidden by their religion; and the curry stuffs, to which they had been accustomed, not being procurable for money." Cordiner, Vol. I. p. 183.—Mr. Percival says, p. 108, "that the berry-berry swells the body and legs of the patient to an enormous size, and generally carries him off in twenty-four hours."

year, 86° being the highest and 73° the lowest, at which it has been seen in any season." *

The pettah, or town without the fort, is clean, regular, and larger than that within. It consists of five streets parallel to each other, and each of half a mile in length. These streets are intersected by the same number at right angles. The fronts of the houses are shaded by virandahs, but they want the dense foliage of the portia, which serves to shelter the houses within the fort from the scorching rays of the sun. Many straggling streets, containing houses of smaller dimensions, are built beyond the pettah, and run for several miles into the country. The fort is principally occupied by the English; the pettah by the Dutch and Portuguese; and the ramifications of the suburbs by native Singalese. Mr. Cordiner computes the collective number of inhabitants of the fort, town, and suburbs, of Columbo, at more than 50,000.

The lake which runs at the back of the fort, and forms a circuit of several miles, is divided by a tongue of land, which was denominated Slave Island, from the use to which it was applied by the Dutch. It is now occupied by a mud village, a bazar, a parade, and two gentlemen's seats. The rest is covered with a dark grove of cocoa-nut trees. This slip of land, after crossing the lake, disappears in the wide expanse of the cinnamon plantations, which make a circumference of more than twelve miles.

The neighbourhood of Columbo abounds with beautifully-diversified rides. The scenery is varied by the gentle eminences which are scattered about the plain, and delight is infused by the sight of its exuberant vegetation. But, even in the neighbourhood of this populous town, the wild predominates over the cultivated. The surface is, for the greater part, covered with impenetrable brush-wood; above which trees of an-

* Vol. I. p. 62.

cient growth cast a deeper shade. Some of the most striking and picturesque views are visible from the fort, where Adam's Peak towers into conspicuous notice in the back ground; while, in the more immediate vicinity, the eye is gratified by the sight of thick groves of cocoa-nut and other trees, interspersed with villas and country-seats, with the lake beneath, fringed with shade, and coming close up to the glacis of the fort.*

* The expense of living in Ceylon is represented to be as great as it is in any of the settlements on the continent of India. The expense of servants is much greater, as most of the persons of that description have been brought from the continent. But the native inhabitants of the island will, no doubt, in time be trained to all kinds of domestic employments, which will so far be productive of less expensive establishments. "No bachelor," says Mr. Cordiner, "can keep house at Columbo comfortably, for less than £800 a year: and he may live at Madras for the same sum. A captain, who receives about £500 per annum, finds it extremely difficult to live upon his pay, notwithstanding the benefit of a mess; and a subaltern, who draws about £300, must practise rigid economy to avoid running in debt. Great loads of meat appear upon the tables of the English inhabitants in Ceylon, as well as of those of all parts of India: and this custom proceeds from the economy of housekeeping being entirely trusted to native servants, who estimate the respectability of a dinner by the quantity and largeness of the dishes that are crowded on the board. In houses, where an English lady or gentleman pays any attention to domestic matters, the case is different, and the superior comfort of their living is always strikingly observed. The only advantage which the tables of Europeans possess over those of the same rank in the united kingdom, is the profusion of elegant fruits, which, every day of the year, furnishes a desert. But the relish for those luxuries is soon lost; and an English inhabitant of Ceylon looks with as much indifference on pine apples and oranges, as John Bull does upon hard biscuit. The dainties of the table in greatest estimation there are all imported from London; such as hams, cheese, pickles, and preserves. Claret, imported from England, is generally sold at four pounds per dozen, and is the wine which is most esteemed. That which comes direct from Bourdeaux is sold at thirty-six shillings, and is a purer but weaker wine. Madeira may be purchased at the last-mentioned price. English ale is also a very favourite beverage. The usual mode of living is to rise at day-break, ride for an hour or two in the country, dress, or perhaps bathe, on returning; breakfast at half-past seven o'clock, commence business at nine, and conclude at four. Lounging and dressing fill up the time until half-past five, which is the hour of another ride. Dinner is usually on the table at seven o'clock, and from it the company retire to rest between nine and ten. Many persons are in the habit of sitting down to a repast at one o'clock, which is called tiffen, and is in fact an early dinner. By those, who can command their time, this is esteemed the best hour of the day for eating, as the evening is the most agreeable and wholesome season for enjoying a glass of wine."

CHAP. LI.

The Birth of Birruma (Brahma), Vishnu, and Uritiram. Their separate Offices. Birruma's two Wives; their Descendants. Incarnations of Vishnu. Vedams. Purrannahs. Doctrines respecting the Soul. Effect of Alms-giving. Future Punishments. Giants destroyed by Vishnu.

THE universe* was round as an egg, which being broken, all the ages or worlds appeared. God then manifested his form, or image, towering in immensity. His presence extended through all space. His feet penetrated through the depths of the earth. His stomach was as the earth, his head as the atmosphere, and his eyes as the sun and moon. This was his appearance; but, though he assumed this mode of manifestation, his divinity was the same and unchanged. He was alone in the midst of light. When he touched any thing, the thunder rolled; and, whilst it rolled, the birth of Birruma took place, then that of Vishnu, and next that of Uritiram.

To these three persons the Omnipotent appointed three several offices, to create, to preserve, and to destroy. The office of Birruma is to create, of Vishnu to preserve, of Uritiram to destroy. They are assimilated to the earth, the water, and the fire. If a tree be planted in the

* I have in some places given only a few of the select features, and in others the substance of what the reader may find in Valentyn under this head; but most of what I have omitted is too indefinite to be made distinct and too obscure to be understood. I have, however, produced enough to shew, that the most extravagant superstition and the most exaggerated absurdities may be often rendered subservient to a moral purpose.

earth where there is no water, it will not grow. Birruma and Vishnu are as the water and the earth, Uritiram is as the sun. The scorching heat of the sun burns up the grass.

Birruma had two wives, Sarasupadi and Majahi. The first was a woman of the other world. Majahi, who was of the race of the giants, and herself a giantess, bore a son called Gaxila Iritru. This Gaxila Iritru also married two wives; one of whom was named Tidi, who was a devastri, or goddess of the other world; and Adidi, who was of the race of the giants, and herself a giantess. The first had three-and-thirty millions of children. Adidi proved the mother of nine millions of children; some of whom were of the race of Asmar, or the demon of the air, and others of the race of the giants.

Vishnu underwent ten incarnations, in order to put these nine millions to death, and Uritiram acted as the executioner. Four laws, or vedams, were formed through the assistance of Birruma, that is, Iricu Vedam; Ediri, or Tirru Vedam; Sama Vedam; and Adarana Vedam. Iricu Vedam regards Birruma, Tirru Vedam relates to Vishnu, Sama Vedam to Uritiram, and Adarana Vedam to the giants.

Iricu Vedam exhibits the modes of imprecation; Ediri Vedam relates to ecclesiastical rites and ceremonies; Sama Vedam is to shew the way of truth respecting God: Adarana Vedam is to teach the arts of the devil, and the worship of devils.

Demuni, a godly man, and entitled Vedaviagaram, composed eighteen purrannahs, or expositions of these four laws; in which he appears to have taught, amongst other things, that, after death, the soul had to traverse two oceans, one of which was of blood, and the other of fire. The readiest way to secure a safe passage over these tremendous seas, was to give alms, particularly to the Brahmins. These alms were not to be given with grudging parsimony, but with cheerful liberality. Thus good works were to serve as boats or ships to transport the soul to the shore which lies beyond the regions of blood and fire.

The alms and good works which a man's children or friends did in his name after his death, would not escape the observation of the all-seeing sun, who would transport the stock of merit, to which they might amount, to the place of his departed soul.

Thus people were invited to marry, in order to have children, through whose aid they might acquire so much merit, as, after an interval of punishment, to be rescued from hell and removed to a state of glory.

Some said that a man would obtain salvation and happiness in a future life only by those alms which he gave with his own hands.

When a man died, his good and his evil deeds were summed up in the presence of God. If his good works turned the scale, a state of glory was his recompense: but, if his sins were greater than his good deeds, hell was to be his portion; and from that hell, if he had no posterity, he had no chance of deliverance.

Some thought that those who are tormented in hell, which they call Jamalocon, had a certain prescribed period of punishment to undergo, after which they would be removed to a happier state. But they also taught, that there are some who are plunged into a dark abyss, which they call Autes Tappes, out of which there is no return for ever and ever. The inmates of this place of misery never enjoy an interval of unconsciousness or oblivion, but are incessantly agonized by every species of woe, and every variety of suffering.

In this mythology of the Singalese, which appears, in a great measure, a transcript from that of the Hindoos, the giants are often represented as disturbing the harmony of the world, which is again restored by Vishnu, under some of his numerous transformations. For instance, on one occasion a giant named Sanguxura is said to have seized one of the laws of Birruma, and to have conveyed it to the world which is near the earth. This was perceived by Vishnu, who was then enjoying his repose in a sea of milk. Vishnu, after searching for the giant through the whole sea in the form of a fish, at last detected the depredator, opened his stomach, took out the law, and delivered it to Birruma.

Another giant, named Vaquira Tenda, once rolled up the world like a scroll, and drew it beneath the earth, when Vishnu following the same track in the form of a hog, killed the giant, and restored things to their ancient state.

A giant, who was at the same time a king, and named Irannian, issued an order that he should be worshipped as a god; for that there was no God but he. This giant king had a son named Pradaladan, who worshipped God alone, and refused to acknowledge his father to be God. In order to punish this disobedience, his father ordered him to be taken to the top of a high hill and thrown into the sea; but this immersion in the deep did not subdue the resolution of the refractory prince. His father then ordered him to be bound to a pillar of stone, and scourged with rods. After he had undergone this discipline, his father asked him if his God was in the pillar? The son answered, that God was present in every part of the whole world, and was in the pillar as well as in every other place. Vishnu, now practising one of his transformations, opened the stomach of Irannian with a needle, which caused his death.

In one instance Vishnu, in the shape of a dwarfish Brahmin, requested of the giant Mavili three hands' breadth of earth, on which he might build a house. This was promised; when Vishnu, towering to the heavens, and stretching the palm of one of his hands over the earth, and the other over the sky, asked where he should obtain the third hand's breadth to make up the complement? Mavili then throwing himself upon the earth, told him to measure it upon his back, when Vishnu setting his foot upon the rear of Mavili, pushed him into the abyss under the earth.

CHAP. LII.

Metaphysical Speculations uncertain; Moral Truths essentially the same in all Parts of the World. Moral Lessons of the Singalese and Malabars.

IT is painful to contemplate the labyrinth of folly, in which men are apt to bewilder themselves when they speculate upon subjects which are placed beyond the limits of the human understanding. Where revelation is wanting, we have no other light, by which to direct our way, than that of reason, analogy, and experience; but these are usually deemed too humble auxiliaries in points of theological research; and the imagination, operating under the influence of inflamed or fanaticised feeling, is usually preferred to more cautious inference, and more sober investigation.

But, though men are apt to rush into such a vortex of absurdity in matters of theological speculation, yet it is very pleasing at the same time to know, that, when they reflect on moral rules of conduct and the common duties of life, they all form the same, or nearly the same, opinions, and proceed to the same results. Here, indeed, they do not attempt to mount into regions beyond mortal vision, or suffer the mind to be hurried into a state of clouds and darkness by the whirlwind of the imagination. They tread on sure and solid ground; and reason and common sense afford a clear and satisfactory light upon the way.

The moral duties of life must be the same in all parts of the world; as they arise out of the nature of man, and the relations in which he is placed. Now this nature is every where the same, whether the skin be black or white, or the latitude hot or cold; and, though the social relations may be diversified, they must still, in all nations and circumstances, be virtually homogeneous. The relations of husband and wife, father and son, brother and sister, with all the kindred ties, the sympathies of friendship, the mutual dependence of the rich and the poor, the governors and the governed, cannot be essentially different at the equator and the pole. Truth, justice, and benevolence, are essentially the same in their nature, their obligations, and importance, in India and in Europe, in the Island of Ceylon and in that of Great Britain; and, therefore, when the natives of these different regions talk of moral duties, they will be found to coincide in a much higher degree than in questions which leave more room for uncertain conjecture and fanciful speculation.

After contemplating some of the wild and incoherent fictions of the Singalese and Malabars on points of inscrutable ambiguity, the reader will, I think, be pleased with the perusal of some of their moral lessons, which I am now going to submit to his inspection. The following is called the Nidi Shastram; and the precepts appear to be selected from several laws, or vedas, and delivered in that tone of authority which is employed by a legislator, or a person delivering rules of conduct, of which he is impressed by the truth, and conscious of the importance.

He who gives alms, should do it with discrimination. That which is good for one person, may not be so for another. But let no negligence appear in doing the works of love.

Death makes no distinction between the rich and the poor, but only between the just and the unjust, though all are born to die.

The good and the bad are respectively doomed to experience the good or the evil of their doings; and this effect would take place, even though one hundred millions of years might intervene.

Every person, who is about to engage in any work, should first well consider what it is that he is going to undertake. If he makes the attempt without this previous consideration, it shall turn out ill, as happened to the wife of a Brahmin, who, with thoughtless fondness, fed a mongoos till he burst.

The money which a man has taken pains to amass, and the house which he has laboured to build, shall not go with him when he dies. His relations or his friends may accompany his ashes to the grave; but the good or the evil which he does, is what alone is inseparably attached to him after death.

A covetous man heaps up money, which he neither uses himself, nor distributes for the use of others; but a liberal man, who amasses money, provides for his own wants, and gives it to him * who needs.

A learned man can be rightly appreciated only by another learned man,† and by no other person; as a barren woman cannot tell the pains of parturition.

* Christianity says, "Take heed, and beware of covetousness; for a man's life consisteth not in the abundance of the things which he possesseth."—"Provide yourselves bags which wax not old, a treasure in the heavens that faileth not, where no thief approacheth, neither moth corrupteth." Luke, xii. 15. 33.

The following two concluding lines of one of Martial's Epigrams are well known and deservedly admired:

> Extra fortunam est quidquid donatur amicis
> Quas dederis, solas semper habebis opes.—Ep. 43. lib. 5.

† Great sagacity is evinced in this remark. It is strikingly just; and I must own that I was much surprised to meet with it in these moral observations of the Singalese. No man, who does not know by experience the toils of literary research, and the travail of intellectual parturition, can estimate them as they ought. I have often remarked, with painful emotions, the flippant manner in which men talk of the more laborious exertions of the mind, and of the facility and promptitude with which they affect to determine that they may be produced. They have no congenial sympathy, no kind feeling for the man who has wearied his eyes, debilitated his nerves, and impaired his strength, by

A refined and elegant phraseology is thrown away on the earthy substance of coarse stupidity and lumpish ignorance. It is as unsuitable as it would be to bind a garland of roses round the neck of an ape.

The good which is done to bad men is often productive of injury, as the milk which is given to a snake is converted into poison.

If men will make a comparison between a bad man and a snake, they find that the former is the worse of the two. When a snake bites, a cure may be effected by medicine and regimen; but no one can convert a bad man into a good.

The sun rises in the east, and travels into the west, and great is the variation in the heat of his rays; but the word of a good man is not subject to instability or change.

A man of low origin, but of exalted sentiments and good life, ought to be treated as a relation; but a relation of base mind and profligate conduct should be considered as a stranger.

A woman who, in the management of her house, is gentle as a slave, who in understanding is fit for a counsellor, who in patience equals the earth, who in beauty rivals an Houry, who in the nuptial bed is like a ********, who in providing for the wants of her husband resembles an anxious mother—she who possesses all these qualifications is the perfection of her sex.

---

keeping the mental faculties continually on the stretch. In fact, none but literary men can properly understand the nature, or estimate the effect, of literary toil. Ignorance cannot judge rightly, except by guess, and consequently by accident, upon any subject; but how is ignorance to criticize its opposite, to estimate the products of the higher or even the lower order of intellects; or to determine the difference between a wise man and a fool? Yet what is it but ignorance which is always accompanied with presumption, which in general appreciates the merit, and apportions the reward, of literary exertion?

The excavation which is made by the white ant, the honey which is collected by the bee, and the money which men acquire to distribute in charity, increase more and more every day.

If you make a bed in a garden of camphor mingled with musk, and sow it with garlic, though you pour over it a thousand pots of rose-water, the smell of the garlick will remain.

Ilaximi, or good fortune, dwells with those who speak truth; fame and a good name with those who have much knowledge. The arts dwell in a man of sagacity; wisdom is the characteristic of him who gives alms according to the degree of his prosperity.

The animosity of two persons shall be terminated when one of them dies. The beauty and youth of a woman shall vanish when she is the mother of children. The poverty of the poor shall be at an end when they shall learn to minister to the wants of each other.

A man who meets a carriage must go on one side of the road; he must keep five yards out of the way of a horse, and ten out of that of an elephant; but he should keep a thousand yards out of the path of a malicious man, and leave the neighbourhood where he dwells.

The power of a Brahmin is in his knowledge; of a woman in her beauty; of a soldier in his courage. The power of a devotee, or jogi, is proved by his avoiding covetousness and dissimulation.

Who has no corn is without money; who has no brothers is without power; who has no cow has nothing good to eat. Who has no son has no satisfaction.

Where a daughter is to be disposed of in marriage, the father seeks a wise man, and the mother a rich. Friends advise a man of rank and family; the bride desires a man of good person and agreeable behaviour.

Sickness is caused by water; sin by women; and destruction by depravity.

To marry two wives; to beg alms by the way; to sow corn in two villages; to become surety for another; or to be evidence for another; —to do these five things is to bring vexation upon one's self.

To conquer a fever a man must go without meat; to conquer his wife, he must learn to sleep alone; to become master of the law, he must study it for ever; to overcome his enemy, he must submit to his will, or minister to his wants.*

It is not good to play with another, whom you wish to preserve a friend, nor to put money in his hand, nor to go into his house when he is out of the way. He must observe these three things, who will preserve another for his friend.

He who is sympathizing and kind-hearted to the good, who makes them objects of preference; who, when he sees a bad man avoids his company, and who delights in those who fear God and work righteousness, is worthy of respect and reverence.

He who is born blind cannot distinguish the difference of precious stones. An impotent man cannot enjoy the intercourse of his wife. The crow cannot rival the beauty of the peacock. A barren woman cannot tell the pains of child-bearing. A poor man knows not the taste of good things. A dog cannot tell the magnanimity of a lion; nor can a fool taste the sweets of virtue.

* The Chinese philosophers assert, that the most wicked may be reclaimed by repeated obligations. Du Halde's China, I. 285. The Christian injunction is, Overcome evil with good. Cleobulus said "That we ought to do good to our friends to make them more friendly, and to our enemies to convert them into friends."—Diog Laert, Lib. I. Cap. IV.

The earth has its intervals of suspended vegetation. Flowers lose their bloom, and pleasures their zest. The low are exalted, and the high brought low. When the Brahmins cease to do good, they begin to do evil. Women despise their husbands. Children despise their parents. Hence vice and misery abound, and piety is banished from the haunts of human life.

A covetous man has no friends. A sensual man throws off reserve and shame. He who is seized with a thirst for wisdom, troubles himself not about what he shall eat nor where he shall repose. A man who has a strong feeling of hunger, goes not in quest of dainties; nor does he wait till the hour of his regular repast.

When a man promises any thing to another, he should perform what he undertakes with instantaneous alacrity. If he puts it off for a day, he ought to do three times as much as he promised to perform. If he puts it off for a month, he shall pay a hundred fold for the delay. If he puts it off for half a year, he ought to recompense the disappointment a thousand fold. But, if he does not perform his promise within a year, he shall go to hell.*

A bad man is found in vicious company. A hog wallows in the mire.

* Massinger, in his "Maid of Honour," says, "Speed doubles the benefit," which is a good rendering of the Latin maxim. "Bis dat qui cito dat." But the Greeks have an epigram on speedy benefits, as opposed to benefits long deferred, which expresses the sentiment with great beauty and truth.

Ωκειαι χαριτες γλυκερωτεραι, ην δε βραδυνη
Πασα χαρις κενεη, μηδε λεγοιτο χαρις.
Sweet is the boon, which no delay attends;
But tardy bounty only half befriends.

The following lines are in Ausonius,

Gratia que tarda est in grataest; gratia namque
Cum fieri properat, gratia grata magis.

Ep. LXXXI.

But a good man delights only in what is gratifying to the mind and heart; just as if you set milk and water before a partridge, it will leave the water and drink the milk.

A man who is wise and learned, but without virtue, shall be despised.

The water of a well, the shadow of a walnut tree, the house of a poor man, and the bosom of a woman, are warm when it is cold, and cool and refreshing when it is hot.

A swine has seven or eight young at a time, an elephant one every twelve years, in order to afford delight to kings. In the same manner, where there is a good and fortunate son in a family, it is a great joy to the father in his old age.

With respect to money, there is trouble in the acquisition, trouble in the possession, trouble in the distribution, and trouble in the loss. Thus money is a source of trouble and woe.*

The Italians say,

" Dono molto aspettato, e venduto non donato.

The Singalese moralists appear very forcibly to have felt the cruelty of procrastination in the performance of promised favours or stipulated benefits; for they would not otherwise have condemned the offender to so severe a doom. It is certain that promises belong to the higher order of moral obligations, and the performance comes under that principle of equity, which withholds not from another what is his due, but gives to every man his own. What one individual has promised to another is no longer his own. The detention therefore beyond the necessity of the circumstances is a species of injustice. To put off the performance of a promise, where you have an opportunity of performing it, is the same as not paying a debt when it is due; and the injustice is aggravated by the cruelty of blasting hopes that you have caused to bloom, and of withering expectations, which you have nurtured into life.

* Juvenal says,

Tantis parta malis cura majore metuque
Servantur, misera est magni custodia census.

Sat. XIV. 302, 3.

A man who is thoroughly vicious cannot be made good, as garlic will not lose its smell, though it is enveloped in perfume.

When calamity lowers, when poverty assails, in the pains of sickness, and in the perils of death, a wise man will not be cast down, nor be afraid.

When a pagoda is demolished, or a well filled up, when a king has lost his throne, when a cow has become lean, or a Brahmin poor, he, who restores these to their former state, shall have four times as much merit as the person to whom they first owed their former prosperity.

A man of good disposition shall reap no advantage from associating with an individual of a bad; but a good man shall be benefited by the company of another who is good; as the bee increases its sweets by visiting the flowers of the distant water-tank; but the toad, which dwells in the water-tank, cannot discriminate the scent of those flowers.

The ornament of a nightingale is its warbling voice; the ornament of a woman is modesty; the ornament of a Brahmin is erudition; the ornament of a supplicant is patience.

The scorpion has poison in its tail, the gnat has poison in its head, the snake has poison in its teeth, but a bad man has poison in his whole body.

The beauty of a woman is her bosom; the beauty of a scholar is his wisdom.

The tongue of a bad man is more destructive than the scorching heat of the sun, or the devouring flame of the fire.

The bloom of youth, beauty of person, and nobility of birth, where the mind has not been cultivated, are only like the flower which the Malabars call muruco, that has no smell.

Good words are sweet to the ear, and gladdening to the heart; but a foul mouth excites loathing or contempt. When the nightingale sings all listen with delight, but when the ass brays we laugh at the noise.

Those who eat to excess, are the slaves of sensual gratification; and who do an injury to another, from the feeling of rancour* in the heart, are not far from the confines of the grave.

A father who neglects the payment of his debts when he dies, a mother who is a w——, a beautiful wife, or a son, who is a fool, are as enemies to human society.

Property, which is purchased with borrowed money, and money, which is obtined by treachery, shall soon pass away.

He who makes a careful provision against want, who rears a young calf, and lets it drink of the milk, who earns his subsistence by the labour of his hands, who ministers to the necessities of his friends, and keeps a bridle upon his tongue—of these five kinds of persons the posterity shall be multiplied.

If any accident befal the cattle of a Brahmin, he who rescues them from danger, though with the loss of his life, shall go through ten times ten thousand nativities as a Brahmin; and shall afterwards be received amongst the spirits in the realms above.

* The tendency of the malevolent passions is to wear the frame by perpetual inquietude, and to shorten the period of human life. The great Founder of Christianity acted as the best friend of man, even in a physical point of view, indepeudently of all moral excellence and all future consequences, by the stress which he laid on the culture of the benevolent affections, and the pains which he took to encourage their growth in the sanctuary of his church.

An elephant is renowned for its strength; the light shines through the clouds; the darkness of the night is dispersed by means of the full moon. A woman is celebrated for her gentleness; a horse for its swiftness; a house for its hospitality; the tongue for its eloquence. A large meeting is adorned by the presence of a wise man; a family is elevated by means of a good son; all nature is illumined by the sun.

He who has a wife and three sons, two yoke of oxen, ten milch cows, and well-irrigated rice lands, in the middle* of a village, is a happy man.

* I suppose, from their greater security in that situation, from wild beasts and external depredators.

CHAP. LIII.

Some Singalese Proverbs, which are contained in the Book Wessakare Satake; or the Sayings of the Wise.

THE heart of a good and wise man can no more be excited to evil by the incentives of the wicked, than the ocean can be made hot by a brand or a torch.

The rich are not despised on account of their low origin; but the poor are held in no estimation, though their pedigree may tower to the moon.

The possessions which a man has amassed with anxious toil, shall not follow him to the grave, or be his companions in the sepulchre. The kind affections which he has excited, and the friends by whom he was beloved, may attend his remains to the confines of the tomb; but the good or the evil which he has done, shall alone be his fixed and inseparable associate after death.

A wicked man is as a sharp thorn, of which, if you break off the prickles, it can do no harm; and, if you hold no converse with the wicked, their power to corrupt is taken away.

Weigh well the difference of good and evil; and, after sober deliberation, do not do that to another which would be displeasing if done to yourself.

A vessel of water is filled by a succession of drops; and wisdom, virtue, and riches, are the effects of minute accumulation and unremitting perseverance.

A covetous man has two sources of inquietude,—first, how to amass money; and, secondly, how to use it.

The good which is done to a good man, however small it may be, shall not be forgotten, but remain engraved in the heart, like letters cut in marble; but the greatest good which can be done to a bad man, shall vanish from his thoughts like the track of a ship in the waters.

There is no greater friend than the knowledge which each person has of his own proper calling; there is no greater enemy than sickness; no greater love than that of one's own children; and no greater power than that which we have from God.

Avoid both the friendship and the enmity of the wicked; for his enmity is like a scorching fire, which burns those who come near it; and his friendship is like an extinguished cinder, which begrimes those by whom it is touched.

As a green and flourishing plant may be bent by the gardener, so may the wise be inclined by good arguments to be good; but no reasoning can alter the purpose of a fool; as a tough and stubborn tree may be broken, but cannot be bent.

The culture which men bestow upon the roots and the trunk of a tree, shall be repaid in the fruit which grows at the top; and what good men do in the earth beneath, shall be recompensed in heaven above.

The moon throws her light over the evil as well as the good, and men should be bountiful not only to the good but to the evil.

If you have lived for some time in a state of friendship with a bad man, consider him always as a snake coiled round your arm, and watching an opportunity to bite.

The time will come when the face will be furrowed with wrinkles, when the hair will turn grey, and the limbs become feeble; but the amiable qualities of mankind delight by the verdure of perpetual youth.

Though men are continually beholding the fall of the lofty, and the destruction of the great, yet some are no sooner elevated to wealth and power, than a dense darkness seems to cover their eyes; for which visual disease no better collyrium can be devised than a precipitation from their towering eminence to a low estate.

It is better to be deaf than to hear our actions the topic of merited reproach. Better is it to be blind, than to have our own unrighteousness stare us in the face. Better is it to be changed into a log or a stone, than to perpetrate murder, or any similar enormity. Better is it to be without understanding, than to employ it in contriving evil and perpetrating wickedness.

As an elephant, pushing against a huge rock with his teeth, is more likely to break his teeth than to move the rock; so a poor man can gain nothing by contending with a great.

When good is requited with evil, the good is changed into evil; as cold water is made hot by being set upon the fire.

Good precedes evil, and evil good; and thus good and evil amongst men are like the wheel of a carriage, that is perpetually turning round.

There are three things by which a man may know a fool: 1. He attempts to execute whatever he wills or conceives, without money or means. 2. He wrestles without any strength in his limbs. 3. He disputes without knowledge or understanding.

There are four things by which a man may know a fool: 1. He goes into any one's house, to which he has no invitation, and where he has no business. 2. He prates incessantly, when he ought to hold his tongue. 3. He bestows praise on others when it is out of place. 4. He praises himself, where no praise is due.

Regard the wife of your neighbour as your own mother; the goods of another as a potsherd;* the life of another as your own: he who observes these rules shall hereafter be recompensed.

A kokila's (or nightingale's) beauty consists in her song; the beauty of a wife in her modesty; the beauty of a scholar in his knowledge; the beauty of a tapasserea, or teacher, in gentle benignity.

A man of noble birth, and interesting form, but who is not endowed with understanding, may be compared with an erebadugas, a certain tree, which bears a fine red flower, but without any smell.

It is not well with a beggar if he is not satisfied with what is set before

* That is, Do not covet the goods of another, any more than you would if they had no more value than a fragment of baked clay, or any thing the most worthless and contemptible. If we long and passionately desire what belongs to another, integrity will soon be corrupted at the very root; and the principle must finally give way to the force of such a constantly-operating temptation. What we violently desire, it will not be long before we attempt to procure; and when one single violation of probity has been perpetrated, who will say where the evil will end? Every species of injustice is a precipice, with few chances of escape; and perdition frowns beneath. Jesus affirmed, He that is unjust in the least, is unjust also in much. The Latin poet says,

——de mille fabæ modiis cum surripis unum;
Damnum est, non facinus mihi pacto lenius isto.

him, nor with a king if his desires are not bounded by the territory he possesses. It is not well with a w—— if she is ashamed, nor with a modest woman if she is without shame.

That which is already done cannot be prevented; ponder well, therefore, what you are going to do; for, otherwise, the pangs of anguish will prey upon your soul.

The wise make perpetual additions to their stock of knowledge; but fools loiter, slumber, bicker, and fight.

Let not your speech be redundant or impertinent; do not love without well knowing the individual; do not be more angry than the occasion will justify, or threaten what you have not power to execute. The wise are known by the observance of these rules.

Do good though there should be no future state; for, though there may be no such state, still the good you do must be good rather than evil; but, if you do evil, it will prove a source of woe if there be a future state.

A king, in the exaltation of sovereign power, is not comparable to a man of transcendent wisdom; for, though a king may receive more homage within the territory over which his authority extends, yet a wise man receives the applause, and excites the respect of the whole world.

The sorrow, which a man feels from the consciousness of ignorance, is like the joy* of heaven.

* It is a sorrow of this kind which often generates an unextinguishable thirst for the acquisition of knowledge; and, therefore, though it be sorrow for the time, it is soon converted into the joy of higher intelligences in brighter spheres.

The rich have little trouble,* the beneficent find nothing difficult† to perform. The country of the learned is in every region of the globe. The eloquent convert their enemies into their friends.

These persons are not formed for the acquisition of knowledge—the dull, the sickly, the sluggard, and the voluptuary.

Of the good or the evil which befals us, we ought not to ascribe the origin to this person or to that; for nothing can befal us which is not from God.

When the good are precipitated into indigence, they ought not to suffer their integrity to be shaken, but to preserve it as immoveable as a column of adamant.

There is poison in a serpent, but there is more venom in a wicked man; for there are remedies for the one, but there is no cure for the other.

* "Little trouble" about procuring the means of subsistence, in procuring which the majority of mankind are so anxiously occupied. The accumulations of wealth are principally to be desired for the means of beneficence which they afford, and the leisure for intellectual improvement which they procure. The more property there is in a country, the more full and deep may be, and ought to be, the reservoir of charity for every species of human woe; and, at the same time, the greater number of individuals may be exonerated from the more laborious corporeal occupations and employments, to devote themselves to the acquisition of knowledge and the enlargement of science. If no individual had more than enough for his own wants, we should be on the verge of barbarism. In proportion as property is augmented and diffused, we escape from the dreary horizon of savage wretchedness, and pass into the sunny region of civilization, of literature, and of joy.

Largior hic campos æther et lumine vestit
Purpureo.

† "Nothing difficult to perform;" for beneficence conciliates zealous friends and grateful auxiliaries. I say nothing about the moral government of the Deity, which I firmly believe to be so arranged as to let no kind action go without its appropriate recompense, either here or hereafter. I have always admired the beautiful scripture sentiment—"He who throws his bread on the waters (of charity), shall find it after many days."

He who has his conversation with the beasts of the field, must eat grass; and he who associates with the wicked shall not find any benefit in their intercourse.

A kind-hearted man makes the little he possesses contribute to the benefit of others, as a well supplies water to him who needs; while a selfish man, out of his abundance, relieves no want, and ministers to no suffering, but is as voracious as the depths of the ocean.

Diligence, in the beginning, is like an enemy; but it is afterwards converted into a friend. On the other hand indolence, which is like a friend in the beginning, proves an enemy in the end. Diligence, at the commencement, may be the poison of delight, though it afterwards becomes the nectar of joy; but indolence, which resembles nectar at first, turns to poison at last.

The air is the region of birds, and the water of fish; the king is the refuge of the poor, and children find protection in their cries.*

The river produces a variety of fish and flowers; but though they proceed from the same water, they have a different taste and smell.

Learning which is abused degenerates into folly. More food than is necessary is difficult of digestion. An old man, who is married to a young wife, is full of inquietude.

Out of ten men you shall find one that is brave; out of a hundred, one that is learned; but, out of a thousand learned, only one who is eloquent.

* Whose heart does not melt at the sight of infancy in agony, and of youth in tears? The strength of a child is in the sympathy it excites.

CHAP. LIV.

Short Lessons and Moral Maxims of the Singalese and Malabars, taken from the Malabar Book, Connevendam.

BE zealous in doing acts of charity.
Learn to command your anger.
Be not negligent* in what you are about.
Do not divulge all that you know.
Be not prodigal of your money.
Despise not the knowledge of reading or arithmetic.
To be devout is to be humble.
When you eat, think of the poor. †
Think not lightly of a conformity to the customs of those with whom you live.
Neglect not the habit of prayer.
Avoid filthy talking.
Diminish not aught of the stipulated recompense.
Do not mention all that you see.
Be contented with what you have.
Weigh well your words, and avoid ambiguity of expression.

---

* What you do, do with all your might. Do not suffer your attention to be diverted from that by which it ought, at the time, to be engaged. Intellectual proficiency, and indeed success, in general, in whatever we undertake depend very much upon the observance of this rule. A flitting, desultory occupation of the mind may not be so unproductive as vacancy of mind; but it is almost as abortive with respect to great attainments or to solid benefit.

† This would be a short grace, but could there be a better? Where I was at school, the master's grace used to be "Benedictus benedicat," which breathes a similar sentiment, and impresses, even in the social hour, a devout remembrance of those who are in want. The Latinity may be rather ecclesiastical than Ciceronian, but the maxim is worthy of its origin in the Christian school. "Whoso hath this world's goods and seeth that his brother have need, and shutteth up his bowels of compassion from him, how dwelleth the love of God in him?"

Do not build a great house.
Keep company with the good.
Cherish your father and mother.
Forget not a good action.
Sow, plant, and reap, in the proper season.
In the administration of justice spurn a bribe.
Do not attempt what you cannot execute.
Do not play with a snake.
Sleep not on a bed of down.
Be not bitter in your speech.
Do nothing which is unseemly.
Learn when you are young.
Forget not the mother who fondled you at her breast.
Indulge not in much sleep.
Do no injustice.
Cherish the spirit of prayer.
Seek peace all your life long.
Abstain from evil.
Despise not your condition.
Desert not those whom you have engaged to befriend.*
Shrink even from the semblance of injustice.
Attend to every thing that is worthy of observation.
Have no fellowship with men of bad principles.
Covet not the gains of iniquity.
Praise not yourself.
Be patient.
Hold fast your integrity.
Indulge not in severity of reproof, or acrimony of invective.
Forget not your native land.

---

* Perform the promises you have made, and disappoint not the expectations you have excited. Where expectations have been deliberately excited, they assume, in a moral point of view, the sacred nature of promises; and the performance is an act of similar obligation. People are too apt to be inconsiderate in their professions of friendship; but no friendship should be professed where it is not really felt; and where it has been professed and confidence has consequently been reposed, it should not be lightly or capriciously relinquished. If we strip friendship of its inviolable sanctity and reduce it to the common level of casual acquaintanceship, we take from human life one of those ingredients which is best fitted to sweeten the cup of human woe. A man's enmities should be ephemeral, but his friendships should be immortal. His animosities should vanish with the setting sun; but his kind affections should last for ever and ever.

Say nothing that is prejudicial to another.
Abstain from throwing the dice.
Whatever you do, do with all your might.
Know the principles of those with whom you associate.
Abstain from turning another into ridicule.
Lend no ear to the tales of detraction.
Have no acquaintance with a sluggard.
Conduct yourself like an honourable man.
Shew submission and reverence to the supreme God.
Forsake not those whom you have caused to rely on you for support.
Oppose the progress of iniquity.
Do not give way to despondency.
Punish with equity and moderation.
Be not induced to scoff by the forbearance of the Deity.
Live peaceably with your neighbours.
Give no ear to licentious women.
Never forget a benefit received.
Do not begin that which you see no likelihood of bringing to a conclusion.
Be steadfast in well-doing.
Conform to the customs of the country in which you live.
Forsake not the land of your fathers.*
Play not in the water.
Speak softly or deliberately.
Learn a variety of arts.
Let integrity be the rule of your conduct.

* This is a text, on which many wholesome homilies might be preached in the present day. The cosmopolite, who affects that his country is the world, that is, who has no heart in any country under heaven, may pretend that it is a mere prejudice to love the land of our fathers, and to venerate the sod that covers the ashes of our progenitors;—but my philosophy was never of that cast; for, even if the love of country were a prejudice, if all the patriotic sentiments were only delusions, still this prejudice, and these delusions are productive of so much good, and contribute so much to augment the sum of social enjoyment, that I should wish them for ever to be nurtured by our education, and invigorated by our habits, to be cherished, like our fondest sympathies, when we are young, that they may cling to our bosoms with an inseparable tenacity when we are old. My bosom approves the exulting glow of the Lacedemonian, when he exclaimed—

Σπαρτα μοι Σπαρτα κυδιανειρα πατρις;

And I would wish every Englishman to think of his native Albion with the same generous transport, the same enthusiastic preference.

Do no bad works.
Let no unbecoming or obscene words proceed out of your mouth.
Do not favour the production of sickness by excess.
Be not the organ of tale-bearing or calumny.
Have no intercourse with the perfidious.
Be not busy in criticising other men's lives or in detecting other men's faults.
Persevere without fear.
Spare no pains in tilling your land.
Honour the great when they are good, but respect the good when they are not great.
Throw off the tyranny of care.
A good life is the earnest of endless good.
Praise that which is praiseworthy.
Be not variable and inconstant in your friendships or your principles.
Do not offer any opportunity of triumph to your enemies.
Be not loquacious.
Eat not voraciously.
Stand not in any man's way.
Be not the familiar companion of the irascible.
Cherish the friendship of the virtuous.
Listen to the words of the wise.
Set not your foot in a brothel.
Speak considerately and distinctly.
Control your lusts.
Let your words be without dissimulation.
Be not hasty in betting.
When your means are good, and your purpose is just, let nothing shake your resolution.
Treat no man despitefully.
Make no enemies.
Waste neither the evening nor the morning in the luxury of sleep.
In doing your duty aim at perfection.*

* In the assemblage of sagacious remarks and wholesome admonitions in the three preceding chapters, as well as in that which immediately follows, I have in general faithfully preserved the sense of the original, though I have in a few instances unravelled the knotty tissue of the sentiment in order to render it more plain to the understanding. I have, at the same time, taken great pains to transplant their various beauties into the English idiom. How far I have succeeded the reader must determine.

CHAP. LV.

Sayings of a Female Sage.

OUR father and mother are our first acquaintance when we come into the world.

It is a good thing to erect buildings for the worship of God.

There is no beneficence more meritorious than that which a man shews to his own household.

He, who gives grudgingly, shall be taught better by adversity.

To eat little is good for the health of the body.

To quarrel with one's fellow-citizens is the way to perdition.

Grammar and arithmetic are as precious as both the eyes.

To do what is commanded is like medicine to the sick.

Do not lightly forsake him whom you have engaged to befriend.

The works of a religious man are to do good, and to teach others to do it.

He, who does not abstain from evil-speaking, shall mar his fortune.

Be diligent in improving your condition.

Filthy speaking does not become the mouth of a virtuous man.

It is a glorious sight to behold a woman of invincible fidelity.

Do not let the mind dwell on what you cannot obtain.

Use plain language with plain men.

He, who is busy in criticising the faults of his friends, has no friendship in his heart.

He, who is sagacious and diligent, seldom fails of his purpose.

Depart from him who gives you bad advice.

To listen to good counsel, and to put it in practice, is like laying up riches.

Wisdom in the mind is better than money in the hand.

The friendship of the great is succour in the time of need.

An informer, or tale-bearer, is like the blast, that kindles the fire and spreads the flame.

If you pronounce against justice, you will have every one your enemy.

The beauty of children consists in their obedience.

The great and rich should be in the place of parents to the lowly and the indigent.

He who can govern his anger is more eminent in the moral scale than all the devout.

Attend to the culture of the earth before you think of personal decoration.
Do not give your friends reason to suspect the sincerity of your friendship.
Litigation and gaming bring many to want.
He, who thinks of benefits received, will forget an injury done.*
A good name is better than any thing else.
Though you have but little still be thankful to God.
He who is happy is rich enough.
He who follows idleness shall find it the path to distress.
What sanctuary merits more confidence than our mother's breast?
The death of a good wife is as if all a man's substance were consumed by fire.
Immoderate sorrow causes great mischief.
A proud woman brings distress upon her family.
If God be with you all harm shall keep away.
He whose expences are greater than his receipts shall come to poverty at last.
It is better to earn your bread by the sweat of your brow than to be dependant on another man.
Use not violent reproof and bitter expostulations with your friends.
Disunion occasions embarrassment.
As long as you live at peace with your neighbours you have no injury to apprehend.
He, who is perpetually finding fault, is not heeded at last; as the water-snake in the fields is habitually seen till it ceases to be feared.
Do not build a house where good water is not to be had.
Do not act without deliberation.
Let the wise and the good be the objects of your reverence.
No deception exceeds that which is found in the human heart.
That prayer is good which is breathed from the soul.
Do not forsake the truth though it should cost you your life.
A liar is never esteemed.
The righteous fast is that which restrains our appetites and vanquishes our lusts.
The industry of a man is seen in his cultivation of the earth.
Live on good terms with your wife.
Where there is depravity and malice there is neither friendship nor benevolence.

---

* One injury will, sometimes, obliterate the sense of many benefits; but this is to suffer one resentful feeling to vanquish numerous claims to benevolent regard. The mind should never be suffered to dwell upon injuries; but it should never cease to make benefits the subject of tender recollection. The principle of gratitude, which is one of the most lovely ramifications of the great trunk of benevolence, would thus repress the growth of every adverse sentiment. According to the admonition of the poet, benefits should be written in marble, but injuries in the dust.

Do not grieve your father and mother by vicious conversation.
Inconstancy of mind is the characteristic of woman.
When you make a long journey, find a place of rest before the sun goes down.
Do not fix your heart upon any thing that is vicious.
Though you have but little do not neglect the offices of friendship.*
Where there is no rain there can be no harvest.
Thunder and lightning go before rain.
The rock makes the pilot.†
The conversation of the wicked is a fountain of mischief.
Men sleep well when the mind is at ease.
To earn your bread by the sweat of your brow is a praise-worthy act.
Keep your hands from the bosom of harlots.
Let what you say be distinct and clear.
There is no greater enemy than sensual excess.
Be on your guard against the blandishments of women.
A disbelief in futurity nips the buds of beneficence.
A passionate man has neither moderation nor constancy.
A generous mind will not ask alms.
It is a glorious thing when wisdom is associated with affluence.
The upright escape the regrets of a bad conscience.
Let no station make you forget God.

---

* No circumstances can justify a cold-hearted selfishness. The sympathies of friendship and of love may flourish in the most inclement atmosphere, and in the most rugged soil; and he, in whose bosom they are not found, however he may be wanting in wealth, is more wanting in humanity. The excuses which men make for omissions of beneficence, are very multiform and various; but they all usually resolve themselves into a narrow selfishness, however they are coloured over with hues of different character.—One man excuses himself by his present needs; another by his future apprehensions. One is too sensual to have any thing to spare; another is too provident not to be more affected by the most remote contingencies which refer to himself, than by the most pressing wants of his kindred or acquaintance. One man has numerous sons and daughters; and his heart is a frozen surface to the touch of distressed relatives and indigent friends. He does not consider that, though it is a bounden duty to provide for sons and daughters, yet those sons and daughters are only self under another name; and that he who confines all his beneficence to their exclusive good, may still be the most selfish of human beings. Beneficence is not pure and holy till it passes the region of self; and instead of being restricted in its activity to a man's own family, steps over the threshold, and scatters blessings amongst neighbours and friends.

† A dangerous navigation makes dexterous seamen. Difficulties cause excellence; they exercise sagacity and elicit skill.

In the four preceding chapters, which contain the moral lessons and ancient proverbs of the Singalese, the reader will, I feel confident, be impressed with the good sense, the prudential sagacity, and, in many instances, the sound piety, which pervade the remarks of these idolatrous heathens. Though in many of their religious ceremonies and speculative opinions, they are oppressed by the most degrading superstition, yet no perversion of reason, no obliquity of judgment, no want of discrimination or sagacity, are found in the notions which some of their sages have displayed on the relative duties of life; and on those actions and habits which it becomes men most to practise and to cultivate for their own good, as well as for that of the community to which they belong. Some, indeed, of their remarks are equally distinguished by the truth, the beauty, and the energy of the sentiment. I believe that they are now exhibited for the first time in our vernacular idiom; and, as proverbs constitute no small part of the moral wisdom of nations, I trust that I have rendered no unacceptable service to my countrymen, by having naturalised these Singalese exotics amongst the popular stock of our moral literature.

CHAP. LVI.

Offices, Casts, and miscellaneous Particulars.

CORAAL. A coraal * is the overseer or president of a corle, or county, who has two, three, or four attacoraals under him, according to the size of the corle, which is sometimes divided into three or four pattus, or districts. He has, moreover, from six to eight lascaryns, pamideas, or messengers, subject to his orders. The attacoraals are to see that the commands of the coraal are duly executed.

Cariacoranno, or the majoraals, may be denominated the bailiffs of a village. They vary from one or two to six or more, according to the size, culture, and population of the village.† It is their business to attend to the payment of the annual imposts; to see that the land is sowed

* I follow the authority of Valentyn in these names and explanations. Some changes may have taken place in the interior administration of the provinces: but, as I intend this work not merely to gratify the curiosity of persons in this country, but of those Englishmen who are resident in Ceylon, I did not think it right to omit any thing which tends to throw light on the past as well as the present state of the island. I have preserved most of the names as they are found in Valentyn; and I thought this better than to make any alterations, which might be less agreeable to the genius and pronunciation of the Singalese. I regret my ignorance of the last-mentioned language, as it might probably have enabled me to render this work much less imperfect, and even to have corrected errors, into which I may have been inadvertently led by my authorities.

† In a part of Valentyn's work, entitled, "Extract uyt de Consideratien van de Heer van Rheede over Ceylon, &c." dated in the year 1677, which contains a great deal of valuable information relative to the state of the island at that time, it is said that a gamma, or village, is composed of several hamlets; a pattu, or district, of several villages; a corle, or county, of several pattus; and a dessaveny, or province, of several corles.

and the harvest got in at the proper time; and, along with other services which the locality may suggest, to render a good account to the lord or proprietor of the soil. When the lord visits the village, it is their duty to take care that he is provided with suitable lodgings, that his apartment is hung with white calico, and his stool covered with the same. It is, at the same time, part of their office to furnish him twice a day with adreckes, or ready-dressed victuals, and with peyndus, or undressed victuals, as the lord shall appoint, and for as many days as has been customary, or is compatible with the size and resources of the village. These majoraals are of five denominations, of which one is of somewhat more consideration than the rest. They are—hitihamis, japamis, pati rannearu, gamneralearu, vitarannearu.

LIANNO is the same as the clerk or scribe of the village, who keeps an account, which he gives to the lord, of all the products and dues of the village.

CANGANEME. This officer musters the people of the village, and calls them together when there is any work to be done.

MANANNA, a measurer of grain. When the harvest has been got in, it is his business to measure out that grain which is a common stock to the different proprietors. He was also particularly to measure the corn that was due as a rent or impost to the king.

GAMHEWAJA. A village lascaryn, who, at the orders of the vidaan of the village, calls the people together, and goes from house to house to announce on what day they are to meet.

HAINDES. These execute the work that is to be done in a village; and work, by turns, for the king or the proprietor.

COOLIES. Porters of all kinds of burdens and goods, and bearers of the palanquins. These coolies* are of the cast or race of the vellalas, who sprang up in the time of the Portuguese. Before their time there were no coolies among the vellalas, but only among the inferior casts.

The King Surievankse. This denotes that he is a descendant of the sun, or of Vigea Raja, the first King of Ceylon, the fabulous origin of whose family has already been described.

The cast Karawo, or that of the fishermen, comprises the following subdivisions:

1. Karawo.
2. Barudel-karawo.
3. Dandu-karawo.
4. Moru-karawo.
5. Kespe-karawo.
6. Kadul-karawo.
7. Tock-keulo.
8. Godo-keulo.
9. Indimal-keulo.

These nine subdivisions of the karawos have each their peculiar kind of fishing instruments; and each is obliged to adhere to his own, according to ancient custom.

Karawo, are the principal fishermen, out of whom they appoint their hiefs according to their intrepidity and enterprise. There are amongst them modeliaars, mohamdirans, araatsjes, kangenys, and other officers of considerable importance. They may go out to sea with their nets, but must not fish either with rod or line.

* In the considerations of Vander Rheede, it is said to be part of the duty of the coolies to carry the various products belonging to the lord out of the field to the storehouse or granary, which no one else is bound to do, and this they perform for no other recompense than a portion of rice.

Barudel-karawo. These may not make use of casting nets, which they call barudel or wisudel, either in the sea or the rivers.

Dandu-karawo. These may fish in the sea only with an angling rod, which they make of the bamboo.

Moru-karawo. These employ nets made of hemp in catching scate (squalus), from which they extract an oil. They subsist by the sale of this, and are not permitted to take any other kind of fish.

Kespe-karawo, who subsist by the tortoises (schildpadden), which they catch with a large net.

Cadul-karawo make the sails of their fishing boats of a dark red colour, which they extract from the bark of the cajou-tree.

Tock-keulo. These are not permitted to launch into the sea, or to frequent the salt water at the mouths of rivers. They fish with a peculiar kind of net, of which they are restricted to the use.

Godo-keulo may not fish in the ocean, but at the mouths of rivers, or in inlets of the sea. Their fishing-tackle is also of a peculiar construction, which is minutely described in Valentyn.

Indimal-keulo, manufacture lines and nets from the bark of the cocoa-nut tree, which they sell to the fishermen. They catch fish in the rivers with baskets and little nets. On their annual festival they are not permitted to make use of the flowers or majang of the cocoa-nut tree, but only of the date, which they call Indimal.

These three last species of fishermen constitute the lowest casts among them, with whom the rest may neither eat nor form any connexion.

The highest classes or ranks of fishermen participate in the privileges of the vellalas. The washermen are under an obligation to wash their clothes. On their solemn festival, they may spread a white cloth where they eat, cover the stool on which they sit with white, and hang the apartment with the same. They may also carry a torch or flambeau, which they term dawalpandam. They also display a white flag, with the device of a particular fish in the centre, and this distinction the higher ranks reserve to themselves, and do not permit to their inferiors. These fishermen may carry an umbrella of the tallipot, and within their own lands are allowed to have white calico spread before their feet. They have military officers amongst their number, and some may fill the place of adigar if they have merited it by their conduct. They are honoured by the king with different titles, according to their offices; and are carried in palanquins, while little drums are beat on the way, with other circumstances of ceremonious parade.

The cast of chiandos, or duravos, has ten subdivisions, each of which has its peculiar occupations, and differs more or less in rank from the rest.

1. Magul duravo, who are employed in catching, or in taming elephants; also as lascaryns, and in offices of other kinds.

2. Nattanbovo are a degree lower than the first, but with few points of discrimination.

3. Niello, carry the knives, or instruments of their trade, fastened with a cord round the waist, as also the vessel in which they put the toddy they collect. They wear a little bell about the middle, in order to give notice to the cast of vellalas to avoid passing under the tree of which they are at the top.

4. Usanno. These who are also drawers of toddy, besides performing the offices of the niellos, and wearing a little bell about the middle, serve as coolies to carry burthens.

5. Weedy. These are a degree lower than the last.

6. Cottu. A still inferior gradation; but when Valentyn wrote, he says, there were none either of these or of the preceding subdivision upon the island.

7. Cutang wolle-etto. In this class both the men and women are dancers, kept for the pagodas, but who exhibit their skill in other places where they are ordered.

8. Arambeo. Dancers exclusively appropriated to the service of the pagoda.

9. Ackerammo. Manufacturers of rope, or thread, from the bark of the cocoa-nut. They also serve to blow the bellows in the smith's forge; to hammer the metal, and to assist in other works.

10. Agunmady. These are not held in the same estimation as the preceding classes. None of the rest will eat, or have any intercourse with them. They play on a sort of globular instrument, or drum, which they hold in one hand and beat with the other.

The two first subdivisions of this cast of chiandos have the privilege of using white* linen, or calico, and have an addealanchody, or flag, with a red lion represented in the middle of a white ground, with other distinctions, from which their inferiors are debarred.

Navandannajo, or artificers, who, though performing different handicraft operations, constitute only one cast in rank. Half of them may display hangings of white calico at their festivals, and carry a flag with the device of an ape, called anumanta.

Achiary, smiths; baddallo, silversmiths; wadduwo, carpenters; liane waduwo, turners; ridiceto ancarao, inlayers of gold and silver; adatketeancarao, workers in ivory and cabinet-makers; galwaduwo, stone-cut-

* Knox says, p. 131, "The signs of higher or meaner ranks, are wearing of doublets, or going bare-backed without them; the length of their cloth below their knees; their sitting on stools, or on blocks, or mats spread on the ground, and in their caps."

ters; ratneenderecarao, jewellers; iwaduwo, arrow-makers; sittereo, painters; lacuruwo, smelters.—These artificers eat together, and intermarry with each other.

Hannalio, tailors, who work for the lord of the land. The washermen wash for them, but do not eat with them. They do not enjoy the privilege of white linen without the permission of the king.

Hommaru, shoemakers. Of these, Valentyn says, there are none at this time in Candy.

Ambetteo, shavers or barbers. One of them must always accompany the lord of the land. The washermen wash for them, but do not eat with them; but they have the privilege of white linen.

Cubello, potters; are attached to the pagodas and villages, and must furnish earthen vessels for the lord. They have their dureas, or overseers; and pay a personal, or poll-tax, called deccum. The washermen wash for them, but do not eat with them; and they have not the privilege of white linen.

Weenawo, elephant-catchers. They follow the track of these animals, drive them into the snare, and put them to death in any perilous emergency. The washermen wash for them, but eat not with them, nor have they the privilege of white linen.

Haly or chialias, cinnamon peelers. The washermen do not wash for them; but they have others, called hinnevo, who are employed for this purpose. They have not the honour of white linen.

Hangarema, who make sugar from the sap of the palm, or borassus flabelliformis. The hinnevos wash for them, and they are excluded from the privilege of white linen.

Hunno or chinambero, lime-burners; the head of whom, or the hunu-dewea, usually plasters the walls, and superintends the rest. Some of them white wash the house of the lord once or twice a week. They are also to furnish purified lime, for chewing with the areca nut, or betel leaf.

Deccum carao. These, who pay an annual poll-tax, have to keep up the lime furnace, to supply fuel, and to tend it till the process is finished. They do not possess the privilege of wearing white linen; and the cast of the pallys wash for them.

Hunu kattanno, are employed in felling trees in the woods, and in procuring fuel for the lime-kilns.

Hunugambadu, are peasants, who fodder and take care of the cattle, and have a particular durea, or superintendent. The coolies who dwell in the villages belong to this cast.

Rodawo,* are washermen, who are obliged to wash for the superior casts, and also for the caraos and chiandos, with whom they eat; though they also wash for the tailors, potters, and shavers, but they must not eat with these, nor go to their festivals. They do not enjoy the privilege of white linen, and they wash for themselves. Amongst the washers are painters, who pay deccum, or a poll-tax.

Berreways, tablinjenos, or tom-tom players, amongst whom there are dancers, lime-burners, mowers, and deccum-caraos,† who have their manquedams, or superintendents, whom they denominate ulewalia. They do not eat with the low casts; and are distributed through the villages. They do not enjoy the honour of white linen; and the pallys wash for them.

* Knox calls them ruddaughs.

† Payers of an annual poll-tax.

Heeri. These have their vidane, or chief. Their office is to fell all kinds of trees, to carry the ammunition in war, and to act as pioneers in clearing the way. They do not enjoy the honour of white linen; and a particular cast, called gangavo, wash for them.

Olias, are dancers, who provide the lord with oil for burning in the night, and keep his mansion clean during the day. They also assist in tending the elephants. They have not the honour of white linen, and the gangavos wash for them.

Pally, wash for the lime-burners abovementioned and, like the four following casts, constitute a degraded and despised race.

Hinnivo, are washers for the cast of chialias, abovementioned. They also provide green food for the elephant stalls.

Gangavo, wash for the casts heeri and olias.

Paduvo, have amongst them payers of the poll-tax, lascaryns and coolies, who carry palanquins.

Palleru, banditti or free booters, who live in woods or caverns.

Hiene Jaty and Antere Jaty, two casts of the lowest order, not reckoned amongst the rest, and more despised than all the rest. The first of these two casts, who are sometimes called kinneas, weave fine mats, with which they pay their deccum or poll-tax. The second, who are at other times denominated rodias, are the lowest of all in rank, have no vidanes or heads. They dwell in a sort of low cabins, without walls or supports, but the roof resting on the ground. They eat dead animals, and make ropes of the hides of cows and buffaloes, of which they form snares to catch elephants, &c. They may not wear the smallest rag of white linen on their heads, and must tie up their hair in a bunch at the top.

Mantris, counsellors: they give advice in affairs of importance, and on other occasions, are next in the government to the king, on whose death one of the mantris conducts the government for the son if he is a minor; and, if there be no heir, he acts as regent with the rest of the counsellors, till another king is appointed. From these mantris they take their priests, those who minister in their pagodas, their doctors, surgeons, teachers, prophets, astrologers, and devotees.

Walinde or chittys, traders or merchants. In the diverse matters of purchase or sale, a chitty is called in, who is bound on all occasions to traffic for the king. Of these chittys there are four divisions or classes, who deal in different commodities.

The chittys trade in all kinds of drugs, linen, and domestic utensils.

The caver chittys deal in gold and silver, which they assay and estimate.

The comety chittys deal in fruits, grain, vegetables, and ready-dressed eatables.

The waligi chittys deal in all kinds of corals, in rings, bracelets, and metallic ornaments.

These four kinds of traders, says Valentyn, speak the same language and employ the same characters. They were not originally natives of Ceylon, but came over from the opposite coast. They do not eat or intermarry with each other, or at least the higher class with the lower, except in cases where money intervenes to compensate the disparity of rank. But the lower casts are well content to eat with the higher, and to marry their daughters.

Gowi or vellalas. These two words, the first of which is Singalese, and the other Malabar, both mean a cultivator of land. There are several subdivisions of this cast, of which the four principal are the following:

The epithet handaeruvo or hondrew, meaning honourable or immaculate, is sometimes added to the name.

1. Bandares or adassing, are those who appear at court as dukes, counts, or princes of the royal family.
2. Mantriunu, who officiate at court as supreme or privy counsellors to the king.*
3. Maeudellyperu. These consist principally of military officers, modeliars, adigars, and dessaves.
4. Gowiperu; include both military persons and cultivators of the land.

Besides the above, there are still nine other sorts of vellalas, whose duty it is to perform different services for the king, both at court and in the country.

1. Wanneweddas; hunters, or persons living in the woods, of whom there are two sorts; one wearing leaves about the body, and the other the bark of a tree made soft for the purpose. Their houses are principally formed of the leaves of trees. Some of them were subject to the Dutch Company, and they paid an annual tribute of elephants with teeth. They eat the flesh of the elk, the deer, &c. which they preserve in honey in the hollow of a tree Their principal property consists of their bows and arrows. When they want a fresh supply of arrows, they take as much iron as is necessary, with a pattern of the arrow which they want, and lay it at night before the smith's door, along with a haunch of the elk or the deer. They then wait three or four days, till they think the work is done; when they return by night to the same place; and, if they find the arrows ready, they leave another portion of venison, and

* These appear to constitute a class of the mantris mentioned above.

go away without saying a word to any body. But, if the smith does not comply with their wishes, they spare no pains to make him repent of his neglect.

2. Diegaranno, are those who collect precious stones from the beds of rivers and torrents.

3. Mallaccarao, supply the court daily with flowers.

4. Dalae murecarao, furnish betel and areca.

5. Hunkiricarao, supply the court daily with milk.

6. Dadeweddas, hunters, or procurers of game.

7. Goddegarranno, who turn up the soil in search of precious stones.

8. Batgamwella Etto, are those who sow the seed in the royal domains.

9. Gombaducarao are peasants, who attend the cows, and supply the king with grain and other articles.

These numerous subdivisions constitute only one cast of vellalas; but the superiors, who are only a degree higher than the rest, will not eat with the inferior members at their festivals, or on other occasions, nor permit them to have their daughters in marriage; though money, as has been previously intimated, will sometimes alter their sentiments with respect to matrimonial connexions. They sow and mow,* and the principal difference between them consists in the offices which they have at court, and about the person of the sovereign.

In cases of a coronation, the crown was put upon the king's head by four persons of the four principal casts.

Valentyn mentions the following officers as existing in his time under the dessave of Matura.

* Knox says, p. 192, "Husbandry is the great employment: in this the best men labour; nor is it held any disgrace, for men of the greatest quality to do any work, either at home, or in the field, if it be for themselves, but to work for hire with them, is reckoned for a great shame; and very few are here to be found that will work so; but he that goes under the notion of a gentleman, may dispense with all works, except carrying, for carrying is accounted the most slave-like work of all."

1. The vice or deputy dessave, who had then the name of adigar, took care that every thing which the dessave ordered should be performed, and whom he acquainted with every thing that occurred. He attended to the interest of every part of the country, taking care that no one should suffer by the oppression of the inferior chiefs. This adigar was also to take care of all dues imposed for the service of the lord.

2. Modeliar has a meaning similar to that of captain. He was at the head of three or four nantches, or companies of lascaryns, each of which companies consisted of one aratsche, two canganes, and twenty-four lascaryns or soldiers, who were always to be ready for service, and to relieve each other at intervals of fourteen or thirty days.

3. Mohotirales, or mahatiars, certain writers, of whom there were four under the dessave of Matura. The attepatte mahatiar was continually present with the dessave, to whom he officiated as secretary, copying all olas or papers, letters, decrees, and ordinances.

The attepatte mahatiar was to keep an account of the pay or support allotted to the officers and lascaryns, with that of the artificers in the province of Matura, to register what each of them received from the lord, and the free perwenies which they possessed by inheritance. The other mahatiars had their peculiar offices, and were employed in collecting portions of the taxes or revenue. New mahatiars were appointed every year by the dessave, in order to prevent collusion in their conduct, and keep a check upon their proceedings.

4. Tupairale, or the interpreter of the dessave of Matura, who made him acquainted with the complaints and interests of the inhabitants.

5. Apohamis. This properly designated no office, but the descendants of black chiefs, who were named apohamis. They were attendants at the court, and some of them were put at the head of two companies of lascaryns.

6. Mohamdirams are chiefs over companies of lascaryns. They serve as a guard, and must take the field wherever they are commanded.

7 Badde corene, or cornerale. This officer is under the adigar. He is at the head of two companies of lascaryns, performs guard, and is en-

tirely subject to the orders of the adigar. He is to be always ready to march along with his men at a moment's notice, whenever their services may be required.

8. Aratsche resembles a serjeant, each having one company of lascaryns under him, while they are at the same time under their respective officers.

9. Canganys, corporals under the aratsches.

10. Lascaryns, soldiers who receive support, and are to be always ready to serve under their chiefs.

The king was the acknowledged lord of the soil, which he distributed in portions to the inhabitants, to descend by inheritance, and to be held as fiefs. Every man had enough allotted for his support; but for which he was bound to perform certain services, and the obligation was limited by the possession.

The king gave away no lands, without reserving to himself some seignorial rights or tokens of proprietorship, which he received every year under different names, and in the form of tributary acknowledgments.

Tupely are pieces of white linen, which are spun by the wives and children of the higher casts, and manufactured by the Singalese weavers. An impost of this kind was annually paid to the king by persons of the greatest consideration, who, doing homage to his majesty, made him a new tender of their obedience and services, as if they were going for the first time to receive their fiefs.

Angebadde are the poll-taxes, which the lower casts paid to the king. Each individual of these casts was liable to this imposition from the age of fifteen to sixty; and, besides this, they were obliged to furnish certain

* Valentyn, p. 268, from the Considerations on Ceylon by Vander Rheede.

portions of iron, sugar, and cinnamon. But the cinnamon-peelers paid no pecuniary tax, but provided a certain portion of cinnamon free of expense, and another portion at a certain price.

Wattabadea, is a tax upon the land, or upon the cocoa or areca-nut trees, according to the numbers they contain.

Pollee, is an impost upon the fruit trees, which is collected three times in the year, and does not altogether amount to a tenth of the produce. But little equality is said to have been observed in the original imposition of this tax, and one place paid much more than another. Of the taxes called otto and anda, the first amounted to the tenth sheaf, and the second to the half of the produce after the deduction of the seed. The best and most fruitful lands were often oppressed by this tax, which operated as a great impediment to cultivation; but it probably took place only on estates that were farmed more immediately for the benefit of the king.

Devel, are gardens and lands in the villages, which, being reserved on account of the king, were left for the use of the officers or magistrates of the village, and to defray the expenses which they might incur.

Madaspo, is a tax of little value, which the village chiefs paid annually to the crown, not amounting to more than six Dutch stivers for each village, and serving principally as an acknowledgment, to keep alive the recollection that the lands were derived from the king.

Motette, are gardens and lands which the crown had not given away or alienated, but employed as a fund of favour or reward. These lands were gratuitously cultivated by the villagers, and exempted from taxes.

Morales, is a mortuary belonging to the king, which amounted to one-third part of the moveables of the deceased.

CHAP. LVII.

List of Singalese Sovereigns, from the earliest Period to the Commencement of the Eighteenth Century.

VIGEA Raja, who appears to have been descended from a Siamese chief, is commonly reputed the first king, or emperor of Ceylon. His daughter, who is fabled to have been carried off by a lion, had a son and daughter.

The Prince Singa Bahu Comara, and the Princess Singa Valli Comara, whose marriage is said to have been productive of thirty-two sons, of whom the eldest, Vigea Comara, mounted the throne. The commencement of the reign of Vigea Comara is placed in the year of our era 106; but if, according to this account, he were the great grandson of Vigea Raja, the first reputed sovereign of the island, the arrival of the latter prince must have been long posterior to the date which I see assigned to it by a gentleman who is said to be eminently learned in the Singalese literature and language. In the account of the Singalese casts which Mr. Tolfrey gave to Lord Valentia,* he says—"Vigea Raja arrived in Ceylon in the fifty-sixth year of the era of the last Boudhou, that is 2290 years ago; the present (meaning 1804) being the year of Boudhou, 2346." Without attempting to clear the way, where so little

* It is printed at the end of the first volume of his lordship's Travels. There appears to be a great chasm in the list of sovereigns between Vigea Raja and Vigea Comara. I have numbered them from the last.

light is afforded, through this labyrinth of chronological difficulties, I shall content myself with exhibiting the succession of Singalese sovereigns with the length of their reigns, as it appears in Valentyn, whose authority has been principally followed in the preceding history.

		Reigned. Years.	M.	D.	Anno	to Anno
1.	Vigea Comara, or as he is named by others Vigea Bahu Comara	30	0	0	106	136
2.	Tissanaon Ameti	1	0	0	136	137
3.	Simit Comara	22	0	0	137	159
4.	Pandoe Vassaja	13	0	0	159	172
	(Others extend his reign to 30 years.)					
5.	Abeia Comara	20	0	0	172	192
6.	Saguganatissa	17	0	0	192	209
7.	Digagamunu	37	0	0	209	246
8.	Pandu Cabaja	33	0	0	246	279
9.	Mutta, or Motta Singa Raja	60	0	0	279	339
10.	Deveni Petissa Maha Raja	40	0	0	339	379
11.	Suratissanum	11	0	0	379	389
12.	Two adventurers from Malabar	22	0	0	389	411
13.	Assalanam Raja	14	0	0	411	425
14.	Etalunam, or Etalanam Raja	44	10	10	425	469
15.	Jattalatissa Guelinitissa Raja	20	0	0	469	489
16.	Goloeumbera, or Ambera Raja	10	0	0	489	499
17.	Ganatissa Raja	4	0	0	499	503
18.	Kingdom still governed in his name	30	0	0	503	533
19.	Dutugenunu Maha Raja	24	0	0	533	557
20.	Sedetissa Raja	18	0	0	557	575
21.	Tullenam Raja	1	9	10	575	577
22.	Lemenetissa Raja	39	8½	0	577	617
23.	Caluman Raja	16	0	0	617	633
24	Walagam Bahu Raja	0	8	0	633	634
25.	Five Malabar princes	36	0	0	634	670
26.	Valla Gambu or Vallagam Bahu Raja	12	5	0	670	683
27.	Choranga Raja	26	0	0	683	709
28.	Bemmenitissa	12	0	0	709	721
29.	Maha Delia Deliatissa	14	0	0	721	735
30.	Chorawa Raja	12	0	0	735	747
31.	Cudda Tissa Raja	3	0	0	747	750
32.	Anularan Bissava	1	0	0	750	751
33.	Culavaon	1	1	0	751	753

	Reigned. Years.	M.	D.	Anno	to Anno
34. Tomo	0	4	0	753	753
35. Malulan Tissa	26	0	0	753	779
36. Batian, or Batta Raja	28	0	0	779	807
37. Madilimanna Raja	12	0	0	807	819
38. Adague Muvene, or Munu Raja	9	8	0	819	829
39. Cada Ambera Raja	6	0	0	829	835
40. Nalabissava	6	0	0	835	841
41. Elunna, or Clunna Raja	6	0	0	841	847
42. Sanda Muhunu, or Sandamu Hunu Raja	6	0	0	847	853
43. Asnapa Raja	41	0	0	853	894
44. Vacnelisanam Raja	3	0	0	894	897
45. Bapa Raja	12	0	0	897	909
46. Gajá Bahu	22	0	0	909	931
47. Mana, or Maria Raja	16	0	0	931	947
48. Hama Tissa Raja	26	0	0	947	973
49. Cuda Raja	31	0	0	973	1004
50. Veni Tissa Raja	22	0	0	1004	1026
51. Ambaheraman Raja	6	0	0	1026	1032
52. Sirina, or Suina Raja	2	0	0	1032	1034
53. Vierdu, or Vejemdu Raja	6	0	0	1034	1040
54. Sanga Tissa Raja	11	0	0	1040	1051
55. Siri, or Suisanga Bodi Raja	22	0	0	1051	1073
56. Leminie Golu Amba Raja	13	0	0	1073	1086
57. Guwelaguwem, or Quelaguwem Dettatissa	10	0	0	1086	1096
58. Malasen, or Mahason Raja	24	0	0	1096	1120
59. Quitissiriamenaon Raja	28	0	0	1120	1148
60. Deva Tissa Raja	9	0	0	1148	1157
61. Rajas Raja	31	0	0	1157	1188
62. Utapissa Maram Raja	26	0	0	1188	1220
63. Scnam Raja	6	1	0	1220	1227
64. Lemini Tissa Raja	6	0	0	1227	1233
65. Visenam Caralsoo Raja	6	0	0	1233	1239
66. Seven Malabar princes	27	0	0	1239	1266
67. Dacem Gulia Raja	18	0	0	1266	1284
68. Comara Dahai Raja	29	0	0	1284	1313
69. Lemini Patissa Raja	1	0	0	1313	1314
70. Amlam Heranam Raja	13	0	0	1314	1327
71. Dajulsen Raja	0	6	0	1327	1327
72. Dalam Agali Raja	20	0	0	1327	1347

		Reigned Years.	M.	D.	Anno	to Anno
73.	Cadda Ginitsirmenam Raja - - - - -	31	0	0	1347	1378
74.	Semini Raja - - - - - - -	3	0	0	1378	1381
75.	Melisinganam Salandana Raja - - - - -	9	0	0	1381	1390
76.	Acbora Raja - - - - - - -	6	0	0	1390	1396
77.	Acboraja - - - - - - - -	51	0	0	1396	1447
78.	Dos Raja - - - - - - -	6	0	0	1447	1453
79.	Rucculei Praccaram Bahu Raja - - -	55	0	0	1453	1508
80.	Jaga Vira Praccaram Bahu - - - -	7	0	0	1508	1515
81.	Maha Pandita Praccaram Bahu Raja - - -	1	0	0	1515	1516
82.	Vira Praccaram Bahu - - - - - -	20	0	0	1516	1536
83.	Darma Praccaram Bahu - - - -	25	0	0	1536	1561
84.	Viga Bahu - - - - - - -	8	0	0	1561	1569
85.	Bowaneca Bahu Mahu Raja - - - -	11	0	0	1569	1580
86.	Darma Palla Raja - - - - - -	10	0	0	1580	1590
87.	Don Philippo - - - - - - -	very short time				1590
88.	Raja Singa Raja - - - - - -	3	0	0	1590	1593
89.	Fimata Darma Suria, or Don John - - -	11	0	0	1593	1604
90.	Cenuwieraat - - - - - - -	28	0	0	1604	1632
91.	Raja Singa Raja - - - - - -	65	0	0	1632	1687
92.	Fimala Darma Suria Maha Raja - - -	20	0	0	1687	1707
93.	Wira Praccaram Narendra Singa - - -	—	–	–	1707	—

THE END.

J. F. Dove, Printer, St. John's Square.

AN

HISTORICAL RELATION

OF THE

ISLAND OF CEYLON,

IN THE

EAST INDIES:

TOGETHER WITH

AN ACCOUNT OF THE DETAINING IN CAPTIVITY THE AUTHOR, AND DIVERS OTHER ENGLISHMEN NOW LIVING THERE; AND OF THE AUTHOR'S MIRACULOUS ESCAPE.

BY ROBERT KNOX,

A CAPTIVE THERE NEAR TWENTY YEARS.

ILLUSTRATED WITH FIGURES, AND A MAP OF THE ISLAND.

LONDON:

PRINTED FOR JOSEPH MAWMAN, LUDGATE STREET,

BY J. F. DOVE, ST. JOHN'S SQUARE.

1817.

TO THE RIGHT WORSHIPFUL

TO THE RIGHT WORSHIPFUL

The Governor, the Deputy Governor, and Four-and-Twenty Committees of the Honourable East India Company, viz.

Sir Josiah Child, Baronet, Governor.
Thomas Papilion, Esq. Deputy.

The Right Honourable George Earl of Berkley,
Sir Joseph Ashe, Baronet,
Sir Samuel Barnardiston, Bart.
Mr. Christopher Boone,
Mr. Thomas Canham,
Colonel John Clerke,
Mr. John Cudworth,
John Dubois, Esq.
Sir James Edwards, Knight, and Alderman,
Richard Hutchinson, Esq.
Mr. Joseph Herne,
Mr. William Hedges,
Sir John Lawrence, Knight, and Alderman,
Mr. Nathaniel Letton,
Sir John Moore, Knight and Alderman,
Samuel Moyer, Esq.
Mr. John Morden,
Mr. John Paige,
Edward Rudge, Esq.
Mr. Jeremy Sambrooke,
Mr. William Sedgwick,
Robert Thomson, Esq.
Samuel Thomson, Esq.
James Ward, Esq.

RIGHT WORSHIPFUL,

WHAT I formerly presented you in writing, having, in pursuance of your commands, now somewhat dressed, by the help of the printer and graver, I a second time humbly tender to you. 'Tis, I confess, at best, too mean a return for your great kindness to me; yet I hope you will not deny it a favourable acceptance, since it is the whole return I made from the Indies, after twenty years stay there, having brought home nothing else; but

Who is also wholly at your

Service and Command,

ROBERT KNOX.

London, 1st of August, 1681.

At the Court of Committees for the East-India Company, the 10th of August, 1681.

WE esteem Captain Knox a man of truth and integrity, and that his relations and accounts of the Island of Ceylon, (which some of us have lately perused in manuscripts) are worthy of credit, and therefore encouraged him to make the same public.

ROBERT BLACKBOURNE, *Secretary.*

By Order of the said Court.

August 8th, 1681.

MR. CHISWELL,

I perused Captain Knox's description of the Isle of Ceylon, which seems to be written with great truth and integrity; and the subject being new, containing an account of a people and country little known to us—I conceive it may give great satisfaction to the curious, and may be well worth your publishing.

CHR. WREN.

PREFACE.

How much of the present knowledge of the parts of the world is owing to late discoveries, may be judged by comparing the modern with the ancient accounts thereof; though possibly many such histories may have been written in former ages, yet few have escaped the injury of time, so as to be handed safe to us. 'Twas many ages, possibly before writing was known, then known to a few, and made use of by fewer, and fewest employed it to this purpose. Add to this, that such as were written remained, for the most part, imprisoned in the cells of some library or study, accessible to a small number of mankind, and regarded by a less, which after perished with the place, or the decay of their own substance. This we may judge from the loss of those many writings mentioned by Pliny, and other of the ancients; and we had yet found fewer, if the art of printing, first invented about two hundred and forty years since, had not secured most that lasted to that time. Since which, that loss has been repaired by a vast number of new accessions, which, besides the satisfaction they have given to curious and inquisitive men, by increasing their knowledge, have excited many more to the like attempts, not only of making, but of publishing also their discoveries: but I am not ignorant still, that as discoveries have been this way preserved, so many others have been lost, to the great detriment of the public. It were very desirable, therefore, that the causes of these and other defects being known, some remedies might be found, to prevent the like losses for the future.

The principal causes, I conceive, may be these:

First, The want of sufficient instructions to seamen and travellers, to shew them what is pertinent and considerable to be observed in their voyages and abodes, and how to make their observations, and keep registers or accounts of them.

Next, The want of some public encouragement for such as shall perform such instructions.

Thirdly, the want of fit persons both to promote and disperse such instructions to persons fitted to engage, and careful to collect returns, and compose them into histories; by examining the persons more at large upon those and other particulars; and by separating what is pertinent from what is not so, and to be rejected; who should have also wherewith to gratify every one according to his performances.

Fourthly, The want of some easy way to have all such printed: first singly, and afterwards divers of them together. It having been found that many small tracts are lost after printing, as well as many that are never printed; upon which account we are much obliged to Mr. Haclute and Mr. Purchas, for preserving many such in their works.

Fifthly, The want of taking care to collect all such relations of voyages, and account of countries, as have been published in other languages, and translating them either into English, or (which will be of more general use) into Latin, the learned language of Europe; there being many such in other countries hardly ever heard of in England.

The difficulties of removing which defects is not so great, but that it might easily fall even within the compass of a private ability to remove, if at least public authority would but countenance the design; how much less then would it be, if the same would afford also some moderate encouragement and reward?

The Royal Society of London, for Improving Natural Knowledge, has not been wanting in preparing and dispersing instructions to this end; and is ready still to promote it, if the public would allow a recompense to the undertakers. The desirableness and facility of this undertaking may, I hope, in a short time, produce the expedients also. In the interim, all means should be used, to try what may be obtained from the generosity of such as have had the opportunities of knowing foreign countries.

There are but few who, though they know much, can yet be persuaded they know any thing worth communicating, and because the things are common and well known to them, are apt to think them so to the rest of mankind: this prejudice has done much mischief in this particular, as well as in many other, and must be first removed. There are others, that are conscious enough of their own knowledge, and yet, either for want of ability to write well, or of use to compose, or of time to study and digest, or out of modesty and fear to be in print, or because they think they know not enough to make a volume, or for not being prompted to, or earnestly solicited for it, neglect to do it; others delay to do it so long, till they have forgotten what they intended. Such as these importunity would prevail upon to disclose their knowledge, if fitting persons were found to discourse and ask them questions, and to compile the answers into a history. Of this kind was lately produced, in High Dutch, a History of Greenland, by Dr. Fogelius, of Hamborough, from the information of Frederick Martin, who had made several voyages to that place, in the doing of which he made use of the instruction given by the Royal Society.

'Tis much to be wondered that we should, to this day, want a good history of most of our West Indian Plantations. Ligon has done well for the Barbadoes, and somewhat has been done for the Summer Islands, Virginia, &c. But how far are all these short, even of the knowledge of these and other places of the West Indies, which may be obtained from divers knowing planters now residing in London? and how easy were it to obtain what is defective, from some ingenious persons now resident upon the places, if some way were found to gratify them for their performances. However, till such be found, 'tis to be hoped, that the kind acceptance only the public shall give to this present work, may excite several other ingenious and knowing men to follow this generous example of Captain Knox; who, though he could bring away nothing almost upon his back, or in his purse, did yet transport the whole kingdom of Candy Uda in his head; and by writing and publishing this his knowledge, has freely given it to his country, and to you, reader, in particular.

'Twas not, I confess, without the earnest solicitations and endeavours of myself, and some others of his friends, obtained from him; but this uneasiness of parting with it was not for want of generosity and freedom enough in communicating whatever he knew or had observed, but from that usual prejudice of modesty, and too mean an opinion of his own knowledge and abilities, of doing any thing should be worthy the view of the public: and, had he found leisure to compose it, he could have filled a much greater volume with useful and pertinent, as well as unusual and strange observations. He could have enriched it with a more particular description of many of their curious plants, fruits, birds, fishes, insects, minerals, stones; and told you many more of the medicinal, and other uses of them, in trades and manufactures. He could have given you a complete dictionary of their language; understanding and speaking it as well as his mother tongue; but his occasions would not permit him to do more at present. Yet the civil usage this his first-born meets with among his countrymen, may, it is hoped, oblige him to gratify them with further discoveries and observations in his future travels.

To conclude, he has in this history given you a taste of his observations; in which most readers, though of very differing gusts, may find somewhat very pleasant to their palate. The statesman, divine, physician, lawyer, merchant, mechanic, husbandman, may select something for their entertainment: the philosopher and historian much more. I believe, at least, all that love truth will be pleased; for, from that little conversation I had with him, I conceive him to be no ways prejudiced or biassed by interest, affection or hatred, fear or hopes, or the vain-glory of telling strange things, so as to make him swerve from the truth of matter of fact: and for his opportunity of being informed, any one may satisfy himself, when he understands his almost twenty years abode and converse among them. His skill in the language and customs of the people, his way of employment in travelling and trading over all parts of the kingdom; add to this his breeding, till nineteen years of age, under his father, a captain for the East India Company, and his own natural and acquired parts; but, above all, his good reputation, which may be judged from the employment that Worshipful Company have now freely bestowed upon him; having made him commander of the Tarquin merchant, and entrusted him to undertake a voyage to Tarquin.

Read, therefore, the book itself, and you will find yourself taken captive indeed; but used more kindly by the author, than he himself was by the natives.

After a general view of the sea coasts, he will lead you into the country by the watches, through the thorny gates, then conduct you round upon the mountains that encompass and fortify the whole kingdom, and by the way carry you to the top of Hommalet or Adam's Peak; from those he will descend with you, and shew you their chief cities and towns, and pass through them into the country, and there acquaint you with their husbandry; then entertain you with the fruits, flowers, herbs, roots, plants, and trees; and, by the way, shelter you from sun and rain with a fan made of the talipat leaf. Then shew you their beasts, birds, fish, serpents, insects; and, last of all, their commodities. From hence he will carry you to court, and shew you the king in the several estates of his life; and acquaint you with his way of governing, revenues, treasures, officers, governors, military strength, wars: and, by the way, entertain you with an account of the late rebellion against him: after which he will bring you acquainted with the inhabitants themselves, whence you may know their different hu mours, ranks, and qualities. Then you may visit their temples, such as they are, and see the foppery of their priests, religious opinions and practices, both in their worship and festivals; and afterwards go home to their houses, and be acquainted with their conversation and entertainment; see their housewifery, furniture, finery; and understand how they breed and dispose of their children in marriage; and in what employments and recreations they pass their time. Then you may acquaint yourself with their language, learning, laws, and, if you please, with their magic and juggling; and, last of all, with their diseases, sickness, death, and manner of burial. After which he will give you a full account of the reason of his own going to, and detainment in the the Island of Ceylon and kingdom of Candy Uda; and of all his various conditions, and the accidents that befel him there, during nineteen years and an half's abode among them; and by what ways and means at last he made his escape, and returned safe into England, in September last, 1680.

ROBERT HOOKE.

Aug. 1, 1681.

CEYLON
ACCORDING TO THE LATEST SURVEY.
Engraved
for Knox's History of the Island.
Published by J. Mawman, 1st July, 1816.
East 80° Longitude
81°
North 6° Latitude
9°
8°
7°
GULF OF MANAAR
BAY OF BENGAL
CANDIAN TERRITORY
MANGUL
NOURECALAVA
KONDEUDA
BINLANA
HOT CORLE
MAULALY
PROVINCE OF THREE CORLES
CANDI OUVAH
MENDE
JALLE
ALLACOLY
SAFFRAGAM CORLE
CADDUACATTA
CANDUCARRE
DISTRICT OF MANAR
DISTRICT OF PUTTELAM AND CHILAW
DISTRICT OF COLOMBO
DISTRICT OF CALTURA
DISTRICT OF GALLE
DISTRICT OF MATURA
DISTRICT OF MAGAMPATTOO
DISTRICT OF THE WANNEY
DISTRICT OF TRINCOMALLE
DISTRICT OF BATTICALOA
COLOMBO
Negombo
Chilaw
POINT DE GALLE
Trincomalle
Batticaloa
Adams Peak
Tank Padivilcolom
Minery Lake
New Candi
Candaly Lake
Delft Island
Amsterdam
Rotterdam
Karidive
Scale of British Miles
Scale of Dutch Miles
East 80° Longitude
81°

AN

HISTORICAL RELATION

OF

CEYLON,

AN

ISLAND IN THE EAST INDIES.

PART I.

CHAP. I.

A General Description of the Island.

How this Island lies with respect unto the neighbouring countries I shall not speak at all, that being to be seen in our ordinary sea cards, which describe those parts; and but little concerning the maritime parts of it, now under the jurisdiction of the Dutch: my design being to relate such things only that are new and unknown unto these European nations. It is the inland country, therefore, I chiefly intend to write of, which is yet

counties, excepting six, Tammanquod, Vellas, Paunoa, Hotteracourly, Hotcurly, and Neurecalava, lie upon hills fruitful and well watered; and therefore they are called in one word Conde Uda, which signifies, On Top of the Hills, and the king is styled, the king of Conde Uda.

Each country divided by woods.

All these counties are divided each from other by great woods; which none may fell, being preserved for fortifications. In most of them there are watches kept constantly, but in troublesome times in all.

The country hilly, but enriched with rivers.

The land is full of hills, but exceedingly well watered, there being many pure and clear rivers running through them; which falling down about their lands is a very great benefit for the country in respect to their rice, their chief sustenance. These rivers are generally very rocky, and so unnavigable. In them are great quantities of fish, and the greater for want of skill in the people to catch them. The main river of all is called Mavelagonga; which proceeds out of the mountain, called Adam's Peak (of which afterwards); it runs through the whole land northward, and falls into the sea at Trenkimalay; it may be an arrow's flight over in breadth, but not navigable, by reason of the many rocks and great falls in it: towards the sea it is full of alligators, but on the mountains none at all.

The great river Mavelagonga described.

It is so deep, that unless it be mighty dry weather a man cannot wade over it, unless towards the head of it. They use little canoes to pass over it: but there are no bridges built over it, being so broad; and the stream in time of rains (which in this country are very great) runs so high, that they cannot make them; neither if they could, would it be permitted: for the king careth not to make his country easy to travel, but desires to keep it intricate. This river runs within a mile or less of the city of Candy. In some places of it, full of rocks; in others, clear for three or four miles.

There is another good large river running through Cotemul, and falls into that before mentioned. There are divers other brave rivers that water the country, though none navigable for the cause abovesaid.

The land is generally covered with woods, excepting the kingdom of Ovuah, and the counties of Oudipallet and Dolusbaug, which are naturally somewhat clear of them. Woody.

It is most populous about the middle, least near about by the sea: how it is with those parts under the Hollander I know not. The northern parts are somewhat sickly, by reason of bad water, the rest very healthful. Where most populous and healthful.

The valleys between their hills are many of them quagmires, and most of them full of brave springs of pure water: which watery valleys are the best sort of land for their corn, as requiring much moisture, as shall be told in its place. The nature of the valleys.

On the south side of Conde Uda is a hill, supposed to be the highest on this Island, called, in the Chingulay language, Hamalell; but, by the Portuguese and the European nations, Adam's Peak. It is sharp like a sugar loaf, and on the top a flat stone with the print of a foot like a man's on it, but far bigger, being about too feet long. The people of this land count it meritorious to go and worship this impression; and generally about their new The great hill, Adam's Peak, described.

year, which is in March, they, men, women, and children, go up this vast and high mountain to worship: the manner of which I shall write hereafter, when I come to describe their religion. Out of this mountain arise many fine rivers, which run through the land, some to the westward, some to the southward, and the main river, viz. Mavelagonga before mentioned, to the northward.

The natural strength of this kingdom.

This kingdom of Conde Uda is strongly fortified by nature; for which way soever you enter into it, you must ascend vast and high mountains, and descend little or nothing. The ways are many, but very narrow, so that but one can go abreast. The hills are covered with wood and great rocks; so that it is scarce possible to get up any where, but only in the paths; in all which there are gates made of thorns, the one at the bottom, the other at the top of the hills, and two or three men always set to watch, who are to examine all that come and go, and see what they carry, that letters may not be conveyed, nor prisoners or other slaves run away. These watches, in case of opposition, are to call out to the towns near, who are to assist them. They oftentimes have no arms, for they are the people of the next towns: but their weapons to stop people are to charge them in the king's name; which disobeyed, is so severely punished, that none dare resist. These watches are but as sentinels to give notice; for, in case of war and danger, the king sends commanders and soldiers to lie here: but of this enough—these things being more proper to be related, when we come to discourse of the policy and strength of the kingdom.

The difference of the seasons in this country.

The one part of this Island differs very much from the other, both in respect of the seasons and the soil: for when the westwardly winds blow, then it rains on the west side of the Island; and that is the season for them to till their grounds: and, at the same time on the east side is very fair and dry weather, and the time of their harvest. On the contrary, when the east winds blow, it is tilling time for those that inhabit the east parts, and harvest to those on the west: so that harvest is here in one part or other all the year long. These rains and this dry weather do part themselves about the middle of the land, as oftentimes I have seen—being on the one side of a mountain, called Cauragashing, rainy and wet weather, and, as soon as I came on the other, dry, and so exceeding hot, that I could scarcely walk on the ground, being, as the manner there is, barefoot.

What parts have most rain.

It rains far more in the high lands of Conde Uda, than in the low lands beneath the hills. The north end of this Island is much subject to dry weather. I have known it for five or six years together so dry, (having no rains, and there is no other means of water but that, being but three springs of running water, that I know, or ever heard of) that they could not plough nor sow, and scarcely could dig wells deep enough to get water to drink; and, when they got it, its taste was brackish. At which time in other parts there wanted not rain; whither the northern people were forced to come to buy food. Let this suffice to have spoken of the countries, soil, and nature of this Island in general. I will proceed to speak of the cities and towns of it, together with some other remarkable matters thereunto belonging.

CHAP. II.

Concerning the Chief Cities and Towns of this Island.

The most eminent cities are five.

IN this Island are several places, where they say formerly stood cities, and still retain the name, though little or nothing of building be now to be seen: but yet there are five cities now standing, which are the most eminent, and where the king hath palaces and goods; yet even these, all of them, except that wherein his person is, are ruined and fallen to decay.

Candy.

The first is the city of Candy, so generally called by the Christians, probably from Conde, which, in the Chingulay's language, signifies hills, for among them it is situated; but by the inhabitants called Hingodagul-neure; as much as to say, the city of the Chingulay people, and Mauneur, signifying the chief, or royal city. This is the chief or metropolitical city of the whole Island. It is placed in the midst of the Island in Tattanour, bravely situate for all conveniences, excellently well watered. The king's palace stands on the east corner of the city, as is customary in this land for the king's palaces to stand. This city is three-square like a triangle, but no artificial strength about it, unless on the south-side, which is the easiest and openest way to it, they have long since cast up a bank of earth cross the valley from one hill to the other; which, nevertheless, is not so steep but that a man may easily go over it any where: it may be some twenty feet in height. In every way to come to this city, about two or three miles off from it, are thorn-gates and watches to examine all that go and come: it is environed round with hills. The great river coming down from Adam's Peak runs within less than a mile of it on the west side: it has oftentimes been burnt by the Portuguese in their former invasions of this Island, together with the king's palace and the temples; insomuch that the king has been fain to pay them a tribute of three elephants *per annum.* The king left this city about twenty years ago, and never since has come at it; so that it is now quite gone to decay.

A second city is Nellemby-neur, lying in Oudipollat, south of Candy, some twelve miles distance. Unto this the king retired, and here kept his court, when he forsook Candy. **Nellemby.**

Thirdly, The city Allout-neur, on the north-east of Candy. **Allout-neur.** Here this king was born; here also he keeps great store of corn and salt, &c. against war or trouble. This is situate in the country of Bintan, which land I have never been at, but have taken **The country of Bintan described.** a view of from the top of a mountain: it seems to be smooth land, and not much hilly; the great river runneth through the midst of it. It is all over covered with mighty woods and abundance of deer; but much subject to dry weather and sickness. In these woods is a sort of wild people inhabiting, whom we shall speak of in their place.

Fourthly, Badoula, eastward from Candy some two days **Badoula.** journey, the second city in this land. The Portuguese, in time of war, burnt it down to the ground. The palace here is quite ruined; the pagodas only remain in good repair.

The province of Ouvah.

This city stands in the kingdom or province of Ouvah, which is a country well watered, the land not smooth, neither the hills very high; wood very scarce, but what they plant about their houses: but great plenty of cattle; their land void of wood, being the more apt for grazing. If these cattle be carried to any other parts in this Island they will commonly die, the reason whereof no man can tell; only they conjecture it is occasioned by a kind of small tree or shrub, that grows in all countries but in Ouvah, the touch or scent of which may be poison to the Ouvah cattle, though it is not so to other. The tree hath a pretty physical smell like an apothecaries shop, but no sort of cattle will eat it. In this country grows the best tobacco that is on this land. Rice is more plenty here than most other things.

Digligy, the place of the king's constant residence.

The fifth city is Digligy-neur, towards the east of Candy, lying in the country of Hevahatts; where the king, ever since he was routed from Nellemby, in the rebellion anno 1664, hath held his court. The situation of this place is very rocky and mountainous, the lands barren; so that hardly a worse place could be found out in the whole Island. Yet the king chose it, partly because it lies about the middle of his kingdom, but chiefly for his safety; having the great mountain Gauluda behind his palace, unto which he fled for safety in the rebellion, being not only high, but on the top of it lie three towns, and corn fields, whence he may have necessary supplies; and, it is so fenced with steep cliffs, rocks, and woods, that a few men here will be able to defend themselves against a great army.

Gauluda.

Many ruins of cities.

There are, besides those already mentioned, several other ruinous places, that do still retain the name of cities, where kings have reigned, though now little footsteps remaining of them. At the north-end of this king's dominions is one of these ruinous cities, called Anurodgburro, where they say ninety kings have reigned, the spirits of whom they hold now to be saints in glory, having merited it by making pagodas and stone pillars and images to the honour of their gods, whereof there are many yet remaining; which the Chingulayes count very meritorious to worship, and the next way to heaven. Near by is a river, by which we came when we made our escape; all along which is abundance of hewed stones, some long for pillars, some broad for paving. Over this river there have been three stone bridges built upon stone pillars, but now are fallen down; and the country all desolate without inhabitants. At this city of Anurodgburro is a watch kept, beyond which are no more people that yield obedience to the King of Candy. This place is above ninety miles to the northward of the city of Candy. In these northern parts there are no hills, nor but two or three springs of running water; so that their corn ripeneth with the help of rain.

Anurodgburro.

The nature of the northern parts.

There is a port in the country of Portaloon, lying on the west side of this Island, whence part of the king's country is supplied with salt and fish; where they have some small trade with the Dutch, who have a fort upon the point to prevent boats from coming. But the eastern parts being too far and hilly to drive cattle thither for salt, God's providence hath provided them a place on the east side nearer them, which, in their language, they call Leawava, where the easterly winds blowing, the sea beats in, and in westwardly winds (being then fair weather there) it becomes salt, and that in such abundance, that they have as much as they please to fetch. This place of Leawava is so con-

The port of Portaloon: it affords salt.

Leawava affords salt in abundance.

Described.

trived by the providence of the Almighty Creator, that neither the Portuguese nor Dutch, in all the time of their wars, could ever prevent this people from having the benefit of this salt, which is the principal thing that they esteem in time of trouble or war; and most of them do keep by them a store of salt against such times. It is, as I have heard, environed with hills on the land side, and by sea not convenient for ships to ride; and very sickly, which they do impute to the power of a great god, who dwelleth near by, in a town they call Cotteragon, standing in the road, to whom all that go to fetch salt, both small and great, must give an offering. The name and power of this god striketh such terror into the Chingulays, that those, who otherwise are enemies to this king, and have served both Portuguese and Dutch against him, yet would never assist either to make invasions this way.

Their towns how built.

Having said thus much concerning the cities and other eminent places of this kingdom, I will now add a little concerning their towns. The best are those that do belong to their idols, wherein stand their dewals or temples. They do not care to make streets by building their houses together in rows, but each man lives by himself in his own plantation, having a hedge it may be, and a ditch round about him, to keep out cattle. Their towns are always placed some distance from the highways; for they care not that their towns should be a thoroughfare for all people, but only for those that have business with them. They are not very big; in some may be forty, in some fifty houses, and in some above a hundred; and in some again not above eight or ten.

Many lie in ruins, and

And, as I said before of their cities, so I must of their towns, that there are many of them here and there lie desolate, occasioned by their voluntary forsaking them, which they often do, in case many of them fall sick, and two or three die soon after one another; for this they conclude to happen from the hand of the devil: whereupon they all leave their town and go to another, thinking thereby to avoid him; thus relinquishing both their houses and lands too. Yet afterwards, when they think the devil hath departed the place, some will sometimes come back and re-assume their lands again.

forsaken, and upon what occasion.

CHAP. III.

Of their Corn, with their Manner of Husbandry.

The product and commodities of the country.

HAVING discoursed hitherto of the country, method will require that I proceed now to the products of it: viz. their fruits, plants, beasts, birds, and other creatures, minerals, commodities, &c. whereof I must declare, once for all, that I do not pretend to write an exact and perfect treatise, my time and leisure not permitting me so to do; but only to give a relation of some of the chief of these things, and as it were a taste of them, according as they that occur to my memory while I am writing. I shall first begin with their corn, as being the staff of their country.

Corn of divers sorts.

They have divers sorts of corn, though all different from ours. And here I shall first speak of their rice, the choice and flower of all their corn, and then concerning the other inferior kinds among them.

Rice.

Of rice they have several sorts, and called by several names, according to the different times of their ripening: however, in taste little disagreeing from one another. Some will require seven months before it come to maturity, called mauvi; some six, hauteal; others will ripen in five, honorowal; others in four, henit; and others in three, aulfancol: the price of these is one and the same. That which is soonest ripe, is most savoury to the taste; but yieldeth the least increase. It may be asked then, why any other sort of rice is sown, but that which is longest a ripening, seeing it brings in most profit? In answer to this, you must know, that all these sorts of rice do absolutely require water to grow in, all the while they stand; so that the inhabitants take great pains in procuring and saving water for their grounds, and in making conveyances of water from their rivers and ponds into their lands, which they are very ingenious in; also in levelling their corn lands, which must be as smooth as a bowling green, that the water may cover all over. Neither are their steep and hilly lands incapable of being thus overflown with water; for the doing of which they use this art: they level these hills into narrow alleys, some three, some eight feet wide, one beneath another, according to the steepness of the hills, working and digging them in that fashion, that they lie smooth and flat, like so many stairs up the hills, one above another. The waters at the top of the hills falling downwards are let into these alleys, and so successively, by running out of one into the other, water all; first the higher lands, and then the lower. The highest alleys have such a quantity of water as may suffice to cover them, the rest runs over unto the next, and that, having its proportion, unto the next, and so by degrees it falls into all these hanging parcels of ground: these waters last sometimes a longer, and sometimes a shorter season. Now the rice they sow is according as they foresee their stock of water will last. It will sometimes last them two or three, or four or five months, more or less; the rice, therefore, they choose to cast into the ground, is of that sort that may answer the duration of the water: for all this crop would be spoilt if the water should fail them before their corn grew ripe. If they foresee their water will hold out long, then they sow the best and most profitable rice, viz. that which is longest a ripening; but, if it will not, they must be content to sow of the worser sorts; that is, those

Grows in water.

Their ingenuity in watering their corn lands.

Why they do not always sow the best kind of rice.

that are sooner ripe. Again, they are forced sometimes to sow this younger rice, for preventing the damage it might otherwise meet with, if it should stand longer: for their fields are all in common; which, after they have sown, they enclose till harvest. But as soon as the corn first sown becomes ripe, when the owner has reaped it, it is lawful for him to break down his fences, and let in his cattle for grazing; which would prove a great mischief to that corn that required to stand a month or two longer. Therefore, if they are constrained to sow later than the rest, either through want, or sloth, or any other impediment, yet they make use of that kind of rice that will become ripe equal with that first sown. And so they all observe one time of reaping to prevent their corn being trampled down or eaten up by the cattle. Thus they time their corn to their harvest; some sowing sooner, some later, but all reaping together, unless they be fields that are enclosed by themselves, and peculiar to one man.

They sow at different times, but reap together.

Their artificial pools.

Where there are no springs or rivers to furnish them with water, as it is in the northern parts, where there are but two or three springs, they supply this defect by saving of rain water; which they do by casting up great banks in convenient places, to stop and contain the rains that fall, and so save it till they have occasion to let it out into their fields: they are made rounding like a C, or half moon; every town has one of these ponds, which, if they can but get filled with water, they count their corn is as good as in the barn. It was no small work to the ancient inhabitants to make all these banks, of which there is a great number; being some two, some three fathoms in height, and in length, some above a mile, some less—not all of a size. They are now grown over with great trees, and so seem natural hills.

When they would use the water, they cut a gap in one end of the bank, and so draw the water by little and little, as they have occasion for the watering their corn: these ponds in dry weather dry up quite. If they should dig these ponds deep, it would not be so convenient for them; it would, indeed, contain the water well, but would not so well nor in such plenty empty out itself into their grounds. In these ponds are alligators, which, when the water is dried up, depart into the woods, and down to the rivers; and in the time of rains come up again into the ponds. They are but small, nor do use to catch people; nevertheless they stand in some fear of them. The corn they sow in these parts is of that sort that is soonest ripe, fearing lest their waters should fail. As the water dries out of these ponds, they make use of them for fields, treading the mud with buffaloes, and then sowing rice thereon, and frequently casting up water with scoops on it. I have hitherto spoken of those rices that require to grow in water.

Alligators harbour in them.

They sow corn on the mud.

There is yet another sort of rice, which will ripen though it stand not always in water: and this sort of corn serves for those places, where they cannot bring their waters to overflow; this will grow with the rains that fall; but is not esteemed equal with the others, and differs both in scent and taste from that which groweth in the watery fields.

A sort of rice that grows without water.

The ordinary season of seed time is in the months of July and August, and their harvest in or about February; but for land that is well watered, they regard no season; the season is all the year long. When they till their grounds, or reap their corn, they do it by whole towns, generally, all helping each other for attoms, as they call it; that is, that they may help them

The seasons of seed time and harvest.

as much, or as many days again in their fields, which accordingly they will do. They plough only with a crooked piece of wood, something like an elbow, which roots up the ground, as uneven as if it were done by hogs, and then they overflow it with water.

A particular description of their husbandry.

But if any be so curious as to know more particularly how they order and prepare their lands, and sow their corn, take this account of it. But before we go to work, it will be convenient first to describe the tools. To begin therefore with their plough.

Their plough.

I said before it was a crooked piece of wood; it is but little bigger than a man's arm, one end whereof is to hold by, and the other to root up the ground. In the hollow of this plough is a piece of wood fastened some three or four inches thick, equal with the breadth of the plough: and at the end of the plough is fixed an iron plate to keep the wood from wearing. There is a beam let into that part of it that the ploughman holds in his hand, to which they make their buffaloes fast to drag it.

The convenience of these ploughs.

These ploughs are proper for this country, because they are lighter, and so may be the more easy for turning, the fields being short, so that they could not turn with longer, and, if heavier, they would sink and be unruly in the mud. These ploughs bury not the grass as ours do, and there is no need they should, for their endeavour is only to root up the ground, and so they overflow it with water, and this rots the grass.

Their first ploughing.

They plough twice before they sow. But before they begin the first time, they let in water upon their land, to make it more soft and pliable for the plough. After it is once ploughed, they make up their banks. For if otherwise they should let it alone

The manner of their Ploughing

Smith, sc. 63 H. Holborn

The manner of smoothing their Fields

London: Published May 10th 1816. by J. Mawman

till after the second ploughing, it would be mere mud, and not hard enough to use for banking. Now these banks are greatly necessary, not only for paths for the people to go upon through the fields, who otherwise must go in the mud, it may be knee deep; but chiefly to keep in and contain their water, which by the help of these banks they overflow their grounds with. These banks they make as smooth with the backside of their houghs, as a bricklayer can smooth a wall with his trowel: for in this they are very neat. These banks are usually not above a foot over.

Their banks, and use of them

After the land is thus ploughed and the banks finished, it is laid under water again for some time, till they go to ploughing the second time. Now it is exceeding muddy, so that the trampling of the cattle that draws the plough, does as much good as the plough; for the more muddy the better. Sometimes they use no plough this second time, but only drive their cattle over to make the ground the muddier.

Their second ploughing.

Their lands being thus ordered, they still keep them overflowed with water, that the weeds and grass may rot. Then they take their corn and lay it a soak in water a whole night, and the next day take it out, and lay it in a heap, and cover it with green leaves, and so let it lie some five or six days to make it grow. Then they take and wet it again, and lay it in a heap covered over with leaves as before, and so it grows and shoots out with blades and roots. In the mean time while this is thus a growing, they prepare their ground for sowing; which is thus: they have a board about four foot long, which they drag over their land by a yoke of buffaloes, not flat ways, but upon the edge of it. The use of which is, that it jumbles the earth and weeds together,

How they prepare their seed-corn.

And their land after it is ploughed.

and also levels and makes the grounds smooth and even, that so the water (for the ground is all this while under water) may stand equal in all places. And wheresoever there is any little hummock standing out of the water, which they may easily see by their eye, with the help of this board they break and lay even. And so it stands overflown while their seed is growing, and become fit to sow, which usually is eight days after they lay it in soak.

When the seed is ready to sow, they drain out all the water, and with little boards of about a foot and a half long, fastened upon long poles, they trim the land over again, laying it very smooth, making small furrows all along, that in case rain or other waters should come in, it might drain away; for more water now would endanger rotting the corn. And then they sow their corn, which they do with very exact evenness, strewing it with their hands, just as we strew salt upon meat.

Their manner of sowing.

And thus it stands without any water, till such time as the corn be grown some three or four inches above the ground. There were certain gaps made in the banks to let out the water, these are now stopped to keep it in; which is not only to nourish the corn, but to kill the weeds: for they keep their fields as clean as a garden without a weed. Then when the corn is grown about a span high, the women come and weed it, and pull it up where it grew too thick, and transplant it where it wants. And so it stands overflown till the corn be ripe, when they let out the water again to make it dry for reaping. They never use any dung, but their manner of plowing and soaking of their ground serves instead thereof.

How they manure and order their young corn.

Smith, sc. 63 H. Holborn

The manner of treading out their Rice

London: Published May 10th 1816. by J. Murray

At reaping they are excellent good, just after the English manner. The whole town, as I said before, as they join together in tilling, so in their harvest also; for all fall in together in reaping one man's field, and so to the next, until every man's corn be down. And the custom is, that every man, during the reaping of his corn, finds all the rest with victuals. The womens work is to gather up the corn after the reapers, and carry it altogether.

Their manner of reaping.

They use not threshing, but tread out their corn with cattle, which is a far quicker and easier way. They may tread out in a day forty or fifty bushels at least with the help of half a dozen cattle.

They tread out their corn with cattle.

When they are to tread their corn they choose a convenient adjoining place. Here they lay out a round piece of ground some twenty or five and twenty feet over, from which they cut away the upper turf. Then certain ceremonies are used. First, they adorn this place with ashes made into flowers and branches, and round circles. Then they take divers strange shells, and pieces of iron, and some sorts of wood, and a bunch of betel nuts, (which are reserved for such purposes) and lay all these in the very middle of the pit, and a large stone upon them. Then the women, whose proper work it is, bring each their burthen of reaped corn upon their heads, and go round in the pit three times, and then fling it down. And after this without any more ado, bring in the rest of the corn as fast as they can. For this labour, and that of weeding, the women have a fee due to them, which they call *warapol*, that is, as much corn as shall cover the stone and the other conjuration instruments at the bottom of the pit.

The ceremonies they use when the corn is to be trodden.

They will frequently carry away their new reaped corn into the pit, and tread it out presently as soon as they have cut it down, to secure it from the rains, which in some parts are very great and often; and barns they have none big enough. But in other places not so much given to rains, they will sometimes set it up in a cock, and let it stand some months.

How they unhusk their rice.

They unshale their rice from its outward husk by beating it in a mortar, or on the ground more often; but some of these sorts of rice must first be boiled in the husk, otherwise in beating it will break to powder. The which rice, as it is accounted, so I by experience have found, to be the wholsomest; this they beat again the second time to take off a bran from it; and after that it becomes white. And thus much concerning rice-corn.

Other sorts of corn among them.

Besides this, though far inferior to it, there are divers other sorts of corn which serve the people for food in the absence of rice, which will scarcely hold out with many of them above half the year. (Coracan.) There is coracan, which is a small seed like mustard-seed; this they grind to meal or beat in a mortar, and so make cakes of it, baking it upon the coals in a potsheard, or dress it otherwise. If they, which are not used to it, eat it, it will gripe their bellies; when they are minded to grind it, they have for their mill two round stones, which they turn with their hands by the help of a stick: there are several sorts of this corn. Some will ripen in three months, and some require four. If the ground be good, it yields a great increase, and grows both on the hills and in the plains. (Tauna.) There is another corn called tanna; it is much eaten in the northern parts, in Conde Uda, but little sown. It is as small as the former, but yieldeth a far greater increase. From one grain may spring up two, three, four, or

five stalks, according as the ground is, on each stalk one ear, that contains thousands of grains. I think it gives the greatest increase of any one seed in the world. Each husbandman sows not above a pottle at a seeds-time. It grows up two foot, or two foot and an half from the ground. The way of gathering it when ripe, is, that the women (whose office it is) go and crop off the ears with their hands, and bring them home in baskets. They only take off the ears of coracan also, but they being tough, are cut off with knives. This tanna must be parched in a pan, and then is beaten in a mortar to unhusk it. It will boil like rice, but swell far more; the taste not bad but very dry, and accounted wholesome; the fashion flattish, the colour yellow and very lovely to the eye. It ripens in four months, some sorts of it in three. There are also divers other sorts, which grow on dry land (as the former) and ripen with the rain. Asmoung, a corn Moung.
somewhat like vetches, growing in a cod. Omb, a small seed, Omb.
boiled and eaten as rice. It has an operation pretty strange, which is, that when it is new it will make them that eat it like drunk, sick and spue; and this only when it is sown in some grounds, for in all it will not have this effect; and, being old, none will have it. Minere, a small seed. Boumas, we call them garavances. Tolla, a seed used to make oil, with which they anoint themselves; and sometimes they will parch it and eat it with jaggory, a kind of brown sugar. And thus much of their corn.

CHAP. IV.

Of their Fruits and Trees.

Great variety of fruits, and dilicious.

OF fruits here are great plenty and variety, and far more might be if they did esteem or nourish them. Pleasant fruits to eat ripe they care not at all to do. They look only after those that may fill the belly, and satisfy their hunger when their corn is spent, or to make it go the further. These only they plant, the other fruits of pleasure plant themselves, the seeds of the ripe fruits shedding and falling on the ground naturally spring up again. They have all fruits that grow in India. Most sorts of these delicious fruits they gather before they be ripe, and boil them to make carrees, to use the Portuguese word, that is somewhat to eat with and relish their rice. But wheresoever there is any fruit better than ordinary, the ponudecarso, or officers of the country, will tie a string about the tree in the king's name with three knots on the end thereof, and then no man, not the owner himself, dares presume under pain of some great punishment, if not death, to touch them. And when they are ripe, they are wrapped in white cloth, and carried to him who is governor of that country wherein they grow: and if they be without any defect or blemish, then being wrapped up again in white cloth, he presents them to the king. But the owner, in whose ground they grow is paid nothing at all for them: it is well if he be not compelled to carry them himself into the bargain, unto the king, be it never so far. These are reasons why the people regard not to plant more than just to keep them alive.

The best fruits, wherever they grow, reserved for the king.

But to specify some of the chief of the fruits in request among them. I begin with their betel-nuts: the trees that bear them grow only on the south and west sides of this Island. They do not grow wild, they are only in their towns, and there like unto woods without any inclosures to distinguish one man's trees from another's; but, by marks of great trees, hummacks, or rocks, each man knows his own; they plant them not, but the nuts being ripe fall down in the grass, and so grow up to trees: they are very straight and tall, few bigger than the calf of a man's leg; the nuts grow in bunches at the top, and being ripe look red and very lovely like a pleasing fruit: when they gather them, they lay them in heaps until the shell be somewhat rotted, and then dry them in the sun, and afterwards shell them with a sharp stick one and one at a time. These trees will yield some 500, some a 1000, some 1500 nuts, and some but three or four hundred; they bear but once a year generally, but commonly there are green nuts enough to eat all the year long; the leaves of it are somewhat like those of a cocoa-nut tree, they are five or six feet long, and have other lesser leaves growing out of the sides of them, like the feathers on each side of a quill. The Chingulays call the large leaves the boughs, and the leaves on the sides the leaves; they fall off every year, and the skin upon which they grow with them; these skins grow upon the body of the tree, and the leaves grow out on them; they also clap about the buds or blossoms which bear the nuts, and as the buds swell, so this skin-cover gives way to them, till at length it falls quite off with the great leaf on it; it is somewhat like unto leather, and of great use unto the country people: it serves them instead of basons to eat their rice in, and when they go a journey to tie up their provisions; for in these skins or leaves they can tie up any liquid substance, as oil or water, doubling it in the middle, and rolling it in the two

Betel-nuts.

The trees.

The fruit.

The leaves.

The skins, and their use.

sides, almost like a purse. For bigness, they are according to the trees, some bigger, some less; ordinarily they are about two feet in length, and a foot and an half in breadth. In this country there are no inns to go to, and therefore their manner, when they travel, is to carry ready dressed what provisions they can, which they make up in these leaves. The trees within have only a kind of pith, and will split from one end to the other; the wood is hard and very strong; they use it for laths for their houses, and also for rails for their hedges, which are only stakes stuck in the ground, and rails tied along with rattans, or other withs growing in the woods. Money is not very plentiful in this land; but by means of these nuts, which is a great commodity to carry to the coasts of Coromandel, they furnish themselves with all things they want. The common price of nuts, when there was a trade, as there was when I came first on this land, is 20,000 for one dollar; but now they lie and grow, or rot in the ground under the trees. Some of these nuts do differ much from others in their operation, having this effect, that they will make people drunk and giddy headed, and give them some stools, if they eat them green.

The wood.

The profit the fruit yields.

Jacks.

There is another fruit, which we call jacks; the inhabitants when they are young call them *polos*, before they be full ripe *cose*; and when ripe, *warracha* or *vellas*: but with this difference, the warracha is hard, but the vellas as soft as pap, both looking alike to the eye no difference; but they are distinct trees. These are a great help to the people, and a great part of their food. They grow upon a large tree; the fruit is as big as a good peck loaf, the outside prickly like an hedge-hog, and of a greenish colour; there are in them seeds or kernels, or eggs, as the Chingulayes call them, which lie dispersed in the fruit like seeds in a cucumber: they usually gather them before they be full ripe, boring an hole in them, and, feeling of the kernel, they know if they be ripe enough for their purpose; then being cut in pieces, they boil them, and eat to save rice and fill their bellies: they eat them as we would do turnips or cabbage, and taste and smell much like the latter; one may suffice six or seven men. When they are ripe they are sweet and good to eat raw. The kernels do much resemble chesnuts both in colour and taste, and are almost as good: the poor people will boil or roast them in the embers, there being usually a good heap of them lying in a corner by the fire side; and, when they go a journey, they will put them in a bag for their provisions by the way. One jack may contain three pints or two quarts of these seeds or kernels. When they cut these jacks, there comes running out a white thick substance, like tar, and will stick just like birdlime, which the boys make use of to catch birds, which they call cola, or blood of the cos: some will mix this with the flower of rice, and it will eat like eggs.

Jombo.

Another fruit there is which I never saw in any other parts of India, they call it jombo; in taste it is like to an apple, full of juice, and pleasant to the palate, and not unwholesome to the body, and to the eye, no fruit more amiable, being white, and delicately coloured with red, as if it were painted.

Other fruits found in the woods.

Also in the wild woods are several sorts of pretty fruits, as murros, round in shape, and as big as a cherry, and sweet to the taste; dongs, nearest like to a black cherry; ambelos, like to barberries; carolla cabella, cabela pooke, and pollas, these are like to little plums, and very well tasted; paragidde, like to our pears, and many more such like fruits.

Fruits common with other parts of India.

Here are also, of Indian fruits, cocoa nuts; plantains also and bananas of divers and sundry sorts, which are distinguished by the taste as well as by the names; rare sweet oranges and sour ones, limes, but no lemons, such as ours are; pautaurings, in taste all one with a lemon, but much bigger than a man's two fists, right citrons, and a small sort of sweet oranges. Here are several other sorts of lemons, and oranges, mangoes of several sorts, and some very good and sweet to eat. In this sort of fruit the king much delights, and hath them brought to him from all parts of the Island. Pine apples also grow there, sugar canes, water melons, pomegranates, grapes both black and white, mirablins, codjeus, and several others.

There are three other trees that must not here be omitted; which, though they bear no eatable fruit, yet the leaves of the one, and the juice of the other, and the bark of the third, are very renowned, and of great benefit.

The tallipot; the rare uses of the leaf.

The first is the tallipot; it is as big and tall as a ship's mast, and very straight, bearing only leaves, which are of great use and benefit to this people; one single leaf being so broad and large, that it will cover some fifteen or twenty men, and keep them dry when it rains. The leaf being dried is very strong, and limber, and most wonderfully made for mens convenience to carry along with them; for, though this leaf be thus broad when it is open, yet it will fold close like a lady's fan, and then it is no bigger than a man's arm: it is wonderfully light: they cut them into pieces, and carry them in their hands. The whole leaf spread is round almost like a circle, but being cut in pieces for use, are near like unto a triangle: they lay them upon their heads as they travel, with the peaked end foremost, which is convenient to

The manner of their sheltering themselves from the rain, by the Talipat leaf

London: Published May 10th 1816, by J. Mawman

make their way through the boughs and thickets. When the sun is vehement hot, they use them to shade themselves from the heat: soldiers all carry them; for, besides the benefit of keeping them dry in case it rain upon the march, these leaves make their tents to lie under in the night. A marvellous mercy which Almighty God hath bestowed upon this poor and naked people in this rainy country! one of these I brought with me into England: these leaves will grow on the top of the tree after the manner of a cocoa. It bears no kind of fruit until the last year of its life, and then it comes out on the top, and spreads abroad in great branches, all full first of yellow blossoms, most lovely and beautiful to behold, but smell very strong, and then it comes to a fruit round and very hard, as big as our largest cherries, but good only for seed to set: and though this tree bears but once, it makes amends, bearing such great abundance, that one tree will yield seed enough for a country. If these tress stand near any houses, the smell of the blossoms so much annoys them, that they, regarding not the seed, forthwith cut them down. This tree is within a pith only, which is very good to eat if they cut the tree down before it runs to seed: they beat it in mortars to flour, and bake cakes of it; which taste much like to white bread: it serves them instead of corn before their harvest be ripe. The pith good to eat.

The next tree is the kettule: it groweth straight, but not so tall or big as the cocoa nut tree; the inside nothing but a white pith, as the former. It yieldeth a sort of liquor, which they call tellegie: it is rarely sweet and pleasing to the palate, and as wholesome to the body, but no stronger than water: they take it down from the tree twice, and from some good trees thrice, in a day. An ordinary tree will yield some three, some four gallons The kettule yields a deliciousjuice.

in a day, some more and some less; the which liquor they boil, and make a kind of brown sugar, called jaggory; but if they will use their skill, they can make it as white as the second best sugar, and for any use: it is but little inferior to ordinary sugar. The manner how they take this liquor from the tree is thus:—when the tree is come to maturity, first out of the very top there cometh out a bud, which, if they let it grow, will bear a round fruit, which is the seed it yieldeth, but is only good to set for increase. This bud they cut and prepare, by putting to it several sorts of things, as salt, pepper, lemons, garlic, leaves, &c. which keeps it at a stand, and suffers it not to ripen. So they daily cut a thin slice off the end, and the liquor drops down in a pot, which they hang to catch it.

The skin bears strings as strong as wire.

It bears a leaf like to that of a betel nut tree, which is fastened to a skin as the betel nut leaves were, only this skin is hard and stubborn, like a piece of board: the skin is all full of strings as strong as wire; they use them to make ropes withal. As long as the tree is growing, the leaves shed; but when the tree is come to its full growth, they remain many years upon the tree before they fall; and when they fall, there are no new ones come again: the top bud, as it ripens and withers, other buds come out lower and lower every year till they come to the bottom of the boughs, and then it hath done bearing, and so may stand seven or ten years, and then dies.

The wood; its nature and use.

The wood of this tree is not above three inches thick, mighty strong and hard to cut in two, but very apt to split from top to bottom; a very heavy wood: they make pestles of it to beat their rice with, the colour black, but looks not like natural wood, but as if it were composed of divers pieces. The buds of this tree, as also of the cocoa, and betel nut tree, are excellent in taste, resembling walnuts or almonds.

I proceed to the third tree, which is the cinnamon, in their language corunda gauhah; it grows wild in the woods as other trees, and by them no more esteemed; it is most on the west side of the great river Mavela-gonga. It is much as plenty as hazel in England; in some places a great deal, in some little, and in some none at all. The trees are not very great, but sizeable: the cinnamon is the bark or rind, when it is on the tree it looks whitish; they scrape it and pull it off, and dry it in the sun: they take it only from off the smaller trees, although the bark of the greater is as sweet to the smell and as strong to the taste. The wood has no smell, in colour white, and soft like fir, which for any use they cut down, favouring them no more than other wild trees in the wood: the leaf much resembles the laurel, both in colour and thickness; the difference is, whereas the laurel hath but one straight rib throughout, whereon the green spreads itself on each side; the cinnamon hath three by which the leaf stretches forth itself. When the young leaves come out, they look purely red, like scarlet; break or bruise them, and they will smell more like cloves than cinnamon. It bears a fruit, which is ripe in September, much like an acorn, but smaller; it neither tastes nor smells much like the bark, but being boiled in water, it will yield an oil swimming on the top, which, when cold, is as hard as tallow, and as white, and smelleth excellently well. They use it for ointments for aches and pains, and to burn in their lamps to give light in their houses; but they make no candles of it, neither are candles used by any but the king.

The cinnamon tree. The bark. The wood. The leaf. The fruit.

Here are many sorts of trees that bear berries to make oil of, both in the woods and gardens; but not eatable, but used only for their lamps.

There are many other trees remarkable either for their strangeness, or use, or both. Of these I shall mention a few.

The orula, the fruit good for physic and dying.

The orula, a tree as big as an apple tree, bears a berry somewhat like an olive, but sharper at each end; its skin is of a reddish green colour, which covereth an hard stone. They make use of it for physic in purges, and also to dye black colour, which they do after this manner: they take the fruit and break it to pieces in mortars, and put it thus beaten into water; and after it has been soaking a day or two, it changeth the water, that it looks like beer, then they dip their cloth in it, or what they mean to dye, and dry it in the sun, and then they dip it in black mud, and so let it lie about an hour, then take it and wash it in water: now it will appear of a pale black: then being dry, they dip it again into the aforesaid dye, and it becomes a very good black.

This water will brighten rusty iron, and serve instead of ink.

Another use there is of this water. It is this: let any rusty iron lie a whole night in it, and it will become bright, and the water look black like ink, insomuch, that men may write with it. These trees grow but in some parts of the land, and nothing near so plentiful as cinnamon. The berries the druggists in the city there, do sell in their shops.

The dounekaia.

The dounekaia gauhah, a shrub, bears leaves as broad as two fingers, and six or eight feet long, on both sides of them set full of thorns, and a streak of thorns runs through the middle. These leaves they split to weave mats withal. The tree bears a bud above a span long, tapering somewhat like a sugar-loaf. Leaves cover this bud, folding it about like the leaves of a cabbage; which leaves smell rarely sweet, and look of a lovely yellow colour like gold. This bud blows into divers bunches of flowers, spreading itself open like a plume of feathers, each flower whitish, but very small. The roots of this shrub they use for ropes, splitting them into thongs, and then making them into ropes.

The capita gauhah is a shrub never bigger than a man's arm. The wood, rind, and leaves, have all a physical smell, and they do sometimes make use of it for physic. The leaf is of a bright green, roundish, rough, and as big as the palm of a hand. No sort of cattle will eat it; no, not the goats, that will sometimes brouze upon rank poison. There is abundance of these trees every where, and they grow in all countries but in Ouvah; and this is supposed to be the cause that the Ouvah cattle die when they are brought thence to any other country. They attribute it to the smell of this tree, of such a venomous nature it is to beasts; and, therefore, to destroy their fleas, or to keep their houses clear of them, they sweep them with brooms made of this shrub. It is excellent good for firing, and will burn when it is green. There are no other coals the goldsmiths use, but what are made of this wood. The Capita.

Rattans grow in great abundance upon this island: they run like honey-suckles, either upon the ground or up trees, as it happens, near twenty fathom in length. There is a kind of a shell or skin grows over the rattan, and encloseth it round, which serves for a case to cover and defend it when tender. This skin is so full of prickles and thorns, that you cannot touch it. As Rattans.

the rattan grows longer and stronger, this case grows ripe and falls off, prickles and shell and all.

Its fruit. It bears fruit in clusters just like bunches of grapes, and as big. Every particular berry is covered with a husk like a gooseberry, which is soft, yellow, and scaly, like the scales of a fish, handsome to look upon. This husk being cracked and broken, within grows a plumb of a whitish colour; within the plumb a stone, having meat about it. The people gather and boil them, to make sour pottage to quench the thirst.

Canes. Canes grow just like rattans, and bear a fruit like them; the difference only is, that the canes are larger.

The betel tree. The tree that bears the betel-leaf, which is so much loved and eaten in these parts, grows like ivy, twining about trees or poles which they stick in the ground for it to run up by; and as the betel grows, the poles grow also. The form of the leaf is longish, the end somewhat sharp, broadest next to the stalk, of a bright green, very smooth, just like a pepper leaf, only different in the colour, the pepper leaf being of a dark green. It bears a fruit just like long pepper, but not good for seed, for it falls off and rots upon the ground. But when they are minded to propagate it, they plant the sprigs, which will grow.

The bo-ganhah, or god-tree. I shall mention but one tree more as famous and highly set by as any of the rest, if not more, though it bear no fruit, the benefit consisting chiefly in the holiness of it. This tree they call Bogauhah; we, the god-tree. It is very great and spreading, the leaves always shake like an asp. They have a very great veneration for these trees, worshipping them, upon a tradition, that the Buddou, a great god among them, when he was upon the earth, did use to sit under this kind of trees. There are many of these trees, which they plant all the land over, and have more care of than of any other. They pave round about them like a key; sweep often under them to keep them clean; they light lamps, and set up their images under them; and a stone table is placed under some of them to lay their sacrifices on. They set them every where in towns and highways, where any convenient places are; they serve also for shade to travellers. They will also set them in memorial of persons deceased, to wit, there where their bodies were burnt. It is held meritorious to plant them, which, they say, he that does shall die within a short while after, and go to heaven: but the oldest men only that are nearest death in the course of nature, do plant them, and none else; the younger sort desiring to live a little longer in this world before they go to the other.

CHAP. V.

Of their Roots, Plants, Herbs, and Flowers.

Roots for food.

SOME of these are for food, and some for medicine: I begin with their roots, with which the jacks before mentioned, being many, and generally bearing well, are a great help towards the sustenance of this people; these by the Chingulays by a general name are called alloes, by the Portuguese and us inyames; they are of divers and sundry sorts, some they plant, and some grow wild; those that grow wild in the woods are as good, only they are more scarce and grow deeper, and so more difficult to be plucked up: it would be to no purpose to mention their particular names; I shall only speak a little in general of them: they serve both for food, and for carrees, that is, sauce, or for a relish to their rice: but they make many a meal of them alone to lengthen out their rice, or for want of it: and of these there is no want to those that will take pains but to set them, and cheap enough to those that will buy.

The manner of their growing.

There are two sorts of these alloes: some require trees or sticks to run upon; others require neither; of the former sort, some will run up to the tops of very large trees, and spread out very full of branches, and bear great bunches of blossoms, but no use made of them; the leaves die every year, but the roots grow still, which some of them will do to a prodigious bigness within a year or two's time, becoming as big as a man's waist;

the fashion of them somewhat roundish, rugged, and uneven, and in divers odd shapes, like a log of cleft wood: they have a very good, savory, mellow taste.

Of those that do not run up on trees, there are likewise sundry sorts; they bear a long stalk and a broad leaf; the fashion of these roots are somewhat roundish, some grow out like a man's fingers, which they call angul-alloes, as much as to say finger-roots; some are of a white colour, some of a red.

Those that grow in the woods run deeper into the earth, they run up trees also: some bear blossoms somewhat like hops, and they may be as big as a man's arm.

For herbs to boil and eat with butter they have excellent good ones, and several sorts: some of them are six months growing to maturity, the stalk as high as a man can reach, and being boiled almost as good as asparagus; there are of this sort, some having leaves and stalks as red as blood, some green: some the leaves green, and the stalk very white. Boiling herbs.

They have several other sorts of fruits which they dress and eat with their rice, and taste very savoury, called carowela, wattacul, morango, cacorehouns, &c. the which I cannot compare to any things that grow here in England. Fruits for sauce.

They have of our English herbs and plants, colworts, carrots, radishes, fennel, balsam, spearmint, mustard; these, excepting the two last, are not the natural product of the land, but they are transplanted hither; by which I perceive all other European plants would grow there: they have also fern, Indian corn; seve- European herbs and plants among them.

ral sorts of beans as good as those in England; right cucumbers, calabasses, and several sorts of pumkins, &c. The Dutch on that Island in their gardens have lettuce, rosemary, sage, and all other herbs and salladings that we have in these countries.

Herbs for medicine.

Nor are they worse supplied with medicinal herbs: the woods are their apothecaries shops, where with herbs, leaves, and the rinds of trees they make all their physic and plaisters, with which sometimes they will do notable cures. I will not here enter into a larger discourse of the medical virtues of their plants, &c. of which there are hundreds: only as a specimen thereof, and likewise of their skill to use them, I will relate a passage or two:—A neighbour of mine, a Chingulay, would undertake to cure a broken leg or arm by application of some herbs that grow in the woods, and that with that speed, that the broken bone, after it was set, should knit by the time one might boil a pot of rice and three carrees, that is about an hour and a half, or two hours; and I knew a man who told me he was thus cured. They will cure an imposthume in the throat with the rind of a tree called amaranga, (whereof I myself had the experience); by chewing it for a day or two after it is prepared, and swallowing the spittle; I was well in a day and a night, though before I was exceedingly ill, and could not swallow my victuals.

Their flowers.

Of flowers they have great varieties, growing wild, for they plant them not; there are roses red and white, scented like ours; several sorts of sweet smelling flowers, which the young men and women gather to tie in their hairs to perfume them; they tie up their hair in a bunch behind, and enclose the flowers therein.

There is one flower deserves to be mentioned for the rarity and use of it, they call it a sindric-mal; there are of them some of a murry colour, and some white; its nature is, to open about four o'clock in the evening, and so continueth open all night until the morning, when it closeth up itself till four o'clock again; some will transplant them out of the woods into the gardens to serve them instead of a clock, when it is cloudy that they cannot see the sun.

A flower that serves instead of a dial.

There is another white flower like our jasmine, well scented; they call them picha-mauls, which the king hath a parcel of brought to him every morning, wrapped in a white cloth, hanging upon a staff, and carried by people, whose peculiar office this is: all people that meet these flowers, out of respect to the king, for whose use they are, must turn out of the way; and so they must for all other things that go to the king, being wrapped up in white cloth; these officers hold land of the king for this service: their office is, also, to plant these flowers, which they usually do near the rivers where they most delight to grow: nay, they have power to plant them in any man's ground, and enclose that ground when they have done it for the sole use of their flowers to grow in: which inclosures they will keep up for several years, until the ground becomes so worn, that the flowers will thrive there no longer, and then the owners resume their own lands again.

Hop-mauls are flowers growing upon great trees, which bear nothing else, they are rarely sweet scented; this is the chief flower the young people use, and is of greatest value among them.

CHAP. VI.

Of their Beasts, Tame and Wild. Insects.

What beasts the country produceth.

HAVING spoken concerning the trees and plants of this Island, we will now go on to speak of the living creatures on it; viz. their beasts, insects, birds, fish, serpents, &c. useful or noxious; and we begin first with their beasts:—they have cows, buffaloes, hogs, goats, deer, hares, dogs, jackals, apes, tigers, bears, elephants, and other wild beasts; lions, wolves, horses, asses, and sheep, thay have none; deer are in great abundance in the woods, and of several sorts, from the largeness of a cow or buffalo, to the smallness of a hare; for here is a creature in this land no bigger, but in every part rightly resembleth a deer, it is called meminna, of colour grey, with white spots, and good meat.

Deer no bigger than hares.

Other creatures rare in their kind.

Here are also wild buffaloes; also a sort of beast they call gauvera, so much resembling a bull, that I think it one of that kind; his back stands up with a sharp ridge; all his four feet white up half his legs; I never saw but one, which was kept among the king's creatures; here was a black tygre catched and brought to the king, and afterwards a deer, milk white; both which he very much esteemed: there being no more either before or since ever heard of in that land.

The way how a wild deer was caught.

If any desire to know how this white deer was caught, it was thus:—this deer was observed to come on evenings with the rest of the herd to a great pond to drink; the people that were ordered to catch this deer, fenced the pond round and plain about it with high stakes, leaving only one wide gap; the men after this done lay in ambush, each with his bundle of stakes ready cut: in the evening the deer came with the rest of the herd to drink according to their want: as soon as they were entered within the stakes, the men in ambush fell to their work, which was to fence in the gap left, which, there being little less than a thousand men, they soon did; and so all the herd were easily caught, and this among the rest.

The king hath also an elephant, spotted or speckled all the body over, which was lately caught; and though he hath many and very stately elephants, and many more as he pleases, yet he prefers this before them all; and since I am fallen upon discourse of the elephant, the creature that this country is famed for above any in India, I will detain myself a little longer upon it. Of their elephants.

I will first relate the manner of taking them, and afterwards their sagacity, with other things that occur to my memory concerning them; this beast, though he be so big and wise, yet he is easily caught; when the king commands to catch elephants, after they have found them they like, that is such as have teeth: for though there be many in the woods, yet but few have teeth, and they males only: unto these they drive some she-elephants, which they bring with them for the purpose; which, when once the males have got a sight of, they will never leave, but follow them wheresoever they go; and the females are so used to it, that they will do whatsoever is wished, either by a word or a beck their keepers bid them; and so they delude them along through towns and The way of catching elephants.

countries, through the streets of the city, even to the very gates of the king's palace; where sometimes they seize upon them by snares, and sometimes, by driving them into a kind of pound, they catch them. After they have brought the elephant which is not yet caught, together with the she, into the king's presence, if it likes him not, he commands to let him go: if it does, he appoints him some certain place near unto the city, where they are to drive him with the females: for without them it is not possible to make him stay; and to keep him in that place until the king's further order and pleasure is to catch him, which perhaps may not be in two or three or four years; all which time there are great men with soldiers appointed to watch there about him: and if he should chance to stray a little out of his bounds set by the king, immediately they bring him back, fearing the king's displeasure, which is no less than death itself: here those elephants do, and may do, great damage to the country, by eating up their corn, and trampling it with their broad feet, and throwing down their cocoa-nut trees, and oftentimes their houses too, and they may not resist them: it is thought this is done by the king to punish them that lie under his displeasure; and if you ask what becomes of these elephants at last—sometimes after they have thus kept watch over them two or three years, and destroyed the country in this manner, the king will send order to carry them into the woods, and let them go free: for he caught them not for any use or benefit he hath by them, but only for his recreation and pastime.

The understanding of elephants. Their nature.

As he is the greatest in body, so in understanding also. For he will do any thing that his keeper bids him, which is possible for a beast not having hands to do. And as the Chingulays report, they bear the greatest love to their young of all irrational creatures; for the shes are alike tender of any ones young ones as of their own : where there are many she-elephants together, the young ones go and suck of any, as well as of their mothers : and if a young one be in distress, and should cry out, they will all in general run to the help and aid thereof; and if they be going over a river, as here be some somewhat broad, and the streams run very swift, they will all with their trunks assist and help to convey the young ones over. They take great delight to lie and tumble in the water, and will swim excellently well. Their teeth they never shed: neither will they ever breed tame ones with tame ones; but to ease themselves of the trouble to bring them meat, they will tie their two fore-feet together, and put them into the woods, where meeting with the wild ones, they conceive, and go one year with young.

It is their constant practice to shove down with their heads great trees, which they love to eat, when they be too high, and they cannot otherwise reach the boughs. Wild ones will run much faster than a man, but tame ones not. The people stand in fear of them, and oftentimes are killed by them. They do them also great damage in their grounds by night, coming into their fields and eating up their corn, and likewise their cocoa-nut trees, &c. So that in towns near unto the woods, where are plenty of them, the people are forced to watch their corn all night, and also their outyards and plantations; into which being once entered, with eating and trampling they will do much harm before they can get them out: who oftentimes when by lighting of torches, and hollowing, they will not go out, take their bows and go and shoot them, but not without some hazard, for sometimes the elephant runs upon them and kills them : for fear of which they will not adventure unless there be trees, about which they may dodge to defend themselves. And although here be

The damage they do.

both bears and tigers in these woods, yet they are not so fierce, as commonly to assault people: travellers and way-faring men go more in fear of elephants than of any other beasts.

Serve the king for executing malefactors.

The king makes use of them for executioners: they will run their teeth through the body, and then tear it in pieces, and throw it limb from limb. They have sharp iron with a socket with three edges, which they put on their teeth at such times; for the elephants that are kept have all the ends of their teeth cut to make them grow the better, and they do grow out again.

Their diseases.

At some uncertain seasons the males have an infirmity come on them, that they will be stark mad, so that none can rule them. Many times it so comes to pass that they with their keepers on their backs, run raging until they throw them down and kill them: but commonly there is notice of it before, by an oil that will run out of their cheeks, which, when that appears, immediately they chain them fast to great trees by the legs. For this infirmity they use no medicine, neither is he sick; but the females are never subject to this.

The sport they make.

The keepers of the king's elephants sometimes make a sport with them after this manner. They will command an elephant to take up water which he does, and stands with it in his trunk, till they command him to squirt it out at some body; which he immediately will do, it may be a whole paleful together, and with such a force, that a man can hardly stand against it.

Ants of divers sorts.

There are ants of several sorts, and some worthy our remark.

First of all, there are coumbias, a sort of small reddish ants like ours in England.

P. 44

Smith sc. 85 H. Holborn

An Execution by an Elephant

London: Published by J. Mawman May 10th 1816

Secondly, the tale-coumbias, as small as the former, but blackish. These usually live in hollow trees or rotten wood, and will sting most terribly.

Thirdly, the dimbios, great red ants. These make their nests upon the boughs of great trees, bringing the leaves together in clusters, it may be as big as a man's head; in which they lay their eggs and breed. There will be oftentimes many nests of these upon one tree, insomuch that the people are afraid to go up to gather the fruits, lest they should be stung by them.

A fourth sort of ants are those they call coura-atch. They are great and black, living in the ground. Their daily practice is to bring up dirt out of the ground, making great hollow holes in the earth, somewhat resembling cony-burrows; only these are less, and run straight downwards for some way, and then turn away into divers paths under ground. In many places of the land there are so many of these holes, that cattle are ready to break their legs as they go. These do not sting.

A fifth is the coddia. This ant is of an excellent bright black, and as large as any of the former. They dwell always in the ground; and their usual practice is, to be travelling in great multitudes, but I do not know where they are going, nor what their business is; but they pass, and repass some forwards and some backwards in great haste, seemingly as full of employment as people that pass along the streets. These ants will bite desperately, as bad as if a man were burnt with a coal of fire. But they are of a noble nature: for they will not begin; and you may stand by them, if you do not tread upon them nor disturb them. The reason of their bite is thus terribly painful, is this;

How these coddia's come to sting so terribly.

formerly these ants went to ask a wife of the Noya, a venomous and noble kind of snake; and because they had such a high spirit to dare to offer to be related to such a generous creature, they had this virtue bestowed upon them, that they should sting after this manner. And if they had obtained a wife of the Noya, they would have had the privilege to have stung full as bad as he. This is a current fable among the Chingulays: though undoubtedly they chiefly regard the wisdom that is concealed under this, and the rest of their fables.

These ants a very mischievous sort.

There is a sixth sort called vaeos. These are more numerous than any of the former. All the whole earth doth swarm with them. They are of a middle size, between the greatest and the least, the hinder part white, and the head red. They eat and devour all that they can come at; as besides food, cloth, wood, thatch of houses, and every thing excepting iron and stone. So that the people cannot set any thing upon the ground within their houses for them. They creep up the walls of their houses and build an arch made of dirt over themselves all the way as they climb, be it never so high. And if this arch or vault chance to be broken, they all, how high soever they were, come back again to mend up the breach, which being finished they proceed forwards again, eating every thing they come at in their way. This vermin do exceedingly annoy the Chingulays, insomuch that they are continually looking upon any thing they value, to see if any of these vaeos have been at it; which they may easily perceive by this case of dirt, which they cannot go up any where without building as they go. And wheresoever this is seen, no doubt the ants are there.

In places where there are no houses, and they can eat nothing belonging to the people, they will raise great hills like huts, some four or five or six feet high; which are so hard and strong, that it would be work enough to dig them down with pick-axes. These humbosses are built with a pure refined clay by the ingenious builders. The people use this clay to make their earthen gods of, because it is so pure and fine. The curious buildings of the Vaeos.

This sort of creatures as they increase in multitudes, so they die in multitudes also: for when they come to maturity they have wings, and in the evening, after the going down of the sun, (never before) all these that are fledged and ripe will issue forth in such vast numbers, that they do almost darken the sky, flying to such a height as they go out of sight, and so keep flying till they fall down dead at last upon the earth. The birds that tarry up late, and are not yet gone to roost, fly among them, and make good suppers of them. The manner of their death.

The people in this land never feed their poultry: but they feed upon these ants, which, by scraping among the leaves and dirt, they can never want; and they delight in them above rice or any thing else. Besides all these ants already mentioned, there are divers other distinct sorts of them.

But we will proceed to a more beneficial insect, the bee; of which there be three sorts. The first are the meemasses, which are the right English bees: they build in hollow trees, or hollow holes in the ground, which the vaeos have made; into which holes the men blow with their mouths, and the bees presently fly out; and then they put in their hands and pull out the combs, which they put in pots or vessels, and carry Bees of several kinds.

away. They are not afraid of their stinging in the least, nor do they arm themselves with any clothes against them.

Bees that build on trees like birds.

The second are the bamburos, larger and of a brighter colour than our English bees; their honey is thin, like water, comparatively. They make their combs upon limbs of trees, open and visible to the eye, generally of a great height. At time of year, whole towns, forty or fifty in company together, will go out into the woods, and gather this honey, and come home laden with it for their use.

The third sort they call connameia, signifying a blind bee. They are small like a fly, and black; they build in hollow trees; and their honey somewhat tarrish: and they make such small quantities of it, that the people little regard it. The boys will sometimes cut a hole and take it out.

The people eat the bees as well as their honey.

When they meet with any swarms of bees hanging on any tree, they will hold torches under to make them drop; and so catch them and carry them home; which they boil and eat, and esteem excellent food.

Leaches that lie in the grass, and creep on travellers legs.

There is a sort of leaches of the nature of ours, only differing in colour and bigness; for they are of a dark reddish colour like the skin of bacon, and as big as a goose quill; in length, some two or three inches. At first, when they are young, they are no bigger than a horse hair, so that they can scarce be seen. In dry weather none of them appear, but immediately upon the fall of rains, the grass and woods are full of them. These leaches seize upon the legs of travellers, who, going barefoot, according to the custom of that land have them hanging upon their legs in multitudes, which suck their blood till

P. 49

A Wanderow

Smith, sc. 83 H. Holborn

A Rillow

London: Published May 10th 1816, by J. Mawman

their bellies are full, and then drop off. They come in such quantities, that the people cannot pull them off so fast as they crawl on: the blood runs pouring down their legs all the way they go, and it is no little smart neither; so that they would willingly be without them if they could, especially those that have sores on their legs; for they all gather to the sore.

Some, therefore, will tie a piece of lemon and salt in a rag, and fasten it unto a stick, and ever and anon strike it upon their legs to make the leaches drop off: others will scrape them off with a reed, cut flat and sharp in the fashion of a knife; but this is so troublesome, and they come on again so fast and so numerous, that it is not worth their while: and generally they suffer them to bite, and remain on their legs during their journey; and they do the more patiently permit them, because it is so wholesome for them. When they come to their journey's end, they rub all their legs with ashes, and so clear themselves of them at once; but still the blood will remain dropping a great while after. But they are most annoyed by them when they go out to stool at night, being small and of the colour of their bodies, so that they can neither see nor feel to pull them off; and these, though they be in such quantities in some of these countries, yet in others there are none at all, nor ever were known to have been. But besides these there are water leaches the same with ours.

The remedies they use against them.

Monkeys, of which there are abundance in the woods, and of divers sorts; some so large as our English spaniel dogs, of a darkish grey colour, and black faces, with great white beards round from ear to ear, which makes them shew just like old men. There is another sort just of the same bigness, but differ in co-

Apes and monkeys of divers kinds

lour, being milk-white both in body and face, having great beards like the others; of this sort of white ones there is not such plenty: but both these sorts do but little mischief, keeping in the woods, eating only leaves and buds of trees; but when they are caught they will eat any thing: this sort they call, in their language, wanderows. There is yet another sort of apes, of which there is great abundance, who, coming with such multitudes, do a great deal of mischief to the corn that groweth in the woods, so that they are fain all the day long to keep watch to scare them out: and so soon as they are gone to fray them away at one end of the field, others, who wait for such an opportunity, come skipping in at the other; and, before they can turn, will fill both bellies and hands full, to carry away with them; and to stand all round to guard their fields is more than they can do. This sort of monkeys have no beards, white faces, and long hair on the top of their heads, which parteth and hangeth down like a man's. These are so impudent that they will come into the gardens and eat such fruit as grows there; they call these rillowes: the flesh of all these sorts of apes they account good to eat. There are several sorts of squirrels also, which they do eat when they can catch them.

Before I make an end of my discourse of their beasts, it may be worth while to relate the ways they use to catch them; at which they are very crafty.

How they catch wild beasts.

For the catching of deer, or other wild beasts, they have this ingenious device: in dark moons when there are drisling rains, they go about this design: they have a basket made with canes, somewhat like unto a funnel, in which they put a potsheard with fire in it, together with a certain wood which they have growing there, full of sap like pitch, and that will burn like a pitch-barrel. This being kindled in the potsheard flames, gives an exceeding light. They carry it upon their heads with the flame foremost; the basket hiding him that is under it, and those that come behind it. In their hands they carry three or four small bells, which they tingle as they go, that the noise of their steps should not be heard. Behind the man that carries the light, go men with bows and arrows; and so they go walking along the plains, and by the pond sides, where they think the deer will come out to feed; which, when they see the light, stand still and stare upon it, seeing only the light, and hearing nothing but the tingling of the bells.

The eyes of the deer, or other cattle, first appear to them glistering like stars of light or diamonds; and by their long experience they will distinguish one beast from another by their eyes. All creatures, as deer, hares, elephants, bears, &c. excepting only wild hogs, will stand still, wondering at this strange sight, till the people come as near as they do desire, and so let fly their arrows upon them: and by this means they seldom go but they catch something. The blades of their hunting arrows are at least a foot, or a foot and a half long; and the length of the staff of their arrows is a rian, that is, about two cubits.

Again, they will observe where a deer's haunt is, to break over their hedges into the corn grounds: there they will set a sharp pole, like a spear, full against the haunt; so that the deer, when she leaps over, thrusts herself upon the point of it. If a tiger chance to come into their grounds and kill a cow, they will take notice of the place through which he passed, and set a cross bow there ready charged: the tiger coming that way again, touches something that is fastened to the trigger of the cross bow, and so it discharges upon him.

How they take the wild boar.

The wild hog is of all other the hardest to be caught; and it is dangerous to attempt the catching of him. For the people make valour to consist in three things: one is to fight against the enemy; another, to hunt the elephant; and the third to catch hogs. Yet sometimes by their art they entrap them; and that they do after this manner: they dig a hole in the earth, of a convenient depth, and fix divers sharp stakes in the bottom of it; then they cover it over lightly with earth and leaves, and plant thereupon roots which the hog loves, as potatoes, or such like which will grow there; and the pit remains, it may be sometimes months or half a year, till at last a hog comes, and while he is rooting, his weight betrays him, and in he falls.

Again, sometimes they will set a falling trap of an exceeding weight, and under it plant roots, and such like things, which the hog delights in. There are contrivances under the weeds and leaves; which, when he goes to eat, by touching or treading upon something fastened to the trap, it falls down upon him: these are made so artificially, that people sometimes have been caught and destroyed by them. Once such a trap, in my remembrance, fell upon three women and killed them; who, having been stealing cotton in a plantation, and fearing to be caught, went to creep out at a hole where this trap stood.

And thus I have related some of their ways of taking wild cattle: they are good also at catching birds and vermin; in fine, they are the most cunning people in the world for such kind of traps and gins; and all of them they make only by the help of their knives, with green sticks and withs that grow in the woods. And so much of their beasts.

CHAP. VII.

Of their Birds, Fish, Serpents, and Commodities.

IN the next place I will entertain you with some relation of the other living creatures among them. I begin with their birds. In that land there are crows, sparrows, tom-tits, snipes, just like those in England, wood pigeons also, but not great flocks of any sorts, as we have, only of crows and pigeons. I have seen there birds just like woodcocks and partridges, but they are scarce; great many wild peacocks, small green parrots, but not very good to talk. But here is another bird, in their language called mal-cowda, which, with teaching, will speak excellently well: it is black, with yellow gills, about the bigness of a blackbird: and another sort there is, of the same bigness, called cau-cowda, yellow like gold, very beautiful to the eye, which also might be taught to speak.

Their birds.

Such as will be taught to speak.

Here are other sorts of small birds, not much bigger than a sparrow, very lovely to look on, but I think good for nothing else: some being in colour white like snow, and their tail about one foot in length, and their heads black like jet, with a tuft like a plume of feathers standing upright thereon. There are others of the same sort, only differing in colour, being reddish, like a ripe orange, and on the head a plume of black feathers standing up. I suppose one may be the cock, and the other the hen.

Such as are beautiful for colour.

A strange bird.

Here is a sort of bird they call carlo, which never lighteth on the ground, but always sits on very high trees; he is as big as a swan, the colour black, the legs very short, the head monstrous, his bill very long, a little rounding like a hawk's, and white on each side of the head, like ears; on the top of the crown groweth out a white thing, something like to the comb of a cock: commonly they keep four or five of them together, and always are hopping from bough to bough; they are seldem silent, but continually make a roaring noise, somewhat like the quacking of a duck, that they may be heard at least a mile off; the reason they thus cry, the Chingulays say, is for rain, that they may drink. The bodies of these fowls are good to eat.

Water fowls resembling ducks and swans.

Here is a sort of bird very much resembling a duck, but not very plentiful; and another sort of fowl as big as a duck, coal black, which liveth altogether upon fish. It is admirable to see how long they will remain under water, and at what a distance they will rise again. Besides these, there are many other kinds of birds, much larger than swans, which keep about the ponds and marshes to catch fish, but the people eat them not: Nature hath endowed them with an admirable understanding; they are not to be catched by the alligators, though there be many of them in those waters.

Peacocks.

The peacocks in rainy weather are sometimes hunted and caught by dogs; for their feathers being wet they are incapable of flying far.

The king keeps fowl.

The king hath geese, ducks, turkeys, pigeons, which he keeps tame; but none else may. Turkeys he delights not in, because they change the colour of their heads: neither doth he kill any

Smith, sc. 83 H. Holborn

Their manner of Fishing

London · Published May 10th 1816 — by J. Mawman

of these to eat, nor any other creature of what sort soever, and he hath many that he keeps tame.

They have no want of fish, and those good ones too. All little rivers and streams running through the valleys are full of small fish, but the boys and others wanting something to eat with their rice, do continually catch them before they come to maturity: nay, all their ponds are full of them, which, in dry weather drying up, the people catch multitudes of them in this manner: —they have a kind of basket made of small sticks, so close that the fish cannot get through; it is broad at bottom, and narrow at top, like a funnel, the hole big enough for a man to thrust his arm in, wide at the mouth about two or three feet; these baskets they jobb down, and the ends stick in the mud, which often happen upon a fish; when they do, they feel it by the fish beating itself against the sides; then they put in their hands and take them out, and rieve a rattan through their gills, and so let them drag after them. One end of this rattan is stuck in the fisher's girdle, and the other knotted, that the fish should not slip off: which, when it is full, he discharges himself of them by carrying them ashore. Nay, every ditch and little plash of water but ancle deep hath fish in it.

Their fish.

How they catch them in ponds.

The great river, Mavela-gonga abounds exceedingly with them: some of them as big as salmons; but the people have little understanding in the way of taking them. In very dry weather, they stretch a with over the river, which they hang full of boughs of trees to scare the fish. This with thus hung they drag down with the stream, and to leeward they place fish-pots between the rocks, and so drive the fish into them. Nets or other ways they have few or none.

How they catch fish in the river.

Fish kept and fed for the king's pleasure.

At a passage-place, near to the city of Candy, the fish formerly have been nourished and fed by the king's order, to keep them there for his majesty's pleasure; whither, having used to be thus provided for, notwithstanding floods and strong streams, they will still resort, and are so tame, that I have seen them eat out of men's hands; but death it is to them that presume to catch them. The people passing over here will commonly feed them with some of their rice, accounting it a piece of charity so to do, and pleasure to see them eat it. In many other places also there are fish thus fed and kept only for the king's recreation; for he will never let any be caught for his use.

Serpents. The pimberah of a prodigious bigness.

Of serpents there are these sorts. The pimberah, the body whereof is as big as a man's middle, and of a length proportionable. It is not swift, but by subtilty will catch his prey, which are deer or other cattle. He lies in the path where the deer use to pass, and as they go, he clasps hold of them by a kind of peg that grows in his tail, with which he strikes them. He will swallow a roebuck whole, horns and all; so that it happens sometimes that the horns run through his belly and kill him. A stag was caught by one of these pimberahs, which seized him by the buttock, and held him so fast, that he could not get away, but ran a few steps this way and that way. An Indian seeing the stag run thus, supposed him in a snare, and having a gun shot him, at which he gave so strong a jerk, that it pulled the serpent's head off, while his tail was encompassing a tree to hold the stag the better.

The polonga.

There is another venomous snake called polongo, the most venomous of all, that kills cattle. Two sorts of them I have seen, the one green, the other of a reddish grey, full of white rings along the sides, and about five or six feet long.

Another poisonous snake there is, called noya, of a greyish colour, about four feet long. This will stand with half his body upright two or three hours together, and spread his head broad open, where there appears like as it were a pair of spectacles painted on it. The Indians call this noy-rogerati, that is, a king's snake, that will do no harm. But if the polonga and the noya meet together, they cease not fighting till one hath killed the other. The noya.

The reason and original of this fatal enmity between these two serpents, is this, according to a fable among the Chingu-lays. These two chanced to meet in a dry season, when water was scarce. The polonga, being almost famished for thirst, asked the noya, where he might go to find a little water: the noya a little before had met with a bowl of water, in which a child lay playing; as it is usual among this people to wash their children in a bowl of water, and there leave them to tumble and play in it. Here the noya quenched his thirst; but, as he was drinking, the child that lay in the bowl, out of his innocency and play, hit him on the head with his hand, which the noya made no matter of, but bare patiently, knowing it was not done out of any malice; and having drank as much as sufficed him, went away without doing the child any harm. The fable of the noya and polonga.

Being minded to direct the polonga to this bowl, but desirous withal to preserve the child, he told him, that he knew of water, but that he was such a surly hasty creature, that he was fearful to let him know where it was, lest he might do some mischief. Making him therefore promise that he would not, he then told him, that at such a place there was a bowl of water with a child playing in it, and that probably the child might, as he was tumbling, give him a pat on the head, as he had done to him before, but charged him nevertheless not to hurt the child; which the polonga, having promised, went his way towards the water as the noya had directed him. The noya, knowing his touchy disposition, went after him, fearing he might do the child a mischief, and that thereby he himself might be deprived of the like benefit afterwards. It fell out as he feared. For as the polonga drank, the child patted him on the head, and he in his hasty humour bit him on the hand and killed him. The noya seeing this, was resolved to be revenged, and so reproaching him for his baseness, fought him so long till he had killed him, and after that devoured him; which to this day they ever do, always fight when they meet, and the conqueror eats the body of the vanquished. Hence the proverb among the Chingulays, when they see two men irreconcileable, they compare them to the polonga and noya, and say, noya polonga waghe, like a noya and polonga.

The Carowala. There is the carowala, about two feet in length, very poisonous, that lurks in the holes and thatch of houses. The cats will seize these and kill and eat them.

Gerende. Other snakes there are, called gerende, whereof there are many, but not venomous. Of the former there are but a few in comparison. These last mentioned, the greatest mischief they do is to destroy young birds and eggs, and young hares. Rabbits cannot be kept here to run wild, because of these and other vermin, such as polecats, ferrets, weazels, &c.

Hickanella, much like a lizard, venomous, but seldom bites unless provoked; these lie in the thatch of the houses. Hickanella.

There is a spider, called democulo, very long, black, and hairy, speckled and glistering. Its body is as big as a man's fist, with feet proportionable. These are very poisonous; and they keep in hollow trees and holes. Men bitten with them will not die, but the pain will for some time put them out of their senses. A great spider.

Cattle are often bit by some of these snakes, and as often found dead of them, though not eaten. Treading upon them sleeping, or the like, may be the cause of it. When the people are bitten by any of these, they are cured by charms and medicines, if taken and applied in time.

There are also a sort of water snakes they call duberia, but harmless.

Alligators may be reduced hither; there be many of them. Of which we have said somewhat before.

There is a creature here called kobberaguion, resembling an alligator. The biggest may be five or six feet long, speckled black and white. He lives most upon the land, but will take the water and dive under it: hath a long blue forked tongue like a sting, which he puts forth and hisseth and gapeth, but doth not bite nor sting, though the appearance of him would scare Kobberaguion, a creature like an alligator.

those that knew not what he was. He is not afraid of people, but will lie gaping and hissing at them in the way, and will scarce stir out of it. He will come and eat carrion with the dogs and jackals, and will not be scared away by them; but if they come near to bark or snap at him, with his tail, which is about an ell long, like a whip, he will so lash them, that they will run away and howl. This creature is not eatable.

Tolla guion. But there is the tolla guion, very like the former, which is eaten, and reckoned excellent meat. The Chingulays say it is the best sort of flesh; and, for this reason, that if you eat other flesh at the same time you eat of this, and have occasion to vomit, you will never vomit out this though you vomit all the other. This creature eats not carrion, but only leaves and herbs; is less of size than the kobbera-guion, and blackish; lives in hollow trees and holes in the humbosses; and I suppose is the same with that which in the West Indies they call the guiana.

The people eat rats. This country has its vermin also. They have a sort of rats, they call musk-rats, because they smell strong of musk. These the inhabitants do not eat of, but of all other sort of rats they do.

Before I conclude my discourse of the growth and product of this country, it will not be improper to reduce under this head its precious stones, minerals, and other commodities. Of which I shall briefly speak, and so make an end of this first part.

Precious stones. In this island are several sorts of precious stones, which the king, for his part, has enough, and so careth not to have more discovery made. For in certain places, where they are known to be, are sharp poles set up fixed in the ground, signifying, that none, upon pain of being stuck and impaled upon those poles, presume so much as to go that way. Also there are certain rivers, out of which, it is generally reported, they do take rubies and sapphires for the king's use, and cat's eyes; and I have seen several pretty coloured stones, some as big as cherry-stones, some as buttons, and transparent, but understood not what they were. Rubies and sapphires I myself have seen here.

Minerals and other commodities.

Here is iron and crystal in great plenty. Salt-petre they can make. Brimstone, some say, is here, but the king will not have it discovered. Steel they can make of their iron. Ebony in great abundance, with choice of tall and large timber. Cardamums, jaggory, rack, oil, black lead, turmeric, salt, rice, betel-nuts, musk, wax, pepper; which last grows here very well, and might be in great plenty if it had a vend; and the peculiar commodity of the island, cinnamon. Wild cattle and wild honey in great plenty in the woods; it lies in holes or hollow trees, free for any that will take the pains to get it. Elephant's teeth and cotton; of which there is good plenty growing in their own grounds, sufficient to make them good and strong cloth for their own use, and also to sell to the people of the Uplands, where cotton is not so plenty. All these things the land affords, and it might do it in much greater quantity if the people were but laborious and industrious: but that they are not, for the Chingulays are naturally a people given to sloth and laziness; if they can but any ways live, they abhor to work; only what their necessities force them to do, they do, that is, to get food and raiment. Yet in this I must a little vindicate them; for

The people discouraged from industry by the tyranny they are under.

what indeed should they do with more than food and raiment, seeing, as their estates increase, so do their taxes also? And although the people be generally covetous, spending but little, scraping together what they can, yet such is the government they are under, that they are afraid to be known to have any thing, lest it be taken away from them. Neither have they any encouragement for their industry, having no vend by traffic and commerce for what they have got.

PART II.

CHAP. I.

Of the present King of Candy.

HITHERTO I have treated of the country, with the provisions and wealth of it; our next discourse shall be of the political government there exercised. And here order will lead us to speak first of the king, and matters relating to him. The government of this island.

Anciently this country consisted of nine kingdoms, all which had their several kings; but now, by the vicissitude of times and things, they are all reduced under one king, who is an absolute tyrant, and rules the most arbitrarily of any king in the world. We will first speak of him as to his personal capacity, and next as to his political.

In his personal capacity are to be considered his birth and parentage, his person, his relations, his state, his manners, his pleasures and recreations, his religion.

The king's lineage.

Radga-Singa is his name, which signifies a lion-king. He is not of the right descent of the royal blood; for the former king deceased, leaving his queen a widow, and two young princes, which he had issue by her. She was a Christian, having been baptized by the Portugueze, and named Dona Catharina. She afterwards married to the chief-priest, whom, in their language, they call tirinanxy; and by him had this son, the present king. The tirinanx, his father, reigned and ruled the land during the minority of the young princes: but being aged he divided the country between the three princes by lot, intending Conde Uda, which is the best part of the land, for his own son, Radga-Singa; which was obtained by this device. The names of the three kingdoms, being written on three papers, were put into a pot, and one was appointed, who knew the matter, to take them out, and deliver them one to each, beginning with the eldest, craftily delivering that which had Conde Uda written in it unto Radga Singa; and so it came to pass according to the old king's determination. All these three, in the beginning of their reigns, joined together against the Portugueze, but soon after fell out amongst themselves, and this king, in the end, prevailed, and got all the country. Danna Polla Rodgerah, the youngest, king of Mautoly, being overthrown, fled down to the Portugueze to Columba, who sent him to Goa, where he died. The other, named Comaure-Singa, king of Ouvah, died in Candy.

His person, mien, and habit.

As to the person of the present king. He is not tall, but very well set, nor of the clearest colour of their complexion, but somewhat of the blackest; great rolling eyes, turning them and looking every way, always moving them; a brisk bold look, a great swelling belly, and very lively in his actions and be-

Smith, sc 63 H.Holborn

Rajah Singah, the King of Ceylon

London: Published May 10th 1818—by J. Mawman

haviour; somewhat bald, not having much hair upon his head, and that grey; a large comely beard, with great whiskers; in conclusion, a very comely man. He bears his years well, being between seventy and eighty years of age; and though an old man, yet appears not to be like one neither in countenance nor action. His apparel is very strange and wonderful, not after his own country fashion, or any other, being made after his own invention. On his head he wears a cap with four corners like a Jesuit's, three tier high, and a feather standing upright before, like that in the head of a fore-horse in a team; a long band hanging down his back in the Portugueze fashion; his doublet after so strange a shape that I cannot well describe it, the body of one, and the sleeves of another; he wears long breeches to his ancles, shoes, and stockings. He doth not always keep to one fashion, but changes as his fancy leads him; but always when he comes abroad, his sword hangs by his side in a belt over his shoulder; which no Chingulays dare wear, only white men may: a gold hilt, and scabbard most of beaten gold. Commonly he holdeth in his hand a small cane, painted of divers colours, and towards the lower end set round about with such stones as he hath and pleaseth, with a head of gold.

His queen and children.

His right and lawful queen, who was a Malabar, brought from the coast, is still living, but hath not been with him, as is known, this twenty years, remaining in the city of Candy, where he left her: she wants, indeed, neither maintenance nor attendance, but never comes out of the palace. Several noblemen's daughters hold land for this service, viz. to come to her court in their turns to wait upon her majesty. She bear him a prince, but what became of him shall hereafter be shewn. He had also a daughter by her, she came also in her youth to a piteous and unfortunate death, as I shall relate in its place.

His palace; situation and description of it.

He keeps his court at Digligy-neur, whither he fled in a rebellion against him. His palace stands adjoining to a great hill, which was before-mentioned: near unto that part of the hill next abutting upon his court, none dares presume to set his foot, that being for his safeguard to fly unto in time of need. The palace is walled about with a clay wall, and thatched, to prevent the clay being melted by the rains, which are great and violent. Within this wall it is all full of houses, most of which are low and thatched; but some are two stories high, and tiled very handsomely, with open galleries for air, railed about with turned banisters, one ebony, and one painted, but not much prospect, standing between two hills; and indeed the king lives there not so much for pleasure as security. The palace itself hath many large and stately gates two leaved; these gates, with their posts, excellently carved; the iron-work thereunto belonging, as bolts and locks, all rarely engraven. The windows inlaid with silver plates and ebony. On the top of the houses of his palace and treasury stand earthern pots at each corner, which are for ornament; or, which is a newer fashion, something made of earth resembling flowers and brambles; and no houses beside, except temples, may have these placed upon them. The contrivance of his palace is, as I may say, like Woodstock bower, with many turnings and windings, and doors, he himself having ordered and contrived all these buildings, and the manner of them. At all the doors and passages stand watches; and they who thus give attendance are not to pass without special order from one place to another, but are to remain in that place, or at that gate where the king hath appointed them. By means of these contrivances it is not easy to know in what part or place his person is, neither doth he care they should.

He has strong watches night and day about his court; and they are his grandees, who themselves in person watch in certain places where the king himself appoints them; and they dare not be absent from thence, without it be to go to eat, or upon such like occasions. At night they all have their set places within the court, where they cannot come to the speech of the other; neither dare they that are near together, or in sight one of the other, so much as come and sit together, and talk to pass away the nights. All these great men have soldiers under them, and they are also to come by turns to watch at the court. But at night, as their masters and commanders watch within the walls, so they must watch without, in outward courts and guards; neither dare any of them be seen within with their commanders. At the end of every watch there are a multitude of trumpets and drums to make a noise; which is to keep his people waking, and for the honour of his majesty. There are also elephants, which are appointed all night to stand and watch, lest there should be any tumult; which, if there should, could presently trample down a multitude. Strong guards about his court.

He hath also a guard of cofferies, or negroes, in whom he imposeth more confidence than in his own people. These are to watch at his chamber door, and next his person. Next his own person negroes watch.

At uncertain times he will send out a spy by night, to see what watch is kept; who, once finding one of the great men asleep, took his cap, his sword, and other arms, and brought them to Spies sent out at night.

the king; who afterwards restored them to the owner again, reproving him, and bidding him take more heed for the future. These spies also are to hear and see what passes; neither is there any thing said or done but he has notice of it. Formerly he used in the nights to disguise himself and walk abroad in the streets to see all passages, but now he will not adventure so to do.

His attendants.

Most of his attendants are boys and young men, that are well favoured, and of good parentage. For the supplying himself with these, he gives order to his dissavas, or governors of the country, to pick and choose out boys that are comely and of good descent, and send them to the court. These boys go bare headed, with long hair hanging down their backs. Not that he is guilty of sodomy, nor did I ever hear the sin so much as mentioned among them.

Handsome women belong to his kitchen.

He hath many women belonging to his kitchen, choosing to have his meat dressed by them. Several times he hath sent into the countries a command to gather handsome young women of the Chingulays to recruit his kitchen, with no exceptions, whether married or unmarried; and those that are chosen for that service never return back again. Once since my being on the land, all the Portugueze women that were young and white were sent for to the court, no matter whether maids or wives; where some remained until now, and some that were not amiable in his sight were sent home; and some, having purchased his displeasure, were cast into a river, which is his manner of executing women; and some sent prisoners in the country, being none admitted to speech or sight of them.

Concubines he keepeth not many; some are within his palace; and those, whose office is about his kitchen, are reported to be so; which is not improbable, seeing he admits none but them that are young and very handsome to the employment. Other of his women dwell in towns near to the city, into which no stranger is permitted to go, nay, it is dangerous to approach near. These towns have this privilege, that if any slave flee from his master and come hither, he is safe and free from his master's service, but still remains a slave there to them.

His women, and the privilege of the towns where they live.

Sometimes he walketh about his palace, where there are certain pedestals of stone whitened with lime and laid in oil, so that they look purely white, made and set up in divers places; here he stands when he comes forth, that he might be above the rest of the people, and see about him. But when he is minded to go abroad, though it be never so little a way, and he seldom or never goes far, order is given, some time before, for all soldiers of his guards, which are a great many, it may be thousands, together with a Dutch and Portugueze captain, with their flags and soldiers, drummers, trumpeters, pipers, singers, and all belonging, as elephants, horses, falconers with their falcons, and many others, to stand at the gate in a readiness to attend his pleasure; and though he means not to come forth, yet they must wait in this manner until he give order that they may depart to their houses. Commonly all this assembly are gathered together at the palace three or four times before he comes out once; and oftentimes he comes out when none there are aware of it, with only those that attend on his person within his palace. And then when it is heard that his majesty is come forth, they all run ready to break their necks, and place themselves at a distance to guard his person and wait his pleasure. Some-

His state when he walks in his palace, or goes abroad.

times, but very seldom, he comes forth riding upon a horse or elephant; but usually he is brought out in a palenkeen, which is nothing so well made as in other parts of India. The ends of the bambou it is carried by are largely tipped with silver, and curiously wrought and engraven; for he hath very good workmen of that profession.

The place where he goeth, when he comes thus abroad, is to a banqueting-house built by a pond side, which he has made. It is not above a musket shot from his palace; where he goeth for his diversion. Which I shall by and bye more particularly relate.

His reception of ambassadors.

Another instance of his state and grandeur will appear in his reception of ambassadors, who are received with great honour and show. First he sends several of his great men to meet them with great trains of soldiers, the ways all cut broad, and the grass pared away for many miles; drums, and trumpets, and pipes, and flags going before him. Victuals and all sorts of varieties are daily brought to them, and continue to be so all the time they are in the land, and all at free-cost; for the custom here is, ambassadors, stay they never so long, are maintained at the king's cost and charges; and, being in the city, have their victuals brought them out from the king's palace ready dressed. Presents, goods, or whatsoever they please to bring with them, the king prepareth men to carry. And when they are come to the house that is prepared for them, which is hung top and sides with white calico, they are kept under a guard, and great commanders with soldiers appointed to watch at their gates, which is accounted a great honour. But these guards dare not permit any to come to the speech of them, for the king careth not that any should talk with ambassadors but himself, with whom he taketh great delight to have conference, and to see them brought before him in fine apparel, their swords by their sides with great state and honour; and that the ambassadors may see and take notice of the greatness of his majesty. And after they have been there some time, he gives them both men and handsome young maids for their servants, to attend and also to accompany them; often causing them to be brought into his presence to see his sports and pastimes, and not caring to send them away; but in a very familiar manner entertaining discourse with them.

His delight in them.

CHAP. II.

Concerning the King's Manners, Vices, Recreations, Religion.

UNDER the consideration of his manners will fall his temperance, his ambition and pride, his policy and dissimulation, his cruel and bloody disposition.

Sparing in his Diet.

He is temperate both in his diet and his lust. Of the former, I am informed by those that have attended on his person in his palace, that though he hath all sorts of varieties the land affords brought to his table, yet his chief fare is herbs and ripe pleasant fruits, and this but once a day. Whatsoever is brought for him to eat or drink is covered with a white cloth, and whoever brings it hath a mufler tied about his mouth, lest he should breathe upon the king's food. The king's manner of eating is thus: He sits upon a stool before a small table, covered with a white cloth, all alone. He eats on a green-plantain leaf laid in a gold bason. There are twenty or thirty dishes prepared for him, which are brought into his dining room; and which of these dishes the king pleases to call for, a nobleman, appointed for that service, takes a portion of, and reaches in a ladle to the king's bason. This person also waits with a muffler about his mouth.

After what manner he eats.

Chaste himself, and re-

And as he is abstemious in his eating, so in the use of women.

If he useth them it is unknown, and with great secrecy. He hath not had the company of his queen this twenty years; to wit, since he went from Candy, where he left her. He allows not in his court whoredom or adultery; and many times, when he hears of the misdemeanours of some of his nobles in regard of women, he not only executes them, but severely punisheth the women, if known; and he hath so many spies, that there is but little done which he knows not of. And often he gives command to expel all the women out of the city, not one to remain; but by little and little, when they think his wrath is appeased, they do creep in again. But no women of any quality dare presume; and, if they would, they cannot, the watches having charge given them not to let them pass. Some have been taken concealed under man's apparel, and what became of them all may judge, for they never went home again. Rebellion does not more displease this king than for his nobles to have to do with women; therefore, when any are admitted to his court to wait upon him, they are not permitted to enjoy the company of their wives, no more than any other women: neither hath he suffered any for near this twenty years to have their wives in the city, except slaves or inferior servants.

quires his attendants to be so.

Indeed, he was once guilty of an act, that seemed to argue him a man of most unbridled lust; for he had a daughter that was with child by himself; but in childbed both died. But this manner of incest is allowable in kings, if it be only to beget a right royal issue, which can only be gotten that way; but in all other it is held abominable, and severely punished; and here they have a common and usual proverb—none can reproach the king nor the beggar. The one being so high, that none dare; and the other so low, that nothing can shame or reproach them.

He committed incest, but such as was allowable.

His pride. How the people address to the king.

His pride and affectation of honour is unmeasurable; which appears in his people's manner of address to him, which he either commands or allows of. When they come before him they fall flat down on their faces to the ground three several times, and then they sit with their legs under them upon their knees all the time they are in his presence; and, when he bids them to absent, they go backwards until they are out of sight, or a great distance from him: but of Christian people, indeed, he requires no more than to kneel with their hats off before him.

They give him divine worship.

Nay, he takes on him all the ceremonies and solemnities of honour which they shew unto their gods; making his account, that as he is now their king, so hereafter he shall be one of their gods; and the people did call him god. Formerly, since my being on that land, he used not to come out of his palace into the sight of the people but very seldom, out of state and haughtiness of spirit, but now of later times he comes forth daily: and, although he be near fourscore years of age, yet his greatest delight is in honour and majesty, being mostly pleased with high and windy titles given him; such as mauhawaul, a phrase importing greatness, but not expressible in our language; hondrewné boudouind, let your majesty be a god. When the king speaks to them, they answer him at every period, oiboa, many lives; baula gaut, the limb of a dog, speaking to the king of themselves: yet now, of late times, since here happened a rebellion against him, he fears to assume to himself the title of god; having visibly seen, and almost felt, that there is a greater power than his ruling on earth, which set the hearts of the people against him; and so hath given command to profane that great name no more, by ascribing it to him.

Pleased with high titles.

In anno 1675, one of the king's greatest and most valiant generals, and that had been notably successful against the Dutch, had done many pieces of good service for the king, expelled the Hollanders out of several forts, taking and killing many of them; this man the king was jealous of, and did resolve to take away his head as a reward of his valour; which he had some private intelligence of, and so fled, being then in camp against the Dutch, and got to Columba with his wife and goods—by which the king had an invaluable loss. Yet the king, out of the height of his stomach, seemed not in the least to be vexed thereat, neither did he regard it; as if it were beneath the quality of such a monarch to be moved with such a trifle: but sent down another general in his place; and, as for the house and estate of him that fled, and whatsoever he left behind him, he let it lie and rot, scorning to esteem or regard it.

An instance or two of the king's haughty stomach.

He slights the defection of one of his best generals.

To give you an instance or two more of this prince's spirit. At the time of new-year, all his subjects, both high and low, do bring him certain presents, or rather taxes, each one a certain rate; which, formerly, he used constantly to take, but of late years, he so abounds with all things, continually putting into his treasury, and but seldom taking out, and that but little, that he thinks scorn to receive these his due revenues, lest his people should think it were out of necessity and want. Nevertheless the great men still, at the new-year, bring their presents day after day before the king at his coming forth, hoping it will please him to accept them; but now of many years he receives them not. His mind is so haughty, that he scorns to seem to value any thing in the world. When tidings are sometimes brought him, that the Dutch have made an invasion into his

He scorns to receive his revenues.

country, although he be well able to expel them, he will not so much as regard it.

The Dutch serve their ends upon his pride by flattering him.

The Dutch, knowing his proud spirit, make their advantage of it, by flattering him with their ambassadors, telling him that they are his majesty's humble subjects and servants; and that it is out of their loyalty to him that they build forts, and keep watches round about his country, to prevent foreign nations and enemies from coming; and that, as they are thus employed in his majesty's service, so it is for sustenance, which they want, that occasioned their coming up into his majesty's country. And thus, by flattering him, and ascribing to him high and honourable titles, which are things he greatly delights in, sometimes they prevail to have the country they have invaded, and he to have the honour. Yet at other times, upon better consideration, he will not be flattered, but falls upon them at unawares, and does them great damage.

The people give way to the king's foul clothes.

Such a veneration does he expect from the people, that whatsoever things are carrying to him, which are known by the white cloth they are wrapped up in, all persons meeting them turn out of the way; not excepting the king's foul clothes: for when they are carried to washing, which is daily, all, even the greatest, rise up as they come by, which is known by being carried on a hand heaved upwards, covered with a painted cloth.

His natural abilities, and deceitful temper.

He is crafty, cautious, a great dissembler, nor doth he want wisdom. He is not passionate in his anger; for with whomsoever he be angry, he will not shew it: neither is he rash or overhasty in any matters, but doth all things with deliberation,

Smith sc. 63 H. Holborn

One Impaled on a Stake

London Published May 10th 1816 by J. Mawman

though but with a little advice; asking counsel of nobody but himself. He accounts it wit and policy to lie and dissemble, that his intents and purposes may the better be concealed; but he abhorreth and punisheth those that lie to him.

Dutch run-aways, whereof there are several come to him, he saith, are rogues, that either have robbed or killed, or else would never run away from their own nation; and, though he receiveth them, yet esteemeth them not. His wise saying concerning run-aways.

He seems to be naturally disposed to cruelty; for he sheds a great deal of blood, and gives no reason for it. His cruelty appears both in the tortures and painful deaths he inflicts, and in the extent of his punishments, viz. upon whole families for the miscarriage of one in them: for when the king is displeased with any, he does not always command to kill them outright, but first to torment them, which is done by cutting and pulling away their flesh by pincers, burning them with hot irons clapped to them, to make them confess of their confederates; and this they do to rid themselves of their torments, confessing far more than ever they saw or knew. After their confession, sometimes he commands to hang their two hands about their necks, and to make them eat their own flesh, and their own mothers to eat of their own children; and so to lead them through the city in public view, to terrify all unto the place of execution, the dogs following to eat them; for they are so accustomed to it, that they, seeing a prisoner led away, follow after. At the place of execution there are always some sticking upon poles, others hanging up in quarters upon trees, besides what lie killed by elephants on the ground, or by other ways. Naturally cruel. The dogs follow prisoners to execution.

This place is always in the greatest highway, that all may see and stand in awe; for which end this is his constant practice.

The king's prisoners; their misery.

Moreover, he hath a great many prisoners, whom he keepeth in chains; some in the common jail, some committed to the custody of great men; and for what or for how long time none dare inquire. Commonly they lie thus two, four, or six years; and some have victuals given them; and some, not having it, must ask leave to go out and beg with a keeper. It is according as the king appoints when they are committed: or some of them, being driven to want, do get food by work, such as sewing, making caps, doublets, purses. This coming once to the king's ears, he said, "I put them there to torment and punish them, not to work and be well maintained;" and so commanded to take away their scissors and needles from them: yet this lasted not long; for afterwards they fell to their work again. Those that have been long there, are permitted to build little shops on the street side against the prison, and to come out in the day-time and sell their work as they make it; but in the night-time are shut up again.

When the streets are to be swept about the palace, they make the prisoners come out in their chains and do it.

And, after all their imprisonment, without any examination, they are carried forth and executed; and these not only the common sort, but even the greatest and most nobly descended in the land; for with whom he is displeased he maketh no difference.

He punishes whole gene-

Nor is his wrath appeased by the execution of the malefactor, but oftentimes he punisheth all his generation; it may be kills them altogether, or gives them all away for slaves. rations for the sake of one.

Thus he often deals with those whose children are his attendants. I mentioned before, that young men of the best families in the land are sought out to wait upon the king in his court: these, after they have served him some small time, and have, as it were, but seen the court, and known his customs and manners, he requiteth them by cutting off their heads, and putting them into their bellies; other faults none do know. Heretofore, as it is reported, he was not so cruel, but now none escape that serves in his palace. Then he recruits his slain out of the countries, by giving orders to his dissavas, or governors, to send him others to court; whither they go like an ox to the slaughter, but with far more heavy hearts; for both they and their parents full well know what end the king's honourable service will bring them to: howbeit there is no remedy. Being thus by order sent unto the court, their own parents must provide for, and maintain them, until the king is pleased to call them to his use, which it may be will not be in some years. Sometimes it happens, that the boys thus brought, before the king makes use of them about his person, are grown too big, and so escape: but those that are employed in this palace enjoy this favour—that all such taxes, customs, or other duties belonging to the king, which their fathers were wont to pay, are released, until such time as they are discharged from the king's employment; which is always either by execution, or by being given to somebody for perpetual bondmen. During the time of the king's favour he is never admitted to go home to visit his parents and friends. The male kind may come to see him, but no women are admitted, be it his mother

The sad condition of young gentlemen that wait on his person.

that bear him; and, after he is killed, though for what no man knows, he is accounted a rebel and traitor against the king; and then his father's house, land, and estate, is seized on for the king; which, after some time, by giving of fees and gifts to the great ones, they do redeem again; and sometimes the whole family and generation perish, as I said before: so that after a lad is taken into the king's palace, his kindred are afraid to acknowledge alliance to him. But these matters may more properly be related when we come to speak of his tyranny.

His pleasure houses.

Sometimes, for his pleasure, he will ride or be carried to his banquetting-house, which is about a musket-shot from his palace. It stands on a little hill, where, with abundance of pains, and many months labour, they have made a little plain, in length not much above an arrow's flight, in breadth less; where, at the head of a small valley, he hath made a bank across to stop the water running down. It is now become a fine pond, and exceeding full of fish. At this place the king hath several houses built according to his own appointment, very handsome, borne up with carved pillars and painted, and round about rails and bannisters turned, one painted and one ebony, like balcony—some standing high upon a wall, being for him to sit in and see sport with his elephants and other beasts, as also for a prospect abroad—others standing over this pond, where he himself sits and feedeth his fish with boiled rice, fruits, and sweetmeats. They are so tame that they will come and eat in his hand; but never doth he suffer any to be caught. This pond is useful for his elephants to wash in. The plain was made for his horses to run upon: for oftentimes he commands his grooms to get up and ride in his presence; and sometimes, for that good service, gives the rider five or ten shillings, and it may be a piece of cloth. Always when he comes forth his horses are brought out ready saddled before him, but he himself mounts them very seldom; all of which he had from the Dutch—some sent to him for presents, and some he hath taken in war. He hath in all some twelve or fourteen; some of which are Persian horses.

His pastimes abroad.

Other pastimes and recreations he hath, (for this is all he minds or regards,) as to make them bring wild elephants out of the wood, and catch them in his presence: the manner how they get them unto the city I have mentioned already. Also, when he comes out of his court, he delights to look upon his hawks, although he never use them for his game; sometimes on his dogs, and tame deer, and tigers, and strange kind of birds and beasts; of both which he hath a great many. Also, he will try his guns, and shoot at marks, which are excellently true, and rarely inlaid with silver, gold, and ivory; for the smiths that make them dare not present them to his hand, not having sufficiently proved them. He hath eight or nine small iron cannon, lately taken from the Dutch, which he hath mounted in field carriages, all rarely carved, and inlaid with silver and brass, and coloured stones, set in convenient places, and painted with images and flowers; but the guns disgrace the carriage. He keeps them in a house on the plain. Upon some festival times he useth them. I think they are set there chiefly for a memorial of his late victories; for he hath many and far better guns of brass that are not so regarded.

His diversion at home.

In his palace he passeth his time with looking upon certain toys and fancies that he hath, and upon his arms and guns, calling in some or other of his great men to see the same, asking them if they have a gun will shoot further than that; and how much steel such a knife, as he will shew them, needs to have in it. He takes great delight in swimming, in which he is very expert; and the custom is, when he goes into the water, that all his attendants that can swim must go in likewise.

His religion.

And now, lastly, for his religion, you cannot expect much from him. Of the religion of his country he makes but a small profession; as perceiving that there is a greater God than those that they, through long custom, have and do worship; and therefore when an impostor, a bastard Moor by nation born in that land, came and publicly set up a new nameless god, as he styled him, and that he was sent to destroy the temples of their gods, the king opposed it not for a good while, as waiting to see which of these gods would prevail, until he saw that he aimed to make himself king, then he allowed of him no longer; as I shall shew more at large hereafter, when I come to speak of the religion of the country.

How he stands affected to the Christian religion.

The Christian religion he doth not in the least persecute or dislike; but rather, as it seems to me, esteems and honours it. As a sign of which take this passage:—when his sister died, for whom he had a very dear affection, there was a very grievous mourning and lamentation made for her throughout the whole nation; all mirth and feasting laid aside, and all possible signs of sorrow expressed; and, in all probability, it was as much as their lives were worth, who should at this time do any thing that might look like joy. This was about Christmas. The Dutch did, notwithstanding, adventure to keep their Christmas by feasting. The news of this was brought to the king, and every body reckoned it would go hard with the Dutch for doing this; but, because it was done at a festival of their religion, the king past it by, and took no notice of it. The value also that he has for the Christian religion will appear from the respect he gives the professors of it, as will be seen afterwards.

CHAP. III.

Of the King's Tyrannical Reign.

WE have all this while considered this king with respect unto his person, temper, and inclinations; now we will speak of him with more immediate respect unto his office and government, as he is a king. And here we will discourse of the manner of his government; of his treasure and revenues; of his great officers; and lastly, of his strength and wars.

His government tyrannical.

As to the manner of his government, it is tyrannical and arbitrary in the highest degree; for he ruleth absolute, and after his own will and pleasure—his own head being his only counsellor. The land all at his disposal; and all the people, from the highest to the lowest, slaves, or very like slaves; both in body and goods wholly at his command. Neither wants he those three virtues of a tyrant—jealousy, dissimulation, and cruelty.

His policy.

But because policy is a necessary endowment of a prince, I will first shew, in an instance or two, that he is not devoid of it.

He farms out his country for service.

The country, being wholly his, the king farms out his land, not for money, but service; and the people enjoy portions of land from the king; and, instead of rent, they have their several appointments: some are to serve the king in his wars, some in their trades, some serve him for labourers, and others are as farmers to furnish his house with the fruits of the ground; and so all things are done without cost, and every man paid for his pains—that is, they have lands for it. Yet all have not watered land enough for their needs; that is, such land as good rice requires to grow in; so that such are fain to sow on dry land, and till other men's fields for a subsistence. These persons are free from payment of taxes; only sometimes, upon extraordinary occasions, they must give a hen, or mat, or such like, to the king's use, forasmuch as they use the wood and water that is in his country; but if any find the duty to be heavy, or too much for them, they may, leaving their house and land, be free from the king's service, as there is a multitude do; and, in my judgment, they live far more at ease, after they have relinquished the king's land, than when they had it.

Many towns are in the king's hand, the inhabitants whereof are to till and manure a quantity of the land, according to their ability, and lay up the corn for the king's use. These towns the king often bestows upon some of his nobles for their encouragement and maintenance, with all the fruits and benefits that before came to the king from them. In each of these towns there is a smith to make and mend the tools of them to whom the king hath granted them, and a potter to fit them with earthern ware, and a washer to wash their clothes, and other men to supply what there is need of; and each one of these hath a piece of land for this their service, whether it be to the king or the lord; but what they do for the other people they are paid for. Thus all that have any place or employment, under the king, are paid without any charge to the king.

His policy to secure himself from assassination or rebellion.

His great endeavour is to secure himself from plots and conspiracies of his people, who are sorely weary of his tyrannical government over them, and do often plot to make away with him; but, by his subtilty and good fortune together, he prevents them; and, for this purpose, he is very vigilant in the night: the noise of trumpets and drums, which he appoints at every watch, hinders both himself and all others from sleeping. In the night also he commonly does most of his business, calling ambassadors before him, and reading the letters; also displacing some of his courtiers, and promoting others, and giving sentence to execute those whom he would have to live no longer; and many times commands to lay hold on and carry away great and noble men, who, until that instant, knew not that they were out of his favour.

Another point of his policy.

His policy is to make his country as intricate and difficult to travel as may be, and therefore forbids the woods to be felled, especially those that divide province from province; and permits no bridges to be made over his rivers, nor the paths to be made wider.

Another, which is to find his people work to do.

He often employs his people in vast works, and that will require years to finish, that he may inure them to slavery, and prevent them from plotting against him, as haply they might do if they were at better leisure: therefore he approves not that his people should be idle; but always finds one thing or other to be done, though the work be to little or no purpose. According to the quantity of the work, so he will appoint the people of one county or of two to come in; and the governor of the said county or counties to be overseer of the work. At such times the soldiers must lay by their swords, and work among the people. These works are either digging down hills, and carrying the earth to fill up valleys; thus to enlarge his court, which standeth between two hills (a more uneven and unhandsome spot of ground he could not well have found in all his kingdom); or else making ways for the water to run into the pond, and elsewhere, for his use in his palace; where he hath it running through in many places unto little ponds, made with lime and stone, and full of fish.

To bring this water to his palace was no small deal of labour; for, not having a more convenient way, they were forced to split a great mountain in twain to bring the water through, and after that to make a bank cross a valley far above a cable's length, and in height above four fathoms, with thickness proportionable to maintain it, for the water to run over the top; which, at first being only earth, the water would often break down; but now both bottom and sides are paved and wrought up with stone. After all this, yet it was at least four or five miles to bring this water in a ditch, and the ground all hills and valleys; so that they were forced to turn and wind, as the water would run: also, when they met with rocks which they could not move, as this ground is full of them, they made great fires with wood upon it, until it was soundly hot; and hereby it became so soft, that they could easily break it with mauls.

A vast work undertaken and finished by the king

This water was that which nourished that country, from whence it was taken: the people of which, ever since, have scarce been able to till their land; which extremity did compel the people of those parts to use a means to acquaint the king how the country was destroyed thereby, and disabled from performing those duties and services, which they owed unto the

The turning this water did great injury to the people.

king; and that there was water sufficient both for his majesty's service, and also to relieve their necessities; which the king took very ill from them, as if they would seem to grudge him a little water: and sure I am, woe be to him, that should mention that matter again.

But he little regards his people's good.

So far is he from regarding the good of his country, that he rather endeavours the destruction thereof: for issue he hath none alive; and, ere long, being of a great age, Nature tells him, he must leave it. Howbeit, no love lost between the king and his people. Yet he daily contriveth and buildeth in his palace like Nebuchadnezzar, wet and dry, day and night, not shewing the least sign of favour to his people; who oftentimes, by such needless employments, are letted from the seasonable times of ploughing and harvest, to their great prejudice, and sometimes utter undoing.

The king by craft at once both pleased and punished the people.

After the rebellion, when the people, that lived at a further distance, saw that the king intended to settle himself near the mountain to which he fled, viz. Digligy, and not to come into the old city again, it being very troublesome and tedious to bring their rents and taxes thither, they all jointly met together, being a great number, and sent an address, to intimate their desires to him; which was with great submission,—That his majesty would not leave them destitute of his presence, which was to them as the sun; that he would not absent himself from them to dwell in a mountain in a desolate country; but, seeing there was no further danger, and all the rebels destroyed, that he would return to his old palace again, vowing all fidelity to him. The king did not like this message, and was somewhat afraid, there being such a tumultuous company met together, and so thought not fit to drive them away, or publicly to declare his displeasure at them, but went to work like a politician; which was, to tell them, that he thanked them for their love and affection towards him; and that he was desirous to dwell among them in such a part of their country as he named; and so bade them all go to work to build him a palace there. The people departed with some satisfaction, and fell to work might and main; and continued at it for near two years together, felling timber, and fetching it out of the woods, laying foundations, hewing stone, till they were almost killed with labour: and, being wrought quite tired, they began to accuse and grumble at one another, for having been the occasion of all this toil. After they had laboured thus a long while, and were all discouraged, and the people quiet, the king sent word to them to leave off. And now it lies unfinished, all the timber brought in rots upon the place, and the building runs to ruin.

And this is the manner how he employs his people; pulling down and building up again, equalling unequal grounds, making sinks under ground for the passage of water through his palace, dragging of great trees out of the wood to make pounds to catch elephants in his presence; although they could catch them with far less labour, and making houses to keep them in, after they are taken. **In what labours he employs his people.**

He stands not upon any villainy to establish himself, or strike terror into his people. This made him cut off his only son, a young man of about fifteen years. After the rebellion, the kingdom being settled in the king's hands again, and knowing that the hearts of the people disaffecting him stood strongly bent to- **He poisons his only son.**

wards the prince; and, fearing his own safety, as the prince grew to riper years, to prevent all, he poisoned him. For about a year after the rebellion, his son was sick; the king takes this opportunity to dispatch him, by pretending to send physic to him to cure him. The people hearing of the death of the prince, according to the custom of the land, when any of the royal blood is deceased, came all in general towards the city where he was, with black, or else very dirty clothes, which is their mourning; the men all bare-headed, the women with their hair loose and hanging about their shoulders, to mourn and lament for the death of their young prince; which the king hearing of, sent this word unto them—that since it was not his fortune to live, to sit on his throne after him, and reign over the land, it would be but in vain to mourn; and a great trouble and let unto the country: and their voluntary good will was taken in as good part as the mourning itself; and so dismissed the assembly, and burned the prince's dead body without ceremonies or solemnities.

The extraordinary lamentation at the death of his sister.

Yet the death of an old sister, which he had, caused no small lamentation. It was she that carried the prince away in the rebellion; which I shall relate by and by. Country after country came up to mourn, giving all signs of extraordinary sadness, both in habit and countenance: the king himself was seen to weep bitterly. The white men also came, which the king took well: insomuch, that the Hollanders, supposing the king himself to be dead, came up to take possession of the country; but, hearing the contrary, and understanding their mistake, returned back again. The king and all his country for more than a year's time went in mourning; and her body was burnt with all the honour and state that could be: yet, notwithstanding all the love and respect he bear unto her, he did not once visit her in all the time of her sickness: and, it is now for certain reported, that there is not one of his generation left.

Once, to try the hearts of his attendants, and to see what they would do, being in the water a swimming, he feigned himself to be in extremity, and near drowning, and cried out for help; upon which two young men, more venturous and forward than the rest, immediately made way and came to his help; who, taking hold of his body, brought him safe to land, at which he seemed to be very glad: putting on his clothes, he went to his palace—then he demanded to know who and which they were that had holpen him out of the water: they, supposing by his speech it was to give them a reward for the good service they had so lately done him, answered, We were they: whereupon he commands to call such a great man, (for it is they whom he appoints always to see execution done by his soldiers) to whom he gave command, saying—Take both these, and lead them to such a place, and cut off their heads, who dared to presume to lay their hands on my person, and did not prostrate themselves rather, that I might lay my hand on them for my relief and safety: and, accordingly, they were executed.

His craft and cruelty shewn at once.

CHAP. IV.

Of his Revenues and Treasure.

The king's rents brought three times in the year.

THREE times in the year they usually carry their rents unto the king. The one is at the new year, called ourida cotamaul: the other is for the first fruits, alleusal cotamaul; and the last is at a certain sacrifice in the month of November, to their god, called ilmoy cotamaul; but, besides these, whatsoever is wanting in the king's house at any other time, and they have it, they must upon the king's order bring it. These rents are but little money, but chiefly corn, rice, or what grows out of the ground.

The first is accompanied with a great festival.

To speak a little of the first time, viz. at the beginning of the new year, when the king's duties are brought him. This new year is always either the 27th, or the 28th, or the 29th of March: at this time, upon a special and good day (for which the astrologers are consulted) the king washes his head, which is a very great solemnity among them. The palace is all adorned with tor-nes, a sort of triumphal arches, that make a very fine show. They are high poles standing in rows before all the gates of the palace, either nine or seven in a row, the middlemost being the highest, and so they fall lower and lower on each side. Through the middle of them there is an arched passage, which serves for a door: on the top of the poles are flags flying, and all about hung full of painted cloth, with images, and figures of men, and beasts, and birds, and flowers; fruits also are hanged up in great order and exactness. On each side of the entrance of the arch stand plantain trees, with bunches of plantains on them, as if they were growing.

There are also in some places single poles, of an exceeding height standing by, with long penons of divers colours flying, and a bell at the end of each, as in the figure B. And now they say, the palace is adorned beyond heaven.

All the army is summoned in to stand and wait at the palace, for the greater state; in the mean time he goes to his washing-houses—houses built on purpose for him to wash in, called oul-pungi: here are baths, and streams, and conveyances of water, and many servants, whose office it is to wait upon the business of these houses: here he washes his head; which, when he has done, he comes forth into public view, where all his militia stand in their arms; then the great guns are fired. Now all the great men, the nobles, and the governors of the country, make their appearance before him with their dackini, their new-year's gifts, which are due and accustomed presents, for persons in their places and offices to give—there is a certain rate for it; their manner of bringing these gifts or rather duties is thus: their servants bring them wrapped up in white cloth to the court, and then they take them at their hands, put them upon their heads, and so come in humble manner, and lay them at the king's feet; these presents are gold, jewels, plate, arms, knives, cloth; each one by a rate according to the place he is in, and the country he hath under him; and most of them are to present a sum of money besides; and, if they can procure any precious stone, or rarity, or any other thing, which they think the king

How the nobles bring their gifts, or duties.

will accept, that also they bring, and glad they are to be honoured with the favour of his acceptance; these new-year's gifts for these many years he thinks scorn to receive, and bids them carry them away again till another time;—thus they come with them time after time presenting them, which he as often refusing: at last they bring them no more.

Inferior persons present their new year's gifts.

All sorts of tradesmen, also, and such as by their skill can any ways get money, at the new year are to pay into the treasury each one a certain rate; which now-a-days he accepts not, though formerly he always did.

What taxes and rents the people pay.

At this and the other times the things which the people carry, as their rents and taxes, are wine, oil, corn, honey, wax, cloth, iron, elephants teeth, tobacco, money; they bring them themselves, and wait at court with them commonly divers months, before they be received;—the great officers tell the king, the people have brought their rents: the king saith,—'Tis well; but, if he give no order withal to receive the things brought (as he seldom does) there is no remedy, but there they must wait with them; and this he doth out of state: the rents and duties brought at the two other times are after the same manner; the great men do only bring theirs once at the new year.

The accidental incomes of the crown.

There are other revenues the king hath, which are accidental, but bring in great wealth; that whensoever any man dies, that hath a stock of cattle, immediately out thence must be paid a bull and a cow with a calf, and a male and female buffalo, which tax they call marral; and there are officers appointed, whose place it is to come and carry them away; also at harvest yearly there is a certain rate of corn to be paid by every man according to the land they hold and enjoy; heretofore the king granted, that, upon payment of a sum of money, they should be clear from this yearly tax of corn so long, till the present possessor died, and the land descended to his son or somebody else; and then the estate became liable again to the forementioned duties; but now of late there is no mention of any discharge by money: so that in time all houses and families in the kingdom will be liable to the payment of this tax of corn; which will bring in no small quantity of provision to the king; only soldiers that are slain in the wars, their lands are free from the payment of this tax; but if they die naturally they are not: the farmers, all in general, besides their measures of corn, pay a certain duty in money, with their rents.

The profits that accrue to the king from corn lands.

If they sell or alienate their inheritances, the king's accustomed duties must not be diminished, whosoever buyeth or enjoyeth them; neither is here any land which doth not either pay, or do some duty to the king; only one case excepted—and that is, if they give or dedicate land to a priest, as an alms or deed of charity in God's name; on that there is never any more tax or duty to be imposed, as being sacrilegious to take ought from one that belongs to the temple. Formerly, the king had the benefit of the trade of two ports—Cortiar and Portalone; unto each of which used to come yearly some twenty or thirty sail of small vessels, which brought considerable customs in; but now the Hollander has deprived him of both, suffering no vessels to come.

Customs of goods imported formerly paid.

The king hath several treasure-houses, and in several places, in cities and towns, where always are guards of soldiers to watch them both day and night. I cannot certainly declare all that is contained in them: there are precious stones, such as his land affords; money, but not very much; cloth, and what he hath got by shipwreck; presents, that have been sent him from other nations; elephants teeth, wax, good store of arms, as guns, bows and arrows, pikes, halberds, swords, ammunition, store of knives, iron, tallipat-leaves, whereof one will cover a large tent, bedsteads, tables, boxes, mats of all sorts. I will not adventure to declare further the contents of his treasuries, lest I may be guilty of a mistake; but, sure I am, he hath plenty of all such things as his lands affords; for he is very provident, and careful to be well furnished with all things; and, what he does abound with, he had rather it should lie and rot, than be embezzled and wasted; that is, distributed among his servants, or slaves; of which he hath great store.

His treasuries.

He has many elephants.

He hath some hundreds of elephants, which he keepeth tame, and could have as many more as he pleaseth; but, although not caught, yet they are all his, and at his command when he pleaseth.

Great treasure thrown into the river formerly.

It is frequently reported, and I suppose is true, that both he and his predecessors, by the distress they have been driven to by the Portuguese, have cast some store of riches into the great river, Mavelagonga, running by the city, in deep holes among rocks, which is irrecoverable, and into a made pond by the palace in the city of Candy, or Hingodegul-neur; wherein are kept to this day two alligators, so that none dare go into the water for fear of being devoured by them; and oftentimes they do destroy cows, that go to drink there; but this pond, by cutting the bank, might easily be drained.

To conclude, the land that is under his jurisdiction is all his, with the people, their estates, and whatsoever it affords, or is therein; but that which he doth chiefly valuc and esteem are toys and novelties—as hawks, horses, dogs, strange birds, and beasts, and particularly a spotted elephant, and good arms, of which he hath no want.

The treasure he most valueth.

CHAP. V.

Of the King's great Officers, and the Governors of the Provinces.

Two greatest officers in the land.

THERE are two, who are the greatest and highest officers in the land; they are called adigars—I may term them chief judges; under whom is the government of the cities, and the countries also in the vacancy of other governors: all people have liberty in default of justice to appeal to these adigars; or, if their causes and differences be not decided by their governors according to their minds.

To these there are many officers and sergeants belonging: all which, to be known, carry staves in their hands like to bandyes, the crooked end uppermost, which none but they dare carry: the sight of which staves, upon what message soever they be sent, signifies as much as the adigar's hand and seal: if the adigar be ignorant in what belongs to his place and office, these men do instruct him what and how to do; the like is in all other places which the king bestows: if they know not what belongs to their places, there are inferior officers under them, that do teach and direct them how to act.

The next great officers.

Next under the adigars are the dissauvas, who are governors over provinces and counties of the land: each province and county has its governor; but all governors are not dissauvas, nor other great officers known by other names or titles, as roterauts, and vidanies; but all these generals, or chief commanders, who have a certain number of soldiers under them. These great men are to provide, that good order be kept in the countries over which they are placed, and that the king's accustomed duty be brought in due season to the court. They have power also to decide controversies between the people of their jurisdiction, and to punish contentions and disorderly persons, which they do chiefly by amercing a fine from them, which is for their profit, for it is their own; and also by committing them to prison: into which, when they are once fallen, no means without money can get them out again. But be the fact never so heinous (murther itself) they can put none to death—the sentence of death being pronounced only by the king. They also are sent upon expeditions in war with their soldiers, and give attendance and watch at court in their appointed stations.

None can put to death but the king

These dissauvas are also to see that the soldiers in their countries do come in due season and order for that purpose.

They are appointed by the king himself, not for life, but during his good pleasure; and, when they are dead or removed, oftentimes their places lay void, sometimes for months, sometimes perhaps for years; during which time the adigar rules and governs those countries; and for his labour receiveth all such income and profits as are accustomed and of right do belong to the governor.

These dissauvas are durante bene plasito

The king, when he advances any one to be dissauvas, or to any other great office, regards not their ability or sufficiency to perform the same; only they must be persons of good rank and

Whom the king makes dissauvas; and their profits and honours.

genteel extraction: and they are all naturally discreet and very solid, and so the fitter for the king's employment. When he first promotes them, he shews them great testimonies of his love and favour, (especially to those that are Christians, in whose service he imposeth greater confidence than in his own people, concluding that they will make more conscience of their ways, and be more faithful in their office) and gives them a sword,—the hilt all carved and inlaid with silver and brass very handsomely, the scabbard also covered with silver—a knife, and halberd; and lastly, a town or towns for their maintenance. The benefit of which is, that all the profits, which before the king received from those towns, now accrues unto the king's officer. These towns are composed of all sorts of trades and people that are necessary for his service, to whom the king hath given them a potter, a smith, a washer; and there is a piece of land, according to the ability of the town, which the townsmen are to till and manure and to lay up the corn for his use: which matters I mentioned before in the third chapter. And, besides the customs or taxes that all other free towns pay to the king, there is a due, but smaller, to be paid to the governor out of them. But these are not all his advantages.

Other benefits belonging to other officers.

When there is a new governor made over any country, it is the custom that that whole country comes up to appear before him at the court, for there his residence is; neither may they come empty handed, but each one must bring his gift or present with him. These also are expected at other times to be brought unto him by the people, though they have no business with him, no suits or causes to be decided: even private soldiers, at their first coming, though to their due watch, must personally appear before their commander; and, if he have nothing else, he must present him with forty leaves of green betle, which he with his own hand receiveth, and they with both their, and delivers into his, which is taken for an honour he vouchsafes them.

They must always reside at court

These governors, nor any other admitted to court into the king's service, are never after to return home, although they are not employed at present, and might be spared—neither are they permitted to enjoy their wives; and they are day and night to stand guard in certain stations, where the king appoints them.

The officers under them.

Courlividani.

Things thus standing with them, they cannot go in person to visit and oversee their several charges themselves. They have therefore several offices under them to do it; the chief of whom is the courlividani. This person, beside his entertainment in the country, unto which he is sent to govern under the dissauva, hath a due revenue, but smaller than that of the governor. His chief business is to rack and hale all that may be for his master, and to see good government; and, if there be any difference or quarrel between one or other, he takes a fine from both, and carrieth to the governor, not regarding equity, but the profit of himself and him that employs him. But he hears their case and determines it; and, if they like not his sentence, they may remove their business unto the governor himself, whose desire is not so much to find out the right of the cause, as that that may be most for his own interest and profit. And these carriages cannot reconcile them much love among the people; but the more they are hated by the people for their rigorous government, the better they please the king: for he cares not that the country should affect the great men.

The dissauvas, by these courlividani, their officers, do op-press and squeeze the people, by laying mulcts upon them for some crimes or misdemeanors, that they will find and lay to their charge. In fine, this officer is the dissauva's chief substitute, who orders and manages all affairs incumbent upon his master.

Congconna. Next to him is congconna, an overseer, who is to oversee all things under the courlividani: but, besides him, there is a courti-achila, like our constable, who is to put that in execution that the governor orders, to dispatch any thing away that the land affords for the king's use, and to send persons to court that are summoned; and, in the discharge of this his office, he may call in the assistance of any man.

Courti-achila.

The Liannah. The next officer under the governor is the liannah. The writer, who reads letters brought, and takes account of all business, and of what is sent away to the court: he is also to keep registers, and to write letters, and to take notice of things happening.

The undia. Next to him is the undia, a word that signifieth a lump: he is a person that gathers the king's money; and so is styled, because he gathereth the king's monies together into a lump.

The monnannah. After him is the monnannah, the measurer: his place is to go and measure the corn that grows upon the king's land, or what other corn belongeth to him.

The power of these officers extends not all a whole county or province over, but to a convenient part or division of it; to wit, so much as they may well manage themselves. And there are several sets of the like officers appointed over other portions of the country, as with us there are divers hundreds or divisions in a county, to each of which are distinct officers belonging.

These officers can exercise their authority throughout the whole division over which they are constituted, excepting some certain towns, that are of exempt jurisdiction; and they are of two sorts. First, such towns as belong to the idol temples and the priests, having been given and bestowed on them long ago by former kings; and secondly, the towns which the king allots to his noblemen and servants. Over these towns, thus given away, neither the fore-mentioned officers, nor the chief magistrate himself, hath any power; but those, to whom they are given, and do belong to, do put in their own officers, who serve to the same purposes as the abovesaid do. Some towns exempt from the dissauva's officers.

But these are not all the officers; there are others, whose place it is, upon the death of any head of a family, to fetch away the king's marrals, harriots as I may call them; viz. a bull and a cow, a male and female buffalo, out of his stock; which is accustomably due to the king, as I have mentioned before—and others, who in harvest time carry away certain measures of corn out of every man's crop, according to the rate of their land. Other officers yet.

These inferior officers commonly get their places by bribery; their children do pretend a right to them after their father's death, and will be preferred before others, greasing the magistrate. These places obtained by bribes.

None of these have their places for life, and no longer than the governor pleaseth; and he pretty often removes them, But remain only during pleasure.

or threatens to do so, upon pretence of some neglects, to get money from them. And the people have this privilege—that upon complaint made of any of these officers, and request that they may be changed, and others made, they must be displaced, and others put in; but not at their choice, but at the choice of the chief magistrate, or owner of the town.

Country courts.

For the hearing complaints, and doing justice among neighbours, here are country courts of judicature, consisting of these officers, together with the head men of the places and towns where the courts are kept; and these are called gom sabbi; as much as to say, town consultations. But if any do not like, and is loath to stand by what they have determined, and think themselves wronged, they may appeal to their head governor that dwells at court; but it is chargeable—for he must have a fee. They may appeal also from him to the adigars, or the chief justices of the kingdom; but whoso gives the greatest bribe, he shall overcome; for it is a common saying in this land,—That he that has money to fee the judge, needs not fear nor care whether his cause be right or not. The greatest punishment that these judges can inflict upon the greatest malefactors is but imprisonment— from which money will release him.

They may appeal.

Appeals to the king.

Some have adventured to appeal to the king sometimes, falling down on the ground before him at his coming forth, which is the manner of their obeisance to him, to complain of injustice. Sometimes he will give order to the great ones to do them right, and sometimes bid them wait, until he is pleased to hear the cause, which is not suddenly—for he is very slow in all his business; neither dare they then depart from the court, having been bidden to stay; where they stay till they are weary, being at expense, so that the remedy is worse than the disease. And sometimes, again, when they thus fall before him, he commands to beat them and put them in chains for troubling of him; and perhaps in that condition they may lay for some years.

How these great officers travel upon public business.

The king's great officers, when they go abroad into the countries about the king's business, they go attended with a number of soldiers armed both before and behind them: their sword, if not by their side, a boy carrieth after him; neither do they carry their swords for their safety or security, (for in travelling here is little or no danger at all,) but it is out of state, and to shew their greatness. The custom is, that all their journey victuals be prepared for them ready dressed; if their business requires haste, then it is brought on a pole on a man's shoulder, the pots that hold it hanging on each end, so that nothing can be spilt out into the road; and this is got ready against the great man's coming: so that they are at no charge for diet—it is brought in at the charge of the country: but, however, this is not for all his soldiers that attend him (they must bring their own provisions with them), but only for himself, and some of his captains.

Their titles and signs of state.

The greatest title that is allowed in the city to be given to the greatest man, is oussary, which signifieth worshipful; but when they are abroad from the king, men call them sihattu and dishondrew, implying honour and excellency. These grandees, whensoever they walk abroad, their manner is in state to lean upon the arm of some man or boy; and the adigar, besides this piece of state, wheresoever he goes, there is one with a great whip, like a coach-whip, goes before him slashing it, that all people may have notice that the adigar is coming.

The misery that succeeds their honour.

But there is something comes after, that makes all the honour and wealth of these great courtiers not at all desirable; and that is, that they are so obnoxious to the king's displeasure; which is a thing so customary, that it is no disgrace for a nobleman to have been in chains; nay, and in the common gaol too. And the great men are as ready, when the king commands, to lay hold on one another, as he to command them; and glad to have the honour to be the king's executioners, hoping to have the place and office of the executed. When any of these are thus dispatched, commonly he cuts off or imprisoneth all the male kind that are near of kin, as sons or brothers, fearing they should plot revenge, and seizes on all the estate; and, as for the family, after examination, with punishment to make them confess where the estate lies, they have monthly allowance out of the same: but the wife, or women-kindred, are now nothing at all in esteem for honourable ladies as they were before. Yet sometimes he will send for the sons or brothers of those whom he hath cut off for traitors, and remand them out of the prisons where he had committed them, and prefer them in honourable employment.

The foolish ambition of the men and women of this country

It is generally reported, and I have seen it so, that those whom he prefers unto the greatest and weightiest employments, are those whom he intends soon to cut off; and contrariwise, those whom he doth affect, and intends to have longer service of, shall not be so laden with places and honours. Howbeit, although they know and see this before their eyes daily, yet their hearts are so haughty and ambitious, that their desires and endeavours are to ascend unto the highest degrees of honour, though that be but one remove from death and utter destruction. And the women's ambition is so great also, that they will put their husbands on to seek for preferment, urging how dishonourable it is for them to sit at home like women, that so they may have respect, and be reputed for great ladies.

CHAP. VI.

Of the King's Strength and Wars.

The king's military affairs.

IT remains now that I speak a little of the king's military affairs. His power consists in the natural strength of his country, in his watches, and in the craft, more than the courage, of his soldiers.

The natural strength of his country.

He hath no artificial forts or castles, but nature hath supplied the want of them; for his whole country of Candy Uda, standing upon such high hills, and those so difficult to pass, is all an impregnable fort; and so is more especially Digligy-neur, his present palace. These places have been already described at large, and therefore I omit speaking any further of them here.

Watches and thorn-gates.

There are constant watches, set in convenient places, in all parts of the country, and thorn-gates; but in time of danger, besides the ordinary watches, in all towns, and in all places, and in every cross road, exceeding thick, that it is not possible for any to pass unobserved. These thorn-gates, which I here mention, and have done before, are made of a sort of thorn-bush or thorn-tree; each stick or branch whereof thrusts out on all sides round about sharp prickles, like iron nails, of three or four inches long: one of these very thorns I have lately seen in the repository at Gresham College. These sticks, or branches, being as big as a good cane, are plaited one very close to another; and so, being fastened and tied to three or four upright spars, are made in the fashion of a door. This is hung upon a door-case some ten or twelve feet high, (so that they may, and do ride through upon elephants) made of three pieces of timber, like a gallows, after this manner Π the thorn-door hanging upon the transverse piece like a shop-window; and so they lift it up, or clap it down, as there is occasion, and tie it with a rope to a cross-bar.

But especially in all roads and passages from the city where the king now inhabits are very strict watches set, which will suffer none to pass not having a passport; which is the print of a seal in clay: it is given at the court to them that have license to go through the watches. The seals are different, according to the profession of the party: as to a soldier, the print of a man with a pike on his shoulder; to a labourer, a man with two bags hanging on each end of a pole upon his shoulder, which is the manner they commonly carry their loads; and to a white man, the passport is the print of a man with a sword by his side, and a hat on his head; and, so many men as there are in the company, so many prints there must be in the clay. There is not half the examination for those that come into the city, as for those that go out, whom they usually search to see what they carry with them. **None to pass from the king's city without passports.**

To speak now of their soldiery, their expeditions, and manner of fight. Besides the dissauvas, spoken of before, who are great generals, there are other great captains—as those they call mote-ralls; as much as to say scribes, because they keep the rolls or registers of certain companies of soldiers, each containing 970 men, who are under their command. Of these mote-ralls there **Their soldiery.**

are four principal; but, besides these, there are smaller commanders over soldiers, who have their places from the king, and are not under the command of the former great ones.

All men of arms wait at court.

All these, both commanders and common soldiers, must wait at the court; but with this difference: the great men must do it continually, each one having his particular watch appointed by the king; but the private soldiers take their turns of watching; and, when they go, they carry all their provisions, for the time of their stay, with them upon their backs. These soldiers are not listed, (listing soldiers being only upon extraordinary occasions) but are by succession, the son after the father: for which service they enjoy certain lands and inheritances, which is instead of wages or pay. This duty, if they omit or neglect, they lose or forfeit their inheritance: or, if they please to be released or discharged, they may, parting with their land; and then their commander placeth another in their room: but so long as the land lies void, he converts the profits to his own proper use; and he that after takes it, gives a bribe to the commander, who yet, nothwithstanding, will not permit him to hold it above two or three years, unless he renew his bribes.

The soldiers have lands allotted them instead of pay.

To prevent the soldiers from ploting.

The soldiers of the high lands, called Candy Uda, are dispersed all over the land; so that one scarcely knows the other, the king not suffering many neighbours and townsmen to be in one company; which hath always heretofore been so ordered for fear of conspiracies.

The manner of sending them out on expeditions.

When the king sends any of these commanders with their armies abroad to war, or otherwise, sometimes they see not his face, but he sends out their orders to them by a messenger; sometimes admits them into his presence, and gives them their orders with his own mouth, but nothing in writing: and, when several of them are sent together upon any design, there is not any one appointed to be chief commander or general over the whole army; but each one, as being chief over his own men, disposeth and ordereth them according to his pleasure; the others do the like; which sometimes begets disagreement among themselves, and by that means their designs are frustrated: neither doth he like or approve, that the great commanders of his soldiers should be very intimate, or good friends, lest they should conspire against him, nor will he allow them to disagree in such a degree, that it be publicly known and observed.

And, when there is any tidings to send the king, they do not send in general, by consent, but each one sends particularly by himself. And their common custom and practice is to inform what they can one against another, thinking thereby to obtain the most favour and good will from the king; by this means, there can be nothing done or said, but he hath notice thereof.

The king requires all the captains singly to send him intelligence of their affairs.

Being in this manner sent forth, they dare not return, although they have performed and finished the business they were sent upon, until he send a special order and command to recal them.

When the war is finished, they may not return without order.

When the armies are sent abroad, as he doth send them very often against the Dutch, it goes very hard with the soldiers, who must carry their victuals and pots to dress it in upon their backs, besides their arms, which are swords, pikes, bows and arrows, and good guns. As for tents—for their armies always lie in the

The condition of the common soldiers.

fields, they carry tallipot leaves, which are very light and convenient, along with them; with these they make their tents, fixing sticks into the ground, and laying other pieces of wood overthwart, after the manner of the roof of an house, and so lay their leaves over all, to shoot the rains off: making these tents stronger or slighter, according to the time of their tarriance. And having spent what provisions they carried out with them, they go home to fetch more: so that after a month or two, a great part of the army is always absent.

He conceals his purpose when he sends out his army.

Whensoever the king sends his armies abroad upon any expedition, the watches beyond them are all secured immediately, to prevent any from passing to carry intelligence to the enemy. The soldiers themselves do not know the design they are sent upon, until they come there; none can know his intentions or meaning by his actions: for sometimes he sends commanders with their soldiers to lie in certain places in the woods until farther order, or until he send ammunition to them; and, perhaps, when they have laid there long enough, he sends for them back again: and, after this manner oftentimes, he catches the Hollanders before they be aware, to their great prejudice and damage: he cares not that his great men should be free spirited or valiant; if there be any better than the rest, them to be sure suddenly he cuts off, lest they might do him any mischief.

Great exploits done, and but little courage.

They work chiefly by stratagems.

In their war there is but little valour used, although they do accomplish many notable exploits; for all they do is by crafty stratagems: they will never meet their enemies in the field, to give them a repulse by battle and force of arms; neither is the enemy like to meet with any opposition at their first goings out to invade the king's coasts, the king's soldiers knowing the adverse forces are at first wary and vigilant, as also well provided with all necessaries; but their usual practice is to waylay them, and stop up the ways before them; there being convenient places in all the roads, which they have contrived for such purposes: and, at these places the woods are not suffered to be felled, but kept to shelter them from the sight of their enemies. Here they lie lurking, and plant their guns between the rocks and trees, with which they do great damage to their enemies before they then are aware: nor can they suddenly rush in upon them, being so well guarded with bushes and rocks before them; through which, before their enemies can get, they flee, carrying their great guns upon their shoulders, and are gone into the woods, where it is impossible to find them, until they come themselves to meet them after the former manner.

Likewise, they prepare against the enemy's coming, great bushy trees, having them ready cut, hanging only by withs which grow in the wood; these, as they march along, they let fall among them with many shots and arrows.

Being sent upon any design, they are very circumspect to keep it hidden from the enemy's knowledge, by suffering only those to pass, who may make for their benefit and advantage; their great endeavour being to take their enemies unprovided and at unawares.

By the long wars first between them and the Portuguese, and since with the Hollander, they have had such ample experience, as hath much improved them in the art of war above what they were formerly; and many of the chief commanders and leaders of their armies are men which formerly served the Portu- **They understand the manner of Christian armies.**

guese against them; by which they come to know the disposition and discipline of Christian armies. Insomuch as they have given the Dutch several overthrows, and taken forts from them, which they had up in the country.

They seldom hazard a battle.

Heretofore for bringing the head of an enemy, the king used to gratify them with some reward, but now the fashion is almost out of use. The ordering of their battle is with great security, there being very few lost in fight: for if they be not almost sure to win the battle, they had rather not fight, than run any hazard of losing it.

If they prove unsuccessful, how he punishes them.

If his men do not successfully accomplish the design he sends them upon, to be sure they shall have a lusty piece of work given them, to take revenge on them: for not using their weapons well, he will exercise them with other tools, houghs, and pickaxes, about his palace; and, during the time they stay to work, they must bring their victuals with them, not having monies there to buy: they cannot carry for above one month; and, when their provisions are all spent, if they will have any more, they must go home and fetch them. But that is not permitted them without giving a fee to the governor or his overseer: neither can they go without his leave; for besides the punishment, the watches, which are in every road from the king's city, will stop and seize them.

CHAP. VII.

A Relation of the Rebellion made against the King.

FOR the conclusion of this part, it will not be improper to relate here a dangerous rising of the people against the king. It happened in the year 1664; about which time appeared a fearful blazing-star. Just at the instant of the rebellion, the star was right over our heads; and one thing I very much wondered at, which was, that whereas, before this rebellion, the tail stood away toward the westward, from which side the rebellion sprung; the very night after (for I very well observed it) the tail was turned and stood away toward the eastward, and by degrees it diminished quite away.

A comet ushered in the rebellion.

At this time, I say, the people of this land, having been long and sore oppressed by this king's unreasonable and cruel government, had contrived a plot against him; which was, to assault the king's court in the night, and to slay him, and to make the prince, his son, king; he being then some twelve or fifteen years of age, who was then with his mother, the queen, in the city of Candy. At this time the king held his court in a city called Nillemby; the situation of which is far inferior to that of Candy, and as far beyond that of Digligy, where he now is. Nillemby lieth some fourteen miles southward of the city of Candy. In the place where this city stands, it is reported by tradition, an hare gave chase after a dog, upon which it was

The intent of the conspirators.

concluded that place was fortunate, and so indeed it proved to the king. It is environed with hills and woods.

How the rebellion began.

The time appointed to put their design in action was the one-and-twentieth of December, 1664, about twelve in the night. And having gotten a select company of men, how many, well I know not, but as is supposed not above two hundred, neither needed they many here, having so many confederates in the court; in the dead of the night they came marching into the city. The watch was thought to be of their confederacy; but if he were not, it was not in his power to resist them. Howbeit afterwards, whether he were not, he was executed for it. The said men, being thus in the city, hastened and came down to the court, and fell upon the great men, which then laid without the palace upon watch; since which, by the king's order, they lie always within the palace; for they were well informed before who were for them, and who not. Many, who before were not entrusted to know of their design, were killed and wounded; and those that could, seeing the slaughter of others, got in unto the king, who was walled about with a clay-wall, thatched; that was all his strength: yet these people feared to assault him, laying still until the morning; at which time the king made way to flee, fearing to stay in his palace, endeavouring to get unto the mountains, and had not with him above fifty persons. There were horses went with him, but the ways were so bad, that he could not ride. They were fain to drive an elephant before him, to break the way through the woods, that the king with his followers might pass.

The king flies.

They pursue him faintly.

As he fled they pursued him, but at a great distance, fearing to approach within shot of him; for he wanted not for excellent good fowling-pieces, which are made there; so he got safe upon a mountain, called Gauluda, some fifteen miles distant, where many of the inhabitants, that were near, resorted to him. Howbeit, had the people of the rebel party been resolute, who were the major part (almost all the land), this hill could not have secured him, but they might have driven him from thence; there being many ways by which they might have ascended. There is not far from hence a high and peaked hill, called Mondamounour, where there is but one way to get up, and that very steep; at the top are great stones hanging in chains, to let fall when need requireth. Had he fled hither, there had been no way to come at him; but he never will adventure to go where he may be stopped in.

The people having thus driven away the old king, marched away to the city of Candy, and proclaimed the prince king; giving out to us English, who were there, that what they had done, they had not done rashly, but upon good consideration, and with good advice; the king, by his evil government having occasioned it, who went about to destroy both them and their country: as in keeping ambassadors, disannulling of trade, detaining of all people that come upon his land, and killing of his subjects and their children, and not suffering them to enjoy nor to see their wives. And all this was contrary to reason; and, as they were informed, to the government of other countries.

They go to the prince and proclaim him king.

The prince being young and tender, and having never been out of the palace, nor ever seen any but those that attended on his person, as it seemed afterwards, was scared to see so many coming and bowing down to him, and telling him that he was

The carriage of the prince.

king, and his father was fled into the mountains: neither did he say or act any thing, as not owning the business, or else not knowing what to say or do. This much discouraged the rebels, to see they had no more thanks for their pains. And so all things stood until the five-and-twentieth of December, at which time they intended to march and fall upon the old king.

Upon the prince's flight the rebels scatter and run.

But in the interim, the king's sister flies away with the prince from the court into the country, near unto the king; which so amazed the rebels, that the money and cloth and plunder which they had taken, and were going to distribute to the strangers, to gain their good will and assistance, they scattered about and fled. Others of their company, seeing the business was overthrown, to make amends for their former fact, turned and fell upon their consorts, killing and taking prisoners all they could. The people were now all up in arms one against another, killing whom they pleased, only saying they were rebels, and taking their goods.

A great man declares for the king.

By this time a great man had drawn out his men, and stood in the field, and there turned and publicly declared for the old king: and so went to catch the rebels that were scattered abroad; who, when he understood that they were all fled, and no whole party or body left to resist him, marched into the city, killing all that he could catch.

For eight or ten days nothing but killing one another to approve themselves good subjects.

And so all revolted, and came back to the king again—whilst he only lay still upon his mountain. The king needed not to take care to catch or execute the rebels; for they themselves, out of their zeal to him, and to make amends for what was passed, imprisoned and killed all they met; the plunder being their own. This continued for some eight or ten days; which the king hearing of, commanded to kill no more, but that whom they took they should imprison, until examination passed; which was not so much to save innocent persons from violence, as that he might have the rebels to torment them, and make them confess of their confederates—for he spared none that seemed guilty: some to this day lay chained in prison, being sequestered of all their estates, and beg for their living. One of the most noted rebels, called Ambom Wellaraul, he sent to Columba, to the Dutch, to execute, supposing they would invent new tortures for him, beyond what he knew of; but they, instead of executing him, cut off his chains, and kindly entertained him, and there he still is in the city of Columba, reserving him for some designs they may hereafter have against the country.

The king could but not be sensible, that it was his rigorous government that had occasioned this rebellion, yet amended it not in the least; but, on the contrary, like to Rehoboam, added yet more to the people's yoke: and, being thus safely reinstated in his kingdom again, and observing that the life of his son gave encouragement to the rebellion, resolved to prevent it for the future, by taking him away; which, upon the next opportunity, he did by poisoning him, which I have related before.

The king poisons his son to prevent a rebellion hereafter.

But one thing there is, that argues him guilty of imprudence and horrible ingratitude—that most of those that went along with him when he fled, of whose loyalty he had such ample experience, he hath since cut off; and that with extreme cruelty too.

His ingratitude.

Another comet, but without any bad effects following it.

In the year 1666, in the month of February, there appeared in this country another comet or stream in the west, the head end under the horizon, much resembling that which was seen in England in the year 1680, in December. The sight of this did much daunt both king and people, having but a year or two before felt the sad event of a blazing-star in this rebellion, which I have now related. The king sent men upon the highest mountains in the land, to look if they could perceive the head of it, which they could not, being still under the horizon. This continued visible about the space of one month; and, by that time it was so diminished, that it could not be seen: but there were no remarkable passages that ensued upon it.

PART III.

CHAP. I.

Concerning the Inhabitants of this Island.

We shall in this part speak of the inhabitants of this country, with their religion and customs, and other things belonging to them.

Besides the Dutch who possess, as I judge, about one fourth of the Island, there are Malabars, that are free denizens, and pay duty to the king for the land they enjoy, as the king's natural subjects do: there are also moors, who are like strangers, and hold no land, but live by carrying goods to the sea-ports, which are now in the Hollanders hands. The sea-ports are inhabited by a mixed people, Malabars and moors, and some that are black, who profess themselves Roman Catholics, and wear crosses, and use beads: some of these are under the Hollander, and pay toll and tribute to then

The several inhabitants of this island.

But I am to speak only of the natural proper people of the Island, which they call Chingulays.

The original of Chingulays. I have asked them whence they derive themselves, but they could not tell. They say their land was first inhabited by devils, of which they have a long fable. I have heard a tradition from some Portuguese here, which was,—That an ancient king of China had a son, who, during his father's reign, proved so very harsh and cruel unto the people, that they, being afraid he might prove a tyrant if he came to the crown, desired the king to banish him, and that he might never succeed; this, that king, to please the people, granted; and so put him, with certain attendants, into a ship, and turned them forth unto the winds, to seek their fortune. The first shore they were cast upon was this Island, which they seated themselves on, and peopled it. But to me nothing is more improbable than this story, because this people and the Chinese have no agreement nor similitude in their features, nor language, nor diet: it is more probable they came from the Malabars; their country lying next, though they do resemble them little or nothing. I know no nation in the world do so exactly resemble the Chingulays as the people of Europe.

Of these natives there be two sorts, wild and tame: I will begin with the former. For, as in these woods there are wild beasts, so wild men also. The land of Bintan is all co-

Wild men. vered with mighty woods, filled with abundance of deer: in this land are many of these wild men; they call them Vaddahs, dwelling near no other inhabitants: they speak the Chingulay's language; they kill deer, and dry the flesh over the fire, and the people of the country come and buy it of them: they never

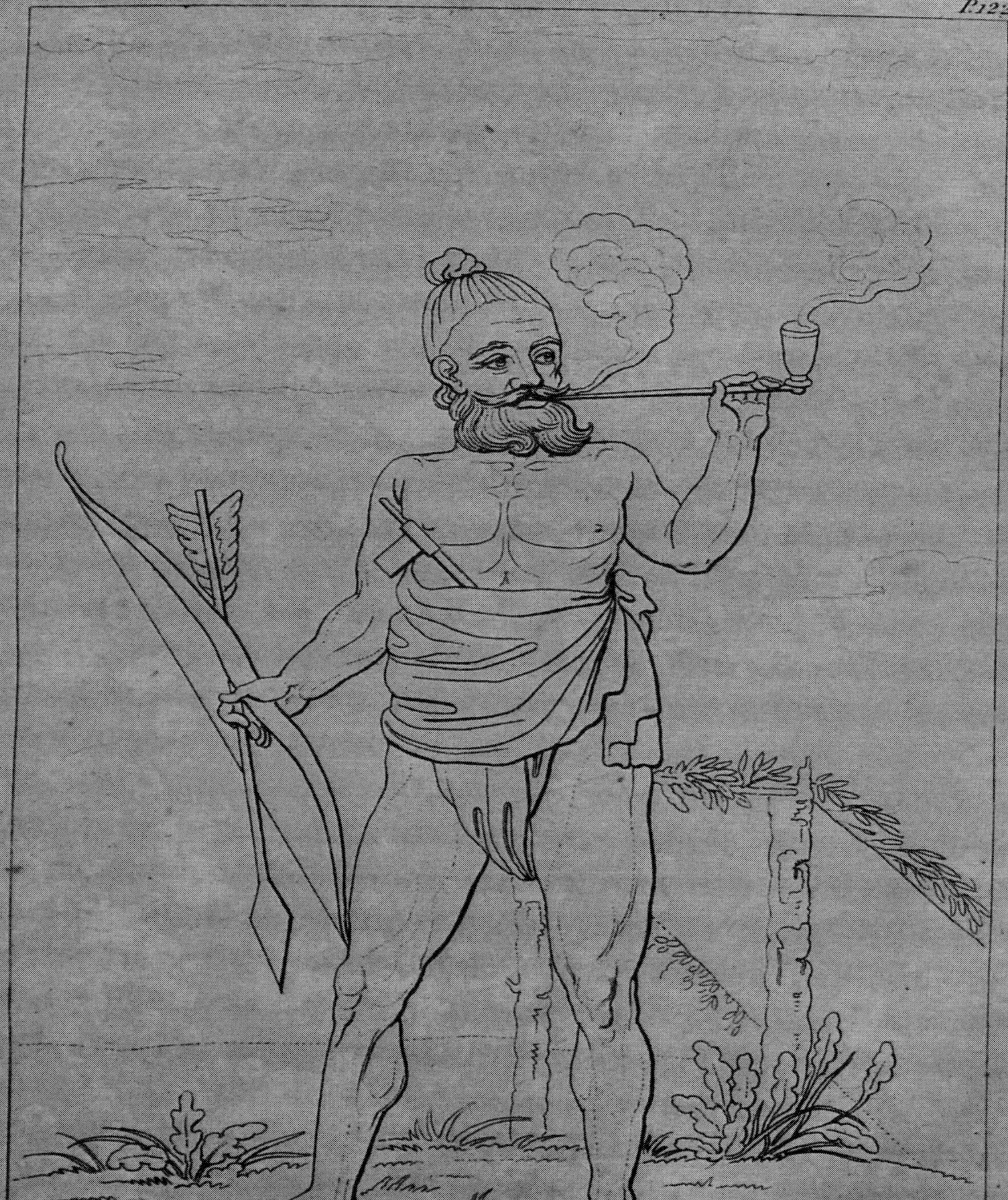

A Vadda, or Wild Man

London Published May 10th 1816. by J. Mawman

till any ground for corn, their food being only flesh; they are very expert with their bows: they have a little axe, which they stick in by their sides, to cut honey out of hollow trees; some few, which are near inhabitants, have commerce with other people: they have no towns nor houses, only live by the waters under a tree, with some boughs cut, and laid round about them, to give notice when any wild beasts come near, which they may hear by their rustling and trampling upon them. Many of these habitations we saw when we fled through the woods; but, God be praised, the Vaddahs were gone.

Some of the tamer sort of these men are in a kind of subjection to the king; for if they can be found, though it must be with a great search in the woods, they will acknowledge his officers, and bring to them elephants' teeth, and honey, and wax, and deer's flesh; but the others, in lieu thereof, do give them as much in arrows, cloth, &c. fearing lest they should otherwise appear no more. By an acknowledgement to the king.

It hath been reported to me by many people, that the wilder sort of them, when they want arrows, will carry their load of flesh in the night, and hang it up in a smith's shop, also a leaf cut in the form they will have their arrows made, and hang by it; which, if the smith do make according to their pattern, they will requite, and bring him more flesh; but, if he make them not, they will do him a mischief one time or other by shooting in the night. If the smith make the arrows, he leaves them in the same place where the Vaddahs hung the flesh. How they bespeak arrows to be made them.

Formerly, in this king's reign, these wild men used to lie in

They violently took away carriers goods.

wait, to catch carriers people, that went down with oxen to trade at the sea-ports, carrying down betel nuts, and bringing up cloth, and would make them to give them such things as they required, or else threatening to shoot them. They, fearing their lives, and not being able to resist, were fain to give them what they asked; or else most certainly they would have had both life and goods too: at which, this king sent many commanders, with soldiers, to catch them, which at length they did; but had not some of themselves proved false to them, being encouraged by large promises, they could never have taken them. The chief being brought before the king, promising amendment, were pardoned; but sent into other woods, with a command not to return thither any more, neither to use their former courses: but soon after their departure, they forsook those woods they were put into, and came to their old haunt again, falling to their former course of life: this the king hearing of, and how they had abused his pardon, gave command either to bring them dead or alive. These Vaddahs knowing now there could be no hope of pardon, would not be taken alive, but were shot by the treachery of their own men. The heads of two of the chiefest were hanged on trees by the city: and ever since they have not presumed to disturb the country, nor the king them, he only desiring their quiet, and not to be against him.

Hourly Vaddahs trade with the people.

About Hourly, the remotest of the king's dominions, there are many of them, that are pretty tame, and come and buy and sell among the people. The king once having occasion of an hasty expedition against the Dutch, the governor summoned them all in to go with him, which they did; and with their bows and arows did as good service as any of the rest; but, afterwards, when they returned home again, they removed far-

One made to serve the king.

ther into the woods, and would be seen no more, for fear of being afterwards prest again to serve the king.

They never cut their hair, but tie it up on their crowns in a bunch. The cloth they use is not broad nor large, but scarcely enough to cover their buttocks. The wilder and tamer sort of them do both observe a religion; they have a god peculiar to themselves. The tamer do build temples; the wild only bring their sacrifice under trees; and, while it is offering, dance round it, both men and women.

Their habit and religion.

They have their bounds in the woods among themselves, and one company of them is not to shoot nor gather honey or fruit beyond those bounds: near the borders stood a jack tree; one Vaddah being gathering some fruit from this tree, another Vaddah of the next division saw him, and told him he had nothing to do to gather jacks from that tree, for that belonged to them: they fell to words, and from words to blows, and one of them shot the other; at which more of them met, and fell to skirmishing so briskly with their bows and arrows, that twenty or thirty were left dead upon the spot.

A skirmish about their bounds.

They are so curious of their arrows, that no smith can please them. The king once, to gratify them for a great present they brought him, gave all of them of his best made arrow-blades, which, nevertheless, would not please their humour; for they went all of them to a rock by a river, and ground them into another form. The arrows they use are of a different fashion from all other, and the Chingulays will not use them.

Curious in their arrows.

How they preserve their flesh. They have a peculiar way by themselves of preserving flesh: they cut a hollow tree and put honey in it, and then fill it up with flesh, and stop it up with clay: which lies for a reserve, to eat in time of want.

How they take elephants. It has usually been told me, that their way of catching elephants is, that when the elephant lies asleep, they strike their axe into the sole of his foot; and, so laming him, he is in their power to take him—but I take this for a fable; because I know the sole of the elephant's foot is so hard, that no axe can pierce it at a blow; and he is so wakeful, that they can have no opportunity to do it.

The dowry they give. Their disposition. For portions with their daughters in marriage they give hunting dogs. They are reported to be courteous. Some of the Chingulays, in discontent, will leave their houses and friends, and go and live among them, where they are civilly entertained: the tamer sort of them, as hath been said, will sometimes appear, and hold some kind of trade with the tame inhabitants; but the wilder, called Ramba Vaddahs, never shew themselves.

A description of a Chingulay. But to come to the civilized inhabitants, whom I am chiefly to treat of; they are a people proper and very well-favoured, beyond all people that I have seen in India, wearing a cloth about their loins, and a doublet, after the English fashion, with little skirts, buttoned at the wrists, and gathered at the shoulders like a shirt; on their heads a red Tunis cap; or, if they have none, another cap, with flaps of the fashion of their country, described in the next chapter, with a handsome short hanger by their side, and a knife sticking in their bosom on the right side.

They are very active and nimble in their limbs, and very ingenious; for, except iron-work, all other things they have need of, they make and do themselves; insomuch, that they all build their own houses. They are crafty and treacherous, not to be trusted upon any protestations—for their manner of speaking is very smooth and courteous; insomuch, that they who are unacquainted with their dispositions and manners, may easily be deceived by them: for they make no account nor conscience of lying, neither is it any shame or disgrace to them, if they be catched in telling lies, it is so customary. They are very vigilant and wakeful, sufficed with very little sleep; very hardy, both for diet and weather—very proud and self-conceited. They take something after the Bramins, with whom they scruple not both to marry and eat; in both which, otherwise, they are exceeding shy and cautious: for there being many ranks or casts among them, they will not match with any inferior to themselves, nor eat meat dressed in any house, but in those only that are of as good a cast or race as themselves; and that which any one hath left, none but those that are near of kin will eat.

Their disposition.

They are not very malicious one towards another; and their anger doth not last long; seldom or never any bloodshed among them in their quarrels: it is not customary to strike, and it is very rare that they give a blow so much as to their slaves, who may very familiarly talk and discourse with their masters: they are very near and covetous, and will pinch their own bellies for profit: very few spendthrifts or bad husbands are to be met with here.

The inhabitants of the mountains differ from those of the low lands.

The natures of the inhabitants of the mountains and low lands are very different; they of the low lands are kind, pitiful, helpful, honest, and plain, compassionating strangers, which we found by our own experience among them: they of the uplands are ill-natured, false, unkind, though outwardly fair, and seemingly courteous, and of more complaisant carriage, speech, and better behaviour, than the low-landers.

Their good opinion of virtue, though they practice it not.

Of all vices, they are least addicted to stealing, the which they do exceedingly hate and abhor; so that there are but few robberies committed among them. They do much extol and commend chastity, temperance, and truth in words and actions, and confess that it is out of weakness and infirmity, that they cannot practice the same, acknowledging that the contrary vices are to be abhorred, being abomination both in the sight of God and man; they do love and delight in those men that are most devout and precise in their matters: as for bearing witness for confirmation in any matters of doubt, a Christian's word will be believed and credited far beyond their own, because, they think, they make more conscience of their words.

Superstitious.

They are very superstitious in making observations of any little accidents, as omens portending good to them or evil; sneezing they reckon to import evil; so that if any chance to sneeze when he is going about his business, he will stop, accounting he shall have ill success if he proceeds: and none may sneeze, cough, nor spit in the king's presence, either because of the ill boding of those actions, or the rudeness of them, or both.

There is a little creature, much like a lizard, which they look upon altogether as a prophet: whatsoever work or business they are going about, if he cries, they will cease for a space, reckoning, he tells them there is a bad planet rules at that instant. They take great notice in a morning, at their first going out, who first appears in their sight; and, if they see a white man, or a big-bellied woman, they hold it fortunate; and, to see any decrepit or deformed people, as unfortunate.

When they travel together, a great many of them, the roads are so narrow, that but one can go abreast; and, if there be twenty of them, there is but one argument or matter discoursed of among them all from the first to the last; and so they go talking along all together, and every one carrieth his provisions on his back for his whole journey. *How they travel.*

In short, in carriage and behaviour they are very grave and stately, like unto the Portugals, in understanding quick and apprehensive, in design subtile and crafty, in discourse courteous, but full of flatteries, naturally inclined to temperance, both in meat and drink, but not to chastity, near and provident in their families, commending good husbandry; in their dispositions not passionate, neither hard to be reconciled again when angry; in their promises very unfaithful, approving lying in themselves, but misliking it in others; delighting in sloth, deferring labour till urgent necessity constrain them, neat in apparel, nice in eating, and not much given to sleep. *A brief character of them.*

As for the women, their habit is a waistcoat of white calico covering their bodies, wrought into flourishes with blue and red, the cloth hanging longer or shorter below their knees, according *The women, their habit and nature.*

to their quality, a piece of silk flung over their heads, jewels in their ears, ornaments about their necks, and arms, and middles. They are in their gait and behaviour very high, stately in their carriage, after the Portugal manner, of whom I think they have learned; yet they hold it no scorn to admit the meanest to come to speech of them. They are very thrifty, and it is a disgrace to them to be prodigal, and their pride and glory to be accounted near and saving: and to praise themselves, they will sometimes say, that scraps and parings will serve them, that the best is for their husbands. The men are not jealous of their wives; for the greatest ladies in the land will frequently talk and discourse with any men they please, although their husbands be in presence. And, although they be so stately, they will lay their hand to such work as is necessary to be done in the house, notwithstanding they have slaves and servants enough to do it. Let this suffice concerning the nature and manners of the people in general: the ensuing chapters will be spent in more particular accounts of them; and, because they stand much upon their birth and gentility, and much of what is afterwards to be related hath reference unto it, I shall speak of the various ranks and degrees of men among them.

CHAP. II.

Concerning their different Honours, Ranks, and Qualities.

AMONG this people there are divers and sundry casts or degrees of quality, which is not according to their riches or places of honour the king promotes them to, but according to their descent and blood: and, whatsoever this honour is, be it higher or lower, it remains hereditary from generation to generation. They abhor to eat or drink, or intermarry, with any of inferior quality to themselves. The signs of higher or meaner ranks, are wearing of doublets, or going bare-backed without them; the length of their cloth below their knees; their sitting on stools, or on blocks or mats spread on the ground, and in their caps.

How they distinguish themselves according to their qualities.

They are especially careful in their marriages, not to match with any inferior cast, but always each within their own rank. Riches cannot prevail with them in the least to marry with those by whom they must eclipse and stain the honour of their family; on which they set a higher price than on their lives. And, if any of the females should be so deluded as to commit folly with one beneath herself, if ever she should appear in the sight of her friends, they would certainly kill her—there being no other way to wipe off the dishonour she hath done the family, but by her own blood.

They never marry beneath their rank.

In case a man lies with a woman of inferior rank.

Yet for the men it is something different: it is not accounted any shame or fault for a man of the highest sort to lay with a woman far inferior to himself; nay, of the very lowest degree, provided he neither eats nor drinks with her, nor takes her home to his house as a wife: but if he should, which I never knew done, he is punished by the magistrate, either by fine or imprisonment, or both; and also, he is utterly excluded from his family, and accounted thenceforward of the same rank and quality that the woman is of whom he hath taken. If the woman be married already, with whom the man of better rank lies, and the husband come and catch them together, how low soever the one be, and high the other, he may kill him, and her too, if he please.

And thus by marrying constantly each rank within itself, the descent and dignity thereof is preserved for ever; and whether the family be high or low it never alters. But to proceed to the particular ranks and degrees of men among them.

Their noblemen.

The highest are their noblemen, called hondrews; which I suppose comes from the word homdrewmé, a title given to the king, signifying majesty; these being honoured people. 'Tis out of this sort alone that the king chooseth his great officers, and whom he employs in his court, and appoints for governors over his country. Riches are not here valued, nor make any the more honourable; for many of the lower sorts do far exceed these hondrews in estates; but it is the birth and parentage that ennobleth.

How distinguished from others.

These are distinguished from others by their names, and the wearing of their cloth, which the men wear half down their legs, and the women to their heels; one end of which cloth the women fling over their shoulders, and with the very end carelessly cover their breasts: whereas, the other sort of women must go naked from the waist upwards, and their clothes not hang down much below their knees, except it be for cold; for then either women or men may throw their cloth over their backs. But then they do excuse it to the hondrews, when they meet them, saying—" Excuse me, it is for warmth."

They are distinguished also by their own country caps, which are of the fashion of mitres; there are two flaps tied up over the top of the crown. If they be hondrews, their caps are all of one colour, either white or blue; if of inferior quality, then the cap and the flaps on each side be of different colours, whereof the flaps are always red. The distinction by caps.

Of these hondrews there be two sorts—the one somewhat inferior to the other as touching marriage; but not in other things. The greatest part of the inhabitants of the land are of the degree of hondrews. Of the hondrews, two sorts.

All Christians, either white or black, are accounted equal with the hondrews. The whites are generally honourable; only it is an abatement of their honour that they eat beef, and wash not after they have been at stool; which things are reckoned with this people an abomination.

Among the noblemen may be mentioned an honour, that the king confers, like unto knighthood; it ceaseth in the person's death, and is not hereditary. The king confers it by putting about their heads a piece of silk, or ribbon, embroidered with An honour like unto knighthood.

gold and silver, and bestowing a title upon them. They are styled mundianna: there are not above two or three of them now in the realm living.

Goldsmiths, blacksmiths carpenters, &c.

Next after the degree of hondrews may be placed goldsmiths, blacksmiths, carpenters, and painters; who are all of one degree and quality. But the hondrews will not eat with them: however, in apparel there is no difference; and they are also privileged to sit on stools, which none of the inferior ranks of people, hereafter mentioned, may do. Heretofore they were accounted almost equal to the inferior sort of hondrews, and they would eat in these artificers houses, but afterwards they were degraded upon this occasion:—It chanced some hondrews came to a smith's shop to have their tools mended: when it came to be dinner time, the smith leaves work, and goes into his house to dine, leaving the hondrews in his shop, who had waited there a great while to have their work done. Now, whether the smith fearing lest their hunger might move them to be so impudent or desperate as to partake with him of his dinner, clapt to his door after him; which was taken so heinously by those hungry people in his shop, that immediately they all went and declared abroad what an affront the smith had put upon them. Whereupon it was decreed and confirmed, that for ever after all the people of that rank should be deposed, and deprived of the honour of having the hondrews to eat in their houses; which decree hath stood in force ever since.

The privilege and state of the smiths.

Nevertheless these smiths take much upon them, especially those who are the king's smiths; that is, such who live in the king's towns, and do his work. These have this privilege, that each has a parcel of towns belonging to them, whom none but they are to work for. The ordinary work they do for them is mending their tools, for which every man pays to his smith a certain rate of corn in harvest time, according to ancient custom; but, if any hath work extraordinary, as making new tools or the like, besides the aforesaid rate of corn, he must pay him for it. In order to this, they come in an humble manner to the smith with a present, being rice, hens, and other sorts of provision, or a bottle of rack, desiring him to appoint his time, when they shall come to have their work done; which, when he hath appointed them, they come at the set time, and bring both coals and iron with them. The smith sits very gravely upon his stool, his anvil before him, with his left hand towards the forge, and little hammer in his right. They themselves, who come with their work, must blow the bellows; and, when the iron is to be beaten with the great maul, he holds it, still sitting upon his stool, and they must hammer it themselves, he only with his little hammer knocking it sometimes into fashion; and, if it be any thing to be filed, he makes them go themselves and grind it upon a stone, that his labour of filing may be the less; and, when they have done it as well as they can, he goes over it again with his file, and finisheth it. That which makes these smiths thus stately is, because the towns-people are compelled to go to their own smith, and none else; and, if they should, that smith is liable to pay damages that should do work for any in another smith's jurisdiction.

All that are of any craft or profession, are accounted of an inferior degree, as elephant catchers, and keepers, who are reckoned equal with the smiths, &c. aforesaid, though they neither eat nor marry together; and these may wear apparel Craftsmen.

as do the hondrews, and sit on stools, but the hondrews eat not with them.

No artificers ever change their trade from generation to generation; but the son is the same as was his father, and the daughter marries only to those of the same craft: and her portion is such tools as are of use, and do belong unto the trade; though the father may give over and above what he pleaseth.

Barbars. Next are the barbars; both the women and men may wear doublets, but not sit on stools, neither will any eat with them.

Potters. Potters yet more inferior, may not wear any doublets, nor their cloth much below the knee, nor sit on stools, neither will any eat with them: but they have this privilege; because they make the pots, that when they are athirst, being at a hondrew's house, they may take his pot, which hath a pipe to it, and pour the water into their mouths themselves; which none other of these inferior degrees may be admitted to do—but they must hold their hands to their mouths and gape, and the hondrews themselves will pour the water in. The potters were at first denied this honour, upon which they jointly agreed to make pots with pipes only for themselves, and would sell none to the hondrews that wanted; whereat being constrained, they condescended to grant them the honour above other inferior people, that they should have the favour to drink out of these spouts at their houses.

Washers. The next are the ruddaughs, washers. Of these there are great numbers. They wash cloths for all people to the degree of a potter; but for none below that degree. Their usual posture is to carry a cloth on their shoulder, both men and women; they use lye in their washing, setting a pot over the fire, holding seven or eight gallons of water, and lay the foul clothes on the top; and the steam of the water goes into the clothes and scalds them: then they take them and carry them to a river side, and instead of rubbing them with their hands, flap them against the rock, and they become very clean; nor doth this tear the clothes at all, as they order it.

Another rank after these are the hungrams, or jaggory-makers; though none will eat with them, yet it is lawful to buy and eat the jaggory they make (which is a kind of sugar), but nothing else. Jaggory-makers.

Another sort among them is the poddah. These are of no trade or craft, but are husbandmen and soldiers, yet are inferior to all that have been named hitherto; for what reason neither I, nor, I think, themselves can tell; only thus it falls to them by succession from their predecessors, and so will ever remain. The poddah

After these are the weavers; who, beside their trade, which is weaving cloth, are astrologers, and tell the people good days and good seasons; and, at the birth of a child, write for them an account of the day, time, and planet, it was born in and under. These accounts they keep with great care all their life-time; by which they know their age, and what success or evil shall befal them. Weavers.

These people also beat drums, and play on pipes, and dance in the temples of their gods, and at their sacrifices: they eat and carry away all such victuals as are offered to their idols; both which to do and take, is accounted to belong to people of a very low degree and quality: these also will eat dead cows.

Basket-makers.

Next to the weavers are the kiddeas or basket-makers, who make fans to fan corn, and baskets of canes, and lace, bedsteads, and stools.

Mat-makers

Then follow the kirinerahs, whose trade is to make fine mats. These men may not wear any thing on their heads—the women of none of these sorts ever do. Of these two last there are but few.

The lower ranks may not assume the habit or names of the higher.

All below the couratto or elephant-men, may not sit on stools, nor wear doublets, except the barbar, nor wear the cloth low down their legs: neither may any of these ranks of people, either man or woman, except the potter and the washer, wear the end of their cloth to cover their bodies, unless they be sick or cold: neither may they presume to be called by the names that the hondrews are called by; nor may they, where they are not known, change themselves by pretending, or seeming to be, higher than nature hath made them: and I think they never do, but own themselves in the rank and quality wherein they were born, and demean themselves accordingly.

All outlandish people are esteemed above the inferior ranks. The names of the hondrews always end in oppow, of others below the degree of the elephant people in adgah.

Slaves.

The slaves may make another rank, for whose maintenance their masters allow them land and cattle, which many of them do so improve, that, except in dignity, they are not far behind their masters, only they are not permitted to have slaves; their masters will not diminish or take away ought, that by their diligence and industry, they have procured, but approve of it, as being persons capable to repose trust in: and, when they do buy, or otherwise get a new slave, they presently provide him a wife, and so put him forward to keep house, and settle, that he may not think of running away. Slaves that are born of hondrew parents, retain the honour of their degree.

There is one sort of people more, and they are the beggars; who, for their transgression, as hereafter shall be shewn, have by former kings been made so low and base, that they can be no lower or baser; and they must and do give such titles and respects to all other people, as are due from other people to kings and princes. Beggars.

The predecessors of these people, from whom they sprang, were dodda vaddahs, which signifies hunters; to whom it did belong to catch and bring venison for the king's table: but, instead of venison they brought man's flesh, unknown; which the king liking so well, commanded to bring him more of the same sort of venison: the king's barbar chanced to know what flesh it was, and discovered it to him; at which the king was so enraged, that he accounted death too good for them; and to punish only those persons that had so offended, not a sufficient recompense for so great an affront and injury as he had sustained by them: forthwith, therefore, he established a decree—that all, both great and small, that were of that rank or tribe, should be expelled from dwelling among the inhabitants of the land, and not be admitted to use or enjoy the benefit of any means, or ways, or callings whatsoever, to provide themselves The reason they became so base and mean a people.

sustenance; but, that they should beg from generation to generation, from door to door, through the kingdom; and to be looked upon and esteemed by all people to be so base and odious, as not possibly to be more.

And they are to this day so detestable to the people, that they are not permitted to fetch water out of their wells; but do take their water out of holes or rivers: neither will any touch them, lest they should be defiled.

And thus they go a begging in whole troops, both men, women, and children, carrying both pots and pans, hens and chickens, and whatsoever they have, in baskets hanging on a pole, at each end one, upon their shoulders. The women never carry any thing; but, when they come to any house to beg, they dance and shew tricks, while the men beat drums: they will turn brass basons on one of their fingers, twirling it round very swift, and wonderfully strange; and they will toss up balls into the air one after another, to the number of nine, and catch them as they fall; and, as fast as they do catch them, still they toss them up again: so that there are always seven up in the air. Also, they will take beads of several colours, and of one size, and put them into their mouths, and then take them one by one out of their mouths again, each colours by themselves; and, with this behaviour, and the high and honourable titles which they give, as to men, your honour, and your majesty; and to women, queens, countesses; and to white men, white of the royal blood, &c. they do beg for their living, and that with so much importunity, as if they had a patent for it from the king, and will not be denied; pretending that it was so ordered and decreed, that by this very means they should be maintained; and, unless they mean to perish with hunger, they cannot accept of a denial. The people, on the other hand, cannot without horrible shame lift up their hand against them to strike or thrust them away; so, rather than to be troubled with their importunity, they will relieve them.

And thus they live, building small hovels in remote places, highways, under trees: and all the land being, as it were of necessity, contributors towards their maintenance, these beggars live without labour, as well, or better, than the other sorts of people; being free from all sorts of service and duties, which all other are compelled to perform for the king:—of them it is only required to make ropes of such cow-hides, as die of themselves, to catch and tie elephants with: by which they have another privilege, to claim the flesh thereof for themselves from the weavers; who, when they meet with any dead cows, use to cut them up and eat them; but, if any of these roudeahs, beggars, see them, they will run to them, and drive them away, offering to beat them with the poles, whereon they carry their baskets; saying to them,—"How can we perform the king's service to make ropes of the hide, if the weavers hack and spoil it?" telling them also—That it is beneath such honourable people as they, to eat such unclean and polluted flesh. By these words, and the fear the weavers are in to be touched by that base people, than which nothing could be more infamous, they are glad to get them away as fast as they can.

They live well.

Their contest with the weavers about dead cows.

These men being so low, that nothing they can do can make them lower, it is not unusual with them to lay with their daughters, or for the son to lay with his mother, as if there were no consanguinity among them.

Incest common among them.

A punishment to deliver noble women to these beggars.

Many times when the king cuts off great and noble men, against whom he is highly incensed, he will deliver their daughters and wives unto this sort of people, reckoning it, as they also account it, to be far worse punishment than any kind of death: this kind of punishment being accounted such horrible cruelty, the king doth usually of his clemency shew them some kind of mercy; and, pitying their distress, commands to carry them to a river side, and there to deliver them into the hands of those, who are far worse than the executioners of death: from whom, if these ladies please to free themselves, they are permitted to leap into the river and be drowned; the which some sometimes will choose to do, rather than to consort with them.

Some of these beggars keep cattle and shoot deer.

There are some of this sort of people which dwell in remote parts, distant from any towns, and keep cattle, and sell them to the Chingulays; also shoot deer, and sell them where they fall in the woods; for, if they should but touch them, none would buy them.

Refuse meat dressed in a barbar's house.

The barbar's information having been the occasion of all this misery upon this people, they in revenge thereof abhor to eat what is dressed in the barbar's house even to this day.

CHAP. III.

Of their Religion, Gods, Temples, Priests.

TO take a more particular view of the state of this country, we shall, first, give some account of their religion, as it justly requires the first place, and then of their other secular concerns.

Under their religion will come to be considered their gods, their temples, their priests, their festivals, sacrifices, and worship, and their doctrines and opinions; and whatsoever other matters occur, that may concern this subject.

Their religion, their gods.

The religion of their country is idolatry. There are many both gods and devils, which they worship, known by particular names, which they call them by. They do acknowledge one to be the Supreme, whom they call Ossa polla maupt Dio, which signifieth the Creator of heaven and earth; and it is he also who still ruleth and governeth the same. This great Supreme God, they hold, sends forth other deities to see his will and pleasure executed in the world; and these are the petty and inferior gods. These, they say, are the souls of good men, who formerly lived upon the earth. There are devils also, who are the inflicters of sickness and misery upon them; and these they hold to be the souls of evil men.

They worship the God that saves souls.

There is another great god, whom they call Buddou, unto whom the salvation of souls belongs. Him they believe once to have come upon the earth; and, when he was here, that he did usually sit under a large shady tree, called bogahah: which trees ever since are accounted holy, and under which, with great solemnities, they do to this day celebrate the ceremonies of his worship. He departed from the earth from the top of the highest mountain on the Island, called Pico Adam; where there is an impression like a foot, which they say is his, as hath been mentioned before.

The sun and moon they repute deities.

The sun and moon they seem to have an opinion to be gods, from the names they sometimes call them by. The sun, in their language, is irri, and the moon, handa: to which they will sometimes add the title haumi, which is a name they give to persons of the greatest honour; and Dio, that signifies God: saying, Irrihaumi, irridio: handahaumi, handa Dio. But to the stars they give not these titles.

Some of their temples of exquisite work

The pagodas, or temples of their gods, are so many, that I cannot number them. Many of them are of rare and exquisite work, built of hewn stone, engraven with images and figures; but by whom, and when, I could not attain to know, the inhabitants themselves being ignorant therein: but, sure I am, they were built by far more ingenious artificers than the Chingulays that now are on the land; for the Portuguese, in their invasions, have defaced some of them, which there is none found that hath skill enough to repair to this day.

The form of their temples.

The fashion of these pagodas are different: some, to wit those that were anciently built, are of better workmanship, as was said before; but those lately erected are far inferior, made only with clay and sticks, and no windows. Some, viz. those belonging to the Buddou, are in the form of a pigeon-house, four square, one story high, and some two; the room above has its idols, as well as that below: some of them are tiled, and some thatched.

In them are idols and images, most monstrous to behold, some of silver, some of brass, and other metals: and also painted sticks, and targets, and most strange kinds of arms, as bills, arrows, spears, and swords. But these arms are not in the Buddou's temples, he being for peace: therefore there are in his temples only images of men, cross-legged, with yellow coats on, like the gonni priests; their hair frizled, and their hands before them, like women: and these, they say, are the spirits of holy men departed. Their temples are adorned with such things as the people's ability and poverty can afford; accounting it the highest point of devotion, bountifully to dedicate such things unto their gods, which in their estimation are most precious.

The shape of their idols.

As for these images, they say they do not own them to be gods themselves, but only figures, representing their gods to their memories; and, as such, they give to them honour and worship.

They worship not the idol, but whom it represents.

Women, having their natural infirmities upon them, may not, neither dare they presume, to come near the temples or houses of their gods: nor the men, if they come out of houses where such women are.

The revenues of the temples, and the honours thereof.

They are dedicated to gods.

Unto each of these pagodas there are great revenues of land belonging, which have been allotted to them by former kings, according to the state of the kingdom: but they have much impaired the revenues of the crown; there being rather more towns belonging to the church than unto the king. These estates of the temples are to supply a daily charge they are at; which is to prepare victuals, or sacrifices, to set before the idols. They have elephants also, as the king has, which serve them for state. Their temples have all sorts of officers belonging to them, as the palace hath.

Most of these pagodas are dedicated to the name and honour of those whom they call dio, or gods: to whom, they say, belong the government on earth, and all things appertaining to this life.

Private chapels.

Besides these public temples, many people do build in their yards private chapels, which are little houses, like to closets; sometimes so small, that they are not above two feet in bigness, but built upon a pillar, three or four feet from the ground, wherein they do place a certain image of the Buddou, that they may have him near them, and to testify their love and service to him: which they do by lighting up candles and lamps in his house, and laying flowers every morning before him; and at sometime they boil victuals, and lay it before him: and, the more they perform such ceremonious service to him here, the more shall be their reward hereafter.

All blessings and good success, they say, come from the hand of God; but sickness and diseases proceed from the devil: not that of himself he hath such absolute power, but as servants

Smith. sc. 63 H. Holborn

A Tirinanxy or Chief Priest

Published May 10th 1816 by J. Mawman

have power, license, and authority from their masters, so they from God.

But the gods will require some to wait at their altars, and the temples men to officiate in them; their priests therefore fall under the next consideration. Of these there are three sorts, according to the three differences of gods among them. And their temples are also called by three different names. The priests.

The first, and highest order of priests, are the tirinanxes, who are the priests of the Buddou god. Their temples are styled vihars. There is a religious house in the city of Digligy, where they dwell, and assemble and consult together about their affairs; which being the meeting place of such holy men, they call it a vihar: also they admit none to come into their order but persons of the most noble birth, and that have learning, and be well bred: of such they admit many. But they do not presently, upon their admission, arrive unto the high degree of a tirinanx; for of these there are but three or four, and they are chose out of all the rest of the order unto this degree. These tirinanxes only live in the vihar, and enjoy great revenues; and are, as it were, the superiors of all the priests, and are made by the king. The first order of them.

Many of the vihars are endowed, and have farms belonging to them; and these tirinanxes are the landlords, unto whom the tenants come at a certain time, and pay in their rents. These farmers live the easiest of any people in the land, for they have nothing to do but at those set times to bring in their dues, and so depart, and to keep in repair certain little vihars in the country. So that the rest of the Chingulays envy them, and say of them, "Though they live easy in this world, they cannot escape unpunished in the life to come, for enjoying the Buddou's land, and doing him so little service for it."

The habit of these priests

All the rest of the order are called gonni. The habit is the same to the whole order, both tirinanxes and gonni. It is a yellow coat, gathered together about their waist, and comes over the left shoulder, girt about with a belt of fine packthread: their heads are shaved, and they go bare-headed, and carry in their hands a round fan, with a wooden handle, which is to keep the sun off their hands.

Their privileges.

They have great benefit and honour: they enjoy their own lands without paying scot or lot, or any taxes to the king. They are honoured in such a measure, that the people, wherever they go, bow down to them as they do to their gods, but themselves bow to none. They have the honour of carrying the tallipot with the broad end over their heads foremost, which none but the king does: wheresoever they come, they have a mat and a white cloth laid over upon a stool for them to sit upon, which is also an honour used only to the king.

What they are prohibited.

They are debarred from laying their hands to any manner of work; and may not marry nor touch women, nor eat but one meal a day, unless it be fruit and rice and water, that they may eat morning and evening; nor must they drink wine. They will eat any lawful flesh that is dressed for them, but they will have no hand in the death of it; as to give order or consent to the killing of it.

They may lay down their order, if they please, which some

do, that they may marry. This is done by pulling off their coat, and flinging it into a river, and washing themselves, head and body, and then they become like other laymen.

When any is religiously disposed, these priests sent for in great ceremony.

There is a benefit that accrueth to them; which is, when any man is minded to provide for his soul, they bring one of these priests under a cloth, held up by four men, unto his house, with drums and pipes, and great solemnity, which only can be done unto the king besides. Then they give him great entertainment, and bestow gifts on him according as they are able; which, after he hath tarried a day or more, they carry for him, and conduct him home with the like solemnities as he came: but the night that he tarries with them he must sing bonna, that is, matter concerning their religion, out of a book made of the leaves of tallipot; and then he tells them the meaning of what he sings, it being in an eloquent style, which the vulgar people do not understand.

None ever used violence toward them before the present king.

Some of these priests, against whom the king took displeasure, were beheaded, afterwards cast into the river; which thing caused amazement in all the people, how the king durst presume to do it towards such holy and reverend persons.

And none heretofore, by any former kings, have ever been so served; being reputed and called sons of Buddou. But the reason the king slew them was because they conspired in the rebellion: they threw aside their habits, and got their swords by their sides.

The second order of their priests

The second order of priests are those called koppuhs, who are the priests that belong to the temples of the other gods:

their temples are called dewals. These are not distinguished by any habit from the rest of the people; no, nor when they are at their worship; only they wear clean clothes, and wash themselves before they go to their service. These are taken out from among the hondrews: they enjoy a piece of land that belongs to the dewal where they officiate, and that is all their benefit, unless they steal somewhat that is dedicated to the gods. They follow their husbandry and employments as other men do; but only when the times of worship are, which usually is every morning and evening, oftener or seldomer, according as the revenue will hold out that belongs to that temple, whereof each is priest. The service is, that when the boiled rice and other victuals are brought to the temple door by others, he takes it, and presents it before the idol: whence, after it hath stood awhile, he brings it out again, and then the drummers, pipers, and other servants that belong to the temple, eat it. These gods have never any flesh brought in sacrifice to them, but any thing else.

The third order.

The third order of priests are the jaddeses, priests of the spirits, which they call dayautaus. Their temples are called covels, which are inferior to the other temples, and have no revenues belonging to them. A man, piously disposed, builds a small house at his own charge, which is the temple, and himself becomes priest thereof. Therein are bills, and swords, and arrows, and shields, and images, painted upon the walls like fierce men. This house is seldom called God's house, but most usually jacco, the devils. Upon some extraordinary festival to the jacco, the jaddese shaves off all his beard.

When they are sick, they dedicate a red cock to the devil;

which they do after this manner. They send for the jaddese to their house, and give him a red cock chicken, which he takes up in his hand, and holds an arrow with it, and dedicates it to the god, by telling him, that if he restore the party to his health, that cock is given to him, and shall be dressed and sacrificed to him in his covel. They then let the cock go among the rest of the poultry, and keep it afterwards, it may be, a year or two; and then they carry it to the temple, or the priest comes for it: for sometimes he will go round about, and fetch a great many cocks together that have been dedicated, telling the owners that he must make a sacrifice to the god; though, it may be, when he hath them, he will go to some other place and convert them into money for his own use, as I myself can witness; we could buy three of them for four-pence halfpenny.

How they dedicate a red cock to the devil.

When the people are minded to inquire any thing of their gods, the priests take up some of the arms and instruments of the gods, that are in the temples upon his shoulder; and then he either feigns himself to be mad, or really is so, which the people call pissowetitch; and then the spirit of the gods is in him, and whatsoever he pronounceth is looked upon as spoken by God himself, and the people will speak to him as if it were the very person of God.

CHAP. IV.

Concerning their Worship and Festivals.

The chief days of worship.

WEDNESDAYS and Saturdays are the days, when people, who have any business with the gods, come and address themselves: that is, either to pray to their god for health, or for their help in some weighty matters, as in war, &c. or to swear concerning any matter in controversy, which is done before the idols.

How they know what god or devil hath made them sick.

But one of their great and frequent businesses with their gods is for the recovery of health. And that god or devil that hath made them sick, in his power only it is to restore them: therefore, when they feel themselves sick or sore—first, they use means to know which god or devil hath been the cause or author thereof; which to find they use these means: with any little stick they make a bow, and on the string thereof they hang a thing they have to cut betel-nuts, somewhat like a pair of scissors; then, holding the stick or bow by both ends, they repeat the names of all, both gods and devils; and, when they come to him who hath afflicted them then the iron on the bow-string will swing: they say by that sign they know their illness proceeds from the power of that god last-named, but I think this happens by the power of the hands that hold it. The god being thus found, to him chiefly they offer their oblations and sacrifices.

The gods of their fortunes.

There are nine deities, which they call gerehah, which are the planets (reckoning in probably the dragon's head and tail); from whom proceed their fortunes: these they reckon so powerful, that if they be ill affected towards any party, neither God nor devil can revoke it.

What worship they give the planets.

When they are disposed to worship these gerehah, they make images of clay, according to the number that stand disaffected towards them, which by certain magic tricks they know: these images, which are made by the weavers, they paint of divers colours, of horrible and monstrous shapes; some with long tusks like a boar, some with horns like a bull—all in a most deformed manner, but something resembling the shape of a man: before them they prostrate victuals, the sick party sitting all the while before them: these ceremonies are always celebrated in the night, with drums, and pipes, and dancing, until almost day; and then they take these images, and cast them out into the high ways to be trampled under foot; and the victuals is taken away, and eaten by the attendants and despicable people that wait there on purpose.

What worship they give devils.

When they worship those whom they call devils, many of whom they hold to be the spirits of some that died heretofore, they make no images for them, as they did for the planets; but only build a new house in their yard, like a barn, very slight, covered only with leaves, and adorn it with branches and flowers: into this house they bring some of the weapons or instruments, which are in the pagods or temples, and place them on stools at one end of the house, which is hanged with cloth for that purpose, and before them on other stools they lay victuals: and all that time of the sacrifice there is drumming,

Who eat the sacrifices.

piping, singing, and dancing; which, being ended, they take the victuals away, and give it to those which drum and pipe, with other beggars and vagabonds—for only such do eat of their sacrifices: not that they do account such things hallowed, and so dare not presume to eat them, but contrariwise they are now looked upon as polluted meat; and, if they should attempt to eat thereof, it would be a reproach to them and their generations.

Their gods are local.

These spirits or gods are local: for those which they worship in one country, or part of the land, are not known or owned to have power over the people in other parts; but each country hath several spirits or devils, that are peculiar to those places, and do domineer over them, and are known by several names they call them by; under whose subjection the people do acknowledge themselves to be; and, as I well perceive, do stand in a greater awe of them, than they do of them whom they call and own to be their gods.

The subjection of this people to the devil.

And indeed it is sad to consider, how this poor people are subjected to the devil, and they themselves acknowledge it their misery, saying their country is so full of devils, and evil spirits, that unless in this manner they should adore them, they would be destroyed by them: Christians they do acknowledge have a prerogative above themselves, and not to be under the power of these infernal spirits.

Sometimes the devil possesses them.

I have many times seen men and women of this people strangely possessed, insomuch that I could judge it nothing else but the effect of the devil's power upon them; and they themselves do acknowledge as much: in the like condition to which

I never saw any that did profess to be a worshipper of the holy name of JESUS. They that are thus possessed, some of them will run mad into the woods, screeching and roaring, but do mischief to none: some will be taken so as to be speechless, shaking, and quaking, and dancing, and will tread upon the fire, and not be hurt; they will also talk idle, like distracted folk.

This may last sometimes two or three months, sometimes two or three days: now, their friends reckoning it to proceed from the devil, do go to him, and promise him a reward if he will cure them: sometimes they are cured, and sometimes die. The people do impute this madness to some breach of promise that the party affected had made to the devil, or else for eating some fruit or betel leaves dedicated to him: for they do dedicate some fruit trees to the devil; and this they do, to prevent people from stealing them, (which few will dare to do after such a dedication) and also to excuse themselves in not bestowing their fruit upon any that might ask or desire it: but, before this dedicated fruit is lawful for them to use, they must carry some of it to the temple.

This for certain I can affirm, that oftentimes the devil doth cry with audible voice in the night; 'tis very shrill, almost like the barking of a dog: this I have often heard myself, but never heard that he did any body any harm. Only this observation the inhabitants of the land have made of this voice, and I have made it also, that either just before, or very suddenly after this voice, always the king cuts off people. To believe that this is the voice of the devil, these reasons urge—because there is no creature known to the inhabitants that cry like it, and because it

The devil's voice often heard.

will on a sudden depart from one place, and make a noise in another, quicker than any fowl could fly; and because the very dogs will tremble and shake when they hear it; and 'tis so accounted by all the people.

This voice is heard only in Candy Uda, and never in the low lands. When the voice is near to a Chingulay's house, he will curse the devil, calling him geremoi goulammah, "beef-eating slave be gone, be damned, cut his nose off, beat him in pieces;" and such like words of raillery, and this they will speak aloud, with noise, and passion, and threatening: this language I have heard them bestow upon the voice; and the voice, upon this, always ceaseth for a while, and seems to depart, being heard at a greater distance.

Their sacrifice to the chief devil.

When smaller devils do fail them, they repair unto the great one; which they do after this manner:—they prepare an offering of victuals ready dressed, one dish whereof is always a red cock; which they do as frequently offer to the devil, as papists do wax candles to saints. This offering they carry out into a remote place in the woods, and prostrate it to the honour and service of the grand devil, before which there are men in horrible disguise, like devils, with bells about their legs, and doublets of a strange fashion, dancing and singing, to call, if it were possible, the devil himself to come and eat of the sacrifices they have brought: the sick party is all the while present.

Their festivals.

I have hitherto spoken of their ordinary and daily worship, and their private and occasional devotions; besides these, they have their solemn and annual festivals: now, of these there are two sorts, some belonging to their gods that govern the earth, and all things referring to this life; and some belonging to the Buddou, whose province is to take care of the soul and future well-being of men.

Festivals to the honour of the gods that govern this world. The great festival in June.

I shall first mention the festivals of the former sort; they are two or three. That they may, therefore, honour these gods, and procure their aid and assistance, they do yearly, in the month of June or July, at a new moon, observe a solemn feast and general meeting, called perahar; but none are compelled—and some go to one pagoda, and some to another. The greatest solemnity is performed in the city of Candy; but, at the same time, the like festival or perahar is observed in divers other cities and towns of the land. The perahar at Candy is ordered after this manner:—

The priest bringeth forth a painted stick, about which strings of flowers are hung, and so it is wrapped in branched silk, some part covered, and some not; before which the people bow down and worship, each one presenting him with an offering, according to his free will. These free-will offerings being received from the people, the priest takes his painted stick on his shoulder, having a cloth tied about his mouth, to keep his breath from defiling this pure piece of wood, and gets up upon an elephant all covered with white cloth, upon which he rides with all the triumph that king and kingdom can afford, through all the streets of the city; but, before him go, first some forty or fifty elephants, with brass bells hanging on each side of them, which tingle as they go.

Next, follow men dressed up like giants, which go dancing

along agreeable to a tradition they have, that anciently they were huge men, that could carry vast burthens, and pull up trees by the roots, &c. after them go a great multitude of drummers, trumpeters, and pipers, which make such a great and loud noise, that nothing else besides them can be heard: then followeth a company of men dancing along, and, after these, women of such casts or trades as are necessary for the service of the pagoda, as potters and washer-women, each cast goeth in companies by themselves, three and three in a row, holding one another by the hand; and between each company go drummers, pipers, and dancers.

After these comes an elephant, with two priests on his back; one whereof is the priest before spoken of, carrying the painted stick on his shoulder, who represents allout neur dio; that is, the god and maker of heaven and earth. The other sits behind him, holding a round thing, like an umbrella, over his head, to keep off sun or rain; then, within a yard after him, on each hand of him, follow two other elephants, mounted with two other priests, with a priest sitting behind, each holding umbrellas as the former; one of them represents cotteragom dio, and the other, potting dio. These three gods that ride here in company, are accounted of all other the greatest and chiefest, each one having his residence in a several pagoda.

Behind go their cook women, with things like whisks in their hands, to scare away flies from them; but very fine, as they can make themselves.

Next, after the gods and their attendants, go some thousands of ladies and gentlewomen, such as are of the best sort of the inhabitants of the land, arrayed in the bravest manner that their ability can afford, and so go hand in hand, three in a row; at which time, all the beauties on Zelone, in their bravery, do go to attend upon their gods, in their progress about the city. Now are the streets also all made clean, and on both sides, all along the streets, poles stuck up, with flags and pennons hanging at the tops of them, and adorned with boughs and branches of cocoa-nut trees, hanging like fringes, and lighted lamps all along on both sides of the street both by day and night.

Last of all go the commanders, sent from the king to see these ceremonies decently performed, with their soldiers after them; and in this manner they ride all round about the city, once by day, and once by night. This festival lasts from the new moon until the full moon.

Formerly, the king himself in person used to ride on horseback, with all his train before him in this solemnity, but now he delights not in these shows.

Always before the gods set out to take their progress, they are set in the pagoda door a good while, that the people may come to worship and bring their offerings unto them; during which time there are dancers, playing and shewing many pretty tricks of activity before him; to see the which, and also to shew themselves in their bravery, occasions more people to resort hither, than otherwise their zeal and devotion would prompt them to do.

Two or three days before the full moon, each of these gods

hath a palanquin carried after them to add unto their honour: in the which there are several pieces of their superstitious relics, and a silver pot; which, just at the hour of full moon, they ride out into a river and dip full of water, which is carried back with them into the temple, where it is kept till the year after, and then flung away; and so the ceremony is ended for that year.

This festival of the gods taking their progress through the city, in the year 1664, the king would not permit to be performed; and that same year the rebellion happened, but never since hath he hindered it.

At this time they have a superstition, which lasteth six or seven days, too foolish to write: it consists in dancing, singing, and juggling; the reason of which is, lest the eyes of the people, or the power of the jaccos, or infernal spirits, might any ways prove prejudicial or noisome to the aforesaid gods in their progress abroad. During the celebration of this great festival, there are no drums allowed to be beaten to any particular gods at any private sacrifice.

The feast in November.

In the month of November, the night when the moon is at the full, there is another great solemn feast, called, in their language, cawtha poujah; which is celebrated only by lighting of lamps round about the pagoda, at which time they stick up the longest poles they can get in the woods, at the doors of the pagods, and of the king's palace, upon which they make contrivances to set lamps in rows one above the other, even unto the very tops of the poles, which they call tornes. To maintain the charge hereof, all the country in general do contribute, and bring in oil. In this poujah, or sacrifice, the king seems to take delight; the reason of which may be, because he participates far more of the honour than the gods do, in whose name it is celebrated: his palace being far more decked and adorned with high poles and lights, than the temples are. This ceremony lasteth but for one night.

The festival in honour of the god of the soul.

And these are their anniversary feasts to the honour of those gods, whose power extends to help them in this life: now follows the manner of their service to the Buddou—who it is, they say, that must save their souls—and the festival in honour of him.

To represent the memorial of him to their eye, they do make small images of silver, brass, and clay, and stone, which they do honour with sacrifices and worship, shewing all the signs of outward reverence which possibly they can. In most places where there are hollow rocks and caves, they do set up images in memorial of this god; unto which they that are devoutly bent, at new and full moons do carry victuals, and worship.

His great festival is in the month of March, at their new year's tide. The places where he is commemorated are two, not temples—but the one a mountain, and the other a tree; either to the one or the other, they at this time go with wives and children, for dignity and merit—one being esteemed equal with the other.

The mountain is at the south end of the country, called Hammalella; but, by Christian people, Adam's Peak, the highest in the whole Island; where, as has been said before, is the print of the Buddou's foot, which he left on the top of that mountain in a rock, from whence he ascended to heaven; unto this footstep they give worship, light up lamps, and offer sacrifices, laying them upon it, as upon an altar. The benefit of the sacrifices that are offered here do belong unto the Moors pilgrims, who come over from the other coast to beg, this having been given them heretofore by a former king; so that, at that season, there are great numbers of them always waiting there to receive their accustomed fees.

The tree is at the north end of the king's dominions at Annarodgburro; this tree, they say, came flying over from the other coast, and there planted itself, as it now stands; under which the Buddou-god, at his being on earth, used, as they say, often to sit. This is now become a place of solemn worship; the due performance whereof they reckon not to be a little meritorious; insomuch that, as they report, ninety kings have since reigned there successively; where, by the ruins that still remain, it appears they sparedot for pains and labour to build temples and high monuments to the honour of this god, as if they had been born only to hew cks and great stones, and lay them up in heaps. These kings are now happy spirits, having merited it by these their labours.

Those, whose ability or necessity serve them not to go to these places, may go to some private vihars nearer.

The high honour they have for this god.

For this god, above all other, they seem to have a high respect and devotion, as will appear by this that follows: ladies and gentlewomen of good quality, will sometimes, in a fit of devotion to the Buddou, go a begging for him. The greatest ladies of all do not indeed go themselves, but send their maids dressed up finely in their stead. These women, taking the image along with them, carry it upon the palm of their hand, covered with a piece of white cloth, and so go to men's houses, and will say, "We come a begging of your charity for the Buddou towards his sacrifice;" and the people are very liberal: they give only of three things to him—either oil for his lamps, or rice for his sacrifice, or money or cotton yarn for his use.

Poor men will often go about begging sustenance for themselves by this means; they will get a book of religion, or a Buddou's image in a case, wrapping both in a white cloth, which they carry with great reverence, and then they beg in the name of the book or the god; and the people bow down to them, and give their charity, either corn, or money, or cotton yarn. Sometimes they will tell the beggar, "What have I to give?" And he will reply, as the saying is, "As much as you can take up between your two fingers is charity." After he has received a gift from any, he pronounceth a great deal of blessing upon him: "Let the blessing of the gods and the Buddou go along with you; let your corn ripen, let your cattle increase, let your life be long," &c.

Some, being devoutly disposed, will make the image of this god at their own charge: for the making whereof they must bountifully reward the founder. Before the eyes are made, it is not accounted a god, but a lump of ordinary metal, and thrown about the shop with no more regard than any thing else: but when the eyes are to be made, the artificer is to have a good gratification, besides the first agreed upon reward.

The eyes being formed, it is thenceforward a god; and then, being brought with honour from the workman's shop, it is dedicated by solemnities and sacrifices, and carried with great state into its shrine or little house, which is before built and prepared for it.

Sometimes a man will order the smith to make this idol; and then, after it is made, will go about with it to a well-disposed people, to contribute toward the wages the smith is to have for making it; and men will freely give towards the charge: and this is looked upon, in the man that appointed the image to be made, as a notable piece of devotion.

I have mentioned the bogahah tree before, which, in memory of this god, they hold sacred, and perform sacrifices, and celebrate religious meetings under;—under this tree, at some convenient distance, about ten or twelve feet at the outmost edge of the platform, they usually build booths or tents; some are made slight only with leaves for the present use, but some are built substantial, with hewn timber and clay walls, which stand many years. These buildings are divided into small tenements for each particular family. The whole town joins, and each man builds his own apartment; so that the building goes quite round like a circle, only one gap is left, which is to pass through to the bogahah tree; and this gap is built over with a kind of portal. The use of these buildings is for the entertainment of the women, who take great delight to come and see these ceremonies, clad in their best and richest apparel. They employ themselves in seeing the dancers, and the jugglers do their tricks, who afterwards by their importunity will get money of them, or a ring off their fingers, or some such matters. Here also they spend their time in eating betel, and in talking with their consorts, and shewing their fine clothes. These solemnities are always in the night, the booths all set round with lamps; nor are they ended in one night, but last three or four, until the full moon, which always puts a period to them.

CHAP. V.

Concerning their Religious Doctrines, Opinions, and Practices.

As to their religion, they are very indifferent.

THERE are few or none zealous in their worship, or have any great matter of esteem for their gods; and they seldom busy themselves in the matters of their religion, until they come to be sick, or very aged. They debar none that will come to see the ceremonies of their worship; and, if a stranger should dislike their way, reprove, or mock at them, for their ignorance and folly, they would acknowledge the same, and laugh at the superstitions of their own devotion; but withal tell you, that they are constrained to do what they do, to keep themselves from the malice and mischiefs that the evil spirits would otherwise do them; with which, they say, their country swarms.

If their gods answer not their desires, they curse them.

Sometimes in their sickness they go to the house of their gods with an offering, with which they present him, intreating his favour and aid to restore them to health. Upon the recovery whereof they promise him not to fail, but to give unto his majesty (for so they entitle him) far greater gifts or rewards, and what they are they do particularly mention; it may be land, a slave, cattle, money, cloth, &c. and so they will discourse, argue, and expostulate with him, as if he were there present in person before them. If, after this, he fails on his part, and cannot restore them to their health, then the fore-promised things are to remain where they were; and, instead of which, perhaps he gets a curse, saying—He doth but cheat and deceive them.

It is an usual saying, and very frequent among them (if their gerahah, which is their fortune, be bad) "What can god do against it." Nay, I have often heard them say, "Give him no sacrifice, but shit in his mouth; what a god is he?" So slight an estimation have they of their idol-gods; and the king far less esteems them: for he doth not in the least give any countenance either to the worshipper, or to the manner of worship. And, God's name be magnified, that hath not suffered him to disturb or molest the Christians in the least in their religion, or ever attempt to force them to comply with the country's idolatry; but, on the contrary, both king and people do generally like the Christian religion better than their own, and respect and honour the Christians, as Christians, and do believe there is a greater God than any they adore: and, in all probability, they would be very easily drawn to the Christian, or any other religion, as will appear by this story following:

They undervalue and revile their gods.

There was lately one among them that pretended himself a prophet, sent to them from a new god, that as yet was nameless; at which the people were amused, especially because he pretended to heal the sick, and do miracles: and presently he was had in high veneration. He gave out it was the command of the new nameless god to spoil and pull down the dewals; that is, the temples of the former gods. This he made a good progress in, with no let or impediment, from king or people. The king all this while inclined neither to one or other, as not regarding such matters, until he might see which of these gods would prevail—the old or the new: for this

A fellow gives out himself for a prophet.

people stand in fear of all that are called gods; and this especially surprised them, because without a name; so contrary to all their old ones, who have names. This new-found god therefore went on boldly and successfully, without control: the people all in general began to admire him thus come among them; and great troops of people daily assembled thither with sacrifices, and to worship him. Whereby, seeing their inclination so strong towards him, he began to perceive it was not only possible, but also easy and probable, to change his priesthood for a kingdom.

His success.

The king sends for one of his priests.

At which time, whether the king began to suspect or not, I cannot say, but he sent for one of his priests to be brought up to the court: for this god had his residence in the country, at Vealbow, in Hotcourly, somewhat remote from the king. This priest having remained at the city some days, the king took a ring from off his finger, and put it in an ivory box, and sent it by three of his great men to him, bidding him to inquire of his nameless god what it was that was therein; which amazed this priest: but he returned this subtle answer—that he was not sent to divine, but to heal the diseases and help the infirmities of the people. Upon which the king gave command to take him and put him in the stocks, under a tree, there to be wet with the rain, and dry again with the sun: which was executed upon him accordingly.

Flies to Columba, pretends himself to be a former king's son.

The chief priest, who was the first inventor of this new god, hearing what the king had done, and fearing what might follow, suddenly dispatched, and carried all, what he had plundered out of the pagods, with him to Columba, and stole one of the king's elephants to carry it upon: where, being arrived, he declares himself to be the son of the King of Mautoly, who was elder brother to this king that now is; and for fear of whom he fled to Columba; being at that time when the Portugals had it, who sent him to Goa, where he died.

This being noised abroad, that he was a prince, made the people flock faster to him than before; which changed both his heart and behaviour from a priest to a king. Insomuch that the Dutch began to be in doubt what this might grow to: who, to prevent the worst, set a watch over him; which he not liking of, took the advantage of the night, and fled with all his followers and attendants up to the king again, and came to the same place where he lay before. Flies from the Dutch.

No sooner had the king notice of his arrival, but immediately he dispatched five of his greatest commanders, with their soldiers, to catch him, and to bring him up to him; which they did, laying both him and all his followers in chains. The king commanded to keep him in a certain pagoda of the Chingulays, until the matter were examined: the people in general much lamenting him, though not able to help. The chief of their churchmen, viz. their gonni-nancies, were all commanded to make their personal appearance at court: which all thought was to see the prince, or priest, should have a legal trial. But, in the mean time, the king commanded to cut him in four quarters, and hang them in places which he appointed—which was done. The king catches and quarters him.

Nevertheless the vulgar people, to this day, do honour and adore the name and memorial of the nameless god; with which, if he could have been content, and not have gone about to usurp The people's opinion still of this new god.

the crown—the king so little regarding religion—he might have lived to die a natural death.

Their doctrines and opinions.

These people do firmly believe a resurrection of the body, and the immortality of souls, and a future state; upon which account they will worship their ancestors. They do believe, that those they call gods are the spirits of men that formerly have lived upon the earth. They hold, that in the other world, those that are good men, though they be poor and mean in this world, yet there they shall become high and eminent; and that wicked men shall be turned into beasts. There is a spider among them that breeds an egg, which she carries under her belly; it is as wide as a groat, and bigger than the body of the spider: this egg is full of young spiders, that breed there—it hangs under her belly wheresoever she goes; and, as their young ones grow to bigness, they eat up the old one. Now, the Chingulays say, that disobedient children shall become spiders in the other world, and their young ones shall eat them up.

They hold that every man's good or bad fortune was predetermined by God, before he was born, according to an usual proverb they have, ollua cottaula tiana—it is written in the head.

The highest points of devotion.

They reckon the chief points of goodness to consist in giving to the priests, in making pudgiahs, sacrifices to their gods, in forbearing shedding the blood of any creature; which to do they call pau boi, a great sin; and in abstaining from eating any flesh at all, because they would not have any hand, or any thing to do, in killing any living thing. They reckon herbs and plants more innocent food. It is religion also to sweep under the bogahah, or god-tree, and keep it clean. It is accounted religion to be just and sober, and chaste and true, and to be endowed with other virtues, as we do account it.

Their charity.

They give to the poor out of a principle of charity, which they extend to foreigners, as well as to their own countrymen: but of every measure of rice they boil in their houses for their families, they will take out a handful, as much as they can gripe, and put into a bag, and keep it by itself, which they call mittahaul; and this they give and distribute to such poor as they please, or as come to their doors.

The privilege of the Moorish beggars.

Nor are they charitable only to the poor of their own nation; but, as I said, to others, and particularly to the Moorish beggars, who are Mahometans by religion: these have a temple in Candy. A certain former king gave this temple this privilege—that every freeholder should contribute a ponnam to it; and these Moors go to every house in the land to receive it: and, if the house be shut, they have power to break it open, and to take of goods to the value of it. They come very confidently when they beg, and they say they come to fulfil the people's charity; and the people do liberally relieve them for charity's sake.

There is only one country in the land, viz. Dolusbaug, that pays not the aforesaid duty to the Moor's temple: and the reason is, that, when they came first to demand, the inhabitants beat them away: for which act they are free from the payment of that ponam; and have also another privilege granted them for the same, that they pay no marral, or harriots, to the king, as other countries do.

These Moors pilgrims have many pieces of land given to them, by well-disposed persons, out of charity, where they build houses and live; and this land becomes theirs from generation to generation, for ever.

They respect Christians; and why?

They lay flowers, out of religion, before their images, every morning and evening; for which images they build little chapels in their yards, as we said before. They carry beads in their hands, on strings, and say so many prayers as they go: which custom, in all probability, they borrowed of the Portuguese. They love a man that makes conscience of his ways: which makes them respect Christians more than any others—because they think they are just, and will not lie. And thus we have finished our discourse of their religion.

CHAP. VI.

Concerning their Houses, Diet, Housewifery, Salutation, Apparel.

HAVING already treated of their religion, we now come to their secular concerns; and first, we will lead you into their houses, and shew you how they live.

Their houses are small, low, thatched cottages, built with sticks daubed with clay, the walls made very smooth; for they are not permitted to build their houses above one story high, neither may they cover with tiles, nor whiten their walls with lime; but there is a clay which is as white, and that they use sometimes. They employ no carpenters or house builders, unless some few noblemen, but each one buildeth his own dwelling; in building whereof there is not so much as a nail used; but, instead of them, every thing which might be nailed is tied with rattans and other strings, which grow in the woods in abundance—whence the builder hath his timber for cutting. The country being warm, many of them will not take pains to clay their walls, but make them of boughs and leaves of trees. The poorest sort have not above one room in their houses, few above two, unless they be great men; neither doth the king allow them to build better. Their houses

They are not nice nor curious in their houses: they have no

No chimneys. chimneys in them, but make their fires in one corner—so that the roof is all blacked with the smoke.

The houses of the better sort. The great people have handsome and commodious houses. They have commonly two buildings, one opposite to the other, joined together on each side with a wall, which makes a square court-yard in the middle: round about against the walls of their houses are banks of clay to sit on, which they often daub over with soft cow-dung to keep them smooth and clean. Their slaves and servants dwell round about without, in other houses, with their wives and children.

Their furniture. Their furniture is but small: a few earthen pots which hang up in slings, made of canes, in the middle of their houses, having no shelves; one or two brass basons to eat in, a stool or two without backs—for none but the king may sit upon a stool with a back: there are also some baskets to put corn in, some mats to spread upon the ground to sleep on, which is the bedding, both for themselves and friends when they come to their houses: also some ebony pestles about four feet long, to beat rice out of the husk, and a wooden mortar to beat it in afterwards to make it white, a hirimony or grater to grate their cocoa nuts with, a flat stone, upon which they grind their pepper and turmeric, &c. with another stone, which they hold in their hands at the same time. They have also in their houses axes, bills, houghs, atches, chissels, and other tools for their use. Tables they have none, but sit and eat on the ground.

How they eat. And now we are mentioning eating, let us take a view of this people at their meals: their diet and ordinary fare is but very mean, as to our account. If they have but rice and salt in their house they reckon they want for nothing; for, with a few green leaves, and the juice of a lemon with pepper and salt, they will make a hearty meal. Beef here may not be eaten, it is abominable. Flesh and fish is somewhat scarce: and that little of it they have, they had rather sell to get money to keep than eat it themselves; neither is there any but outlandish men that will buy any of them. It is they, indeed, do eat the fat and best of the land. Nor is it counted any shame or disgrace to be a niggard and sparing in diet, but rather a credit even to the greatest of them, that they can fare hard, and suffer hunger; which, they say, soldiers ought to be able to endure.

The great ones have always five or six sorts of food at one meal, and of them not above one or two, at most, of flesh or fish, and of them more pottage than meat, after the Portugal fashion; the rest is only what groweth out of the ground. The main substance with which they fill their bellies is rice; the other things are but to give it a relish.

How the great men eat.

If these people were not discouraged from rearing and nourishing of cattle and poultry, provisions might be far more plentiful; for here are many jackals which catch their hens, and some tigers that destroy their cattle: but the greatest of all is the king, whose endeavour is to keep them poor, and in want. For from them that have hens his officers take them for the king's use, giving little or nothing for them; the like they do by hogs. Goats, none are suffered to keep, besides the king, except strangers.

Discouraged from nourishing cattle.

In dressing of their victuals they are not to be discommended;

Cleanly in dressing their meat.

for, generally, they are very cleanly and very handy about the same: and, after one is used to that kind of fare, as they dress it, it is very savoury and good. They sit upon a mat on the ground, and eat: but he, whom they do honour and respect, sits on a stool, and his victuals on another before him.

Their drink, and manner of eating.

Their common drink is only water; and, if they drink rack, it is before they eat, that it may have the more operation upon their bodies: when they drink, they touch not the pot with their mouths, but hold it at a distance, and pour it in. They eat their rice out of china dishes, or brass basons, and they that have not them, on leaves. The carrees, or other sorts of food which they eat with their rice, is kept in the pans it is dressed in, and their wives serve them with it, when they call for it: for it is their duties to wait and serve their husbands while they eat; and, when they have done, do take and eat that which they have left upon their trenchers: during their eating, they neither use nor delight to talk to one another.

Their manner of washing before and after meals.

They always wash their hands and mouths both before and after they have eaten; but, for others to pour the water on their hands, is looked upon as an affront; for, so they do to them, whom they account not worthy to handle their water pot: but, when they wash, with one hand they pour it themselves upon the other. They are very cleanly both in their bodies and heads, which they do very often wash; and also, when they have been at stool, they make use of water.

None must speak while the rice is put into the pot.

But to give you a little of their cookery:—if people being in the room talking together, the woman, being ready to put the rice into the pot, bids them all be silent till she has put it in,

Smith. sc. 43 H.Holborn

Their manner of Eating & Drinking

London: Published May 10th 1816 – by J. Mawman

and then they may proceed with their discourse: for, if they should talk while the rice is putting in, it would not swell.

Sauce made of lemon juice.

At the time of the year that there is most plenty of lemons, they take them and squeeze the juice into an earthen pot, and set over the fire, and boil it so long, till it becomes thick and black like tar: this they set by for their use, and it will keep as long as they please. A very small quantity of it will suffice for sauce: they call it annego.

Their sweetmeats.

They have several sorts of sweetmeats; one they call caown: it is like to a fritter made of rice flour, and jaggory. They make them up in little lumps, and lay them upon a leaf, and then press them with their thumbs, and put them into a frying pan, and fry them in cocoa-nut oil or butter. When the Dutch first came to Columba, the king ordered these caown to be made and sent to them, as a royal treat; and, they say, the Dutch did so much admire them, that they asked if they grew not upon trees, supposing it past the art of man to make such dainties.

Oggulas, another sort of sweetmeats, made of parched rice, jaggory, pepper, cardamum, and a little cinnamons: they roll them up in balls, which will grow hard; these they tie up in bags, and carry them with them when they travel, to eat in afternoons when they are hungry.

Alloways, made much after the former manner, only they are flat, in the fashion of a lozenge; which are good for faintings and thirsty souls to relish their water, and to eat of in afternoons when they are at home. We carried some of these along with us in our travel.

A kind of puddings.

Yacpetties, made of rice flour, and the meat of the cocoa-nut and jaggory; they are made up into small lumps, and so put in a leaf, and laid on a cloth over a pot of boiling water, the stream of which heats that which is laid upon it, and so they are sodden like a pudding: they taste like white bread, almonds, and sugar.

Pitu, which is made thus:—they take flour of coracan, and sprinkle a little water into it, being both put into a large pot for the purpose; then they stir and roll it in the pot with their hands, by which means it crumbles into corns like gun-powder; then they have a pot of boiling water, with a cloth tied over it; and upon this cloth they lay so much of this corn flour as they can conveniently cover with another pot; and so the steam, coming through the cloth, boils it, that it will be much like unto a pudding; and this they use to eat, as they do rice.

The women's housewifery.

The women's housewifery is to beat the rice out of the husk, which they do with an ebony pestle, before mentioned; they lay the rice on the ground, and then beat it, one blow with one hand, and then tossing the pestle into the other, to strike with that; and, at the same time they keep stroke with their feet, (as if they were dancing) to keep up the corn together in one heap; this being done, they beat it again in a wooden mortar to whiten it, as was said before. This work, though it be very hard, belongeth only to the women: as also to fetch both wood and water; the wood they bring upon their heads, the water in an earthen pot, placing it upon their hip: to the women also belongs a small bill to cut herbs, pumpkins, &c. which she is to dress; which bill she lays upon the ground, the edge upwards, and sets herself upon a staff or handle to hold it fast; and, what she meaneth to cut, she lays upon the edge, and shoveth it on it.

When one comes to another's house, being set down, the entertainment is, green leaves, they call bullat, which they eat raw with lime and betel-nut, and tobacco; and, being set awhile, the man of the house will ask the stranger what he comes for, which, if he does not suddenly, the stranger will take exceptions at it, as thinking he is not welcome to him: neither do they ever go one to visit the other, unless it be for their own ends, either to beg or borrow.

How they entertain strangers.

And if kindred, that are very nearly related come together, they have no loving or private conference one with the other, but sit like strangers very solid and grave: and, if they stay above one night, which is the common custom, then they do help and assist the man of the house in any work or service he hath to do.

And kindred.

When any friends go to another's house to visit, they never go empty handed, but carry provisions and sweetmeats with them to their friend: and then he makes them a feast according to his ability; but they never eat of those things which themselves brought:—but there is but little feasting among them, unless at a wedding.

When they visit.

We have been long enough in the house, let us walk abroad, and shew you how the people demean themselves without doors.

When they meet one another, their manner of salutation or obeisance is, to hold forth their two hands, the palms upwards,

Their manner of salutations.

and bow their bodies; but the superior to the inferior holds forth but one hand; and, if the other be much beneath him, he only nods his head: the women salute by holding up both their hands edgeways to their foreheads: the general compliment one to another at first meeting, is to say—Ay; it signifies—How do you: and the other answers—Hundoi; that is, well.

The nobles in their best apparel.

The habit of the men when they appear abroad is after this sort:—the nobles wear doublets of white or blue calico, and about their middle a cloth; a white one next their skin, and a blue one or of some other colour, or painted, over the white: a blue or red sash girt about their loins, and a knife with a carved handle, wrought or inlaid with silver, sticking in their bosom; and a complete short hanger carved and inlaid with brass and silver by their sides—the scabbard most part covered with silver, bravely engraven; a painted cane, and sometimes a tuck in it in their hands, and a boy always bare-headed with long hair hanging down his back waiting upon him, ever holding a small bag in his hand, which is instead of a pocket, wherein is betel-leaves and nuts; which they constantly keep chewing in their mouth, with lime kept in a silver box rarely engraven, which commonly they hold in their hands, in shape like a silver watch.

The fashion of their hair.

The great ones also generally, and spruce young men, do wear their hair long, hanging down behind; but when they do any work, or travel hard, it annoying them, they tie it up behind: heretofore generally they bored holes in their ears, and hung weights in them, to make them grow long, like the Malabars, but this king not boring his, that fashion is almost left off: the men for ornament do wear brass, copper, silver rings on their

Smith, sc. 63 H. Holborn

A Nobleman

Publishd May 10th 1816 - by J. Mawman

Smith sc. 65 H. Holborn

A Gentlewoman

Published May 10th 1816—by J. Mawman

fingers, and, some of the greatest, gold; but none may wear any silk.

But the women in their apparel do far surpass the men, neither are they so curious in clothing themselves as in making their wives fine: the men's pride consists in their attendance, having men bearing arms before and behind them.

The women dressed in their bravery.

In their houses the women regard not much what dress they go in, but so put on their clothes as is most convenient for them to do their work; but when they go abroad, and make themselves fine, they wear a short frock with sleeves to cover their bodies, of fine white calico, wrought with blue and red thread in flowers and branches: on their arms silver bracelets, and their fingers and toes full of silver rings; about their necks, necklaces of beads or silver, curiously wrought and engraven, gilded with gold, hanging down so low as their breasts: in their ears hang ornaments made of silver set with stones, neatly engraven and gilded: their ears they bore when they are young, and roll up cocoa-nut leaves, and put into the holes to stretch them out; by which means they grow so wide, that they stand like round circles on each side of their faces, which they account a great ornament; but in my judgment a great deformity—they being well-featured women.

How they dress their heads.

Their other ornaments and apparel shew very comely on them—their hair they oil with cocoa-nut oil to make it smooth, and comb it all behind: their hair grows not longer than their waist; but, because it is a great ornament to have a great bunch of hair, they have a lock of other hair fastened in a plate of engraved silver and gilded, to tie up with their own in a knot, hanging down half their backs. Their hands are bare, but they carry a scarf of striped or branched silk, or such as they can get, casting it carelessly on their head and shoulders: about their waists they have one or two silver girdles made with wire and silver plate, handsomely engraven, hanging down on each side, one crossing the other behind; and as they walk they chew betel: but, notwithstanding all their bravery, neither man nor woman wears shoes or stockings; that being a royal dress, and only for the king himself.

They commonly borrow their fine clothes.

It is in general a common custom with all sorts of people to borrow apparel or jewels to wear when they go abroad; which, being so customary, is no shame nor disgrace to them, neither do they go about to conceal it; for, among their friends or strangers where they go, they will be talking, saying—"This I borrowed of such an one, and this of another body:" their poverty is so great, that their ability will not reach to buy such apparel as they do desire to wear; which nevertheless is but very mean and ordinary at the best.

CHAP. VII.

Of their Lodging, Bedding, Whoredom, Marriages, and Children.

HAVING been thus entertained with the fine ladies abroad, it is time now to return home to our lodging; and the night coming on, we will lead you to their bed-chambers, and shew you how they sleep—about which they are not very curious: if their house be but one room (as it often is) then the men sleep together at one end, and the women at the other.

Their bed, and how they sleep a-nights.

They have bedsteads laced with canes or rattans, but no testars to them, nor curtains—that the king allows not of: neither have they nor care they for more than one bedstead, which is only for the master of the house to sit, or sleep on: to this bedstead belongs two mats and a straw pillow; the women with the children always lie on the ground on mats by the fire-side: for a pillow she lays a block or such like thing under her mat—but the children have no pillows at all; and for covering and other bedding they use the cloth they wear by day: but always at their feet they will have a fire burning all night, which makes more work for the women, who must fetch it all upon her head; for it is accounted a disgrace for the man to meddle or make with those affairs that properly do belong unto the woman.

They rise in the night.

The younger sort of children, such as go naked by day, creep in under a corner of their mothers' clothes: and, if they feel themselves cold in the night, they rise and blow the fire with their mouths—having no bellows in that country—and so sit and warm themselves thereby.

They are so little given to sleep, that they do rise many times in the night to eat betel and to take tobacco; which done, they lay them down, and sing songs until they fall asleep again.

Children taught to sing at going to bed.

At their first going to bed, it is very seldom that they do pray to God, neither do they ever teach their children so to do; but sometimes will say, Auh Dio; which is, God help or keep me: but they do, instead of that, teach and bid their children to sing songs when they go to bed.

Young people lie at one another's houses.

Where their houses consist but of one room, the children that are of any years always go and sleep in other houses, among their neighbours; which please them better than their own: for so they come to meet with bedfellows; nor doth it displease the parents, if young men, of as good quality as themselves, become acquainted with their daughters, but rather like well of it; knowing that their daughters, by this means, can command the young men to help and assist them in any work or business that they may have occasion to use them in: and they look upon it so far distant from a disgrace, that they will, among their consorts, brag of it, that they have the young men thus at their command.

So that youth are bred up to whoredom: indeed, here are no

public whores allowed by authority. In the city, some that have followed that trade, have oftentimes, by the king's order, been severely punished, by whipping, and having their ears and hair cut off; but, in private, few or none can exempt themselves: and, for the matter of being with child, which many of them do not desire, they very exquisitely can prevent the same.

Nothing so common as whoredom.

Indeed, the public trade would be bad, and hardly maintain them that exercised it, the private one being so great; and though I think they be all whores, yet they abhor the name of vesou, which is whore: neither do they in their anger reproach one another with it, unless they should lay with a man of an inferior quality to themselves; and the woman reckons herself as much obliged to the man for his company, as he does to her for her's. In these affairs the women are very expert (it being their continual practice) to keep their design from the husband's knowledge; though, by his own experience, he cannot be ignorant of women's devices; and, unless he catch them in the act, he doth not much trouble himself to prove himself a cuckold—cuckolds being so common, that it is not here regarded.

They are guilty of the thing, but love not the name.

It is a law here, that if a man catch another in bed with his wife, he may, be it whosoever, kill him and her, if he please. It hath so happened, that the man hath come to the door when another hath been within with his wife; there being no way to escape, the woman has took a pan of hot ashes; and, as she opened the door, her husband being entering, cast them in his eyes, and so she and her bedfellow made an escape.

The man may kill whom he finds in bed with his wife.

To fetch wood out of the woods to burn, and to fetch home

The women's craft to compass and conceal their debauchery.

the cattle is the woman's work; if they cannot have their opportunities at home, now they appoint their meetings, while the husband stays at home holding the child. In the evenings it is common for them, with whom the women be acquainted, to come and wait behind the house, when it is dark, to attend their coming forth to them. To which end they give them notice, either by breaking of a stick, or by putting some betel over the wall, to fall in such places as they have appointed, where she will look to find it; and, when she has such notice, she cannot want an excuse to go forth to meet him.

They bear such love to their bedfellows, that I have known this done:—The husband hath beset the house, and the woman's friend in it, when she hath holpen him to make a hole through the thatch to get out at, which he hath done, and made his escape, and she remain behind to suffer all the blame herself. When other opportunities are wanting to enjoy the company of their paramours whole nights together, they usually take occasion to be discontented, and fall out with their husbands, and so go home to their friends houses to get longer enjoyments; who, to shew their friendship, will not hinder, but further them in what they delight in.

They do treat their friends with the use of their wives or daughters.

In some cases, the men will permit their wives and daughters to lie with other men: and that is, when intimate friends, or great men chance to lodge at their houses, they commonly will send their wives, or daughters, to bear them company in their chamber; neither do they reckon their wives to be whores for lying with them that are as good, or better than themselves.

They do not matter, or regard, whether their wives, at the first marriage, be maids or not; and, for a small reward, the mother will bring her daughter, being a maiden, unto those that do desire her: but it is so much abhorred for women of the high cast, or descent, to admit men of the low cast to have any thing to do with them, that I think they never do it.

The mother for a small reward, prostitutes her daughter.

But enough of this ribaldry; let us turn away to more honest practices; to speak of their marriages, which make the bed lawful: there are not many ceremonies used in or about the same. Here is no wooing for a wife—the parents commonly make the match; and, in their choice, regard more the quality and descent than the beauty: if they are agreed, all is done. The match being thus made, the man carrieth, or sends to the woman, her wedding clothes, which is a cloth containing six or seven yards in length, and a linen waistcoat wrought with blue and red. If the man be so poor that he cannot buy a cloth, it is the custom to borrow one: in case the man with his friends goes and carries it himself, that night they both sleep together, to beget acquaintance one with the other; and then they appoint a day, when he is to come and fetch her home, which is the marriage-day.

Marriages.

No wooing

The day being come, he, attended with his friends, goes to her house, which is always in the evening, and brings provisions and sweetmeats with him according to his ability, towards the charges of the wedding, which is never more than two meals, whereof supper is the first. Then the bride and bridegroom both eat together in one dish; which is to intimate, that they are both of one rank and quality—and sometimes they tie their thumbs together, but not always, and that night go to sleep together.

The bridegroom goes to the bride's house.

How the bridegroom carrieth home his bride.

The next day, having dined, he taketh his bride, and departeth home with her, putting her before him, and he following her, with some of her friends to conduct her; for it is the constant custom and fashion in this land for the husband to follow his wife: the reason whereof is a tradition among them, that a man once going foremost, it happened that his wife was stolen away, and he not aware of it. Being come home the bridegroom makes a feast as he is able.

A ceremony of marriage

Some few days after, her friends usually come to see her, bringing a present of provision with them; and sometimes they use this ceremony—the man is to stand with one end of the woman's cloth about his loins, and she with the other, and then they pour water on both their heads, wetting all their bodies; which being done, they are firmly married to live together, so long as they can agree.

The elder sorts of people usually woo and conclude their marriages as they are in bed together; for when they have lost their maidenheads, they fear not much what man comes to sleep with them, provided he be of as good quality as they, having nothing more to lose: and at the day appointed the man gives the woman her clothes, and so takes her home.

Man and wife may part at pleasure.

But their marriages are but of little force or validity: for if they disagree and mislike one the other, they part without disgrace; yet it stands firmer for the man than for the woman: howbeit, they do leave one the other at their pleasure. They do give according to their ability a portion of cattle, slaves, and money with their daughters; but, if they chance to mislike one another, and part asunder, this portion must be returned again, and then she is fit for another man, being as they account never the worse for wearing.

Both women and men do commonly wed four or five times before they can settle themselves to their contentation. And if they have children when they part, the common law is, the males for the man, and the females for the woman: but many of the women are free from this controversy, being childless. Men and women change till they can please themselves.

In this country, each man, even the greatest, hath but one wife; but a woman often has two husbands: for it is lawful and common with them for two brothers to keep house together with one wife, and the children do acknowledge and call both fathers. Women have two husbands.

So long as the women have their infirmities or flowers upon them, they are accounted very unclean, insomuch that the very house is polluted in that degree, that none will approach near it; and even she herself cares not to conceal it, but calls out to them that come near, that they may avoid her house; but, after she hath washed her head and body, all is purified again. It is lawful for no woman, although they be great men's wives, to sit on a stool in the presence of a man. It is customary for men upon any frivolous account to charge one another in the king's name to do or not to do, according as they would have it. This the women, upon penalty of having their tongues cut out, dare not presume to do. Women unclean. Privileges of men above women.

As it is usual to punish men for faults committed by imprisonment and chains, or by making them stand with a weight on their backs, until they do pay such a sum of money as is demanded, which for ordinary faults may be five or ten shillings; so the punishment, which is inflicted upon women, is to make them stand with a basket of sand upon their heads, so long as they shall think fitting, who appoint the punishment. Punishment by stripes is never used either to men or women, but only to those on whom the king commands them to be laid.

Privileges of women.

Lands of inheritance, which belong to women, are exempted from paying harriots to the king: women pay no custom for things they carry to the sea-ports; neither is any custom paid for what is carried upon any female cattle, cow, or buffalo.

They often destroy new born infants.

They have no midwives, but the neighbouring good women come in and do that office. As soon as the child is born, the father, or some friend, apply themselves to an astrologer, to enquire whether the child be born in a prosperous planet, and a good hour, or in an evil. If it be found to be in an evil, they presently destroy it, either by starving it, letting it lie and die, or by drowning it, putting its head into a vessel of water, or by burying it alive, or else by giving it to some body of the same degree with themselves, who often will take such children, and bring them up by hand with rice and milk; for they say, the child will be unhappy to the parents, but to none else. We have asked them why they will deal so with their poor infants, that came out of their bowels. They will indeed have a kind of regret and trouble at it; but they will say withal, "Why should I bring up a devil in my house?"—For they believe, a child born in an ill hour, will prove a plague and vexation to his parents, by his disobedience and untowardliness.

But seldom a first born.

But it is very rare a first-born is served so; him they love and make much of: but, when they come to have many, then usual it is, by the pretence of the child's being born under an unlucky planet, to kill him. And this is reputed no fault, and no law of the land takes cognizance of it.

In their infancy they have names, whereby one may be called and distinguished from the other; but, when they come to years, it is an affront and shame to them, either men or women, to be called by those names, which they say is to be like unto dogs. Then they change their names into titles, according to the town wherein they were born, or do dwell. Also they have other names, which may be compared to coats of arms, properly and only belonging to that family, by which likewise they are called. Their names

This people are very ambitious of their titles, having but little else that they can boast in: and of names and titles of respect they have great plenty in their language; instances whereof shall be given afterwards. They are ambitious of high titles.

CHAP. VIII.

Of their Employments and Recreations.

IT is full time now, that we relate what course of life the people take, and what means they use for a livelihood; this has been in part already related.

Their trade.

As for commerce and merchandize with foreign nations, there is little or nothing of that now exercised; indeed, in the times when the Portuguese were on this Island, and peace between them and the king, he permitted his people to go and trade with them; the which he would never permit them to do with the Hollander, though they have much sought for it. They have a small traffic among themselves, occasioned from the nature of the Island; for that which one part of the country affords, will not grow in the other—but in one part or other of this land they have enough to sustain themselves, I think, without the help of commodities brought from any other country; exchanging one commodity for another, and carrying what they have to other parts to supply themselves with what they want.

Work not discreditable to the best gentlemen.

But husbandry is the great employment of the country, which is spoken of at large before; in this the best men labour: nor is it held any disgrace for men of the greatest quality to do any work, either at home, or in the field, if it be for themselves, but to work for hire with them, is reckoned for a great shame; and very few are here to be found that will work so: but he that goes under the notion of a gentleman, may dispense with all works, except carrying—that he must get a man to do when there is occasion; for carrying is accounted the most slave-like work of all.

Under their husbandry, it may not be amiss to relate how they geld their cattle: they let them be two or three years old before they go about this work; then casting them, and tying their legs together, they bruise their cods with two sticks tied together at one end, nipping them with the other, and beating them with mallets all to pieces; then they rub over their cods with fresh butter and soot, and so turn them loose, but not suffer them to lie down all that day: by this way they are secured from breeding maggots, and I never knew any die upon this. How they geld their cattle.

Whensoever they have occasion to use glue, they make it after this fashion: they take the curd of milk, and strain the water from it through a cloth; then tying it up in a cloth like a pudding, they put it into boiling water, and let it boil a good while; which done, it will be hard like cheese-curd; then mixing it with lime, use it. If it be not for present use, they will roll up these curds into a ball, which becomes hard, and as they have occasion will scrape some of it off with a knife, and so temper it with lime; this lime with them is as soft as butter. How they make glue.

Their manufactures are few; some calicoes, not so fine as good strong cloth, for their own use—all manner of iron tools for smiths, and carpenters, and husbandmen; all sorts of earthen Their manufactures.

ware, to boil, stew, fry, and fetch water in; goldsmith's work, painter's work, carved work, making steel and good guns, and the like.

But their art in ordering the iron-stone and making iron may deserve to be a little insisted on; for the country affords plenty of iron, which they make of stones, that are in several places of the land—they lay not very deep in the ground; it may be about four, or five, or six feet deep.

How they make iron

First, they take these stones and lay them in a heap, and burn them with wood, which makes them more soft, and fitter for the furnace; when they have so done, they have a kind of furnace made with a white sort of clay, wherein they put a quantity of charcoal, and then these stones on them, and on the top more charcoal: there is a back to the furnace, like as there is to a smith's forge, behind which the man stands that blows; the use of which back is to keep the heat of the fire from him. Behind the furnace they have two logs of wood placed fast in the ground, hollow at the top, like two pots; upon the mouths of these two pieces of hollow wood they tie a piece of a deer's skin, on each pot a piece, with a small hole as big as a man's finger in each skin; in the middle of each skin, a little beside the holes, are two strings tied fast to as many sticks stuck in the ground, like a spring, bending like a bow—this pulls the skin upwards. The man that blows stands with his feet, one on each pot, covering each hole with the soles of his feet; and, as he treads on one pot, and presseth the skin down, he takes his foot off the other, which presently, by the help of the spring, riseth; and the doing so alternately, conveys a great quantity of wind through the pipes into the furnace—for there are also two pipes made of hollow reed, let in to the sides of the pots, that are to conduct the wind like the nose of the bellows into a furnace.

For the ease of the blower, there is a strap that is fastened to two posts, and comes round behind him, on which he leans his back; and he has a stick laid crossways before him, on which he lays both his hands, and so he blows with greater ease: as the stones are thus burning, the dross that is in them melts, and runs out at the bottom, where there is a slanting hole made for the purpose, so big as the lump of iron may pass through: out of this hole, I say, runs out the dross like streams of fire, and the iron remains behind; which, when it is purified, as they think enough, so that there comes no more dross away, they drive this lump of iron through the same sloping hole, then they give it a chop with an axe half through, and so fling it into the water: they so chop it, that it may be seen that it is good iron, for the satisfaction of those that are minded to buy.

For a farewell of their labours, let it not be unacceptable to relate here a piece of their housewifery, and tell you how they make butter. First, they boil the milk, then they turn it into a curd; the next morning they skim off the cream, and drill it in an earthen vessel with a stick, having a cross at the bottom of it, somewhat like a chocolate stick: when the butter is come, they put it in a pan and fry it, to get all the water dry out of it, and so put it into an earthen pot for use. How they make butter.

There are no markets on the Island—some few shops they have in the cities, which sell cloth, rice, salt, tobacco, limes, drugs, fruits, swords, steel, brass, copper, &c. Shops in the city.

Prices of commodities.

As to the prices of commodities, they are sold after this rate:—rice in the city, where it is dearest, is after six quarts for fourpence halfpenny, English, or a small tango, or half a tango; six hens as much; a fat pig the same; a fat hog, three shillings and sixpence, or four shillings—but there are none so big as ours; a fat goat, two and six pence; betel-nuts, 4000, ninepence current price, when a trade.

And, now we are discoursing of their traffic, we will speak a little of their measures, weights, and coin.

Of their measures.

First for measures.—A rian is a cubit, which is with them from the bone on the inside of the elbow to the tip of the fourth finger.—A waddo rian is the carpenter's rule: it is as much as will reach from one elbow to the other; the thumbs touching one the other at the tops, and so stretching out both elbows.

For their corn-measures, the least is a potta, which is to contain as much grain as a man can hold heaped up in his whole hand, palm, and fingers and all: four pottas make a lawful, or statute-measure, called bonder nellia, signifying the king's measure; which is the king's ordinary allowance to a man—that is as much as he can eat in a day; but we Englishmen were allowed two. Four of these bonder nellias make a courney. In fashion it is a handsome turned measure; some of them are made with canes, like a basket; ten of these courneys make a pale, that is, forty measures, which is the usual price in Candy Uda: but in time of harvest two pales for a laree: four of these pales make an ommouna; in which they keep the account of their corn, reckoning by ommounas.

For their weights, their smallest is a collonda—six make just a piece of eight:—they have half collondas, and quarter collondas. When they are to weigh things smaller than a collonda, they weigh them with a kind of red berries, which grow in the woods, and are just like beads — the goldsmiths use them: twenty of these beads make a collonda, and twenty collondas make a pallum. Their weights.

Here is no punishment for those that make less weights and measures: they are more circumspect that their measures be not too big than too little; for money being scarce, corn passeth instead of money, and every man metes by his own measure; which, therefore, he makes as large as he can, or dares; that so when he receives his debt of corn, he may get as much as he can; which, upon this account, would be a great injury to the poorer sort of people, who commonly are the debtors: therefore the adigar's officers will go about the towns to examine the measures by a statute-measure; and where they find great ones they cut them in pieces, and hang them up in the streets to terrify others, and sometimes will amerce a fine upon them that have them. Measures bigger than the statute punishable, but less not —and why.

Of money they have but three sorts that passeth for coin in the king's dominions: the one was coined by the Portugals; the king's arms on one side, and the image of a friar on the other, and by the Chingulays called tangom massa. The value of one is nine-pence English; poddi tangom, or the small tangom, is half as much: there is another sort, which all people by the king's permission may and do make: the shape is like a fish-hook, they stamp what mark or impression on it they please: the silver is purely fine beyond pieces of eight; for, if any sus- Of their coin.

pect the goodness of the plate, it is the custom to burn the money in the fire, red hot, and so put it in water; and, if it be not then purely white, it is not current money.

The third sort of money is the king's proper coin; for none upon pain of death may coin it; it is called a ponnam: it is as small as a spangle; seventy-five make a piece of eight, or a Spanish dollar: but all sorts of money are here very scarce; and they frequently buy and sell by exchanging commodities.

Of their play.

Pass we now from their business to their pastimes and diversions: they have but few sports, neither do they delight in play; only at their new-year they will sport and be merry one with another: their chief play is to bowl cocoa-nuts one against the other, to try which is the hardest. At this time none will work, until their astrologers tell them, it is a good hour to handle their tools; and then both men and women do begin their proper works—the man with his axe, bill, and hough, and the woman with her broom, pestle, and fan to clean her corn.

A play or a sacrifice.

There is another sport, which generally all people used with much delight, being, as they called it, a sacrifice to one of their gods—to wit, potting dio; and the benefit of it is, that it frees the country from grief and diseases; for the beastliness of the exercise they never celebrated it near any town, nor in sight of women, but in a remote place. The manner of the game is thus:—they have two crooked sticks like elbows, one hooked into the other, and so with contrivances they pull with ropes, until the one break the other; some siding with one stick, and some with the other; but never is money laid on either side: upon the breaking of the stick, that party that hath won doth not a little rejoice; which rejoicing is expressed by dancing and singing, and uttering such sordid beastly expressions, together with postures of their bodies, as I omit to write them, as being their shame in acting, and would be mine in rehearsing; for he is at that time most renowned that behaves himself most shamelessly and beast-like.

For the filthiness of it, forbid by the king.

This filthy solemnity was formerly much in use among them; and even the king himself hath spent time in it, but now lately he hath absolutely forbidden it, under penalty of a forfeiture of money; so that now the practice hereof is quite left off.

A cunning stratagem of an officer.

But though it is thus gone into dis-use, yet out of the great delight the people had in it, they of Gompala would revive it again—and did; which, coming to the king's ear, he sent one of his noblemen to take a fine from them for it. The noblemen knew the people would not come to pay a fine, and therefore was fain to go to work by stratagem. Pitching therefore his tents by a pond, he gave order to call all the people to his assistance to catch fish for the king's use; which they were very ready to do, hoping to have the refuse fish for themselves; and, when they were all thus assembled together with their tools and necessary instruments for that purpose, the nobleman charged them all in the king's name according to the country's fashion, which was, by pulling off his cap, and falling down upon the ground three times, that not a man should budge till they had paid such a sum of money, which was so much apiece, for reviving that play that the king had forbid; which they were forced to do before they departed from the pond side; and the money was carried into the king's exchequer.

Tricks and feats of activity.

When they would be merry, and particularly at their great festival in the new moon of June or July, (before mentioned) they have people that shew pretty tricks and feats of activity before them. A man sets a pole of seven or eight feet long upon his breast; a boy gets to the top of this pole, and leans with his belly upon the end of it; and thus the man danceth with the pole on his breast, and the boy on it, and but little holding the pole. A man takes four arrows, with blades about a foot long; they are tied one across another, and so laid upon the end of a pole, which rests upon the man's breast; on a sudden he squats down upon the ground, and the four arrows all fall on the four sides of him, sticking in the ground. Two cross bows stand bent, one opposite to the other, charged with arrows drawn up to the heads; they are placed just so high, as they may fly over a man's back when he lies flat upon the ground; a man danceth between them, and shews tricks; and when he is pleased, he touches a string made fast to both sides their triggers, at which they both instantly discharge, and he falls flat down between them, and the arrows fly over his back, which, if they hit him, undoubtedly fly through his body. A woman takes two naked swords, under each arm one, and another she holds in her mouth, then fetcheth a run, and turns clear over, and never touches the ground till she lights on her feet again, holding all her swords fast. There are divers other diversions of this nature, too large to mention.

At leisure times they meet, and discourse of news.

At their leisure, when their affairs will permit, they commonly meet at places built for strangers and wayfaring men to lodge in, in their language called amblomb, where they sit chewing betel, and looking one upon the other very gravely and solidly, discoursing concerning the affairs at court, between the king and the great men, and what employment the people of the city are busied about: for, as it is the chief of their business to serve the king, so the chief of their discourse is concerning such matters; also they talk of their own affairs, about cattle and husbandry; and, when they meet with outlandish men, they inquire about the laws and government of their country, and if it be like theirs; and what taxes and duties we are bound to pay, and perform to our king, &c.

And this manner of passing their leisure time they account the greatest recreation. Drunkenness they do greatly abhor; neither are there many that do give themselves to it: tobacco, likewise, they account a vice, but yet it is used both by men and women, but more eaten than drunk in pipes. Drunkenness abhorred.

But, above all things, betel leaves they are most fond of, and greatly delight in: when they are going to bed, they first fill their mouths with it, and keep it there until they wake, and then rise and spit it out, and take in more; so that their mouths are no longer clear of it than they are eating their victuals. This is the general practice both of men and women, insomuch, that they would rather want victuals or clothes than be without it; and my long practice in eating it brought me to the same condition. And the reasons why they thus eat it, are, first, because it is wholesome; secondly, to keep their mouths perfumed; for, being chewed, it casts a brave scent; and, thirdly, to make their teeth black—for they abhor white teeth, saying that is like a dog. Their great delight in betel.

The better sort of women, as gentlewomen or ladies, have no other pastime but to sit and chew betel, swallowing the spittle, and spitting out the rest: and when friends come to see and visit one the other, they have as good society thus to sit and chew betel, as we have to drink wine together.

The manner of their eating betel leaves.

But, to describe the particular manner of their eating these leaves:—they carry about with them a small box, filled with wet lime; and, as often as they are minded to eat betel, they take some of this lime, as much as they judge convenient, and spread it thin upon their leaf; then they take some slices of the betel nut, and wrap them up in the leaf, and so eat it, rubbing their teeth therewith ever and anon to make them black: thus they eat it generally; but sometimes they eat it otherwise, according as they please, neither spreading the lime on the leaf, nor rolling up slices of the nut into it; but they will take a little of the lime out of their box, between their fingers, and put it in their mouths, and eat of the nut and the leaf by themselves.

But whensoever they eat of the betel leaf, the lime and the nut always accompany it.

How they make lime.

They have a pretty shift of making their lime, when they chance to need it as they are travelling. They take certain shells, almost resembling snail's shells, which they pick up in fresh-water rivers, washed ashore with the water beating upon the rocks; these shells, mixed with charcoal and fire, they wrap up in a wisp of rice straw, and bind them together in a round bundle, of a convenient bigness, tying all up with green withs, that they may not fall in pieces: by a with, some four feet long, they hold it in their hands, swinging it round over their heads; which motion blows the coals, and makes them burn. And, as they are weary of swinging it in one hand, they shift, and take it in the other; and so keep swinging it for half an hour, or thereabouts; by which time it will be burnt to very good lime, and most part of the straw consumed; but it is still kept together by the green withs: then they take it and wet it in water, and put it into their pots or boxes for their use. The lime made of white stone, burnt in a kiln, they do indifferently use to eat with their leaves, as well as this made of shells, now described.

CHAP. IX.

Of their Laws and Language.

THERE are three things that ingenious men may possibly be inquisitive after, which have not yet been professedly handled—their laws, their language, and their learning.

Their laws.

Concerning the first, here are no laws, but the will of the king; and whatsoever proceeds out of his mouth is an immutable law: nevertheless, they have certain ancient usages and customs that do prevail, and are observed as laws; and, pleading them in their courts, and before their governors, will go a great way.

Lands descend.

To hint some of them, their lands are hereditary, and do descend from parents to their children; but the eldest son, by privilege of birth-right, does not possess and enjoy all the land—but if the father please, he can divide it among his children: yet, in case the eldest son does enjoy the land, then, without dispute, he is to maintain his mother, and her children, until they come to years of ability to provide for themselves.

In case corn receives damage by a neighbour's cattle.

They have a custom in the land of Ouvah, which is a great breeder of cattle, and hath but very little wood, so that they have not wherewith to make hedges; it is, that when they sow their lands, they drive their cattle thence, and watch them all day that they break not into the corn; and at night they tie their cattle, to secure them from straying into the corn lands; otherwise, if one neighbour's cattle eats another neighbour's corn, he must pay the damage.

Those that are lazy and loath to plough, or that are poor and want corn to sow, the custom is, to let out their ground to others to till at ande, that is, at halves; but fees and accustomable dues, taken out by the husbandman that tills it, the owner of the land receives not much above a third part.

For the husband hath divers considerable payments besides his half share of the corn: as namely, first he hath cotoumaun, that is so much corn as they scratch off from the whole heap of trodden corn by drawing a bundle of thorns over it. Secondly, waracool, that is a consideration for the expenses they are at in tilling and sowing; for which there is a rate according to the bigness of the field. Thirdly, warrapoll, that is the corn they leave at the bottom of the heap after they have done fanning: which is the women's fee for their pains in weeding the corn, and in pulling it up where it is too thick, and planting it where it is thin, &c. Fourthly, bolerud, which is the chaff and sweepings of the pit. This sometimes comes to a considerable value, according to the quantity of corn that is trodden. Fifthly, peldorah, which is a piece of corn they leave standing before the watch-house, which is set up in their corn grounds to watch their corn from the wild beasts; and this left standing is the fee for watching. There is yet another due, ockyaul, which belongs to their gods, and is an offering sometimes carried away by the priests, and sometimes they bestow it upon the beggars, and sometimes they will take it and hang it up in their houses, and

The loss of letting out land to till.

at convenient time sacrifice it themselves.' It is one of their measures, which is about half a peck.

The great considera-tion for corn borrowed.

And in the mean time until this corn is ripe, the owner is fain to go a borrowing corn to sustain himself and family, which he pays consideration for: which is, when his own corn is ripe, a bushel and an half for a bushel; that is, at the rate of fifty per cent. Which manner of lending corn is a means that doth maintain many strangers and others; for they who have got a small stock of corn by that profit may competently live upon it, which was the means that Almighty God prepared for my relief and maintenance.

Corn thus lent is somewhat difficult to receive again: for the debtor, being poor, all the creditors will come into the field, when the corn is a sharing, that being the place of payment; and, as soon as it is divided, each one will scramble to get what he can; and, having taken possession of it, from thence the creditor must carry it home himself, be it far or near.

The debt becomes double in two years.

If the debt remains in the debtor's hands two years, it becomes doubled; and from thence forward be it never so long, no more use is to be paid by the law of the land; which act was established by the king in favour of the poor, there having been some whole families made slaves for a bushel of corn.

If the debtor pay not his debt he is liable to be a slave for it.

But yet it is lawful for the creditor missing corn to lay hands on any of his goods; or, if the sum be somewhat considerable, on his cattle or children, first taking out a license from the magistrate so to do; or, if he have none, on himself or his wife, if she came with him to fetch the debt; if not, she is clear from this violence, but his children are not.

If a woman goes away from her husband without his consent, no man may marry her, until he first be married. In lending of money, by the use of it in one year's time it becomes double; and, if the creditor receive not his money at the expiration of the year, but lets it lie in the debtor's hands never so long after, no more than double is to be paid,—the increase never runs up higher as it is in lending corn. If a bond woman has children by a free man, the children are all slaves to her master; but if a bond man has children by a free woman, the children are free; for the children are always as the mother, whether bond or free. No man may cut down a cocoa-nut tree. If any man to a bargain or promise gives a stone in the king's name, it is as firm as hand and seal, and if any after this go back of his word, it will bear an action. If any man be taken stealing, he must restore seven for one, or else be made a slave, if he be not able to pay it. Divers other laws and customs.

It is lawful and customary for a man in necessity to sell or pawn his children, or himself. No man building an house, either in his own or another man's ground, if he be afterwards minded to leave his land, where his house stood, may pull it down again; but must let it stand for the benefit of whosoever comes after him.

For the deciding of matters in controversy, especially of more abstruse cognizance, the parties do both swear before their gods, sometimes in their temples, and sometimes upon more extraordinary occasions in hot oil. For deciding controversies.

Sometimes in their temples. To explain which, take this following relation:—a slave was accused by a merchant to have Swearing in the temples.

robbed his house, whereupon, to clear himself, the slave desired he might swear; so the merchant and slave went both to the temple to swear: the merchant swore positively that the slave had robbed his house, and the slave swore as point blank that he had not robbed his house; and neither of them having any witnesses, God, who knew all things, was desired to shew a judgment upon him that was forsworn. They both departed to their houses, waiting to see upon whom the judgment would fall; in the mean time the slave privately sets the merchant's house on fire, and his house was burnt down to the ground. Then it was clear, by this supposed divine judgment, the merchant was forsworn: the slave presently demands satisfaction for laying theft falsely to his charge; the merchant could not tell what to say to it, but would give him none; the slave was now to take his own satisfaction, as he had opportunity, and his master bids him seize upon the merchant's person, or any other relating to him, and bring them to his house, and there detain them: within a short time after, the slave seeing a kinsman of the merchant's passing by, offers to seize him; but he, rather than be taken, draws his knife, and stabs the slave on the shoulder, and so escapes. In fine, the merchant was fain to bribe the great men to save himself from further damage, and sit down contented with the loss of his goods and house; though the slave was a person of a very bad reputation, and had done divers thefts, and some of his stolen goods he hath brought to me to sell.

The benefit of swearing in hot oil

Sometimes they do decide their debates by swearing in hot oil, which, because it is remarkable, I will relate at large. They are permitted thus to swear in matters of great importance only, as when lawsuits happen about their lands, or when there is no witness; when they are to swear, each party hath a license from the governor for it, written with his hand to it. Then they go and wash their heads and bodies, which is a religious ceremony, and that night they are both confined prisoners in a house with a guard upon them, and a cloth tied over each of their right hands and sealed, least they might use any charm to harden their fingers.

The next morning they are brought out; they then put on clean cloths, and purify themselves, reckoning they come into the presence of God; then they tie to their wrists the leaf wherein the governor's license is, and repair under some bagahah, god tree, and all the officers of the country assemble with a vast number of people besides. Cocoa nuts are brought, and oil is there extracted from them in the sight of the people, that all may see there is no deceit. Also they have a pan of cow-dung and water boiling close by: the oil and cow-dung being both boiling and thoroughly hot, they take a young leaf of a cocoa-nut tree and dip that into the oil, that all may see it is hot: for it singes, and frizzles up, and roars as if you poured water into hot boiling oil, and so they do likewise to the cow-dung. When all are satisfied the oil is hot, the two men come and stand on each side of this boiling oil, and say—The God of heaven and earth is witness, that I did not do this that I am accused of: or, the four sorts of gods be witness, that this land in controversy is mine: and then the other swears quite contrary, but first the accuser always swears; the accused also relates his own innocence, or-his own right and title. The cloths that their hands were bound up in are taken off, and immediately upon using the former words, he dips his two fingers into the hot oil, flinging it out three times, and then goes to the boiling cow-dung, and does the same, and so does the other. Then they tie up their hands again with the cloth, and keep both of them prisoners till the next day, when their hands are looked upon, and their fingers ends rubbed with a cloth, to see if the skin come off; and, from whose fingers the skin comes, he is forsworn, the penalty of which is a great forfeiture to the king, and great satisfaction to the adversary.

I am able to testify, that the fingers of some of these that have thus sworn have been whole from any scald after this use of hot oil; but, whether it be their innocence or their art, that it thus comes to pass, I know not. The penalty of the breach of the laws or customs of this land is at the pleasure of the judge, either amercement or imprisonment, or both.

How they exact fines.

For the taking of fines from men, on whom they are laid, this is their custom: the officers wheresoever they meet the man, stop him in the place, where they take away his sword and knife, and make him pull off his cap and doublet, and there he sits with his keepers by him, till he pays the fine; and, if he delays paying it, they clap a great stone upon his back, in which condition he must remain till he pays it; and, if he doth not pay, they load him with more stones, until his compliance prevent further pains. Another way they have to exact the payment of the fines laid upon them; they take some sprigs of thorns, and draw them between the man's naked legs till he pays; but if he remain obstinate they clap him up in chains.

They have an odd usage among them to recover their debts, which is this: they will sometimes go to the house of their debtor

Smith. sc. 63 H. Holborn

The manner of extorting their Fine

London: Published May 10th 1818. by J. Mawman

with the leaves of neiingala, a certain plant, which is rank poison, and threaten him that they will eat that poison and destroy themselves, unless he will pay him what he owes. The debtor is much afraid of this, and rather than the other should poison himself, will sometimes sell a child to pay the debt; not that the one is tender of the life of the other, but out of care of himself: for, if the party dies of the poison, the other, for whose sake the man poisoned himself, must pay a ransom for his life. By this means, also, they will sometimes threaten to revenge themselves of those with whom they have any contest, and do it too. And, upon the same intent, they will also jump down some steep place, or hang, or make away with themselves, that so they might bring their adversary to great damage.

Of their language.

To speak now a little of their language.—It is a language peculiar to that Island; and I know not any Indian nation that speak it but themselves. There are a few words that are common to the Chingulays and the Malabars, which they might borrow of one another, by intercourse and commerce; but the words are so few, that a Malabar cannot understand a Chingulay, nor on the contrary.

Their language is copious, smooth, elegant, courtly, according as the people that speak it are; who are full of words, titles, and compliments. They have no less than twelve or more titles that they use when they speak to women according to their ranks and qualities.

Titles to women according to their qualities.

Puddeci. *A word for a woman of the lowest condition.*
Kiddekel. *A term of more respect given to a young wench.*

Nanda.	*A term for an inferior woman something in years, signifies also* Ant.
Nandadga.	*A little higher, yet of the like years.*
Nauchere.	*A title may be given to an ordinary woman, still, but yet higher.*
Lamhaumi.	*A title higher than any yet.*
Ettani.	*Higher still.*
Lam-ettani.	*Of more respect.*
Ettanihaumi.	*Higher than that.*
Maugi.	*Proper only to an old woman, but of good quality.*
Maugiwanxi.	*Better than the maugi.*
Comaurehaumi.	*A title due to the greatest ladies.*
Hondreunié.	*Given to the queen or the king.*

So that it is hard to speak to a woman without they know what she is before, lest they might mistake her title. And the women are much pleased with some of the better titles.

Titles given to men.

The men also have various titles, though not so many as the women. People give to them these titles according to the business they have with them. If they come for some favour or kindness to be done them, they bestow the better sort of titles upon them.

They have seven or eight words for thou, or you, which they apply to persons according to their quality, or according as they would honour them. And they are so, topi, umba, umbela, tomnai, tomsi, tomfela, tomnanxi. All these words are gradually one higher than the other.

Their ordinary ploughmen and husbandmen do speak elegantly,

and are full of compliment; and there is no difference between the ability and speech of a countryman and courtier. When any hath a favour to beg of a nobleman, or any business with him, they do not abruptly speak their desires or errand at first, but bring it in with a long harangue of his worth or good disposition or abilities; and this in a very handsome and taking style. They bring up their children to speak after this manner, and use them to go with errands to great men; and they are able to tell their tale very well also.

No difference between a countryman and a courtier for language.

Their speech and manner of address is courtly and becoming.

In their speech the people are bold, without sheepish shamefacedness, and yet no more confidence than is becoming.

The king they call by a name, that signifies somewhat higher than a man, and next to God. But, before the wars, they styled him Dionanxi, which is a title higher than God, by the addition of Nanxi; this title the king took before the rebellion; but since, he forbad it. When they speak to the king concerning themselves, they do not speak in the first person, and say—" I did so, or so; but baulagot, the limb of a dog did it, or will do it." And, when they speak of their children unto the king, they call them " puppies;" as if he ask them " how many children they have?" they say " so many puppy-dogs, and so many puppy-bitches;" by which, by the way, we may conjecture, at the height of the king, and the slavery of the people under him.

Their language in their address to the king.

They have certain words of form and civility, that they use upon occasion: when they come to another man's house, he asks them " What they come for?" which is his civility; and they answer—" Nicamava; I come for nothing:" which is their ordinary

Words of form and civility.

reply, though they do come for something—and upon this they have a fable.

A god came down upon earth one day, and bade all his creatures come before him, and demand what they would have, and it should be granted them: so all the beasts and other creatures came—and one desired strength, and another legs, and another wings, &c. and it was bestowed on them. Then came the white men; the god asked them "What they came for?" And they said, "They desired beauty, and valour, and riches:" it was granted them. At last came the Chingulays—the god required of them, "What they came for?" They answered, "Nicamava—I come for nothing." Then replied he again—"Do you come for nothing; then go away with nothing." And so they for their compliment fared worse than all the rest.

When one proffers something as a gift to another, although it be a thing that he is willing to have, and would be glad to receive, yet he will say, "Eeppa queinda—no, I thank you, how can I be so chargeable to you?" And in the same time, while the words are in his mouth, he reacheth forth his hand to receive it.

Full of words and compliment. Neither are they free or forward to requite them, from whom they have received a gift or good turn, otherwise than with words and windy protestations—the which shall not be wanting; but forwards they are to receive, yet very backward to part with any thing: and, if one neighbour asketh ought of another, or to borrow any thing, which the other is unwilling either to give or lend, they never will plainly deny, by saying,

"I cannot—or will not;" but with dissembling they will excuse themselves, saying, "They have it not; or it is lent abroad already;" although it be with them in the house at the same time.

Their usual manner of swearing in protestations, is by their mother, or by their children, or by their two eyes, oftener than by their gods: but their protestations, be they never so deep, and seem they never so serious, they are not to be regarded, as proceeding more from custom than truth. By whom they swear.

Some of their words of reproach, or raillery, are such as these: one brother will say to another, and that in presence of their mother—"Tomotowoy—go lie with your mother"—the other replies—"Go you and lie with your mother." And the mother will say to the daughter—"Jopi oppota audewind—go lie with your father;" intimating she is good for nothing. They will commend their children, when they can use their tongues in their own defence, by scolding, and say—"Hærri, oppana—well said; valiantly spoken." They will say also in reproach—"Creep between my legs, cut your nose off; if you have five hundred lives you shall be damned." The worst raillery they can give a woman, is to tell her "She has laid with ten sorts of inferior ranks of people, which they will rather die than do." If any thing be stole out of their grounds or plantations, fruit, or the like, they will cry out aloud—"This was done by some low-cast begotten rogue;" or, "She was a whore to some inferior rank who dressed it:" and this language they will continue for half an hour together, though they know not who hath done it: the worst word they use to whites and Christians, is to call them beef-eating slaves. Their raillery.

Proverbs. I shall conclude this discourse of their language, by giving you a taste of their proverbs; some hints of the strain of their speech.

Miris dílah, ingurah gotta—*I have given pepper, and got ginger*—spoken when a man makes a bad exchange; and they use it in reference to the Dutch succeeding the Portuguese in their Island.

Datta horrala badda perind—*Pick your teeth to fill your belly.* Spoken of stingy, niggardly people.

Caula yonawa ruah atti—*To eat before you go forth, is handsome and convenient.* Which they therefore ever do.

Kiallah tiannah, degery illand avah oppala hanguand mordy —*As the saying is, if I come to beg butter-milk, why should I hide my pan.* Which is ordinarily spoken to introduce the business that one man comes to speak to the other about.

Hingonna wellendam cor cottonwat geah par wardenda netta —*A beggar and a trader cannot be lost.* Because they are never out of their way.

Atting mitting delah hottarah harracurnowah—*To lend to another makes him become an enemy*: for he will hate you, if you ask him for it again.

Annuna min yain ecka ourowaying younda eppa—*Go not with a slave in one boat.* It signifies, to have no dealing or correspondence with any one's slave; for if any damage should happen, it would fall upon your head, and by their law you must make it good.

Issara otting bollanowa pos cotting—First look in the hand, afterwards open the mouth. Spoken of a judge who first must have a bribe, before he will pronounce on their side.

Take a ploughman from the plough, and wash off his dirt, and he is fit to rule a kingdom. Spoken of the people of Candy Uda, where there are such eminent persons of the Hondrew rank; and, because of the civility, understanding, and gravity of the poorest men among them.

Nobody can reproach the king and the beggar. Because the former is above the slander of the people, and nothing can be said bad enough of the latter.

Like *noia* and *polonga.* Denoting *irreconcileable enemies.* The story of which two serpents hath been related before.

He that hath money to give to his judge, need not fear, be his cause right or wrong. Because of the corruption of the great men, and their greediness of bribes.

If our gerehah, *fortune be bad, what can God do against it?* Reckoning that none of their gods have power to reverse the fate of an ill planet.

The ague is nothing, but the head-ach is all. That country is very subject to agues, which do especially afflict their heads who have them: I might multiply many more of their proverbial sayings, but let these suffice.

I cannot pretend to give an account of the *grammar* of this tongue: I shall only give a few instances of their words, and leave it to the learned to make their conjectures. First, I will give you some of their *nouns plural*.

Something of their grammar.

Minnia,	*A man.*	Minnis,	*Men.*
Cucula,	*A cock.*	Cuculong,	*Cocks.*
Cole-la,	*A boy.*	Colani,	*Boys.*
Gahah,	*A tree.*	Gos,	*Trees.*
Auhoun,	*A horse.*	Auspio,	*Horses.*
Polaha,	*A young jack.*	Polas,	*Jacks.*

But usually, when they have occasion to speak of many, they express themselves by *numerals* set after the *noun*: as, *dissawva*, two, three, &c.; *an egg*, bittera; *eggs*, bittera cattei; *word for word*, egg many.

Their *verbs* they form after this manner:

Mam conna,	*I eat.*	Caupoudi,	*Let him eat.*
Mam conyum,	*I will eat.*	Caum,	*Let us eat.*
Mam cava,	*I have eat.*	Conda,	*To eat.*
Conowa,	*Eating.*	Caula,	*Eaten.*
Mam denyam,	*I will give.*	Dem,	*Let us give.*
Mam Doun-na,	*I gave.*	Dennowa,	*Giving.*
Dila,	*I have given.*	Dipon,	*Give him.*
Dendi,	*Shall I give?* / *To give.*	Douna, or / Dila tiana,	*Given.*
Mam yonyam,	*I'll go.*	Yonda dipadi,	*Let him go.*

Mam yonda oni,	*I will go.*	Pollatch,	*Gone*—spoken of an ordinary person.
Yong,	*Let us go.*	Polladda,	*Gone*—spoken of a person of great quality.
Yonowa,	*Going.*		
Mam oy,	*I am.*	Mam gia atti,	*I have been,* [atti] signifieth [have.]
Eai,	*He* or *they,* or *he is.*	Gia d endi,	*Let him,* or *give him leave to go.*

A specimen of their words.

Dio,	*God.*	Gani,	*A woman.*
Dio loco,	*Heaven.*	Rodgura,	*A king.*
Jacco,	*The devil.*	Haul,	*Raw rice.*
Narra cauda,	*Hell.*	Bat,	*Boiled rice.*
Aucoi,	*The sky.*	Banglale,	*A table.*
Taurcoi,	*A star.*	Wellau,	*Time.*
Deure,	*Water.*	Wauri,	*Season.*
Gindere,	*Fire.*	Colading,	*Harvest.*
Oppa, Piananah, Oppatchi,	*Father.*	Dua, Donianna,	*Daughter.*
Omma, Ommandea,	*Mother.*	Molla,	*A flower.*
		Gauhah,	*A tree.*
		Courilla,	*A bird.*
Puta, Putandi,	*Son.*	Gom,	*A town.*

Oppuland, *To wash clothes.*
Naund, *To wash the body.*
Pinaund, *To swim.*
Coppaund, *To cut.*

Goumanic, *A journey.*
Gauman corowaund, *To send* word for word, *to cause to do a journey.*

Heuwaycom, *To fight.*
Coraund, As much as to say, *To act the soldier.*

Negatind, *To rise.*
Upaudenowa, *The resurrection.*
Negantind eppa, *Do not rise.*

Horraund, *To bore.*
Hoppacaund, *To bite.*
Coraund, *To do.*
Corowaund, *To cause to be done.*

Heuwoya, Heuwoynanna, Heuwoynanoura, } All words signifying common soldiers, only they are titles one above another; and the two last are as much as to say, gentlemen soldiers.

Mihi, *To die.*
Mich, *Dead.*
Mienyum, *I will die.*
Miœnowa, *Dying.*
Eppa, *Do not.*

Tonnanud, *To build.*
Tannith *Built.*
Tounch̥eroutwitch, *It is finished.*
Na & natti, *No, or not.*

I shall only make one observation from these words, and that is concerning the four first, it is this;—that they have no words of their own language for God and heaven, but in all probability borrowed them from the Portuguese; but, for the two next, the devil and hell, words of their own. They number thus:—

Eckhoi	I.	*Novihoi*	IX.	*Dauhahottoi*	XVII.
Deckhoi	II.	*Dauhoihoi*	X.	*Dauha ot hoi*	XVIII.
Tunhoi	III.	*Eckolauhoi*	XI.	*Dauhanovihoi*	XIX.
Hotterhoi	IV.	*Dolahoi*	XII.	*Vishoi*	XX.
Pauhhoi	V.	*Dauhottunhoi*	XIII.	*Tihoi*	XXX.
Hoyhoi	VI.	*Dauhotterhoi*	XIV.	*Hottalehoi*	XL.
Hothoi	VII.	*Paulohoi*	XV.	*Ponnahoi*	L.
Ot hoi	VIII.	*Dauhossahoi*	XVI.		

CHAP. X.

Concerning their Learning, Astronomy, and Art Magic.

Of their learning.

THEIR learning is but small: all they ordinarily learn is to read and to write; but it is no shame to a man if he can do neither; nor have they any schools wherein they might be taught and instructed in these or any other arts.

Their books are only of their religion, and of physic. Their chief arts are astronomy and magic. They use a language something differing from the vulgar tongue, (like latin to us) which their books are writ in. They learn to write upon sand, spreading it upon the ground, and making it smooth with the hand, and so write the letters with their fingers, to bring their hand in use.

Tallipot leaf used instead of paper.

They write not on paper, for of that they have little or none; but on a tallipot leaf, with an iron bodkin, which makes an impression: this leaf, thus written on, is not folded, but rolled up like ribbon, and somewhat resembles parchment.

Their manner of writing a book.

If they are to write a book, they do it after this manner:—they take the tallipot leaf, and cut it into divers pieces of an equal shape and size, some a foot, some eight inches, some a foot and a half long, and about three fingers broad; then, having thus prepared the leaves, they write in them long ways from the left hand to the right, as we do; when the book is finished they take two pieces of board, which are to serve for the cover of the book: to these boards are fastened two strings, which do pass through every leaf of the book, and these tie it up fast together: as the reader hath read each leaf, he lifts it up, and lays it by, still hanging upon the strings, and so goes to the next leaf, something resembling bills filed upon wire.

The gonnies, who are men of leisure, write many books of bonna; that is, of the ceremonies of their religion; and, will sometimes carry them to great men, as a present, and do expect a reward. The priests write books of bonna.

The king when he sends any warrants or orders to his officers, hath his writings wrapped up in a way proper to himself; and none else do or may fold up their leaves in that manner but he. The king's warrants; how wrapped up.

They write upon the tallipot leaves records or matters of great moment, or that are to be kept and preserved: but, for any ordinary business, as letters, &c. they commonly use another sort of leaf, called taulcole; the leaves of which will bear a better impression than the tallipot; but they are more stubborn, and harder than the other, and will not fold. They write upon two sorts of leaves.

But to speak a little of their astronomy:—they who have understanding in it, and practice it, are the priests of the highest order, of which the king's father was; but, the common sort of astrologers are the weavers: these men can certainly foretel eclipses of the sun and moon: they make leet, that is, almanacks that last for a month; they are written upon a tallipot leaf, a little above a foot long, and two fingers broad; in Their skill in astronomy. Their almanacks.

them are told the age of the moon, and the good seasons and times to begin to plough or to sow, or to go a journey, or to take any work in hand. On this precise time they will be sure to sprinkle their first seed, though they sow all their field it may be a month after: and so they will begin to set forth at the very moment, though possibly they will not go till some days after.

These astronomers tell them also when the old year ends to the very minute; at which time they cease from all work, except the king's, which must not be omitted: they acquaint them also with the good hour of the new year they are to begin work; at which time every man and woman begin to do somewhat in their employment they intend to follow the ensuing year: they have also another season directed them by their astronomers; that is, when to begin to wash their heads, which is assigned to every one according to the time of their nativity—which ceremony they observe very religiously.

The astronomers, or rather astrologers, are skilful in the knowledge of the stars, and planets, of which they reckon nine;—'tis supposed they may add the dragon's head and tail: by which they pretend to foretel all things concerning the health and recovery of sick persons: also concerning the fate of children born; about which the parents do presently consult them, and save their children or kill them, according to the fortunate or unfortunate hour they tell the parents they were born in.

When a person is sick, he carries to these men his nativity, which they call hanna hom pot; upon the perusal of which they tell his destiny: these also direct fit times for beginning journeys, or other undertakings: they are likewise consulted concerning marriages, by looking upon the man and woman's nativity.

They reckon their time from one Saccewarsi, an ancient king: their year consists of 365 days—they begin their year upon our eight-and-twentieth day of March, and sometimes the seven-and-twentieth; and sometimes, but very seldom, on the nine-and-twentieth: the reason of which I conceive to be, to keep it equal to the course of the sun, as our leap-year doth: they call the year ouredah; this they divide into twelve months, named, Wasachmaha, Pomaha, Ahalamoha, Micheneha, Bochmoha, &c.: they divide their months into weeks, each consisting of seven days, called, Fridah, Sandudah, Onghorudah, Bodadah, Braspotindah, Secouradah, Henouradah: the first of which they account a good and a fortunate day to begin to do or undertake any thing; and it falls out upon our Sunday. On their Wednesdays and Saturdays they open their churches, and perform their ceremonies: their day, which they call Dausack, they divide into thirty pays, hours, or parts, and begin their account from the sun rising, and their night also into as many, and begin from sun-setting; so that the fifteenth pay is twelve o'clock at noon; they have a flower, by which they judge of the time, which constantly blows open seven pays before night. Their era, their years, months, weeks, days, and hours.

They have no clocks, hour-glasses, or sun-dials, but keep their time by guess. The king indeed hath a kind of instrument to measure time. It is a copper dish, holding about a pint, with a very small hole in the bottom. This dish they set How they measure their time.

a swimming in an earthen pot of water; the water leaking in at the bottom till the dish be full, it sinks;—and then they take it out, and set it empty on the water again, and that makes one pay. Few or none use this but the king, who keeps a man on purpose to watch it continually;—the people will use it upon some occasions, as if they are to sow their corn at any particular hour, as being the good lucky season, then they make use of the copper pan, to know the time exactly.

Their magic.

They do practise magic:—whereof take these two remarkable instances that might be given.

The plenty of country destroyed by magic.

The country of Neurecalava formerly brought forth great plenty of corn, occasioned by reason of its large waterings. A neighbour kingdom, the kingdom of Cournegal, which lies in Hotcourley, in those times was brought to a great dearth, at which the king sends to the people of Neurecalava, that they would bring a supply of corn to his country, which they did in great store upon beasts in sacks, and arrived at the king's city: and there, for the more expeditious measuring out every householder his proportion of corn, they made a hole in the sacks, and let it run out, still driving on the beasts before them; and all that was shed before every man's house, was to be his share. This exceedingly gratified the king.

Afterwards, the king to requite them asked what they most needed in this country? They answered, "They had plenty of all things, only they wanted cahah mirris;" that is, turmeric and pepper. The king, to gratify them, sent them such a quantity of each as his country could afford. As soon as this was brought to the people of Neurecalava, they went to measure it out to every man his portion; but, finding it of so small a quantity, they resolved to grind it, as they do when they use it with their victuals, and put it into the river to give a seasoning to the water, and every man was to take up his dish of water thus seasoned. From whence Neurecalava had its denomination, viz. from Near, signifying a city, and cahah, that signifies turmeric; and lava, as if it were lalla, put into the river.

The king, hearing of this action of theirs, was offended, in that they so contemned his gift, but concealed his displeasure. Some time after, he took a journey to them; and, being there, desired to know how their country became so very fruitful; they told him, it was the water of the river pent up for their use in a very vast pond, out of which they made trenches to convey the water down into their corn grounds. This pond they made with great art and labour with great stones and earth thrown up a vast length and thickness, in the fashion of a half moon. The king afterwards took his leave of them, and went home, and by the help of his magicians break down this vast dam that kept in the water, and so destroyed the pond. And by this means this fruitful country, wanting her water, is become as ordinary land as the rest, having only what falls out of the sky.

When a robbery is committed—to find the thief, they charm a cocoa-nut, which is done by certain words, and any one can do it that can but utter the charm words: then they thrust a stick into it, and set it either at the door or hole the thief went out at: then one holds the stick with the nut at the end of it, *Their charm to find out a thief.*

and the nut pursues and follows in the tract that the thief went. All the way it is going, they still continue charming, and flinging the blossoms of the betel-nut tree upon it, and at last it will lead to the house or place where the thief is, and run upon his feet. This nut will sometimes go winding hither and thither, and sometimes will stand still; then they follow their charms, strewing on blossoms, and that sets it forward again. This is not enough to find the thief guilty; but, if they intend to prosecute the man upon this discovery, the charmer must swear against him point blank, which he sometimes will do upon the confidence of the truth of his charm, and the supposed thief must either swear or be condemned.

The way to dissolve this charm.

Oftentimes men of courage and metal will get clubs, and beat away the charmer and all his company, and by this means put all to an end. If the thief has the wit to lay his tail by the way, the cocoa-nut, when it comes thither, will stop and run round about it, but go no further. I, doubting the truth hereof, once took the stick, and held it myself, when they were upon this business, but it moved not forward while I held it in my hand, though they strewed their flowers, and used their mutterings to provoke it; but afterwards, when another took it, it went forward. I doubted whether they did not guide it with their hand, but they assured me it guided their hand.

Inscriptions upon rocks.

Here are some ancient writings engraven upon rocks, which poseth all that see them. There are divers great rocks in divers parts in Candy Uda, and in the northern parts. These rocks are cut deep with great letters for the space of some yards, so deep that they may last to the world's end: nobody can read them or make any thing of them;—I have asked Malabars, Gentuses, as well as Chingulays and Moors, but none of them understood them: you walk over some of them. There is an ancient temple, Goddiladenni in Yattanour, stands by one place where there are of these letters. They are probably in memorial of something; but of what we must leav to learned men to spend their conjectures.

CHAP. XI.

Of their Sickness, Death, and Burial.

The diseases this country is subject to.

NOTHING now remains, but to carry you to their sick beds, and to tell you what they do with the bodies of their friends deceased, and their behaviour on these occasions. They live to a great age, very often to fourscore, and hale at that age: the king's sister was near an hundred. They are healthy, and of a sound constitution: the diseases this land is most subject to are agues and fevers, and sometimes to bloody fluxes: the small pox also sometimes happeneth among them, from which they cannot free themselves by all their charms and enchantments, which are oftentimes successful to them in other distempers; therefore they do confess, like the magicians in Egypt, that this is the very finger of Almighty God. They are also subject to aches and pains in their bodies; for the remedy whereof, they have excellent ointments and oils, which they make and keep, to have ready when they have occasion.

Every one a physician to himself.

Here are no professed physicians nor chirurgeons, but all in general have some skill that way, and are physicians and chirurgeons to themselves. Their medicines they make of the leaves that are in the woods, and the bark of trees, with which they purge and vomit themselves, and will do notable cures upon green wounds, and also upon sore eyes.

To give a few hints of their method of physic, and what ingredients they make use of.

For purging, they make use of a tree called dallugauhah: it bears no leaves, nothing but thorns, and is of a soft substance; being cut, there runs out a white thick milk, into which we soak some whole corns of pepper a whole night; the next day the pepper is taken out and washed clean, and then boiled in fair water, with a sour fruit they call goraca, which we shall speak of by and bye; this they drink, and it purgeth very well. This milk is reckoned as rank poison as any thing can be, and yet the goats eat of the tree greedily without harm. To purge.

For a vomit, there is a leaf of a plant called warracole, in colour like a cabbage leaf, but smaller; it grows upon a long stalk, some three feet high; this leaf, as soon as it is broken from the stalk is full of milk, which runs out: in this milk they put a lump of salt, and let it lie a whole night; the next day they take the salt out, which is not dissolved, and wash it clean, then boil a little rice and water together; after 'tis taken off the fire, they put this salt into it, and drink it. To vomit.

There is a strong purge they make, with a berry called jawpolls, which is a little long greenish berry: of itself it is rank poison. They boil it with goraca and pepper in water, and drink a little of the water.

For drawing and healing of sores, they have a leaf called mockinacola: it is very like our tunhoof or ground ivy, only it is a brighter green; it runs along upon the ground, and spreads itself as tunhoof doth. They only take the leaf and clap it upon the sore. To heal sores.

To heal an imposthume

For an imposthume in the throat, they take the rind of the tree amaranga, and bruise and rub it with green turmeric, and wrap it up in a plantain leaf, and bury it in hot ashes, and there let it lie an hour or two till the fire hath well qualified it. Then the patient takes it, and keeps chewing it for a day or two, swallowing the spittle. The virtue of this I myself can testify, being exceedingly ill with a sore throat, and could not swallow; by the use of this I was well within a day and a night.

For a hurt in the eye.

For a sore, or hurt in the eye, they take oulcande-cole, goderacole, two herbs, the juice of each, and woman's milk; and having mingled them, drop them into the eye. I had a thorn of a considerable length run into the grey of my eye, and put me to great pain; the Chingulays advised me to use this means, assuring me how successful it was wont to be; but I was loath to tamper with so tender a place; and, thanks be to God, after some days the thorn fell out of itself.

To cure the itch.

It is a speedy cure of the itch, to take condouro giddi, a fruit of a tree, in form somewhat like a muscle, but bigger: this fruit they cut in slices, and fry it in cocoa-nut oil, and with this oil they anoint the body.

The caudle for lying-in women.

The ordinary caudle for women in child-bed is goraca boiled in water, with pepper and ginger; women in that condition use nothing else. This goraca is a fruit round like an apple, marked with divers creases along the side of it; being ripe, it is within and without, red like blood, but sour; they use this fruit as we do lemons and oranges. The core is sweet and pleasant, but they regarding it not fling it away: if you bite this fruit, it sticks to the teeth like wax or pitch, but their chief use of it is, to boil it with other things, to make them taste sour; they gather them at the time of year, and break the cloves asunder by their fingers; for they, if they be pulled, will part at the creases, and then they lay them in the sun and dry them; being dried they look like men's ears, and so they keep them for their use: two or three of these will give a pleasant sour relish unto a large vessel of any liquid thing. This goraca is in great use among them.

As there are in this country very many poisonous plants, and creatures, so the people have excellent skill in the healing thereof. There is one plant among the rest so strong a venom, that no creature will eat or touch it; and this is the leaf, that the people sometimes carry with them when they go to demand their debts, and threaten their debtors—they will poison themselves before them, unless they will pay them. It is called neiingala, a sprig that springs out of the ground almost like an honeysuckle, but not so big, and bears a curious flower, much like an honeysuckle.

Excellent at the cure of poison.

They are oftentimes stung with venomous serpents, upon which sudden death follows, without speedy help: but, if the bite be taken in time, they can certainly cure themselves, and make nothing of it; which they perform both by herbs and charms, though upon the sting they presently vomit blood. The knowledge of these antidotal herbs they have learned from the mounggoutia, a kind of ferret. This creature, when the noya and he meets, always fight; if he chanceth to be bitten by the serpent, which is very venomous, he runs away to a certain herb and eats it, and so is cured, and then comes back and fights again. The Chingulays, when they see these two things

They easily heal the biting of serpents by herbs.

fighting, do diligently observe them; and, when they see the mounggoutia go away, they take notice of the herbs he eats, and thereby have learned what herbs are proper to cure such venoms.

And charms.

They are skilful also in the use of charms: to cure the stings of serpents, or to prevent them, the noyas they can charm to that pass, that they will take them up in their hands, and carry them in baskets, and handle them, and kiss them without any harm; but the polonga will not hear a charm. They charm other wild and venomous creatures also: as the tiger, that he shall not hurt their cattle.

Not good at healing inward distempers.

But to cure inward diseases they are not excellent; but generally, when they are sick, they apply themselves to their gods; but their chief supplication they make to the devil, as being God's instrument, sent to punish and afflict whom he pleaseth, as I have discoursed at large already.

They both bury and burn their dead.

These people are very loath to die, and as much afraid of the devil in their sickness, whom at such times they chiefly invoke. Being dead, none will come near the house for many days, lest they should be defiled: the better sort burn the dead, because worms and maggots should not eat them; but the poorer sort, who regard not such matters, bury them, making a hole in the woods, and carrying the body wrapped up in a mat, upon a pole on their shoulders, with two or three attending it, and so laying it in without any ceremony, and covering it.

Some days after his decease, if his friends wish well to his soul, they send for a priest to the house, who spends a whole night in praying and singing for the saving of that soul. This priest, besides very good entertainment, in the morning must have great gifts and rewards; and, to encourage them therein, he tells them, that the like bounty and liberality as they shew to him, shall the soul of their departed friend receive in the other world; and so, according to their ability, they freely give unto him such things as they are possessors of: and he, out of his wonderful good nature, refuseth not any thing, be it never so mean. And thus with drums and pipes sounding before him, they conduct him home to his house. They send for a priest to pray for his soul.

Their manner of mourning for the dead is, that all the women that are present do loose their hair, and let it hang down, and with their two hands together behind their heads, do make an hideous noise, crying and roaring as loud as they can, much praising and extolling the virtues of the deceased, though there were none in him; and lamenting their own woeful condition to live without him: thus for three or four mornings they do rise early, and lament in this manner; also on evenings. Meanwhile the men stand still and sigh. How they mourn for the dead.

These women are of a very strong courageous spirit, taking nothing very much to heart, mourning more for fashion than affection, never overwhelmed neither with grief or love: and, when their husbands are dead, all their care is where to get others, which they cannot long be without. The nature of the women.

It may not be unacceptable to relate how they burn their dead. As for persons of inferior quality, they are interred in some convenient places in the woods, there being no set places for burial, carried thither by two or three of their friends, and How they bury.

buried without any more ado. They lay them on their backs, with their heads to the west, and their feet to the east, as we do: then those people go and wash; for they are unclean by handling the dead.

How they burn.

But persons of greater quality are burned, and that with ceremony. When they are dead, they lay them out, and put a cloth over their privy parts, and then wash the body, by taking half a dozen pitchers of water, and pouring upon it: then they cover him with a linen cloth, and so carry him forth to burning; this is, when they burn the body speedily. But otherwise, they cut down a tree that may be proper for their purpose, and hollow it, like a hog-trough, and put the body, being embowelled and embalmed, into it, filled up all about with pepper, and so let it lay in the house, until it be the king's command to carry it out to the burning; for that they dare not do without the king's order, if the person deceased be a courtier. Sometimes the king gives no order in a great while—it may not be at all; therefore, in such cases, that the body may not take up house-room, or annoy them, they dig a hole in the floor of their house, and put hollowed tree and all in, and cover it. If afterwards the king commands to burn the body, they take it up again, in obedience to the king—otherwise there it lies.

Their order for burning is thus: if the body be not thus put into a trough or hollowed tree, it is laid upon one of his bedsteads, which is a great honour among them. This bedstead, with the body on it, or hollowed tree with the body in it, is fastened with poles, and carried upon men's shoulders unto the place of burning, which is some eminent place in the fields

Smith, sc. 63 H. Holborn

The manner of burning their Dead

London: Published May 10th 1816—by J. Mawman

or highways, or where else they please. There they lay it upon a pile of wood some two or three feet high;—then they pile up more wood upon the corpse, lying thus on the bedstead, or in the trough. Over all they have a kind of canopy built, if he be a person of very high quality, covered at top, hung about with painted cloth, and bunches of cocoa-nuts, and green boughs, and so fire is put to it. After all is burnt to ashes, they sweep together the ashes into the manner of a sugar-loaf, and hedge the place round from wild beasts breaking in, and they will sow herbs there. Thus I saw the king's uncle, the chief tirinanx, who was, as it were, the chief primate of all the nation, burned upon a high place, that the blaze might be seen a great way. If they be noblemen, but not of so high quality, there is only a bower erected over them, adorned with plantain trees, and green boughs, and bunches, as before.

How they bury those that die of the small pox.

But if any die of the small pox, be his degree what it will, he must be buried upon thorns, without any further ceremony.

PART IV.

CHAP. I.

Of the Reason of our going to Ceylon, and Detainment there.

The subject of this fourth Part.

In this fourth and last Part I purpose to speak concerning our captivity in this Island; and, during which, in what condition the English have lived there, and the eminent providence of God in my escape thence, together with other matters relating to the Dutch, and other European nations, that dwell and are kept there. All which will afford so much variety, and new matters, that I doubt not but the readers will be entertained with as much delight in perusing these things, as in any else that have been already related. I begin with the unhappy occasion of our going to this country.

Anno 1657, the Ann frigate, of London, Captain Robert Knox, commander, on the one-and-twentieth day of January, set sail out of the Downs, in the service of the Honourable the English East-India Company, bound for Fort St. George, on the coast of Coromandel, to trade one year from port to port in India: which, we having performed, as we were lading of goods to return for England, being in the road of Matlipatan, on the nineteenth day of November, anno 1659, happened such a mighty storm, that in it several ships were cast away, and we were forced to cut our main-mast by the board, which so disabled the ship, that she could not proceed in her voyage: whereupon Cotair, in the Island of Ceylon, being a very commodious bay, fit for our present distress, Thomas Chambers, Esq. (since sir Thomas) the agent at Fort St. George, ordered, that the ship should take in some cloth, and go to Cotair Bay, there to trade, while she lay to set her mast; where being arrived, according to the appointment of those Indian merchants of Porta Nova we carried with us, to whom those goods belonged, they were put ashore, and we minded our business to set another main-mast, and repair our other damages we had sustained by the late storm.

At our first coming thither, we were shy and jealous of the people of the place, by reason our nation never had any commerce or dealing with them; but now, having been there some twenty days, and going ashore and coming on board at our pleasure, without any molestation, the governor of the place also telling us, that we were welcome, as we seemed to ourselves to be, we began to lay aside all suspicious thoughts of the people dwelling thereabouts, who had very kindly entertained us for our money, with such provisions and refreshings as those parts afforded.

They were not jealous of the people, being very courteous.

By this time the king of the country had notice of our being there; and, as I suppose, grew suspicious of us, not having

A pretended message to the captain from the king.

all that while by any message made him acquainted with our intent and purpose in coming; thereupon, he dispatched down a dissauva or general with his army to us; who immediately sent a messenger on board to acquaint the captain with his coming, and desired him to come ashore to him, pretending a letter to him from the king: we saluted the message with firing of guns; and my father, the captain, ordered me, with Mr. John Loveland, merchant of the ship, to go on shore, and wait upon him. When we were come before him, he demanded who we were, and how long we should stay? We told him we were English, and should not stay above twenty or thirty days, and desired permission to trade in his majesty's port. His answer was, the king was glad to hear that the English had come to his country, and had commanded him to assist us as we should desire, and had sent a letter to be delivered to none but to the captain himself.

We were then some twelve miles from the sea-side. Our reply was, that the captain could not leave his ship to come so far; but, if he pleased to come down to the sea-side himself, the captain would immediately wait upon him to receive the letter: upon which the dissauva desired us to stay that day, and on the morrow he would go down with us.

Which being a small request, and we unwilling to displease him, consented to.

The beginning of their suspicions.

The same day at evening, the dissauva sent two of his chief captains to the house where we lay, to tell us, that he was sending a present to the captain, and if we pleased we might send a letter to him: that he would send the present in the night, and himself, with us, follow the next morning. At which we began to suspect, and accordingly concluded to write and advise the captain, not to adventure himself, nor any other on shore, till he saw us: we having writ a letter to this purpose, they took it and went away, but never delivered it.

The captain seized, and seven more.

The next morning, the present, which was cattle, fruit, &c. was brought to the sea-side, and delivered to the captain; the messengers telling him withal, that we were upon the way coming down with the dissauva, who desired his company on shore against his coming, having a letter from the king to deliver into his own hand. Hereupon the captain, mistrusting nothing, came up with his boat into a small river; and, being come ashore, sat down under a tamarind tree, waiting for the dissauva and us. In which time the native soldiers privately surrounded him and men, having no arms with them; and so he was seized on, and seven men with him; yet without any violence or plundering them of any thing: and then they brought them up unto us, carrying the captain in a hammock upon their shoulders.

The long-boat men seized.

The next day after, the long boat's crew, not knowing what had happened, came ashore to cut a tree to make cheeks for the main-mast, and were made prisoners after the same manner, though with more violence: for they being rough, and making resistance, were bound with withs; and so were led away till they came where the people got ropes; which, when our men saw brought to them, they were not a little affrighted: for, being already bound, they concluded there could be no other use for those ropes but to hang them. But the true use of them was to bind them faster, fearing lest the withs might break, and so they were brought up farther into the country; but, afterwards being become more tame, they were loosed. They would not adventure to bring them to us, but quartered them in another house, though in the same town; where, without leave, we could not see one another. The house wherein they kept the captain and us, was all hanged with white calico, which is the greatest honour they can shew to any: but the house wherein the other men were, that were brought up after, was not. They gave us also as good entertainment as the country afforded.

The general's craft to get the ship, as well as the men.

Having thus taken both our boats and eighteen men of us, their next care was, fearing lest the ship should be gone, to secure her; therefore to bring this about, the dissauva told the captain,—that the reason of this their detainment was, that the king intended to send letters and a present to the English nation by him, and therefore that the ship must not go away, till the king was ready to send his messenger and message; and thereupon desired the captain to send on board, to order her stay; and, it being not safe for her to ride in the bay, lest the Dutch might come and fire her, that he should take order for her bringing up into the river:—which advice of his, the captain approved not of. But, concealing his dislike of it, replied—" that unless he could send two of his men on board with his letter and order, those in the ship would not obey him, but speedily would be gone with the ship;" which he, rather than he would run the hazard of the ship's departing, granted; imagining that the captain would order the ship to be brought up into the river, as he had advised, though the captain intended to make another use of this message.

The captain's order to them on board the ship.

Upon which the captain sent two of his men, some Indians accompanying them in a canoe to the ship; the captain ordering them when they were aboard, not to abuse the Indians, but to entertain them very kindly; and afterwards, that setting them ashore, they should keep the canoe to themselves, instead of our two boats which they had gotten from us, and to secure the ship, and wait till further order.

These two men stayed on board, and came not back again: this, together with the ship's not coming up, displeased the dissauva, and he demanded of the captain the reason thereof. His answer was—"That being detained on shore, the men on board would not obey his command." Upon this some days after, the dissauva bid the captain send his son with order to those aboard, that the ship might be brought into the river; but provided that he would be security for my return, which he promised he would. His order to me was, to see the top chains put upon the cables, and the guns shotted; and to tell Mr. John Burford, chief mate, and all the rest, as they valued their lives and liberties, to keep a watch, and not to suffer any boat to come near, after it was dark; and charged me, upon his blessing, and as I should answer it at the great day, not to leave him in this condition, but to return to him again; upon which I solemnly vowed, according to my duty, to be his obedient son.

The captain's second message to his ship.

So having seen all done according to his appointment, I wrote a letter in the name of the company, to clear my father and myself, to this effect—"That they would not obey the captain, nor any other in this matter, but were resolved to stand upon their own defence;" to which they all set their hands. Which done, according to my promise and duty, I returned again, and delivered the letter to the dissauva, who was thereby answered, and afterwards urged the captain no more in that matter, but

The ship's company refuse to bring up the ship.

gave him leave at his pleasure to write for what he pleased to have brought to him from the ship: still pretending the king's order to release us was not yet, but would suddenly come: and so we remained, expecting it about two months, being entertained as formerly with the best diet and accommodation of the country.

The captain orders the ship to depart.

Having continued thus long in suspense, and the time and season of the year spending for the ship to proceed on her voyage to some other place, and our condition being, as we feared, and afterwards found to be, the beginning of a sad captivity, the captain sent order to Mr. John Burford to take the charge of the ship upon him, and to set sail for Porto Nova whence we came, and there to follow the agent's order.

The lading of cloth remained untouched.

If any inquire what became of the cloth of our lading, which we brought thither, they only took an account to see what it was, and so left it where and as it was before, and there it remained until both house and goods rotted, as the people of the same town informed me afterwards.

The probable reason of our surprise.

I impute the main reason of our surprise to our neglect, viz. in not sending a letter and present to the king at our first coming; who, looking upon himself as a great monarch, as he is indeed, requires to be treated with suitable state.

The number of those that were left on the Island.

Thus were sixteen of us left to the mercy of those barbarians, the names of which are as follow:—The captain, Mr. Joseph Loveland, John Gregory, Charles Beard, Roger Gold, Stephen Rutland, Nicolas Mullins, Francis Crutch, John Berry, Ralph Knight, Peter Winn, William Hubbard, Arthur Emery, Richard Varnham, George Smith, and myself. Though our hearts were very heavy, seeing ourselves betrayed into so sad a condition to be forced to dwell among those that knew not God nor his laws; yet so great was the mercy of our gracious God, that he gave us favour in the sight of this people; insomuch, that we lived far better than we could have expected, being prisoners, or rather captives, in the hands of the heathen, from whom we could have expected nothing but very severe usage.

The dissauva departs.

The ship being gone, the king sent to call the dissauva speedily to him, who, upon this order, immediately marched away with his army, leaving us where we were; but concerning us was no order at all.

CHAP. II.

How we were carried up the Country, and disposed of there, and of the Sickness, Sorrow, and Death of the Captain.

They intend to attempt an escape, but are prevented.

THE dissauva with his men, being gone, the people of the town were appointed to guard and secure us until further order; but they carried us some six miles higher into the country, and would not yet adventure to bring the long boat's crew unto us, but kept them by themselves in another town, fearing lest we might make an escape, as certainly we should have attempted it, had they not removed us. There was a small Moor's vessel, which lay in the river, which they had seized on about this time, as we supposed they would have done by our ship if they could have catched her there. This vessel had some forty men belonging to her, who were not made prisoners as we were, but yet lay in the same town;—with those we had concluded, that they should furnish us with arms, and in the night altogether to march down, and get on board of their vessel, and so make our escape; but, being prevented in this design by our departure, we were fain to lay at their mercy.

Their condition commisserated by the people.

In our new quarters our entertainment proved as good as formerly; and, indeed, there was this to mitigate our misery,—that the people were courteous to us, and seemed to pity us; for there is a great difference between the people inhabiting the high lands, or the mountains of Candy, and those of the low lands, where we now are placed, who are of a kinder nature by far than the other: for these countries beneath the mountains formerly were in subjection unto the Portuguese, whereby they have been exercised and acquainted with the customs and manners of Christian people, which, pleasing them far better than their own, have begot and bred in them a kind of love and affection towards strangers, being apt to shew pity and compassion on them in their distress: and you shall hear them oftentimes upbraiding the highlanders for their insolent and rude behaviour.

It was a very sad condition whilst we were all together; yet hitherto, each other's company lessened our sufferings, and was some comfort that we might condole one another; but now it came to pass that we must be separated and placed asunder, one in a village, where we could have none to confer withal or look upon, but the horrible black faces of our heathen enemies, and not understand one word of their language neither: this was a great addition to our grief; yet God was so merciful to us, as not to suffer them to part my father and I.

They are distributed into divers towns.

For it was some sixteen days after our last remove, the king was pleased to send a captain with soldiers to bring us into the country; who brought us, and the other men taken in the long boat, together: which was an heavy meeting; being then, as we well saw, to be carried captives into the mountains. That night we supped together, and the next morning changed our condition into real captivity; howbeit, they gave us many comfortable promises, which we believed not; as, that the king's intent was not to keep us any longer than till another ship came to carry us away. Although we had but very little

An order comes from the king to bring them up into the country.

to carry, God knows, yet they appointed men to carry the clothes that belonged to the captain and officers.

How they were treated on the way in the woods.

We still expected they would plunder us of our clothes, having nothing else to be plundered of: but the Chingulay captain told us, that the king had given order that none should take the value of a thread from us, which indeed they did not: as they brought us up, they were very tender of us, as not to tire us with travelling, bidding us go no faster than we would ourselves: this kindness did somewhat comfort us, the way was plain and easy to travel, through great woods, so that we walked as in an arbour, but desolate of inhabitants; so that for four or five nights, we lay on the ground, with boughs of trees only over our heads. And of victuals twice a day, they gave us as much as we could eat; that is, of rice, salt fish, dried flesh; and sometimes they would shoot deer, and find honey in the trees, good part of which they always brought unto us; and drink we could not want, there being rivers and puddles full of water, as we travelled along.

And in the towns among the inhabitants.

But when we came out of the woods among inhabitants, and were led into their towns, they brought us victuals ready dressed, after their fashion, viz. rice boiled in water, and three other sorts of food, whereof one flesh, and the other two herbs, or such like things that grow in their country, and all kinds of ripe fruit, which we liked very well, and fed heartily upon. Our entertainment all along was at the charge of the country, so we fed like soldiers upon free quarter; yet I think, we gave them good content for all the charge we put them to; which was to have the satisfaction of seeing us eat, sitting on mats upon the ground in their yards, to the public view of all beholders, who greatly admired us, having never seen, nor scarce heard of Englishmen before; it was also great entertainment to them, to observe our manner of eating with spoons, which some of us had, and that we could not take the rice up in our hands, and put it to our mouths without spilling, as they do, nor gaped and poured the water into our mouths out of pots, according to their country's custom. Thus at every town where we came, they used both young and old in great companies to stare upon us.

Being thus brought up all together, somewhat near to the city of Candy—now came an order from the king to separate us, and to place us one in a town; which then seemed to us to be very hard, but it was for the convenience of getting food, being quartered upon the country at their charge.

They are brought near Candy, and there separated.

The captain, Mr. John Loveland, myself, and John Gregory, were parted from the rest, and brought nearer to the city, to be ready when the king should send for us. All the rest were placed one in a town, according to the aforesaid order. Special command also was given from the king, that we all should be well entertained; and, according to the country fare, we had no cause to complain: we four were thus kept together some two months, faring well all the while; but the king minding us not, order came from the great men in court to place us in towns, as the rest were; only my father and I were still permitted to be together, and a great charge given to use us well, and indeed twice a day we had brought unto us as good fare as the country afforded; all the rest had not their provisions brought to them, as we had, but went to eat from house to house, each house taking its turn.

The captain and his son and two more quartered together.

Parted.

How they fared.

The captain and his son placed in Coos-wat.

On the sixteenth of September, 1660, my father and I were placed in a town called Bonder Coos-wat, the situation was very pleasing and commodious, lying about thirty miles to the northward of the city of Candy, in the country called Hotcourly, and distant from the rest of our people a full day's journey. We were removed hither from another town nearer to the city, where the nobles at court, supposing that the king would call for us, had placed us to have us ready. Being thus brought to Bonder Coos-wat, the people put it to our choice, which house we would have to reside in. The country being hot, and their houses dark and dirty, my father chose an open house, having only a roof, but no walls; wherein they placed a cot, or bedstead, only with a mat upon it for him, which in their account is an extraordinary lodging; and for me a mat upon the ground.

Money scarce with them.

Monies at this time was very low with us; for, although we wanted not for opportunity to send for what we would have brought unto us from the ship, yet fearing we should be plundered of it, sent not for any thing, only a pillow for my father; for we held it a point without dispute, that they that made prisoners of our bodies, would not spare to take our goods: my father also alleging, that he had rather his children at home should enjoy them.

But they had good provisions without it.

But to make amends for that, we had our provisions brought us without money, and that twice a day, so much as we could eat, and as good as their country yielded: to wit, a pot of good rice, and three dishes of such things as is accounted good cheer; one always either flesh, fish, or eggs; but not over much of this dish; the other dishes, herbs, pumpkins, or such like, one of which is always made sour.

The town where they were sickly.

The first year that we were brought into this town, this part of the land was extraordinary sickly by agues and fevers, whereof many people died: insomuch, that many times we were forced to remain an hungry—there being none well enough either to boil or bring victuals unto us.

How they passed their time.

We had with us a Practice of Piety, and Mr. Rogers's seven treatises, called the Practice of Christianity; with which companions we did frequently discourse, and, in the cool of the evening, walk abroad in the fields for a refreshing, tired with being all day in our house or prison.

They both fall sick.

This course lasted until God was pleased to visit us both with the country sickness, ague and fever. The sight of my father's misery was far more grievous unto me than the sense of my own, that I must be a spectator of his affliction, and not any ways able to help him: and the sight of me so far augmented his grief, that he would often say, "What have I done, when I charged you to come ashore to me again; your dutifulness to me hath brought you to be a captive. I am old, and cannot long hold out; but you may live to see many days of sorrow, if the mercy of God do not prevent it. But my prayers to God for you shall not be wanting, that for this cause he would visit you with his mercy, and bestow on you a blessing."

Deep grief seizes the captain.

My father's ague lasted not long; but deep grief, daily more and more, increased upon him, which so over-whelmed even his very heart, that with many a bitter sigh he used to utter these words: "These many years, even from my youth, have I used the seas; in which time the Lord God hath delivered me from a multitude of dangers," rehearsing to me what great dangers he had been in, in the Straits by the Turks, and by other enemies, and also in many other places, too large here to insert, and always how merciful God was to him in delivering him out of them all: so that he never knew what it was to be in the hand of an enemy; but now in his old age, when his head was grown grey, to be a captive to the heathen, and to leave his bones in the eastern parts of the world, when it was his hopes and intention, if God permitted him, to finish this voyage, to spend and end the residue of his days at home with his children, in his native country, and to settle me in the ship in his stead—the thoughts of these things did even break his heart.

Their sickness continues.

Upwards of three months my father lay in this manner upon his bed, having under him only a mat, and the carpet he sat upon in the boat when he came ashore, and a small quilt I had to cover him withal. And I had only a mat upon the ground, and a pillow to lay on, and nothing to cover me but the clothes on my back; but, when I was cold, or that my ague came upon me, I used to make a fire, wood costing nothing but the fetching.

Their boy's disobedience adds to their trouble.

We had a black boy my father brought from Porto Nova, to attend upon him, who, seeing his master to be a prisoner in the hands of the people of his own complexion, would not now obey his command, further than what agreed unto his own humour, neither was it then, as we thought, in our power to compel or make him; but it was our ignorance. As for me, my ague now came to a settled course; that is, once in three days, and so continued for sixteen months time.

His excessive sorrow

There appearing now to us no probability whereupon to build any hopes of liberty, the sense of it struck my father into such an agony and strong passion of grief, that once, I well remember, in nine days time, nothing came into his mouth but cold water; neither did he, in three months together, ever rise up out of his bed, but when the course of nature required it: always groaning and sighing in a most piteous manner; which, for me to hear and see come from my dear father, myself also in the same condition, did almost break my heart. But then I felt that doctrine most true, which I had read out of Mr. Rogers's book, "That God is most sweet, when the world is most bitter."

In this manner my father lay until the ninth of February, 1660,–61, by which time he was consumed to an anatomy, having nothing left but skin to cover his bones; yet he often would say, "That the very sound of liberty would so revive him, that it would put strength into his limbs." But it was not the will of Him, to whom we say, "Thy will be done," to have it so.

His discourse and charge to his son before his death.

The evening before his death, he called to me to come near his bed-side, and to sit down by him; at which time also I had a strong fever upon me. This done, he told me, "That he sensibly felt his life departing from him, and was assured, that this night God would deliver him out of this captivity; and that he never thought, in all his life-time, that death could be so easy and welcome to any man, as God had made it to be to him:

and the joys he now felt in himself, he wanted utterance to express to me." He told me, "These were the last words that ever he should speak to me, and bid me well regard, and be sure to remember them, and tell them to my brother and sister, if it pleased God, as he hoped it would, to bring us together in England, where I should find all things settled to my contentation;" relating to me after what manner he had settled his estate, by letters which he sent from Cotiar.

In the first place, and above all, he charged me to serve God, and with a circumspect care to walk in his ways; and then he said, God would bless me and prosper me. And next, he bade me have a care of my brother and sister. And lastly, he gave me a special charge to beware of strong drink, and lewd company, which, as by experience many had found, would change me into another man, so that I should not be myself. It deeply grieved him, he said, to see me in captivity in the prime of my years; and so much the more, because I had chosen rather to suffer captivity with him than to disobey his command, which now he was heartily sorry for, that he had so commanded me, but bade me not repent of obeying the command of my father, seeing for this very thing, he said, God would bless me, and bid me be assured of it, which he doubted not of, viz. that God Almighty would deliver me; which at that time I could not tell how to conceive, seeing but little sign of any such matter. But, blessed be the Name of my most gracious God, who hath so bountifully sustained me ever since, in the land of my captivity, and preserved me alive to see my deceased father's word fulfilled! And truly I was so far from repenting, that I had obeyed the command of my father, and performed the oath and promise I made unto him upon it, that it rather rejoiced me to see that God had given me so much grace.

But though it was a trouble to him, that by his means I was thus made a captive; yet it was a great comfort to him, he said, to have his own son sit by him on his death-bed, and by his hands to be buried; whereas otherwise he could expect no other but to be eaten by dogs, or wild beasts. Then he gave me order concerning his burial—that having no winding sheet, I should pull his shirt over his head, and slip his breeches over his feet, and so wrap him up in the mat he laid upon; and then ceased speaking, and fell into a slumber. This was about eight or nine o'clock in the evening, and about two or three in the morning he gave up the ghost, February the 9th, 1660; being very sensible unto the very instant of his departure. His death.

According to his own appointment, with my own hands I wrapped him up ready for the grave; myself being very sick and weak, and, as I thought, ready to follow after him. Having none but the black boy with me, I bad him ask the people of the town for help to carry my father to the grave, because I could not understand their language; who immediately brought forth a great rope they used to tie their cattle withal, therewith to drag him by the neck into the woods, saying—"They could afford me no other help, unless I would pay for it." This insolency of the heathen grieved me much to see; neither could I, with the boy alone, do what was necessary for his burial, though we had been able to carry the corpse, having not wherewithal to dig a grave, and the ground very dry and hard: yet it was some comfort to me, that I had so much ability as to hire one to help; which at first I would not have spared to have done, had I known their meaning. And burial.

The place where he lies.

By this means, I thank God, in so decent a manner as our present condition would permit, I laid my father's body in the grave; most of which I digged with my own hands—the place being in a wood, on the north side of a corn field, where heretofore we had used often to walk, going up to Handapoul: that division, as I have said, being called Bonder Coos-wat, because formerly it had belonged to the revenues, or jointure of the queen; Bonder implying something relating to the king. It lies towards the north-west of the middle of the Island, in the county of Hotcourly.

Thus was I left desolate, sick, and in captivity, having no earthly comforter, none but only He who looks down from Heaven to hear the groaning of the prisoners, and to shew himself a father of the fatherless, and a present help to them that have no helper.

Upon the captain's death, a message sent his son from court.

The news of my father's death being carried to court, presently two messengers were sent from thence to see me, and to know of me—how, and in what manner my father died, and what he had left: which was a gold ring, a pagoda, and some two or three dollars, and a few old clothes; God knows but a very little, yet it scared me not a little—fearing they would take it away from me, and my want being so great; but they had no such order nor intent. But the chief occasion of their coming was, to renew the former order unto the people of that town; that they should be kind to, and give me good victuals, lest I might die also as my father had done: so for a while I had better entertainment than formerly.

CHAP. III.

How I lived after my Father's Death, and of the Condition of the Rest of the English; and how it fared with them; and of our Interview.

I STILL remained where I was before, having none but the black boy and my ague to bear me company. Never found I more pleasure in reading, meditating, and praying, than now; for there was nothing else could administer to me any comfort, neither had I any other business to be occupied about. I had read my two books so often over, that I had them almost by heart; for my custom was, after dinner, to take a book and go into the fields, and sit under a tree, reading and meditating until evening—excepting the day when my ague came; for then I could scarce hold up my head. Often have I prayed, as Elijah under the juniper tree, that God would take away my life—for it was a burthen to me. His chief employment is reading.

At length, it pleased God, my ague began to be a little moderate; and so by degrees it wore away, after it had held me sixteen months. He loses his ague.

Provisions falling short with me, though rice, I thank God, I never wanted; and monies also growing low, as well to help out a meal as for recreation, sometimes I went with an angle to

How he met with an English Bible in that country.

catch small fish in the brooks, the aforesaid boy being with me. It chanced as I was fishing, an old man passed by, and seeing me, asked of my boy, "If I could read a book?" He answered "Yes." "The reason I ask," said the old man, "is, because I have one I got when the Portuguese lost Columbo; and, if your master please to buy it, I will sell it him:" which, when I heard of, I bid my boy go to his house with him, which was not far off, and bring it to me, making no great account of the matter, supposing it might be some Portuguese book.

The boy having formerly served the English, knew the book; and, as soon as he had got it in his hand, came running with it, calling out to me, "It is a Bible!" It startled me to hear him mention the name of a Bible, for I neither had one, nor scarcely could ever think to see one; upon which I flung down my angle, and went to meet him. The first place the book opened in, after I took it in my hand, was the sixteenth chapter of the Acts; and the first place my eye pitched on, was the thirtieth and one and thirtieth verses—where the jailor asked St. Paul, "What must I do to be saved?" And he answered, saying—"Believe in the Lord Jesus Christ, and thou shalt be saved, and thine house."

Struck into a great passion at the sight of the book.

The sight of this book so rejoiced me, and affrighted me together, that I cannot say which passion was greater; the joy, for that I had got sight of a Bible, or the fear, that I had not enough to buy it; having then but one pagoda in the world, which I willingly would have given for it, had it not been for my boy, who dissuaded me from giving so much; alleging my necessity for money many other ways, and undertaking to procure the book for a far meaner price, provided I would seem to slight it in the sight of the old man. This counsel after I considered, I approved of: my urgent necessities earnestly craving, and my ability being but very small to relieve the same: and however, I thought I could give my piece of gold at the last cast, if other means should fail.

I hope the readers will excuse me, that I hold them so long upon this single passage; for it did so affect me then, that I cannot lightly pass it over as often as I think of it, or have occasion to mention it.

The sight indeed of this Bible so overjoyed me, as if an angel had spoken to me from heaven; to see that my most gracious God had prepared such an extraordinary blessing for me, which I did, and ever shall look upon as miraculous; to bring unto me a Bible in my own native language, and that in such a remote part of the world—where his Name was not so much as known, and where any Englishman was never known to have been before. I looked upon it, as somewhat of the same nature with the Ten Commandments he had given the Israelites out of heaven: it being the thing, for want whereof I had so often mourned, nay, and shed tears too; and, than the enjoyment whereof, there could be no greater joy in the world to me.

Upon the sight of it I left off fishing; God having brought a fish to me that my soul had longed for—and now how to get it, and enjoy the same, all the powers of my soul were employed. I gave God hearty thanks that he had brought it so near me, and most earnestly prayed that he would bestow it on me. Now, it being well towards evening, and not having wherewithal to buy it about me, I departed home, telling the

He casts with himself how to get it.

old man, that in the morning I would send my boy to buy it of him.

All that night I could take no rest for thinking on it, fearing lest I might be disappointed of it. In the morning, as soon as it was day, I sent the boy with a knit cap he had made for me, to buy the book, praying in my heart for good success, which it pleased God to grant; for that cap purchased it, and the boy brought it to me to my great joy, which did not a little comfort me over all my afflictions.

Where the rest of the English were bestowed.

Having said all this concerning my father and myself, it will be time now to think of the rest of our poor countrymen, and to see what is become of them: they were carried into the county of Hotteracourly, westward from the city of Candy, and placed singly, according to the king's order aforesaid, some four, some six miles distant one from the other. It was the king's command concerning them, that the people should give them victuals, and look after them; so they carried each man from house to house to eat, as their turns came to give them victuals—and where they supped, there they lodged that night: their bedding was only a mat upon the ground.

Kept from one another a good while, but after permitted to see each other.

They knew not they were so near to one another a great while, till at length Almighty God was pleased by their grief and heaviness to move those heathen to pity, and take compassion on them; so that they did bring some of them to one another, which joy was but abortive; for no sooner did they begin to feel the comfort of one another's company, but immediately their keepers called upon them, to go from whence they came; fearing they might consult and run away, although Columbo, the nearest port they could fly to, was above two days journey from them. But as it is with wild beasts beginning to grow tame, their liberty increaseth; so it happened to our men—so that at length they might go and see one another at their pleasures, and were less and less watched and regarded: and seeing they did not attempt to run away, they made no matter of it, if they stayed two or three days one with the other.

They all wondered much to see themselves in this condition; to be kept only to eat, and the people of the country giving it unto them, daily expecting when they would put them to work, which they never did, nor dared to do: for the king's order was to feed them well only, and to look after them until he pleased to send for them. This, after some time, made them to change their minds, and not to think themselves slaves any more—but the inhabitants of the land to be their servants, in that they laboured to sustain them.

No manner of work laid upon them.

Which made them to begin to domineer, and would not be content, unless they had such victuals as pleased them; and oftentimes used to throw the pots, victuals, and all at their heads that brought them, which they patiently would bear.

And as they lived here longer, they knew better what privileges they had in belonging unto the king, and being maintained by virtue of his command; and their privileges they made use of to no purpose, as I shall relate an instance or two by and bye; and shewed their English metal.

They begin to pluck up their hearts.

Victuals was the only thing allowed them, but no clothes:

What course they took for clothes.

by this time the clothes they had were almost worn out. This put them to a study what course to take to procure more, when those on their backs were gone. The readiest way that they could devise was this: that whereas they used to take their victuals brought to them ready dressed, they should now take them raw; and so to pinch somewhat out of their bellies, to save to buy clothes for their backs. And so accordingly they concluded to do; and by the favour that God gave them in the sight of the people, by alleging the innocency of their cause, and the extremity of their present condition, having not the least ability to help or relieve themselves, they consented to give them two measures of rice a day each man; one of which is as much as any man can eat in a day, so that the other was to serve for advance towards clothes; for, besides rice, they gave them to eat with it salt, pepper, limes, herbs, pumpkins, cocoa-nuts, flesh a little: these and such like things were their constant fare.

Their fare.

What employment they afterwards followed.

And thus they made a shift to live for some years, until some of them had an insight in knitting caps, by whom all afterwards learned, and it proved to be the chief means and help we all had to relieve our wants. The ordinary price we sold these caps for, was ninepence a piece in value English money, the thread standing us in about threepence; but at length, we plying hard our new learned trade, caps began to abound, and trading grew dead, so that we could not sell them at the former price; which brought several of our nation to great want.

How the English domineered.

The English began now to pluck up their hearts; and, though they were entered into a new condition, they kept their old spirits, especially considering they were the king's men, and quartered by his special order upon the people. When they had obtained to have their allowance raw, if any brought them not their full due, they would go in and plunder their houses of such goods as they found there, and keep them, until they came and brought them their complete allowance to redeem their goods back again.

What satisfaction one of them received from a potter.

Some of our Englishmen have proceeded further yet. One for example went to buy pots of a potter; who, because he would not let him have them at his own price, fell to quarrel, in which the Englishman met with some blows, which he complained of to the magistrate, as being a person that belonged unto the king, and therefore claimed better usage. And the magistrate condemned the potter as guilty in lifting up his hand against him, and sent some of his soldiers to bind him, and then bade the Englishman go and content himself, by paying him in the same coin again, as he had served our countryman, which he did until he was satisfied; and, moreover, ordered him to take the pots he came to buy, and pay nothing. But the law was not so satisfied neither, for the soldiers laid on many blows besides.

A scuffle between the English and natives.

Another time at a certain feast, as they were drinking and wanting wine, they sent money to buy more; but the seller refused to give it them for their money, which they took so heinously, that they unanimously concluded to go and take it by force. Away they went each man with his staff in his hand, and entered the house, and began to drink; which the people not liking of, gathered their forces together, and by blows began to resist them. But the Englishmen bravely behaved themselves, and broke several of their pates; who, with the blood about their ears, went to the city to complain to the great men.

They demanded of them—"If they had ever sold them wine before?" They answered, "Yes." They asked them again, "Why then did they refuse to sell them now?" And that they were well served by the English for denying them drink for their money; and so sent them away laughing at them. Our men got two or three black and blue blows, but they came home with their bellies full of drink for their pains.

The author after a year sees his countrymen

But to return unto myself. It was a full year after my father died, before I had sight of any of my countrymen and fellow-prisoners. Then John Gregory, with much ado, obtained leave to come and see me, which did exceedingly rejoice me; for a great satisfaction it was, both to see a countryman, and also to hear of the welfare of the rest. But he could not be permitted to stay with me above one day. Until then, I knew not punctually where the rest of my countrymen were; but having heard that they were within a day's journey of me, I never ceased importuning the people of the town where I dwelt, to let me go and see them; which, though very loth, yet at last they granted. Being arrived at the nearest Englishman's house, I was joyfully received, and the next day he went and called some of the rest of our countrymen that were near; so that there were some seven or eight of us met together.

Their conference and entertainment.

We gave God thanks for his great mercies towards us, being then, as we did confess, in a far better condition than we could have expected. They were now no more like the prisoners I left them; but were become house-keepers, and knitters of caps, and had changed their habit from breeches to clouts, like the Chingulays. They entertained me with very good cheer in their houses, beyond what I did expect.

He consults with his countrymen for a future livelihood.

My money at the same time almost gone, and clothes in the same condition, it was high time for me now to take some course in hand to get more; therefore I took some advice with them about knitting, my boy having skill therein. Likewise they advised me to take my victuals raw, wherein they found great profit. For all this while, here being no signs of releasing us, it concerned me now to bethink myself how I should live for the future; for neither had I, any more than my countrymen, any allowance for clothes, but victuals only.

Having stayed here some two or three days, we did take leave of one another, hoping to see one another oftener, since now we knew each other's habitations; and I departed to my house, having a keeper with me.

The difficulty he met with of having raw rice.

By this time I began to speak the language of the country, whereby I was enabled the better to speak my mind unto the people that brought me my victuals, which was henceforward not to boil my rice, but to bring it raw, according to the quantity that the other Englishmen had. This occasioned a great deal of disputing and reasoning between us. They alleged, "That I was not as they, being the captain's son, and they but his servants; and therefore, that it was ordered by the great men at court, that my victuals should be daily brought unto me, whereas they went always from house to house for theirs; neither was it fitting for me," they said, "to employ myself in such an inferior office to dress my own meat, being a man that the king had notice of by name, and very suddenly, before I should be aware of it, would send for me into his presence, where I should be highly promoted to some place of honour." In the mean time, they told me, as pretending to give me good counsel, "that it was more for my credit and repute to have my provisions brought unto me ready dressed, as they were before."

He reasons with the people about his allowance.

Although I was yet but a novice in the country, and knew not much of the people, yet plain reason told me, that it was not so much for my good and credit that they pleaded, as for their own benefit: wherefore I returned them this answer—"That if, as they said, I was greater in quality than the rest, and so held in their estimation, it would be but reason to demand a greater allowance; whereas, I desired no more than the other Englishmen had; and, as for the toil and trouble of dressing of it, that would be none to me, for my boy had nothing else to do." And then I alleged several inconveniencies in bringing my victuals ready boiled; as first, that it was not dressed according to my diet, and many times not brought in due season, so that I could not eat when I was an hungry; and the last and chief reason of all was, that I might save a little to serve my necessity of clothing; and rather than want clothes for my back, I must pinch a little out of my belly, and so both go share and share alike. And so at length, thanks be to God, I obtained, though with much ado, to get two measures of rice per day for myself, and one for my boy; also cocoa-nuts, pumpkins, herbs, limes, and such like, enough, besides pepper and salt: and sometimes hens, eggs, or flesh—rice being the main thing they stand upon; for other things they refuse not to give what they have.

He builds him a house

Now having settled all business about my allowance, my next concern was to look after a house more convenient; for my present one was too small to dress my victuals in, and to sleep in too. Thereabouts was a garden of cocoa-nut trees, belonging unto the king—a pleasant situation; this place I made choice of to build me a house in, and discovering my desire to the people, they consented, and came and built it for me; but, before it was finished, their occasions called them away; but my boy and I made an end of it, and whitened the walls with lime, according to my own country fashion; but in doing this I committed a capital offence; for none may white their houses with lime, that being peculiar to royal houses and temples. But being a stranger nothing was made of it, because I did it in ignorance; had it been a native that had so done, it is most probable it would have cost him his head, or at least a great fine.

Being settled in my new house, I began to keep hogs and hens; which, by God's blessing, thrived very well with me, and were a great help unto me. I had also a great benefit by living in this garden: for all the cocoa-nuts that fell down they gave me, which afforded me oil to burn in the lamp, and also to fry my meat in; which oil, being new, is but little inferior to this country butter. Now I learned to knit caps, which skill I quickly attained unto; and, by God's blessing upon the same, I obtained great help and relief thereby. He follows business and thrives.

In this manner we all lived, seeing but very little sign that we might build upon, to look for liberty. The chief of our hopes was, that in process of time, when we were better acquainted, we might run away; which some of our people attempted to do too soon, before they knew well which way to go, and were taken by the inhabitants: for it is the custom of the Chingulays to suspect all white people they meet travelling in the country, to be runaways, and to examine them; and, if they cannot give satisfactory answers, they will lay hold of them, Some attempted running away, but were catched.

and carry them back unto the city; where they will keep them prisoners under a guard of soldiers, in an open house like a barn, with a little victuals sometimes, and sometimes with none at all; where they have no other remedy to help themselves but begging: and in this condition they may lie perhaps for their life time, being so kept for a spectacle unto the people.

Little encouragement for those that bring back runaways.

Though the common way whereby the king gratifies such as catch runaways and bring them up, is not over acceptable; for they are appointed to feed and watch them until he calls for them to be brought before him, at which time his promise is bountifully to reward them. But these promises I never knew performed; neither doth he perhaps ever think of it after. For when the king is made acquainted with the matter, the men that have brought up the prisoner, are in a manner as bad prisoners themselves, not daring to go home to their houses without his leave, but there they must remain. After some years stay, the common manner is, for them to give a fee to the governor of the country, and he will license them to go home, which they must be contented with, instead of the promised reward.

CHAP. IV.

Concerning some other Englishmen detained in that Country.

IN the same captivity with ourselves, on this Island, was another company of Englishmen, who were taken about a year and an half before us, viz. in the year 1758: they were thirteen in number, whose numbers were as follow; viz. Mr. William Vassal, John Merginson, Thomas March ,Thomas Kirby, Rich. Jelf, Gamaliel Gardiner, William Day, Thomas Stapleton, Henry Man, Hugh Smart, Daniel Holstein, an Hamburgher, James Gony, and Henry Bingham. The occasion of their seizure was thus:—the ship these men belonged unto was the Persia merchant, Captain Francis Johnson, commander, which was lost upon the Maldives Islands, but they escaped in their boats; and, passing along by this land, went on shore to recruit and buy provisions, and so were taken. The Chingulays that took them, plundered them of what they had, except their clothes. Yet one of them, John Merginson by name, having cunningly hid his money about him, saved it from the heathen, but from his own countrymen he could not; some of whom knowing of it, set upon him and robbed him of it: but it did them little good, for the king hearing of it, sent and robbed the robbers.

The Persia merchant's men captives before us.

Plundered by the natives.

These men, thus seized, were carried up before the king; of whom he demanded, whether the English had wars with the

Brought up to the king.

Hollanders? they answered, No; or if the English could beat them? they answered—They could, and had done it lately. Then he gave order to give them all some clothes, and to Mr. William Vassal, being the chief of them, a double portion; and out of them made choice of two lads, whom afterwards he sent, and took into his court. Their honours and their ends we shall see by and bye. They were all placed in the city of Candy, and each of them had a new mat given him to sleep on, and their diet was victuals dressed and brought them twice a day from the king's own palace: they had clothes also distributed to them at another time.

So that these men had the advantage of us; for we neither had mats, nor clothes, nor had the honour of being ever brought into the king's presence.

They hoped to obtain liberty, but were mistaken.

This civil reception, upon the first coming up into the city, put these Persia merchantmen in hope, that the king would give them their liberty. There was at that time an old Portuguese father, Padre Vergonse by name, living in the city; with him they discoursed concerning the probability of their liberty, and that the favours the king had shewn them, seemed to be good signs of it; but he told them the plain truth—that it was not customary there to release white men: for saying which, they railed at him, calling him Popish dog, and Jesuitical rogue, supposing he spoke as he wished it might be; but afterward, to their grief, they found it to be true as he told them.

A ridiculous action of these men.

Their entertainment was excellently good, according to the poor condition of the country, but they thought it otherwise, very mean, and not according to the king's order: therefore, that the king might be informed how they were abused, each man took the limb of a hen in his hand, and marched rank and file in order through the streets with it in their hands to the court, as a sign to the great men, whereby they might see how ill they were served; thinking hereby the king might come to hear of their misusage, and so they might have order to be fed better afterwards. But this proved sport to the noblemen, who well knew the fare of the country, laughing at their ignorance, to complain where they had so little cause; and indeed afterwards, they themselves laughed at this action of theirs, and were half ashamed of it, when they came to a better understanding of the nature of the country's diet.

Yet notwithstanding being not used to such short commons of flesh, though they had rice in abundance, and having no money to buy more, they had a desire to kill some cows, that they might eat their bellies full of beef; but made it somewhat a point of conscience, whether it might be lawful or not, to take them without leave: upon which they apply themselves to the old father aforesaid, desiring him to solve this case of conscience, who was very ready to give them a dispensation; and told them, "That forasmuch as the Chingulays were their enemies, and had taken their bodies, it was very lawful for them to satisfy their bodies with their goods." And the better to animate them in this design, bid them bring him a piece, that he might partake with them. So being encouraged by the old father, they went on boldly in their intended business.

They had a mind to beef, and how they got it.

Now if you would have an account of the metal and manfulness of these men, as you have already had a taste of ours, take this passage. The jack fruit the king's officers often gather,

A passage of the courage of the men.

wheresoever it grows, and give to the king's elephants, and they may gather it in any man's grounds, without the owner's leave; being for the king's use. Now these Englishmen were appointed to dwell in a house, that formerly belonged unto a nobleman, whom the king had cut off, and seized upon it. In the ground belonging to this house stood a jack tree, full of fruit: some of the king's men came thither to gather some of them to feed the elephants; but, although the English had free liberty to gather what they could eat, or desire, yet they would permit none but themselves to meddle with them, but took the officers by the shoulders, and turned them out of the garden; although there were more a great many than they could tell what to do with. The great men were so civil, that, notwithstanding this affront, they laid no punishment upon them: but the event of this was, that a few days after they were removed from this house to another, where was a garden, but no trees in it; and, because they would not allow the king a few, they lost all themselves.

Two of his company taken into court.

I mentioned before, two lads of this company, whom the king chose out of for his own service; their names were Hugh Smart, and Henry Man. These being taken into his court, obtained great favour and honour from him, as to be always in his presence; and very often he would kindly and familiarly talk with them concerning their country, what it afforded, and of their king and his strength for war: thus they lived in his favour for some time.

The one out of favour; his end.

Till at length Hugh Smart having a desire to hear news concerning England, privately got to the speech of a Dutch ambassador; of which the king had notice, but would not believe it; supposing the information was given him out of envy to his favourite, but commanded privately to watch him, and if he went again, to catch him there; which he, not being aware of, went again, and was catched: at which, the king was very angry; for he allows none to come to the speech of ambassadors, much less one that served in his presence, and heard and saw all that passed in court. But yet the king dealt very favourably with him; for had it been a Chingulay, there is nothing more sure, than that he should have died for it. But this Englishman's punishment was only to be sent away and kept a prisoner in the mountains without chains, and ordered him to be well used there; where indeed he lived better content than in the king's palace. He took a wife here, and had one son by her, and afterwards died by a mischance; which was thus—as he was gathering a jack from the tree by a crook, it fell down upon his side, and bruised him so, that it killed him.

Henry Man, the other, yet remained in favour, and was promoted to be chief over all the king's servants that attended on him in his palace. It happened one day that he broke one of the king's China dishes, which made him so sore afraid, that he fled for sanctuary into a vehar, a temple where the chief priests always dwell, and hold their consultations. This did not a little displease the king; this act of his supposing him to be of opinion that those priests were able to secure him against the king's displeasure. However he, shewing reverence to their order, would not violently fetch him from thence, but sent a kind message to the Englishman, bidding him not to be afraid for so small a matter as a dish; (and it is probable had he not added this fault, he might have escaped without punishment) and that he should come and act in his place as formerly. At which message he came forth; and immediately as the king had given

The other out of favour, and lamentable death.

order, they took hold of him, and bound his arms above the elbows behind, which is their fashion of binding men: in which manner he lay all that night, being bound so hard, that his arms swelled, and the ropes cut through the flesh into the bones. The next day, the king commanded a nobleman to loose the ropes off his arms, and put chains on his legs, and keep him in his house, and there feed him and cure him.

Thus he lay some six months, and was cured, but had no strength in his arms, and then was taken into his office again, and had as much favour from the king as before; who seemed much to lament him for his folly, thus to procure his own ruin.

Not long after, he again offended the king; which as it is reported was thus. A Portuguese had been sent for to the city, to be employed in the king's service; to which service he had no stomach at all, and was greatly afraid of, as he justly might be. For the avoiding therefore of it, he sends a letter to this English courtier, wherein he entreated him to use his interest to excuse him to the king. The Englishman could not read the letter, being writ in the Portuguese tongue, but gave it to another to read; which, when he knew the contents of, thought it not safe for him to meddle in that business, and so concealed the letter. The person to whom the Englishman had given it to read, some time after informed the king thereof: whereupon both the Portuguese that sent the letter, and the Englishman to whom it was sent, and the third person that read it, because he informed no sooner, were all three at one time, and in one place, torn in pieces by elephants.

After this execution, the king, supposing that we might be

either discontented in ourselves, or discountenanced by the people of the land, sent special order to all parts where we dwelt, that we should be of good cheer, and not be discouraged, neither abused by the natives.

The king sends special order concerning their good usage.

Thus jealous is the king of letters, and allows none to come or go. We have seen how dear it cost poor Henry Man;—Mr. William Vassal, another of the Persia-merchant men, was therefore more wary of some letters he had, and came off better.

This man had received several letters, and it was known abroad that he had; which he fearing lest the king should hear of, thought it most convenient and safe to go to the court and present them himself, that so he might plead in his own defence to the king, which he did. He acknowledged to him that he had received letters, and that they came to his hands a pretty while ago, but withal pretended excuses and reasons to clear himself;—as first, "That when he received them, he knew not that it was against the law and manner of the country: and when he did know, he took council of a Portuguese priest, who was now dead, being old, and as he thought well-experienced in the country. But he advised him to defer a while the carrying them unto the king until a more convenient season. After this he did attempt, he said, to bring them unto the king, but could not be permitted to have entrance through the watches; so that until now he could not have opportunity to present them."

Mr. Vassal's prudence upon the receipt of letters.

The king at the hearing hereof, seemed not to be displeased in the least, but bid him read them, which he did in the English

The king bids him read his letters.

language, as they were writ; and the king sat very attentive, as if he had understood every word. After they were read, the king gave Vassal a letter he had intercepted, sent to us from Sir Edward Winter, then agent at Fort St. George, and asked the news and contents thereof, which Mr. Vassal informed him at large of. It was concerning the victory we had gained over the Dutch, when Obdam, Admiral of Holland, was slain, and concerning the number of our ships in that fight, being there specified to be an hundred and fifty sail. The king enquired much after the number of guns and men they carried. The number of men he computed to be, one ship with another, about three hundred per ship. At that rate, the king demanded of him, how many that was in all, which Mr. Vassal went about to cast up in the sand with his finger; but, before he had made his figures, the king had done it by head, and bid him desist, saying it was 45,000.

The king pleased to hear of England's victory over Holland.

This news of the Hollanders overthrow, and the English victory, much delighted the king, and he enquired into it very particularly. Then the king pretended he would send a letter to the English nation, and bade Mr. Vassal inform him of a trusty bearer, which he was very forward to do, and named one of the best which he had made trial of. One of the great men there present, objected against him, saying, he was insufficient, and asked him if he knew no other: at which Vassal suspected their design, which was, to learn who had brought those letters to him, and so framed his answer accordingly, which was, that he knew no other.

Private discourse between the king and Vassal.

There was much other discourse passed between the king and him at this time, in the Portuguese tongue; which, what it was,

I could never get out of him, the king having commanded him to keep it secret; and he saith, he hath sworn to himself not to divulge it, till he is out of the king's hands. At parting, the king told him for secrecy, he would send him home privately, or otherwise he would have dismissed him with drums and honour. But after this the king never sent for him again, and the man that he named as fit and able to carry the king's letter, was sent away prisoner to be kept in chains in the country. It is supposed that they concluded him to have been the man that brought Vassal his letters. And thus much of the captivity and condition of the Persia-merchant men.

CHAP. V.

Concerning the Means that were used for our Deliverance, and what happened to us in the Rebellion, and how we were settled afterwards.

Means made to the king for our liberty.

ALL of us in this manner remained until the year 1664; at which time arrived a letter, on our behalf to the king, from the Right Worshipful Sir Edward Winter, governor of Fort St. George, and agent there. The Dutch ambassador also at that time, by a commission from the governor of Columba, treated with the king for us. With Sir Edward's message the king was much pleased, and with the Dutch's mediation so prevailed with, that he promised he would send us away.

Upon which they all met at the city.

Upon this, he commanded us all to be brought to the city; whither when we came, we were very joyful not only upon the hopes of our liberty, but also upon the sight of one another; for several of us had not seen the others since we were first parted. Here also we met with the Persia-merchant men, whom, until this time we had not seen; so that we were nine and twenty English in all.

Word sent them from the court, that they had their liberty.

Some few days after our arrival at the city, we were all called to the court; at which time, standing all of us in one of the palace court-yards, the nobles, by command from the king, came forth and told us, that it was His Majesty's pleasure to grant unto us our liberty, and to send us home to our country, and that we should not any more look upon ourselves as prisoners or detained men, at which we bowed our heads and thanked His Majesty. They told us, moreover, that the king was intended to send us either with the Dutch ambassador, or by the boat which Sir Edward Winter had sent; and that it was His Majesty's good will to grant us our choice. We humbly referred it to His Majesty's pleasure; they answered; His Majesty could and would do his pleasure, but his will was to know our minds. After a short consultation we answered, since it was His Majesty's pleasure to grant us our choice, with many thanks and obeisance, we chose to go with the Dutch ambassador, fearing the boat's insufficiency, she having, as we were well sensible, laid there a great while; and, if we had chosen the boat, the danger of going that way might have served them for a put off to us, and a plea to detain us still out of care of us. And again, had we refused the ambassador's kindness at this time, for the future, if these things succeeded not with us now, we could never have expected any more aid or friendship from that nation.

In the next place, they told us, it was the king's pleasure to let us understand, that all those that were willing to stay and serve His Majesty should have very great rewards, as towns, monies, slaves, and places of honour, conferred upon them; which all in general refused.

All in general refuse the king's service.

Then we were bidden to absent while they returned our answers to the king. By and by there came order to call us in one at a time, where the former promises were repeated to every one of us of great favours, honours, and rewards, from the king, to those that were willing to stay with him: and after each one had given his answer, he was sent into a corner in the court, and then another called, and so all round, one after another; they inquiring particularly concerning each man's trade and office—handicrafts-men and trumpeters being most desired by the king. We being thus particularly examined again, there was not one of us was tempted by the king's rewards, but all in general refused the king's honourable employment, choosing rather to go to our native country: by which we purchased the king's displeasure.

Commanded still to wait at the palace, during which, a rebellion breaks out.

After this they told us we must wait at the palace gate daily; it being the king's pleasure, that we should make our personal appearance before him: in this manner we waited many days. At length happened a thing which he least suspected; viz. a general rebellion of his people against him, who assaulted his palace in the night; but their hearts failed them, daring not to enter into the apartment where his person was; for if they had had courage enough, they might have taken him there: for he stayed in his palace until the morninig, and then fled into the mountains, and escaped their hands; but more through their cowardliness than his valour. This rebellion I have related at large in the second part; whither he that desires to know more of it may have recourse: only I shall mention here a few things concerning ourselves, who were gotten into the midst of these broils and combustions, being all of us now waiting upon the king in the city.

They are in the midst of it, and in great danger.

It was a great and marvellous mercy of Almighty God, to bring us safe through these dangers; for it so happened all along that we were in the very midst. Before they gave the assault on the king's palace, they were consulting to lay hands on us, fearing lest we might be prejudicial to their business, in joining to the help and assistance of the king against them; for, though we were but few in comparison, yet the name of white men was somewhat dreadful to them. Whereupon at first their counsels were to cut us off; but others among them advised that it would be better to let us alone; for that we being ignorant of their designs, as indeed we were, and at quiet in our several lodgings, could not be provided to hurt or endanger them; but otherwise if they should lay hands on us, it would certainly come to the king's ears and alarm him, and then all would be frustrated and overthrown. This some of their own party have related to us since. These counsels were not given out of any secret good will any of them bore to us (as I believe), but proceeded from the over-ruling hand of God, who put those things into their hearts for our safety and preservation. The people of the city, whence the king fled, ran away also, leaving their houses and goods behind them; where we found good prey and plunder, being permitted to ransack the houses of all such as were fled away with the king.

The rebels having driven away the king, and marching to the city of Candy to the prince, carried us along with them; the chief of their party telling us, that we should now be of good cheer, for what they had done upon very good advisement they had done, the king's ill government having given an occasion to it; who went about to destroy both them and their country, and particularly insisted upon such things as might be most plausible to strangers; such as keeping ambassadors, discouraging trade, detaining of foreigners that come upon his land, besides his cruelties towards themselves that were his natural people. All

The rebels take the English with them.

which, they told us, they had been informed, was contrary to the government of other countries; and now so soon as their business was settled, they assured us, they would detain none that were minded to go to their own countries.

They design to engage the English with them.

Being now at Candy, on Christmas-day of all the days in the year, they sent to call us to the court, and gave us some money and clothes first, to make us the more willing to take arms, which they intended them to deliver unto us, and to go with them upon a design, to fall upon the old king in the place whither he was fled. But in the very interim of time, God being merciful unto us, the prince with his aunt fled; which so amazed and discouraged them, that the money and clothes which they were distributing to us, and other strangers, to gain us over to them, they scattered about the court, and fled themselves: and now followed nothing but cutting one another's throats, to make themselves appear the more loyal subjects, and make amends for their former rebellion.

They resolve neither to meddle or make.

We, for our parts, little thinking in what danger we were, fell in to scramble among the rest, to get what we could of the monies that were strewed about, being then in great necessity and want; for the allowance which formerly we had, was in this disturbance lost; and so we remained without it for some three months, the want of which this money did help to supply. Having gotten what we could at the court, we made way to get out of the hurly burly to our lodgings; intending, as we were strangers, and prisoners, neither to meddle, nor make, on the one side or the other; being well satisfied, if God would but permit us quietly to sit, and eat such a Christmas dinner together as he had prepared for us.

For our parts we had no other dealings with the rebels, than to desire them to permit us to go to our native country, which liberty they promised we should not want long: but, being sent for by them to the court, we durst not but go, and they giving us such things as we wanted, we could not refuse to take them: but the day being turned, put us into great fear, doubting how the king would take it at our hands, from whom we knew this could not be hid.

The day being turned they fear the king.

Into our houses we got safely; but no sooner were we there, but immediately we were called again by a great man, who had drawn out his men, and stood in the field. This man we thought had been one of the rebels, who, to secure himself upon this change, had intended to run away down to Columbo, to the Dutch; which made us repair to him the more cheerfully, leaving our meat a roasting on the spit. But it proved otherwise; for no sooner had he gotten us unto him, but he proclaimed himself for the old king, and forthwith he and his company taking us with him, marched away to fight or seize the rebels, but meeting none, went into the city, and there dismissed us, saying, "He would acquaint the king, how willing and ready we were to fight for him, if need had required," although, God knows, it was the least of our thoughts and intents; yet God brought it to pass for our good, for when the king was informed of what we had received of the rebels, this piece of good service that we had done, or rather were supposed to have done, was also told unto him; at the hearing of which, himself justified us to be innocent, saying, "Since my absence, who was there that would give them victuals? And, "It was mere want that made them to take what they did." Thus the words of the king's own mouth

But he justifies them.

acquitted us; and, when the sword devoured on every side, yet, by the providence of God, not one hair of our heads perished.

They are driven to beg in the highways.

The tumults being appeased, and the rebellion vanished, the king was settled in his throne again. And all this happened in five days time. We were now greatly necessitated for food, and wanted some fresh orders from the king's mouth for our future subsistence; so that having no other remedy, we were fain to go and lay in the high way that leads to the city a begging; for the people would not let us go any nearer towards the king, as we would have done. There therefore we lay, that the king might come to the knowledge of us, and give command for our allowance again; by which means we obtained our purpose: for, having laid there some two months, the king was pleased to appoint our quarters in the country as formerly, not mentioning a word of sending us away, as he had made us believe before the rebellion.

Sent into new quarters there, and their pensions settled again.

Now we were all sent away indeed, but not into our own country, but into new quarters; which being God would have to be no better, we were glad it was so well, being sore a weary of laying in this manner. For some three months time we had no manner of allowance. We were all now placed one in a town as formerly, together with the Persia-merchant men also, who hitherto had lived in the city of Candy, and had their provisions brought them out of the king's palace ready dressed. These were now sent away with us into the country; and as strict a charge was given for our good entertainment as before.

Fall to trading, and have more freedom.

We were thus dispersed about the towns here one and there another, for the more convenient receiving our allowance, and for the greater ease of the people. And now we were far better to pass than heretofore, having the language, and being acquainted with the manners and customs of the people, and had the same proportion of victuals, and the like respect as formerly. And now they fall into employment as they please, either husbandry or merchandizing, or knitting of caps, being altogether free to do what they will themselves, and go where they will, excepting running away ; and, for that end, we are not permitted to go down to the sea, but we may travel all about the country, and no man regards us ; for, though the people some of the first years of our captivity would scarcely let us go any whither, and had an eye upon us afterwards; yet, in process of time, all their suspicions of our going away wore off; especially when several of the English had built them houses, and others had taken them wives, by whom they had children, to the number of eighteen living, when I came away.

Having said all this in general of the English people there, I will now continue a further account of myself.

CHAP. VI.

A Continuation of the Author's Condition after the Rebellion. Purchaseth a Piece of Land.

The author at his new quarters builds him another house.

MY hap was to be quartered in a country called Handapon-down, lying to the westward of the city of Candy; which place liked me very well, being much nearer to the sea than where I dwelt before, which gave me some probable hopes, that in time I might chance to make an escape. But in the mean time to free myself from the suspicion of the people, who watched me by night and by day, had an eye to all my actions, I went to work with the help of some of my neighbours, to build me another house upon the bank of a river, and entrenched it round with a ditch, and planted an hedge, and so began to settle myself, and followed my business in knitting, and going about the countries a trading, seeming to be very well contented in this condition.

The people counsel him to marry.

Lying so long at the city without allowance, I had spent all to some seven shillings, which served me for a stock to set up again in these new quarters: and, by the blessing of my most gracious God, which never failed me in all my undertakings, I soon came to be well furnished with what that country afforded, insomuch that my neighbours and townsmen no more suspected my running away, but earnestly advised me to marry, saying, "It would be an ease and help to me;" knowing that I then dressed my victuals myself, having turned my boy to seek his fortune when we were at the city. They urged also, "That it was not convenient for a young man as I was to live so solitarily alone in a house; and, if it should so come to pass, that the king should send me hereafter to my own country, their manner of marriage," they said, "was not like ours; and I might without any offence discharge my wife and go away."

I seemed not altogether to slight their counsel, that they might the less suspect I had any thoughts of mine own country; but told them—"That as yet I was not sufficiently stocked, and also, that I would look for one that I could love;" though in my heart I never purposed any such matter; but, on the contrary, did heartily abhor all thoughts tending that way. Which he seemed to listen to.

In this place I lived two years; and all that time could not get one likely occasion of running for it; for I thought it better to forbear running too great a hazard by being over-hasty to escape, than to deprive myself of all hopes for the future, when time and experience would be a great help to me. Here he lived two years.

In the year 1766, the Hollanders came up and built a fort just below me—there being but a ridge of mountains between them and me; but though so near, I could not come to them, a watch being kept at every passage. The king sent down against them two great commanders with their armies; but, being not strong enough to expel them, they lay in these watches to stop them from coming up higher.—The name of this fort was called Arrandery; which, although they could not prevent the Dutch from building at that time, yet, some years after, when they were not aware, they fell upon it and took it; and brought A fort built near him, but afterward taken by the king all the people of it up to Candy, where those that remained alive of them were when I came from thence.

He and three more removed thence.

In this country of Hotteracourly, where the Dutch had built this fort, were four Englishmen placed, whereof I was one. All whom the king immediately upon the news of the Dutch's invasion, sent order to bring up out of the danger of the war into Candy Uda, fearing that which we were indeed intended to do—viz. to run away.

This invasion happening so unexpectedly, and our removal so sudden, I was forced to leave behind me that little estate which God had given me, lying scattered abroad in betel-nuts, the great commodity of that country which I was then parting from: and much ado I had to get my clothes brought along with me, the enemies, as they called them, but my friends, being so near. And thus was I carried out of the country as poor as I came into it, leaving all the fruits of my labour and industry behind me; which called to my remembrance the words of Job: —" Naked came I into this world, and naked shall I return: God gave, and God hath taken away, blessed be the name of the Lord."

Settled in a dismal place.

We all four were brought up together into a town on the top of a mountain, called Laggendenny; where I, and my dear friend and fellow prisoner, and fellow batchelor, Mr. John Loveland, lived together in one house. For, by this time, not many of our people were as we, that is, single men; but, seeing so little hopes, despaired of their liberty, and had taken wives or bedfellows.

At our first coming into this town, we were very much dismayed, it being one of the most dismal places that I have seen upon that land. It stands alone upon the top of a mountain, and no other town near it, and not above four or five houses in it; and, oftentimes into this town did the king use to send such malefactors as he was minded suddenly to cut off. Upon these accounts, our being brought to this place could not but scare us; and the more, because it was the king's special order and command to place us in this very town.

A comfortable message from the king concerning us.

But this our trouble and dejection (thanks be to God) lasted but a day. For the king seemed to apprehend into what a fit of fear and sorrow this our remove would cast us, and to be sensible how sadly we must needs take it, to change a sweet and pleasant country, such as Handapondown and the country adjacent was, for this most sad and dismal mountain. And, therefore, the next day came a comfortable message from the king's own mouth, sent by no less man than he who had the chief power and command over those people who were appointed to give us our victuals where we were. This message, which, as he said himself, he was ordered by the king to deliver to the people in our hearing, was this:—that they should not think that we were malefactors, that is, such who, having incurred the king's displeasure, were sent to be kept prisoners there—but men whom his majesty did highly esteem, and meant to promote to great honour in his service, and that they should respect us as such, and entertain us accordingly. And if their ability would not reach thereunto, it was the king's order, he said, to bid them sell their cattle and goods; and, when that was done, their wives and children, rather than we should want of our due allowance, which he ordered should be as formerly we used to have; and if we had not houses thatched, and sufficient for us to dwell in, he said we should change, and take theirs.

Placed there to punish the people for a crime.

This kind order from the king coming so suddenly, did not a little comfort and encourage us; for then we did perceive the king's purpose and intent in placing us in those remote parts was not to punish us, but them; that we might be his instruments to plague and take revenge of that people, who, it seems, had plundered the king's palace in the time of the late rebellion, when he left it and fled; for this town lies near unto the same; and their office lying about the court, they had the fairer opportunity of plundering it. For the service they are to perform to the king, is, to carry his pallanquin when he pleaseth to ride therein, and also to bring milk every morning to the court, being keepers of the king's cattle.

Weary of this place

In this town we remained some three years, by which time we were grown quite weary of the place, and the place and people also grown weary of us, who were but troublesome guests to them; for, having such great authority given us over them, we would not lose it; and, being four of us in call one of another, we would not permit or suffer them to domineer over us. Being thus tired with one another's company, and the king's order being of an old date, we used all means we could to clear ourselves of one another; often repairing unto the court to seek to obtain a license that we might be removed and placed any where else: but there was none that durst grant it, because it was the king's peculiar command, and special appointment, that we must abide in that very town.

During the time of our stay here, we had our victuals brought us in good order and due season; the inhabitants having such a charge given them by their governor, and he from the king, durst not do otherwise: so that we had but little to do, only to dress and eat, and sit down to knit.

I had used the utmost of my skill and endeavour to get a licence to go down to my former quarters, all things being now pretty well settled, hoping that I might recover some of my old debts; but by no means could I obtain it. The denial of so reasonable a desire put me upon taking leave. I was well acquainted with the way, but yet I hired a man to go with me, without which I could not get through the watches; for, although I was the master, and he the man, yet when we came into the watches, he was the keeper, and I the prisoner: and by this means we passed without being suspected.

By a piece of craft he gets down to his old quarters.

Being come into my old quarters, by pretending that this man was sent down from the magistrate to see that my debts and demands might be duly paid and discharged, I chanced to recover some of them, and the rest gave over for lost; for I never more looked after them. And so I began the world anew, and by the blessing of God was again pretty well recruited before I left this town.

Began the world anew the third time.

In the time of my residence here, I chanced to hear of a small piece of land that was to be sold, about which I made very diligent inquiry; for, although I was sore a weary of living in this town, yet I could not get out of it, not having other new quarters appointed me, unless I could provide a place for myself to remove to; which now God had put into my hand. As for the king's command, I dreaded it not much, having

Plots to remove himself.

found by observation, that the king's orders wear away by time, and the neglect of them comes at last to be unregarded. However, I was resolved to put it to a hazard, come what will.

Is encouraged to buy a piece of land.

Although I had been now some seven or eight years in this land, and by this time came to know pretty well the customs and constitutions of the nation, yet I would not trust my own knowledge, but to prevent the worst, I went to the governor of that same country where the land lay, to desire his advice, whether or no I might lawfully buy that small piece of land. He inquired whose, and what land it was? I informed him, that it had been formerly dedicated to a priest, and he, at his death, had left it to his grandson, who, for want, was forced to sell it. Understanding this, the governor approved of the business, and encouraged me to buy it, saying, that such kinds of lands only were lawful here to be bought and sold, and that this was not in the least litigious.

The situation and condition of it.

Having gotten both his consent and advice, I went on cheerfully with my purchase. The place also liked me wonderous well; it being a point of land standing into a corn field, so that corn fields were on three sides of it, and just before my door a little corn ground belonging thereto, and very well watered. In the ground, besides eight cocoa-nut trees, there were all sorts of fruit trees the country afforded; but, it had been so long desolate, that it was all overgrown with bushes, and no sign of a house therein.

Buys it.

The price of this land was five-and-twenty larees, that is, five dollars, a great sum of money in the account of this country: yet, thanks be to God, who had so far enabled me after my late and great loss, that I was strong enough to lay this down. The terms of purchase being concluded on between us, a writing was made upon a leaf after that country manner, witnessed by seven or eight men of the best quality in the town; which was delivered to me, and I paid the money, and then took possession of the land:—it lies some ten miles to the southward of the city of Candy, in the county of Oudaneur, in the town of Elledat.

Now I went about building an house upon my land, and was assisted by three of my countrymen that dwelt near by, Roger Gold, Ralph Knight, and Stephen Rutland, and in a short time we finished it. The country people were all well pleased to see us thus busy ourselves about buying of land and building of houses, thinking it would tie our minds the faster to their country, and make us think the less upon our own. **Builds an house on it.**

Though I had built my new house, yet I durst not leave my old quarters in Laggendenny, but wait until a more convenient time fell out for that purpose; I went away, therefore, to my old home, and left my aforesaid three English neighbours to inhabit it in my absence. Not long after I found a fit season to be gone to my estate at Elledat; and, upon my going, the rest left the town also, and went and dwelt elsewhere, each one where he best liked: but, by this means we all lost a privilege which we had before; which was, that our victuals was brought unto us, and now we were forced to go and fetch them ourselves, the people alleging (true enough) that they were not bound to carry our provisions about the country after us. **Leaves Laggendenny.**

Being settled in my new house, I began to plant my ground

Settled at his new purchase, with three more living with him.

full of all sorts of fruit trees; and, by the blessing of God, all grew and prospered, and yielded me great plenty, and good increase, sufficient both for me and for those that dwelt with me. For the three Englishmen I left at my house, when I departed back to Laggendenny, still lived with me; we were all single men, and we agreed very well together, and were helpful to one another; and, for their help and assistance of me, I freely granted them liberty to use and enjoy whatsoever the ground afforded, as much as myself. And, with a joint consent it was concluded amongst us, that only single men and batchelors should dwell there, and such as would not be conformable to this present agreement, should depart and absent himself from our society, and also forfeit his right and claim to the forementioned privilege, that is, to be cut off from all benefit of whatsoever the trees and ground afforded.

I thought fit to make such a covenant, to exclude women from coming in amongst us, to prevent all strife and dissention, and to make all possible provision for the keeping up love and quietness among ourselves.

In this manner we four lived together some two years very lovingly and contentedly, not an ill word passing between us. We used to take turns in keeping at home, while the rest went forth about their business; for our house stood alone, and no neighbour near it, therefore we always left one within; the rest of the Englishmen lived round about us, some four or five miles distant, some more; so that we were, as it were, within reach of one another, which made us like our present situation the more.

Thus we lived upon the mountains, being round about us beset with watches, most of our people being now married: so that now all talk and suspicion of our running away was now laid aside; neither, indeed, was it scarce possible: the effect of which was, that now we could walk from one to the other, or where we would upon the mountains, no man molesting or disturbing us in the least: so that we began to go about a pedling, and trading in the country farther towards the northward, carrying our caps about to sell. Their freedom and trade.

By this time, two of our company, seeing but little hopes of liberty, thought it too hard a task thus to lead a single life, and married: which, when they had done, according to the former agreement, departed from us; so that our company was now reduced to two, viz. myself and Stephen Rutland, whose inclination and resolution was as stedfast as mine against marriage; and we parted not to the last, but came away together. His family reduced to two.

CHAP. VII.

A Return to the Rest of the English, with some further Accounts of them, and some further Discourse of the Author's Course of Life.

Confer together about the lawfulness of marrying with the native women.

LET us now make a visit to the rest of our countrymen, and see how they do. They, reckoning themselves in for their lives, in order to their future settlement, were generally disposed to marry: concerning which, we have had many and sundry disputes among ourselves; as particularly concerning the lawfulness of matching with heathens and idolators, and whether the Chingulays marriages were any better than living in whoredom; there being no Christian priests to join them together, and it being allowed by their laws to change their wives, and take others as often as they pleased. But these cases we solved for our own advantage, after this manner—That we were but flesh and blood, and that it is said, it is better to marry than to burn, and that as far as we could see, we were cut off from all marriages any where else, even for our life time; and therefore, that we must marry with these, or with none at all. And, when the people in scripture were forbidden to take wives of strangers, it was then when they might intermarry with their own people, and so no necessity lay upon them; and that when they could not, there are examples in the Old Testament upon record, that they took wives of the daughters of the lands wherein they dwelt. These reasons being urged, there was none among us, that could object ought against them, especially if those that were minded to marry women here, did take them for their wives during their lives, as some of them say, they do; and most of the women they marry are such as do profess themselves to be Christians.

As for mine own part, however lawful these marriages might be, yet I judged it far more convenient for me to abstain, and that it more redounded to my good; having always a reviving hope in me, that my God had not forsaken me, but according to his gracious promise to the Jews in the thirtieth chapter of Deuteronomy, and the beginning, "would turn my captivity, and bring me into the land of my fathers." These, and such like meditations, together with my prayers to God, kept me from that unequal yoke of unbelievers, which several of my countrymen and fellow prisoners put themselves under. He resolves upon a single life.

By this time our people having plied their business hard, had almost knit themselves out of work; and now caps were become a very dead commodity, which was the chief stay they had heretofore to trust to; so that now most of them betook themselves to other employments; some to husbandry, plowing ground, and sowing rice, and keeping cattle; others stilled rack to sell—others went about the country a trading: for that which one part of the land affords, is a good commodity to carry to another that wants it. And thus with the help of a little allowance, they make a shift to subsist. Most of their wives spin cotton yarn, which is a great help to them for clothing, and at spare times also knit. What employments they follow.

After this manner, by the blessing of God, our nation hath lived, and still doth, in as good fashion as any other people or The respect and credit they live in.

nation whatsoever, that are strangers here, or as any of the natives themselves, only the grandees and courtiers excepted. This I speak to the praise and glory of our God, who loves the stranger in giving him food and raiment, and that hath been pleased to give us favour and a good repute in the sight of our enemies. We cannot complain for want of justice, in any wrongs we have sustained by the people, or that our cause hath been discountenanced; but rather we have been favoured above the natives themselves.

A Chingulay punished for beating an Englishman.

One of our men happened to be beaten by his neighbour, at which we were all very much concerned, taking it as a reproach to our nation, and fearing it might embolden others to do the like by the rest of us: therefore with joint consent we all concluded to go to the court to complain, and to desire satisfaction from the adigar, which we did. Upon this the man who had beat the Englishman was summoned in to appear before him; who seeing so many of us there, and fearing the cause will go very hard with him, to make the judge his friend, gave him a bribe: he having received it, would have shifted off the punishment of the malefactor; but we, day after day, followed him from house to court, and from place to place, wherever he went, demanding justice and satisfaction for the wrong we received, shewing the black and blue blows upon the Englishman's shoulders to all the rest of the noblemen at court. He, fearing therefore, lest the king might be acquainted herewith, was forced, though much against his will, to clap the Chingulay in chains; in which condition after he got him, he released him not till besides the former fee he had given him another.

Lately was Richard Varnham taken into the king's service,

and held as honourable an employment as ever any Christian had in my time, being commander of nine hundred and seventy soldiers, and set over all the great guns; and, besides this, several towns were under him, a place of no less profit than honour. The king gave him an excellent silver sword and halberd, the like to which the king never gave to any white man in my time: but he had the good luck to die a natural death: for had not that prevented, in all probability he should have followed the two Englishmen that served him, spoken of before.

An Englishman preferred at court.

Some years since, some of our nation took up arms under the king; which happened upon this occasion:—The Hollanders had a small fort in the king's country, called Bibligom Fort. This the king minded to take and demolish, sent his army to besiege it; but being pretty strong, for there were about ninety Dutchmen in it, besides a good number of black soldiers, and four guns on each point one; being in this condition, it held out. Some of the great men informed the king of several Dutch runaways in his land, that might be trusted, not daring to turn again for fear of the gallows, who might help to reduce the fort; and that also there were white men of other nations that had wives and children, from whom they would not run—and these might do him good service. Unto this advice the king inclined.

The English serve the king in his wars.

Whereupon the king made a declaration to invite the foreign nations into his service against Bibligom Fort; that he would compel none, but such as were willing of their own free accord, the king would take it kindly, and they should be well rewarded. Now there entered into the king's service upon this expedition some of all nations, both Portuguese, Dutch, and English, about the number of thirty. To all that took arms he gave to the value of twenty shillings in money, and three pieces of calico for clothes, and commanded them to wear breeches, hats, and doublets—a great honour there. The king intended a Dutchman, who had been an old servant to him, to be captain over them all; but the Portuguese, not caring to be under the command of a Dutchman, desired a captain of their own nation, which the king granted—studying to please them at this time: but the English being but six, were too few to have a captain over them, and so were forced, some to serve under the Dutch, and some under the Portuguese captain. There were no more of the English, because, being left at their liberty, they thought it safest to dwell at home, and cared not much to take arms under a heathen against Christians.

Who now live miserably.

They were all ready to go, their arms and ammunition ready, with guns prepared to send down; but, before they went, tidings came that the fort yielded at the king's mercy. After this, the Whites thought they had got an advantage of the king, in having these gifts for nothing, but the king did not intend to part with them so; but kept them to watch at his gate; and now they are reduced to great poverty and necessity—for since the king's first gift, they have never received any pay or allowance, though they have often made their addresses to him to supply their wants, signifying their forwardness to serve him faithfully. He speaks them fair, and tells them he will consider them, but does not in the least regard them. Many of them since, after three or four years service, have been glad to get other poor run away Dutchmen to serve in their steads, giving them as much money and clothes as they received of the king before, that so they might get free to come home to their wives and children.

The Dutch captain would afterwards have forced the rest of

the English to have come under him, and called them traitors because they would not, and threatened them. But they scorned him, and bid him do his worst, but would never be persuaded to be soldiers under him; saying, that it was not so much his zeal to the king's service, as his own pride to make himself greater, by having more men under him.

I will now turn to the progress of my own story. It was now about the year 1672, I related before, that my family was reduced to two, myself and one honest man more; we lived solitarily and contentedly, being well settled in a good house of my own. Now we fell to breeding up goats; we began with two, but, by the blessing of God, they soon came to a good many, and their flesh served us instead of mutton. We kept hens and hogs also; and seeing no sudden likelihood of liberty, we went about to make all things handsome and convenient about us, which might be serviceable to us while we lived there, and might farther our liberty whensoever we should see an occasion to attempt it, which it did, in taking away all suspicion from the people concerning us; who not having wives as the other's had, they might well think, lay the readier to take any advantage to make an escape; which indeed we two did plot and consult about, between ourselves, with all imaginable privacy, longbefore we got away; and therefore, we laboured by all means to hide our designs, and to free them from so much as suspicion.

He returns to speak of himself. Plots and consults about an escape.

We had now brought our house and ground to such a perfection, that few noblemen's seats in the land did excel us. On each side was a great thorn gate for entrance, which is the manner in that country: the gates of the city are of the same. We built also another house in the yard all open for air, for

A description of his house.

ourselves to sit in, or any neighbours that came, to talk with us; for seldom should we be alone, our neighbours oftener frequenting our house than we desired, out of whom to be sure we could pick no profit; for their coming is always either to beg or borrow; for although we were strangers and prisoners in their land, yet they would confess that Almighty God had dealt far more bountifully with us than with them, in that we had a far greater plenty of all things than they.

He takes up a new trade and thrives on it.

I now began to set up a new trade; for the trade of knitting was grown dead, and husbandry I could not follow, not having a wife to help and assist me therein, a great part of husbandry properly belonging to the women to manage. Whereupon I perceived a trade in use among them, which was, to lend out corn; the benefit of which is fifty per cent. per annum. This I saw to be the easiest and most profitable way of living, whereupon I took in hand to follow it, and what stock I had I converted into corn or rice in the husk. And now as customers came for corn, I let them have it, to receive, their next harvest, when their own corn was ripe, the same quantity I lent them, and half as much more. But as the profit is great, so is the trouble of getting it in also; for he that useth this trade, must watch when the debtor's field is ripe, and claim his due in time, otherwise other creditors coming before, will seize all upon the account of their debts, and leave no corn at all for those that came later. For these that come thus a borrowing, generally carry none of their corn home when it is ripe; for their creditors ease them of that labour, by coming into their fields and taking it, and commonly they have not half enough to pay what they owe: so that they that miss getting their debts this year, must stay till the next, when it will be double, two measures for one; but the interest never runs up higher, though the debt lie seven years unpaid. By means hereof I was put to a great deal of trouble, and was forced to watch early and late to get my debts, and many times miss of them after all my pains. Howbeit, when my stock did increase that I had dealings with many, I mattered not if I lost in some places; the profit of the rest was sufficient to bear that out.

And thus, by the blessing of God, my little was increased to a great deal; for he had blessed me so, that I was able to lend to my enemies, and had no need to borrow of them; so that I might use the words of Jacob, not out of pride of myself, but thankfulness to God, "That he brought me hither with my staff and blessed me so here, that I became two bands.

His allowance paid him out of the king's store-houses.

For some years together after I removed to my own house from Laggen Denny, the people from whence I came continued my allowance that I had when I lived among them. But now in plain terms they told me, "They could give it me no more, and that I was better able to live without it, than they to give it me," which, though I knew to be true, yet I thought not fit to lose that portion of allowance, which the king was pleased to allot me; therefore I went to court, and appealed to the adigar, to whom such matters did belong: who, upon consideration of the people's poor condition, appointed me monthly to come to him at the king's palace, for a ticket to receive my allowance out of the king's store-houses.

Hereby I was brought into great danger, out of which I had much ado to escape, and that with the loss of my allowance for ever after. I shall relate the manner of it in the next chapter.

CHAP. VIII.

How the Author had like to have been received into the King's Service, and what Means he used to avoid it. He meditates and attempts an Escape, but is often prevented.

He voluntarily forgoes his pension.

THIS frequent appearance at the court, and waiting there for my tickets, brought me to be taken notice of by the great men; insomuch, that they wondered I had been all this while forgotten, and never been brought before the king, being so fit, as they would suppose me, for his use and service, saying, "That from henceforward I should fare better than the allowance amounted to, as soon as the king was made acquainted with me;—which words of theirs served instead of a ticket: whereupon, fearing I should suddenly be brought unto the king—which thing I most of all feared, and least desired; and, hoping that out of sight might prove out of mind, I resolved to forsake the court, and never more ask for tickets, especially seeing God had dealt so bountifully with me as to give me ability to live well enough without them:—as when Israel had eaten of the corn of Canaan, the manna ceased; so when I was driven to forego my allowance that had all this while sustained me in this wilderness, God otherways provided for me.

Summoned before the king.

From this time forward to the time of my flight out of the land, which was five years, I neither had nor demanded any allowance—and glad I was that I could escape so; but I must have more trouble first. For some four or five days after my last coming from court, there came a soldier to me, sent from the adigar with an order in writing under his hand, "that upon sight thereof I should immediately dispatch and come to the court to make my personal appearance before the king; and, in case of any delay, the officers of the country were thereby authorized and commanded to assist the bearer, and to see the same order speedily performed."

The chief occasion of this had been a person, not long before my near neighbour and acquaintance, Oua Matteral by name, who knew my manner of life, and had often been at my house, but now was taken in and employed at court; and he out of friendship and good will to me was one of the chief actors in this business, that he might bring me to preferment at court.

He is informed that he is to be preferred at court.

Upon the abovesaid summons there was no remedy, but to court I must go; where I first applied myself to my said old neighbour, Oua Motteral, who was the occasion of sending for me. I signified to him—that I was come in obedience to the warrant, and I desired to know the reason why I was sent for? to which he answered—"Here is good news for you; you are to appear in the king's presence, where you will find great favour and honourable entertainment, far more than any of your countrymen yet here found." Which the great man thought would be a strong inducement to persuade me joyfully to accept of the king's employments: but, this was the thing I always most dreaded and endeavoured to shun, knowing that being taken into court would be a means to cut off all hopes of liberty from me—which was the thing I esteemed equal unto life itself.

But resolves to refuse it.

Seeing myself brought unto this pass, wherein I had no earthly helper, I recommended my cause to God, desiring him, in whose hands are the hearts of kings and princes, to divert the business; and my cause being just and right I was resolved to persist in a denial. My case seemed to me to be like that of the four lepers at the gate of Samaria,—no avoiding of death for me. If out of ambition and honour I should have embraced the king's service, besides the depriving myself of all hopes of liberty, in the end I must be put to death, as happens to all that serve him; and to deny his service could be but death, and it seemed to me to be the better death of the two. For if I should be put to death only because I refused his service, I should be pitied as one that died innocently; but if I should be executed in his service, however innocent I was, I should be certainly reckoned a rebel and a traitor, as they all are whom he commands to be cut off.

The answer he makes to the great man.

Upon these considerations having thus set my resolutions, as God enabled me, I returned him this answer: first—" That the English nation, to whom I belonged, had never done any violence or wrong to their king, either in word or deed. Secondly, that the causes of my coming on their land was not like to that of other nations, who were either enemies taken in war, or such as by reason of poverty or distress, were driven to sue for relief out of the king's bountiful liberality, or such as fled for the fear of deserved punishment; whereas, as they all well knew, I came not upon any of these causes, but upon account of trade, and came ashore to receive the king's orders, which we understood were come concerning us; and to render an account to the dissauva of the reasons and occasions of our coming into the king's port: and that by the grief and sorrow I had undergone by being so long detained from my native country, (but, for which I thanked the king's majesty, without want of any thing) I scarcely enjoyed myself; for my heart was always absent from my body." Hereunto adding my insufficiency and inability for such honourable employment, being subject to many infirmities and diseases of body.

To this he replied,—" Cannot you read and write English? servile labour the king requireth not of you." I answered,— " When I came ashore I was but young, and that which then I knew, now I had forgot for want of practice, having had neither ink nor paper ever since I came ashore. I urged, moreover, that it was contrary to the custom and practice of all kings and princes upon the earth to keep and detain men that came into their countries upon such peaceable accounts as we did; much less to compel them to serve them beyond their power and ability."

He is sent to another great officer.

At my first coming before him he looked very pleasingly, and spake with a smiling countenance to me: but now his smiles were turned into frowns, and his pleasing looks into bended brows; and, in rough language, he bad me be gone and tell my tale to the adigar—which immediately I did; but he being busy did not much regard me, and I was glad of it, that I might absent the court. But I durst not go out of the city. Sore afraid I was that evil would befal me, and the best I could expect was to be put in chains. All my refuge was prayer to God, whose hand was not shortened that it could not save; and would make all things work together for good to them that trust in him. From him only did I expect help and deliverance in this time of need.

He stays in the city expecting his doom.

In this manner I lodged in an Englishman's house that dwelt in the city about ten days, maintaining myself at my own charge; waiting with a sorrowful heart, and daily expecting to hear my doom. In the meantime, my countrymen and acquaintance, some of them blamed me for refusing so fair a proffer; whereby I might not only have lived well myself, but also have been helpful unto my poor countrymen and friends: others of them pitying me, expecting as I did nothing but a wrathful sentence from so cruel a tyrant, if God did not prevent; and Richard Varnham, who was at this time a great man about the king, was not a little scared to see me run the hazard of what might ensue, rather than be partaker with him in the felicities of the court.

He goes home, but is sent for again.

It being chargeable thus to lie at the city, and hearing nothing more of my business, I took leave without asking, and went home to my house, which was but a day's distance, to get some victuals to carry with me and to return again. But soon after I came home I was sent for again; so I took my load of victuals with me, and arrrived at the city, but went not to the court, but to my former lodging, where I staid as formerly, until I had spent all my provisions: and, by the good hand of my God upon me, I never heard any more of that matter, neither came I any more into the presence of the great men at court, but dwelt in my own plantation upon what God provided for me by my labour and industry.

Having escaped the court service, falls to his former course of life.

For now I returned to my former course of life, dressing my victuals daily with mine own hands, fetching both wood and water upon mine own back—and this, for ought I could see to the contrary, I was like to continue for my life time. This I could do for the present; but I began to consider how helpless I should be, if it should please God I should live till I grew old and feeble. So I entered upon a consultation with myself for the providing against this. One way was the getting of me a wife, but that I was resolved never to do. Then I began to inquire for some poor body to live with me, to dress my victuals for me, that I might live at a little more ease, but could not find any to my mind. Whereupon I considered, that there was no better way than to take one of my poor countrymen's children, whom I might bring up to learn both my own language and religion. And this might be not only charity to the child, but a kindness to myself also afterwards: and several there were that would be glad to be eased of their charge, having more than they could well maintain. A child therefore I took, by whose aptness, ingenuity, and company, as I was much delighted at present, so afterwards I hoped to be served.

It was about the year 1673; although I had now lived many years in this land, and, God be praised, I wanted for nothing the land afforded, yet I could not forget my native country, England; and lamented, under the famine of God's word and sacraments, the want whereof I found greater than all earthly wants: and my daily and fervent prayers to God were, in his good time, to restore me to the enjoyment of them.

I and my companion were still meditating upon our escape and the means to compass it, which our pedling about the country did greatly forward and promote; for, speaking well the language, and going with our commodities from place to place, we used often to entertain discourse with the country people, viz. concerning the ways and countries, and where

Their pedling forwarded their escape.

there were most and fewest inhabitants, and where and how the watches laid from one country to another; and what commodities were proper to carry from one part to the other, pretending we would from time to time go from one place to another, to furnish ourselves with ware that the respective places afforded. None doubted but we had made these inquiries for the sake of our trade, but ourselves had other designs in them. Neither was there the least suspicion of us for these our questions; all supposing I would never run away and leave such an estate as in their accounts and esteem I had.

Their most probable course to take was northwards.

By diligent enquiry I had come to understand, that the easiest and most probable way to make an escape was by travelling to the northward, that part of the land being least inhabited. Therefore we furnished ourselves with such wares as were vendible in those parts; as tobacco, pepper, garlic, combs, all sorts of iron ware, &c.; and, being laden with these things, we two set forth, bending our course towards the northern parts of the Island, knowing very little of the way; and the ways of this country generally are intricate and difficult; here being no great highways that run through the land, but a multitude of little paths; some from one town to another, some into the fields, and some into the woods, where they sow their corn; and the whole country covered with woods, that a man cannot see any thing but just before him. And that which makes them most difficult of all is, that the ways shift and alter, new ways often made and old ways stopped up:—for they cut down woods and sow the ground; and, having got one crop off from it they leave it, and wood soon grows over it again: and in case a road went through those woods they stop it, and contrive another way; neither do they regard though it goes two or three miles about: and to ask and inquire the way for us white men is dangerous, it occasioning the people to suspect us. And, the Chingulays themselves never travel in countries where they are not experienced in the ways without a guide, it being so difficult; and there was no getting a guide to conduct us down to the sea.

But we made a shift to travel from Candy Uda downwards towards the north from town to town; happening at a place at last which I knew before, having been brought up formerly from Cooswat that way, to descend the hill called Bocaul, where there is no watch, but in time of great disturbance. Thus, by the providence of God, we passed all difficulties until we came into the county of Neurecalava, which are the lowest parts that belong to this king; and some three days journey from the place whence we came. They get three days journey northward.

We were not a little glad that we were gotten so far onwards in our way, but yet at this time we could go no farther; for our ware was all sold, and we could pretend no more excuses; and also we had been out so long that it might cause our townsmen to come and look after us, it being the first time that we had been so long absent from home. But return back again.

In this manner we went into these northern parts eight or ten times, and once got as far as Hourly, a town in the extremities of the king's dominions, but yet we could not attain our purpose. For this northern country being much subject to dry weather, and having no springs, we were fain to drink of ponds of rain water, wherein the cattle lie and tumble, which would They often attempted to fly this way, but still hindered.

be so thick and muddy, that the very filth would hang in our beards when we drank. This did not agree with our bodies, being used to drink pure spring water only; by which means, when we first used those parts, we used often to be sick of violent fevers and agues, when we came home. Which diseases happened not only to us, but to all other people that dwelt upon the mountains, as we did, whensoever they went down into those places; and commonly the major part of those that fall sick, dies; at which the Chingulays are so scared, that it is very seldom they do adventure their bodies down thither; neither truly would I have done it, were it not for those future hopes, which God of his mercy did at length accomplish. For both of us smarted sufficiently by those severe fevers we got, when we should both lay sick together, and one not able to help the other;—insomuch, that our countrymen and neighbours used to ask us, if we went thither purposing to destroy ourselves, they little thinking, and we not daring to tell them, our intent and design.

In those parts is bad water, but they had an antidote against it.

At length we learned an antidote and counter poison against the filthy venomous water, which so operated by the blessing of God, that after the use thereof we had no more sickness. It is only a dry leaf; they call it in Portuguese Banga, beaten to powder with some of the country jaggory; and this we eat morning and evening upon an empty stomach. It intoxicates the brain, and makes one giddy, without any other operation, either by stool or vomit.

They still improve in the knowledge of their way.

Thus every voyage we gathered more experience, and got lower down, for this is a large and spacious country. We travelled to and fro where the ways led us, according to their own proverb, "The beggar and the merchant is never out of his way;" because the one begs, and the other trades wherever they go. Thus we used to ramble until we had sold all our ware, and then went home for more;—and by these means we grew acquainted both with the people and the paths.

In these parts I met with my black boy, whom I had divers years before turned away, who had now wife and children. He proved a great help to me in directing me in the ways, for he had lived many years in these parts. Perceiving him to be able, and also in a very poor and sad condition, not able to maintain his family, I adventured once to ask him if a good reward would not be welcome to him, for guiding us two down to the Dutch; which, having done he might return again, and nobody the wiser: at which proposition he seemed to be very joyful, and promised to undertake the same, only at this time for reasons he alleged, which to me seemed probable, as that it was harvest time, and many people about, it could not so safely and conveniently be done now, as it might be some two months after.

Meets with his black boy in these parts, who was to guide him to the Dutch.

The business was concluded upon, and the time appointed between us; but so it fell out, that at the very precise time, all things being ready to depart on the morrow, it pleased God, whose time was not yet come, to strike me with a most grievous pain in the hollow on my right side, that for five days together I was not able to stir from the fire side, but by warming it and fomenting and chafing it I got a little ease.

Afterwards, as soon as I was recovered and got strength, we went down and carried one Englishman more with us for com-

But disappointed.

pany, for our better security, seeing we must travel in the night upon our flight. But though we took him with us, we dared not to tell him of our design, because he had a wife, intending not to acquaint him with it till the business was just ready to be put into action. But when we came, expecting to meet with our guide, he was gone into another country, and we knew not where to find him, and we knew not how to run away without him. Thus we were disappointed that time.

But as formerly, we went to and fro until we had sold our ware; and so returned home again, and delivered the man to his wife, but never told him any thing of our intended design, fearing lest, if he knew it, he might acquaint her with it, and so all our purposes coming to be revealed, might be overthrown for ever afterwards. For we were resolved by God's help still to persevere in our design.

An extraordinary drought for three or four years together.

Some eight or nine years one after another we followed this trade, going down into this country on purpose to seek to get beyond the inhabitants, and so to run away through the woods to the Hollanders. Three or four years together the dry weather prevented us, when the country was almost starved for want of rain—all which time they never tilled the ground. The wells also were almost all dry; so that in the towns we could scarcely get water to drink, or victuals to eat, which affrighted us at those times from running into the woods, lest we might perish for thirst. All this while upon the mountains, where our dwelling was, there was no want of rain.

We found it an inconvenience when we came three of us down together, reckoning it might give occasion to the people to suspect our design, and so prevent us from going thither again. Some of the English that followed such a trade as we had been down that way with their commodities; but, having felt the smart of that country's sickness, would go there no more, finding as much profit in nearer and easier journeys. But we still persisted in our courses this way, having some greater matter to do here than to sell wares, viz. to find out this northern discovery, which in God's good time we did effect.

CHAP. IX.

How the Author began his Escape, and got onward of his Way about an hundred Miles.

Their last and successful attempt.

HAVING often gone this way to seek for liberty, but could not yet find it, we again set forth to try what success God Almighty would now give us; in the year 1679, on the two-and-twentieth of September, furnished with such arms as we could well carry with safety and secrecy, which were knives and small axes; we carried also several sorts of ware to sell as formerly: the moon being seven-and-twenty days old, which we had so contrived, that we might have a light moon, to see the better to run away by—having left an old man at home, whom I had hired to live with me, to look after my house and goats.

The way they went.

We went down at the hill Bocawl, where there was now no watch, and but seldom any; from thence down to the town of Bonder Cooswat, where my father died, and by the town of Nicavar, which is the last town belonging to Hotcurly in that road. From thence forward the towns stand thin—for it was sixteen miles to the next town called Parroah, which lay in the country of Neure-Cawlava, and all the way through a wilderness called Parroah Mocolane, full of wild elephants, tigers, and bears.

They design for Anarodgburro.

Now we set our design for Anarodgburro, which is the lowest place inhabited belonging to the King of Candy; where there is a watch always kept, and nearer than twelve or fourteen miles of this town as yet we never had been.

When we came into the midst of this country, we heard that the governor thereof had sent officers from the court to dispatch away the king's revenues and duties to the city, and that they were now come into the country; which put us into no small fear, lest if they saw us they should send us back again: wherefore we edged away into the westernmost parts of Ecpoulpot, being a remote part of that country wherein we now are; and there we sat to knitting until we heard they were gone; but this caused us to overshoot our time, the moon spending so fast. But as soon as we heard they were departed out of the country, we went onwards of our journey, having kept most of our ware for a pretence to have an occasion to go further; and having bought a good parcel of cotton yarn to knit caps withal, the rest of our ware we gave out, was to buy dried flesh with, which only in those lower parts is to be sold.

They turn out of the way to avoid the king's officers.

Our way now lay necessarily through the chief governor's yard at Colliwilla, who dwells there purposely to see and examine all that go and come. This greatly distressed us. First, because he was a stranger to us, and one whom we had never seen. And secondly, because there was no other way to escape him: and plain reason would tell him, that we, being prisoners, were without our bounds. Whereupon we concluded, that our best way would be to go boldly and resolutely to his house, and not to seem daunted in the least; or to look as if we did distrust him to disallow of our journey, but to shew such a behaviour as if we had authority to travel where we would.

Forced to pass through the chief governor's yard.

So we went forward, and were forced to inquire and ask

The method they used to prevent his suspicion of them.

the way to his house, having never been so far this way before. I brought from home with me knives with fine carved handles, and a red Tunis cap purposely to sell or give him, if occasion required, knowing before, that we must pass by him; and all along, as we went, that we might be the less suspected, we sold caps and other ware, to be paid for at our return homewards. There were many cross paths to and fro to his house, yet, by God's providence we happened in the right road: and, having reached his house, according to the country manner, we went and sat down in the open house, which kind of houses are built on purpose for the reception of strangers: whither, not long after, the great man himself came and sat down by us; to whom we presented a small parcel of tobacco, and some betel: and, before he asked us the cause of our coming, we shewed him the ware we brought for him, and the cotton yarn which we had trucked about the country; telling him withal how the case stood with us: viz. that we had a charge greater than the king's allowance would maintain; and, that because dried flesh was the chief commodity of that part, we told him, that missing of the lading which we used to carry back, we were glad to come thither to see if we could make it up with dried flesh; and, therefore, if he would please to supply us either for such ware as we had brought, or else for our money, it would be a great favour, the which would oblige us for the future to bring him any necessaries that he should name unto us, when we should come again unto those parts, as we used to do very often; and, that we could furnish him, having dealings, and being acquainted with the best artificers in Candy.

At which he replied, that he was sorry we were come at such a dry time, wherein they could not catch deer; but if some rain fell he would soon dispatch us with our ladings of flesh. But, however, he bade us go about the towns, and see whether there might be any or no, though he thought there was none. This answer of his pleased us wondrous well, both because by this we saw he suspected us not, and because he told us there was no dried flesh to be got: for it was one of our greatest fears that we should get our lading too soon, for then we could not have had an excuse to go further. And, as yet, we could not possibly fly; having still six miles further to the northward to go before we could attempt it; that is, to Anarodgburro.

From Anarodgburro it is two days journey further, through a desolate wilderness, before there is any more inhabitants; and, these inhabitants are neither under this king nor the Dutch; but are Malabars, and under a prince of their own. These people we were sorely afraid of, lest they might seize us and send us back; there being a correspondence between this prince and the King of Candy: wherefore it was our endeavour by all means to shun them, lest, according to the old proverb,—We might leap out of the frying-pan into the fire.

Their danger by reason of the ways they were to pass.

But we must take care of that as well as we could when we came among them, for as yet our care was to get to Anarodgburro; where, although it was our desire to get, yet we would not seem to be too hasty, lest it might occasion suspicion; but lay where we were two or three days: and one staid at the governor's house a knitting, whilst the others went about among the towns to see for flesh. The ponds in the country being now dry, there was fish everywhere in abundance, which they dry like red herrings over a fire.

They still remain at the governor's, to prevent suspicion.

They offered to sell us store of them; but they, we told them, would not turn to so good profit as flesh. The which we said, we would have, though we staid ten days longer for it. For here we could live as cheap, and earn as much as if we were at home, by our knitting: so we seemed to them as if we were not in any haste.

An accident that now created them great fear.

In the mean time happened an accident which put us to a great fright: for the king having newly clapped up several persons of quality, whereof my old neighbour Ova Motteral that sent for me to court was one, sent down soldiers to this high sheriff or governor, at whose house we now were, to give him orders to set a secure guard at the watches that no suspicious person might pass. This he did to prevent the relations of these imprisoned persons from making an escape, who through fear of the king might attempt it. This is always the king's custom to do, but it put us into an exceeding fear, lest it might beget an admiration in these soldiers to see white men so low down; which indeed is not customary nor allowed of, and so they might send us up again: which, doubtless they would have done, had it not been of God, by this means, and after this manner, to deliver us. Especially considering that the king's command came just at that time, and so expressly to keep a secure guard at the watches; and that, in that very way that we always proposed to go in: so that it seemed scarcely possible for us to pass afterwards, though we should get off fairly at present with the soldiers.

But get fairly rid of it.

Which we did: for they having delivered their message departed, shewing themselves very kind and civil unto us.

And we seemed to lament for our hard fortune, that we were not ready to go upwards with them in their good company; for we were neighbours, dwelling in one and the same county. However, we bid them carry our commendations to our countrymen, the English; with whom they were acquainted, and so bid them farewell. And glad we were when they were gone from us. And the next day in the morning we resolved, God willing, to set forward: but we thought not fit to tell our host the governor of it, till the very instant of our departure; that he might not have any time to deliberate concerning us.

That night, he being disposed to be merry, sent for people whose trade it is to dance and shew tricks, to come to his house to entertain him with their sports. The beholding them spent most part of the night; which, we merrily called our old host's civility to us at our last parting: as it proved indeed, though he, honest man, then, little dreamed of any such thing.

The morning being come we first took care to fill our bellies; then we packed up those things which were necessary for our journey, to carry with us; and the rest of our goods, cotton yarn, and cloth, and other things, that we would not encumber ourselves withal, we bound up in a bundle; intending to leave them behind us. This being done, I went to the governor, and carried him four or five charges of gunpowder, a thing somewhat scarce with them; intreating him, rather than we should be disappointed of flesh, to make use of that, and shoot some deer: which he was very willing to accept of; and to us it could be no ways profitable, not

They get away fairly from the governor.

2 T

having a gun. While we, we told him, would make a step to Anarodgburro to see what flesh we could procure there. In the mean time, according as we had laid the business, came Stephen with a bundle of goods, desiring to leave them in his house till we came back; which he was ready to grant us leave to do. And seeing us leave such a parcel of goods, though, God knows, but of little account in themselves, yet of considerable value in that land, he could not suppose otherwise but that we were intended to return again. Thus we took our leaves, and immediately departed, not giving him time to consider with himself, or consult with others about us: and he, like a good-natured man, bid us heartily farewell.

Although we knew not the way to this town, having never been there in all our lives, and durst not ask, lest it might breed suspicion; we went on confidently through a desolate wood; and happened to go very right, and came out directly at the place.

In their way they meet with a river which they found for their purpose.

But in our way before we arrived hither, we came up with a small river which run through the woods, called by the Chingulays, Malwat Oyah; the which we viewed well, and judged it might be a probable guide to carry us down to the sea, if a better did not present. Howbeit we thought good to try first the way we were taking; and to go onward towards Anarodgburro, that being the shortest and easiest way to get to the coast; and this river being just under our lee, ready to serve and assist us if other means failed.

They come to Anarodg-

To Anarodgburro therefore we came, called also Neur Waug,

which is not so much a particular single town, as a territory. It is a vast great plain, the like I never saw in all that Island; in the midst whereof is a lake which may be a mile over; not natural, but made by art, as other ponds in the country, to serve them to water their corn grounds. This plain is encompassed round with woods, and small towns among them on every side inhabited by Malabars; a distinct people from the Chingulays. But these towns we could not see till we came in among them. Being come out through the woods into this plain we stood looking and staring round about us, but knew not which way to go: at length we heard a cock crow, which was a sure sign to us that there was a town hard by; into which we were resolved to enter: for, standing thus amazed, was the ready way to be taken up for suspicious persons; especially, because white men never come down so low.

burro. This place described.

Being entered into this town, we sat ourselves under a tree and proclaimed our wares; for we feared to rush into their yards as we used to do at other places, lest we should scare them. The people stood amazed as soon as they saw us, being originally Malabars, though subjects of Candy; nor could they understand the Chingulay language in which we spake to them. And we stood looking one upon another until there came one that could speak the Chingulay tongue, who asked us "From whence we came?" We told him "From Candy Uda." But they believed us not; supposing that we came up from the Dutch:—from Manaar. So they brought us before their governor; he not speaking Chingulay, spake to us by an interpreter: and, to know the truth, whether we came from the place we pretended, he inquired about news at court, demanded—"Who were governors of such and such

The people stand amazed at them.

They are examined by the governor of the place.

countries? and what was become of some certain noblemen whom the king had lately cut off? and also, what the common people were employed about at court?" for it is seldom that they are idle. To all which we gave satisfactory answers. Then he inquired of us—"Who gave us leave to come down so low?" We told him—"That privilege was given us by the king himself full fifteen years since, at his palace at Nellemby; when he caused it to be declared unto us, that we were no longer prisoners:" and, (which indeed was our own addition) that we were free to enjoy the benefit of trade in all his dominions.

To prove and confirm the truth of which, we alleged the distance of the way that we were now come from home, being near a hundred miles; passing through several countries, where we met with several governors and officers in their respective jurisdictions; who, had they not been well sensible of these privileges granted us, would not have allowed us to pass through their countries:—all which officers we described to him by name. And also, that now we came from the high sheriff's house at Colliwilla, where we had been these three days; and there heard of the order that was come to secure the watches: which was not for fear of the running away of white men, but of the Chingulays. These reasons gave him full satisfaction that we were innocent traders; seeing also, the commodities that we had brought with us, this further confirmed his opinion concerning us.

Provide things necessary for their flight.

The people were very glad of our coming, and gave us an end of an open house to lie in: but at present they had no dried flesh, but desired us to stay two or three days and we should not fail: which we were very ready to consent to, hoping by that time to come to a knowledge of the way, and to learn where about the watch was placed. To prevent the least surmise that we were plotting to run away, we agreed that Stephen should stay in the house by the things, while I with some few went abroad; pretending to inquire for dried flesh to carry back with us to Candy: but, intending to make discoveries of the way, and provide necessaries for our flight: as rice, a brass pot to boil our rice in; a little dried flesh to eat; and a deer's-skin to make us shoes of. And, by the providence of my gracious God, all these things I happened upon and bought; but, as our goodhap was, deer's-flesh we could meet with none: so that we had time enough to fit ourselves; all people thinking that we staid only to buy flesh.

They find it not safe to proceed farther this way.

Here we staid three days; during which he had found the great road that runs down towards Jafnapatan; one of the northern ports belonging to the Dutch, which road we judged led also towards Manaar, a Dutch northern port also, which was the place we endeavoured to get to; lying above two or three days journey distant from us. But in this road there was a watch lay, which must be passed. Where this watch was placed it was necessary for us punctually to know, and to endeavour to get a sight of it: and, if we could do this, our intent was to go unseen by night, the people being then afraid to travel; and, being come up to the watch, to slip aside into the woods, and so go on until we were past it, and then strike into the road again. But this project came to nothing, because I could not, without suspicion and danger, go and view this watch, which laid some four or five miles below this plain, and so far I could not frame any business to go.

But several inconveniencies we saw here, insomuch that we found it would not be safe for us to go down in this road; for, if we should have slipt away from them by night, in the morning we should be missed; and then most surely they would go that way to chace us, and ten to one overtake us, being but one night before them. Also, we knew not whether or no it might lead us into the country of the Malabar prince, of whom we were much afraid.

Then resolving to let the great road alone, we thought of going right down through the woods, and steer our course by the sun and moon; but, the ground being so dry, we feared we should not meet with water; so we declined that counsel also. Thus, being in doubt, we prayed to God to direct us, and to put it into our hearts which way to take. Then, after a consultation between ourselves, all things considered, we concluded it the best course to go back to Malwat Oyah; the river we had well viewed, that lay in our way as we came hither. And back thither we resolved to repair.

Resolve to go back to the river they lately passed.

CHAP. X.

The Author's Progress in his Flight from Anarodgburro, into the Woods, until their Arrival in the Malabars Country.

NOW God of his mercy having prospered our design hitherto, for which we blessed his holy Name, our next care was how to come off clear from the people of Anarodgburro, that they might not presently miss us, and so pursue after us; which, if they should do, there would have been no escaping them. For from this town to Colliwilla, where the sheriff lived, with whom we left our goods, they are as well acquainted in the woods as in the paths. And when we came away we must tell the people that we were going thither, because there is no other way but that. Now our fear was, lest upon some occasion or other any men might chance to travel that way soon after we were gone, and not finding us at Colliwilla, might conclude, as they could do no otherwise, that we were run into the woods. Therefore to avoid this danger, we staid in the town till it was so late, that we knew none durst venture to travel afterwards, for fear of wild beasts; by which means we were sure to gain a night's travel at least, if they should chance to pursue us.

They depart back again towards the river.

So we took our leaves of the governor, who kindly gave us a pot of milk to drink for a farewell, we telling him, "We were returning back to the sheriff at Colliwilla, to whom we had given some gunpowder when we came from him, to shoot us

But first take their leave of the governor here.

some deer, and we doubted not but by that time we should get to him, he would have provided flesh enough for our lading home." Thus bidding him and the rest of the neighbours farewell, we departed, they giving us the civility of their accustomed prayers, Diabec; that is, God bless or keep you.

They begin their flight.

It was now the twelfth day of October, on a Sunday, the moon eighteen days old. We were well furnished with all things needful, which we could get, viz. ten days provision, rice, flesh, pepper, salt, a bason to boil our victuals in, two calabasses to fetch water, two great tallipats for tents, big enough to sleep under if it should rain, jaggory and sweet-meats, which we brought from home with us, tobacco also, and betel, tinder-boxes, two or three for failing, and a deer's skin to make us shoes, to prevent any thorns running into our feet as we travelled through the woods, for our greatest trust under God was to our feet. Our weapons were, each man a small axe fastened to a long staff in our hands, and a good knife by our sides; which were sufficient, with God's help, to defend us from the assaults of either tiger or bear; and as for elephants there is no standing against them, but the best defence is to flee from them.

In this posture and equipage we marched forward. When we were come within a mile of this river, it being about four in the evening, we began to fear lest any of the people of Anarodgburro, from whence we came, should follow us to Colliwilla; which place we never intended to come at more, the river along which we intended to go laying on this side of it. That we might be secure therefore that no people came after us, we sat down upon a rock by a hole that was full of water in the highway, until it was so late, that we were sure no people durst travel. In case any had come after us, and seen us sitting there and gotten no further, we intended to tell them, that one of us was taken sick by the way, and therefore not able to go. But it was our happy chance there came none. So about sun-dawn we took up our sacks of provisions, and marched forward for the river, which under God we had pitched upon to be our guide down to the sea.

They come to the river along which they resolved to go.

Being come at the river, we left the road, and struck into the woods by the river side. We were exceeding careful not to tread on the sand or soft ground, lest our footsteps should be seen; and, where it could not be avoided, we went backwards; so that by the print of our feet, it seemed as if we had gone the contrary way. We were now gotten a good way into the wood, when it grew dark and began to rain, so that we thought it best to pitch our tents, and get wood for firing, before it was all wet, and too dark to find it;—which we did, and kindled a fire.

Which they travel along by till it was dark.

Then we began to fit ourselves for our journey against the moon arose. All our sale-wares which we had left we cast away, (for we took care not to sell too much) keeping only provisions and what was very necessary for our journey. About our feet we tied pieces of deers hide to prevent thorns and stumps annoying our feet. We always used to travel bare-foot, but now being to travel by night and in the woods, we feared so to do; for if our feet should fail us now, we were quite undone. And by the time we had well fitted ourselves, and were refreshed with a morsel of Portuguese sweet-meats, the moon began to shine. So having commended ourselves into the hands of the Almighty, we took up our provisions upon our shoulders, and set forward, and travelled some three or four hours, but with a great deal of

Now they fit themselves for their journey.

difficulty; for the trees being thick, the moon gave but little light through—but our resolution was to keep going.

Meeting with an elephant they took up for that night.

Now it was our chance to meet with an elephant in our way just before us, which we tried, but could not scare away; so he forced us to stay. We kindled a fire and sat down, and took a pipe of tobacco, waiting till morning. Then we looked round about us, and it appeared all like a wilderness, and no signs that people ever had been there, which put us in great hopes that we had gained our passage, and were past all the inhabitants. Whereupon we concluded, that we were now in no danger of being seen, and might travel in the day securely. There was only one great road in our way, which led to Portaloon from the towns which by and bye we fell into; this road therefore we were shy of, lest when we passed it over, some passengers travelling in it, might see us; and this road we were in expectance about this time to meet withal, secure, as I said before, of all other danger of people. But the river winding about to the northward, brought us into the midst of a parcel of towns called Tissea Wava, before we were aware; for the country being all woods, we could not discern where there were towns, until we came within the hearing of them. That which betrayed us into this danger was, that meeting with a path, which only led from one town to another, we concluded it to be that great road above-mentioned; and so having past it over, we supposed the danger we might encounter in being seen, was also past over with it; but we were mistaken—for going further we still met with other paths, which we crossed over, still hoping one or other of them was that great road; but at last we perceived our error; viz. that they were only paths that went from one town to another.

They fall in among towns before they are aware,

And so while we were avoiding men and towns, we ran into the midst of them. This was a great trouble to us, hearing the noise of people round about us, and knew not how to avoid them; into whose hands we knew if we had fallen, they would have carried us up to the king, besides beating and plundering us to boot.

We knew before that these towns were here away; but had we known that this river turned and run in among them, we should never have undertaken the enterprize. But now to go back, after we had newly passed so many paths, and fields, and places where people did resort, we thought not advisable; and that the danger in so doing might be greater than in going forward—and had we known so much then, as afterwards did appear to us, it had been safer for us to have gone on, than to have hid there as we did: which we then thought was the best course we could take for the present extremity; viz. to secure ourselves in secret until night, and then to run through in the dark. All that we now wanted was a hole to creep in to lie close, for the woods thereabouts were thin, and no shrubs or bushes, under which we might be concealed.

We heard the noise of people on every side, and expected every moment to see some of them to our great terror; and it is not easy to say in what danger, and in what apprehension of it we were: it was not safe for us to stir backwards or forwards, for fear of running among people, and it was as unsafe to stand still where we were, lest somebody might spy us; and where to find covert we could not tell. Looking about us in these straits, we spied a great tree by us, which, for the bigness thereof, 'tis probable might be hollow; to which we went, and found it so:

Their fright lest they should be seen.

Hid themselves in a hollow tree.

It was like a tub, some three feet high; into it immediately we both crept, and made a shift to sit there for several hours; though very uneasy, and all in mud and wet. But, however, it did greatly comfort us in the fright and amazement we were in.

They get safely over this danger.

So soon as it began to grow dark we came creeping out of our hollow tree, and put for it as fast as our legs could carry us; and then we crossed that great road, which all the day before we did expect to come up with; keeping close by the river side, and going so long till dark night stopped us. We kept going the longer, because we heard the voice of men hollowing towards evening, which created us a fresh disturbance; thinking them to be people that were coming to chace us. But at length we heard elephants behind us, between us and the voice; which we knew by the noise of cracking the boughs and small trees which they break down and eat. These elephants were a very good guard behind us; and were, methought, like the darkness that came between Israel and the Egyptians. For, the people we knew, would not dare to go forwards hearing elephants before them.

They dress meat, and lay down to sleep.

In this security we pitched our tents by the river side, and boiled rice and roasted flesh for our supper, for we were very hungry; and so, commending ourselves to God's keeping, laid down to sleep. The voice which we heard still continued, which lasting so long, we knew what it meant; it was nothing but the hollowing of people that lay to watch the corn fields, to scare away the wild beasts out of their corn. Thus we past Monday.

But, nevertheless, next morning, so soon as the moon shone out bright, to prevent the worst, we took up our packs, and were gone—being past all the tame inhabitants, with whom we had no more trouble; but the next day we feared we should come among the wild ones; for these woods are full of them; of these we were as much afraid as of the other: for they would have carried us back to the king, where we should be kept prisoners; but these, we feared, would have shot us, not standing to hear us plead for ourselves.

They fear wild men, which these woods abound with.

And indeed all along, as we went by the sides of the river, till we came to the Malabar inhabitants, had been the tents of wild men, made only of boughs of trees: but, God be praised, they were all gone, though but very lately before we came; as we perceived by the bones of cattle, and shells of fruit, which lay scattered about. We supposed that want of water had driven them out of the country down to the river side; but since it had rained a shower or two they were gone again. Once about noon, sitting down upon a rock by the river side, to take a pipe of tobacco and rest ourselves, we had almost been discovered by the women of these wild people, coming down, as I suppose, to wash themselves in the river; who being many of them, came talking and laughing together. At the first hearing of the noise, being a good distance, we marvelled what it was: sitting still and listening, it came nearer, a little above where we sat; and at last we could plainly distinguish it to be the voices of women and children: whereupon we thought it no boot to sit longer, since we could escape undiscovered, and so took up our bags, and fled as fast as we could.

They meet with many of their tents.

Very near falling upon the wild people.

Thus we kept travelling every day, from morning till night,

What kind of travelling they had.

still along by the river side, which turned and winded very crooked. In some places it would be pretty good travelling, and but few bushes and thorns, and in others a great many. So that our shoulders and arms were all of a gore, being grievously torn and scratched; for we had nothing on us but a clout about our middles, and our victuals on our shoulders, and in our hands a tallipat and an axe.

Some account of this river.

The lower we came down this river the less water, so that sometimes we could go a mile or two upon the sand; and, in some places, three or four rivers would all meet together. When it happened so, and was noon, the sun over our head, and the water not running, we could not tell which to follow, but were forced to stay till the sun was fallen, thereby to judge of our course. We often met with bears, hogs, deer, and wild buffaloes, but all ran so soon as they saw us; but elephants we met with no more than that I mentioned before. The river is exceeding full of aligators, all along as we went; the upper part of it nothing but rocks. Here and there, by the side of this river is a world of hewn stone pillars, standing upright, and other heaps of hewn stones, which I suppose formerly were buildings; and in three or four places are the ruins of bridges, built of stone; some remains of them yet standing upon stone pillars. In many places are points built out into the river like wharfs, all of hewn stone; which, I suppose, have been built for kings to sit upon for pleasure. For, I cannot think they ever were employed for traffic by water, the river being so full of rocks that boats could never come up into it.

Ruins.

The woods hereabouts.

The woods in all these northern parts are short and shrubbed, and so they are by the river side, and the lower the worse; and the grounds so also.

In the evenings we used to pitch our tent, and make a great fire both before and behind us, that the wild beasts might have notice where we lay, and we used to hear the voices of all sorts of them; but, thanks be to God, none ever came near to hurt us. Yet we were the more wary of them, because once a tiger shewed us a cheat; for, having bought a deer, and having nothing to salt it up in, we packed it up in the hide thereof salted, and laid it under a bench in an open house on which I lay that night, and Stephen laid just by it on the ground; and, some three people more lay then in the same house; and, in the said house a great fire, and another in the yard: yet a tiger came in the night, and carried deer and hide, and all away. But we missing it concluded it was a thief. We called up the people that lay by us, and told them what had happened: who informed us that it was a tiger; and with a torch they went to see which way he had gone, and presently found some of it, which he let drop by the way. When it was day we went further, and picked more which was scattered, till we came to the hide itself; which remained uneaten. **How they secured themselves a-nights against wild beasts.**

We had now travelled till Thursday afternoon, when we crossed the river called Coronda-Oyah, which was then quite dry;—this parts the king's country from the Malabars. We saw no sign of inhabitants here; the woods began to be very full of thorns and shrubby bushes, with clifts and broken land; so that we could not possibly go into the woods: but now the river grew better, being clear of rocks and dry, water only standing in holes. So we marched along in the river upon the sand. Hereabouts are far more elephants than higher up; by day we saw none, but by night the river is full of them. **They pass the river that divides the king's country from the Malabars.**

After four or five days travel they come among inhabitants.

Friday, about nine or ten in the morning, we came among the inhabitants; for then we saw the footing of people on the sand, and tame cattle with bells about their necks. Yet we kept on our way right down the river, knowing no other course to take to shun the people. And, as we went still forward, we saw Coracan corn sowed in the woods, but neither towns nor people; nor so much as the voice of man. But yet we were somewhat dismayed, knowing that we were now in a country inhabited by Malabars. The wanniounay, or prince of this people, for fear pays tribute to the Dutch; but stands far more affected towards the King of Candy: which made our care the greater to keep ourselves out of his hands; fearing, lest if he did not keep us himself, he might send us up to our old master. So that great was our terror again; lest, meeting with people we might be discovered :—yet there was no means now left us how to avoid the danger of being seen. The woods were so bad, that we could not possibly travel in them for thorns; and to travel by night was impossible, it being a dark moon; and, the river a-nights so full of elephants and other wild beasts coming to drink, as we did both hear and see, laying upon the banks with a fire by us. They came in such numbers, because there was water for them no where else to be had; the ponds and holes of water, nay, the river itself in many places being dry.

But do what they can to avoid them.

As yet undiscovered.

There was therefore no other way to be taken but to travel on in the river :—so down we went into the sand, and put on as fast as we could set our legs to the ground; seeing no people (nor I think nobody us), only buffaloes in abundance in the water.

CHAP. XI.

Being in the Malabar Territories, how they encountered two Men, and what passed between them. And of their getting safe unto the Dutch Fort. And their Reception there, and at the Island Manaar, until their embarking for Columbo.

THUS we went on till about three of the clock, afternoon. At which time coming about a point, we came up with two Bramins on a sudden, who were sitting under a tree boiling rice. We were within forty paces of them; when they saw us they were amazed at us, and as much afraid of us as we were of them. Now we thought it better policy to treat with them than to flee from them; fearing they might have bows and arrows, whereas we were armed only with axes in our hands, and knives by our sides; or else that they might raise the country and pursue us. So we made a stand, and in the Chingulay language asked their leave to come near to treat with them; but they did not understand it. But being risen up spake to us in the Malabar tongue, which we could not understand. Then still standing at a distance, we intimated our minds to them by signs, beckoning with our hand, which they answered in the same language. Then offering to go towards them, and seeing them to be naked men and no arms near them, we laid our axes upon the ground with our bags, lest we might scare them, if we had come up to them with those weapons in our hands, and so went towards them with

They meet with two Malabars, to whom they relate their condition.

only our knives by our sides: by signs with our hands, shewing them our bloody backs, we made them understand whence we came, and whither we were going. Which when they perceived they seemed to commiserate our condition, and greatly to admire at such a miracle which God had brought to pass: and as they talked one to another they lifted up thir hands and faces towards heaven, often repeating Tombrane, which is God in the Malabar tongue.

They are courteous to them.

And by their signs we understood they would have us bring our bags and axes nearer; which we had no sooner done, but they brought the rice and herbs which they had boiled for themselves to us, and bad us eat; which we were not fitted to do, having not long before eaten a hearty dinner of better fare; yet could not but thankfully accept of their compassion and kindness, and eat as much as we could; and, in requital of their courtesy, we gave them some of our tobacco; which after much entreating they did receive, and it pleased them exceedingly.

But loath to conduct them to the Hollanders.

After these civilities passed on either side, we began by signs to desire them to go with us and shew us the way to the Dutch Fort; which they were very unwilling to do, saying, as by signs and some few words which we could understand, that our greatest danger was past, and that by night we might get into the Hollander's dominions. Yet we being weary with our tedious journey, and desirous to have a guide, shewed them money to the value of five shillings, being all I had; and offered it them to go with us. Which, together with our great importunity so prevailed, that one of them took it; and, leaving his fellow to carry their baggage, he went with us about one mile, and then began to take his leave of us, and to return: which we supposed was to get more from us. Having therefore no more money, we gave him a red Tunis cap and a knife; for which he went a mile farther, and then as before would leave us, signifying to us, that we were out of danger, and he could go no further.

Now we had no more left to give him, but began to perceive, that what we had parted withal to him, was but flung away; and although we might have taken all from him again, being alone in the wood, yet we feared to do it, lest thereby we might exasperate him, and so he might give notice of us to the people; but bad him farewel, after he had conducted us about four or five miles. And we kept on our journey down the river as before, until it was night, and lodged upon a bank under a tree: but were in the way of the elephants; for in the night they came and had like to have disturbed us, so that for the preservation we were forced to fling fire brands at them to scare them away.

In danger of elephants.

The next morning being Saturday as soon as it was light, having eaten to strengthen us, as horses do oats before they travel, we set forth going still down the river; the sand was dry and loose, and so very tedious to go upon: by the side we could not go, being all overgrown with bushes. The land hereabouts was as smooth as a bowling-green, but the grass clean burnt up for want of rain.

Having travelled about two hours, we saw a man walking in the river before, whom we would gladly have shunned, but well could not; for he walked down the river as we did,

They overtake another man, who tells them they were in the Dutch dominions.

but at a very slow rate, which much hindered us. But we considering upon the distance we had come, since we left the Bramin, and comparing with what he had told us, we concluded we were in the Hollander's jurisdiction, and so amended our pace to overtake the man before us; whom we, perceiving to be free from timorousness at the sight of us, concluded he had used to see white men: whereupon we asked him to whom he belonged? He, speaking the Chingulay language, answered—to the Dutch; and also, that all the country was under their command, and that we were out of all danger, and that the fort of Arrepa was but some six miles off; which did not a little rejoice us. We told him, we were of that nation, and had made our escape from Candy, where we had been many years kept in captivity; and, having nothing to give him ourselves, we told him, that it was not to be doubted, but the chief commander at that fort would bountifully reward him, if he would go with us, and direct us thither. But, whether he doubted of that, or no, or whether he expected something in hand, he excused himself—pretending earnest and urgent occasions that he could not defer; but advised us to leave the river, because it winds so much about, and turn up without fear to the towns, where the people would direct us the way to the fort.

They arrive at Arrepa Fort.

Upon his advice we struck up a path that came down to the river, intending to go to a town, but could find none; and there were so many cross paths that we could not tell which way to go—and the land here so exceedingly low and level, that we could see no other thing but trees. For, although I got up a tree to look if I could see the Dutch fort, or discern any houses, yet I could not; and the sun being right over our heads, neither could that direct us; insomuch that we wished ourselves again in our old friend, the river. So after so much wandering up and down, we sat down under a tree waiting until the sun was fallen, or some people came by; which, not long after, three or four Malabars did: one of which could speak a little Portuguese. We told these men we were Hollanders, supposing they would be the more willing to go with us, but they proved of the same temper with the rest before mentioned; for until I gave one of them a small knife to cut betel nuts, he would not go with us—but for the lucre of that he conducted us to a town: from whence they sent a man with us to the next, and so we passed from town to town until we arrived at the fort called Arrepa; it being about four of the clock on Saturday afternoon, October the 18th, 1679; which day God grant us grace that we may never forget—when he was pleased to give us so great a deliverance from such a long captivity of nineteen years and six months, and odd days, being taken prisoner when I was nineteen years old, and continued upon the mountains among the heathen, till I attained to eight and thirty.

He travels a-nights in the woods without fear, and slept securely.

In this my flight through the woods, I cannot but take notice, with some wonder and great thankfulness, that this travelling by night in a desolate wilderness, was little or nothing dreadful to me, whereas formerly the very thoughts of it would seem to dread me; and in the night when I laid down to rest with wild beasts round me, I slept as soundly and securely as ever I did at home in my own house: which courage and peace I look upon to be the immediate gift of God to me upon my earnest prayers; which, at that time, he poured into my heart in great measure and fervency: after which, I found myself freed from those frights and fears, which usually possessed my heart at other times.

In short, I look upon the whole business as a miraculous Providence, and that the hand of God did eminently appear to me, as it did of old to his people Israel in the like circumstances, in leading and conducting me through this dreadful wilderness, and not to suffer any evil to approach nigh unto me.

Entertained very kindly.

The Hollanders much wondered at our arrival, it being so strange that any should escape from Candy, and entertained us very kindly that night; and the next morning, being Sunday, sent a corporal with us to Manaar, and a black man to carry our few things.

Sent to Manaar. Received by the captain of the castle.

At Manaar we were brought before the captain of the castle, the chief governor being absent; who, when we came in was just risen from dinner: he received us with a great deal of kindness, and bade us sit down to eat. It seemed not a little strange to us, who had dwelt so long in straw cottages among the black heathen, and used to sit on the ground, and eat our meat on leaves; now to sit on chairs, and eat out of China dishes at a table—where were great varieties, and a fair and sumptuous house inhabited by white and Christian people; we being then in such habit and guise, our natural colour excepted, that we seemed not fit to eat with his servants, no nor his slaves.

Who intended them to sail the next day to Jafnapatan.

After dinner the captain enquired concerning the affairs of the king and country, and the condition of their ambassadors and people there; to all which we gave them true and satisfactory answers. Then he told us, that to-morrow there was a sloop to sail to Jafnapatan, in which he would send us to the commander or governor, from whence we might have passage to Fort St. George, or any other place on that coast, according to our desire. After this, he gave us some money, bidding us go to the castle, to drink and be merry with our countrymen there: for all which kindness, giving him many thanks in the Portuguese language, we took our leaves of him.

Here they meet with a Scotch and Irish man.

When we came to the court of guard at the castle, we asked the soldiers if there were no Englishmen among them. Immediately there came forth two men to us, the one a Scotchman, named Andrew Brown; the other an Irishman, whose name was Francis Hodges; who, after very kind salutes, carried us unto their lodgings in the castle, and entertained us very nobly, according to their ability, with rack and tobacco.

The people flock to see them.

The news of our arrival being spread in the town, the people came flocking to see us—a strange and wonderful sight! and some to enquire about their husbands, sons, and relations, which were prisoners in Candy.

In the evening, a gentleman of the town sent to invite us to his house, where we were gallantly entertained both with victuals and lodging.

They are ordered a longer stay.

The next day being Monday, ready to embark for Jafnapatan, came order from the captain and council, that we must stay until the commander of Jafnapatan, who was daily expected, came thither; which we could not deny to do: and order was given to the victuallers of the soldiers to provide for us. The Scotch and Irish man were very glad of this order, that they might have our company longer; and would not suffer us to spend the captain's benevolence in their company, but spent freely upon us at their own charges. Thanks be to God we both continued in health at the time of our escape; but, within three days after we came to Manaar, my companion fell very sick, that I thought I should have lost him.

They embark for Columbo.

Thus we remained some ten days, at which time the expected commander arrived, and was received with great ceremonies of state. The next day we went before him to receive his orders concerning us; which were, to be ready to go with him on the morrow to Columbo, there being a ship that had long waited in that road to carry him, in which we embarked with him for Columbo. At our coming on board to go to sea, we could not but expect to be sea sick, being now as fresh men, having so long disused the sea; but it proved otherwise, and we were not in the least stirred.

CHAP. XII.

Their Arrival at Columbo, and Entertainment there: their Departure thence to Batavia, and from thence to Bantam; whence they set sail for England.

BEING arrived safely at Columbo, before the ship came to an anchor, there came a barge on board, to carry the commander ashore; but, being late in the evening, and my consort sick of an ague and fever, we thought it better for us to stay until morning, to have a day before us. The next morning we bid the skipper farewell, and went ashore in the first boat, going straight to the court of guard; where all the soldiers came staring upon us, wondering to see white men in Chingulay habit. We asked them, If there were no Englishmen among them? they told us, There were none—but that in the city there were several:—a trumpeter being hard by, who had formerly sailed in English ships, hearing of us, came and invited us to his chamber, and entertained my consort, being sick of his ague in his own bed. **They are wondered at at Columbo.**

This strange news of our arrival from Candy was presently spread all about the city, and all the Englishmen that were there immediately come to bid us welcome out of our long captivity; with whom we consulted how to come to speech of the governor; upon which one of them went and acquainted the captain of the guard, of our being on shore; which the captain **Ordered to appear before the governor.**

understanding, went and informed the governor thereof—who sent us answer, that to-morrow we should come before him.

Treated by English there.

After my consort's fit was over, our countrymen and their friends invited us abroad, to walk and see the city; we, being barefooted, and in the Chingulay habit, with great long beards, the people much wondered at us, and came flocking to see who, and what we were; so that we had a great train of people about us as we walked in the streets. After we had walked to and fro, and had seen the city, they carried us to their landlady's house, where we were kindly treated both with victuals and drink, and returned to the trumpeter's chamber, as he had desired us when we went out. In the evening came a boy from the governor's house, to tell us, that the governor invited us to come to supper at his house: but we, having dined late with our countrymen and their friends, had no room to receive the governor's kindness, and so lodged that night at the trumpeter's.

They come into the governor's presence. His state.

The next morning, the governor, whose name was Ricklof Van Gons, son of Ricklof Van Gons, general of Batavia, sent for us to his house, whom we found standing in a large and stately room, paved with black and white stones, and only the commander, who brought us from Manaar, standing by him, who was to succeed him in the government of that place. On the further side of the room stood three of the chief captains, bareheaded. First, he bid us welcome out of our long captivity, and told us—that we were free men, and that he should have been glad if he could have been an instrument to redeem us sooner, having endeavoured as much for us as for his own people. For all which we thanked him heartily, telling him, we knew it to be true.

The governor perceiving I could speak the Portugueze tongue, began to inquire concerning the affairs of the king and country very particularly, and oftentimes asked about such matters as he himself knew better than I. To all his questions my too much experience enabled me to give a satisfactory reply. Some of the most remarkable matters he demanded of me were these :— Matters the governor inquired of.

First, they inquired much about the reason and intent of our coming to Cuttiar? To which I answered them at large. Then they asked, If the King of Candy had any issue? I told them, As report went, he had none. And, Who were the greatest in the realm next to him? I answered, There were none of renown left—the king had destroyed them all.—How the hearts of the people stood affected? I answered, " Much against their king, he being so cruel."—If we had never been brought into his presence? I told them, " No, nor had ever had a near sight of him."—What strength he had for war? I answered, Not well able to assault them, by reason the hearts of his people were not true to him; but that the strength of his country consisted in mountains and woods, as much as in the people.

What army he could raise upon occasion? I answered, I knew not well, but as I thought about thirty thousand men.

Why he would not make peace with them, they so much sueing for it, and sending presents to please him? I answered, " I was not one of his council, and knew not his meaning."

But they demanded of me, What I thought might be the reason or occasion of it? I answered, " Living securely in the mountains, he feareth none; and for traffic he regardeth it not."

Which way was best and most secure to send spies or intelligence to Candy? I told them, "By the way that goeth to Jafniputtan, and by some of that country people, who have great correspondence with the people of Neurecaulava, one of the king's countries."

What I thought would become of that land after this king's decease? I told them, "I thought, he having no issue, it might fall into their hands."

How many Englishmen had served the king, and what became of them? which I gave them an account of.

Whether I had any acquaintance or discourse with the great men at court? I answered, "That I was too small to have any friendship or intimacy, or hold discourse with them."

How the common people used to talk concerning them? I answered, "They used much to commend their justice and good government in the territories, and over the people belonging unto them."

Whether the king did take counsel of any, or rule and act only by his own will and pleasure? I answered, "I was a stranger at court, and how could I know that?"

But, they asked further, What was my opinion? I replied,

" He is so great, that there is none great enough to give him counsel."

Concerning the French, If the king knew not of their coming before they came? I answered, " I thought not; because their coming seemed strange and wonderful unto the people."

How they had proceeded in treating with the king? I answered, as shall be related hereafter, when I come to speak of the French detained in this land.

If I knew any way or means to be used, whereby the prisoners in Candy might be set free? I told them, Means, I knew none, unless they could do it by war.

Also, they enquired about the manner of executing those whom the king commands to be put to death? They enquired also very curiously concerning the manner of our surprizal, and entertainment, or usage among them—and in what parts of the land we had our residence; and particularly concerning myself, in what parts of the land, and how long in each I had dwelt, and after what manner I lived there, and of my age; and in what part or place when God sends me home, I should take up my abode? To all which I gave answers.

They desired to know also, how many Englishmen there were yet remaining behind? I gave them an account of sixteen men, and also of eighteen children born there. They much enquired concerning their ambassadors detained there, and of their behaviour and manner of living; also what the king allowed them for maintenance—and concerning several officers of quality, prisoners there: and in general about all the rest of their nation; and what countenance the king shewed to those Dutchmen that came running away to him? I answered, "The Dutch runaways the king looks upon as rogues." And concerning the Portugueze they enquired also: I told them, the Portugueze were about some fifty or threescore persons, and six or seven of those Europe men born.

They asked me, moreover, how we had made our escape, and which way, and by what towns we passed, and how long we were in our journey? To all which I answered at large.

The governor desires him to go to Batavia.

Then the governor asked me, what was my intent and desire? I told him, to have passage to our own nation at fort St. GEORGE. To which he answered, that suddenly there would be no convenient opportunity. But his desire was that we would go with him to Batavia, where the general his father would be very glad to see us, which was not in our power to deny. Then he commanded to call a Dutch captain, who was over the countries adjacent, subject to their jurisdiction. To him he gave order to take us home to his house, and there well to entertain us, and also to send for a tailor to make us clothes. Upon which I told him, his kindness shewn us already was more than we could have desired; it would be a sufficient favour now to supply us with a little money upon a bill to be paid at fort St. George, that we might therewith clothe ourselves. To which he answered, that he would not deny me any sum I should demand, and clothe us upon his own account besides. For which we humbly thanked his lordship; and so took our leaves of him, and went home with the aforesaid captain.

Clothes them.

The governor presently sent me money by his steward for expenses when we walked abroad in the city. We were nobly entertained without lack of any thing all the time we staid at Columbo My consort's ague increased, and grew very bad; but the chief chirurgeon by order daily came to see him, and gave him such potions of physic, that by God's blessing he soon after recovered.

Sends them money.

And a chirurgeon.

During my being here, I writ a letter to my fellow prisoners I left behind me in Candy: wherein I described at large the way we went, so that they might plainly understand the same. Which I finding to be safe and secure, advised them, when God permitted, to steer the same course. This letter I left with the new governor, and desired him, when opportunity presented, to send it to them. Who said he would have it copied out into Dutch for the benefit of their prisoners there, and promised to send both together.

The author writes a letter to the English at Candy.

The governor seemed to be pleased with my aforesaid relations and replies to his demands, insomuch, that he afterwards appointed one that well understood Portugueze to write down all the former particulars. Which being done, for further satisfaction they brought me pen and paper, desiring me to write the same that I had related to them in English, and sign it with my hand, which I was not unwilling to do.

The former demands and answers penned down in Portugueze by the governor's order.

Upon the governor's departure there were great and royal feasts made: to which he always sent for me. Here were exceeding great varieties of food, wine, and sweetmeats, and music. Some two and twenty days after our arrival at Co-

They embark for Batavia.

lumbo, the governor went on board ship to sail to Batavia, and took us with him. At which time there were many scores of ordnance fired. We sailed all the way with flag and penant under it, being out both day and night, in a ship of about eight hundred tuns burthen; and a soldier standing armed sentinel at the cabin door both night and day. He so far favoured me, that I was in his own mess, and eat at his table; where every meal we had ten or twelve dishes of meat with variety of wine. We set sail from Columbo the four and twentieth of November, and the fifth of January anchored in Batavia road.

His friendly reception at Batavia with the governor.

As we came to greater men so we found greater kindness; for the General of Batavia's reception of us and favours to us exceeded (if possible) those of the governor his son. As soon as we came before him, seeming to be very glad, he took me by the hand, and bad us heartily welcome, thanking God on our behalf that had appeared so miraculously in our deliverance; telling us withal, that he had omitted no means for our redemption, and that if it had laid in his power, we should long before have had our liberty. I humbly thanked his excellency, and said, that I knew it to be true; and that though it missed of an effect, yet his good will was not the less, neither were our obligations, being ever bound to thank and pray for him.

Furnishes them with the clothes and money.

Then his own tailor was ordered to take measure of us, and furnish us with two suits of apparel. He gave us also money for tobacco and betel, and to spend in the city. All the time we staid there, our quarters were in the captain of the castle's house. And oftentimes the general would send for me to his own table, at which sat only himself and lady, who was all bespangled with diamonds and pearls. Sometimes his sons and daughters-in-law, with some other strangers, did eat with him; the trumpet sounding all the while. We finding ourselves thus kindly entertained, and our habits changed, saw that we were no more captives in Candy, nor yet prisoners elsewhere; therefore cut off our beards, which we had brought with us out of our captivity; for until then we cut them not; God having rolled away the reproach of Candy from us.

Here also they did examine me again concerning the passages of Candy, causing all to be writ down which I said, and requiring my hand to the same: which I refused, as I had done before, and upon the same account, because I understood not the Dutch language. Whereupon they persuaded me to write a certificate upon another paper under my hand, that what I had informed them of was true: which I did. This examination was taken by two secretaries, who were appointed to demand answers of me concerning the King of Ceylon and his country; which they committed to writing from my mouth.

The general's youngest son being to go home admiral of the ships this year, the general kindly offered us passage upon their ships, promising me entertainment at his son's own table, as the Governor of Columbo had given me in my voyage hither. Which offer he made me, he said, that I might better satisfy their company in Holland concerning the affairs of Ceylon, which they would be very glad to know.

Offer him passage in their ships.

Come home from Bantam in the Cæsar.

At this time came two English merchants hither from Bantam, with whom the general was pleased to permit us to go. But when we came to Bantam, the English agent very kindly entertained us, and being not willing that we should go to the Dutch for passage, since God had brought us to our own nation, ordered our passage in the good ship Cæsar, lying then in the road bound for England, the land of our nativity, and our long wished-for port: where, by the good providence of God, we arrived safe in the month of September.

CHAP. XIII.

Concerning some other Nations, and chiefly Europeans, that now live in this Island. Portugueze, Dutch.

HAVING said all this concerning the English people, it may not be unacceptable to give some account of other whites, who either voluntarily or by constraint inhabit there. And they are, besides the English already spoken of, Portugueze, Dutch, and French. But before I enter upon discourse of any of these, I shall detain my readers a little with another nation inhabiting in this land, I mean, the Malabars; both because they are strangers and derive themselves from another country, and also because I have had occasion to mention them sometimes in this book.

Concerning Malabars that inhabit in this Island. Their territories.

These Malabars then are voluntary inhabitants in this Island, and have a country here; though the limits of it are but small: it lies to the northward of the king's coasts, betwixt him and the Hollander. Corunda Wy river parts it from the king's territories. Through this country we passed, when we made our escape. The language they speak is peculiar to themselves; so that a Chingulay cannot understand them, nor they a Chingulay.

Their prince.

They have a prince over them, called Coilat Wannea, that

is independent either upon the King of Candy on one hand, or the Dutch on the other, only that he pays an acknowledgment to the Hollanders, who have endeavoured to subdue him by wars, but they cannot yet do it: yet they have brought him to be a tributary to them, viz. to pay a certain rate of elephants per annum. The king and this prince maintain a friendship and correspondence together. And when the king lately sent an army against the Hollanders, this prince let them pass through his country; and went himself in person to direct the king's people, when they took one or two forts from them.

The people how governed.

The people are in great subjection under him: they pay him rather greater taxes than the Chingulays do to their king. But he is nothing so cruel. He victualleth his soldiers during the time they are upon the guard, either about the palace or abroad in the wars—they are now fed at his charge: whereas it is contrary in the king's country; for the Chingulay soldiers bear their own expenses. He hath a certain rate out of every land that is sown, which is to maintain his charge.

Their commodities and trade.

The commodities of this country are, elephants, honey, butter, milk, wax, cows, wild cattle: of the three last great abundance. As for corn it is more scarce than in the Chingulay's country; neither have they any cotton. But they come up into Neure Caulava yearly with great droves of cattle, and lade both corn and cotton. And to buy these they bring up cloth made of the same cotton, which they make better than the Chingulays; also they bring salt and salt fish, and brass basons, and other commodities, which they get of the Hollander: because the king permits not his people to have any manner of trade with the Hollander: so they receive the Dutch commodities at the second hand.

We now proceed unto the European nations. And we begin with the Portugueze, who deserve the first place, being the oldest standers there.

Concerning the Portugueze.

The sea-coasts round about the Island were formerly under their power and government, and so held for many years. In which time many of the natives became Christians, and learned the Portugueze tongue. Which to this day is much spoken in that land: for even the king himself understands and speaks it excellently well. The Portugueze have often made invasions throughout the whole land, even to Candy, the metropolis of the Island; which they have burnt more than once, with the palace and the temples: and so formidable have they been, that the king hath been forced to turn tributary to them, paying them three elephants per annum. However the middle of this Island, viz. Candy Uda, standing upon mountains, and so strongly fortified by nature, could never be brought into subjection by them, much less by any other, but hath always been under the power of their own kings.

Their power and interest in this Island formerly.

There were great and long wars between the King of Ceylon and the Portugueze: and many of the brave Portugal generals are still in memory among them: of whom I shall relate some passages presently. Great vexation they gave the king by their irruptions into his dominions, and the mischiefs they did him, though oftentimes with great loss on their side. Great battles have been lost and won between them, with great destruction of men on both parts. But being greatly distressed

The great wars between the king and them, force him to send in for the Hollanders.

at last, he sent and called in the Hollander to his aid. By whose seasonable assistance, together with his own arms, the king totally dispossessed the Portugueze, and routed them out of the land: whose rooms the Dutch now occupy, paying themselves for their pains.

The king invites the Portugueze to live in his country.

At the surrender of Columbo, which was the last place the Portugueze held, the king made proclamation, that all Portugueze, which would come unto him, should be well entertained: which accordingly many did, with their whole families, wives, children, and servants, choosing rather to be under him than the Duch, and divers of them are alive to this day, living in Candy Uda; and others are born there. To all whom he alloweth monthly maintenance; yea also, and provisions for their slaves and servants, which they brought up with them. This people are privileged to travel the countries above all other whites, as knowing they will not run away. Also when there was a trade at the sea ports, they are permitted to go down with commodities, clear from all customs and duties. Besides these who came voluntarily to live under the king, there are others whom he took prisoners. The Portugueze of the best quality the king took into his service, who are most of them since cut off, according to his kind custom towards his courtiers. The rest of them have allowance from that king, and follow husbandry, trading about the country, stilling rack, keeping taverns; the women sew womens waistcoats, and men sew mens doublets for sale.

Their privileges,

Their generals.

I shall now mention some of the last Portugueze generals, all within this present king's reign, with some passages concerning them.

Constantine Sa, general of the Portugal's army in Ceylon, when the Portugueze had footing in this land, was very successful against this present king. He run quite through the Island unto the royal city itself, which he set on fire with the temples therein; insomuch that the king sent a message to him, signifying that he was willing to become his tributary. But he proudly sent him word back again, that that would not serve his turn, "He should not only be tributary, but slave to his master, the King of Portugal." This the King of Candy could not brook, being of an high stomach, and said, "He would fight to the last drop of blood rather than stoop to that." There were at this time many commanders in the general's army who were natural Chingulays; with these the king dealt secretly, assuring them, that if they would turn on his side, he would gratify them with very ample rewards. The king's promises took effect, and they all revolted from the general. The king now daring not to trust the revolted, to make trial of their truth and fidelity, put them in the forefront of his battle, and commanded them to give the first onset. The king at that time might have twenty or thirty thousand men in the field; who, taking their opportunity, set upon the Portugueze army, and gave them such a total overthrow, that as they report in that country, not one of them escaped. The general seeing that defeat, and himself like to be taken, called his black boy to give him water to drink, and snatching the knife that stuck by his boy's side, stabbed himself with it.

Constantine Sa.

He loses a victory and stabs himself.

Another general after him was Lewis Tissera; he swore he would make the king eat coracan tallipa, that is a kind of hasty pudding, made of water and the coracan flower, which is reckoned the worst fare of that Island. The king afterwards

Lewis Tissera served as he intended to serve the king.

took this Lewis Tissera, and put him in chains in the common goal, and made him eat of the same fare; and there is a ballad of this man and this passage, sung much among the common people there to this day.

Simon Caree of a cruel mind.

Their next general was Simon Caree, a natural Chingulay, but baptized. He is said to be a great commander. When he had got any victory over the Chingulays, he did exercise great cruelty. He would make the women beat their own children in their mortars, wherein they used to beat their corn.

Gasper Figari splits men in the middle.

Gasper Figari had a Portugueze father and Chingulays mother. He was the last general they had in this country, and a brave soldier, but degenerated not from his predecessors in cruelty. He would hang up the people by the heels, and split them down the middle. He had his axe wrapped up in a white cloth, which he carried with him into the field to execute those he suspected to be false to him, or that ran away. Smaller malefactors he was merciful to, cutting off only their right hands; several, whom he hath so served, are yet living, whom I have seen.

His policy.

This Gasper came up one day to fight against the king, and the king resolved to fight him. The general fixed his camp at Motaupul in Hotteracourly, and in order to the king's coming down to meet the Portugueze, preparation was made for him at a place called Cota Coppul, which might be ten or twelve miles distant from the Portugueze army. Gasper knew of the place by some spies; but of the time of the king's coming he was informed that it was a day sooner than it really happened. According to this information he resolved privately to march thither, and come upon him in the night unawares. And because he knew the king was a politician, and would have his spies abroad to watch the general's motions, the general sent for all the drummers and pipers to play and dance in his camp, that thereby the king's spies might not suspect that he was upon the march, but merry and secure in his camp. In the mean time, having set all his people to their dancing and drumming, he left a small party there to secure the baggage, and away he goes in the night with his army, and arrives to Catta Coppul, intending to fall upon the king; but when he came thither, he found the king was not yet come; but into the king's tents he went, and sits him down in the seat appointed for the king. Here he heard where the king was with his camp, which being not far off, he marched thither in the morning and fell upon him, and gave him one of the greatest routs that ever he had. The king himself made a narrow escape; for, had it not been for a Dutch company, which the Dutch had sent a little before for his guard, who after his own army fled, turned head and stopped the Portugueze for a while, he had been seized. The Portugueze general was so near the king, that he called after him, Houre; that is brother, stay, I would speak with you: but the king being got a top of the hills, was safe; and so Gaspar retired to his quarters.

Gives the king a great overthrow.

This gallant expert commander, that had so often vanquished the Chingulays, could not cope with another European nation; for when the Hollanders came to besiege Columbo, he was sent against them with his army. They told him before he went, that now he must look to himself, for he was not now to fight against Chingulays, but against soldiers that would look him in the face: but he made nothing of them, and said he would

Loses Columbo, and taken prisoner.

serve them as he had served the Chingulays. The Hollanders met him, and they fought, but had before contrived a stratagem, which he was not aware of: they had placed some field-pieces in the rear of their army, and after a small skirmish they retreated as if they had been worsted, which was only to draw the Portugueze nearer upon their guns; which, when they had brought them in shot of, they opened on a sudden to the right and left, and fired upon them, and so routed them, and drove them into Columbo. This Gaspar was in the city when it was taken, and himself taken prisoner; who wás afterwards sent to Goa, where he died: and so much of the Portugueze.

The Dutch, the occasion of their coming in.

The Dutch succeeded the Portugueze; the first occasion of whose coming into this land was, that the present king being wearied and overmatched with the Portugueze, sent for them into his aid long ago from Batavia; and they did him good service, but they feathered their own nests by the means, and are now possessed of all the sea coasts, and considerable territories thereunto adjoining.

The king, their implacable enemy, and why.

The king of the country keeps up an irreconcileable war against them; the occasion of which is said to be this: upon the besieging of Columbo, which was about the year 1655, it was concluded upon between the king and the Dutch, that their enemies, the Portugueze, being expelled thence, the city was to be delivered up by the Dutch into the king's hands; whereupon the king himself in person with all his power went down to this war, to assist and join with the Hollanders, without whose help, as is generally reported, the Dutch could not have taken the city; but being surrendered to them, and they gotten into it, the king lay looking when they would come, according to their former articles, and put him into possession of it; meanwhile they turned on a sudden and fell upon him, contrary to his expectation, (whether the king had first broke word with them) and took bag and baggage from him; which provoked him in so high a manner, that he maintains a constant hostility against them, detains their ambassadors, and forbids his people, upon pain of death, to hold commerce with them.

So that the Dutch have enough to do to maintain those places which they have. Oftentimes the king, at unawares, falls upon them and does them great spoil, sometimes giving no quarter, but cutting off the heads of whomsoever he catches, which are brought up and hung upon trees near the city; many of which I have seen. Sometimes he brings up his prisoners alive, and keeps them by the highway sides, a spectacle to the people in memory of his victories over them: many of these are now living there in a most miserable condition, having but a very small allowance from him, so that they are forced to be, and it is a favour when they can get leave to go abroad and do it.

The damage the king does them.

The Dutch, therefore, not being able to deal with him by the sword, being unacquainted with the woods, and Chingulays manner of fighting, do endeavour for peace with them all they can, dispatching divers ambassadors to him, and sending great presents, by carrying letters to him in great state, wrapped up in silks wrought with gold and silver, bearing them all the way upon their heads in token of great honour, honouring him with great and high titles, subscribing themselves his subjects and servants, telling him, the forts they build are out of loyalty to him, to secure his majesty's country from foreign enemies; and, that when they come up into his country, it is to seek

The means they use to obtain peace with him.

maintenance. And by these flatteries and submissions they sometimes obtain to keep what they have gotten from him; and sometimes nothing will prevail, he neither regarding their ambassadors nor receiving their presents, but taking his opportunities, on a sudden, of setting on them by his forces.

How he took Bibligom Fort.

His craft and success in taking Bibligom Fort, in the county of Habberagon, may deserve to be mentioned. The Chingulays had besieged the fort, and knowing the Dutch had no water there, but all they had was conveyed through a trench, wrought under ground, from a river near by, they besieged them so close, and planted so many guns towards the mouth of this trench, that they could not come out to fetch water. They cut down wood also, and made bundles of faggots therewith, which they piled up round about their fort at some distance, and every night removed them nearer and nearer, so that their works became higher than the fort. Their main intent by these faggot-works, was to have brought them just under the fort, and then to have set it on fire, the walls of the fort being for the most part of wood. There was also a Bo-gahah tree, growing just by the fort, on which they planted guns, and shot right down into them. The houses in the fort being thatched, they shot also fire-arrows among them, so that the beseiged were forced to pull off the straw from their houses, which proved a great inconvenience to them being a rainy season, so that they lay open to the weather and cold. The Dutch finding themselves in this extremity desired quarter, which was granted them at the king's mercy. They came out and laid down their arms, all but the officers, who still wore theirs. None were plundered of any thing they had about them. The fort they demolished to the ground, and brought up the four guns to the king's palace, where they, among others, stand mounted in very brave carriages before his gate.

The Dutch were brought two or three days journey from the fort, into the country they call Owyah, and there were placed with a guard about them, having but a small allowance appointed them; insomuch, that afterwards having spent what they had, they perished for hunger; so that of about ninety Hollanders taken prisoners, there were not above five and twenty living when I came away.

Several ambassadors detained by the king.

There are several white ambassadors, besides other Chingulay people, by whom the Dutch have sent letters and presents to the king, whom he keeps from returning back again. They are all bestowed in several houses, with soldiers to guard them; and though they are not in chains, yet none is permitted to come to them or speak with them, it not being the custom of that land for any to come to the speech of ambassadors. Their allowance is brought them ready dressed, out of the king's palace, being all sorts of varieties that the land affords. After they have remained in this condition some years, the guards are somewhat slackened, and the soldiers that are to watch them grow remiss in their duty, so that now the ambassadors walk about the streets, and any body goes to their houses and talks with them; that is, after they have been so long in the country, that all their news is stale and grown out of date. But this liberty is only winked at, not allowed. When they have been there a great while, the king usually gives them slaves, both men and women, the more to alienate their minds from their own country, and that they may stay with him with the more willingness and content. For his design is, to make them, if he can inclineable to serve him ; as he prevailed with one of these ambassadors to do for the love of a woman. The manner of it I shall relate immediately.

There are five ambassadors whom he hath thus detained since my coming there ; of each of whom I shall speak a little, besides two whom he sent away voluntarily.

The first ambassador there detained since the author's remembrance.

The first of these was sent up by the Hollanders some time before the rebellion against the king ; who had detained him in the city. After the rebellion the king sent for him, to him, to the mountain of Gauluda, whither he had retreated from the rebels. The king not long after removed to Digligy, where he now keeps his court ; but left the ambassador at Gauluda, remaining by himself with a guard of soldiers. In this uncomfortable condition, upon a dismal mountain, void of all society, he continued many days. During which time a Chingulay and his wife falls out, and she being discontented with her husband, to escape from him, flies to this ambassador's house for shelter. The woman being somewhat beautiful, he fell greatly in love with her ; and, to obtain her, he sent to the king and proferred him his service if he would permit him to enjoy her company ; which the king was very willing and glad to do, having now obtained that which he had long aimed at ;—to get him into his service.

His preferment and death.

Hereupon the king sent him word that he granted his desire, and withal sent to both of them rich apparel, and to her many jewels and bracelets of gold and silver. Suddenly after there was a great house prepared for them in the city, furnished with all kinds of furniture out of the king's treasure and at his proper costs and charges: which being finished, he was brought away from his mountain into it; but from thenceforward never saw his wife more, according to the custom of court. And he was entertained in the king's service, and made courtalbad; which is chief over all the smiths and carpenters in Candy Uda. Some short time after, the king was about to send his forces against a fort of the Hollanders, called Arundery, built by them in the year 1666. He, though in the king's service, yet being a well-wisher to his country, had privately sent a letter of advice to the Dutch concerning the king's intention and purpose:—an answer to which was intercepted, and brought to the king; wherein thanks was returned him from the Dutch for his loyalty to his own nation, and that they would accordingly prepare for the king's assault. The king having this letter, sent for him and bade him read it; which he excused, pretending it was so written that he could not:—whererеupon, immediately another Dutchman was sent for, who read it before the king, and told him the contents of it. At which it is reported the king should say—"Beia pas mettandi hitta pas ettandi." That is, He serves me for fear, and them for love; or, his fear is here, and his love is there; and forthwith commanded to carry him forth to execution: which was accordingly done upon him. 'Tis generally said, that this letter was framed by somebody on purpose to ruin him.

The next ambassador dying there, his body is sent down to Columbo in great state.

The next ambassador after him was Hendrick Draak; a fine gentleman, and good friend of the English. This was he who was commissioned in the year 1664 of intercede with the king on the behalf of the English, that they might have liberty to go home; and with him they were made to believe they should return: which happened at the same time that Sir Edward Winter sent his letters to the king for us; which I have already spoke of in the fifth chapter of this part. This ambassador was much in the king's favour, with whom he was detained till he died. And then the king sent his body down to Columbo, carried in a pallenkine, with great state and lamentation; and accompanied with his great commanders and many soldiers.

The third ambassador gets away by his resolution.

Some time after the loss of the fort of Arrundery, which was about the year 1670, the Dutch sent up another ambassador to see if he could obtain a peace, which was the first time their ambassadors began to bring up letters upon their heads in token of extraordinary reverence. This man was much favoured by the king, and was entertained with great ceremony and honour, clothing him in Chingulay habit; which I never knew done before or since. But being weary of his long stay, and of the delays that were made, having often made motions to go down, and still he was deferred from day to day; at length he made a resolution, that if he had not leave to go by such a day, he would go without it, saying—"That the former ambassador who died there, died like a woman; but it should be seen that he would die like a man." At the appointed day he girt on his sword, and repaired to the gates of the king's palace, pulling off his hat, and making his obeisance as if the king were present before him; and thanking him for the favours and honours he had done him, and so took his leave. And there being some Englishmen present, he generously gave them some money to drink his health; and, in this resolute manner departed, with some two or three black servants that attended on him. The upshot of this was, that the king not being willing to prevent his resolution by violence, sent one of his noblemen to conduct him down; and so he had the good fortune to get home safely to Columbo.

The fourth was of a milder nature.

The next ambassador after him was John Baptista;—a man of a milder spirit than the former, endeavouring to please and shew compliance with the king. He obtained many favours of the king, and several slaves, both men and women; and, living well, with servants about him, is the more patient in waiting the king's leisure till he pleaseth to send him home.

The fifth brings a lion to the king, as a present.

The last ambassador that came up while I was there, brought up a lion; which the Dutch thought would be the most acceptable present they could send to the king, as indeed did all others;—it was but a whelp. But the king did never receive it, supposing it not so famous, as he had heard by report lions were. This man with his lion was brought up and kept in the county of Oudapollat, near twenty miles from the king's court; where he remained about a year, in which time the lion died. The ambassador being weary of living thus like a prisoner, with a guard always upon him, often attempted to go back, seeing the king would not permit him audience; but the guards would not let him. Having divers times made disturbances in this manner to get away home, the king commanded to bring him up into the city, to an house that was prepared for him, standing some distance from the court: where, having waited many days, and seeing no sign of audience, he resolved to make his appearance before the king by force; which he attempted to do, when the king was abroad taking his pleasure. The soldiers of his guard immediately ran, and acquainted the noblemen at court of his coming; who delayed not to acquaint the king thereof: whereupon the king gave order forthwith to meet him; and, where they met him, in that same place to stop him till further order; and there they kept him, not letting him go either forward or backward. In this manner and place he remained for three days, when the king sent order that he might return to his house whence he came. This the king did to tame him; but afterwards he was pleased to call him before him; and there he remained when I left the country, maintained with plenty of provisions at the king's charge.

The number of Dutch there.

The number of Dutch now living there may be about fifty or sixty; some whereof are ambassadors, some prisoners of war; some runaways, and malefactors that have escaped the hand of justice, and got away from the Dutch quarters: to all whom are allotted respective allowances; but the runaways have the least, the king not loving such, though giving them entertainment.

They follow their vice of drinking.

The Dutch here love drink, and practise their proper vice in this country. One, who was a great man in the court, would sometimes come into the king's presence half disguised with drink, which the king often past over; but once asked him—"Why do you thus disorder yourself; that when I send for you about my business, you are not in a capacity to serve me?" He boldly replied, "That as soon as his mother took away her milk from him, she supplied it with wine; and, ever since," saith he, "I have used myself to it." With this answer the king seemed pleased; and, indeed, the rest of the white men are generally of the same temper; insomuch, that the Chingulays have a saying,—" That wine is as natural to white men, as milk to children."

The Chingulays prejudiced against the Dutch, and why.

All differences of ranks and qualities are disregarded among those Chingulay people that are under the Dutch; neither do the Dutch make any distinction between the hondrews, and the low inferior casts of men: and permit them to go in the same habit, and sit upon stools, as well as the best hondrews; and the lower ranks may eat, and intermarry with the higher, without any punishment, or any cognizance taken of it: which is a matter that the Chingulays in Candy Uda are much offended with the Dutch for; and makes them think, that they themselves are sprung from some mean rank and extract. And this prejudiceth this people against them, that they have not such an esteem for them:—for, to a Chingulay, his rank and honour is as dear as his life. And thus much of the Dutch.

CHAP. XIV.

Concerning the French: with some Enquiries what should make the King detain White Men as he does: and how the Christian Religion is maintained among the Christians there.

The French come hither with a fleet.

ABOUT the year 1672, or 73, there came fourteen sail of great ships from the King of France to settle a trade here. Monsieur De la Hay, admiral, put in with his fleet into the port of Cottiar: from whence he sent up three men by way of embassy to the King of Candy; whom he entertained very nobly, and gave every one of them a chain of gold about their necks, and a sword all inlaid with silver, and a gun; and afterwards sent one of them down to the admiral with his answer; which encouraged him to send up others: that is, an ambassador and six more, who were to reside there till the return of the fleet back again, being about to sail to the coast.

To whom the king sends provisions, and helps them to build a fort.

To the fleet the king sent all manner of provision, as much as his ability could afford: and, not only permitted, but assisted them to build a fort in the bay; which they manned partly with their own people, and partly with Chingulays, whom the king sent and lent the French. But, the admiral finding that the king's provisions, and what else could be bought in the Island would not suffice for so great a fleet, was forced to depart for the coast of Coromandel; promising the king, by the ambassador afore-mentioned, speedily to return again: so, leaving some of his men with the king's supplies to keep the fort till his return, he weighed anchor and set sail; but never came back again. Some reported they were destroyed by a storm—others by the Dutch. The admiral had sent up to the king great presents, but he would not presently receive them, that it might not seem as if he wanted any thing, or were greedy of things brought him: but, since the French returned not according to their promise, he scorned ever after to receive them. At first he neglected the presents out of state, and ever since out of anger and indignation. This French fort at Cottiar was a little after easily taken by the Dutch.

But to return to the ambassador and his retinue; he rode up from Cottiar on horseback, which was very grand in that country: and, being with his company gotten somewhat short of the city, was appointed there to stay until a house should be prepared in the city for their entertainment. When it was signified to him that their house was ready for their reception, they were conducted forward by certain noblemen sent by the king, carrying with them a present for his majesty. The ambassador came riding on horseback into the city; which the noblemen observing, dissuaded him from, and advised him to walk on foot; telling him—it was not allowable, nor the custom; but he regarding them not, rode by the palace gate. It offended the king, but he took not much notice of it for the present.

The French ambassador offends the king.

The ambassador alighted at his lodgings, where he and his companions were nobly entertained, provisions sent them ready dressed out of the king's palace three times a day—great plenty they had of all things the country afforded. After some time the king sent to him to come to his audience. In great state he was conducted to the court, accompanied with several of the

He refuses to wait longer for audience.

nobles that were sent to him. Coming thus to the court in the night, as it is the king's usual manner at that season to send for foreign ministers, and give them audience, he waited th er some small time—about two hours or less, the king not yet admitting him; which he took in such great disdain, and for such an affront, that he was made to stay at all, much more so long—that he would tarry no longer, but went towards his lodging. Some about the court observing this, would have stopped him by elephants that stood in the court, turning them before the gate through which he was to pass: but he would not so be stopped, but laid his hand upon his sword, as if he meant to make his way by the elephants; the people seeing his resolution, called away the elephants, and let him pass.

Which more displeased the king. Clapped in chains.

As soon as the king heard of it, he was highly displeased; insomuch, that he commanded some of his officers, that they should go and beat them, and clap them in chains: which was immediately done to all excepting the two gentlemen that were first sent up by the admiral; for these were not touched, the king reckoning they did not belong to this ambassador; neither were they now in his company, excepting that one of them in the combustion got a few blows: they were likewise disarmed, and so have continued ever since. Upon this, the gentlemen attendants upon the ambassador, made their complaints to the captain of their guards, excusing themselves, and laying all the blame upon their ambassador; urging, "That they were his attendants, and a soldier must obey his commander, and go where he appoints him." Which sayings being told the king, he approved thereof, and commanded them out of chains—the ambassador still remaining in them, and so continued for six months: after which he was released of his chains by means of the intreaties his own men made to the great men in his behalf.

The rest of the Frenchmen, seeing how the ambassador's imprudent carriage had brought them to this misery, refused any longer to dwell with him. And each of them by the king's permission dwells by himself in the city, being maintained at the king's charge. Three of these, whose names were Monsieur Du Plessy, son to a gentleman of note in France, and Jean Bloom, the third whose name I cannot tell, but was the ambassador's boy, the king appointed to look to his best horse, kept in the palace. This horse some time after died, as it is supposed of old age; which extremely troubled the king, and, imagining they had been instrumental to his death by their carelessness, he commanded them, Monsieur Du Plessy and Jean Bloom to be carried away into the mountains, and kept prisoners in chains, where they remained when I came thence.

The rest of the French refuse to dwell with the ambassador.

The rest of them follow employments; some whereof still rack, and keep the greatest taverns in the city.

Lately, a little before I came from the Island, the king understanding the disagreements and differences that were still kept on foot betwixt the ambassador and the rest of his company, disliked it, and used these means to make them friends. He sent for them all, the ambassador and the rest, and told them, that it was not seemly for persons as they were, at such a distance from their own country, to quarrel and fall out, and that if they had any love for God, or the King of France, or himself, that they should go home with the ambassador, and

The king uses means to reconcile the French to their ambassador.

agree and live together. They went back together, not daring to disobey the king: and, as soon as they were at home, the king sent a banquet after them of sweetmeats and fruits to eat together. They did eat the king's banquet, but it would not make the reconcilement; for, after they had done, each man went home and dwelt in their own houses as they did before. It was thought that this carriage would offend the king, and that he would at least take away their allowance: and it is probable before this time the king hath taken vengeance on them. But the ambassador's carriage is so imperious, that they would rather venture whatsoever might follow, than be subject to him: and in this case I left them.

The author acquaints the French ambassador in London with the condition of these men.

Since my return to England, I presumed by a letter to inform the French ambassador then in London of the abovesaid matters, thinking myself bound in conscience and Christian charity to do my endeavour, that their friends knowing their condition, may use means for their deliverance. The letter ran thus:

"These may acquaint your excellency that, having been a prisoner in the Island of Ceylon, under the king of that country near twenty years; by means of this, my long detainment there, I became acquainted with the French ambassador, and the other gentlemen, his retinue, being in all eight persons; who was sent to treat with the said king in the year 1672, by Monsieur De la Hay; who came with a fleet to the port of Cottiar; or, Trinkemalay, from whence he sent these gentlemen. And, knowing that from thence it is scarce possible to send any letters or notice to other parts; for, in all the time of my captivity I could never send one word, whereby my friends here might come to hear of my condition; until, with one more I made an escape, leaving sixteen Englishmen yet there. The kindness I have received from those French gentlemen, as also my compassion for them, being detained in the same place with me, hath obliged and constrained me, to presume to trouble your lordship with this paper; not knowing any other means whereby I might convey notice to their friends and relations, which is all the service I am able to perform for them. The ambassador's name I know not; there is a kinsman of his called Monsieur le Serle, and a young gentleman called Monsieur du Plessy; and another, named Monsieur la Roche; the rest by name I know not. And then an account of them is given, according to what I have mentioned above. I shall not presume to be farther tedious to your honour; craving pardon for my boldness, which my affection to those gentlemen, being detained in the same land with me, hath occasioned; concerning whom, if your lordship be pleased farther to be informed, I shall be both willing and ready to be,

"Yours," &c.

The ambassador, upon the receipt of this, desired to speak with me. Upon whom I waited; and he, after some speech with me, told me he would send word into France of it, and gave me thanks for this my kindness to his countrymen.

It may be worth some inquiry what the reason might be,

An inquiry into the reason of this king's detaining Europeans.

that the king detains the European people as he does; it cannot be out of hope of profit or advantage; for they are so far from bringing him any, that they are a very great charge—being all maintained either by him or his people. Neither is it in the power of money to redeem any one, for that he neither needs nor values; which makes me conclude, that it is not out of profit, nor envy, or ill-will; but out of love and favour that he keeps them, delighting in their company, and to have them ready at his command. For, he is very ambitious of the service of these men, and winks at many of their failings, more than he uses to do towards his natural subjects: as may appear from a company of white soldiers he hath, who upon their watch used to be very negligent; one lying drunk here, and another there. Which remissness in his own soldiers he would scarce have endured, but it would have cost them their lives. But with these he uses more craft than severity to make them more watchful.

The king's gentleness towards his white soldiers.

They watch at his magazine.

These soldiers are under two captains, the one a Dutchman, and the other a Portugueze: they are appointed to guard one of the king's magazines, where they always keep sentinel both by day and night. This is a pretty good distance from the court, and here it was the king contrived their station, that they might swear and swagger out of his hearing, and that no body might disturb them, nor they no body. The Dutch captain lies at one side of the gate, and the Portugueze at the other.

How craftily the king corrected their negligence.

Once the king to employ these his white soldiers, and to honour them by letting them see what an assurance he reposed in them, sent one of his boys thither to be kept prisoner, which they were very proud of. They kept him two years, in which time he had learnt both the Dutch and Portugueze language. Afterwards the king retook the boy into his service, and within a short time after executed him. But the king's reason in sending this boy to be kept by these soldiers was, probably not as they supposed, and as the king himself outwardly pretended; viz.—to shew how much he confided in them, but out of design to make them look the better to their watch, which their debauchery made them very remiss in. For the prisoners hands only were in chains, and not his legs; so that his possibility of running away, having his legs at liberty, concerned them to be circumspect and wakeful: and they knew if he had escaped, it were as much as their lives were worth. By this crafty and kind way did the king correct the negligence of his white soldiers.

Indeed his inclinations are much towards the Europeans, making them his great officers, accounting them more faithful and trusty than his own people; with these he often discourses concerning the affairs of their countries, and promotes them to places far above their ability, and sometimes their degree or desert; and indeed all over the land they do bear as it were a natural respect and reverence to white men, inasmuch as black they hold to be inferior to white: and they say the gods are white, and that the souls of the blessed after the resurrection shall be white; and therefore that black is a rejected and accursed colour. **The king's inclinations are towards white men.** **The colour of white honoured in this land.**

And as further signs of the king's favour to them, there are many privileges, which white men have and enjoy, as tolerated **Their privilege above the natives.**

or allowed them from the king, which I suppose may proceed from the aforesaid consideration; as to wear any manner of apparel, either gold, silver, or silk, shoes and stockings, a shoulder belt and sword; their houses may be whitened with lime, and many such like things—all which the Chingulays are not permitted to do.

The king loves to send and talk with them.

He will sometimes send for them into his presence, and discourse familiarly with them, and entertain them with great civility, especially white ambassadors. They are greatly chargeable unto his country, but he regards it not in the least, so that the people are more like slaves unto us than we unto the king; insomuch that they are inforced by his command to bring us maintenance; whose poverty is so great oftentimes, that for want of what they supply us with, themselves, their wives, and children, are forced to suffer hunger, this being as a due tax imposed upon them to pay unto us. Neither can they by any power or authority refuse the payment hereof to us; for, in my own hearing, the people once complaining of their poverty and inability to give us any longer our allowance, the magistrate or governor replied, it was the king's special command, and who durst disannul it; and if otherwise they could not supply us with our maintenance, he bade them sell their wives and children rather than we should want of our due. Such is the favour that Almighty God hath given Christian people in the sight of this heathen king, whose entertainment and usage of them is thus favourable.

How they maintain Christianity among them.

If any enquire into the religious exercise and worship practised among the Christians here, I am sorry I must say it, I can give but a slender account; for they have no churches and no priests, and so no meetings together on the Lord's days for divine worship, but each one reads and prays at his own house as he is disposed. They sanctify the day chiefly by refraining work and meeting together at drinking-houses. They continue the practice of baptism; and there being no priests, they baptize their children themselves with water, and use the words, "In the name of the Father, and of the Son, and of the Holy Ghost," and give them Christian names. They have their friends about them at such a time, and make a small feast according to their ability, and some teach their children to say their prayers, and to read, and some do not.

Indeed their religion at the best is but negative, that is, they are not heathen, they do not comply with the idolatry here practised, and they profess themselves Christians in a general manner, which appear by their names, and by their beads and crosses that some of them wear about their necks: nor indeed can I wholly clear them from compliance with the religion of the country. For some of them when they are sick do use the ceremonies which the heathen do in the like case, as in making idols of clay, and setting them up in their houses, and offering rice to them, and having weavers to dance before them. But they are ashamed to be known to do this; and I have known none to do it, but such as are Indians born. Yet I never knew any of them, that do inwardly in heart and conscience incline to the ways of the heathen, but perfectly abhor them; nor have there been any, I ever heard of, that came to their temples upon any religious account, but only

In some things they comply with the worship of the heathen.

An old priest used to eat of their sacrifices.

would stand by and look on; without it were one old priest named Padre Vergonse, a Genoeze born, and of the Jesuits order, who would go to the temples, and eat with the weavers and other ordinary people of the sacrifices offered to the idols: but with this apology for himself, that he eat it as common meat, and as God's creature, and that it was never the worse for their superstition that had past upon it. But however this may reflect upon the father, another thing may be related for his honour. There happened two priests to fall into the hands of the king; on whom he conferred great honours; for, having laid aside their habits, they kept about his person, and were the greatest favourites at court. The king one day sent for Vergonse, and asked him, "If it would not be better for him to lay aside his old coat and cap, and to do as the other two priests had done, and receive honour from him." He replied to the king, "that he boasted more in that old habit and the name of Jesus, than in all the honour that he could do him." And so refused the king's honour. The king valued the father for this saying. He had a pretty library about him, and died in his bed of old age: whereas the two other priests in the king's service died miserably, one of a canker, and the other was slain. The old priest had about thirty or forty books, which the king, they say, seized on after his death, and keeps.

The king permitted the Portugueze to build a church.

These priests, and more lived there, but all deceased, excepting Vergonse, before my time. The king allowed them to build a church; which they did, and the Portugueze assembled there, but they made no better than a bawdy-house of it; for which cause the king commanded to pull it down.

Although here be protestants and papists, yet here are no differences kept up among them; but they are as good friends, as if there were no such parties. And there is no other distinction of religion there, but only heathens and Christians; and we usually say, we Christians.

THE END.

J. F. Dove, Printer, St. John's Square.